Research Methods

Research Methods

Information, Systems, and Contexts

Second Edition

Kirsty Williamson
Graeme Johanson
Editors

Chandos Publishing is an imprint of Elsevier
50 Hampshire Street, 5th Floor, Cambridge, MA 02139, United States
The Boulevard, Langford Lane, Kidlington, OX5 1GB, United Kingdom

British Library Cataloguing-in-Publication Data
A catalogue record for this book is available from the British Library

Library of Congress Cataloging-in-Publication Data
A catalog record for this book is available from the Library of Congress

ISBN: 978-0-08-102220-7 (print)
ISBN: 978-0-08-102221-4 (online)

For information on all Chandos Publishing publications
visit our website at https://www.elsevier.com/books-and-journals

Working together
to grow libraries in
developing countries

www.elsevier.com • www.bookaid.org

Publisher: Glyn Jones
Acquisition Editor: Glyn Jones
Editorial Project Manager: Katie Chan
Production Project Manager: Debasish Ghosh
Cover Designer: Miles Hitchen

Typeset by MPS Limited, Chennai, India

Contents

Section V: Information Research: Reflections on Past and Future........535

Chapter 23: The future of information research 537

Kirsty Williamson, Graeme Johanson, Alex Byrne, Lisa M. Given,
Mary Anne Kennan and Gillian Oliver

Concluding reflections: The research journey..............................565

Donald Schauder

List of contributors

Nargiza Bekmamedova
Embry-Riddle Aeronautical University Asia, Singapore

Alex Byrne
NSW State Librarian, Australia

Dubravka Cecez-Kecmanovic
University of NSW, Australia

Anne J. Gilliland
University of California Los Angeles, United States

Lisa M. Given
Swinburne University of Technology, Australia

Gaby Haddow
Curtin University, Australia

James E. Herring
Charles Sturt University, Australia

Graeme Johanson
Monash University, Australia

Mary Anne Kennan
Charles Sturt University, Australia

Sue McKemmish
Monash University, Australia

Gillian Oliver
Monash University, Australia

Donald Schauder
Monash University, Australia

Paul Scifleet
Swinburne University of Technology, Austraila

Graeme Shanks
University of Melbourne, Australia

Judithe Sheard
Monash University, Australia

Kerry Tanner
Monash University, Australia

Kim M. Thompson
Charles Sturt University, Australia

Ron Weber
Monash University and University of Queensland, Australia

Kirsty Williamson
Monash University and Charles Sturt University, Australia

Acknowledgements

Our thanks go to colleagues who have contributed chapters to this second edition of *Research Methods: Information, Systems, and Contexts*. We were lucky that all the contributors to the first edition of the book were available and willing to revise and update the chapters for the new edition. We have two new authors, both significant contributors to a new chapter, on the future of information research. Our thanks go to them as well. We have very much appreciated the expert knowledge of all authors: their diverse approaches, their personal styles, and their patience with the complex processes involved in creating a book aimed at meeting the range of needs in the fields in which we work and research. The authors are mostly academics working at a range of Australian universities: several from Monash University Caulfield School of Information Technology; two from the School of Information Studies at Charles Sturt University, two from Swinburne University, plus scholars from three other Australian universities (University of New South Wales, University of Melbourne, and Curtin University in Western Australia) as well as one from University of California Los Angeles (UCLA). An additional author for the second edition is Dr Alex Byrne who has been one of Australia's leading library practitioners, as well as a well-regarded researcher.

We very much appreciate the assistance we received from our specialist reviewers for the first edition. They gave willingly of their time to help us ensure that the chapters are of the highest standard. Mary Anne Kennan not only reviewed two chapters but gave us support in several other ways. Other reviewers were James Herring (four reviews), Sigrid McCausland (two reviews), Yeslam Al-Saggaf (two reviews), Ron Weber, Sue McKemmish, Frada Burstein, Donald Schauder, Rebecca French, Kim Thompson, Joy McGregor, John Arnold, Christopher Cook, and Simon (sic) of the University of Newcastle. The new chapter for the second edition was reviewed by the authors involved, all of them experienced researchers.

We also thank Dr Rebecca French who, at the time of writing the first edition, was a Monash University PhD student. Rebecca made a valuable written contribution to the book. We are also grateful to a more recent Monash PhD graduate, Dr Joanne Mihelcic, who agreed to her thesis being used as an example in the second edition's new chapter and who also provided advice about RMIT University's new Digital Ethnographic Research Centre. Professor Lisa M. Given deserves credit for the idea for the title which we believe encapsulates the scope of the book. She also wrote the forewords for both editions of the book.

Our personal editor, Penny Whitten, has played a very important role in the minutiae of the creation of the first and second editions of this book, as well as the first editor's original research methods book (2000 & 2002). She has been indispensable to us in so many ways and we acknowledge her contribution with gratitude. She has many years of experience working in information fields, as well as in editing, and thus added topical value to her other qualities of perceptiveness and efficiency. She has supported us cheerfully through the long process of producing books of a high standard. We cannot praise her too highly.

We acknowledge, with gratitude, our original publisher, Rick Ryan of Tilde University Press, who produced a high-quality first edition of the book and graciously allowed Elsevier to take over the second edition. We thank Dr Glyn Jones, our Elsevier publisher and his production team, headed by Katie Chan, for their support and for the opportunity to revise and extend our original work.

Finally, we thank our spouses, Geoff Williamson and Turid Foyn-Johanson, for their support and tolerance while we devoted considerable amounts of time to our prolonged writing and editing.

To some extent preparing a book is like planning a long hike or journey; although the terrain and experience are basically familiar and anticipated, inevitably one diverges into rarely-visited territory at times. Supplies and resources can be assembled, but not every eventuality along the way can be envisaged. It has been a treat for the editors to share and to benefit from mutual intellectual exploration with fellow authors.

Kirsty Williamson
Monash University and Charles Sturt Univesity, Australia

Graeme Johanson
Monash University, Australia

About the editors

Williamson, Kirsty: Dr (Christina) Kirsty Williamson is an adjunct senior research fellow at Monash University and Charles Sturt University in Australia. For many years she was the Director of the research group, Information and Telecommunications Needs Research (ITNR), a joint initiative of both universities. Since the early 1990s she has undertaken many research projects, with her principal area of research being human information behaviour. Her research has been funded by a range of different organisations including the principal funding body of Australian Universities, the Australian Research Council (ARC). As well as two editions of an earlier research methods book, *Research Methods for Students, Academics and Professionals: Information Management and Systems*, she has many journal articles to her credit, including five in the highly ranked *Library & Information Science Research.*

Johanson, Graeme: Associate Professor Graeme Johanson has undertaken academic research for 45 years. His initial interest in archives, historical documents, and oral history led him to work as a librarian in research institutions for ten years before becoming an academic. His PhD deals with cultural commerce, emergent publishing laws, and distributed imperial values. He has undertaken many funded research projects about the evaluation and use of information and communications technologies for the benefit of developing countries and marginalised groups of people. Until recently he was Associate Dean Research Training, Faculty of Information Technology, Monash University, and he continues to supervise postgraduate students.

About the authors

Bekmamedova, Nargiza: Dr Nargiza Bekmamedova is an Assistant Professor in the Department of Business at the Embry-Riddle Aeronautical University Asia. Her teaching and research interests include business information systems, information systems project management and implementation, information security ontologies and risk management strategies. She has presented at a number of conferences including the International Conference on Information Systems and the European Conference on Information Systems, with publications resulting. She was awarded best research paper at the Australasian Conference on Information Systems and regularly reviews for leading information systems and information security journals and conferences.

Byrne, Alex: Dr Alex Byrne is a professional librarian, researcher and writer with deep interest in the roles of memory institutions, the complexity of issues relating to Indigenous peoples and transmission of knowledge. He was the State Librarian and Chief Executive of the State Library of New South Wales from 2011 to his retirement in 2016 following positions in library and university executive management around Australia, most recently at the University of Technology, Sydney. Alex served for a decade in leadership positions with the International Federation of Library Associations and Institutions — the world body for libraries — including President from 2005 to 2007. He has contributed to and chaired many associations and committees in the library, information and information technology sector including the Council of Australian University Librarians and National and State Libraries Australasia, the consortium of the primary libraries in each jurisdiction of Australia and New Zealand. The author of more than 300 professional papers, he is especially proud of leading the development of the *Aboriginal and Torres Strait Islander Protocols for Libraries, Archives and Information Services*, a landmark guide to interaction with Indigenous peoples first published in 1995. His contributions to the profession, to culture and to human rights have been recognised through a number of honours including the HCL Anderson Award of the Australian Library and Information Association, the Honorary Fellowship of the International Federation of Library Associations and Institutions, both in 2015, and Chevalier des Artes et des Lettres from the Republic of France in 2016. Alex enjoys travel, especially in remote areas, drawing and printmaking, and — inevitably — reading.

Cecez-Kecmanovic, Dubravka: Dubravka Cecez-Kecmanovic is Professor of Information Systems at the UNSW Business School, University of New South

Wales, Sydney, Australia. Her research interests include theoretical and methodological developments in understanding information systems, organisations and society. She has published in *MIS Quarterly, Information Systems Journal; Journal of Information Technology; European Journal of Information System; Information Technology and People, Information & Management;* and presented at leading Information Systems conferences. She is Senior Editor of *Journal of the Association of Information Systems* and *Information Systems Journal.*

Gilliland, Anne: Anne J. Gilliland is Professor and Director of the Archival Studies specialisation in the Department of Information Studies at the University of California Los Angeles (UCLA). She is also the Director of the global Archival Education and Research Initiative (AERI), a Fellow of the Society of American Archivists and an Honorary Research Fellow of the Centre for Global Research, RMIT University in Melbourne. Her recent work addresses recordkeeping and archival systems and practices in support of human rights and daily life in post-conflict, refugee and diasporic contexts, particularly in the countries emerging out of the former Yugoslavia; the role of community memory in promoting reconciliation in the wake of ethnic conflict; digital recordkeeping and archival informatics; archival metadata and metadata politics; and research methods and design in archival studies.

Given, Lisa M.: Lisa M. Given, PhD, is Associate Dean, Research and Development in the Faculty of Health, Arts and Design, Swinburne University of Technology. She is an Adjunct Professor in the School of Information Studies, Charles Sturt University, and in Humanities Computing (Faculty of Arts) and the Faculty of Education at the University of Alberta (Canada). A former Director of the International Institute for Qualitative Methodology, Lisa has received numerous research grants and awards and has published widely on topics related to individuals' information behaviours and qualitative inquiry. She has also served on the College of the Australian Research Council. Her research interests include the social construction of knowledge, web usability, spatial analysis, information literacy, research methods, and information issues in the context of higher education. Lisa is the author of *100 Questions (and Answers) About Qualitative Research Methods* (Sage, 2016) and the editor of *The Sage Encyclopedia of Qualitative Research Methods* (2008).

Haddow, Gaby: Dr Gaby Haddow is a Senior Lecturer at Curtin University. She teaches research methods in the Department of Information Studies and supervises research students. Gaby has published widely in national and international journals, with a focus on bibliometrics and research assessment in the social sciences and humanities, and the communication of research to practice. In 2012, Gaby was appointed co-editor of the *Australian Academic & Research Libraries,* now the *Journal of the Australian Library & Information Association.* She was nominated as a member of the IFLA Library Theory and Research Section in 2015.

Herring, James: Dr James Herring is an internationally acclaimed authority on information literacy and has used grounded theory in a number of studies relating to information literacy in schools, including students' use of the web. His ground-breaking research (including the development of a grounded theory) into aspects of the transfer of information literacy practices in schools has led researchers and practitioners to recognise transfer as a key issue. He is the author of eleven books and numerous articles on information and communications technologies in schools, information literacy and school libraries. James Herring retired from Charles Sturt University in 2012.

Johanson, Graeme: Associate Professor Graeme Johanson has undertaken academic research for 45 years. His initial interest in archives, historical documents, and oral history led him to work as a librarian in research institutions for ten years before becoming an academic. His PhD deals with cultural commerce, emergent publishing laws, and distributed imperial values. He has undertaken many funded research projects about the evaluation and use of information and communications technologies for the benefit of developing countries and marginalised groups of people. Until recently he was Associate Dean Research Training, Faculty of Information Technology, Monash University, and he continues to supervise postgraduate students.

Kennan, Mary Anne: Dr Mary Anne Kennan is Associate Head of the School of Information Studies at Charles Sturt University. Her areas of research include scholarly communication and open access, research data sharing and management, and the relationship of information services to social inclusion. Her present teaching focusses on research data management, a foundations subject for the information sciences and research methods and methodologies. Mary Anne is Co-editor of the *Journal of the Australian Library and Information Association*, and on the editorial boards of *Webology* and the *International Journal of Actor-Network Theory and Technological Innovation*.

McKemmish, Sue: Sue McKemmish is Associate Dean of Graduate Research in the Faculty of Information Technology, Chair of Archival Systems, and a lead researcher in the Centre for Organisational and Social Informatics at Monash University. She is a leading records continuum theorist who has engaged in research and standards initiatives relating to the use of metadata in records and archival systems, information resource discovery and smart information portals. Her current research focusses on archives and human rights, the participatory archive, archival autonomy and agency, rights in records, community and Indigenous archiving, and the development of inclusive archival educational programs to meet the needs of diverse communities.

Oliver, Gillian: Gillian Oliver is Associate Professor of Information Management at Monash University in Australia. Previously she led teaching and research into archives and records at Victoria University of Wellington and the Open Polytechnic of New Zealand. Her professional practice background spans information management in the United Kingdom, Germany and New Zealand. Her research interests reflect these experiences, focusing on the information cultures of organisations. She is the co-author (with Fiorella Foscarini) of the book *Records Management and Information Culture: Tackling the People Problem* (Facet, 2014) and is currently leading research funded by the International Council on Archives (ICA) to develop an information culture toolkit for archival authorities.

Schauder, Donald: Donald Schauder (BA DipLib Rhodes, MA Sheffield, MEd PhD Melbourne, FALIA, MACS) is Emeritus Professor of Information Management, and former Associate Dean (Research) in the Faculty of Information Technology at Monash University. These academic roles continued his long involvement with university-based research as a Library Director, first at the University of Natal then RMIT University. Don pioneered e-publishing of Australian research databases as founder of INFORMIT Electronic Publishing. He promoted research in social computing as co-founder of VICNET: Victoria's Network, as founder-chair of Monash University's Centre for Community Networking Research (CCNR), as Chair of Information and Telecommunication Needs Research (ITNR) and as a member of the Australian Government's delegation to the United Nations World Summit on the Information Society.

Scifleet, Paul: Dr Paul Scifleet is a Lecturer with Swinburne University of Technology, Melbourne, Victoria. He has previously held positions with the Discipline of Business Information Systems at the University of Sydney and the School of Information Systems, Technology and Management at the University of New South Wales. More recently, he was a Visiting Scholar with the Information School at the University of Sheffield, the Royal School Library and Information Science, Copenhagen, and Research Fellow with the School of Information Studies, Charles Sturt University. Paul's research focusses on enterprise information management and consumer information systems; most particularly on the challenges that present at the interface between consumers and organisations as the conditions for information management change in the digital economy. He approaches his research from the interpretive tradition and is enthusiastic about the use of methods for qualitative content analysis that inform our understanding of digital networks and the changing dimensions of documenting society digitally.

Shanks, Graeme: Graeme Shanks is a Professorial Fellow in the Department of Computing and Information Systems at the University of Melbourne. His research interests include business analytics, the implementation and impact of information systems, data quality, conceptual modelling and case study research in information systems. Graeme has published widely in information systems journals and conferences. He is a Senior Editor of the *Journal of Information Technology*. Prior to becoming an academic, Graeme worked for a number of years as programmer, programmer-analyst and project leader in several large organisations.

Sheard, Judithe: Associate Professor Judithe (Judy) Sheard is Head of the Faculty of Information Technology at the Caulfield campus. She is Vice Chair of the ACM Special Interest Group in Computer Science Education. Her areas of research activity include pedagogical and epistemological issues in the use of educational technology; educational use of Web 2.0; teaching and learning of programming; plagiarism in tertiary education; and promoting knowledge of the history of computing. An active member of the international computing education research community, she has designed and taught quantitative research methods courses to doctoral students and chaired doctoral consortiums in several countries.

Tanner, Kerry: Dr Kerry Tanner has been an information management educator (senior lecturer) and researcher in the Monash University Faculty of Information Technology (IT) since 2000. Prior to that she lectured at RMIT (1979–1999) and at Melbourne State College (1977–1978). Her teaching fields have encompassed most areas of the information management curriculum, including research methods. Research projects she has undertaken have utilised both quantitative and qualitative methods, for instance, surveys of information professionals' continuing professional development, secondary students' and tertiary students' library usage habits, managers' information needs, and organisations' IT outsourcing practices. She has undertaken qualitative research in the fields of knowledge management and community informatics.

Thompson, Kim M.: Dr Kim M. Thompson is a Senior Lecturer in the School of Information Studies at Charles Sturt University. Her areas of teaching and research interest include information poverty, information cultures, and international information access issues. She has published a book about digital inclusion along with many articles about digital governance, information management, information poverty, and social-cultural influences on access. She earned a Bachelor's degree in English at Brigham Young University and received both her Master's and Doctorate of Library and Information Studies from Florida State University.

Weber, Ron: Ron Weber is Emeritus Professor at Monash University and a part-time professor at The University of Queensland. In 2013, he was Pro Vice-Chancellor of Monash South Africa, and from 2004–2012 he was Dean, Faculty of Information Technology, Monash University. Prior to joining Monash University, he was Professor of Information Systems and Research Director in the Faculty of Business, Economics and Law at The University of Queensland. Ron has held visiting appointments at the University of Alberta, University of British Columbia, City University of Hong Kong, University of Minnesota, Nanyang Technological

University (Singapore), New York University, and University of Otago, New Zealand. From 2002–2004, he was Editor-in-Chief of the *MIS Quarterly*. He has had a longstanding interest in the 'sciences of the artificial' and the ways they have motivated the emergence of design-science research methods.

Williamson, Kirsty: Dr (Christina) Kirsty Williamson is an adjunct senior research fellow at Monash University and Charles Sturt University in Australia. For many years she was the Director of the research group, Information and Telecommunications Needs Research (ITNR), a joint initiative of both universities. Since the early 1990s she has undertaken many research projects, with her principal area of research being human information behaviour. Her research has been funded by a range of different organisations including the principal funding body of Australian Universities, the Australian Research Council (ARC). As well as two editions of an earlier research methods book, *Research Methods for Students, Academics and Professionals: Information Management and Systems*, she has many journal articles to her credit, including five in the highly ranked *Library & Information Science Research*.

Foreword

Let me begin with an important self-disclosure: I am a methodologist. I have devoted much of my career to the exploration of research practice, alongside my research focus on individuals' information behaviours. Having served as Director of the International Institute for Qualitative Methodology, having edited *The Sage Encyclopedia of Qualitative Research Methods* (2008), having written *100 Questions (and Answers) About Qualitative Research* (Sage, 2016), and having received the Association for Library and Information Science Education (ALISE) Best Methodology Paper award on two separate occasions, I consider myself to be a methods geek. And yet, I have been searching – for years – for an inclusive, thoughtful and balanced resource that would address key issues in information science research practice. For many years, I taught graduate-level subjects in research methods, advised dozens of PhD and Masters thesis students, and guided other students and information science practitioners on the appropriate ways to conceptualise, design and implement their research. I also hosted a round-table discussion for many years at the ALISE Annual Conference, where scholars who are engaged in the teaching of research methods (including thesis supervision) can discuss the joys and struggles of this task. In talking to my colleagues at other institutions, around the globe, I see that we have all struggled with this same challenge, that is, finding an appropriate, all-in-one resource addressing research issues specific to the discipline.

At long last I have found just the resource!

Now, I know what you're thinking. Yes, there are a number of existing resources that find their ways onto syllabi or are referenced by information science scholars in their work (such as Vaughan's (2001) *Statistical Methods for the Information Professional*, Pickard's (2013) *Research Methods in Information* or Connaway and Radford (2016) *Research Methods in Library and Information Science*). However, many of these are limited in particular ways and not always appropriate for general discussions of research practice. Finding a resource that addresses both quantitative and qualitative paradigms, appropriately, can be a struggle. Similarly, many of the available research-related texts are focussed on introductory-level skills, with little in-depth examination of the key issues at play in contemporary information science research. Other texts may address the 'library' context, with little attention paid to the range of diverse contexts that shape our research. A number of resources also focus on practitioner-researchers, with little guidance for academic staff working in universities. Finally, it is important to note that many of the available texts used in the discipline provide little in the way of research examples drawn from the writers' own research; here, the authors have included copious references to their own research projects and data, making this a unique contribution to the field.

The book that you are about to read provides a fresh perspective on research in information science. In the sections that follow I will walk through the goals and intentions of the book, addressing some of the key decisions that informed its design. There is something for everyone here — whether you are new to research in the discipline, or whether you are a seasoned scholar, looking for new and inspiring ideas. Enjoy!

What will you find in this book?

Dr Kirsty Williamson published two previous editions of a research methods book, focused on information management and systems (2000 & 2002). In 2013, came her new research methods book, titled *Research Methods: Information, Systems, and Contexts*, with Monash University's Associate Professor Graeme Johanson as co-editor, published by Tilde University Press. Now they have an updated and expanded edition of this book, with a new publisher.

The editors (who reviewed each chapter, carefully and in-depth) are highly experienced and accomplished academics in Australia, working at Monash University's Faculty of Information Technology. Dr Williamson is also an adjunct senior researcher in the School of Information Studies at Charles Sturt University. Although the book follows Australian spelling conventions, the content is universal; information science researchers working in Canada, the United Kingdom, the United States, Sweden and other countries will find that this book addresses key issues of interest to us all. That said, readers may find that terms used to represent specific subfields of study (such as 'information management' or 'information systems') reflect the authors' own training and geography. We continue to struggle with the labels we give to specific areas of study within the discipline, so readers are encouraged to consider this context when reviewing specific terms.

Although the structure of the earlier books has been maintained (i.e., separating methods from techniques), the chapters in this new edition present updated versions of works that were first crafted in 2013. The end result is a diverse range of information science perspectives (including, for example, archives, records, information management, librarianship) and an equally diverse authorship. The chapters generally focus on social sciences approaches to research practice, with some humanities influences (e.g., discourse analysis) — in keeping with the nature of the discipline — and with some interesting areas of overlap, and difference, among the approaches. The editors have also included a comprehensive index to guide readers through specific topics and people discussed across the various chapters, as well as a very useful glossary of key terms. Each chapter was reviewed by a content expert in the discipline, in addition to the editors' own thorough review of the material. This new edition includes a new chapter that explores the future of information research in the three interconnecting fields; here, a team of six authors has worked together to explore future research methodologies, including the influence of 'big data', the impact of cultural differences on future research, the relationship of research to professional practice, and other issues and topics that will feature prominently in years to come.

One significant area of difference, worth noting, between the chapters is in the area of terminology. The terms used to describe research practice are contested across all social sciences, sciences, health and humanities disciplines — and information science is no different. In reading through this collection, it is important to keep this in mind, to guide your way through the content. One of the great struggles for researchers is to identify the conceptual differences between epistemology, paradigm, methodology, method, technique, and many other key terms. One of my favourite resources in this regard is Michael Crotty's *The Foundations of Social Research* (1998). Crotty defined the differences in this way:

- *Methods:* the techniques or procedures used to gather and analyse data related to some research question or hypothesis.

- *Methodology*: the strategy, plan of action, process or design lying behind the choice and use of particular methods and linking the choice and use of methods to the desired outcomes.

- *Theoretical perspective*: the philosophical stance informing the methodology and thus providing a context for the process and grounding its logic and criteria.

- *Epistemology*: the theory of knowledge embedded in the theoretical perspective and thereby in the methodology (Crotty, 1998, p. 3).

Others have defined these concepts in similar ways (see, e.g., Schensul, 2008a; Schensul, 2008b). However, the labels used to represent these concepts are not applied consistently in research publications. One's discipline, research training and geography will have an impact on how concepts are defined and labelled. Researchers and students must find their own paths through the terminology landscape as they read the literature and engage in their work, no matter the discipline. Indeed, Williamson and Johanson suggest that readers think about the terms in these ways as they read through each chapter:

- *Methodology*: theory of method; a set of principles of methods. Methodology is the entire framework or design of the research: the choice of paradigm, methods, and tools or techniques to explore research questions and make knowledge claims.

- *Research method*: provides a design for undertaking research, which is underpinned with theoretical explanation of its value and use. Techniques for data gathering and sample selection, as well as processing and interpreting data, are usually included as part of this design.
- *Research technique*: is a procedure or tool for undertaking research processes, e.g., selecting samples, collecting and analysing data.

In reviewing these concepts, you may find that Crotty's (1998) notions of 'epistemology' and 'theoretical perspective' are closely aligned to this collection's use of the term 'methodology'. Similarly, Crotty's term 'methodology' is comparable to the 'research method' label used here, while his term 'methods' is aligned to what Williamson and Johanson call 'research technique'. Although many of my students and colleagues have struggled to make sense of these terms over the years, I find the opportunities for dialogue around the concepts underlying these labels to be well worth the struggle.

These terms are also important to note in relation to the structure of the book, as specific techniques (such as individual interviews) can be used with a number of different methods. Similarly, other terms (such as grounded theory, discourse analysis or participant observation) can be regarded as methods and/or techniques. Chapters included in this volume should not be considered as 'blueprints' for specific methods or techniques or the definitive word on terminology. Given the word length that authors were encouraged to respect, the chapters best serve as a key starting point for specific approaches to research practice, with many examples included. Readers will certainly want to explore each of these in more depth, supplementing the content presented here with the hundreds of handbooks, guides and other research resources that have been published across disciplines. Overall, the contextualisation of each research approach within the discipline of information science makes each of these chapters an ideal overview of the key issues to consider in engaging in specific techniques, methods, methodologies and paradigms in the field. With each chapter readers will find an extensive list of references to guide further reading on the specific topics.

In considering the readings that are referenced here it is also worth noting that the editors have (rightly) taken the view that it is important to include some older material when discussing research practice. Some research methods fundamentals do not change over time. In this volume you will find some foundational work by key figures (e.g., Spradley, 1979, 1980), including some of the interesting dialogues and debates that have had a tremendous influence on shaping research practice (e.g., Denzin & Lincoln, 1994).

Chapter overviews

In approaching the reading of this collection of research chapters, let's return for a moment to the structure. The book is generally organised in a logical (some might say, linear) fashion, starting with key foundational concepts, running through the implementation of research projects, and closing with topics related to dissemination. In this way, the book is quite a straightforward read, leading scholars through the typical progress of the research enterprise. The first section includes five chapters on 'foundations and framing'. The first two chapters (Williamson) discuss key concepts and steps in the research process (from exploring the meaning of 'epistemology', to understanding how to create 'hypotheses'). The last three chapters group the subfields of the discipline into three distinct areas: 1) information research (Johanson and Williamson), which examines key topics in library and information studies (such as information literacy and information behaviour); 2) archives and records research (Sue McKemmish, Monash University and Anne Gilliland, University of California, Los Angeles), which provides a brief history of these areas of work in the past 25 years; and 3) information systems and knowledge management (Dubravka Cecez-Kecmanovic, University of New South Wales and Mary Anne Kennan, Charles Sturt University), which examines the methodological landscape of these areas. Although some readers may take issue with how the subfields have been grouped (and will note that the subfields covered here are not exhaustive), the three chapters work as a complementary set, providing a very comprehensive picture of much of the research across information science.

The next section presents an overview of key 'research methods' (or 'methodologies', to use Crotty's (1998) terminology). Here, you will find chapters on survey designs (Kerry Tanner, Monash University), case study (Graeme Shanks, University of Melbourne and Nargiza Bekmamedova, Embry-Riddle Aeronautical University Asia), action research (Williamson), constructivist grounded theory (James Herring, Charles Sturt University), bibliometrics (Gaby Haddow, Curtin University), design-science (Ron Weber, Monash University), historical research (Johanson), ethnography (Williamson) and experimental research (Tanner).

The five chapters that follow explore various topics related to 'data collection and data analysis' across the quantitative and qualitative paradigms. Dr Williamson has authored three of these chapters, demonstrating her expertise in many areas of research technique: populations and samples; questionnaires, interviews and focus groups; and, observation. The fourth chapter focusses, specifically, on quantitative analysis (Judithe Sheard, Monash University), while the fifth chapter explores qualitative analysis. This last chapter brings Kirsty Williamson, myself, and my colleague at Swinburne University of Technology, Paul Scifleet, together to explore qualitative analysis, generally, as well as content analysis and discourse analysis, specifically.

The fourth section, of the book is titled 'research practice and communication'. Here, three chapters explore ethical research practices (Johanson), research data management (Kennan), dissemination (Kennan and Thompson, Charles Sturt University). These chapters ground the discussion in many of the key decisions that researchers must make about their own practices.

The final section of the book reflects on the past and future of research methods in a totally new chapter as well as in the 'concluding reflections', updated from the first edition. In the new chapter (Williamson, Johanson, Byrne, Given, Kennan, and Oliver), there is also some reflection on the past because, as we know, the past affects the future. While the authors do not claim to have a crystal ball, they have examined emerging trends to take an educated guess about what the future may hold. In his 'Concluding Reflections: The Research Journey', Professor Emeritus Donald Schauder (Monash University) notes that the book is designed to guide information science researchers "to undertake the kind of research that extends understanding of how information, the very 'stuff' of communicative action and memory, influences individuals and social collectivities large and small".

Researchers and practitioners alike will find their research questions and approaches reflected in these pages, with the certainty of something new for everyone. The end result is an engaging set of chapters that will challenge your thinking about the information science discipline, the research we have done in the past, and our research agendas – and practices – for the future.

Lisa M. Given
Swinburne University of Technology, Australia

References

Connaway, L. S., & Radford, M. L. (2016). *Research methods in library and information science* (6th ed.). Santa Barbara, CA: Libraries Unlimited.

Crotty, M. (1998). *The foundations of social research.* London: Sage Publications.

Denzin, N. K., & Lincoln, Y. S. (1994). *The handbook of qualitative research.* Thousand Oaks, CA: Sage.

Given, L. M. (2016). *100 questions (and answers) about qualitative research.* Thousand Oaks, CA: Sage.

Given, L. M. (Ed.). (2008). *The Sage encyclopedia of qualitative research methods.* Thousand Oaks, CA: Sage.

Pickard, A. J. (2013). *Research methods in information* (2nd ed.). London: Facet.

Schensul, J. (2008a). Methodology. In L. M. Given (Ed.), *The Sage encyclopedia of qualitative research methods* (pp. 517–522). Thousand Oaks, CA: Sage.

Schensul, J. (2008b). Methods. In L. M. Given (Ed.), *The Sage encyclopedia of qualitative research methods* (pp. 522–527). Thousand Oaks, CA: Sage.

Spradley, J. P. (1979). *The ethnographic interview.* New York: Holt, Rhinehart & Winston.

Spradley, J. P. (1980). *Participant observation.* New York: Holt, Rhinehart & Winston.

Vaughan, L. (2001). *Statistical methods for the information professional: A practical, painless approach to understanding, using and interpreting statistics.* Medford, NJ: Information Today.

Williamson, K. (Ed.). (2000). *Research methods for students and professionals: Information management and systems.* Wagga Wagga, NSW: Centre for Information Studies, Charles Sturt University.

Williamson, K. (Ed.). (2002). *Research methods for students, academics and professionals: Information management and systems* (2nd ed.). Wagga Wagga, NSW: Centre for Information Studies, Charles Sturt University.

Williamson, K., & Johanson, G. (Eds.). (2013). *Research methods: Information, systems and contexts.* Prahran, VIC: Tilde University Press.

Section I

Foundations and Framing

In this section, Chapters 1–5 introduce the frameworks and concepts for thinking about research, including major philosophies and their associated paradigms. The fundamentals of research planning, including the iterative steps required, are also discussed. Introductions to research in the three discipline areas covered by the book provide a major contribution in this section.

Chapter 1

Research concepts

Kirsty Williamson

Monash University and Charles Sturt University, Australia

This chapter explores the major philosophical debates in the research field, and introduces and explains key research terms and concepts. A major argument is that an understanding of 'methodology', not only methods and techniques, is important for researchers. The major philosophical traditions discussed are positivism and interpretivism, which can also be described as umbrella paradigms that encompass, firstly, positivist and post-positivist paradigms, and, secondly, constructivist and phenomenological paradigms. The critical theory paradigm, although more closely associated with interpretivism, is discussed separately. Other strands to the chapter include an exploration of the ways in which the term, qualitative research, has been applied; and a discussion of the concept of mixed methods research.

Research Methods: Information, Systems, and Contexts. DOI: http://dx.doi.org/10.1016/B978-0-08-102220-7.00001-7

Introduction

It is important to understand that there is a range of ways of conceptualising the foundations of research. I believe that understanding the ways in which research is not only conducted, but also conceptualised, is important and rewarding. Doing so yourself will make you aware of the implication of the methods choices you make and will provide you with deeper insight for understanding the implications of your research findings. You will thus be able to think in terms of 'research methodology', not just methods and techniques or tools. *Methodology*, the theory of method, implies making theoretical research choices, which this chapter sets out to help you do. The term is often misused in that many researchers "collapse methodology into methods" (Dervin, 2005, p. 26). Methodology is the entire framework or design of the research: the choice of paradigm, methods and tools or techniques to explore research questions and to create new knowledge.

You may find the variety of approaches to be daunting at first, especially because the use of terminology is fluid. Nevertheless, as I said in my research methods book (Williamson, 2002, p. 38), it is important for researchers to accept, and deal with, the fluidity and rich diversity of terminology and approaches. Case and Given (2016) provide a useful discussion, highlighting terminological and conceptual issues particularly with regard to information seeking research, including information needs and information behaviour.

The following discussion is intended to present research concepts simply and clearly. Should you want to delve deeply, and consider multiple viewpoints, I recommend *The Handbook of Qualitative Research* (1994 & 2000) and *The Sage Handbook of Qualitative Research* (2005 & 2011), all edited by Denzin and Lincoln.[1] Each of the editions is very different and warrants scrutiny (by the undaunted!) in its own right. The changes in thinking over time, especially of the editors themselves, are also interesting. *Sage Research Methods Online* is also a useful resource but you will need to access it through your academic library.

Williamson, Burstein and McKemmish (2002) discussed the two major philosophies or traditions of research, labelled *positivist* and *interpretivist* (also written as *interpretive*), which are also sometimes referred to as 'paradigms'. This is the dichotomous approach where the labels represent opposing groups each believing that theirs is the only reliable means of acquiring knowledge about social phenomena. However, in the third edition of *The Sage Handbook of Qualitative Research*, Denzin and Lincoln (2005) talked about all research being 'interpretive', that is, "it is guided by the researcher's set of beliefs and feelings

---

[1] The chapters in each of these tomes are reprinted in three-volume paperback editions a few years after the original publication. The reprint volumes are titled: *The Landscape of Qualitative Research: Theories and Issues; Strategies of Inquiry;* and *Collecting and Interpreting Qualitative Materials.*

about the world and how it should be understood and studied" (p. 22). In other words, all research is guided by beliefs about *ontology* and *epistemology*. Ontology is defined in Chapter 5: *The methodological landscape* as "the nature and existence of social reality". In research terms, it "refers to the claims or assumptions that a particular approach to social enquiry makes about the nature of social reality – claims about what exists, what it looks like, what units make it up and how these units interact with each other" (Blaikie, 1993, p. 6). It is important to note here that the assumptions under discussion are based on the social world as being different from the physical world, the domain of science.

The two major positions within ontology are termed *realist* and *nominalist* (Neuman, 2014). According to Neuman, "a realist assumes that the 'real world' exists independently of humans and their interpretations of it", while the *critical realist* takes precautions to control the effect of interpretations on the grounds of their modified position "that it is not easy to capture reality directly" as it can "easily become distorted or muddied" (p. 94). At the other end of the spectrum, the nominalist believes that experience of the so-called real world "is always occurring through a lens or scheme of interpretations and inner subjectivity" (p. 94). The epistemological function is rooted in ontological assumptions. Epistemology is the theory of knowledge; a concern with what constitutes knowledge and how knowledge is formed.

This chapter focusses principally on research and theoretical concepts. A glossary is included later in the book.

Research paradigms

Denzin and Lincoln (2005, p. 22) suggested that "the net that contains the researcher's epistemological, ontological, and methodological premises may be termed a *paradigm* or an interpretive framework". A much cited definition of the key term paradigm is that it is "a set of interrelated assumptions about the social world which provides a philosophical and conceptual framework for the systematic study of that world" (Kuhn, 1970, p. 10). Bates (2005) saw meta-theory as closely related to this definition of paradigm: "Metatheory can be seen as the philosophy behind the theory, the fundamental set of ideas about how phenomena of interest in a particular field should be thought about and researched" (p. 2).[2] The major research paradigms used in the fields under discussion in this book are positivism, post-positivism, interpretivism and critical theory. Interpretivism is considered here as an umbrella paradigm, encompassing a range of other paradigms. Critical theory also involves a complex range of

---

[2] Bates (1999) has characterised information science as a meta-field. Her discussion of this, along with the associated concept of the 'double hermeneutic' (Giddens, 1984), are discussed in Chapter 4: *Archival and recordkeeping research: Past, present and future.*

approaches, for example, critical feminist and postmodern. As implied above, the positivist and interpretivist traditions of research have, by and large, been considered to be very different; in fact, dichotomous, with debate about them having taken place since at least the mid-nineteenth century (Hammersley, 1992, p. 39). Now the boundaries are not always seen as clear-cut. As also implied above, the debate is fundamentally *epistemological*, which means that it is concerned with questions such as: 'What constitutes knowledge?' and 'How is knowledge formed?'

Reasoning styles

Before discussing positivism and interpretivism, it is necessary to examine two different styles of reasoning, 'deductive' and 'inductive'. The former is broadly associated with the scientific, or positivist, approach to research; the latter with interpretivist approaches. The examples, below, are slightly modified from those used in my earlier research methods book, in the chapter by Williamson *et al.* (2002, pp. 26–27).

Deductive reasoning is linked with the hypothesis-testing approach to research. With deductive reasoning, the argument moves from general principles to particular instances. An example is as follows:

1. People who are aged 60 and over are less likely than younger people to be users of the internet.
2. Tom Carter is aged 75.
3. Therefore Tom Carter is less likely than someone aged 25 to be a user of the internet.

In this example (a syllogism), the first two statements are the premises, and include a general and a specific statement. The third statement, or conclusion, is specific. The truth of the premises guarantees the truth of the conclusion. Positivist researchers often deduce hypotheses from the literature for testing in their studies.

Inductive reasoning begins with particular instances and concludes with general statements or principles. An example is: *Tom Carter, Jim Brown and Pam Eliot, who are all aged 60 and over, are not users of the internet.* If there were many other instances which were identical and only a few that were not, it could be concluded: *People who are aged 60 and over are unlikely to be users of the internet.*

Inductive reasoning is associated with the generation of hypotheses and also of theory of a more complex nature, as occurs in grounded theory. With the inductive approach, field work and observations occur initially and hypotheses, or theory, are developed. Thus if the data were to show that a large majority of people aged 60 and over were not using the internet (in comparison with those aged under 60), it could be hypothesised that, at this time, *older people (60 aged and over) are less likely than younger people (aged under 60) to be users of the internet.* If it were also found that there were variations according to a range of factors and/or contexts, theory might be generated to help understand these findings and as a basis for further research.

Positivism

The term *positivist* was first used in 1830 by the philosopher Comte, one of the founding fathers of sociology. Later, in the 1920s, a brand of positivism known as logical positivism was developed by a group of scholars known as the Vienna circle, members of which moved to the USA in the 1930s. Proclaiming the benefits of science, seen as 'value-free' (Cecez-Kecmanovic, 2011), this group began the movement to apply scientific research methods to the social sciences. Like scientific researchers, positivist researchers seek to link cause and effect (Dick, 1991, p. 232) and consider that knowledge can only be based on what can be observed and experienced (empiricism).

Positivists, also sometimes referred to as 'rationalists' (Guba, 1981) or 'realists' (as discussed above), believe that there is a 'reality', or truth, to be discovered. In order to make this discovery, 'measurement' and 'objectivity' are key positivist tenets. The focus is on quantitative data, deductive reasoning and generalisability or "the extent to which the findings and conclusions of one particular study can be applied to other similar situations or settings or the population at large" (Gilliland & McKemmish, 2004, p. 172). Positivist researchers usually begin with theories and models, single out certain variables for study and predict their relationships by framing hypotheses which are then tested. The assumption is that researchers are independent of the subjects or objects of their inquiry (Guba, 1981, p. 77). Generalisations, "enduring truth statements that are context free" (Guba, 1981, p. 77), are eventually made.

The positivist approach combines "deductive logic with precise empirical observations of individual behaviour in order to discover and confirm a set of probabilistic causal laws that can be used to predict general patterns of human activity" (Neuman, 2014, p. 97). This search for general laws, central to the positivist approach, is termed *nomothetic*, which means literally "pertaining to the search for general laws" (*Macquarie Dictionary*, 1987, p. 1158). The elements of the process of positivist research, as illustrated in Figure 1.1, combine mostly in a linear manner (except in the earlier stages).

The aim of positivist researchers is to verify their hypotheses (Guba & Lincoln, 2005, p. 196). This is despite the stance of Popper (1959), originally writing in 1934, who emphasised that hypotheses can only be refuted with certainty; they can only be considered true as long as they are not proven to be false. It is best, nevertheless, to take the approach that hypotheses and theories are **supported** by the data, **not** proved. The required degree of 'proof' – to use a legal dictum – is the balance of probabilities, rather than beyond reasonable doubt. Connaway and Powell (2010, pp. 47–60) provide a detailed discussion of the processes involved in the positivist research process, which they refer to as the scientific method.

Common positivist research designs are 'experimental design', with its emphasis on cause and effect, and 'survey', which must be carried out according to scientific principles. For example, the sample must be randomly selected according to the scientific definition: where each element in the sample must have an equal and independent chance of being included. Also important are the principles of validity and reliability. The former is concerned with accuracy of various kinds. For example, *internal validity* refers to the extent to which a research instrument measures what it is designed to measure. *External validity* refers to the extent to which findings are generalisable. *Reliability* is concerned with obtaining consistent, stable research results when the study is repeated, that is with replication. Connaway and Powell (2010, pp. 60–67) discuss these concepts in considerable depth.

Figure 1.1 Positivist research process

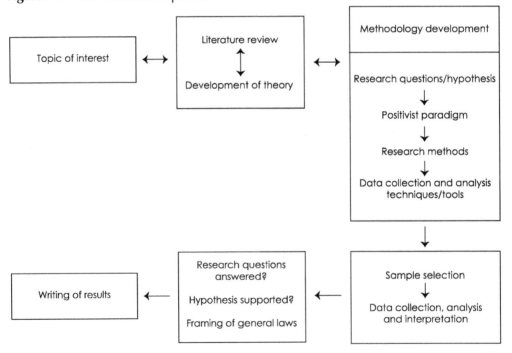

Post-positivism

Although *post-positivists* assume that reality exists, in keeping with the 'critical realist' position they believe it is not easy to discover. This is because "only partially objective accounts of the world can be produced, for all methods for examining such accounts are flawed" (Denzin & Lincoln, 2005, p. 27). Post-positivists therefore believe that reality must be subjected to the widest possible critical examination. Qualitative methods are seen as important in achieving this goal. Research methods involve the use of more natural settings and the soliciting of *emic* (or insider) views, as opposed to a reliance on outsider or the *etic* perspective. While post-positivists develop hypotheses, they sometimes use propositions instead. Propositions are broad statements drawn from theory or "a theoretical statement that two or more factors or concepts are related and the type of relationship it is" (Neuman, 2014, p. 68), A proposition may be considered by some researchers as sufficient for comparison with empirical evidence or data. Other researchers might prefer to use hypotheses which are more specifically formulated statements that are empirically testable. The now frequently-used term, 'knowledge claim', appears to be in tune with the opinion of Popper, discussed above: non-falsified hypotheses are considered "probable facts or laws" (Guba & Lincoln, 2005, p. 196), in other words, a claim for the time being. Post-positivism has some similarities with interpretivist perspectives (discussed below).

If you are interested in understanding the post-positivist approach further, Wildemuth (2009) provides two examples of post-positivist research.

Interpretivism: Its paradigms and research designs

Interpretivism, which I labelled an 'umbrella term' in my first research methods book, receives lengthier discussion here than positivism. This is because there are a number of approaches, also often labelled as *paradigms*, fitting within the ambit of the broader paradigm, interpretivism, also referred to as the naturalistic inquiry paradigm (Guba, 1981). These include constructivism and phenomenology, both of which are discussed further below. To add to the confusion, Denzin and Lincoln (2005, p. 22) discussed constructivism rather than interpretivism as one of their four major paradigms, the others being positivism, post-positivism and critical theory. In my first research methods book, I treated *critical theory* as a paradigm within the interpretivist umbrella. This time critical theory will be treated as a paradigm in its own right, the more common approach in the literature.

Emerging from hermeneutics, an intellectual tradition concerned originally with the interpretation of texts but later of social life, all interpretivist approaches share an interest in the meanings and experiences of human being. Since the central tenet of interpretivism is that people are constantly involved in interpreting their ever-changing world, researchers who are interpretivists believe that the social world is constructed by people (the nominalist position) and is therefore different from the world of nature. They favour *naturalistic inquiry* (where field work usually takes place in a natural setting), embrace an inductive style of reasoning, emphasise qualitative data and are aware of the impact of context.

Because of their belief in the role played by people, the key task of interpretivist researchers is to come to understand how the various participants in a social setting construct their world (Glesne & Peshkin, 1992, p. 6). As recognised by interpretivists, people invariably have different perspectives which means that researchers need to learn to deal with what are referred to as 'multiple realities'. Guba and Lincoln (1981) described the latter as the layers of an onion, nesting within or complementing each other: "Each layer provides a different perspective of reality, and none can be considered more 'true' than any other" (p. 57). These multiple realities are gauged through an exploration of the beliefs, feelings and interpretations of research participants, who are also sometimes referred to as actors. In contrast to the positivist approach, interpretivists espouse the view that researchers and participants are interrelated, with each influencing each other (Guba, 1981, p. 77). This is in keeping with Giddens' (1984) view:

> For their part, lay actors are social theorists, whose theories help to constitute the activities and institutions that are the object of study of specialized social observers or social scientists. There is no clear dividing line between informed sociological reflection carried on by lay actors and similar endeavours on the part of specialists. I do not want to deny that there are dividing lines, but they are inevitably fuzzy, and social scientists have no absolute monopoly either upon innovative theories or upon empirical investigations of what they study (Giddens, 1984, pp. xxxii-xxxiii).

Giddens' suggestion of the 'blurring of boundaries' between lay actor and social scientists has implications for the traditional constructs of 'researcher' and 'researched'. These are particularly addressed by participatory action research (see Chapter 8: *Action research*) and postmodern approaches to ethnography, for example, autoethnography (see Chapter 13).

Good interpretivist researchers are aware that there can be difficulties in understanding fully the perspectives of others very different from themselves. Glesne and Peshkin (1992) discussed this problem at length, also examining the impact of postmodernism.

> The researcher becomes the main research instrument as he or she observes, asks questions and interacts with research participants. The concern with researcher objectivity is replaced by a focus on the impact of subjectivity on the research process. ... [Postmodernists look] carefully for ways in which the historical and cultural context shapes the researcher's preconceptions. Postmodernists are particularly concerned with issues of 'intersubjectivity', that is, how researcher and researched affect each other (pp. 6 & 10).

As Sutton (1993, p. 423) pointed out: "one can understand something observed only through the tinted lens of one's own experience." He saw the fact that the researcher inevitably has a point of view as a strength, as a source of insight and understanding, as long as there is an awareness of it (p. 425).

Good interpretivist researchers therefore record the perspectives of participants as accurately as possible, sometimes providing them with some opportunity to comment on what has been recorded about them (referred to as 'member checking'). They then "develop concepts, insights and understanding from patterns in the data" (Reneker, 1993, p. 499), attempting not to allow "initial interpretations to overly confine analytical possibilities" (Patton, 2015, p. 524). There is an assumption that generalisations are not possible, the aim being to develop *idiographic* knowledge, focussing on differences as much as similarities in perspectives, "the consensus and the dissonance" (Williamson 2006, p. 131). For further discussion of the issue of generalisations in interpretivist research, see Chapter 15: *Populations and samples*.

A rigorous process developed for this kind of inductive research is *grounded theory* where theory is built literally from the ground upwards, that is, from the data of participants. Original proponents of grounded theory were Glaser and Strauss (1967). Much later, a constructivist approach to grounded theory was developed (Charmaz, 2014) and is discussed in Chapter 9: *Constructivist grounded theory.*

Other interpretivist methods include ethnography and phenomenography, the former of which, in its many variations, is discussed in Chapter 13: *Ethnographic research. Ethnography* or *participant observation* is a key method used by interpretivists. Originally developed by anthropologists for the study of culture, it has now been adapted by some researchers to encompass a range of techniques to enable rich description of the views, experiences and behaviour of research participants (Bow, 2002). Techniques used by ethnographers include interviews – individual and focus group – observation, and examination of documents. As Saule (2002, pp. 184–185) stated, ethnography is validated through triangulation – the use of multiple methods and theoretical constructs to add rigour, breadth and depth to a study.

Phenomenography, according to Edwards (2007, p. 88, citing a combination of Marton, 1988, p. 179 and Marton, 1986, p. 31), is "a research method adopted for mapping the qualitatively different ways in which people experience, conceptualise, perceive, and understand various aspects of, and phenomena in, the world around them". Edwards pointed out that it is not individual experiences that matter, but rather "the collective experiences of the group who are considered in an attempt to find the distinctly different ways of seeing the experience" (p. 88). A description of a phenomenographic study is included as one of the examples of methodology in Chapter 2: *The fundamentals of research planning.*

Interpretivist paradigms

The interpretivist paradigms discussed here are constructivism (personal construct theory and social constructionism) and phenomenology.

Constructivism

One of several interpretivist paradigms, constructivism is concerned with the ways in which people construct their worlds. Constructivist researchers investigate constructions or meanings about broad concepts such as cultural values; or more specific issues or ideas, for example, the possible ingredients of the dynamic, creative public library of the future and how to create it. They commonly use ethnographic techniques, such as interviews and observation. There are two major constructivist approaches, one focussing on individual, personal constructions; the other on shared meanings or social constructions. It is important to note the slightly different labels usually applied, viz., personal *constructivists* and social *constructionists*, with the umbrella term for both being *constructivist*.

Personal constructivists, of whom Kelly (1963) was an early and key exemplar, believe people make sense of their world on an individual basis, that is, they personally construct reality, with each person's reality differing to some extent from another person's. Some later cognitive researchers in the information-seeking field are theoretically closest to this form of constructivism. They were those who moved beyond study of external, observable behaviour to try to understand individuals from their own points of view. Brenda Dervin's 'sense making' theory, for example, Dervin (1992) and Dervin and Nilan (1986), are examples. Carol Kuhlthau (2004) is a prominent researcher in the library and information studies/science (LIS) field.

Social constructionists place emphasis on people developing meanings for their activities together, that is, socially constructing reality, as analysed in the famous book, *The Social Construction of Reality* (Berger & Luckman, 1967). Shared meanings are seen to be developed through social processes involving people, language and religion. According to Schwandt (2000, p. 197), "we do not construct our interpretations in isolation but against a backdrop of shared understandings, practices, language, and so forth". Language is considered very important as "we produce and organise social reality together by using language" (Talja, Tuominen & Savolainen, 2005, p. 89).

Constructivist grounded theory is a method linked to the constructivist paradigm. It was developed by Charmaz (2003 & 2014) who postulated that, unlike the original grounded theory, constructivist grounded theory is not 'objectivist'. In keeping with the view that the social world is constructed by people, it "recognises that the viewer creates the data and ensuing analysis through interaction with the viewed" and therefore the data do not provide a window on an objective reality (Charmaz, 2003, p. 273). Thus, there is recognition that researchers' backgrounds will influence their interpretations of the data. They cannot avoid being influenced by 'disciplinary emphases' and 'perceptual proclivities' (p. 259). There is "acceptance that researchers shape their data collection and redirect their analysis as new issues emerge" (p. 271).

Phenomenology

Although phenomenology has seldom been used in information research, it is an important philosophical approach because of its influence on the general interpretivist proposition that individuals interpret phenomena.

Like phenomenography, phenomenology has human experience as its object but, whereas the former is an empirical method for exploring the different ways in which people experience phenomena, phenomenology is philosophically based, supposedly penetrating the essences of human experiences by focussing on phenomena or the "things themselves" (Sutton, 1993, p. 414). It "aims to capture the richness of experience, the fullness of all the ways in which a person experiences and describes the phenomena of interest" (Marton & Booth, 1997, p. 117). According to Marton and Booth, the founder of modern phenomenology, Edmund Husserl, saw it as "logically preceding the empirical sciences, aimed at clarifying their experiential foundations" (p. 117). Husserl set out "to investigate the structures of consciousness that make it possible to apprehend an empirical world" (Holstein & Gubrium, 2005, p. 485).

Patton (2015) emphasised that phenomenology requires the description, explication, and interpretation of experience: "There is no separate (or objective) reality for people. There is only what they know their experience is and means. The subjective experience incorporates the objective thing and a person's reality" (p. 116).

Smith, Flowers and Larkins (2009) provide a useful introduction to phenomenology in both a theoretical and practical sense as attested by Gorichanaz (2015) who used interpretative phenomenological analysis as a key component of his research design for information research. Gorichanaz's work is interesting in that it also draws on autoethnography which will be discussed in Chapter 13.

Interpretivist research designs

The need to be open and responsive to the setting as well as the participants involved in their studies, means that interpretivist researchers are much less linear in their approach than are positivist researchers. Interpretivist research designs are mainly based on inductive reasoning and tend to be *iterative,* with various elements in the research being interwoven: the development of one influences decisions about the others. The literature review is still usually developed for background understanding of the topic and some tentative theory may be considered by researchers without imposing pre-existing expectations. Research questions are developed, although they will usually be less specific and more flexible than in a positivist study, allowing for adjustment if new insights emerge as data are collected and analysed. Data analysis takes place on an on-going basis, not just at the conclusion of the study. Figure 1.2 illustrates the interpretivist research process, emphasising the interconnectedness especially within the sample selection/data collection/data analysis/theory development stage.

Figure 1.2 Interpretivist research process

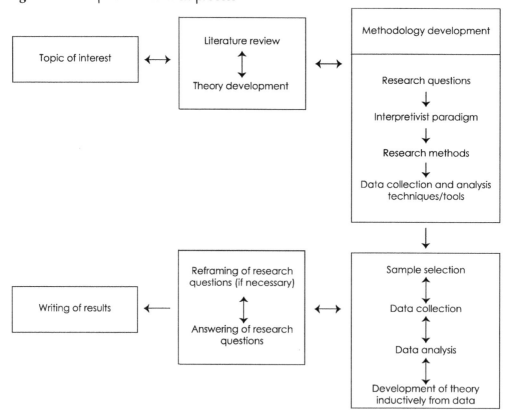

In comparing Figures 1.1 and 1.2, there are notable differences apart from the iterative nature of the latter, indicated by the two-way arrows. There is no mention of hypotheses in Figure 1.2 as they are not part of the repertoire of interpretivists; nor of generalisation which, as mentioned above, is not a goal of interpretivist studies. In contrast to positivism, there are also not the same demands about the capacity to replicate research. There is recognition that certain phenomena are confined in time and place, and that the particular styles of observation and explanation relevant in one case may not be capable of repetition. Samples tend to be quite small and the need for random sampling is not emphasised or required as in the positivist paradigm. The form of sampling which is popular in interpretive research is *purposive sampling*, a term which literally means a sample suited to the purposes of the study. Purposive sampling is not intended to be representative or typical but governed by what is important and relevant to the study. *Theoretical sampling* is defined as the process of selecting "incidents, slices of life, time periods, or people on the basis of their potential manifestation or representation of important theoretical constructs" (Patton, 2015, p. 288). There are different approaches to theoretical sampling, which is widely used in grounded theory. See, for example, Chapter 9.

Nevertheless, interpretivist research needs to be rigorous. In interpretivist research, validity and reliability are constructed rather differently than they are in positivist research. In discussing qualitative research design, Maxwell (2013) explained validity in terms of a researcher's openness to alternative explanations. He identified a key validity threat as researcher bias where the findings are constrained by pre-conceived ideas and do not emerge idiographically from the data. Reliability in positivist terms is more difficult where each context is likely to be quite different.

Guba (1981) discussed rigour in terms of 'trustworthiness' of findings and proposed four constructs which he considered to be comparable to those used by positivists to establish rigour:

1. *Credibility*, ensuring that findings and interpretations reflect the multiple realities of research participants, is the equivalent of internal validity (p. 80).

2. *Transferability*, where there are some similarities between contexts, meaning that some findings may be transferable, is comparable to external validity (p. 81).

3. *Dependability*, comparable to the positivist construct of reliability where consistent, stable results are obtained over time, focusses on the fact that, with the acceptance of multiple realities and varying contexts, there will be variance but that this must be tracked and explained. For this to happen, research design must be reported in detail (p. 81).

4. *Confirmability*, is related to positivist 'objectivity', where researchers are independent of their subjects or objects. Since interpretivists accept that researchers and participants are interrelated, researchers need to establish that the results are not the results of their own biases, interests and perspectives (p. 80).

The role of *triangulation* plays an important part in all four of these constructs and therefore in establishing trustworthiness. Triangulation involves the use of multiple methods of data collection, multiple sources of data, and theoretical constructs. Shenton (2004) provides an in-depth discussion of the four constructs, including the ways in which researchers can address these criteria.

Critical theory

Critical theorists share similarities with interpretivists in that they are critical of positivist approaches and believe that reality is interpreted or constructed by social actors as individuals or in social groups. Nevertheless, they have some points of disagreement with interpretivists and mix nomothetic and idiographic approaches (Neuman, 2014, p. 110). One key difference is that:

> a critical social theory is concerned in particular with issues of power and justice and the ways that the economy, matters of race, class, and gender, ideologies, discourses, education, religion and other social institutions, and cultural dynamics interact to construct a social system (Kincheloe & McLaren, 2003, pp. 436–437).

Critical emancipation has been a key role of critical researchers who attempt "to expose the forces that prevent individuals and groups from shaping the decisions that crucially affect their lives" (p. 437). There are strong links between critical theory, postmodernism and postcolonialism. Thus critical theorists see interpretivists as "being too subjective and relativist, treating people's ideas as more important than actual conditions (e.g., real poverty, oppression, violence)"... [and focussing] "too much on localized, microlevel, short-term settings while ignoring the broader and long-term structural conditions" (Neuman, 2014, p. 110). Neuman summarises what he terms 'critical social science': "A critical process of inquiry that goes beyond surface illusions to uncover the real structures in the material world in order to help people change conditions and build a better world for themselves" (p. 110).

In relation to information systems research, Cecez-Kecmanovic (2001) pointed to the differences between the approaches of interpretive researchers and critical theorists. Whereas interpretive researchers seek to understand and describe the influences on an information system in context, "critical IS researchers go further to expose inherent conflicts and contradictions, hidden structures and mechanisms accountable for these influences" (p. 143). This includes attempts to "deceive, manipulate, exploit, dominate and disempower people" through information systems design (p. 143).

Other conceptual approaches

Not everyone who favours either quantitative or qualitative methods (or a combination thereof) espouses, or may even be aware of, the paradigms, with their implications, outlined above – at least not precisely as discussed. This chapter partly aims to persuade you that understanding the full complexity of 'methodology' is important but, in reality, some researchers simply label their research quantitative, qualitative or mixed methods research, without explaining the theoretical foundations. In addition to the terminological problem, there is a wide variety of views about how the landscape of research should be configured. This is particularly evident in the field of inquiry labelled 'qualitative research' which, because of the range of methods and techniques available, is widely discussed in the literature. (See, e.g., Denzin & Lincoln, 1994, 2000, 2005, 2011; Given, 2008; Gorman & Clayton, 1997, 2005; Marshall & Rossman, 2016; Maxwell, 2013; Mellon, 1990; Patton, 2015.) Maxwell (2013) provides a step-by-step guide to planning qualitative research. The two-volume *Sage Encyclopedia of Qualitative Research Methods* (Given, 2008) is particularly useful where multi-disciplinary projects – spanning the humanities, social and health sciences – are involved.

Qualitative research

While Denzin and Lincoln (2003) emphasised the 'interpretive' nature of qualitative research, theirs is a broad, historical conceptualisation and is not synonymous with interpretivist research. For them, "qualitative research is a field in its own right... 'crosscutting' disciplines, fields, and subject matters" (p. 3). Other comments they made were that qualitative research "is difficult to define clearly", "has no theory or paradigm that is distinctly its own" (p. 9), and historically is surrounded by:

> a complex, interconnected family of terms, concepts, and assumptions ... [that] include the traditions associated with foundationalism, positivism, postpostivism, poststructuralism, and the many qualitative research perspectives, and/or methods, connected to cultural and interpretive studies (p. 3).

Surprisingly positivism is listed here, especially since Denzin and Lincoln (2003) critiqued the views about reality on which positivist research is based, making it seem at odds (as indeed it is) with the interpretive approach with its emphasis on the "value-laden nature of inquiry" (p. 13). But, viewed historically, the earliest ethnographers were positivist qualitative researchers who "asserted that through a scientific and rigorous analysis, universal truths could be discerned that lay beneath the superficial diversities of different culture" (Saule, 2002, p. 179). As noted above, Charmaz (2014) labelled the original grounded theory (Glaser & Strauss, 1967) and the later version (Strauss & Corbin, 1998) as 'objectivist'. As also noted above, particularly post-positivists place an emphasis on qualitative research (Myers, 1997; Denzin & Lincoln, 1994).

Denzin and Lincoln (2003) spoke of qualitative research as using "a variety of empirical materials – case study; personal experience; introspection; life story; interview; artifacts; cultural texts and productions; observational, historical, interactional, and visual texts" (p. 5). At another point, they stated that qualitative researchers "draw upon and utilize the approaches, methods, and techniques of ethnomethodology, phenomenology, hermeneutics, feminism, rhizomatics, deconstructionism, ethnography, interviews, psychoanalysis, cultural studies, survey research, and participant observation, among others" (p. 10). In other words, all forms, methods and practices of social inquiry can come under the banner of 'qualitative research'.

Not all writers agree with Denzin and Lincoln's portrayal of qualitative research. For example, Gorman and Clayton (1997), in their handbook of qualitative research for the information professional stated that the qualitative approach "lies within the interpretivist paradigm, which focuses on social constructs" (p. 23). My view, as stated in Williamson (2007, p. 6), is that the terms 'positivist' and 'interpretivist' distinguish two different epistemological views: first, of researchers who believe that there is a measurable social reality and, second, of those who postulate that reality is constructed by individuals and groups. While data are most likely to be quantitative with positivist researchers and qualitative with interpretivists, this will not be exclusively the case. Understanding this distinction enables researchers to gauge whether they think there is an objective reality for a particular set of phenomena; or whether the associated meanings are constructed by people. The use of qualitative data by those with the former mindset does not mean that the study is necessarily interpretivist. As Myers (1997) expressed it: "the word 'qualitative' is not a synonym for 'interpretive' – qualitative research may or may not be interpretive, depending upon the underlying philosophical assumptions of the researcher". In other words, it is the approach to the research and how data are used that make the distinction. The labeling of research simply by the type of data collected (as do Creswell (2003), Gorman and Clayton (1997) and Gorman and Clayton (2005), for example) is often inadequate. I agree with Greene and Caracelli's (2003) point, which I present again below, in relation to mixed methods: "there is merit in different paradigmatic traditions" (p. 107). Being aware of paradigmatic distinctions will sharpen your powers of discernment and deepen your understanding.

I also believe, however, that the paradigms should not be 'straight-jackets'. Accommodation is required for those who postulate that there are some aspects of life, although not all, which are measurable and see the findings from the study of these aspects to be generalisable (given sufficient rigour in data collection), at least at a particular point in time. They are likely to favour the use of mixed paradigms, and of quantitative or qualitative methods as appropriate. However, there is always a need to understand, and explicate lucidly, the philosophical assumptions of chosen research methods and techniques. Cecez-Kecmanovic (2011) presented a cogent argument for the return to a focus on 'research methodology'. This means not just the selection of research methods and techniques, but concern with "the ontological, epistemological, and normative assumptions behind research methods and their inherent limitations". These assumptions need to be made overt.

Mixed methods research

As with other research conceptualisations, there is a lack of agreement about what constitutes mixed methods research. At the simplest level, it involves the use of quantitative and qualitative methods in the same study. The use of mixed methods is a popular approach with some researchers who believe that this is a good way to gain a deeper understanding of issues and experience. For example, Ford (1987) suggested that it is possible for researchers to use either quantitative or qualitative approaches, or both, according to the research problem, or problems, under consideration. He made a strong case for integration because the use of different kinds of thinking involved in positivist and interpretivist approaches make a full understanding of topics more likely.

Other writers, while appreciating the benefits of mixed methods research, have urged consideration of the assumptions behind different epistemologies which constitute "different ways of seeing, knowing, and valuing" (Greene & Caracelli 2003, p. 107). Because of the different nature and role of various paradigms, Greene and Caracelli argued that mixed methods research should be undertaken "in a thoughtful and defensible manner" (p. 94). Mellon (1990) postulated that methodologies can be profitably combined, but warned that great care needs to be taken because they "are separate and distinct from one another, with different purposes, methods and outcomes" (p. 5). Morse (2003) also saw value in mixed methods but warned of the need for awareness that the *ad hoc* mixing of strategies or methods may lead to the violation of methodological assumptions.

Greene and Caracelli (2003) reviewed a small sample of social research and concluded that "inquiry decisions are rarely, if ever, consciously rooted in philosophical assumptions or beliefs" (p. 107). This also appears to be the case in single method research although, along with Greene and Caracelli (p. 95), I have argued (Williamson, 2002, p. 58) that all researchers have some kind of mental model of the social world, whether or not they are consciously aware of it, or make it explicit. Greene and Caracelli lamented this lack of philosophical underpinnings, proposing that:

> there is merit in different paradigmatic traditions in that each has something valuable to offer to our understanding of our complex social world. If such differences are not attended to in practice, then the full potential of mixed methods inquiry will remain unfulfilled (p. 107).

An example of mixed methods research, using different paradigms as well as methods, is presented in Chapter 2.

Matching research questions to appropriate designs

A golden rule for all researchers is that choosing an appropriate research design should be based on the kinds of research questions that will be the focus of the research, that is, the questions should be determined first before the research design is considered. One approach is to consider whether a question implies measurement or whether straightforward, factual information is involved. Such questions may begin with 'what', 'who', 'how many', 'how much', 'where', 'when' which can often be measured at a particular point in time. For example, 'what' are the rules for eligibility for the aged pension in Australia? The rules may change over time, but they can be reliably ascertained (barring misinterpretation) on a particular day of a specific year. What proportion of a random sample (assuming it is a true random sample) of Victorians bought *The Age* newspaper on a particular date? This can be reliably measured and positivist concepts of measurement are appropriate. On the other hand, complex questions, which involve 'why', 'how', and in some cases 'what', lend themselves to in-depth exploration (Williamson, 2002, p. 34). If the proposed research asks a series of complex questions, where it will be not possible to measure and obtain an objective result, then an interpretivist paradigm and qualitative data collection should be chosen. For example, the questions of one of my PhD students focussed on the information needs and information seeking of the very oldest people in society, people in the Fourth Age. He, appropriately, chose a constructivist paradigm along with interpretivist ethnography. It would have been impossible to obtain reliable survey results from a random sample of this population and in-depth perceptions would have been impossible without the use of techniques associated with an ethnographic approach, viz., interviews and observation.

It must be noted that for some researchers, whose goal is eventually 'measurement' and 'generalisation', 'why' and 'how' questions need to be answered in an initial, exploratory stage. For example, Shanks, Rouse and Arnott (1993) suggested that:

> exploratory research (sometimes termed formulative research) is aimed at formulating more precise questions that future research can answer. It is used in the theory-building stage of research. Exploratory researchers frequently use qualitative research methods such as case studies and phenomenological studies (p. 7).

Conclusion

The three major research paradigms in the social sciences are broadly labelled positivism, interpretivism and critical theory. The first attempts to apply scientific methods to the social sciences, and is most usually associated with deductive reasoning and quantitative data collection. Because of their use of natural settings and greater emphasis on qualitative data collection, post-positivists have some characteristics in common with interpretivists, although they still believe that there is a reality which can be measured. Interpretivists, on the other hand, are concerned with meanings constructed by individuals and groups, use principally inductive reasoning and collect qualitative data. The interpretivist umbrella paradigm, sometimes called the naturalistic inquiry paradigm, includes other paradigms such as constructivism and phenomenology. Critical theory, while having more in common with interpretivists than positivists, stands apart in its emphasis on changing the structures of society and empowering disadvantaged groups.

Another way of conceptualising research approaches is through the labels, nomothetic (concerned with discovery of general laws) or idiographic (concerned with the individual). Bates (2005, p. 8) saw this as "the most fundamental orienting strategies of all". Bates (pp. 10−12) provides a deep discussion of meta-theories in LIS in relation to whether they are nomothetic, idiographic or mixed approaches.

To many researchers, combined paradigmatic and methodological approaches are acceptable, and even desirable. There is a strong case to argue that research designs should be matched to the questions to be investigated. Triangulation is a popular approach which enables the checking of findings by the use of different data-collection methods, sources and using different theoretical constructs. Whatever approach is chosen, I urge researchers to apply 'methodological' thinking, making clear the theoretical assumptions regarding the choices that are made.

References

Bates, M. J. (1999). The invisible substrate of Information Science. *Journal of the American Society for Information Science, 50*(12), 1043−1050.

Bates, M. J. (2005). An introduction to theories, metatheories and models. In K. E. Fisher, S. Erdelez, & E. F. McKechnie (Eds.), *Theories of information behavior* (pp. 1−24). Medford, NJ: Information Today.

Berger, P. L., & Luckmann, T. (1967). *The social construction of reality: A treatise in the sociology of knowledge.* New York: Anchor Press.

Blaikie, N. (1993). *Approaches to social enquiry.* Cambridge: Polity Press.

Bow, A. (2002). Ethnographic techniques. In K. Williamson (Ed.), *Research methods for students, academics and professionals: Information management and systems* (2nd ed., pp. 265−279). Wagga Wagga, NSW: Centre for Information Studies, Charles Sturt University.

Case, D. O., & Given, L. M. (2016). *Looking for information: A survey of research on information seeking, needs and behavior* (4th ed.). Bingley, UK: Emerald.

Cecez-Kecmanovic, D. (2001). Doing critical IS research: The question of methodology. In E. Trauth (Ed.), *Qualitative research in information science: Issues and trends* (pp. 142–163). Hershey, PA: Idea Group Publishing.

Cecez-Kecmanovic, D. (2011). *On methods, methodologies and how they matter*. Paper presented at the European Conference on Information Systems. Retrieved from http://aisel.aisnet.org/ecis2011/233/.

Charmaz, K. (2003). Grounded theory: Objectivist and constructivist methods. In N. K. Denzin, & Y. S. Lincoln (Eds.), *Strategies of qualitative inquiry* (2nd ed., pp. 249–291). Thousand Oaks, CA: Sage.

Charmaz, K. (2014). *Constructing grounded theory: A practical guide through qualitative analysis* (2nd ed.). London: Sage.

Connaway, L. S., & Powell, R. (2010). *Basic research methods for librarians* (5th ed.). Santa Barbara, CA: Libraries Unlimited.

Creswell, J. (2003). *Research design: Qualitative, quantitative, and mixed method approaches* (2nd ed.). Thousand Oaks, CA: Sage.

Denzin, N. K., & Lincoln, Y. S. (1994). *The handbook of qualitative research*. Thousand Oaks, CA: Sage.

Denzin, N. K., & Lincoln, Y. S. (2000). *The handbook of qualitative research* (2nd ed.). Thousand Oaks, CA: Sage.

Denzin, N. K., & Lincoln, Y. S. (2003). Introduction: The discipline and practice of qualitative research. In N. K. Denzin, & Y. S. Lincoln (Eds.), *Strategies of qualitative inquiry* (2nd ed., pp. 1–45). Thousand Oaks, CA: Sage.

Denzin, N. K., & Lincoln, Y. S. (2005). *The Sage handbook of qualitative research* (3rd ed.). Los Angeles: Sage.

Denzin, N. K., & Lincoln, Y. S. (2011). *The Sage handbook of qualitative research* (4th ed.). Los Angeles: Sage.

Dervin, B. (1992). From the mind's eye of the user: The sense-making qualitative-quantitative methodology. In J. D. Glazier, &. In R. R. Powell (Ed.), *Qualitative research in information management* (pp. 61–84). Englewood, CO: Libraries Unlimited.

Dervin, B. (2005). What methodology does to theory. In K. E. Fisher, S. Erdelez, & E. F. McKechnie (Eds.), *Theories of information behavior* (pp. 25–36). Medford, NJ: Information Today.

Dervin, B., & Nilan, M. (1986). Information needs and uses. *Annual Review of Information Science and Technology (ARIST), 21,* 3–33.

Dick, A. I. (1991). Influence of positivism on the designs of scientific techniques. Implications for library and information science techniques. *South African Journal of Library and Information Science, 59*(4), 231–239.

Edwards, S. (2007). Phenomenography: 'Follow the yellow brick road!'. In S. Lipu, K. Williamson, & A. Lloyd. (Eds.), *Exploring methods in information literacy research* (pp. 87–110). Wagga Wagga, NSW: Centre for Information Studies, Charles Sturt University.

Ford, N. (1987). Research and practice in librarianship: A cognitive view. In B. Katz, & R. Kinder (Eds.), *Current trends in information research and theory* (pp. 21–47). New York: Haworth.

Giddens, A. (1984). *The constitution of society: Outline of the theory of structuration.* Berkeley, CA: University of California Press.

Gilliland, A., & McKemmish, S. (2004). Building an infrastructure for archival research. *Archival Science*, 4(3–4), 149–199.

Given, L. M. (2008). *Sage Encyclopedia of qualitative research methods.* Thousand Oaks, CA: Sage.

Glaser, B. G. & Strauss, A. L. (1967). *The discovery of grounded theory: Strategies of qualitative research.* Chicago: Aldine.

Glesne, C. & Peshkin, A. (1992). *Becoming qualitative researchers: An introduction.* White Plains, NY: Longman Publishing Group.

Gorichanaz, T. (2015). Information on the run: experiencing information during an ultramarathon. *Information Research: An International Electronic Journal*, 20(4). Retrieved from http://www.informationr.net/ir/20-4/paper697.html#.WHf6uXrzJnk.

Gorman, G. E., & Clayton, P. (1997). *Qualitative research for the information professional: A practical handbook.* London: Library Association Publishing.

Gorman, G. E., & Clayton, P. (2005). *Qualitative research for the information professional: A practical handbook* (2nd ed.). London: Facet.

Greene, J. C., & Caracelli, V. J. (2003). Making paradigmatic sense of mixed methods practice. In A. Tashakkori, & C. Teddlie (Eds.), *Handbook of mixed methods in social and behavioral research* (pp. 91–110). Thousand Oaks, CA: Sage.

Guba, E. G. (1981). Criteria for assessing the trustworthiness of naturalistic inquiries. *Educational Communication and Technology*, 29(2), 75–91.

Guba, E. G., & Lincoln, Y. S. (1981). *Effective evaluation.* San Francisco: Jossey-Bass.

Guba, E. G., & Lincoln, Y. S. (2005). Paradigmatic controversies, contradictions, and emerging influences. In N. K. Denzin, & Y. S. Lincoln (Eds.), *The Sage handbook of qualitative research* (3rd ed., pp. 191–215). Thousand Oaks, CA: Sage.

Hammersley, M. (1992). Deconstructing the qualitative-quantitative divide. In J. Brannen (Ed.), *Mixing methods: Qualitative and quantitative research* (pp. 39–55). Aldershot, Hants: Avebury.

Holstein, J. A., & Gubrium, J. K. (2005). Interpretive practice and social action. In N. K. Denzin, & Y. S. Lincoln (Eds.), *The Sage handbook of qualitative research* (3rd ed., pp. 483–505). Los Angeles: Sage.

Kelly, G. (1963). *A theory of personality: The psychology of personal constructs.* New York: W. W. Norton.

Kincheloe, J. L., & McLaren, P. (2003). Rethinking critical theory and qualitative research. In N. K. Denzin, & Y. S. Lincoln (Eds.), *The landscape of qualitative research: Theories and issues* (2nd ed., pp. 433–488). Thousand Oaks, CA: Sage Publications.

Kuhlthau, C. C. (2004). *Seeking meaning: A process approach to library and informaiton services* (2nd ed.). Westport, CT: Libraries Unlimited.

Kuhn, T. S. (1970). *The structure of scientific revolutions* (2nd ed.). Chicago: University of Chicago Press.

Marshall, C. & Rossman, G. B. (2016). *Designing qualitative research* (6th ed.). Thousand Oaks, CA: Sage Publications.

Marton, F., & Booth, S. (1997). *Learning and awareness*. Mahwah, NJ: Lawrence Erbaum Associates.

Maxwell, J. A. (2013). *Qualitative research design: an interactive approach* (3rd ed.). Thousand Oaks, CA: Sage Publications.

Mellon, C. (1990). *Naturalistic inquiry for library science: Methods and applications for research, evaluation and teaching*. New York: Greenwood Press.

Morse, J. M. (2003). Principles of mixed methods and multimethod research design. In A. Tashakkori, & C. Teddlie (Eds.), *Handbook of mixed methods in social and behavioral research* (pp. 189–208). Thousand Oaks, CA: Sage.

Myers, M. (1997). Qualitative research in information systems. *MIS Quarterly, 21*(2), 241–242.

Neuman, W. L. (2014). *Social research methods: Qualitative and quantitative approaches* (7th ed.). Harlow, Essex: Pearson New International.

Patton, M. Q. (2015). *Qualitative research and evaluation methods* (4th ed.). Los Angeles, CA: Sage Publications.

Popper, K. R. S. (1959). *The logic of scientific discovery*. London: Hutchinson.

Reneker, M. H. (1993). A qualitative study of information seeking among members of an academic community: Methodological issues and problems'. *Library Quarterly, 63*(4), 487–507.

Saule, S. (2002). Ethnography. In K. Williamson (Ed.), *Research methods for students, academics and professionals: Information management and systems* (2nd ed., pp. 177–193). Wagga Wagga, NSW: Centre for Information Studies, Charles Sturt University.

Schwandt, T. (2000). Three epistemological stances for qualitative inquiry: interpretivism, hermeneutics, and constructionism. In N. K. Denzin, & Y. S. Lincoln (Eds.), *Handbook of qualitative research* (2nd ed., pp. 189–213). Thousand Oaks, CA: Sage Publications.

Shanks, G., Rouse, A., & Arnott, D. (1993). *A review of approaches to research and scholarship in information systems*. Caulfield, VIC: Department of Information Systems, Monash University.

Shenton, A. K. (2004). Strategies for ensuring trustworthiness in qualitative research projects. *Education for Information, 22*, 63–75.

Smith, J. A., Flowers, P., & Larkin, M. (2009). *Interpretative phenomenological analysis: Theory, method and research*. London: Sage.

Strauss, A., & Corbin, J. (1998). *Basics of qualitative research: Grounded theory procedures and techniques* (2nd ed.). Newbury Park, CA: Sage.

Sutton, B. (1993). The rationale for qualitative research: A review of principles and theoretical foundations. *Library Quarterly, 63*(4), 411–429.

Talja, S., Tuominen, K., & Savolainen, R. (2005). "Isms" in information science: constructivism, collectivism and constructionism. *Journal of Documentation, 61*(1), 79–101.

Wildemuth, B. M. (2009). *Applications of social research methods to questions in information and library science*. Westport, CT: Libraries Unlimited.

Williamson, K. (Ed.). (2002). *Research methods for students, academics and professionals: Information management and systems*. Wagga Wagga, NSW: Centre for Information Studies, Charles Sturt University.

Williamson, K. (2006). Research in constructivist frameworks using ethnographic techniques. *Library Trends, 55*(1), 83–101.

Williamson, K. (2007). The broad methodological contexts of information literacy research. In S. Lipu, K. Williamson, & A. Lloyd (Eds.), *Research methods in information literacy research* (pp. 1–12). Wagga Wagga, NSW: Centre for Information Studies, Charles Sturt University.

Williamson, K., Burstein, F., & McKemmish, S. (2002). The two major traditions of research. In K. Williamson (Ed.), *Research methods for students, academics and professionals: Information management and systems* (2nd ed., pp. 25–47). Wagga Wagga, NSW: Centre for Information Studies, Charles Sturt University.

Chapter 2

The fundamentals of research planning

Kirsty Williamson

Monash University and Charles Sturt University, Australia

The fundamentals of research planning need considerable attention for successful research outcomes. This chapter discusses the iterative steps required as part of that research planning. It begins with selection of a topic or research problem and then discusses hypotheses and research questions, providing guidance for their development. Examples of research questions/hypotheses are provided for positivist/quantitative studies; research questions for interpretivist/qualitative research, mixed methods and critical ethnography; and matching methodologies for all four sets of questions. The literature review section outlines steps for the writing of a high-quality, critical literature review. The final section discusses the importance of theory, gives examples of different kinds of theories and provides an example of theory development in a PhD study.

Research Methods: Information, Systems, and Contexts. DOI: http://dx.doi.org/10.1016/B978-0-08-102220-7.00002-9

Introduction

The beginning stages of a research project require considerable planning and preparation. Regardless of the research paradigms involved, before empirical work can begin, a number of different steps must be completed. The diagrams illustrating the positivist and interpretivist research processes in Chapter 1: *Research concepts*, show beginning steps, most of which need to take place simultaneously. Once you have a topic of interest, you need to read widely to find other research that has been done on that topic, including both theoretical and empirical research. Gradually you will begin to focus your project, define your research problem and develop your hypotheses if appropriate, or formulate your research questions. Even if undertaking grounded theory, where your theory will be literally built from the ground upwards, that is, will be constructed from your findings, you need to read widely and be knowledgeable about relevant theoretical and empirical work. You will write a preliminary literature review in which the proposed theoretical underpinnings for your project should be explored.

According to the advice regarding the matching of research questions to designs, only when you have a clear research focus and questions should you decide on appropriate methodology (paradigm/s, method/s and technique/s). Realistically, however, researchers' backgrounds and cognitive styles will predispose them to favour particular approaches. As Bates (2005, p. 8) stated: "We are all drawn to the sort of research and thinking that works best for us, that is most harmonious with the way our minds work." If you have a predisposition to favour certain approaches, you will need to consider the kinds of questions that are suited to those approaches as you do your preliminary work.

Matching research designs to research questions is very much part of the fundamentals of research planning. Methodologies for archives and records, and information systems and knowledge management are included in the chapters devoted to those disciplines (Chapter 4: *Archival and recordkeeping research* and Chapter 5: *The methodological landscape*). This chapter includes examples of questions and matching methodologies for what we label 'information research'. It must be emphasised that the initial steps in research planning cannot be undertaken in a linear fashion. The process needs to be iterative, although choosing a topic is clearly important to making initial progress. Research questions for interpretive research may be varied as data are collected, revealing insights that have emerged from the study.

Choosing a topic

In choosing a topic for a major project, such as a PhD study, it is very important to consider what will maintain your interest over a long period of time. Genuine engagement with your topic is crucial for good research outcomes. It is also a good idea to consider your present levels of knowledge, experience and skills. The need for the research to add to knowledge, and not just to reinvent the wheel, is a fundamental requirement. Literature searching is a key element as it identifies where the gaps lie in your area of interest. As Morse (1998, p. 57) stated: "Researchable questions often become apparent when one reads the literature." Research students need to discuss their topics with their supervisors who can often provide insights.

Perhaps you will begin with a broad idea emanating from experience of life, including in the workplace, and then turn to the literature, or to an expert in a field, to explore what research has already been undertaken. Just because there is a body of work that is focussed on your area of interest, does not mean that there are not gaps or other possibilities for examining an issue from a different perspective. Connaway and Powell, 2010, p. 44) made the point that:

> A problem does not have to be entirely new and unresearched in order to be worthy of investigation. Some of the most important research builds on and improves or refines previous research. The degree of uniqueness desired will in part depend upon the purposes of the research.

Problems which emerge from a workplace situation can still involve conceptual thinking; indeed, ideas and theoretical concepts are needed to bring innovative approaches to problems and their solution, and to ensure the dissemination of those ideas to other professionals in the field.

The next step, after the problem has been identified, is to formulate viable and manageable research questions or, if you are choosing a positivist paradigm, you may wish to develop hypotheses.

Hypothesis development and an example of hypothesis use

Hypotheses are often used as part of positivist research. This section discusses the development of hypotheses and provides an example of the use of hypotheses from the literature.

Hypotheses: Definitions and types

Hypotheses are usually used in the positivist paradigm. Neuman (2014, p. 68) defined a hypothesis as: "an empirically testable version of a proposition. It is a tentative statement about a relationship ... By empirically evaluating a hypothesis, we learn whether a theoretical proposition is supported". Sorting out the various ways in which hypotheses are labelled can be confusing. To begin, it is important to understand the difference between independent and dependent variables. Neuman discussed these in terms of "their location in a causal relationship or chain of causality" (p. 180). He explained that the *independent variable* is "the cause variable or the force or condition that acts on something else" (p. 180). The *dependent variable* is "the effect, result, or outcome of another variable" (p. 181). In the example of hypothesis use, below, all the initial variables are the independent ones, all predicted to affect 'user satisfaction', the dependent variable.

There are two key types of hypothesis: null and alternative:

> **Null hypothesis:** *A hypothesis stating that there is no significant effect of an independent variable on a dependent variable.*
>
> **Alternative hypothesis:** *A hypothesis paired with the null hypothesis that says an independent variable has a significant effect on a dependent variable* (Neuman, 2014, p. 185).

It is very important to avoid double-barrelled hypotheses, where there are two or more independent variables. This is because the interactive effect of two or more independent variables will be unclear if not separated when the hypothesis is empirically tested.

Other labels that are applied to hypotheses include 'operational', an example of which is provided by Burns (2000, p. 109): "There is a significant relationship between reading ability for nine-year-old children living in major cities in NSW as measured by standardised reading test X and parental attitudes to education as measured by attitude test Y." Connaway and Powell (2010) would call this a 'directional hypothesis'.

You will note that the term 'significant' is used by Burns (2000). Good researchers will not claim a null hypothesis to be supported or that there is a relationship between variables without conducting tests of statistical significance. This issue is discussed further in Chapter 18: *Quantitative data analysis.*

An example of hypothesis use from the literature

Al-Maskari and Sanderson (2010) believed that user satisfaction

> can be influenced by several factors such as system effectiveness, user effectiveness, user effort, and user characteristics and expectations. Therefore information retrieval evaluators should consider all these factors in obtaining user satisfaction and in using it as a criterion of system effectiveness (p. 869).

To investigate these factors, the researchers developed the following hypotheses to test, using them in place of research questions. The ways in which the hypotheses were derived from the literature is described in detail by the authors, which you can check for yourself if you choose to do so.

Hypothesis 1: System effectiveness influences user satisfaction

Hypothesis 2: User effectiveness influences user satisfaction

Hypothesis 3: User effort influences user satisfaction

Hypothesis 4: User characteristic influences user satisfaction (Al-Maskari & Sanderson, 2010, pp. 861-862).

The examples from Al-Maskari and Sanderson (2010) are of alternative hypotheses. Were they to have used null hypotheses they would have stated them in opposite terms, for example, System effectiveness does not influence user satisfaction.

Formulating research questions and matching them to methodologies

When I taught research methods, and was trying to help students formulate clear research questions, I asked them to work out one or two key questions and then a series of sub-questions, all of which should fit within the ambit of the key question/s. I found this exercise helped them to focus their thinking and their questions and prevented the inclusion of unrelated or tangential questions. The exploration of the literature needs to be undertaken in conjunction with this process. It is very important to understand the way in which other researchers have viewed the topic, if at all, and to take into account other research. Maybe there has been quite a lot of research undertaken on your topic of interest, but approaches have been mainly positivist/ quantitative and, in your opinion, there is not yet a deep understanding of the issues involved. Conversely, you may believe that the broader, generalisable approach is missing. Thus you will be thinking about methodological questions as you develop your questions and, later, need to make sure that you match your questions to your methodology (not just your method and techniques, as explained in Chapter 1). Theory formulation also plays a part; in other words, there is an iterative process involved. Logical consistency and explicated interdependence of all parts of all components are essential.

The suggestions for a process for setting questions was originally outlined in Williamson (2002, p. 53) and is repeated here.

Step 1: Write down your broad area of interest.

Step 2: Write down a specific sub-area of this broad area in which you have a particular interest. Try to formulate a question based on this.

Step 3: List five to eight unanswered questions you have in respect to the specific sub-area.

You need to scrutinise your questions carefully to make sure they are communicating exactly what you mean. Consult with others. Note that questions may relate to your sample. For example, if the main focus of your study is the factors influencing library use, sub-questions might include the differences between males and females, or the differences between certain age groups in the sample. More experienced researchers are unlikely to follow this suggestion for the actual setting of questions, but they will still work through the other parts of the initial iterative planning process. Developing a mind map may assist in this process. Remember that questions for an interpretivist study may be tentative and may change as your study progresses, although you should always begin with some questions which will provide focus and an intellectual challenge.

The following are examples that have been drawn from the literature, illustrating the kinds of questions suited, first, to a positivist/quantitative approach; second, to an interpretivist/qualitative approach, although here there is also a 'mixed methods' example; and third, to critical theory/ethnography. The methodologies linked to these sets of questions are also presented and explained. The emphasis in all these discussions is on the appropriateness of the choice of methodology for the research questions involved. Methodology, as explained in Chapter 1, includes not only how research is conducted, but also how it is conceptualised. It includes paradigmatic framework, method and techniques (or data collection and analysis tools). Each example includes a consideration of possible alternative approaches. PhD students often include a discussion of the options available to them for the investigation of their research questions and the reasons for the particular choices they have made.

The critical theory (critical ethnography) example is from the information systems field, although it could just as easily been undertaken by researchers with an information management/library and information studies (LIS) background, given that it is about computer-mediated communication. As mentioned in the foreword, the two fields have much in common.

Questions and methodology for a positivist/quantitative study

As mentioned in Chapter 1, questions suited to a positivist/quantitative study are those where measurement can reliably provide an objective answer, generalisable to the population on which the study is based. Cause and effect are often explored; for instance, the authors below discuss whether age affects online searching.

Borgman, Hirsh, Walter and Gallagher (1995)

Although this study was undertaken some time ago, it is a good example of a useful application of a positivist approach to research in the information field.

Borgman *et al.* (1995) were interested in understanding more about children's information-seeking abilities at a stage of development when schools were adopting computers for classroom instruction. They emphasised that surprisingly little research had been done "at the nexus of libraries and education, addressing questions of how to automate libraries for children in ways consonant with their learning, cognitive development, and curriculum" (p. 663). Thus they wanted to address questions of how to automate libraries for children in ways consonant with their learning, cognitive development, and curriculum. Their research questions were:

1. How do children search for topics in an automated library catalog?

2. Are children able to use a hierarchical, browsing, recognition-based system effectively? Is such searching behavior related to age, sex, or computer experience?

3. Are children able to use a keyword, Boolean retrieval system effectively? Is such searching behaviour related to age, sex, or computer experience?

4. How does search behavior vary between browsing and keyword systems? (Borgman *et al.*, 1995, p. 668)

Note that there are 'how' questions here and that other interpretation is involved to some extent, for example, in defining what 'to use' involves. As mentioned in Chapter 1, there is always interpretation involved in research. Nevertheless, these questions are objectively measureable and the findings generalisable to the population of the study if correct positivist procedure is used.

The positivist paradigm and experimental method were chosen for this project for reasons that can be surmised, rather than being spelled out by the authors.

a) Two of the research questions focussed on the effect of certain independent variables, for example, age and sex, on a dependent variable, for example, use of information retrieval systems. Experimental design (a positivist approach) would need to be used to answer these questions.

b) A superficial consideration of the other research questions might indicate that particularly the first 'how' question might invite exploration of individual approaches and perceptions, suited to an interpretivist approach. However, the second 'how' question definitely implies 'measurement' in that it brings in a comparison of browsing and keyword systems. Effective use of the systems involved also implies the need to 'measure' success.

Methodology

There were four experiments involved in the project, involving two schools (University Elementary School and Open School) and Los Angeles Public Library.

Each of the experiments involved between 32 and 34 children, a total of 131 subjects. (Note that positivist researchers normally refer to 'subjects' and interpretivists to 'participants'.) The samples, which were balanced according to age and sex as far as possible, were randomly selected from multiple classes in each age group, within the range (9–12). Random sample selection is an essential element of positivist research. The numbers in the individual experiments were adequate for the statistical tests which this kind of research requires. (For discussion of statistical tests in quantitative research, see Chapter 18.)

As indicated above, experimental design involves the investigation of the effect of dependent variables on independent variables. In the case of this research, the independent variables were age, sex, and computer experience and the dependent variables "browsing and keyword catalog retrieval systems" (Borgman, *et al.*, 1995, p. 670). A number of variables were 'controlled', also common in experimental research. (For detailed discussion of experimental design, see Chapter 14: *Experimental research*.)

Another element of positivist research designs, as discussed in Chapter 1, is the development of a theoretical framework to underpin the research. In the case of Borgman *et al.*, having reviewed the literature on children's use of information retrieval systems, they outlined an alternative information retrieval model for children. The major system used in the experiments was Science Library Catalog, which was based on the premises the researchers had developed. The system was tested in different environments and adapted over the four experiments, as well as compared to two different keyword systems. The researchers did not develop specific hypotheses, considering that too little was known to do this. As they expressed their approach:

> We are relying on approaches common in human-computer interaction research, to construct a prototype system based on our theories of children's information retrieval behaviour, test the children on the system, then refine both the system and our theories (Borgman *et al.*, 1995, p. 669).

Findings and conclusions

The results are outlined in detail in Borgman *et al.* (1995, pp. 671-676). The researchers believed that "taken as whole, the set of experiments shows several interesting trends in children's searching behavior on both the Science Library Catalog and keyword OPAC systems" (p. 676). The discussion section sets out, very specifically, to answer the research questions. Amongst the conclusions, the authors postulated that they had made substantial progress toward the goal of understanding

> children's information-searching behavior sufficiently to design a
> system with powerful searching mechanisms that build on children's

natural tendencies to explore, that can be used without prior training, and is within their range of skills and knowledge (Borgman *et al.*, 1995, p. 681).

Possible alternative approaches

Given the research questions involved in this project, other ways of undertaking the research do not spring easily to mind. One possibility could be action research (within an interpretivist framework). Children could have been involved in trialling various information retrieval systems with a focus being on their views about how each one worked for them and what improvements could be made. A number of cycles could have been included. However it would have been difficult, if not impossible, to include such a large sample and obtain the comparative results (e.g., of age groups and systems) achieved by what appears to have been a clearly thought out and executed set of experiments. In the experimental research, attitudes to each of the systems were measured with Likert scales, which did not explore the reasons for the answers as could be obtained through action research. However, four focus groups, drawn from the same population, and intended to parallel the children in the experiment, were held at the conclusion of the experiments. These provided qualitative data with additional useful insights.

Questions and methodologies for interpretivist/qualitative studies

As discussed in Chapter 1, more complex questions, where the meanings of people are likely to differ, are suited to an interpretivist/qualitative approach. For the first example below a phenomenographic method was used. For the second example, the approach was broadly ethnographic (in a constructivist framework). There was also a minor quantitative component, although this did not meet all the criteria of the positivist paradigm.

(1) Bruce, Stoodley and Pham's (2009) phenomenographic study

Bruce *et al.* (2009) were interested in exploring how doctoral candidates "'see' or 'constitute' the fields of research in which they are engaged" (p. 203). The field of research which they chose was 'information technology' where they examined the different ways in which research students experienced "their object(s) of study and their research field or territory" (p. 203). The aim of the project was: "to investigate aspects of the collective awareness of information technology (IT) research amongst doctoral candidates in that field" (p. 205). It is useful to note that the various terms, 'see', 'constitute' and 'understand' refer to the phenomenographic construction of experience. There was a series of research questions, focussed on three different features of IT research:

1. IT research. What does it mean to do IT research? What is it that makes a project identifiably IT research?

2. Their research object(s). How do IT research students see the 'things' underpinning their research? How do they collectively constitute or 'shape' the objects of IT research? What kinds of shared understandings do they have of their research object? How do their understandings differ?

3. Their research field, or territory. What are the features of the field? What are its boundaries as students see them. (p. 205)

The reasons that a phenomenographic approach, within an interpretivist framework, was chosen for this study are:

a) Phenomenography is an empirical method for exploring the ways in which people experience phenomena. As can be seen from the research questions, the focus of the project was the ways in which students were aware of various issues concerned with their current project as well as their field of study.

b) The focus of phenomenography is on collective experiences, although these may differ amongst a group of people. An explicit aim of the Bruce *et al.* (2009) study was to look at shared understandings as well as differences amongst the students. (See the second set of questions, above.)

c) The approach had been used successfully in earlier studies into learning about information technology concepts and phenomena (p. 205). The same research team had previously used phenomenographic research to investigate "the significance and value of IT research", in 2004, and "different ways of seeing IT objects and territories", in 2005 (Bruce *et al.*, 2009, p. 204). Both projects focussed on the collective awareness of IT researchers. The new project was on the same topic, with the target group different but closely related to the original one. Part of the rationale of the new project was that it "allows us to compare students' views with those of experienced researchers. The differences between the two groups provide useful insights for higher degree supervisors inducting new researchers into the IT research community" (p. 204).

Methodology

As all researchers need to do in reporting their work, Bruce *et al.* discussed the way in which their methodology works. Phenomenographic research, following Marton and Booth (1997), describes findings in terms of *categories*, which includes the central focus of each way of experiencing a phenomenon: "A change in focus ... signals a change in category" (Bruce *et al.*, 2009, p. 207). The *perceptual boundaries* represent the boundaries of awareness, "beyond which participants do not see" (p. 207). The *structure of awareness* for each category includes the focus and the perceptual boundary. The interaction between the object (phenomenon) and those experiencing it is central to the approach: "In phenomenographic research, the term 'experience' is used to refer to the constitution of a phenomenon in the interaction between 'perceiving subjects' and an 'appearing object'" (p. 206).

Categories are developed through an iterative process of analysis. They do not represent individual participants, but rather the varied ways of constituting phenomena, "discernible across the group" (p. 207). Thus individuals, amongst a group of participants, can contribute to the description of more than one category.[1]

In terms of the specific project being described, the small sample (eighteen doctoral students) was purposively, or purposefully, selected; in other words, a sample suited to the purposes of the research. Purposeful samples are commonly used in interpretivist research. (See Chapter 15: *Populations and samples* for a discussion of various types of sampling.) Bruce *et al.* (2009) briefly described and summarised the sample in a succinct table (p. 206). Likewise, the data collection and analysis are concisely outlined (pp. 206-208). The word-length constraints of journal articles often call upon skills in economically describing method, as in this instance.

Findings and conclusions

The findings are comprehensively presented (pp. 208-215), with identification and discussion of seven different ways of constituting the object and territory of IT research by doctoral candidates. For each of the seven categories, the focus described the research object and the perceptual boundary delineated the research territory. The authors then bring in their points of comparison "with outcomes from previous investigations of IT researchers' collective awareness" (p. 216). They concluded that:

> Looking at doctoral candidates' views of IT research has provided insights into how their views compare with those of more experienced researchers; revealing significant differences across all categories except one and suggesting the need for ongoing conversations about the meaning of those differences (Bruce *et al.*, 2009, p. 220).

---

[1] For a detailed explanation of phenomenographic research, readers are referred to the present article as well as to Bruce, Pham & Stoodley (2004), Pham, Bruce & Stoodley (2005) and to the work of Ference Marton, one of the founders of phenomenography, for example, Marton (1986), Marton and Booth (1997). Edwards (2007) provides a clear, simple outline of the approach.

Possible alternative approaches

There are several pointers indicating why the paradigm for this research needed to be interpretivist. It would be impossible to explore the meanings of doctoral students in the required depth using the measurement approach of the positivist paradigm. Even post-positivism, which encourages qualitative data, would not be appropriate. There was no specific theory to be tested and the categories were "developed through an ongoing iterative process of analysis" (Bruce *et al.*, 2009, p. 207). As Bruce *et al.* (p. 207) stated, "the categories of description ... are analytical constructs that represent the different ways of constituting IT research, as established through the interrelation between researchers and data". The results were not generalisable to all doctoral students, although theoretical generalisations would be possible. It would also be impossible to carry out such in depth research with a large sample. Indeed, Patton (2015, p. 264) postulated that:

> perhaps nothing better captures the differences between quantitative and qualitative [interpretivist] methods than the different logics that undergird sampling approaches. Qualitative inquiry typically focuses in depth on relatively small samples. ... Quantitative methods typically depend on larger samples selected randomly... [and which] will permit confident generalization from the sample to a larger population.

Nevertheless, another interpretivist approach could be considered. A constructivist framework and ethnographic method could have been an option. This approach also enables the exploration of similarities and differences in participants' views. The different style of analysis used in this type of research, however, would not have produced categories of description, or analytical constructs, very specifically focussed on different ways of experiencing, in the same way that the phenomenographic analysis did. Phenomenography is therefore well tailored to the aims of the research and research questions.

(2) Williamson's and Williamson and Kingsford Smith's mixed methods

Kirsty Williamson and Dimity Kingsford Smith received an Australian Research Council (ARC) Discovery Grant for a three-year project (2005–2007). They were interested in gathering more information about how people make investment decisions in online markets, particularly their use of information in the process. This was the focus of interest to Williamson, the information specialist. Kingsford Smith is a Professor of Law with a particular interest in how these processes are regulated and managed. Regulation of online investments is more likely to work if it is under-pinned by understanding the attitudes and experiences of investors. Publications from the project included Kingsford Smith and Williamson (2004),

Williamson (2008), and Williamson and Kingsford Smith (2010). The generous funding from the ARC enabled an ambitious project which had the following initial research questions relevant to this book. While interpretivist research questions can be changed as data are collected, these questions remained those used for the study.

1. What sources of information are used by online investors and how often? (quantitative questions)

2. What are the key sources of information used by investors and the reasons for their importance (e.g., type of content, currency, ease of access)? (qualitative questions)

3. Do preferred sources change according to the specific investment task? (qualitative question)

4. What is the extent of use, and perceived value, of the following for investment information? (a) search engines on the internet (b) internet websites (c) the media (newspapers, magazines, radio and TV) (d) interpersonal sources (family, friends and acquaintances) (e) professional advisors. (qualitative questions)

5. Do investors have a sense of information overload? (qualitative question)

6. Do they feel that they undertake systematic analysis using information? (qualitative question)

7. What can be gleaned about level of risk taking in relation to the extent of information seeking? (qualitative question). (Williamson, 2008)

The reasons why mixed methods were appropriate for the research are as follows.

a) A survey, with a large number of respondents, was appropriate for answering the first research question. The researchers wanted to obtain a broad picture of the types of information sources used by a range of online investors, along with the frequency of use.

b) The other research questions were complex and required the in-depth exploration only possible with a small sample and a qualitative (interpretivist) approach. For example, the researchers were interested in the *reasons* for the use of key sources, not possible to understand reliably through the box-ticking process of a self-administered questionnaire.

Methodology

The researchers adopted a mixed method approach with regard to both research philosophy and method but tried to do it "in a thoughtful and defensible manner" (Greene & Caracelli 2003), as discussed in Chapter 1. Following Morse (2003), they determined that the 'theoretical drive' of their project was qualitative (interpretivist), that is, that this component would play the major part in answering the research questions, but their goal was to respect both positivist and interpretivist paradigms (Williamson & Kingsford Smith, 2010, p. 45).

The quantitative component

The quantitative data were used to provide the 'broad picture' of investing and information-seeking behaviour. For this component, major Australian online investing companies put the survey questionnaire up on their websites, thus inviting their clients to take part. This resulted in the target sample of at least 500 respondents being easily reached and exceeded (total of 520). Apart from demographics, questions all focussed on frequency of (a) various types of online investment activity and (b) information source use. Analysis involved only simple frequency counts on an Excel spreadsheet. The sample was large enough to enable cross-tabulation of variables, such as 'age' by use of particular information sources, but the researchers were not interested in this level of statistical detail. They reported only the numbers and percentages of respondents for each variable, sufficient to ascertain the most frequently used information sources, a major goal of the survey. (Note: people who fill in questionnaires are usually referred to as 'respondents'.) Moreover, the researchers were aware that this component fell short regarding positivist rigour. For example, although the sample was large, it had not been randomly selected. Care therefore was taken to avoid generalisation to all online investors.

The most important outcome of the survey was that it provided a large number of potential interviewees. "Almost 200 respondents offered to be interviewed, providing a large and varied pool of people from which to build a balanced, purposive sample" (Williamson & Kingsford Smith 2010, p. 46). Purposive/purposeful sampling is discussed above and in Chapter 15.

The qualitative component

The researchers were interested in the "perceptions, values, beliefs and the 'meanings' online investors constructed around information needs, seeking and use related to OLI [online investment] outcomes" (Williamson & Kingsford Smith, 2010, p. 47). They therefore adopted an interpretivist/ constructivist approach to explore the information behaviour of online investors. Although not spelled out in their publications, the researchers were influenced by both personal construct theory (Kelly, 1963) and social constructionist approaches (Berger & Luckmann, 1967; Schwandt, 2000) (discussed in Chapter 1). They expressed their views in this way: "Since Australian online investors have an interest in common and live with a similar range of cultural influences, both macro and micro, they are likely to have at least some shared needs, understandings and information behaviors" (Williamson & Kingsford Smith, 2010, p. 47). Differences were also expected. Thus the researchers were looking for both consensus and dissonance regarding the role of information in investing and how information services could be improved.

The method used within this constructivist framework was broadly ethnographic, influenced by Bow's (2002) well-researched argument: that ethnography or participant observation can be undertaken in flexible ways, for example, combining techniques such as interviews and observation, emphasising some techniques over others, or leaving some techniques out altogether. The principal technique was the individual interview, combined with responses to the questionnaire. A small sample of 26 investors was purposively selected from the 200 survey volunteers. Processes of data collection and analysis are detailed in Williamson and Kingsford Smith (2010, pp. 47–51).

Williamson (2005) discussed this use of ethnographic techniques in constructivist frameworks in more detail, using the pilot of the online investment project as an example. (See also, Chapter 13: *Ethnographic research).*

Findings and conclusions

The findings for both the quantitative and qualitative components are comprehensively discussed in Williamson and Kingsford Smith (2010, pp. 51-65). Profiles of each interviewee's questionnaire responses were prepared prior to the interviews and read out as interviewers moved through the questions with each person. Not only did this set the scene for the in-depth questions, but also enabled the researchers to check the level of accuracy of the survey results and to critique the effectiveness of the questionnaire. Williamson and Kingsford Smith considered that the discrepancies they picked up during this exercise "should prove salutary for other developers of survey instruments" (p. 50). These are discussed more fully in Williamson (2008).

In their conclusions, Williamson and Kingsford Smith (2010) reflected on multi-disciplinary advantages of their project. Through the combination of information seeking and legal research, unique insights emerged as expertise from two perspectives was brought to bear. The outcomes showed that, while online investors remain vulnerable, they are amenable to investor education, part of which should focus on information literacy.

Possible alternative approaches

A mixed methods approach was appropriate to this study. On the one hand, the quantitative component enabled the researchers to gain a broad picture of Australian online investment from a large sample. A high-quality purposive sample for the qualitative component, from across Australia, was possible because of the large pool of volunteers from the survey. Without the survey component, building a quality purposive sample would not have been possible. On the other hand, the 'drilling down' enabled by the interviews resulted in a depth of data which could not have been obtained if only a survey had been used. Both components were essential to the outcomes of the research. Alternatives to the methods used do not appear to be available.

Questions and methodology for a critical ethnography (based on critical theory)

With the information systems (IS) research examined here (Cecez-Kecmanovic, 2001), the researchers initially began to undertake an interpretive ethnography. The study set out to examine a consultation with staff, by the President of University X, about how restructuring of the university should occur to deal with Australian Federal Government funding cuts. The consultation began in late 1996 and took place through computer-mediated-communication (CMC). The initial purpose of the research was "to explore, document, and interpret the use and appropriation of CMCs in the consultative process focusing on different social and cultural contexts (within groups and at the University level)" (p. 151). When it became apparent that a true consultation was not taking place, but that most staff were taking part without realising this, it was decided that critical ethnography would be a more appropriate methodology and the research questions changed as a result. By this stage, the researchers had decided that the methods applied to date "were not sufficient to make sense of what was going on via CMC" and that they needed "to gain deeper understanding of the process" (p. 151). The following became some of the research questions:

1. How do participants use language to express themselves in email messages and how do such email *linguistic acts* produce a particular type of action?

2. In what ways do such communicative practices (the linguistic acts and social actions of participants) shape discourse?

3. How do participants frame perceptions and problems to be resolved, establish personal and collective identities, legitimise power relations and the production of organisational knowledge?

4. To what extent are such communicative practices enabled and assisted by the particular features of CMC used (Cecez-Kecmanovic, 2001, p. 152).

These new questions were designed to go beyond ethnographic research in its descriptive sense. They were framed to attempt to understand how the President could "use CMC instrumentally to conceal his strategic intent" (p. 155), while staff also used CMC to achieve their own goals. The researchers were therefore engaged in "critical thinking about IS" (p. 160).

Methodology

At the time that the researchers perceived the need for a change of direction for their research, Cecez-Kecmanovic (2001) and colleagues recognised the opportunity to apply Habermas' theory of communicative action. This provided the researchers with a much needed guide and influenced the development of their new research questions. Habermas' theory enabled the researchers to "explore what linguistic expressions or acts (as Habermas calls them) *mean* but also what they *do* and what they *produce* in the life-world of participants" (p. 151). This put a different complexion on the interpretation of the staff emails:

> In this context the purpose of hermeneutic interpretation became to develop understanding of communicative practices in CMC and reveal hidden forms of distorted communication that impacted upon the lifeworld of the participants (Cecez-Kecmanovic, 2001, p. 151).

After the new research questions were articulated and the decision to use Habermas' critical theory made, the research method had to be chosen:

> We adopted critical ethnography to help us discover how an apparently open and participative CMC discussion was in effect undemocratic; how CMC, introduced as a means for accessibility of information and transparency of process, in fact enabled distorted communication, disempowerment of participants, and preservation of the existing power structure (Cecez-Kecmanovic, 2001, pp. 152–153).

Unlike the other examples discussed in this chapter, Cecez-Kecmanovic's (2001) does not spell out, precisely, the method used after the change of approach. Rather Cecez-Kecmanovic was interested in exploring the relationship between theory and methodological strategies. Here you will not find a blueprint for conducting critical ethnography, but rather a deep, stimulating discussion of issues in the use of methodology which is not commonly used in information systems research (nor in LIS). Elsewhere critical ethnography has been described as an "emergent process, involving a dialogue between the ethnographer and the people in the setting" (Myers, 1999, p. 8), exactly the approach of Cecez-Kecmanovic (2001). With critical theory, researchers are "open to scrutiny otherwise hidden agendas, power centers and assumptions that inhibit, repress, and constrain. Critical scholarship requires commonsense assumptions be questioned" (Thomas, 1993, pp. 2–3).

With Cecez-Kecmanovic's (2001) research, we know that the staff emails were reinterpreted in light of the new questions and framework and that being "very much aware of the uncertainty and fragility of our interpretations" (p. 153), the researchers conducted their interviews with participants and non-participants as a dialogue, sharing with them "interpretations and explanations of critical issues trying to achieve mutual understanding" (p. 153).

Possible alternative approaches

This study is particularly interesting because of the perceptiveness and adaptability of the researchers as they perceived the changed circumstances of their research context. It provides an excellent example of the links between research context, research questions and methodology. Alternative approaches cannot be suggested.

The literature review

The literature search and review should take place as the research questions and matching methodologies are developed. This involves identifying, locating, synthesising, and analysing the conceptual (theoretical) literature, as well as completed research reports, journal articles, conference papers, books, theses, and other materials about the specific problem or problems of a research topic. It is important that a literature review should include evaluative and critical judgements about the literature, and that it should present a comparison of ideas and research findings, tying them together. If the positivist paradigm is to be used for the research, the theoretical framework for the study should emerge from the literature review. Interpretivists may also propose a tentative theoretical framework although they will not set out to 'test' this framework.

The literature review has a crucial role in research. It provides a background, a framework and a context for a study, indicating relationships to other studies. It also assists the researcher in understanding the problem and its context. Marshall and Rossman (2016) discussed the role of the literature review in their book, *Designing Qualitative Research*, in which the process for developing a research proposal receives emphasis.

As already pointed out, the literature review plays an important role in the generation of theory and in the formulation and refinement of research questions and hypotheses. In addition, a thorough search of the literature enables the researcher to identify the gaps in previous research and thus to justify a proposed study in relation to a demonstrated need. Pointing out the gaps in the literature, through the literature review, is very important.

A further role of the literature review is documenting research results already available for the topic. Researchers can then use these results for comparison with the findings of their own studies. In this way, the findings of the new research are placed in the context of the findings of past research.

Undertaking a literature search

Because of the discipline areas to which this book relates, many readers will be trained in retrieval of information. Given the vast range of possible sources of literature, it is not possible to include more than a brief mention of the literature search. It is important not to limit your thinking to your own disciplinary field. There is much to gain from thinking laterally to other fields (depending on your topic).

The World Wide Web is now an important source of material but should be used in conjunction with other sources. *Google,* or even *Google Scholar,* will not lead to a comprehensive search. Remember that universities provide full text access to electronic journals not available on open access, although there is a variation in the levels and topics of their subscriptions. Some electronic journals provide their own search engines. For example, I was able to find two good examples of the positivist research approach in the highly regarded *Journal of the American Society of Information Science and Technology (JASIST)* – now *Journal of the Association for Information Science and Technology* – by searching for 'experiment' in the Monash University database. Above all, use *Wikipedia* only as a starting point, if at all. There are very few thesis examiners who accept *Wikipedia* articles as authoritative sources.

Sometimes you may be lucky enough to find a review article which gives a detailed coverage of the literature of your topic. If you are initially lucky enough to locate one or more recent key articles, the bibliographies of these will very often lead you to other relevant terms. If you are writing a literature review, you should try to include a range of literature – not all books, journal articles or internet sites, for example. Remember to look for theses, conference papers, working papers, lecture notes and government or industry reports, if relevant. Pickard (2013, pp. 25-38) gives useful advice regarding approaches to literature searching.

It is important to remember to update your literature review, late in the project as there could be new literature emerge as the project evolves. Indeed a literature review, though required in the early stages, should ideally be expanded and updated as the project proceeds.

Basic steps for writing a literature review

Below is a list of basic steps for writing a literature review as recorded in my research methods book (Williamson, 2002, p. 63).

1. Categorise your literature into subject/topic areas. Categories should be clearly related to your research questions.
2. Begin with an introduction to the topic including its significance and importance.
3. End the introduction with an overview of the contents of the review.
4. Organise the body of the review under headings which relate to your research questions.

5.   Critically analyse the relevant literature — conceptual, research and anecdotal — under those headings.

6.   Write a conclusion which draws the threads together, indicating the gaps in the literature and other reasons why research, or further research, is needed. The key concepts for the proposed research should be highlighted.

7.   End with the research questions which the proposed research will investigate.

8.   Check that you have written a critical and evaluative literature review. For example, did you examine the quality of the research which you discussed? Or did you simply assume that the findings were useful and valid? Did you simply report the views of other authors, rather than questioning and evaluating those views?

9.   Finally, ask yourself the question: "Are there prominent authors who are often cited on your topic by others and whom you have not included?" If you are unable to answer in the negative, you need to be sure of your reasons and perhaps include an explanatory statement in the review.

Theoretical frameworks

Consideration of theory, informed by the literature review, will also be taking place, iteratively. Not only are theoretical concepts important in the choice and discussion of research methodology; *theory* plays other roles in research. Emphasising that research is about finding ways of 'seeing', Schauder (2002, p. 325) cited Skeat (1887, p. 503) to point out that the derivation of the word 'theory' is from the Greek word meaning 'to see' or 'to behold'. Even if you decide to undertake a grounded theory, where you will construct theory or theories from your own data, it is important to understand relevant theoretical concepts that will enable you to build a rich theory of your own. (See Chapter 9: *Constructivist grounded theory* for discussion of the role of theory development in that method.) If you are undertaking deductive, positivist research, theory construction prior to empirical research will be important. As already mentioned, reading and reviewing the literature is an integral part of theory development.

Social theory "condenses and organizes knowledge about the social world. We can also think of it as a type of systematic 'story telling' that explains how some aspect of the social world works and why" (Neuman, 2014, p. 57). Thinking in general terms about what theory is, I proposed (Williamson, 2002, p. 58) that "we develop theories all the time in our everyday lives, for example, to account for someone's behaviour or explain certain problems that we face". I gave an example from a putative public library workplace:

> Suppose staff from a particular public library observe that the children's collection of the library is used less than would be expected

(or they believe that is the case). Their theory of why this is so could include the fact that there are very good school libraries in the area; and that the area is basically working class with the result that parents do not encourage their children to use the library as much as middle-class parents do. They might develop other theories about what can be done to change the situation (Williamson, 2002, p. 58).

Neuman (2014) also discussed social theories in general terms, including the fact that "we all encounter social theories in daily life, although few are explicit or labeled as such" (p. 57). At another point he postulated:

> Theories are not static. We are constantly modifying older theories and developing new ones. Theories come in many shapes and sizes. Some are broad systems of thought while others are narrow and specific explanations of one particular issue. At their core, we use social theories to organize and systematize our thinking and to deepen and extend understanding. Because they organize knowledge, theories also become a way to communicate effectively with one another (Neuman, 2014, p. 57).

Theories can be simple or deep, local or global. Weber (2012), addressing the concept of theory in the information systems field, provides in-depth perspectives. His view is that the articulation of high-quality theory enhances scholars' knowledge in the domain covered by the theory and "can enhance practitioners' capabilities to operate effectively and efficiently" in particular domains (p. 2). His broad definition is that "theories provide a *representation* of how a subset of real-world phenomena should be described" (p. 3). Weber provides a framework and criteria that can be used to evaluate the quality of theories in the information systems field. Chapter 7: *Case study research in information systems*, also briefly discusses theory in information systems research.

Theory development

We are fortunate in the LIS field to have a book devoted to the "theories of information behavior" (Fisher, Erdelez & McKechnie, 2005). The editors conceptualised "information behavior as including how people need, seek, manage, give and use information in different contexts" (p. xix). This book provides a useful overview of theory development in an important area of LIS and may provide ideas for theory development.

In the first chapter of *Theories of Information Behavior*, Bates (2005) distinguished the terms meta-theory, theory and models, pointing out differences which are not always acknowledged. Initially she provided the following definition of *metatheory* from *Webster's Unabridged Dictionary*: "A theory concerned with the investigation, analysis or description of theory itself" (p. 1). In summarising definitions of *theory* she stated: The core meaning "centers around the idea of a developed understanding, an explanation, for some phenomenon" (p. 2). In defining *model*, she cited the *American Heritage Dictionary* (1969): "A tentative ideational structure used as a testing device" (p. 2). Later she made the point that "models sometimes stand as theoretical beacons for years, guiding and directing research in a field, before the research finally matures to the point of producing something closer to a true theory" (p. 3).

As noted in Chapter 1, Bates provided a more specific definition of meta-theory, a definition she saw as comparable to Kuhn's definition of 'paradigm': "Metatheory can be seen as the philosophy behind the theory, the fundamental set of ideas about how phenomena of interest in a particular field should be thought about and researched" (Bates, 2005, p. 2). Indeed, she provided examples of meta-theories often indistinguishable from the paradigms discussed in Chapter 1 of this book.

There are many other meta-theories, which could also be described as macro-theories and which have had broad impact in the field of social research. Earlier meta-theories emanated from classic sociological theorists such as Marx, Durkheim and Weber. There are also well regarded meta-theories, concerned with broad societal analysis, from eminent modern theorists some of whom have also influenced the major meta-theories (paradigms) as discussed by Bates (2005) and in Chapter 1 of this book. Examples are from Pierre Bourdieu's cultural theory of action of which the *habitus* concept is a part (Joyce, 2005, p. 349); Anthony Giddens' *structuration theory*; and the *theory of communicative action* (Jürgen Habermas). All of these meta-theories have been directly used in information research. For example Bourdieu's (1984) concept of *habitus* provided an important part of Savolainen's (1995; 2005) *Everyday Life Information Seeking (ELIS)* model:

> Habitus can be defined as a socially and culturally determined system of thinking, perception, and evaluation, internalized by the individual. Habitus is a relatively stable system of dispositions by which individuals integrate their experiences and evaluate the importance of various choices, for example, the preference of information sources and channels (Savolainen, 2005, p. 143).

Williamson, Schauder, Wright and Stockfeld (2002) used Giddens' (1984) structuration theory in their exploration of the use of action research within an interpretivist framework. Structuration theory provides an account of the reproduction of culture across time and space, blending well with the constructivist perspectives of the authors. "Culture comprises both objective and subjective perspectives and the kinds of knowledge implied by both" (Williamson *et al.*, 2002, p. 12).

An example of the use of Habermas's theory of communicative action comes from the information systems discipline. Janson and Cecez-Kecmanovic (2005) used the theory to provide an explanatory framework in e-commerce research, the objectives of which included "to explain how the changes in social conditions brought about by B2C [business-to-consumer] e-commerce – such as public availability of information and equality of access to information – impact actors, their social behaviour and trade practices" (p. 312). The authors interpreted "buyers' and sellers' commercial transactions as social actions" (p. 312). Since Habermas's theory emphasises discourse ethics and the concept of justice in democracy (Benoît, 2005), it has also been used in computer mediated communications since it can explain the democratising potential of services such as email and intranets (Janson & Cecez-Kecmanovic, 2005, p. 314). Benoît (2005) stated that the theory has also been applied in information seeking and information behaviour. "Casting information seeking as a communicative action raises questions of interpretation, meaning, truth, and responsible agency" (p. 101). As noted above, Cecez-Kecmanovic (2001) used Habermas's theory of communicative action in her research focussed on the use of CMCs.

While novice researchers may not feel equal to incorporating one of these meta-theories into their own theoretical frameworks, they can provide stimulation. There are also other highly regarded theorists who are more specific in their theorising. As Leckie (2005) expressed:

> Towards the other end of the spectrum are theorists with a more finely grained and specialized theoretical perspective, such as Carol Kuhlthau (2004) and Elfreda Chatman (1999), who focus upon the micro-processes of daily life in particular cultural contexts and social settings (p. 158).

The work of these theorists/researchers, although still complex, is easier to use by the less experienced researcher. Both integrate a range of concepts into their own theoretically strong research and provide excellent models for theory building. Chatman (1999) brought her theoretical strands together in *A theory of life in the round* following her study of women in a maximum security prison. She had studied other small-world settings, such as women in a retirement village (Chatman, 1992). Her approach to deriving theory is presented in 'Framing social life in theory and research' (Chatman, 2000). Originally a keynote address at an Information Seeking in Context conference, this is a fascinating exploration of how Chatman formulated many concepts and frameworks over her career, beginning with 'small world', for which she acknowledged others who had gone before her in addressing this idea. She outlined how her original research question "has driven me to several conceptual frameworks and even the creation of several of my own" (Chatman, 2000, p. 4).

Kuhlthau's (2004) theory of the *information search process* was based on George Kelly's (1963) personal construct theory and Vygotsky's (1978) "zone of proximal development" (Kuhlthau, 2005). Julien and Williamson (2011) noted that Kuhlthau's work has been extensively cited, as well as used by practitioners. Clearly "practitioners have found Kuhlthau's theoretical contributions, incorporating both information seeking and information literacy concepts, to provide a very useful foundation for their information literacy instructional work".

An example of theory development

Rebecca French, a PhD student at Monash University at the time of the writing of the first edition of this book (2012), and now a graduate, grappled with theory development in an admirable way as I, one of her supervisors, attest. In Box 2.1 she outlines her theoretical journey.

Box 2.1

Example of theory development: Bricolage and welfare worker information behaviour

At the beginning of my PhD, I had identified that my particular research interest was in the community non-profit sector, in particular a focus on the welfare workers who work in this sector. I chose the research field of information behaviour because, not only was it an area which had been little studied in the welfare sector, but it was also an area of expertise for my supervisors.

I initially thought about the level of analysis. I was interested in the practices of individual workers, with interactions at a team, organisational and sector level being important but not the primary focus. I also wanted to take an ethnographic approach, immersing myself in the work of a small number of workers for an extended period of time. While I had a particular method in mind (video ethnography) I needed to remain responsive to the environment in which I was working, changing my combination of techniques (involving interviews, observation and a personal journal) as required.

Taking this approach naturally influenced which theoretical frames of reference I used. I have deliberately drawn on the research and thinking of researchers outside my initial focus of study, which brought a theoretical depth to my model building somewhat lacking in the field itself. For example, while I initially critically reviewed information behaviour and information-seeking models extant in the literature, I also reviewed a wide range of papers and monographs, particularly overarching key theories or key thinkers in the field. Authors such as Giddens (Structuration Theory), Polanyi (Tacit Knowledge) and Levi-Strauss (Bricolage) were key to developing my thinking. In particular, the concept of bricolage (taking a dynamic, fluid approach to work using the resources to hand, and relying on pre-existing knowledge) seemed to be potentially useful, given how the literature described the work of people employed in the welfare sector. It confirmed my own experience of working in the sector. While this process sounds smooth in retrospect, there was actually much time spent struggling to see the connections between sometimes very different theoretical areas.

After the initial foray into the theoretical arena, I decided to take a grounded theory approach, with data collection, data analysis and theory building occurring in an iterative, cyclical manner. At a practical level, this meant that insights from interviews or observations of study participants influenced the development of ideas which could then direct further questioning or observation. Ideas from data analysis led to changes in the focus of the research, with the concept of bricolage becoming far more prominent to the research than initially planned. Indeed, as the fieldwork progressed and I revisited the bricolage literature, I began to see that I could potentially develop a framework of bricolage in welfare work, while also critically analysing the concept of bricolage generally.

At a practical level, I found that it was important to give myself time between intensive periods of interview and observation, not only to transcribe and do an initial coding of the data, but to read through the data, think and talk about it. These discussions with colleagues, together with extensive use of memos (some reflective, some quite theoretical) were a vital part of the linkage between data and theory, one of the most challenging tasks undertaken during this PhD. I also found that regular concept mapping (through mind maps or Venn diagrams) was a very useful way of not only seeing the range of key concepts for myself, but was a very useful communication tool when meeting with my supervisors. An example of one of my Venn diagrams is below the box. I went through many stages of model-building and diagramming, sometimes on my own, and at other times with colleagues. I found that there was power for me in using a pen and paper as a tool when developing my thinking – sometimes models drawn on a computer were not enough.

This diagramming and modelling, together with discussions, memoing, critical analysis and re-analysis of literature, led to the beginnings of a model of bricolage in welfare work which has moved away from mapping an informational process, to focussing on a cluster of tools which the worker selects and enacts.

It is important to think of what may be in and out of scope in your research in relation to your theory building. I have continued to review the scope throughout the life of the project, even while writing up the thesis itself. Scope can change to ensure that the project is realistic in terms of the timeline, but can also be revisited in the light of data analysis and theory building. Even within the scope, different theoretical concepts can go in and out of focus as the theory-building progresses.

The stories I have just shared can make the journey of the research project seem like a straight road. However, if I were to visualise my journey, I would actually see it as a winding path. At times, you can feel quite lost, and unsure of the best way ahead. It is an emotional journey, with times when I lost confidence in the value and contribution of the research. It was important at these times to keep talking through these issues with my supervisors and fellow students. Just knowing that this was a common experience of all the researchers I talked to was helpful.

An example of concept mapping

Rebecca French found Venn diagrams can be a useful tool for exploring interrelationships between different thematic elements in a research study, and can be used a pre-cursor for later theoretical development. Figure 2.1 below is an example of a Venn diagram created at the mid-point of the data analysis phase of the research. It explores the relationship between welfare worker information behaviour (shown in the central circle) and four key themes that were identified during data analysis. The influence of particular factors on welfare worker information behaviour is indicated by the relative size of the circle. Examples of workers engaging in bricolage were frequent, many of which involved some form of information behaviour, as seen by the positioning of the bricolage circle over the top of the central circle There were far fewer instances of information resource seeking, where a worker actively searched for new information resources, hence the small size of its circle. The culture of the welfare professions was also influential, with the presence of an oral storytelling culture amongst these professions impacting on the type of information behaviour observed (focussed on sharing of information through talking to colleagues rather than use of internet searches, for example). The organisation's information culture seemed to have a

Figure 2.1 Example of a Venn diagram concept map.

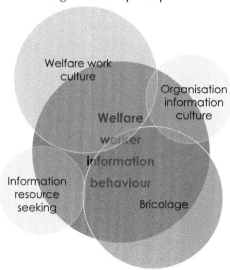

lesser impact. Bricolage and welfare work culture influence each other, as shown by the overlap between the two concepts in the figure.

For more details of Rebecca French's innovative theory, see French and Williamson (2016).

Conclusion

It is important that researchers pay close attention to research planning. Before methodology can be selected and fieldwork can begin, a suitable topic needs to be selected and refined; the literature must be searched and at least preliminarily reviewed; research questions need to be developed. None of these are discrete steps. If a researcher already has a topic in mind, at least the refinement and focus of this should occur through reading the literature. The research questions will be developed as the literature is explored and the preliminary review is written. If the plan to test theory (in positivist style), the researcher will need to develop this prior to field work. If grounded theory is planned, it is still a good idea to consider some possible theoretical concepts that might assist, as Rebecca French's example indicates.

References

Al-Maskari, A., & Sanderson, M. (2010). A review of factors influencing user satisfaction in information retrieval. *Journal of the American Society of Information Science and Technology, 61*(5), 859–868.

Bates, M. J. (2005). An introduction to theories, metatheories and models. In K. E. Fisher, S. Erdelez, & E. F. McKechnie (Eds.), *Theories of information behavior* (pp. 1–24). Medford, NJ: Information Today.

Benoît, G. (2005). Communicative action. In K. E. Fisher, S. Erdelez, & E. F. McKechnie (Eds.), *Theories of information behavior* (pp. 99–103). Medford, NJ: Information Today.

Berger, P. L., & Luckmann, T. (1967). *The social construction of reality: A treatise in the sociology of knowledge*. New York: Anchor Press.

Borgman, C. L., Hirsh, S. G., Walter, V. A., & Gallagher, A. L. (1995). Children's searching behavior on browsing and keyword online catalogs: The science library catalog project. *Journal for the American Society for Information Science, 46*(9), 663–684.

Bourdieu, P. (1984). *Distinction: A social critique of the judgement of taste*. London: Routledge.

Bow, A. (2002). Ethnographic techniques. In K. Williamson (Ed.), *Research methods for students, academics and professionals: Information management and systems* (2nd ed., pp. 265–279). Wagga Wagga, NSW: Centre for Information Studies, Charles Sturt University.

Bruce, C., Pham, B., & Stoodley, I. (2004). Constituting the significance and value of research: Views from information technology academics and industry professionals. *Studies in Higher Education, 29*(2), 210–239.

Bruce, C., Stoodley, I., & Pham, B. (2009). Doctoral students' experience of information technology research. *Studies in Higher Education, 34*(2), 203–221.

Burns, R. B. (2000). *Introduction to research methods* (4th ed.). Frenchs Forest, NSW: Longman.

Cecez-Kecmanovic, D. (2001). Doing critical IS research: The question of methodology. In E. Trauth (Ed.), *Qualitative research in information systems: Issues and trends* (pp. 142–163). Hershey, PA: Idea Group Publishing.

Chatman, E. A. (1992). *The information world of retired women*. Westport, CT: Greenwood Press.

Chatman, E. A. (1999). A theory of life in the round. *Journal for the American Society for Information Science, 50*, 207–217.

Chatman, E. A. (2000). Framing social life in theory and research. *The New Review of Information Behaviour Research: Studies of Information Seeking in Context, 1*, 3–17.

Connaway, L. S., & Powell, R. (2010). *Basic research methods for librarians* (5th ed.). Santa Barbara, CA: Libraries Unlimited.

Edwards, S. (2007). Phenomenography: 'Follow the yellow brick road'! In S. Lipu, K. Williamson, & A. Lloyd (Eds.), *Exploring methods in information literacy research* (pp. 87–110). Wagga Wagga, NSW: Centre for Information Studies, Charles Sturt University.

Fisher, K. E., Erdelez, S., & McKechnie, L. F. (Eds.). (2005). *Theories of information behavior*. Medford, NJ: Information Today.

French, R., & Williamson, K. (2016). Conceptualising welfare workers as information bricoleurs: Theory building using literature analysis, organisational ethnography and grounded theory analysis. *Information Research: An International Electronic Journal, 21*(4). Retrieved from http://www.informationr.net/ir/21-4/isic/isic1605.html.

Giddens, A. (1984). *The constitution of society: Outline of the theory of structuration.* Berkeley, CA: University of California Press.

Greene, J. C., & Caracelli, V. J. (2003). Making paradigmatic sense of mixed methods practice. In A. Tashakkori, & C. Teddlie (Eds.), *Handbook of mixed methods in social and behavioral research* (pp. 91–110). Thousand Oaks, CA: Sage.

Janson, M., & Cecez-Kecmanovic, D. (2005). Making sense of e-commerce as social action. *Information Technology & People, 18*(4), 311–342.

Joyce, S. (2005). Symbolic violence. In K. E. Fisher, S. Erdelez, & E. F. McKechnie (Eds.), *Theories of information behavior* (pp. 349–353). Medford, NJ: Information Today.

Julien, H., & Williamson, K. (2011). Discourse and practice in information literacy and information seeking: Gaps and opportunities. *Information Research: An International Electronic Journal, 16*(1). Retrieved from http://informationr.net/ir/16-1/isic2.html.

Kelly, G. (1963). *A theory of personality: The psychology of personal constructs.* New York: W. W. Norton.

Kingsford Smith, D., & Williamson, K. (2004). How do online investors seek information, and what does this mean for regulation? *Journal of Information, Law and Technology, 2*. Retrieved from http://www2.warwick.ac.uk/fac/soc/law/elj/jilt/2004_2/kingsford-smithandwilliamson/.

Kuhlthau, C. C. (2004). *Seeking meaning: A process approach to library and information services* (2nd ed.). Westport, CT: Libraries Unlimited.

Kuhlthau, C. C. (2005). Kuhlthau's information search process. In K. E. Fisher, S. Erdelez, & E. F. McKechnie (Eds.), *Theories of information behavior* (pp. 230–234). Medford, NJ: Information Today.

Leckie, G. (2005). General model of the information seeking of professionals. In K. E. Fisher, S. Erdelez, & E. F. McKechnie (Eds.), *Theories of information behavior* (pp. 158–163). Medford, NJ: Information Today.

Marshall, C. R., & Rossman, G. B. (2016). *Designing qualitative research.* (6th ed.). Thousand Oaks, CA: Sage.

Marton, F. (1986). Phenomenography: Exploring different conceptions of reality. In D. Fetterman (Ed.), *Qualitative approaches to evaluation in education: The silent revolution* (pp. 176–205). New York: Praeger.

Marton, F., & Booth, S. (1997). *Learning and awareness.* Mahwah, NJ: Lawrence Erbaum Associates.

Morse, J. M. (1998). Designing funded qualitative research. In N. K. Denzin, & Y. S. Lincoln (Eds.), *Strategies of qualitative inquiry* (pp. 56–85). Thousand Oaks: Sage.

Morse, J. M. (2003). Principles of mixed methods and multimethod research design. In A. Tashakkori, & C. Teddlie (Eds.), *Handbook of mixed methods in social and behavioral research* (pp. 189–208). Thousand Oaks, CA: Sage.

Myers, M. (1999). Investigating information systems with ethnographic research. *Communications of the Association for Information Systems, 2*(Article 23), 1–19. Retrieved from http://aisel.aisnet.org/cais/vol2/iss1/23/.

Neuman, W. L. (2014). *Social research methods: Qualitative and quantitative approaches* (7th ed.). Harlow, Essex: Pearson New International.

Patton, M. Q. (2015). *Qualitative research and evaluation methods* (4th ed.). Los Angeles, CA: Sage Publications.

Pham, B., Bruce, C., & Stoodley, I. (2005). Constituting information technology research: The experience of IT researchers. *Higher Education Research and Development, 24*(3), 215–232.

Pickard, A. J. (2013). *Research methods in information* (2nd ed.). Chicago: Neal-Schuman.

Savolainen, R. (1995). Everyday life information seeking: Approaching information seeking in the context of 'way of life'. *Library & Information Science Research, 17,* 259–294.

Savolainen, R. (2005). Everyday life information seeking. In K. E. Fisher, S. Erdelez, & E. F. McKechnie (Eds.), *Theories of information behavior* (pp. 143–148). Medford, NJ: Information Today.

Schauder, D. (2002). Postcript: Seven questions for information management and systems researchers. In K. Williamson (Ed.), *Research methods for students, academics and professionals: Information management and systems* (2nd ed., pp. 323–329). Wagga Wagga, NSW: Centre for Information Studies, Charles Sturt University.

Schwandt, T. (2000). Three epistemological stances for qualitative inquiry: Interpretivism, hermeneutics, and constructionism. In N. K. Denzin, & Y. S. Lincoln (Eds.), *Handbook of qualitative research* (2nd ed., pp. 189–213). Thousand Oaks, CA: Sage.

Thomas, J. (1993). *Doing critical ethnography.* Newbury Park, CA: Sage.

Vygotsky, L. (1978). *Mind in society: The development of higher psychological processes.* Cambridge, MA: Harvard University Press.

Weber, R. (2012). Evaluating and developing theories in the information systems discipline. *Journal of the Association of Information Systems, 13*(1), 1–30.

Williamson, K. (Ed.). (2002). *Research methods for students, academics and professionals: Information management and systems* (2nd ed.). Wagga Wagga, NSW: Centre for Information Studies, Charles Sturt University.

Williamson, K. (2005). Ecological theory of human information behavior. In K. E. Fisher, S. Erdelez, & E. F. McKechnie (Eds.), *Theories of information behavior* (pp. 128–132). Medford, NJ: Information Today.

Williamson, K. (2008). Where information is paramount: A mixed methods, multidisciplinary investigation of Australian online investors. *Information Research: An International Electronic Journal, 13*(4). Available from http://www.informationr.net/ir/13-4/paper365.html.

Williamson, K., & Kingsford Smith, D. (2010). Empowered or vulnerable? The role of information for Australian online investors. *Canadian Journal of Information and Library Science, 34*(1), 39–81.

Williamson, K., Schauder, D., Wright, S., & Stockfeld, L. (2002). Oxymoron or a successful mixed marriage? A discussion of the use of action research within an interpretivist framework. *Qualitative Research Journal, 2*(1), 7–17. Retrieved from http://www.stiy.com/qualitative/1AQR2002.pdf#page=7.

Chapter 3

Information research

Patterns and practice

Graeme Johanson[1] and Kirsty Williamson[2]

[1]Monash University, Australia [2]Monash University and Charles Sturt University, Australia

This chapter describes research in the information professions, in library and information science/studies (LIS), and associated disciplines. Within those disciplines, powerful themes of significant research include human information behaviour, especially information literacy, and a much wider range of methodologies than in earlier years. The chapter identifies the main topics of research by academics employed in universities, and by information professionals mainly employed by organisational information providers. Recent moves by governments to measure and control the quantity and quality of research have forcibly heightened awareness of research productivity. Tensions are explored between open access to and commercial constraints on knowledge, the good and bad that content analysis can reveal, and the pros and cons of collaboration within the disciplines, and beyond them. Research harnesses and respects the massive influences of information and communications technologies, while at the same time it helps to humanise and explain their dominance.

Research Methods: Information, Systems, and Contexts. DOI: http://dx.doi.org/10.1016/B978-0-08-102220-7.00003-0

Introduction

It cannot be assumed that research progresses in any predictable direction at a steady pace, although a casual observer might believe that to be the case. There are bursts of activity, too many (sometimes competing) interests, and too much to know and to research, for a prescriptive plan or preconceived agenda to be followed slavishly. Bold research must deal with risk, uncertainty, challenge, practical problems, non-trivial questions, significant consequences, the latest technical applications, new methods, and careful investment of available resources, including expertise (Buckland, 2003).

There are many names for the activities associated with research into the seeking, collection, understanding, organisation, and use of information (Myburgh, 2005), and the fields which conduct such research activities. While the frequency of use of the word 'libraries' declined in research publications and the names of university departments, 'information' grew in popularity (Wilson, Boell, Kennan & Willard, 2011). There are slight variations to the names of active disciplinary groupings (Hjørland, 2000), and 'information' and 'information technology' are now part and parcel of most of them.

If one explores the essential elements of research and practice, they deal with: information repositories (libraries, archives, records, digital resources); print and analog objects; how people seek information ('human information behaviour'); structures for their creation and dissemination; systems for the organisation of knowledge; how people use systems and repositories as individuals, or in groups, or in organisations for specific objectives for learning, planning, leisure and decision-making; and the most effective means for retrieving information (Meadows, 2008; Rochester & Vakkari, 2003). Because "the concept of information has entered the vocabulary of the physical and biological sciences" – and many other fields – Bawden (2008) noted that there is now a "unique opportunity for the insights of information science to be 'exported' to other disciplines" (p. 424).

Research focussed on the internet and other new technologies, including the World Wide Web and networking on social media (rapidly gathering momentum), has become very common in recent years. Also of increasing importance is the study of human information behaviour, often referred to as just 'information behaviour'. Information behaviour is defined as "how people need, seek, manage, give and use information in different contexts" (Fisher, Erdelez, & McKechnie, 2005, p. xix). This area of research has been particularly linked to the Information Seeking in Context conferences, inaugurated in 1996 and held biennially ever since. Another growing research area is community informatics, with its annual international conferences and emphases on the development of geographical or virtual inclusive communities by means of information and communications technologies (Gurstein, 2007). Community informatics includes several cognate disciplines (including information research) which have a concern for personal, social, cultural and economic improvement in the not-for-profit sector.

Because of the diversity of the field under consideration, we have decided to adopt the simple label 'information research' for this chapter, in spite of its non-specificity and the fact that such a label can include research into both archives and records and information systems, which are covered separately in the next two chapters. As was pointed out in the foreword to this book, there are synergies and overlaps between the information systems field and other areas of information research. There are also many differences, meaning that a separate chapter for information systems research is warranted (Chapter 5: *The methodological landscape*). The same is the case for a separate archives and records research chapter (Chapter 4: *Archival and recordkeeping research*). Knowledge management can be viewed from a range of perspectives and it has been decided to emphasise the 'information systems' perspective in this book. Knowledge management is therefore briefly discussed in Chapter 5. The present chapter, on information research, emphasising aspects of information management/library and information studies/science (LIS), provides an overview of research in the field, rather than a detailed discussion of methodological issues – because these were addressed in Chapter 2: *The fundamentals of research planning*.

Information research dimensions

In view of the vast amount of information available to billions of users, it is hardly surprising that extensive research is required to help to access, arrange, seek, use and understand information well. 'Information' and its by-products are increasingly at the heart of major inventions, discoveries and human developments (Kucier, 2010). Information plays a crucial role in the lives of individuals, groups and societies. The corollary must be that research focussed on information – undertaken particularly by university academics, information professionals, and organisational information providers – is also of great importance. Researchers examine, re-evaluate, integrate, extend, discard and replace the work of others who went before (Rayward, 1990). Researchers make use of prior research invariably; information and knowledge build on themselves.

What is information research?

Information research deals with all aspects of information. It includes analysis of the structure and delivery of information. Academic research can be theoretically based, or it may aim to develop theory inductively, but is more likely to be applied than basic. Information professionals manage information, monitor the emergence of fresh knowledge and plunge into the maelstrom of the endless re-creation, redistribution, re-dissemination and re-use of knowledge, and try to help others to steer through it in useful directions. Increasingly they are part of multiple communities of knowledge and social discourse (Buckland, 2003).

Human information behaviour, or information behaviour (mentioned above), is the major research area which emphasises information needs, seeking of information including use of sources, information use and information literacy. The catalyst for the original change of emphasis from information systems to information users was a review article by Dervin and Nilan (1986), eventually leading to a burgeoning in human information behaviour research. Wilson (2016) wrote of a shift of focus occurring from about 2000 – from a focus on what information humans 'need' to how they 'behave' in relation to sources and systems when seeking information. The field grew rapidly. Recently, automated information systems have added another dimension to the research scope, an interest in 'information receiving' (Long, Stewart, Cunningham, Warmack, & McElfish, 2016).

Academic and professional research

Academics, employed by universities, are major producers of research, although information professionals are also contributors as they conduct their own research in order to improve their practice. Practical research is a theme that recurs throughout this book, and is reviewed in the final chapter (Chapter 23: *The future of information research*). Information professionals are particularly interested in information users, their needs, their levels of satisfaction, and ways of assisting them with their information literacy. An example is Visser (2007), who undertook research as a teacher librarian focussed on 'information literacy development in the electronic age' – discussed in Chapter 8: *Action research.* Teacher librarians have been particularly interested in research concerning collaboration between teachers and teacher librarians (e.g., Haycock, 2007). Information professionals also collaborate with academic researchers, although the precise extent of collaboration is hard to identify. One example is the study of information literacy needs of research students at Monash University, which was undertaken by the University's Information Literacy Librarian, together with academic colleagues (Williamson, Bernath, Wright, & Sullivan, 2007). Another is the study, undertaken by practitioners and academic researchers, which recommended that academics assist librarians transform the pedagogy of information literacy to suit the special needs of students in the sector known as vocational education and training (Youens, Johanson, Pang, & Sullivan, 2007). Further discussion of practitioner/ professional research is discussed in Chapter 23 as well as below.

Until 1985, in the LIS field, only 1.6 percent of researchers employed qualitative methods (Järvelin & Vakkari, 1993). Academic research is now more often qualitative (interpretivist), although positivist, quantitative research continues on a smaller scale (Davis & Wilson, 2004). There is now a greater variety of other approaches than in earlier times, with methods such as phenomenography, action research, ethnography, grounded theory/constructivist grounded theory being commonly used. Mixing positivist and interpretivist approaches is becoming more common in Australian research projects in the field of LIS (Middleton & Yates, 2014). An example is Williamson and Kingsford Smith (2010), which is discussed in Chapter 2. As Bates (2005) pointed out, there is no compunction to adopt either a positivist or a subjectivist approach alone for any research problem: both can provide useful insights. (Note that Bates uses the label 'subjectivist' rather than interpretivist.)

The organisations, groups, individuals or other entities of interest to academic information researchers in universities cover a very wide variety. They include different types of libraries — national, academic, school, special and public — together with their users (staff and students); other organisations, e.g., archives, business, local government and not-for-profit organisations which sometimes represent non-mainstream groups, for example, self-help groups such as Arthritis Australia, disability groups, neighbourhood houses, environmental voluntary groups; e-repositories developed by a range of organisations; various internet components, for example, the World Wide Web and e-mail, and the users thereof; and groups which represent particular members of the community, for example, older people, young people, people with disabilities, online personal investors, women with breast cancer, migrants, refugees, and rural and remote residents. Much of the research has a human information behaviour focus, as discussed below.

Issues of research quantity and quality

Quality of research has always been a fundamental preoccupation of researchers. One of the recent developments affecting research worldwide is the intervention by governments in order to improve research productivity and to try to ensure that public funding invested in research will deliver real benefits to the wider community. They are assisted by various citation indexes that provide article citations and journal rankings. (See Chapter 10: *Bibliometric research*.) The many international rankings of research feed into university rankings such as the Shanghai Jiao Tong University Academic Ranking of World Universities, The Times Higher Education World University Rankings and the QS World University Rankings. Governments which fund public universities have tried to develop objective measures of the quantity and quality of publishing outputs of research academics, with variable success (Meadows, 2008). Thomson's *Web of Science* and *Scopus* have been relied on increasingly for measurement in assessment processes. *Google* also collates article citations in its product *Google Scholar*.

In Australia, formal government assessment of research began in 2006 with the proposal for a Research Quality Framework (RQF). In preparation for this evaluation exercise, university academics, with the support of professional and scholarly peak bodies such as the Australian Library and Information Association and the Australian Academy of the Humanities, developed the key field of research (FoR) codes for disciplines. Since then periodic changes of federal government have resulted in alterations to the criteria to evaluate academic output. The latest university assessment process is Excellence in Research for Australia (ERA). Academics also contribute to the annual Higher Education Research Data Collection (HERDC), for which universities are financially rewarded as they are for completion of higher degrees by research. The government has undertaken many investigations into the preferred methods for matching output with funding, and will continue to do so no doubt.

Any system of evaluation will find it hard to categorise LIS which field is, by nature, inclusive and multi-disciplinary. The general FoR code for LIS is 'library and information studies'. Sub-codes are health, social and community informatics; human information behaviour; information retrieval and web research; informetrics; librarianship; organisation of information and knowledge resources; and records and information management (business records associated with information management). The human information behaviour code would be applied to publications about information seeking and information literacy. An article on bibliometrics would receive the informetrics code, as it is concerned with the study of quantitative aspects of information, and the government tabulates it as such.

Many other potential problems with any measurement system which depends on hard-and-fast categories can be easily imagined, not the least of which are that the schema must accommodate changes over time, and that they can discourage international collaboration (because of different codes – or absence of them – in different parts of the world) (Cooper & Poletti, 2011). Each Australian university, indeed individual faculties, create their own local rewards to researchers for complying with the criteria.

Changes in government policy with regard to research publications and their impact will concern those individual researchers choosing where and when to broadcast publicly their progress and results.

Other methods of identifying research strengths and approaches

Apart from the categories and codes developed in response to government requirements, which help in identifying research areas considered important to a field, there are other ways of highlighting research interests and strengths. One is to use content analysis of professional journal articles to discover the topics which have caught the attention of information researchers over decades. As a research method, content analysis began in the 1930s in libraries. Content analysis studies the content of text in detail to determine authorship, authenticity, or significant meaning, assisted by computer scanning. It is rarely used for non-journal publications, e.g., for books, chapters in books, or reports; they are less indexed, and therefore were not so easily identified in the past. As the experienced researcher Meadows (2008, p. 1) stated confidently: "The development of information science research – as with most science and social science subjects – is reflected reasonably well by the changing nature of the research papers published in its leading journals." Ironically, the academic discipline which gave the world bibliometrics and scientometrics endures its increasing use for critical external surveillance. Meek calls are sometimes made for broader, internal, professional peer evaluation as an alternative (Aviles & Ramirez, 2015).

Various earlier studies showed that information retrieval, information services, and information seeking (now human information behaviour) were popularly published research areas (Rochester & Vakkari, 2003), as were information for competitive advantage, information behaviour in organisations, user satisfaction with systems, networking, the universal service obligation in telecommunications policies, computer applications, and knowledge management (Maceviciute & Wilson, 2002). The prominence of library history research indicated by an even earlier content analysis (Rochester, 1995) has diminished. A later study added the World Wide Web, computer applications, and online information retrieval (González-Alcaide, Castelló-Cogollos, Navarro-Molina, Aleixandre-Benavent, & Zurián, 2008).

Identifying important distributors is another way to assess significant research in a field. A stalwart for research dissemination for many years is the Association for Information Science and Technology (formerly the American Society for Information Science and Technology), by means of its primary outlet, *The Journal of the Association for Information Science and Technology* (*JASIST*), and its predecessors. It is an extremely prestigious journal.

Constants and fashions in research topic choices

As revealed above, major problems in discussing popular research topics are the variable terminology and the boundaries of the discipline areas considered. It is not difficult to discern topics that have endured over time. Examples include information retrieval, information seeking/information behaviour, and archives and records management. Research into censorship by libraries has been a popular theme in information research around the world for many decades, but has faded (Dick, 2007; Oppenheim & Smith, 2004). Since the terrorist fears in the US deriving from the events of 2001, serious concern about government censorship and invasion of privacy has revived among information researchers. Changes in fashions can also be observed in choice of research topics (Gilliland, McKemmish & Lau, 2016). For example, total quality management occupied the attention of information professionals and researchers for a decade, and mostly faded, but it still attracts serious investigation by researchers in non-Western countries with emerging information services (Moghaddam & Moballeghi 2008; Yang & Zhu, 2005). Fads do not detract from the importance of expressed professional concerns as providing grist to a researcher's mill, because they are a reflection of practical problems that require solutions in the workplace. Thus in the virtual world, digital preservation (Corrado & Sandy 2016) and metadata have become very important areas of research which are under-resourced (Gilliland, McKemmish & Lau, 2016).

Human information behaviour research

Human information behaviour, or information behaviour as it is commonly called, is a field of academic research that has burgeoned exceptionally in recent years. Interest in this area has been sustained over a long period of time, albeit under different labels, so the current enthusiasm cannot be regarded as a 'fashion'. The broad label, information behaviour, came to subsume the previous narrower topics of information needs, information seeking (including use of information sources), information use, and information literacy. The common term for this group of topics was previously 'information-seeking behaviour'. Nevertheless, there is a new, competing label: information practice. Savolainen (2007) analysed the "umbrella concepts of information-seeking studies", which he labelled as 'information behaviour' and 'information practice'. Examining a considerable number of sources from the information-seeking literature from the 1960s onwards, he found that the concept of 'information behaviour' extends back to the mid-1960s (p. 112), whereas "more detailed discussion" about the information practice approach only began "in the first decade of the twenty-first century" (p. 119). His conclusion was that discourse on information behaviour is mainly associated with the cognitive viewpoint, "while information practice is mainly inspired by the ideas of social constructionism" (p. 109). Regardless of labels, the popularity of this area is unquestioned. For example, information literacy is a very popular topic of research in Australia and, indeed worldwide (Boon, 2005; Clyde & Oberg, 2004). Chapter 9: *Constructivist grounded theory*, uses an information literacy study in three state high schools in rural Australia as its example.

An even earlier label for this field of research was 'user studies' which was of particular interest to information professionals keen to understand the needs of their service users. Before the 1970s, the research approach in this area was primarily positivist, trying to measure the features of the information user with scientific precision (Bawden, 2008). Case and Given (2016) provided a detailed overview of the field as it developed into a focus on information behaviour, and Wilson (2008) charted the growth of the field as a subject of academic research, particularly as a topic for research at PhD level and beyond. The field grew ten-fold in the sixteen years to 2006. "The development of the field has thus led to a division between the needs of academia for theoretically grounded work, and the needs of the field of practice for guidance for service development" (Wilson, 2008, p. 457). This 'discourse disconnect' between scholars and information professionals has been discussed more recently by Julien and Williamson (2011) with regard to information literacy research. Their view was that information literacy scholars have tended to be attracted to theoretical discussions, largely of no interest to practitioners. Moreover, Julien, Pecoskie, & Reed (2011, p. 19) reported that the proportions of researchers and practitioners contributing to the literature in the information behaviour area have reversed, with researchers now being the major contributors.

Theories of information behaviour

The importance of the field of information behaviour research is underlined by the key publication, *Theories of Information Behavior* (Fisher *et al.*, 2005). In their introduction, the editors stated:

> information behavior researchers are among the highest users of theory within library and information science research ... Also theory use in information behavior is growing with an increasing number of theories being developed from within the field (p. xx).

The book includes short chapters on 72 meta-theories, theories and models, the majority of which were drawn from the social sciences (31 percent) and from library and information science (51.2 percent), with small percentages from computer science and the humanities. It provides many original suggestions about how the theories might be used. Several of the theories from the book are discussed in the theory section of Chapter 2.

Information management research in organisations

It is not uncommon for information educators to be based in university faculties which are devoted to management, business and economics, or for information graduates to work as information researchers in large enterprises, whether in government or business. Their emphasis is on research in what is termed 'information management' or 'business intelligence' (Wilson, 2002). 'Management' permeated the language of information studies from the 1980s (Meadows, 2008; Wilson *et al.*, 2011). An excellent example of a company profiting from business intelligence is IBISWorld (2017), which began in 1971. It charges a fee to provide information for strategic planning and research purposes, employing 25 researchers, some of whom are graduates of information management schools. It now has branches in the UK, USA, and China, as well as in Australia, where it began (Brynko, 2006). Whether or not a government department or a business has a library as such, most organisations of the size of medium enterprises, or larger, have a group of specialists or a unit with an information research role (Calvo-Mora, Navarro-García, Rey-Moreno, & Periañez-Cristobal, 2016). It is seen as essential, and the in-house value of good quality information has been researched extensively.

Consultants are used widely for specific problem solving, as they are in most industries, and it is said that their research is less rigorous than what scholarly standards require (Case & Given, 2016). They focus on achieving practical outcomes, as is suggested by lists of topics from consulting companies themselves: information strategies, electronic document management, business process reviews, systems and storage audits, development and implementation of standards, and risk analysis (Park & Chung, 2016).

Research sharing across disciplines and collaboration

As noted above, it is common for information researchers to use a range of methods, and to collaborate with other disciplines, with the result that it can be hard to differentiate distinctive approaches. The boundaries between information management, LIS, knowledge management, data management, archives and recordkeeping, and information systems are blurred. The increasing requirement for global perspectives on most research topics demands broader understandings. Research projects can no longer afford to function in geographical or intellectual isolation, or to ignore developing regions of the world (Johanson, 2012).

Information researchers benefit by borrowing methodologies and theories from many other (sometimes overlapping) areas and may include: knowledge management, anthropology, psychology, sociology, cultural studies, science and technology studies, organisational development, operations research, business intelligence, information systems, human computer interaction, web computing, community informatics, development informatics, media studies, and other disciplines. They also give back. In other words, the information fields borrow from particularly social science disciplines, which in turn borrow from them. There is collaboration across disciplines. For example, Kirsty Williamson collaborated with two Professors of Law to undertake research which focussed on the role of information in online investment (Williamson & Kingsford Smith, 2010). She has also collaborated with information systems and information technology specialists. Another project set out to determine the importance of the personal uses of information and communications technologies by poor Chinese migrant labourers in northern Italy — for information for personal well-being, job-seeking, and financial management. For this project, the first author of this chapter teamed up with two Professors of Economics and a Professor of Anthropology (Guercini, Dei Ottati, Baldassar, & Johanson, 2017). A fine example of cross-fertilisation is found in the life-work of the Australian Professor John Weckert, who has devoted his career to connecting the philosophy of ethics to aspects of information technology. He has worked with LIS researchers (Williamson, Kennan, Johanson, & Weckert, 2016). His research relates closely also to information systems, and to business and economics (e.g., Weckert & Lucas, 2013).

Nevertheless, the formation of trans-disciplinary groups irritates purist theorists (Lehmann & Quilling, 2011). Narrow compartmentalisation also suits bureaucratic administration; the politics of funding and the more powerful influence of some disciplines over others (Gilliland & McKemmish, 2004) are never far from the minds of research grant applicants (Hill, 2016). The introduction of major government research assessment exercises poses further impediments, as discussed above. Yet there are all-round benefits from collaboration, whether it is a simple process of just importing or exporting knowledge or a closer working relationship. Collaboration is a strength to the extent that it can combine talent, add cachet and breadth of achievement, and create greater ability to resolve complex problems. But it can also be a weakness in the sense that the foci of a particular field may be dissipated within a single project.

An example of successful research collaboration between information management and archives and recordkeeping occurred with the creation of the Continuum Model, a theory about the creation and diffusion of information over time and space in various formats (Borgland & Oberg, 2008; Schauder, Johanson, & Stillman, 2005). It originated from a merger of researchers into one university department (Upward, 2000) and has been widely adopted by research communities globally (e.g., Desrochers, 2015, pp. 63-64). Unfortunately, many information researchers do not take a strong interest in their own underlying philosophical assumptions.

The role of research in professional practice

As indicated above, information researchers have always undertaken some research associated with their practice. Their professional associations have had some influence on research priorities by partnering and sometimes funding projects, and providing an audience for reception of the research results via conferences and journals; yet the associations have declining memberships (Agarwal & Islam, 2016). The decline continues. Collaboration and enquiry are part of the professional ethos of librarians but, to the extent that they engage in postgraduate study themselves, it is normally in selective coursework for professional development (Obaseki, Ibrahim & Momoh, 2010) or a Master of Business Administration (MBA) (Rupp, 2013). A content analysis of recent professional publications by Julien *et al.* (2011) showed that practitioners are contributing less to the research literature than they did in earlier years, at least in the key area of information behaviour research, as noted above. Julien *et al.* called for LIS educators to strengthen research training for LIS graduates. A strong case can be mounted for the importance of research to professional practice, as it is in Chapter 23.

Importance of research to professional practice

Williamson (2002) provided the following summary of why research in professional practice should be undertaken:

- to assist in understanding the problems and issues that arise in the workplace;
- to add to knowledge in the field and/or provide solutions to problems;
- to maintain dynamic and appropriate services;
- to meet requirements of accountability — research is important in the age of accountability as it can assist in policy formulation and provide data to justify present funding or increased funding;
- to maintain and improve professional status — it is generally believed that high status research assists in improving the status of a profession; and
- to provide a body of research findings and theory to inform practitioners — professionals therefore need to be intelligent, critical consumers of research (Williamson, 2002, p. 12).

The last point is related to the development of evidence-based library and information practice. Other points in the list are elucidated below.

Evidence-based library and information practice (EBLIP)

The concept of evidence-based librarianship and, subsequently, evidence-based practice and EBLIP, originated with an article in the *Bulletin of the Medical Library Association*, written by Eldredge (2000), in which he discussed the potential for the core characteristics of evidence-based medicine and evidence-based health care to be adapted to health sciences librarianship. Since that time, there has been considerable discussion of EBLIP in the literature and the commencement of an open access, peer-reviewed journal, *Evidence Based Library and Information Practice* which began publication in 2006 (Lazarow, 2007). Indeed, by 2002, a number of different definitions of EBL had appeared in the literature (Partridge & Hallam, 2007) to the point that Booth (2002) compiled a list of 'consensually-based' defining characteristics of evidence-based librarianship:

- a context of day to day decision making;
- an emphasis on improving the quality of the professional practice;
- a pragmatic focus on the 'best available evidence';

- incorporation of the user perspective;
- acceptance of a broad range of quantitative and qualitative designs;
- access to the process of EBP and its products (Booth, 2002, p. 54).

This list omitted, however, the role within EBLIP for librarians to produce their own research results. Also in 2002, Crumley and Koufogiannakis provided a definition of EBL which encouraged librarians "to conduct high quality qualitative and quantitative research" (p. 62). Eldredge (2006) followed his initial contributions by providing a series of five steps, which he saw as analogous to the scientific method:

1. formulate a clearly-defined, relevant, and answerable question;
2. search for an answer to both the published and unpublished literature, plus any other authoritative resources, for the best available evidence;
3. critically appraise the evidence;
4. assess the relative value of expected benefits and costs of any decided upon action plan; and
5. evaluate the effectiveness of the action plan (Eldredge, 2006, p. 342).

Whether EBLIP represents a new research activity, or is derivative and/or a matter of fresh emphasis on 'evidence', is open for discussion. EBLIP certainly has its supporters. It is a useful concept from the viewpoint of encouraging information practitioners to be critical consumers of research and to use the research findings of others, as well as their own, to improve their practice. The literature on how evidence-based practice has been used in LIS is expanding (Partridge & Hallam, 2007). Nevertheless there are detractors as Partridge, Edwards and Thorpe (2010) discussed. A thoughtful critique of the evidence-based model of information literacy research was undertaken by Lazarow (2007) who raised questions regarding the emphasis in evidence-based practice on research conducted according to the scientific method, the role of context and culture, whether evidence-based practice is capable of addressing complex questions, and the role in it of values and politics. Given's (2007) view was that "qualitative research [is still] pushed to the edges of EBLIP ... due to the imposition of inappropriate [quantitative] expectations" (p. 16).

The axiomatic relationship between research and professional practice

Key elements in the definition of a 'profession' are the requirements for a 'mode of enquiry', 'a body of evidence', and 'a valuative stance', all important elements of any research enquiry (Becher, 2001; Freidson, 1986). The mode of enquiry assumes that a profession has a way to examine and investigate issues in its field. The body of evidence relates to special forms of acceptable data, and repositories of them, to assist the professional researcher in the discipline. The valuative stance refers to a set of ethical practices that are essential to research and professional behaviour. (See Chapter 20: *Ethical research practices*.) It can be argued that the idea of a profession and research cannot be separated. Myburgh (2005) argued that understanding ways of thinking is fundamental to professional action.

Experts in information, who know a lot about knowing, might be called 'applied epistemologists'. They understand the importance of knowledge, of ideas and theories, the expressions of human experience, the values of informing and being informed. From their own work practices, they develop a respect for the techniques and guiding principles of others. They have unique opportunities to observe, assist and influence research, and to create new knowledge.

There are many constructive connections between research and professional practice. Practising professionals benefit from understanding up-to-date research findings, which can improve the effectiveness of their work and provide them with reflective insights as well as generalised understandings to enrich their professional experience. Practical workplace problems frequently suggest researchable solutions. For example, early in this century, Australian public librarians, along with those from other developed countries, began to be concerned about the impact of the retirement of the baby boomers on public libraries. Researchers, who were members of Information and Telecommunications Needs Research (ITNR) — a research group affiliated with Monash and Charles Sturt Universities — were partnered by librarians to undertake research about this problem (Williamson *et al.*, 2006; & Williamson, Bannister, & Sullivan, 2010).

Research dissemination

Dissemination is crucial for all fields of research endeavour. It is a professional norm that beneficial insights and new discoveries should be communicated in the public interest. Which research is disseminated in a particular field, and which withheld, and how it is done, indicate a great deal about the successes, transparency, service orientation, status, and importance of a research field.

Research dissemination practices

Analysis of the content of professional and academic journals can provide an indication of research dissemination practices. In Australia in LIS more of the content of Australian publications are authored by practitioners and fewer by academics. Australian academic researchers publish in overseas outlets more than local professionals (Middleton & Yates, 2014).

One problem for publishing in LIS is that there were too many journal titles where research was and can be published — there were 469 different titles available in the period 1959–2008 (Wilson *et al.*, 2011). Not all can be of high quality. There are still more than 488 journal titles which publish library and information research internationally (ProQuest, 2016). The number of titles has increased by almost two per cent per annum over the past five years.

Other criticisms are that too often 'research' in published accounts are over-personalised and anecdotal (Williams, 2009), taking a particularist and shallow approach of "How we did our case study well" (Haddow, 2011) rather than presenting thorough, broad-ranging investigations of prior knowledge, fresh hypotheses, applied theory, and rigorous use of trustworthy research designs (Rayward, 1990; Weber, 2012).

On the positive side, dissemination analysis shows that more authors are collaborating with each other than before, resulting in increasing international research links and readership of articles; the research quality has improved; and trans-disciplinary authorship and expertise (encompassing co-authors from other disciplines) have grown (Willard, Kennan, Wilson & White, 2008). For more discussion of research dissemination choices, and the role of peer review, see Chapter 22: *Research dissemination.*

Scholarly communication and open access: The role of researchers

The average cost to researchers and libraries of research journals, in any format, grows at about six percent per annum, more than the average global budget of the libraries themselves and more than the average increase in the cost of books (Bosch, & Henderson, 2016). Traditional journal publishers try to maintain high levels of profit in spite of the widespread online access to other sources of research information. The world's largest journal publishers benefit from a profit margin of 35 per cent annually, more than the world's largest bank or Facebook (Hu, 2016).

Much research has focussed on the irony that many academics and other researchers undertake research with the assistance of government funding, write the results up as journal articles for a few large journal publishing companies, for no profit, then libraries in research institutions buy the journals back at high prices (Steele, 2012). The heated tension between commercial profit-making and ethical provision of public knowledge is thoroughly articulated in much recent published research. Organisations like UNESCO (OASIS, 2009; Das, 2008) and professional associations (such as Information for Social Change, in association with the Chartered Institute of Library and Information Professionals) align together on the side of open access. In Australia, some research on these issues has also been undertaken (e.g., AOASG, 2016; OASPA, 2016). Chapter 22 discusses 'open access' and 'peer review' further.

Add to the manifest net financial loss to public institutions, as mentioned, the fact that academic authors frequently review unpublished articles for no fee for the benefit of the journal publishers (Eve, 2012), and sometimes pay to get their own articles into publication in the first place (Bergstrom & Bergstrom, 2012), and a strong reaction is inevitable. Librarians and academic authors have responded to the inequity by boycotting mainstream journal publishers, by refusing to buy their products or to write for them (Gowers, 2012), by establishing free electronic journals (Harzing & Adler, 2016), and by supporting online repositories (including archives) of articles and research papers which anyone on the internet can access at no cost. Funders of research are starting to insist that research findings resulting from their public support must be available to any interested reader for no fee. Research which quantifies usage suggests that online articles are more frequently used than print articles, and cost less to produce (Thelwall, 2008). It is speculated that journals may disappear entirely as a form of publication (Morrison, 2016) thanks to expanding open access online sources, and the dismemberment of formal documents.

Impacts of information technology

Technology has had a dramatic impact on access to information in every field of research endeavour. This is particularly the case in the information field because research here is partly responsible for charting and explaining the impacts of IT and assisting in the solutions to the new problems which occur as new technological applications become available. They go hand in glove.

Technological opportunities

Up to the turn of the last century, researchers depended heavily not only on personal search and management skills, but also on institutions which collected publications, documents, records, artistic expressions, and artefacts. Libraries, archives, galleries and museums are well-known symbols of scholarly and civic status. These days a virtual repository or shared database may well act as a substitute, and a well-designed website and search engine may provide access as a simulation of the service of the personal information provider of yore (Cram, 2011). Whether the organisation of managed information is made of bricks and mortar today, or is conceived of as entirely virtual or hybrid (Marcum, 2003), there will always be a need for collecting and disseminating public knowledge quickly, widely and equitably on request (Meadows, 2008). An excellent example of the use of technology to support research is Trove, a project of the National Library of Australia, which uses thousands of volunteers to help to digitise the content of old newspapers and magazines, among other items, in its collections (Hart, 2011). As the managers of Trove explained, the system demonstrates the value of common open standards across cultural institutions, and shared understanding that data should be open and accessible (Alam & Campbell, 2016).

Historians find huge potential in the use of Trove for mapping uniquely Australian trends in the past (Clark, 2016).

Transformations resulting from IT

Information technology has changed the way that information as a unit of analysis can be described by researchers. The piece of information is no longer just a concrete object which might provide data, nor the content of a publication, nor a tangible document (Buckland, 1999). It can be simply a digital trace of an electronic transaction, or an automatically-created bit of metadata. What is capable of being researched has been transformed by digitisation. (Gilliland & McKemmish, 2004; Rheingold, 1985). So has the immeasurable explosion of collected data.

Contrary to a few gloomy predictions of not so long ago, information and communications technologies and electronic objects have transformed workplaces in unexpected ways – which warrant thorough research. Some has been undertaken, in the form of the Delphi study, a method which seeks to elicit from experts what is probable and desirable in the future. In one study, 77 percent of 40 experts from the US, Canada, Western Europe, Central Europe, and Israel believed that probably the traditional library would be transformed, but that it would not disappear altogether. Of the group, 85 percent believed that, because of the arrival of instant access for users of information, it was desirable for information managers to thoroughly immerse themselves in understanding information-seeking behaviour, and become involved in training information users in good use; and 95 percent believed it was desirable that information managers become more assertive in promoting their skills (Baruchson-Arbib & Bronstein, 2002). A recent Australian study of libraries, archives, galleries and museums, used the Delphi method. Notably it concluded that one important desirable professional quality in future will be "the ability to research", as well as "problem solving, critical thinking and critical analysis" (Howard, Partridge, Hughes, & Oliver, 2016, p. 13).

Resisting technological determinism

When information and communications technologies began to demonstrate their enormous influence on information professionals in the 1980s, there was a tendency for technologists to promote their hardware, software, and applications as 'magic bullets' for any research problem (Buckland, 2003). At times the information researcher felt pressured into finding a 'problem' that would best fit an available pre-existing technical 'solution'. Buckland (2003, p. 680) explained that "technological modernism was a dominant influence in Western society from the late nineteenth century to the present and … the influence on and in librarianship has been greatly underestimated". Fortunately, such a top-down approach has been resisted by researchers who welcome the advantages of information technologies, but who give primacy to the underlying assumption that they must serve human needs and expectations first and foremost. The user comes first (Davenport, 2008).

Conclusion

This chapter has provided an overview of information research, broadly spanning many types of research. Unlike the other two discipline chapters, Chapter 4 and Chapter 5, this chapter does not discuss methodological issues in depth. Examples of methodology use in the information field are not dealt with here, but in Chapter 2 where they are related to the development of research questions. The researcher involved in the critical theory example, in Chapter 2, is from the information systems field (also one of the authors of Chapter 5), thus providing an example of the inter-relationships of the fields covered in this book.

The chapter has shown that on some fronts information research has posted modest victories. For example, we now know much more about seekers and users of information, and not just about the systems for information provision, where earlier research had concentrated. Individuals, and society more broadly, benefit materially and emotionally from an enhanced understanding of how people expect, find, manage, provide and use information better than ever before. Information research into the cost-benefits of information services and institutions has led to advocacy for the wider incorporation of intangible measures of the values of social inclusion. Free and open access to knowledge is mostly accepted as a global human right. Research into the benefits of information and communications technologies have led to personal, social, and economic improvements around the world. The benefits will increase. The alliance of information research with other disciplinary groups may seemingly dissipate a research focus, and add an extra burden to the work agendas of information researchers in the short term, but ultimately it will foster constructive relationships which sustain innovation, mutual fulfillment and symbiotic growth.

References

Agarwal, N. K., & Islam, M. A. (2016). How can professional associations continue to stay relevant? Knowledge Management to the rescue. *Proceedings of the Association for Information Science and Technology, 53*(1). Retrieved from http://onlinelibrary. wiley.com/doi/10.1002/pra2.2016.14505301028/pdf.

Alam, S. L., & Campbell, J. (2016). Understanding the temporality of organizational motivation for crowdsourcing. *Scandinavian Journal of Information Systems, 28*(1), 91–120.

Australasian Open Access Strategy Group (AOASG). (2016). What is open access? Retrieved from https://aoasg.org.au/what-is-open-access/.

Aviles, F.P., & Ramirez, I.S. (2015). Evaluating the internationality of scholarly communications in information science publications. *iConference 2015 Proceedings*. Retrieved from https://www.ideals.illinois.edu/bitstream/handle/2142/73769/477_ready.pdf?sequence=2.

Baruchson-Arbib, S., & Bronstein, J. (2002). A view to the future of the library and information science profession: A Delphi study. *Journal of the American Society for Information Science and Technology, 53*(5), 397–408.

Bates, M. J. (2005). Information and knowledge: An evolutionary framework for information science. *Information Research: An International Electronic Journal, 10*(4). Retrieved from http://informationR.net/ir/10-4/paper239.html.

Bawden, D. (2008). Smoother pebbles and the shoulders of giants: The developing foundations of information science. *Journal of Information Science, 34*(4), 415–426.

Becher, T. (2001). *Academic tribes and territories: intellectual enquiry and the culture of discipline*. Buckingham: Open University Press.

Bergstrom, T. C., & Bergstrom, C. T. (2012). Can 'author pays' journals compete with 'reader pays'? *Nature*, 11 February. Retrieved from http://www.nature.com/nature/focus/accessdebate/22.html.

Boon, S. (2005). *UK academics' conceptions of, and pedagogy for, information literacy: University of Sheffield*. Retrieved from http://dis.shef.ac.uk/literacy/project/progress.html.

Booth, A. (2002). From EBM to EBL: Two steps forward or one step back? *Medical Reference Services Quarterly, 21*(3), 51–64.

Borgland, E. A. M., & Oberg, L.-M. (2008). How are records used in organizations? *Information Research: An International Electronic Journal, 13*(2), 79–102. Retrieved from http://InformationR.net/ir/13-2/paper341.html.

Bosch, S., & Henderson, K. (2016, April 21). Fracking the ecosystem; periodicals price survey 2016. *Library Journal*. Retrieved from http://lj.libraryjournal.com/2016/04/publishing/fracking-the-ecosystem-periodicals-price-survey-2016/.

Brynko, B. (2006). IBISWorld; a pioneer in business data. *Information Today, 23*(9), 30–31.

Buckland, M. K. (1999). Form, meaning and structure of knowledge selection systems. *Proceedings of ISK099, Lyon, France, October 21-22 1999*. Retrieved from http://people.ischool.berkeley.edu/~buckland/lyon.html.

Buckland, M. K. (2003). The grand challenges for library research. *Library Trends, 51*(4), 675–686.

Calvo-Mora, A., Navarro-García, A., Rey-Moreno, M., & Periañez-Cristobal, R. (2016). Excellence management practices, knowledge management and key business results in large organisations and SMEs: A multi-group analysis. *European Management Journal, 34*(6), 661–673.

Case, D. O., & Given, L. M. (2016). *Looking for information: A survey of research on information seeking, needs, and behavior*. Bingley, UK: Emerald.

Clark, A. (2016). *Private lives, public history*. Carlton, VIC: Melbourne University Press.

Clyde, L. A., & Oberg, D. (2004). *LIS journals as a source of evidence for evidence-based practice: The case of school libraries worldwide*. Paper presented at the 70th IFLA General Conference and Council, 22–27 August, 2004, Buenos Aires, Argentina. Retrieved from http://archive.ifla.org/IV/ifla70/papers/051e-Clyde_Oberg.pdf.

Cooper, S., & Poletti, A. (2011). The new ERA of journal ranking; the consequences of Australia's fraught encounter with 'quality'. *Australian Universities' Review*, 53(1), 57–65.

Corrado, E. M., & Sandy, H. M. (2016). *Digital preservation for libraries, archives, and museums*. Lanham, MD: Rowman & Littlefield.

Cram, J. (2011). Public librarian? Is there an app for that? *The Australian Library Journal*, 60(4), 323–325.

Crumley, E., & Koufogiannakis, D. (2002). Developing evidence-based librarianship: Practical steps for implementation. *Health Information and Libraries Journal*, 19(2), 61–70.

Das, A. K. (2008). *Open access to knowledge and information: Scholarly literature and digital library initiatives – the South Asian scenario*. New Delhi, India.

Davenport, E. (2008). Social informatics and sociotechnical research – a view from the UK. *Journal of Information Science*, 4(4), 519–530.

Davis, M., & Wilson, C. S. (2004). *Research applications in information management: The case of informetric research in Australia*. Paper presented at the Research Applications in Information and Library Studies Seminar, 20 September, 2004, Brisbane, QLD.

Dervin, B., & Nilan, M. (1986). Information needs and uses. *Annual Review of Information Science and Technology*, 21, 3–33.

Desrochers, P. (2015). *La théorie sociale de la connaissance et la gestion du patrimoine documentaire à l'ère numérique* (PhD thesis). Université de Montréal, Montreal, Canada.

Dick, A. (2007). Censorship and reading practices of political prisoners in South Africa, 1960–1990. *Innovation*, 35(December), 24.

Eldredge, J. D. (2000). Evidence-based librarianship: An overview. *Bulletin of the Medical Library Association*, 88(4), 289–302.

Eldredge, J. D. (2006). Evidence-based librarianship: The EBL process. *Library Hi Tech*, 24(3), 341–354.

Eve, M. P. (2012, Februrary 8). Open access journals: Are we asking the right questions? *The Guardian*. Retrieved from http://www.guardian.co.uk/higher-education-network/blog/2012/feb/08/open-access-journals-elsevier-boycott.

Fisher, K. E., Erdelez, S., & McKechnie, L. F. (Eds.). (2005). *Theories of information behavior*. Medford, NJ: Information Today.

Freidson, E. (1986). *Professional powers: A study of the institutionalization of formal knowledge*. Chicago: University of Chicago Press.

Gilliland, A. J., & McKemmish, S. (2004). Building an infrastructure for archival research. *Archival Science, 4*(3-4), 149–197.

Gilliland, A. J., McKemmish, S., & Lau, A. J (Eds.). (2016). *Research in the archival multiverse*. Melbourne: Monash University Publishing.

Given, L. (2007). Evidence-based practice and qualitative research: A primer for Library and information professionals. *Evidence Based Library and Information Practice, 2*(1), 15–22.

González-Alcaide, G., Castelló-Cogollos, L., Navarro-Molina, C., Aleixandre-Benavent, R., & Zurián, J. C. V. (2008). Library and information science research areas: Analysis of journal articles in LISA. *Journal of the American Society of Information Science and Technology, 59*(1), 150–154.

Gowers, T. (2012). Elsevier – my part in its downfall. Retrieved from http://gowers. wordpress.com/2012/01/21/elsevier-my-part-in-its-downfall/.

Guercini, S., Dei Ottati, G., Baldassar, L., & Johanson, G. (Eds.). (2017). *Native and immigrant entrepreneurship; Lessons for local liabilities in globalization from the Prato case study*. London: Springer.

Gurstein, M. (2007). *What is community informatics (and why does it matter)?* Milan, Italy: Polymetrica.

Haddow, G. (2011). 'Glad tidings, testimony and research': Sixty years of *The Australian Library Journal*. *The Australian Library Journal, 60*(4), 280–290.

Hart, N. I. (2011). In search of the trout cod. Retrieved from https://arrc.com.au/ research/in-search-of-the-trout-cod-2/.

Harzing, A.-W., & Adler, N. J. (2016). Disseminating knowledge: from potential to reality—new Open-Access journals collide with convention. *Academy of Management and Learning and Education, 15*(1), 140–156.

Haycock, K. (2007). Collaboration: Critical success factors for student learning. *School Libraries Worldwide, 13*(1), 25–35.

Hill, S. (2016). Assessing (for) impact: Future assessment of the societal impact of research. *Palgrave Communications, 2*(Article 16073). Retrieved from http://www. palgrave-journals.com/articles/palcomms201673.

Hjørland, B. (2000). Library and information science: Practice, theory, and philosophical basis. *Information Processing and Management, 36*(3), 501–531.

Howard, K., Partridge, H. L., Hughes, H. E., & Oliver, G. (2016). Passion trumps pay: A study of the future skills requirements of information professionals in galleries, libraries, archives and museums in Australia. *Information Research: An International Electronic Journal, 21*(2). Retrieved from http://InformationR.net/ir/ 21-2/paper74.html.

Hu, J. C. (2016, January 26). Academics want you to read their work for free. *The Atlantic*. Retrieved from http://www.theatlantic.com/science/archive/2016/01/ elsevier-academic-publishing-petition/427059/.

IBISWorld. (2017). *IBISWorld industry data wizard.* Retrieved from https://www. ibisworld.com.au/.

Järvelin, K. & Vakkari, P. (1993). The evolution of library and information science 1965 1985: a content analysis of journal articles. *Information Processing & Management, 29*(1), 129−144.

Johanson, G. (2012). Delineating the meaning and value of development informatics. In J. Steyn, & G. Johanson (Eds.), *ICTs and sustainable solutions for the digital divide: Theory and perspectives* (pp. 1−18). New York: Information Science Reference.

Julien, H., Pecoskie, J. L., & Reed, K. (2011). Trends in information behavior research, 1999−2008: A content analysis. *Library & Information Science Research, 33*(1), 19−24.

Julien, H., & Williamson, K. (2011). Discourse and practice in information literacy and information seeking: Gaps and opportunities. *Information Research: An International Electronic Journal, 16*(1). Retrieved from http://informationr.net/ir/ 16-1/isic2.html.

Kucier, K. (2010, February 25). Data, data everywhere. *The Economist.* Retrieved from http://www.economist.com/node/15557443.

Lazarow, M. (2007). The evidence-based model of information literacy research: A critique. In S. Lipu, K. Williamson, & A. Lloyd (Eds.), *Exploring methods in information literacy research* (pp. 171−183). Wagga Wagga, NSW: Centre for Information Studies, Charles Sturt University.

Lehmann, H., & Quilling, R. (2011). Why are there not more grounded theories in information systems research? *Alternation, Special edition 4,* 350−364.

Long, C. R., Stewart, M. K., Cunningham, T. V., Warmack, T. S., & McElfish, P. A. (2016). Health research participants' preferences for receiving research results. *Clinical Trials, 13*(6), 582−591.

Maceviciute, E., & Wilson, T. D. (2002). The development of the information management research area. *Information Research: An International Electronic Journal, 7*(3). Retrieved from http://InformationR.net/ir/7-3/paper133.html.

Marcum, D. B. (2003). Research questions for the digital era library. *Library Trends, 51* (4), 636−689.

Meadows, J. (2008). Fifty years of UK research in information science. *Journal of Information Science, 34*(4), 403−414.

Middleton, M., & Yates, C. (2014). *ALIA/LIS research environmental scan report.* Canberra: Australian Library and Information Association.

Moghaddam, G. G., & Moballeghi, M. (2008). Total quality management in library and information sectors. *The Electronic Library, 26*(6), 912−922.

Morrison, H. (2016). Small scholar-led scholarly journals: Can they survive and thrive in an open access future? *Learned Publishing, 29*(2), 83−88.

Myburgh, S. (2005). *The new information professional: How to thrive in the information age doing what you love.* Oxford: Chandos.

Open Access Scholarly Information Sourcebook (OASIS). (2009). Practical steps for implementing open access. Retrieved from http://www.openoasis.org/index.php?option = com_content&view= article&id=254&Itemid=256.

Open Access Scholarly Publishers Association (OASPA). (2016). *Predatory publishers.* Retrieved from http://guides.is.uwa.edu.au/c.php?g = 325342&p = 2178782.

Obaseki, T. I., Ibrahim, S. D., & Momoh, J. N. (2010). Scientific research in librarianship: A panacea for library development in Nigeria. *Library Philosophy and Practice.* Retrieved from http://digitalcommons.unl.edu/libphilprac/439/.

Oppenheim, C., & Smith, V. (2004). Censorship in libraries. *Information Services & Use,* 24(4), 159–170.

Park, Y. G., & Chung, Y. K. (2016). A Study on the analysis of the factors for the introduction of the management for records in public enterprises. *Journal of Records Management and Archives Society of South Korea,* 16(2), 1–28.

Partridge, H., Edwards, S. L., & Thorpe, C. (2010). Evidence-based practice: Information professionals' experience of information literacy in the workplace. In A. Lloyd, & S. Talja (Eds.), *Practising information literacy: Bringing theories of learning, practice and information literacy together* (pp. 273–297). Wagga Wagga, NSW: Centre for Information Studies, Charles Sturt University.

Partridge, H., & Hallam, G. (2007). Evidence-based practice and information literacy. In S. Lipu, K. Williamson, & A. Lloyd (Eds.), *Exploring methods in information literacy research* (pp. 149–170). Wagga Wagga, NSW: Centre for Information Studies, Charles Sturt University.

ProQuest. (2016). Library and Information Science Abstracts (LISA): About. Retrieved from http://proquest.libguides.com/lisa.

Rayward, W. B. (1990). Scholarly publishing in journals of library and information science. *The Australian Library Journal,* 39(May), 127–133.

Rheingold, H. (1985). Tools for thought: The people and ideas of the next computer revolution. Retrieved from http://www.rheingold.com/texts/tft/6.html.

Rochester, M. K. (1995). Library and information science research in Australia 1985-1994. *Australian Academic & Research Libraries,* 26(3), 163–170.

Rochester, M. K., & Vakkari, P. (2003). *International library and information science research: A comparison of national trends.* The Hague, The Netherlands: IFLA.

Rupp, N. (2013). 'How I spent my summer vacation (and all my other free time) earning an MBA'. In C. Smallwood, K. Harrod, V. Gubnitskaia, & R. P. Holley (Eds.), *Continuing education for librarians: Essays on career improvement through classes, workshops, conferences and more* (pp. 22–27). Jefferson, NC: McFarland & Company.

Savolainen, R. (2007). Information behaviour and information practice: reviewing the 'umbrella concepts' of information-seeking studies. *The Library Quarterly,* 77(2), 109–132.

Schauder, D., Johanson, G., & Stillman, L. (2005). Sustaining a community network: The information continuum: E-democracy and the case of VICNET. *The Journal of Community Informatics,* 1(2), 79–102.

Steele, C. (2012, January 25). Scholarly licence to print money. *The Australian*. Retrieved from http://www.theaustralian.com.au/higher-education/opinion/scholarly-licence-to-print-money/story-e6frgcko-1226252771554.

Thelwall, M. (2008). Bibliometrics to webometrics. *Journal of Information Science, 34*(4), 605−621.

Upward, F. (2000). Modelling the continuum as paradigm shift in recordkeeping and archiving processes, and beyond: A personal reflection. *Records Management Journal, 10*(3), 115−139.

Visser, K. (2007). Action research. In S. Lipu, K. Williamson, & A. Lloyd (Eds.), *Exploring methods in information literacy research* (pp. 111−132). Wagga Wagga, NSW: Centre for Information Studies, Charles Sturt University.

Weber, R. (2012). Evaluating and developing theories in the information systems discipline. *Journal of the Association of Information Systems, 13*(1), 1−30.

Weckert, J., & Lucas, R. (Eds.). (2013). *Professionalism in the information and communication technology industry*. Canberra: ANU Press.

Willard, P., Kennan, M. A., Wilson, C. S., & White, H. D. (2008). Publication by Australian LIS academics and practitioners: A preliminary investigation. *Australian Academic & Research Libraries, 39*(2), 65−78.

Williams, R. V. (2009). Enhancing the cultural record: Recent trends in the history of information science and technology. *Libraries and the Cultural Record, 44*(3), 326−342.

Williamson, K. (Ed.). (2002). *Research methods for students, academics and professionals: Information management and systems* (2nd ed.). Wagga Wagga, NSW: Centre for Information Studies, Charles Sturt University.

Williamson, K., Bannister, M., Makin, L., Johanson, G., Schauder, D., & Sullivan, J. (2006). 'Wanting it now': Baby boomers and the public library of the future. *The Australian Library Journal, 55*(1), 54−72.

Williamson, K., Bannister, M., & Sullivan, J. (2010). The crossover generation: Baby boomers and the role of the public library. *Journal of Librarianship and Information Science, 42*(3), 179−190.

Williamson, K., Bernath, V., Wright, S., & Sullivan, J. (2007). Research students in the electronic age: Impacts of changing information behaviour on information literacy needs. *Communications in Information Literacy, 1*(2), 47−63.

Williamson, K., Kennan, M. A., Johanson, G., & Weckert, J. (2016). Data sharing for the advancement of science: Overcoming barriers for citizen scientists. *Journal of the Association for Information Science and Technology, 67*(10), 2392−2403.

Williamson, K., & Kingsford Smith, D. (2010). Empowered or vulnerable? The role of information for Australian online investors. *Canadian Journal of Information and Library Science, 34*(1), 39−81.

Wilson, C. S., Boell, S. K., Kennan, M. A., & Willard, P. (2011). Publications of Australian LIS academics in databases. *Australian Academic & Research Libraries, 42*(3), 211−230.

Wilson, T. D. (2002). Information management. In J. Feather, & P. Sturges (Eds.). *The International encyclopedia of information and library science.* London: Routledge. Retrieved from http://www.informationr.net/tdw/publ/papers/ encyclopedia_entry.html.

Wilson, T. D. (2008). The information user: Past, present and future. *Journal of Information Science, 34*(4), 457–464.

Wilson, T. D. (2016). A general theory of human information behaviour. *Information Research: An International Electronic Journal, 21*(4). Retrieved from http:// InformationR.net/ir/21-4/isic/isic1601.html.

Yang, L. Y., & Zhu, H. K. (2005). An experiment on digital library based on the method of TQM system. *Journal of Zhejiang University, 6A*(11), 1362–1366.

Youens, Z., Johanson, G., Pang, N., & Sullivan, A. (2007). *Towards a learning commons: Modelling a transformation of library services and information resource provision in the Vocational Education Sector.* Melbourne: The Victorian Association of TAFE Libraries (VATL).

Chapter 4

Archival and recordkeeping research

Past, present and future

Anne J. Gilliland[1] and Sue McKemmish[2]

[1]University of California Los Angeles, United States [2]Monash University, Australia

The chapter provides an overview of research in the archival multiverse, reviewing and reflecting upon historical developments, current trends and future directions. It chronicles the rapid diversification and expansion of archival and recordkeeping research over the past three decades with the development of important research and education infrastructure. It presents philosophical and theoretical frameworks that have been drawn from archival science and other fields, particularly those that support the exploration of records and recordkeeping as they exist in multiple cultural and social contexts. Common and emergent methodological stances are discussed and archival and recordkeeping research methods and techniques are identified and defined, including those derived and adapted from other disciplines The purpose is to promote their rigorous application, and provide sources for the teaching of research methods for professional and research careers. The chapter concludes with recommendations for how to sustain and extend archival and recordkeeping research to address the needs of our societies, organisations and communities.

Research Methods: Information, Systems, and Contexts. DOI: http://dx.doi.org/10.1016/B978-0-08-102220-7.00004-2

Introduction

This chapter provides an overview of contemporary archival and recordkeeping research in the archival multiverse, which:

> encompasses the pluralism of evidentiary texts, memory-keeping practices and institutions, bureaucratic and personal motivations, community perspectives and needs, and cultural and legal constructs with which archival professionals and academics must be prepared, through graduate education, to engage (PACG, 2011, p. 73).

The chapter uses the terms 'archival' and 'recordkeeping' throughout to include all aspects of archival science as more traditionally understood through life cycle ideas, as well as all aspects of the creation, management, use, and social embeddedness of records that are delineated in the records continuum and other emerging models. The concept of 'archival and recordkeeping research' is similarly broadly construed and includes research on archival and recordkeeping topics being undertaken in ancillary fields. The term 'evidentiary texts' is inclusive of records as they exist in multiple cultural contexts (i.e., the societal record), because the term 'records' could be read as pertaining only to institutional/bureaucratic forms of recordkeeping (PACG, 2011, p. 73). 'The Archive' encompasses broad philosophical and cultural notions of the archive in society and its societal functions, while 'the archive(s)' refers to narrower professional constructions as they relate to records, the repository responsible for their management, and the practices and services associated with that management.

Research plays an indispensable role in ensuring the growth, self-knowledge, and general wellbeing of any field. It builds theories and models that provide frameworks for practice and contextualise it. As well as developing the professional knowledge base and skills, research leads to a heightened understanding of the field's ethos and societal roles and how these have evolved over time. It promotes critical enquiry and analysis, as well as reflection upon and evaluation of theories, literature and practices. Research helps to facilitate standardisation, planning and assessment by identifying and building benchmark data within and across research areas, institutional and community settings, and local and national jurisdictions. It also challenges and transforms existing paradigms, constructs and practices. It promotes nuanced responsiveness to social, technological and intellectual developments. Overall, research supports more rigorous and sophisticated conceptualisation, articulation and assessment of the field's central precepts and practices.

This chapter demonstrates how archival science has emerged as a meta-field that cuts across so-called 'content disciplines' and whose research analyses the *processes and domains* associated with relevant professional activities (Bates, 1999).

The meta-field is permeated by notions of the archival multiverse and its researchers increasingly question:

> whether archival ideas and practices developed over centuries in response to the needs and modalities of large and powerful bureaucracies and scholarly repositories are relevant or effective when applied in other cultural and organisational contexts, for example those that are grass roots, Indigenous, transnational, or emergent (PACG, 2011, p. 70);

[and]

> how ... we move from an archival universe dominated by one cultural paradigm to an Archival Multiverse; from a world constructed in terms of "the one" and "the other" to a world of multiple ways of knowing and practicing, of multiple narratives co-existing in one space (PACG, 2011, p. 73).

Historical developments, current trends, future directions

This section reviews the archival and recordkeeping research landscape, pointing to historical developments and future directions. Over the past three decades, the field has experienced unprecedented growth worldwide within the academy and the profession, spurred on by technological and educational developments and social and intellectual movements. A more mature archival research consciousness has emerged in the academy and in practice with an unparalleled diversification of research themes. There has also been a significant expansion of the field's research front, with an increasing number of large, collaborative research endeavours involving major international, national and local partnerships with archival institutions, the archival and recordkeeping profession, researchers from other disciplines, government, business and not-for-profit sector organisations, and communities. The building of new archival theories and models similarly indicates a growing maturity and scholarly awareness that the constructs of the Archive and archive(s) provide rich loci for research and theorising.

Growing diversity of research themes

Table 4.1 summarises three different characterisations of the landscape of archival research over this period. Couture and Ducharme (2005) analysed forty articles published in five North American and international archival professional journals, from 1988 to 1998. In a special issue of *Archival Science* on research methods, Gilliland and McKemmish (2004) reported on major and emergent areas of archival research, referencing not only professional journals but also new research journals, conference proceedings, and the growing number of research monographs.

Table 4.1 Characterising the archival research landscape

Couture & Ducharme (1998 & 2005)	Gilliland & McKemmish (2004)	McKemmish (2016)
■ Archives and archival science – the nature of the Archive, archival goals and the usefulness of archives ■ Archives and society – the role and place of archives, archival science and the profession ■ Archival issues – ethics, access, privacy ■ Archival functions ■ History of archives and archival science ■ Management of archival programs and services ■ Technologies ■ Types of media and archives; electronic records ■ Types of archival institutions	Building; evaluating, reflecting on: ■ Archival education ■ Archival history ■ Archival media ■ Archival practice ■ Archival research methods and techniques ■ Archival systems ■ Archival theory, ideas and concepts ■ Archival tools and technology ■ Archival use and usability (by specific user groups) ■ Archives and recordkeeping metadata ■ Archives and recordkeeping policy ■ Development of descriptive models and schemas ■ Electronic recordkeeping ■ Ethnography of archival collaboration ■ Ethnography of archival practice ■ Ethnography of the archive ■ Impact on the record of organisational and technological change and vice versa	■ Anthropologicalcollecting and repatriation of data and archives ■ Archaeological recordkeeping ■ Archival advocacy and activism ■ Archival affect, agency, autonomy ■ Archival description and recordkeeping metadata ■ Archival education and pedagogy ■ Archival implications of social media ■ Archival literacy ■ Archives and postcoloniality, decolonisation of the Archive ■ Art-as-archive-as-art ■ Arts and performing arts archives ■ Business records and recordkeeping ■ Big data and open data ■ Co-design of systems ■ Community recordkeeping practices ■ Community-based archives and community-centric archival policy and practices ■ Criminal justice, counter-terrorism, surveillance and recordkeeping

Couture & Ducharme (1998 & 2005)	Gilliland & McKemmish (2004)	McKemmish (2016)
	- Psychology and ethnology of recordkeeping and use, including socialisation into document creation and use - Sociology and politics of the record and recordkeeping. Emergent areas of research related to archival globalisation: - Exploration of ways to diversify the archival paradigm and understand associated power and empowerment issues - Assessment of the impact of global research and international standards emanating from research upon local archival traditlions and theory, as well as marginalised communities - Postcolonial issues: 'The West vs. the Rest' - Evaluation, comparison and potential reconciliation of conflicting conceptual models and descriptive schema - Records law and policy, including reconciliation of different traditions - Ontological, semantic, and ethnomethodological issues relating to	- Critical archival and recordkeeping studies - Diasporic, expatriate and displaced records and identity - Digital curation - Diplomatics in digital and other contexts - Digital forensics and knowledge recovery - Digital heritage convergences - Digital humanities convergences - Digitisation and policy concerns - Electronic recordkeeping systems - Evidence studies - Gender, sexuality and archives and recordkeeping - Globalisation and other global concerns - Health records and recordkeeping - History of archives and archival practices - Imagined records and archival imaginaries - Indigenous knowledge, culture and the Archive - Legislative analysis - Memory and identity studies - Metadata modelling - Moving image archives - Museum archives

Couture & Ducharme (1998 & 2005)	Gilliland & McKemmish (2004)	McKemmish (2016)
	• developing understanding of emergent media forms • Addressing terminological difference within the archival field and between it and other fields interested in some of the same issues.	• Participatory archiving • Personal recordkeeping and digital archives • Policy concerns: privacy, access, security, etc. • Recordkeeping informatics • Records in post-conflict recovery and justice • Rights in records for victims, refugees, etc. • Scientific recordkeeping and data archives • Social justice and human rights archives • The social life of records and documents • Transformative research by and with Indigenous and other communities • Trusted digital repositories, records in the Cloud, distributed recordkeeping systems.

McKemmish (2016) reviewed more recent thematic trends in archival scholarship based on the contents of the annual 2009–2016 Archival Education and Research Institutes (AERI, n.d.), research published in leading archival journals (*The American Archivist, Archival Science, Archivaria, Archives and Manuscripts, Records Management Journal*) and *Research in the Archival Multiverse* (Gilliland, McKemmish & Lau, 2016).

Until the mid-1990s, much of the archival discourse focussed on the archive(s) as an institution that systematically promotes, preserves and makes accessible memory, culture and identity in the form of bureaucratic and social evidence. With reference to this construction, much of the research reported from this period is fairly narrowly focussed on archival best practice, management and enabling technologies. The later studies indicate subsequent major shifts in the types of research being undertaken. There is growing engagement with issues that span organisational, disciplinary, cultural and national boundaries or are raised by globalisation and transnational movement and technologies. Collaborations with professional, industry and big data communities continue on technology, policy, data and conceptual concerns (e.g., the nature of trust and trusted systems and repositories in the digital world). At the same time, critically-framed participatory and partnership approaches in the areas of community and Indigenous archives and recordkeeping, grounded in an ethos of equity, rights and community-identified research needs, have come to the forefront. Moreover, critical theoretical issues and developing technological capabilities have encouraged convergence with the cultural heritage sector and digital humanities (Caswell, 2016).

The research trajectory reflected in Table 4.1 speaks to a maturing research culture that is responsive to the complexity and changing boundaries and ideas of the world in which archival and recordkeeping activities are situated. Innovative approaches range from social justice activism, decolonising approaches, humanistic contemplation, performance and aesthetics, policy analysis and development, and social scientific analysis, to ontological modelling and systems analysis and design. At the same time, the trend towards trans-disciplinary and trans-institutional collaborations tackling multiple facets of priority research problems continues. Research on societal grand challenges such as climate change, sustainable communities, peace and security, social justice and social inclusion, called out by the Archival Education and Research Initiative (AERI), highlights the complexity, inter-relatedness, scale and immediacy of problems confronting archives as well as the ways in which archives and recordkeeping are integral to such challenges (Gilliland, 2015 & 2016b).

Expanding research front

Historically, most archival and recordkeeping research was individually or institutionally based. As already noted, there has been a major shift to collaborative research situated locally, nationally, trans-nationally, and even globally. There has also been a more conscious bridging of academia and practice, and of basic and applied research, especially in the digital arena. Many of these collaborative partnerships have resulted in the publication of policies, standards and strategies that have set a benchmark for archives and recordkeeping best practices.

Archival and recordkeeping researchers have also been involved as participants in wider multi-disciplinary collaborative research relating to the preservation of digital objects (Day, 1999; Gilliland, 2014), the building of digital libraries (D'Avolio, *et al.*, 2005), digital healthcare (Smart Information Portals, n.d.), digital asset management, digital government, digital humanities, digital heritage work, and resource discovery.

Partnership research in community settings, with funding from granting bodies and philanthropic foundations, has included the Monash Trust and Technology Project (McKemmish, Faulkhead & Russell, 2011) addressing the archiving of oral memory and the relationship between Indigenous communities and government archives; the Monash Country Lines Archive (n.d.) of animations of the story lines of Australian Indigenous communities (Bradley & Yanyuwa families, 2010), and research on archives and the rights of the child (Evans, McKemmish, Daniels, & McCarthy, 2015). Other prominent community archives research has brought together local communities and scholars at University College London (Flinn, 2010) and the University of California, Los Angeles (Caswell, Migoni, Geraci, & Cifor, 2016).

Archival theory and model building

The greater diversity and the expanding research front reflect in part the impact of the so-called 'archival turn', first evident in postmodern and postcolonial discourses in disciplines like anthropology, literature and history (Ketelaar, 2016). It encouraged researchers in archival science to contemplate the societal implications and effects of archives and recordkeeping. Critical theory (discussed in Chapter 1: *Research concepts*) provides a framework for theorising about both the role of the Archive in social conditions and forces such as colonialism, oppression, marginalisation and abuse of human rights, and the part that it might play in postcolonial, post-trauma and post-conflict societies.

The archival literature has been replete for many decades with expository and discursive writings on the nature of archival theory and how it can or cannot be distinguished from praxis. In the 1980s and 1990s there was considerable intellectual ferment internationally in two areas: the historical articulation and adoption of archival principles such as *respect des fonds* and *provenance* (Carucci, 1992; Nesmith, 1993) and the manifold re-examinations of appraisal theory in response to Hans Booms' reflections on archival appraisal with reference to communism, the rise of social history and the proliferation of records created through new technologies (Booms, 1987; Menne-Haritz, 1994). More recently, researchers influenced by cultural theorists such as Appadurai, have applied participatory design ideas to conceptualising participatory appraisal and archiving (Huvila, 2008; Shilton and Srinivasan, 2007).

An international cadre of archival scholars, including Brothman (1999 & 2001), Cook (1997 & 2001c), Harris (2001), Ketelaar (1999 & 2000), Nesmith (1999 & 2002), and Upward (1996 & 1997) began a movement re-thinking and debating the theories and models that informed archival practice for most of the twentieth century. Their postmodern, postcustodial writing has been influenced by philosophers such as Foucault and by Derridean archiviology, "a general science of the archive, of everything that can happen to the economy of memory and to its substrates, traces, documents …" (Derrida, 1995, p. 34). Their work represents a conscious archival theory-building movement. Upward's records continuum theory and related models, in particular, introduced a sophisticated and robust approach to building an archival ontology and epistemology that can be applied in multiple and increasingly complex contexts (McKemmish, Reed, & Upward, 2009; Upward, McKemmish, & Reed, 2011). Critical archiving, recordkeeping and practice are emerging at the nexus of continuum and critical theories (Evans, McKemmish, & Rolan, 2017).

Responding to social and political developments around the globe, and human rights and social justice movements, other scholars today are engaging critical theory in a more radical re-thinking of archival theory, roles and practices (Caswell & Cifor, 2016; Day, Lau, & Sellie, 2017). Increasingly the Archive is being explored as a contested, political space, a societal concept associated with the promotion of asymmetrical power, grand narratives, nationalism, surveillance, and the omission, diminution or silencing of alternate narratives (Faulkhead, 2009; Ketelaar, 2002; McKemmish, Iacovino, Ketelaar, Castan, & Russell, 2011; Punzalan & Caswell, 2016; Stoler, 2009). Interdisciplinary areas such as race and ethnicity, gender and sexual orientation, and Indigenous and subaltern studies, are also addressing the role of the Archive (Caswell, Cifor, & Ramirez, 2016; Cifor, 2016; Drake, 2014; Rawson, 2009). At the same time, war crimes tribunals, truth commissions, and reparations and reconciliation efforts increasingly employ records and archives as key instruments in human rights and social justice efforts (Blanco-Rivera, 2009; Caswell, 2011; Harris, 2007; McKemmish, Iacovino, Ketelaar, Castan, & Russell, 2011). A theoretical base for postcolonial archival studies and the decolonisation of the Archive is emerging, situated in the larger discourses on postcolonialism and postcoloniality (Burton, 2005). Ethnic and critical race studies, transnational approaches and theories of the diaspora are informing the re-conceptualisation of the Archive in a trans-disciplinary, multicultural, pluralistic, and increasingly interconnected and globalised world (Campt, 2012; Dunbar, 2006; Gilliland & Halilovich, 2017; Kaplan, 2000; Wurl, 2005).

Research programs and research infrastructure

This section discusses the development of archival research infrastructure over the past three decades.

Research education

In some places in the world, such as the US and Europe, there has long been a tradition of practising archivists holding doctoral degrees, often in history. From the early 1990s, partly in response to the need to grapple with the impact of new technologies, increasing numbers of students and professionals have pursued doctoral degrees through academic programs in archival science. These programs have expanded and diversified in response to increasing demand for professional qualifications, archival and recordkeeping research to support practice, and new career faculty members who will be state-of-the-art scholars as well as educators. Rising numbers of recent doctoral graduates have contributed to increasingly rigorous research being disseminated through a growing number of conferences and scholarly publications, as well as the growing diversity of research topics and methods. The centrality of archival and recordkeeping professionals in institution-based research and development initiatives, as well as in collaborative research projects, highlight the important role of archival education programs. These programs prepare future professionals to conduct, evaluate, and read research that relates to their areas of professional activity, and equip them with knowledge about archival concepts, practices, policies and technologies (Gilliland, 2016a).

Targeted research agendas and funding programs

Funding is critical to nurturing sustained and purposeful research. At national and international levels, scholars play an important role in working with government funding agencies and the professional community to identify priority research areas. US, Canadian, UK, European and Australian government funding agencies have encouraged collaborative work, and the willingness of archival institutions, records programs, private foundations, the profession and partner communities to sponsor and provide matching funding, in-kind resources and test beds has been critical to securing major grants. Beginning in the 1990s, unprecedented amounts of funding supported research on the management and long-term preservation of electronic records in international, national and institutional settings. The pioneering 1991 report from the US National Historical Publications and Records Commission (NHPRC), *Research Issues in Electronic Records*, set the research agenda for NHPRC funding initiatives. They included the Pittsburgh and Indiana University projects (Bantin, 1998; Bearman, 1994), the US contribution to InterPARES, and the Archivists' Workbench. In Canada, the Social Sciences and Humanities Research Council supported University of British

Columbia based projects, including InterPARES (with major sponsorship from national archival institutions and other professional associations, consortia, and smaller repositories worldwide). The Australian Research Council has funded major collaborative research on recordkeeping metadata with matching inputs from national and state archival institutions and professional associations. In the context of the growing convergence between the research interests of digital archives, digital libraries, digital preservation, and metadata development communities, the US National Science Foundation, and the UK's Joint Information Systems Committee (JISC, 2006) have contributed substantial funds to research on the preservation of digital materials, digital/data curation and cyberinfrastructure (American Council of Learned Societies, 2006; National Science Board, 2005; and National Science and Technology Council, 2009). European initiatives like ERPANET and DRAMBORA (the Digital Repository Audit Method Based on Risk Assessment) have been funded through Digital Preservation Europe (DPE). Another major source of funds is through the European Union Frameworks for Research and Technological Development such as the recent Horizon 2020. Research in digital humanities and in not-for-profit and community settings has also been funded by government and philanthropic foundations. Research funding is increasingly available for archival research relating to post-conflict societies, in part as an outcome of the 2005 UN Joinet/Ohrentlicher Principles to combat impunity and in part through philanthropic and other interests such as Swisspeace (2013), the United States Institute of Peace, and the Soros Foundation.

Scholarly venues

A research front cannot be sustained without robust ways for researchers to exchange ideas and research findings, work together to build research capacity and infrastructure, and nurture future generations of archival educators and researchers. Up until 2008, archival academics and researchers were only likely to gather in periodic pre-conferences before the meetings of the major professional societies and at events sponsored by the Section on Archival Education and Training of the International Council on Archives (ICA-SAE). Since then, summer schools for regional doctoral students have been held in Europe, for example, as part of Memornet in Finland (Sormunen, 2012) and at the University of Zadar in Croatia (APAE, 2016; RAMS, 2013). In 2008, the US Institute of Museum and Library Services provided initial funding for the week-long annual Archival Education and Research Institutes, (AERI), which have subsequently become self-sustaining. The latter development has demonstrated the importance of dedicated venues to present and gain feedback on research, learn about innovative methodological approaches, strategise research priorities, and collaborate on building needed research infrastructure. Another telling development has been the rapid increase in the number of scholarly forums in which archival research can be published, and the publication of archival research in journals and conference proceedings in many other fields.

Evolving research ethos and culture

As the field's research ethos and culture evolve, important questions arise relating to professional and disciplinary values, and the principles, knowledge and skill sets that archival and recordkeeping researchers need to bring to their work. How can the field ensure that its research is rigorous, eligible and available for peer review, able to withstand scrutiny by the public and funding bodies, and compliant with professional, institutional, and funding body requirements for ethical conduct? How does the development of a more robust ethical framework for archival and recordkeeping research fit with the professional codes of ethics and value statements (Gilliland, 2011; 2015 & 2017)? Collaborative, community-centric, trans-disciplinary and international research, and increasing concern about protecting vulnerable research populations bring new challenges, including exposure to institutional review boards or community-based ethics committees. These processes typically require the submission of a detailed research protocol, data gathering instruments, draft informed consent letters, and statements about how the rights, privacy and non-coercion of individuals referred to in gathered data will be ensured during and after the project, as well as in any resulting publications and presentations. Researchers need to become familiar with ethical processes and practice, and the ethical philosophies and frameworks that underpin them.

The ethical conduct of research becomes even more complicated when working with multiple funding agencies, institutions and national jurisdictions, and in partnerships involving diverse cultural beliefs and world-views, and researchers from several disciplines. Complex issues of intellectual property, acknowledgement of the contributions of the various parties, rights of all participants in the research data and publications, and ownership of outcomes arise. Working with communities, especially vulnerable communities, requires respectful negotiation of what constitutes ethical research behaviour in terms of the culture and values of all involved. Difficulties associated with often incommensurate infrastructures and resource bases need to be addressed. Negotiated partnership agreements need to address issues relating to the ownership of research data, other data rights, appropriate research protocols, the co-creation of knowledge, and the co-authorship and modes of dissemination of research outcomes. At the same time researchers must guard against the misappropriation of community knowledge through research processes that might be considered ethical in a traditional academic context (Lau, Gilliland, & Anderson, 2012).

Philosophical and theoretical frameworks for research

The increasing emphasis on rigour in research design, combining multiple methodological approaches within a single project, and the explicit choice of methods and techniques that are likely to yield the most insightful outcomes, is evidence of a growing maturity in the archival research culture. It also reflects the impact of professional and doctoral education in research methods and design and the requirements of peer-reviewed research journals and conferences. This section explores the philosophical and theoretical frameworks in which archival and recordkeeping research is conducted, while the following section discusses commonly used methodologies, models, methods, and techniques.

Positivism, interpretivism and critical theory

Chapter 1 discusses how until recently the dominant research paradigms in the social sciences have been positivism and interpretivism, and critiques how they have been constructed as binary opposites. It points to the association of particular research methodologies, methods and techniques with different paradigms, e.g., positivist researchers tend to favour quantitative and experiment-based research, while interpretivists are more likely to use qualitative methods. Increasingly research methodologies, methods and techniques are used *across* these paradigms, albeit applied and evaluated in different ways. They are also used in combination in mixed methods research. Chapter 1 also points to the emergence of critical theory as a third paradigm, another option for framing research in the archival and recordkeeping field. Chapter 5: *The methodological landscape* provides an explication of the three different approaches and their defining characteristics.

The broader intellectual context of the differing approaches to research encompasses modern and postmodern philosophical, anthropological, sociological, and historiographical thinking, including explorations of the nature of theory itself. This is clearly illustrated in the different understandings and interpretations of the record and the archive that underpin archival and recordkeeping research. The interpretive and critical paradigms encompass a spectrum of approaches that are linked to constructivism, structuralism, critical theory and cultural studies, and has in recent years been strongly influenced by postmodernism, and increasingly also postcolonial ideas. Mortenson (1999) argued that: "when the positivist conception of science is abandoned, new forms of archival theory emerge" (p. 1), theory that is better understood as "reflections on or criticism of existing practices" (p. 20), displaying "sensitivity to context and history" (p. 21). Positivist researchers tend to espouse notions of the record and the archive(s) associated with ideas about the objective and fixed nature of records, and the impartial and neutral roles played by archivists in their preservation. By contrast, interpretivist researchers focus on the contingent nature of records, the diverse and changing contexts in which they are created, managed and used, and the formative role played by recordkeepers and archivists. Their views are influenced by anthropological thinking about records as cultures of documentation. Critical archival researchers see the Archive and the archive(s), the processes that shape both, and the world views embedded in archival systems of classification as manifesting the power configurations, memory and evidence paradigms of particular times and places (Stoler, 2002). Postmodern ideas about records view them as both fixed and mutable, "always in a process of becoming", fixed in terms of content and structure, but linked to ever-broadening layers of contextual metadata that manages their meanings, and enables their accessibility and usability as they move through "spacetime" (McKemmish, 2005, p. 9). The archive(s) and often also the Archive, conceptualised as by-product or residue, and as an historical artefact fully formed and circumscribed in the positivist tradition, is seen as constantly evolving and changing shape – a dynamic, performative entity in postmodern frameworks.

As also discussed in Chapter 1, 'post' ways of seeing challenge the dualism inherent in positivism versus interpretivism, the theoretical-inductive versus the empirical-deductive, and quantitative versus qualitative approaches. MacNeil (2004) has explored the way in which the creative tension between the two paradigms was manifest in the first and second phases of InterPARES, speculating on how far the research moved beyond the paradigms in the triangulation of methods. The power of moving beyond such binary oppositions is suggested by Harris (2001, p. 42) when referring to the global and the local/Indigenous:

> It is in the both/and, the holding of these apparent opposites in creative tension, that there is liberation. For instance, a liberation for the Indigenous in being open to engagement with the dynamics of globalisation. A liberation for the global in respecting the Indigenous.

In emergent archival and recordkeeping research, liberation may well require the counter-intuitive application of what appear to be the opposites of interpretive and positivist approaches to studying archival phenomena. In part this may lead us to redefine, even refigure, the phenomena of interest to us. In part it may lead to understandings that some phenomena in our world behave in ways that are susceptible to being seen from a positivist perspective, while others are more readily understood from an interpretivist viewpoint. And perhaps the creative tension generated will lead us to yet other ways of seeing.

Double hermeneutics

Giddens coined the term 'the double hermeneutic' to refer to the "mutual interpretative interplay between social science and those whose activities compose its subject matter" (Giddens, 1984, p. xxxii), pointing to a blurring or even renegotiation of the boundaries between the observer and the observed. Schauder

(2002, p. 307) has characterised the 'mind bending' aspect of the double hermeneutic involved in research in the information meta-disciplines thus:

> It is yet another manifestation of the toughness of information management and systems research that what is studied – information phenomena – are in essence the same as how they are studied – the 'tools' used to study them. Both are constituted of processes of modelling.

Thus information researchers, in studying how people create a model or representation of knowledge, in turn create information models or knowledge representations that explain the models they are studying: "what information management and systems researchers are modelling is other people's information modelling!" (Schauder 2002, p. 308).

While the construct of the Archive is itself an object of study, it provides the evidence for the study of other phenomena. Yet another manifestation of the double hermeneutic emerges in archival and recordkeeping research in community settings when definitions of community that rest on a shared identity and a sense of belonging to a collective are considered. Ketelaar has depicted every community as a *community of memory* wherein collective identity is linked to a community recognising itself:

> through its memory of a common past ... To be a community, family, a religious community, a profession involves an embeddedness in its past and, consequently, in the memory texts [in any form, written, oral, as well as physical] through which that past is mediated (Ketelaar, 2005b, p. 44).

Research methodologies, design, methods and techniques

In this section, methodologies, modes, methods and techniques commonly used in archival and recordkeeping research, as well as emergent approaches, are discussed with reference to research designs and case studies exemplifying their use. The discussion is supported by tables that name and articulate methods and techniques being used in archival and recordkeeping research, including those derived and adapted from other disciplines. The aim of this section is to promote their rigorous application, provide literary warrant for those wishing to use them, and serve as a reference source for the teaching of research methods for professional and research careers in archival science.

Methodologies

There is often confusion over the meaning and scope of research 'methodologies', 'methods' and 'techniques'. Simply put, methodologies are the epistemological paradigms, the normative assumptions and ontologies which frame the researcher's approach to 'knowing' and investigating their world.

There are two prevalent methodologies in the archival world. First, the set of ideas formulated about Archive Science since the Enlightenment and influenced by modern, scientific thinking and positivism: that archives are unconscious and therefore objective by-products of bureaucratic activity, that records follow a predictable lifecycle and that custody is integral to archival management. And second, the Records Continuum approach, influenced by postmodern thinking, and increasingly by critical theory, and viewing recordkeeping as a continually interacting and evolving set of contingent activities with individual, institutional and societal aspects. The continuum approach allows for broad definitions of what is a record and for postcustodial, postcolonial notions of the Archive.

In response to societal challenges relating to social justice and inclusion, a new archival methodology is emerging. Influenced by postcolonial, post-conflict, and subaltern approaches, and the 'archival turn', it is concerned with ideas about decolonising and pluralising the Archive. It is closely associated with inclusive, participatory models of archival and recordkeeping practice and education (Lau, *et al.*, 2012; PACG, 2011) and community partnership research. Participatory, inclusive, reflexive research approaches engage researchers and community members in decision-making from conception to dissemination of the research. They aim to reposition those hitherto regarded as subjects of the research to active participants working in partnership with researchers, challenging more traditional constructs of data ownership, intellectual property, authorship and rights in research outcomes, and the unequal power relationships that are embedded in them.

Methods and techniques

The growing diversity of methods used to examine complex and emergent phenomena within the archival multiverse can be grouped into three categories as presented in the tables below. They name and define methods and techniques, suggest possible applications, and provide examples of their application in archival and recordkeeping research. Further discussion of several of these and detailed case studies can be found in Gilliland, *et al.* (2016).

Table 4.2 includes general research methods and techniques that might be considered at this point to be generic in the social sciences, computing and information sciences, and humanities.

Table 4.3 includes adapted research methods and techniques, borrowed from other fields but adapted and extended for use in recordkeeping and archival research.

Table 4.2 General research methods and techniques

Method/Technique	Definition	Potential applications and examples
Action research	See Chapter 8: *Action research: Theory and practice*.	Particularly relevant to collaborative research and development projects involving university, institutional, community and professional partnerships where archival institutions, recordkeeping programs or communities are the locus of the research.
Participatory action research	Based on "fundamental differences in our understanding of the nature of inquiry, not simply methodological niceties" (Reason & Bradbury, 2008, p. 4). "A participatory perspective asks us to be both situated and reflexive, to be explicit about the perspective from which knowledge is created, to see inquiry as a process of coming to know" (Reason & Bradbury 2001, p. 7).	Aims to solve practical problems (action), and generate new knowledge (research). May use case studies, ethnography and system analysis & design research methods and techniques. Participatory action research often employs second generation grounded theory approaches to data collection and analysis, as well as auto-ethnography, user-sensitive and value-sensitive design approaches. Examples include: ▪ InterPARES (InterPARES, n.d.) ▪ Clever Recordkeeping Metadata project (Evans, McKemmish & Reed, 2009) ▪ Monash Country Lines Archive (MCLA, n.d.).
Case studies	See Chapter 7: *Case study research in information systems*.	In-depth studies of a single 'case' or comparative studies of multiple 'cases' that aim to generate rich pictures and insights that might be transferable to other cases. In 'comparative archivistics' (Ketelaar, 1997), case studies and ethnographies are used to explore differences in recordkeeping cultures and practice.

Method/Technique	Definition	Potential applications and examples
		Examples include: - case studies of recordkeeping accountability (Cox & Wallace, 2002) - archival custody and memory in the US Virgin Islands (Bastian, 2003) - impact of recordkeeping and national cultures on recordkeeping in three educational institutions in different countries (Oliver, 2004) - electronic recordkeeping systems in multiple contexts (InterPARES, n.d.) - economics and politics of international preservation collaborations (Dong, 2012).
Constructivist grounded theory (also known as second generation grounded theory)	See Chapter 9: *Constructivist grounded theory: A 21st century research methodology.*	Used in exploratory research where little is known about a particular situation or phenomenon and new theory is developed or existing theories advanced. Used in participatory and community-based research projects to develop rich understandings of personal and community recordkeeping behaviours, recordkeeping and archival needs, and conceptualising the Archive in communities. Used to explore new phenomena and technologies, e.g., social media.

Method/Technique	Definition	Potential applications and examples
		Examples include: ■ early research on electronic records, e.g. University of Pittsburgh project on Functional Requirements for Electronic Recordkeeping (Bearman, 1994), the Indiana University Electronic Records Project (Bantin, 1998) ■ Indigenous archiving projects (McKemmish, Faulkhead & Russell, 2011) ■ multiple narratives and views in archival appraisal (Bunn, 2016).
Content and discourse analysis	See Chapter 19: *Qualitative data analysis*.	Analysis of professional and scholarly discourse to identify paradigm shifts and establish trends in theory and practice. Analysis of the development of policy and laws. Identification of counter- or submerged narratives.
Concept analysis	"A technique that treats concepts as classes of objects, events, properties, or relationships. The technique involves precisely defining the meaning of a given concept by identifying and specifying the conditions under which any entity or phenomenon is (or could be) classified" (Furner 2004, p. 233).	Analysis of constructs of the archive. Examples include: ■ history of archival ideas (Cook, 1997) ■ Derrida and the Archive (Brothman, 1999) ■ analysis of the concept of evidence (Furner, 2004) ■ nexus between recordkeeping, law and ethics (Iacovino, 2004) ■ exploration of archives, power, and memory (Ketelaar, 2005a).

Method/Technique	Definition	Potential applications and examples
Historiography	See Chapter 12: *Historical research.*	Historical studies of archival science, recordkeeping and archival practice, archival institutions, the profession, development of national or regional archival traditions, key figures in the profession. Examples include: ▪ history of Australian recordkeeping (Piggott, 1998) ▪ Lester Cappon, the relationship of history, archives, and scholarship (Cox, 2004) ▪ archival knowledge cultures in Europe, 1400–1900 (Head, 2010 & 2016) ▪ Waldo Gifford Leland (Wosh, 2011).
Surveys, interviews and focus groups	See Chapter 6: *Survey designs, and* Chapter 16: *Questionnaires, individual interviews and focus group interviews.*	Extensively used for data collection, in particular in action research, case studies, second generation grounded theory approaches, ethnography and systems analysis and design research (see examples in those sections). Examples include: ▪ user information seeking practices (Sundqvist, 2016) ▪ archival professional personality types (Craig, 2000; Pederson, 2002).

Table 4.3 Adapted research methods and techniques

Method/Technique	Definition	Potential applications and examples
Archival information retrieval	Information retrieval research employs mathematical and property-based models, and correctness measures (e.g., recall, precision, fall-out).	Furner and Gilliland (2016) discuss its application to archival work. Examples include: ■ pioneering work on online finding aids (Daniels & Yakel, 2010).
Bibliometrics & sociometrics	See Chapter 10: *Bibliometric research.* Sociometrics is a quantitative method for studying social relationships, networks and patterns of interactions, and revealing hidden structures such as invisible colleges, subgroups, alliances, ideological agreement, and dominant individuals (Moreno, 1951).	Can be adapted for use in analysing recordkeeping practice, e.g., through an analysis of the occurrence of certain data elements in records, or consistency of linkages between data elements; discerning patterns of influence and interaction in institutional and professional collaborations; or revealing patterns of use. Useful in studies that reflect on the research trajectory of the field, e.g., citation analyses to explore trends and influences in the archival discourse; identification of patterns of collaboration between key researchers and the transmission of ideas; tracing the influence of particular academic programs, their faculty and graduates. Examples include: ■ citation analyses to explore impact of computing on archival science (Gilliland-Swetland, 1992) ■ metrics applied to user studies (Yakel, 2004) ■ how archivists learn to appraise (Anderson, 2016).

Method/Technique	Definition	Potential applications and examples
Design-science	See Chapter 11: *Design-science research.* Design-science research focuses on developing innovative artefacts to solve a class or classes of problems.	Research is most often situated within a positivist paradigm, but also has potential to be used in interpretivist and critical research (particularly in the co-design of participatory systems). Examples include: ▪ the socio-technical and human contexts of systems (Iivari & Venable, 2009) ▪ designing interoperable online archiving and recordkeeping systems (Rolan, 2017).
Ethnography & ethnology Ethnography of the Archive	See Chapter 13: *Ethnographic research.* Ethnology involves cross-cultural and comparative study of the origin of human cultures, including social structure, language, religion and technology, and social change, often using multiple pre-existing ethnographies (Geertz, 1973; Monaghan & Just, 2000).	In-depth, comparative and cross-cultural studies of recordkeeping and archiving practice in different national and cultural contexts. Studies of recordkeeping and archival communities of practice. Studies of role of national archival authorities in democratic societies. In-depth studies of archival practices such as reference services. Community-based fieldwork studies of archival issues in the socio-cultural realm of record creation, management, preservation and use. Studies of cultures of documentation, record and archive forms, formative recordkeeping and archiving processes, world views manifested in their classification, the power configurations they reflect, and associated memory and evidence paradigms.

Method/Technique	Definition	Potential applications and examples
		Examples include: - recordkeeping and radiology (Yakel, 2001) - records as infrastructure in science laboratories (Shankar, 2004) - preservation practices (Gracy, 2016) - archival reference services (Trace, 2006) - remembering in an Afro-Mexican community (White, 2008) - colonial cultures of documentation (Stoler, 2009) - ethnography of artists in the archive (Carbone, 2015).
Expert systems	Elicitation and codification of expert domain knowledge into a knowledge representation scheme or set of rules enables tasks or decision-making normally requiring human experts to be automatically implemented through an expert system (Gilliland, 2016c).	Potential applications include automating or semi-automating online reference inquiries, applying archival description rules, creating metadata and making appraisal decisions. Examples include: - eliciting cultural ontologies in archives (Srinivasan, Pepe, & Rodriquez, 2009).
Indigenous methods	Indigenous research design and methods which fully engage with community, and are guided by principles of respect and reciprocity, and community protocols	Examples include: - designing "culturally safe to explore narratives of Koorie Victoria (Faulkhead, 2016) - an ethical community research approach to explore the archival needs of an Aboriginal community (Thorpe, 2016).

Method/Technique	Definition	Potential applications and examples
Metadata modelling, mapping and instantiation	Modelling and mapping metadata sets enabling precise definition and structuring, and graphical means of representation. Meta-mapping establishes equivalences and correspondences between metadata sets, as well as identifying gaps and inconsistencies. Metadata concept-mapping identifies major concepts and illustrate their inter-relationships. Instantiation systematically uses examples to populate models in order to test their validity, and highlight areas for further investigation and development (McKemmish, Acland, Ward, & Reed, 1999).	Use of formal modelling and mapping techniques in developing, structuring, testing and validating recordkeeping metadata sets and standards. Formal modelling of meta-maps to enable automatic translation between recordkeeping metadata sets, including those implemented in legacy systems. Used with systems analysis and design method. Examples include: • Australian SPIRT Recordkeeping Metadata Schema project (McKemmish et al., 1999) • Clever Recordkeeping Metadata and InterPARES MADRAS projects (see citations below).
Systems analysis, design and development	Involves cycles of system conceptualising, user needs analysis, prototyping and reflective evaluation (Burstein, 2002). Can be used to investigate concepts and constructs, allowing exploration of the interface between theoretical concepts and their practical realisation (Evans & Rouche, 2004). User and value sensitive design (VSD) emerged in the 1990s as approaches to ICT development that consciously and systematically takes into account human needs and values through the design process. VSD uses a tripartite, iterative approach integrating conceptual, empirical and technical investigations (McKemmish, Manaszewicz, Burstein, & Fisher, 2009; Friedman, Kahn, & Borning, 2006).	Extensively used and adapted to investigate the design of systems to support electronic recordkeeping and archiving, and digital archives. Used to develop a model system as a proof of concept or demonstrator of the feasibility of the approach or the underlying theory. Using a prototype as a research artefact to explore new concepts and constructs for digital archiving and participatory, online archives. Using formal activity, entity, relationship, role and data modelling techniques (e.g., IDEF, UML, ORM, DFD, RDF) in iterative, exploratory processes, enabling precise description and structuring of recording and archiving functions and processes.

Method/Technique	Definition	Potential applications and examples
		Examples include: • Victorian Electronic Records Strategy (PROV, 1999) • demonstrator of a metadata broker in a web service environment for the Clever Recordkeeping Metadata Project (Evans et al. 2009) • MADRAS metadata schema registry in InterPARES2 (Gilliland, Rouche, Evans, & Lindberg, 2005) • development of preservation and business recordkeeping models in InterPARES2 (Duranti & Preston, 2008) • the development of digital recordkeeping strategies, standards and policies, e.g. the work undertaken by the Australasian Digital Recordkeeping Initiative (ADRI) in partnership with the International Council on Archives (ICA, 2008).
Visualisation, animation and augmented reality	Virtual heritage modelling, involving three-dimensional (3D) animation and visualisation technologies as well as augmented reality, has enormous potential in archival research and practice.	Research employing virtual heritage modelling, 3D animation and augmented reality to explore innovative use of multimedia and social media technologies in living online archives, archival interfaces, and capturing Indigenous knowledge. Examples include: • the Monash Country Lines Archive project (MCLA, n.d.) which uses 3D animations, visualisations, and 3D representations to capture the dynamics of oral storytelling, intergenerational transmission of knowledge, and active learning.

The examples presented in Table 4.3 point to an increasing sophistication in adapting and extending, even transforming, methods and techniques from other fields over the past two decades. This can be seen in trends relating to the application of bibliometrics and ethnography, and the use of system modelling and design to prototype solutions to challenging recordkeeping problems, as well as the design of artefacts to investigate concepts and constructs, and provide proof of concept.

Table 4.4 includes archival and recordkeeping research methods and techniques that are unique to the archival field, having developed out of archival theory and practice.

The examples in Table 4.4 reflect the maturation and rich potential of archival research methods. Contemporary archival diplomatics has been extensively used in conceptual and applied studies of electronic recordkeeping, and more recently in digital forensics. Adapted from professional practice, functional analysis has become embedded in research practice. Archival literary warrant analysis, pioneered by Duff (1998), has been extended and refined to support a wide range of research in recordkeeping, archival and other fields (McKemmish, Manaszewicz, Burstein & Fisher, 2009).

Reflexivity is another indicator of the growing maturation of the recordkeeping and archival field. As can be seen in the tables, the main methods used include bibliometrics and sociometrics, ethnography, and historiography. Perhaps acknowledging the double hermeneutics in play in archival and recordkeeping research, there is an increasing realisation of the importance of reflexive research practice for individual researchers and research projects. This is particularly the case in interpretivist frameworks, including those using second generation grounded theory, ethnographic studies, and participatory action research. Reflective methods are particularly associated with ethnographic methods, especially autoethnography (Anderson, 2006; Charmaz & Mitchell, 1997), which is used in a variety of social science disciplines to elicit self-reflection and encourage transparency regarding one's own role and reactions by researchers and participants. An example is Štefanac's use of it to contemplate her own practice as a museum archivist in her study of how museum curators describe archival materials in their museums (2017). It can also be applied to reflect the experience of designing and implementing research, and working in collaborative research partnerships.

Designing research

Methods and techniques are the tools available to a researcher to carry out their investigation, observe, and model the phenomena they are studying. They are creatively combined in research design. Designing research encompasses

Table 4.4 Archival and recordkeeping research methods and techniques

Method/Technique	Definition	Potential applications and examples
Archival theory and model building	Systematic building and exposition of new theory, drawing on existing theories, concepts and models, observation, scholarly communication, data derived from other methods, and characterised by reflection, deep thought and a process of gestation of ideas. See Chapter 2: *Fundamentals of research planning*.	Reflection upon and augmentation of archival theory, and development of new theories and theoretical models, e.g., Records Continuum. Theorising about the nature and role of the Archive with reference to postmodern and postcolonial thinking, including exploration of the concept of decolonising the Archive. Developing conceptual and descriptive models of recordkeeping and archival activities and functions such as records creation, appraisal, description, preservation and access. Building conceptual models for describing records in their societal, business, and documentary contexts. Examples include: ▪ appraisal theory (Cook, 1992) ▪ development of theories and models of archival description (Hurley, 1995a, 1995b, 1998 & 2000) ▪ archival hermeneutics (Brown, 1991-2).
Diplomatics	Body of techniques, theories, and principles for analysing the form, function, and genesis of documents, with a particular view to establishing authenticity and reliability (Duranti, 1998).	Analysis of changes and continuity in document forms over time.

Method/Technique	Definition	Potential applications and examples
Contemporary archival diplomatics	In contemporary archival diplomatics, they are applied to electronic and digital records.	Identification of record types in electronic systems. Identification of requirements for preserving reliable, authentic records in electronic and digital systems. Examples include: ■ identification of requirements for reliability and authenticity in electronic records in InterPARES 1 and 2 (Duranti, Eastwood, & MacNeil, 2002; MacNeil, 2004) ■ application of digital diplomatics to digital records forensics (Duranti, 2009).
Functional analysis	Methods and techniques for recordkeeping functional, business analysis and work process analysis. Initially these techniques were developed for use in recordkeeping and archival practice, e.g., in system specification, appraisal and disposal, the development of business and archival classification schemes, the development of access policy.	Developing innovative policy and strategies, new standards and procedures. Identifying how records are created and used within recordkeeping systems. Understanding the societal and organisational mandates that govern recordkeeping. Examples include: ■ research and development projects on functional appraisal and macro-appraisal (Cook, 2001a, 2001b & 2004). Also used extensively in projects using systems analysis & design and metadata modelling methods (see examples in relevant sections of table).

Method/Technique	Definition	Potential applications and examples
Literary warrant analysis	(The term "literary warrant" was first used in 1911 in an article by Wyndham Hulme (Hulme, 1911/1950). Hulme used the term specifically to refer to the fact that the vocabulary of the Library of Congress Classification was empirically based on the warrant supplied by the Library's collection rather than on the warrant supplied by other means such as classification theory and attempts to classify the whole body of knowledge, or by readers' requests.) The literary warrant for professional practice, therefore, is made up of authoritative sources, which are recognised and valued by experts. Such authoritative sources may be found in the law, codes of ethics, standards, the professional and scholarly literature, oral and literary texts, and in domain experts. Analysis of the literary warrant for professional practice establishes the "mandates" for best practice, and identifies its conceptual and theoretical frames of reference (Duff, 1998).	Identification of social mandates for personal recordkeeping through analysis of sociology texts, and creative and reflective writings. Analysis of literary warrant to establish recordkeeping requirements. Analysis of standards, statements of best practice, and research reports to identify recordkeeping metadata requirements. Examples include: ■ functional requirements for recordkeeping (Duff, 1998) ■ evidence and law in recordkeeping (Iacovino, 2004) ■ recordkeeping warrant for metadata schemas (Duff & Cumming, 2016; Evans, McKemmish & Bhoday, 2005) ■ development of InterPARES 2 Literary Warrant Database (Gilliland et al., 2005) ■ evidence of me (McKemmish, 2011).

identification of the research problem, goals and desired outcomes; selecting the methodology with reference to the philosophical and theoretical approaches that frame the research; selecting and integrating appropriate methods; identifying the most effective techniques of data collection and analysis; and iteratively implementing, evaluating and adapting the research design as the research unfolds. It also involves rigorous negotiation and definition of research questions, mixing and matching research methods, triangulation of complementary methods to tease out multi-dimensional problems or questions, and meta-analysis of data collected through a variety of techniques, especially in large multi-disciplinary, collaborative projects. Perusal of the examples in Tables 4.2–4.4 illustrates how the research design of initiatives like InterPARES, the Clever Recordkeeping Metadata project and the Trust and Technology Project mix, match and triangulate a range of methods and techniques. InterPARES is also an intriguing example of research undertaken *across* the positivist and interpretivist paradigms.

Many aspects of research design are classically established by the academic participants in research projects, even in research projects that are undertaken in collaborative partnerships in institutional and community settings. True partnership research, however, engages all participants, non-academic and academic, as partners and key stakeholders from research conception to dissemination. Inclusive design processes are employed within appropriate philosophical approaches and research paradigms. The methods and techniques most commonly used are those associated with participatory action research, second generation grounded theory (also known as constructivist grounded theory), user-centred and value-sensitive design approaches. Examples of this kind of research include the suite of Australian Indigenous community-based partnership projects which explore the archiving and recordkeeping needs of Indigenous Australian communities, and involve Indigenous and non-Indigenous researchers, Indigenous community partners, and the archival community in reconciling research (McKemmish, Faulkhead & Russell, 2011; MCLA, n.d.). The research design utilises user- and value-sensitive approaches to conceptualising, building and reflectively evaluating community archival systems, interfaces and functionalities. These approaches provide a principled way to identify, conceptualise and take into account the values, expectations and needs of community and academic partners, and other stakeholders and users. In-depth interviewing, focus groups, interpretative narratives and structured questionnaires are used to elicit needs and values. Data are analysed using interpretative, qualitative and second generation grounded theory techniques. Relevant sources of literary warrant include the lore, law, protocols, codes of ethics, standards, best practice models, professional and scholarly literature, seminal research findings, and community Elders and domain experts.

Conclusion

This chapter has discussed past, present and future trends in archival and recordkeeping research, and the philosophies, paradigms and methodologies that frame it. It has explored the growing maturation of the field's research ethos and culture, the evolving toolkit of research methods and techniques, and the field's increasingly robust research infrastructure.

We have tracked the emergence of an epistemological and research framework that is self-consciously archival in construction and application, although it is indebted to the epistemologies and methods of other fields, as well as their constructions of the Archive and the archival endeavour. We have also explored how archival methodologies link to broader intellectual, philosophical and theoretical trends, and related shifts in research paradigms. Continued development and maturation of the diversity of research methodologies, designs, methods and techniques in the field will enable examination of complex and emergent phenomena in the archival multiverse. Research on, and publication of, the literary warrant for archival and recordkeeping research methodologies, including methods and techniques, will facilitate deeper understandings of the epistemological lineage behind methods that are being borrowed from other fields. The ways in which these methods are being adapted for archival uses will also emerge, as well as the evolution and maturation of methods that are uniquely archival, having developed out of archival theory and practice. Being more reflexive and explicit about the development of archival and recordkeeping research agendas and the design of research will enable robust, rigorous and ethical research.

The chapter also points to an increasing awareness and shared understanding of the role and importance of archival research in our own and other fields. There is today a robust corpus of researchers with sound conceptual archival knowledge, educated in the conduct of rigorous research, and aware of the potential of transformative research. Nurturing and extending our research partnerships and channels for dissemination of research outcomes enables us to engage in intellectually exciting and productive ways. Inclusive, collaborative research agenda-setting and ongoing research infrastructure development is critical at local, national and international levels to ensure that archival and recordkeeping research makes a major contribution to the challenges our societies face locally and globally, and addresses the short and long-term needs of the discipline and the profession. As we move forward, reaching consensus on research priorities, working out how to articulate them persuasively to potential funding bodies and linking them to societal grand challenges will enable the field to have a greater influence on the priorities of funding agencies. It will also promote focussed, in-depth research and consolidation of results in priority research areas.

References

American Council of Learned Societies. Commission on Cyberinfrastructure for the Humanities and Social Sciences. (2006). *Our cultural commonwealth.* Retrieved from http://www.acls.org/cyberinfrastructure/OurCulturalCommonwealth.pdf.

Anderson, K. (2016). Bibliometric analysis as a tool in understanding the development of archival thought. In A. J. Gilliland, S. McKemmish, & A. J Lau (Eds.), *Research in the archival multiverse* (pp. 811–843). Melbourne: Monash University Press.

Anderson, L. (2006). Analytical ethnography. *Journal of Contemporary Ethnography, 35* (4), 373–395.

Archival Education and Research Initiative (AERI). (n.d.). http://aeri.website.

Authenticity, Provenance, Authority and Evidence (APAE) Conference and School, University of Zadar. (2016). http://apae.unizd.hr/?lang = en.

Bantin, P. C. (1998). Developing a strategy for managing electronic records. The findings of the Indiana University Electronic Records Project. *American Archivist, 61*(2), 328–364.

Bastian, J. A. (2003). *Owning memory. How a Caribbean community lost its archives and found its history.* Westport, CT: Libraries Unlimited.

Bates, M. J. (1999). The invisible substrate of Information Science. *Journal of the American Society for Information Science, 50*(12), 1043–1050.

Bearman, D. (1994). *Electronic evidence. Strategies for managing records in contemporary organizations.* Pittsburgh, PA: Archives and Museum Informatics.

Blanco-Rivera, J. A. (2009). Truth commissions and the construction of collective memory. The Chile experience. In B. Alexander, & J. Bastian (Eds.), *Community archives: The shaping of memory.* London: Facet.

Booms, H. (1987). Society and the formation of a documentary heritage. *Archivaria, 24,* 69–107.

Bradley, J., & Yanyuwa families (2010). *Singing saltwater country.* Sydney: Allen & Unwin.

Brothman, B. (1999). Declining Derrida. Integrity, tensegrity and the preservation of archives from deconstruction. *Archivaria, 48,* 64–88.

Brothman, B. (2001). The past that archives keep. Memory, history, and the preservation of archival records. *Archivaria, 51,* 41–80.

Brown, R. (1991-2). Records acquisition strategy and its theoretical foundation. The case for a concept of archival hermeneutics. *Archivaria, 33,* 34–56.

Bunn, J. (2016). Grounded theory. In A. J. Gilliland, S. McKemmish, & A. J Lau (Eds.), *Research in the archival multiverse* (pp. 516–536). Melbourne: Monash University Press.

Burstein, F. (2002). Systems development in information systems research. In K. Williamson (Ed.), *Research methods for students, academics and professionals:*

Information management and systems (2nd ed., pp. 147–158). Wagga Wagga, NSW: Centre for Information Studies, Charles Sturt University.

Burton, A. (Ed.). (2005). *Archive stories. Facts, fictions and the writing of history.* Durham, NC: Duke University Press.

Campt, T. (2012). *Image matters. Archive, photography, and the African diaspora in Europe.* Durham, NC: Duke University Press.

Carbone, K. (2015). Artists in the archive: An exploratory study of the Artist-in-Residence Program at the City of Portland Archives & Records Center. *Archivaria, 79*, 27–52.

Carucci, P. (1992). Archival science today. Principles, methods and results. In O. Bucci (Ed.), *Archival science on the threshold of the year 2000: Proceedings of the international conference, Macerata, 3–8 September 1990* (pp. 55–68). Ancona: University of Macerata.

Caswell, M. (2011). Khmer Rouge archives: Accountability, truth, and memory in Cambodia. *Archival Science, 11*(1–2), 25–44.

Caswell, M. (2016). 'The Archive' is not an archives: On acknowledging the intellectual contributions of Archival Studies. *Reconstruction: Studies in Contemporary Culture, 16*(1). Retrieved from reconstruction.eserver.org/Issues/161/Caswell.shtml.

Caswell, M., & Cifor, M. (2016). From human rights to feminist ethics: Radical empathy in archives. *Archivaria, 81*, 23–43.

Caswell, M., Cifor, M., & Ramirez, M. H. (2016). 'To suddenly discover yourself existing': Uncovering the affective impact of community archives. *American Archivist, 79*(1), 56–81.

Caswell, M., Migoni, A. A., Geraci, N., & Cifor, M. (2016). 'To be able to imagine otherwise': Community archived and the importance of representation. *Archives and Records.* Retrieved from http://www.tandfonline.com/doi/full/10.1080/23257962.2016.1260445.

Charmaz, K., & Mitchell, K. G., Jr. (1997). The myth of silent authorship: Self, substance and style in ethnographic writing. In R. Hertz (Ed.), *Reflexivity and voice* (pp. 193–215). Thousand Oaks, CA: Sage Publications.

Cifor, M. (2016). Aligning bodies: Collecting, arranging, and describing hatred for a critical queer archives. *Library Trends, 64*(4), 756–775.

Cook, T. (1992). Mind over matter. Towards a new theory of archival appraisal. In B. Craig (Ed.), *The archival imagination: Essays in honour of Hugh A. Taylor* (pp. 38–70). Ottawa: Association of Canadian Archivists.

Cook, T. (1997). What is past is prologue. A history of archival ideas since 1898, and the future paradigm shift. *Archivaria, 43*, 17–63.

Cook, T. (2001a). *Appraisal methodology: Macro-appraisal and functional analysis - Part A: Concepts and theory.* Retrieved from http://www.bac-lac.gc.ca/eng/services/government-information-resources/disposition/records-appraisal-disposition-program/Pages/appraisal-methodology-part-a-concepts-theory.aspx.

Cook, T. (2001b). *Appraisal methodology: Macro-appraisal and functional analysis - Part B: Guidelines for performing an archival appraisal on government records.* Retrieved from http://www.bac-lac.gc.ca/eng/services/government-information-resources/disposition/records-appraisal-disposition-program/Pages/appraisal-methodology-part-b-guidelines.aspx.

Cook, T. (2001c). Archival science and postmodernism. New formulations for old concepts. *Archival Science, 1*(1), 3−24.

Cook, T. (2004). Macro-appraisal and functional analysis. Documenting governance rather than government. *Journal of the Society of Archivists (UK), 25*(1), 5−18.

Couture, C., & Ducharme, D. (2005). Research in archival science. A status report. *Archivaria, 59,* 41−67.

Couture, C., & Ducharme, D. (1998). La recherche en archivistique: Un état de la question. *Archives, 30*(3−4), 11−38.

Cox, R. J. (Ed.). (2004). *Lester J. Cappon and the relationship of history, archives, and scholarship in the golden age of archival theory.* Chicago, IL: Society of American Archivists.

Cox, R. J., & Wallace, D. (Eds.). (2002). *Archives and the public good. Accountability and records in modern society.* Westport, CT: Quorum Books.

Craig, B. L. (2000). Canadian archivists. What types of people are they? *Archivaria, 50,* 79−92.

Daniels, M., & Yakel, E. (2010). Seek and you may find. Successful search in online finding aid systems. *American Archivist, 73*(2), 535−568.

D'Avolio, L. W., Borgmàn, C. L., Champeny, L., Leazer, G. H., Gilliland, A. J., & Millwood, K. A. (2005). From prototype to deployable system: Framing the adoption of digital library services. *Proceedings of the American Society for Information Science and Technology, 42*(1). Retrieved from http://onlinelibrary.wiley.com/doi/10.1002/meet.1450420178/epdf.

Day, M. (1999). Metadata for digital preservation: An update. *Ariadne, 22.* Retrieved from http://www.ariadne.ac.uk/issue22/metadata/.

Day, R. E., Lau, A. J, & Sellie, A. (Eds.). (2017). [Inaugural issue]. *Journal of Critical Library and Information Studies, 1*(1). Retrieved from http://libraryjuicepress.com/journals/index.php/jclis.

Derrida, J. (1995). *Archive fever: A Freudian impression.* (E. Prenowitz, trans.). Chicago, IL: University of Chicago Press.

Dong, L. (2012). The economics and politics of international preservation collaborations. A Malian case study. *Archival Science, 12*(3), 267−285.

Drake, J. M. (2014). Insurgent citizens: The manufacture of police records in post-Katrina New Orleans and its implications for human rights. *Archival Science, 14*(3), 365−380.

Duff, W. M. (1998). Harnessing the power of warrant. *American Archivist, 61*(1), 88−105.

Duff, W., & Cumming, K. (2016). Respect my authority. In A. J. Gilliland, S. McKemmish, & A. J Lau (Eds.), *Research in the archival multiverse* (pp. 456–478). Melbourne: Monash University Press.

Dunbar, A. W. (2006). Introducing critical race theory to the archival discourse. Getting the conversation started. *Archival Science, 6*(1), 109–129.

Duranti, L. (1998). *Diplomatics. New uses for an old science.* Lanham, MD: Society of American Archivists, Association of Canadian Archivists, and Scarecrow Press.

Duranti, L. (2009). From digital diplomatics to digital records forensics. *Archivaria, 68,* 39–66.

Duranti, L., Eastwood, T., & MacNeil, H. (2002). *Preservation of the integrity of electronic records.* Dordrecht: Kluwer Academic Publishing.

Duranti, L., & Preston, R. (Eds.). (2008). International research on permanent authentic records in electronic systems (InterPARES) 2: Experiential, interactive and dynamic records. Padova, Italy: Associazione Nazionale Archivistica Italiana. Retrieved from http://www.interpares.org/ip2/book.cfm.

Evans, J., McKemmish, S., & Bhoday, K. (2005). Create once, use many times. The clever use of recordkeeping metadata for multiple archival purposes. *Archival Science, 5*(1), 17–42.

Evans, J., McKemmish, S., Daniels, E., & McCarthy, G. (2015). Self-determination and archival autonomy: advocating activism. *Archival Science, 15*(4), 337–368.

Evans, J., McKemmish, S., & Reed, B. (2009). Making metadata matter: Outcomes from the Clever Recordkeeping Metadata project. *Archives & Manuscripts, 37*(1), 28–56.

Evans, J., McKemmish, S., & Rolan, G. (2017). Critical archiving and recordkeeping research and practice in the Continuum. *Journal of Critical Library and Information Studies, 1*(2). Retrieved from http://libraryjuicepress.com/journals/index.php/jclis/article/view/35.

Evans, J., & Rouche, N. (2004). Utilizing systems development methods in archival systems research: Building a metadata schema registry. *Archival Science, 4*(3–4), 315–334.

Faulkhead, S. (2009). Connecting through records: Narratives of Koorie Victoria. *Archives and Manuscripts, 37*(2), 60–88.

Faulkhead, S. (2016). Negotiating methodologies: Designing research respectful of academic and Indigenous traditions. In A. J. Gilliland, S. McKemmish, & A. J Lau (Eds.), *Research in the archival multiverse* (pp. 479–515). Melbourne: Monash University Press.

Flinn, A. (2010). Independent community archives and community-generated content: Writing, saving and sharing our histories. *Convergence: The International Journal of Research into New Media Technologies, 16*(1), 39–51.

Friedman, B., Kahn, P. H., Jr., & Borning, A. (2006). Value sensitive design and information systems. In P. Zhang, & D. Galleta (Eds.), *Human-computer interaction and management information systems: Foundations* (pp. 348–372). London: Armonk.

Furner, J. (2004). Conceptual analysis: A method for understanding information as evidence, and evidence as information. *Archival Science, 4*(3–4), 233–265.

Furner, J., & Gilliland, A. J. (2016). Archival IR: Applying and adapting information retrieval approaches in archives and recordkeeping research. In A. J. Gilliland, S. McKemmish, & A. J Lau (Eds.), *Research in the archival multiverse* (pp. 580–630). Melbourne: Monash University Press.

Geertz, C. (1973). *The interpretation of cultures*. New York: Basic Books.

Giddens, A. (1984). *The constitution of society*. Cambridge UK: Polity Press.

Gilliland, A. J. (2011). Neutrality, social justice and the obligations of archival educators and education in the twenty-first century. *Archival Science, 11*(3–4), 193–209.

Gilliland, A. J. (2014). *Fostering high impact* research. *Preservation, Digital Technology & Culture, 42*(2), 54–60.

Gilliland, A. J. (2015). Permeable binaries, societal grand challenges, and the roles of the twenty-first-century archival and recordkeeping profession. *Archifacts*, (December), 12–30.

Gilliland, A. J. (2016a). Archival traditions in the multiverse and their importance for researching situations and situating research. In A. J. Gilliland, S. McKemmish, & A. J Lau (Eds.), *Research in the archival multiverse* (pp. 31–73). Melbourne: Monash University Press.

Gilliland, A. J. (2016b). Building the scholarly base of a field: Reflections on 8 years of AERI. *Preservation, Digital Technology and Culture, 45*(1), 27–31.

Gilliland, A. J. (2016c). Designing expert systems for archival evaluation and processing of computer mediated communications: Frameworks and methods. In A. J. Gilliland, S. McKemmish, & A. J. Lau (Eds.), *Research in the archival multiverse* (pp. 685–721). Melbourne: Monash University Press.

Gilliland, A. J. (2017). 'Dead on arrival'? Impartiality as a measure of archival professionalism in the twenty-first century. In H. van Engen (Ed.), *Values in transition: Perspectives on the future of the archival profession*. The Netherlands: Royal Society of Archivists in the Netherlands (KVAN).

Gilliland, A. J., & Halilovich, H. (2017). Migrating memories: Transdisciplinary pedagogical approaches to teaching about diasporic memory, identity and human rights in Archival Studies. *Archival Science, 17*(1), 79–96.

Gilliland, A. J., & McKemmish, S. (2004). Building an infrastructure for archival research. *Archival Science, 4*(3–4), 149–199.

Gilliland, A. J., McKemmish, S., & Lau, A. J (2016). *Research in the archival multiverse*. Melbourne: Monash University Press.

Gilliland, A. J., Rouche, N., Evans, J., & Lindberg, L. (2005). Towards a twenty-first century metadata infrastructure supporting the creation, preservation and use of trustworthy records. Developing the InterPARES2 Metadata Schema Registry. *Archival Science, 5*(1), 43–78.

Gilliland-Swetland, A. J. (1992). Archivy and the computer. A citation analysis of North American periodical articles. *Archival Issues, 17*(2), 95–112.

Gracy, K. F. (2016). Documenting communities of practice. Making the case for archival ethnography. In A. J. Gilliland, S. McKemmish, & A. J Lau (Eds.), *Research in the archival multiverse* (pp. 868–899). Melbourne: Monash University Press.

Harris, V. (2001). Law, evidence and electronic records. A strategic perspective from the global periphery. *Comma, International Journal on Archives, 1–2*, 29–44.

Harris, V. (2007). *Archives and justice. A South African perspective.* Chicago, IL: Society of American Archivists.

Head, R. (Ed.). (2010). Archival knowledge cultures in Europe, 1400–1900. [Special issue]. *Archival Science, 10*(3).

Head, R. (2016). Historical case studies of pre-modern European archives: A comparative approach. In A. J. Gilliland, S. McKemmish, & A. J Lau (Eds.), *Research in the archival multiverse* (pp. 433–455). Melbourne: Monash University Press.

Hulme, E. W. (1950). *Principles of book classification: Reprinted from the Library Association Record.* London: Association of Assistant Librarians (Originally published in 1911).

Hurley, C. (1995a). Ambient functions. Abandoned children to Zoos. *Archivaria, 40,* 21–39.

Hurley, C. (1995b). Problems with provenance. *Archives and Manuscripts, 23*(2), 234–259.

Hurley, C. (1998). The making and keeping of records: (1) What are finding aids for? *Archives and Manuscripts, 26*(1), 57–77.

Hurley, C. (2000). The making and keeping of records: (2) The tyranny of listing. *Archives and Manuscripts, 28*(1), 8–23.

Huvila, I. (2008). Participatory archive. Towards decentralised curation, radical user orientation, and broader contextualization of records management. *Archival Science, 8*(1), 15–36.

Iacovino, L. (2004). Multi-method interdisciplinary research in archival science: The case of recordkeeping, ethics and law. *Archival Science, 4*(3–4), 267–286.

Iivari, J., & Venable, J. (2009). Action research and design science research. Seemingly similar but decisively dissimilar. Paper presented at the European Conference on Information Systems. Retrieved from http://aisel.aisnet.org/cgi/viewcontent.cgi?article = 1025&context = ecis2009.

International Council on Archives. (2008). *Principles and functional requirements for records in electronic office environments.* Retrieved from http://www.ica.org.

International Researchon Permanent Authentic Records in Electronic Systems (InterPARES). (n.d.). http://www.interpares.org/.

Joint Information Systems Committee (JISC). (2006). *Digital preservation briefing paper.* Retrieved from https://www.webarchive.org.uk/wayback/archive/2014061420 2005/http://www.jisc.ac.uk/publications/briefingpapers/2006/pub_digipreser vationbp.aspx.

Kaplan, E. (2000). We are what we collect, we collect what we are. Archives and the construction of identity. *American Archivist, 63*(1), 126–151.

Ketelaar, E. (1997). The difference best postponed? Cultures and comparative archival science. *Archivaria, 44,* 142–148.

Ketelaar, E. (1999). Archivalisation and archiving. *Archives and Manuscripts, 27*(1), 54–61.

Ketelaar, E. (2000). Archivistics research saving the profession. *American Archivist, 63* (2), 322–340.

Ketelaar, E. (2002). Archival temples, archival prisons. Modes of power and protection. *Archival Science, 2*(3–4), 221–238.

Ketelaar, E. (2005a). Recordkeeping and societal power. In S. McKemmish, M. Piggott, B. Reed, & F. Upward (Eds.), *Archives. Recordkeeping in society* (pp. 277–298). Wagga-Wagga, NSW: Centre for Information Studies, Charles Sturt University.

Ketelaar, E. (2005b). Sharing: Collected memories in communities of records. *Archives and Manuscripts, 33*(1), 44–61.

Ketelaar, E. (2016). Archival turns and returns: Studies of the archive. In A. J. Gilliland, S. McKemmish, & A. J Lau (Eds.), *Research in the archival multiverse* (pp. 228–268). Melbourne: Monash University Press.

Lau, A. J, Gilliland, A. J., & Anderson, K. (2012). Naturalizing community engagement in information studies. *Information, Communication & Society, 15*(7), 991–1015.

MacNeil, H. (2004). Contemporary archival diplomatics as a method of inquiry. Lessons learned from two research projects. *Archival Science, 4*(3–4), 199–232.

McKemmish, S. (2005). Traces: Document, record, archive, archives. In S. McKemmish, M. Piggott, B. Reed, & F. Upward (Eds.), *Archives: Recordkeeping in society* (pp. 1–20). Wagga Wagga, NSW: Centre for Information Studies, Charles Sturt University.

McKemmish, S. (2011). Evidence of me in a digital world. In C. A. Lee (Ed.), *I, digital. Personal collections in the digital era* (pp. 115–148). Chicago IL: Society of American Archivists.

McKemmish, S. (2016). *ARK research: The state of the art.* Plenary paper presented at AERI 2016. Kent: Kent State University. Retrieved from https://du1ux2871uqvu. cloudfront.net/sites/default/files/file/AERI%202016%20for%20web%20page% 20%28Read-Only%29.pdf.

McKemmish, S., Acland, G., Ward, N., & Reed, B. (1999). Describing records in context in the continuum: The Australian Recordkeeping Metadata Schema. *Archivaria, 48,* 3–43.

McKemmish, S., Faulkhead, S., & Russell, L. (2011). Distrust in the archive: Reconciling records. *Archival Science*, *11*(3–4), 211–239.

McKemmish, S., Iacovino, L., Ketelaar, E., Castan, M., & Russell, L. (2011). Resetting relationships. Archives and Indigenous human rights in Australia. *Archives and Manuscripts*, *39*(1), 107–114.

McKemmish, S., Manaszewicz, R., Burstein, F., & Fisher, J. (2009). Consumer empowerment through metadata-based information quality reporting: The Breast Cancer Knowledge Online Portal. *Journal of the American Society for Information Science and Technology*, *60*(9), 1792–1807.

McKemmish, S., Reed, B., & Upward, F. (2009). The records continuum. In M. Bates, & M. Maack (Eds.), *Encyclopedia of library and information sciences* (3rd ed., pp. 4447–4459). New York: Taylor & Francis.

Menne-Haritz, A. (1994). Appraisal or documentation. Can we appraise archives by selecting content? *American Archivist*, *57*, 528–542.

Monaghan, J., & Just, P. (2000). *Social and cultural anthropology: A very short introduction*. Oxford: Oxford University Press.

Monash Country Lines Archive(MCLA). (n.d.). http://artsonline.monash.edu.au/countrylines-archive/.

Moreno, J. L. (1951). *Sociometry, experimental method and the science of society. An approach to a new political orientation*. New York: Beacon House.

Mortenson, P. (1999). The place of theory in archival practice. *Archivaria*, *47*, 1–26.

National Science and Technology Council, Interagency Working Group on Digital Data (2009). *Harnessing the power of digital data for science and society*. Washington, DC: National Science and Technology Council.

National Science Board and National Science Foundation (2005). *Long-lived digital data collections. Enabling research and education in the 21st century.*. Washington, DC: National Science Foundation.

Nesmith, T. (Ed.). (1993). *Canadian archival studies and the rediscovery of provenance*. Metuchen, NJ: SAA and ACA.

Nesmith, T. (1999). Still fuzzy, but more accurate. Some thoughts on the 'ghosts' of archival theory. *Archivaria*, *47*, 136–150.

Nesmith, T. (2002). Seeing archives. Postmodernism and the changing intellectual place of archives. *American Archivist*, *65*(1), 24–41.

Oliver, G. (2004). Investigating information culture. Comparative case study research design and methods. *Archival Science*, *4*(3–4), 287–314.

Pederson, A. (2002). Understanding ourselves and others. In S. Hicks, & K. Crowley (Eds.), Archives at risk. Accountability, vulnerability and credibility. *Proceedings of the 1999 conference and annual general meeting of the Australian Society of Archivists, Brisbane, Queensland, 29–31 July 1999* (pp. 61–93). Canberra: Australian Society of Archivists.

Piggott, M. (1998). The history of Australian recordkeeping. A framework for research. *Australian Library Journal, 47*(4), 343–354.

Pluralizing the Archival Curriculum Group (PACG). (2011). Educating for the archival multiverse. *American Archivist, 74*(1), 69–101.

Public Record Office of Victoria (PROV). (1999). *VERS Standard 99/007: Management of electronic records.* Retrieved from http://prov.vic.gov.au/government/vers/standard-2.

Punzalan, R., & Caswell, M. (2016). Critical directions for archival approaches to social justice. *Library Quarterly, 86*(1), 25–42.

Rawson, K. (2009). Accessing transgender // desiring queer(er?) Archival logics. *Archivaria, 68,* 123–140.

Reason, P., & Bradbury, H. (Eds.). (2001). *Handbook of action research: Participative inquiry and practice.* London: Sage Publications.

Reason, P., & Bradbury, H. (Eds.). (2008). *The Sage handbook of action research: Participative inquiry and practice* (2nd ed.). London: Sage Publications.

Records, Archives and Memory Studies (RAMS), Conference and School, University of Zadar. (2013). http://ozk.unizd.hr/rams/.

Rolan, G. (2017). Towards interoperable recordkeeping systems: A meta-model for recordkeeping metadata. *Records Management Quarterly, 27*(2), 125–148.

Schauder, D. (2002). Seven questions for information management and systems researchers. In K. Williamson (Ed.), *Research methods for students, academics and professionals: Information management and systems* (2nd ed., pp. 323–330). Wagga Wagga, NSW: Centre for Information Studies, Charles Sturt University.

Shankar, K. (2004). Recordkeeping in the production of scientific knowledge: An ethnographic study. *Archival Science, 4*(3–4), 367–382.

Shilton, K., & Srinivasan, R. (2007). Participatory appraisal and arrangement for multicultural archival collections. *Archivaria, 63,* 87–101.

Smart Information Portals Publications. (n.d.). http://www.infotech.monash.edu.au/research/about/centres/cosi/projects/sip/publications.html.

Sormunen, E. (2012). FINLAND Memornet Doctoral programme for experts in memory institutions. *Scandinavian Library Quarterly, 45*(3). Retrieved from http://slq.nu/?article = volume-45-no-3-2012-2.

Srinivasan, R., Pepe, A., & Rodriguez, M. (2009). A clustering-based semi-automated technique to build cultural ontologies. *Journal of the American Society of Information Science and Technology, 60*(3), 608–620.

Štefanac, T. (2017). *Conceptualization of archival materials held in museums* (Doctoral dissertation). University of Zadar School of Information Sciences, Croatia.

Stoler, A. (2002). Colonial archives and the arts of governance. *Archival Science, 2* (1–2), 87–109.

Stoler, A. (2009). *Along the archival grain. Epistemic anxieties and colonial common sense.* Princeton, NJ: Princeton University Press.

Sundqvist, A. (2016). Archival mediation: Studying users' interaction with access systems. In A. J. Gilliland, S. McKemmish, & A. J Lau (Eds.), *Research in the archival multiverse* (pp. 558–580). Melbourne: Monash University Press.

Swisspeace. (2013). *A conceptual framework for dealing with the past*. Retrieved from http://archivesproject.swisspeace.ch/fileadmin/user_upload/archivesproject/Publications/DwP_Conceptual_Framework_October2012.pdf.

Thorpe, K. (2016). Aboriginal community archives. In A. J. Gilliland, S. McKemmish, & A. J Lau (Eds.), *Research in the archival multiverse* (pp. 900–934). Melbourne: Monash University Press.

Trace, C. (2006). For love of the game. An ethnographic analysis of archival reference work. *Archives and Manuscripts, 34*(1), 124–143.

Upward, F. (1996). Structuring the records continuum part one. Postcustodial principles and properties. *Archives and Manuscripts, 24*(2), 268–285.

Upward, F. (1997). Structuring the records continuum part two. Structuration theory and recordkeeping. *Archives and Manuscripts, 25*(1), 10–35.

Upward, F., McKemmish, S., & Reed, B. (2011). Archivists and changing social and information apaces: A continuum approach to recordkeeping and archiving in online cultures. *Archivaria, 72*, 197–237.

White, K. (2008). *The dynamics of race and remembering in a 'colorblind' society. A case study of racial paradigms and archival education in Mexico* (Doctoral dissertation). University of California, Los Angeles, CA.

Wosh, P. (2011). *Waldo Gifford Leland and the origins of the American archival profession*. Chicago IL: Society of American Archivists.

Wurl, J. (2005). Ethnicity as provenance. In search of values and principles for documenting the immigrant experience. *Archival Issues, 29*(1), 65–76.

Yakel, E. (2001). The social construction of accountability. Radiologists and their record-keeping practices. *The Information Society, 17*, 233–245.

Yakel, E. (2004). Seeking information, seeking connections, seeking meaning. Genealogists and family historians. *Information Research: An International Electronic Journal, 10*(1). Retrieved from http://www.informationr.net/ir/10-1/paper205.html.

Chapter 5

The methodological landscape

Information systems and knowledge management

Dubravka Cecez-Kecmanovic[1] and Mary Anne Kennan[2]

[1]University of NSW, Australia [2]Charles Sturt University, Australia

This chapter begins with a broad overview of the methodological landscape that distinguishes between three levels: the level of meta-theoretical assumptions where different paradigms are articulated, the level of research methods and the level of research techniques and tools. Different research paradigms are then discussed, making explicit the assumptions that inform them, and the relationships between methodology, theory and method in conducting research. We then build on this analysis illustrating the distinctive nature of the paradigms with examples from three seminal papers from within the same topic domain, information richness. Drawing on these papers, we discuss how the methodological assumptions determine choice of research paradigm, formulation of research questions and selection of methods, and provide practical examples of how this is achieved. The chapter concludes by summarising the arguments for adopting a broader view of research methodology and its importance for achieving greater reflexive awareness of our "unconscious metaphysics" that underlay and influence how we see and research the world.

Research Methods: Information, Systems, and Contexts. DOI: http://dx.doi.org/10.1016/B978-0-08-102220-7.00005-4

Introduction

The purpose of this chapter is to present a broad view of the methodological landscape within which researchers in information systems and knowledge management find pathways in their pursuits of knowledge and scholarship. By discussing methodological issues within such a broad landscape, that not only includes research methods and techniques, but also what lies behind them, the chapter promotes thinking about, and a reflective attitude towards, meta-theoretical assumptions. Drawing researchers' attention to the meta-theoretical assumptions raises awareness of research paradigms and the way they affect methodological choices in information systems and knowledge management (and beyond). There are at least two reasons why this is important for information systems and knowledge management in particular. First, research publications even in their top outlets often avoid dealing with the assumptions and the way they underpin and limit particular research designs and methods. Second, research methods courses are primarily concerned with methods and techniques, that is, *how* to conduct research, without discussing *why* we choose to conduct research in a particular way.

Through research we build knowledge and understanding of phenomena involved in developing, deploying and using information systems and knowledge management systems in organisations and society. As information and knowledge-related fields, information systems and knowledge management investigate a wide range of research problems in order to advance understanding of the adoption of information technologies (IT), as well as the nature of technologically-mediated information and knowledge management, and the ways they enable and limit different forms of organising, governing and community living. This chapter deals specifically with the question of methodology, that is, the ways in which our assumptions about these processes influence how we research them; how we link research problems and questions with particular research methods and techniques to conduct empirical research; and how we create new understanding, develop theoretical accounts and make knowledge claims.

In this chapter we consider information systems and knowledge management as overlapping fields broadly concerned with the development, deployment, adoption and appropriation of IT to automate routine tasks and support individuals, groups and organisations in planning, conducting, and coordinating non-routine, creative and complex tasks and activities.[1] Research in information systems covers a wide range of topics and aims (e.g., Constantinides, Chiasson, & Introna, 2012; Lee, 2010; Willcocks & Lee, 2007). Examples of topics include information systems development, implementation, and assessment (e.g., Cecez-Kecmanovic, Kautz, & Abrahall, 2014; Mumford, 2006); information infrastructure (e.g., Monteiro, Pollock, & Williams, 2014), the social and organisational aspects of information systems (Ellwey & Walsham, 2015; Nandhakumar & Montealegre, 2003), the ethics of information systems (Mingers & Walsham, 2010); power and IT (Jasperson *et al.*, 2002) and many more. Knowledge management research is more explicitly concerned with the nature of knowledge in organisations and how information systems and knowledge-based systems support and enable knowledge creation, discovery, sharing and transfer (Burstein & Linger, 2006; Newell & Galliers, 2006; Schultze & Leidner, 2002; Shollo & Galliers, 2016); furthermore, to examine these issues researchers also investigate organisational learning, social capital, and communities of practice, among others (Timbrell, Delaney, Chan, Yue, & Gable, 2005).

Research methodology is not necessarily a well understood concept and researchers in information systems and knowledge management often struggle in comprehending its meaning and especially its distinction from another important concept – research method (Mingers, 2003). We emphasise here the importance of *methodology* as an overall logic of inquiry that includes a set of assumptions or a paradigm as a foundation for conducting research and selecting and applying research methods and techniques. Research methodology thus enables researchers to make knowledge claims and argue contribution to knowledge. On the other hand, *research method* as a much narrower concept denotes processes, procedures and techniques to conduct empirical studies and collect and analyse data (Cecez-Kecmanovic, 2011). Scholarly articles in information systems and knowledge management are increasingly more focussed on methods and technical issues of data collection and analysis while disregarding broader methodological issues. Reviewers and editors pay particular attention to the elaborate detailing of research methods and techniques with a tacit assumption that the adoption of 'rigorous' and 'reliable'

---

[1] Information systems commonly refer to the appropriation and use of a variety of IT such as "computers, software, databases, communication systems, the Internet, mobile devices and much more, to perform specific tasks, interact with and inform various actors in different organizational or social contexts. Of general interest to the field of IS are therefore all aspects of the development, deployment, implementation, use and impact of IS in organizations and society." (Boell and Cecez-Kecmanovic, 2015, p. 1). Knowledge management is defined more generally as "a range of strategies and practices used in an organization to identify, create, represent, distribute, and enable adoption of insights and experiences. Such insights and experiences comprise knowledge, either embodied in individuals or embedded in organizations as processes or practices" (Knowledge management, 2012). Apart from information systems, knowledge management has been studied within the fields of business administration and management, library and information sciences, computer science, media studies, and public policy and others (Alavi & Leidner, 1999).

research methods is a guarantor of the validity of research outcomes. The quality and validity of research outcomes are often reduced to, and thus judged by, the rigour and reliability of research methods and techniques. This is reinforced by research training that is often focussed on the technical matters, especially in relation to quantitative data analysis and statistical techniques. Assumptions and theoretical foundations that inform research questions and the overall design of the study, and the arguments for selecting particular research method(s) are often ignored.

In this chapter we aim to redress this imbalance, to argue for and demonstrate the importance of research methodology – above and beyond the rigorous application of research methods and techniques – in developing and conducting research projects and producing high quality research results. In order to achieve this we draw from philosophy of science and sociology literature to analyse key aspects of methodology and its meaning and relevance in empirical research. We also discuss how a researcher's view of the world and meta-theoretical foundation influence the type of questions the researcher will ask and also open (as well as limit) potential methodological paths that he or she will choose from. Furthermore we discuss how research questions are developed and how methodological arguments are used to select and justify the research methods to answer the questions. We give examples from information systems and knowledge management research; however the issues covered are also relevant for other social science fields.

This chapter is intended to be relevant and useful for both novice and more experienced researchers. Novice researchers will be introduced to an advanced level of thinking about the assumptions that inform research and the relationship between methodology, theory and method in the conduct of research. For experienced researchers, the chapter provides arguments and examples that might stimulate critical reflection on their research practices, their dealing with methodological issues and choices of, and justification for, particular research methods/techniques.

Methodological landscape

Methodology denotes an overall logic of inquiry involving philosophical assumptions behind an inquiry, the strategy of conducting research such as research design and selection and adoption of research methods and techniques as well as arguments for knowledge construction and justification (Cecez-Kecmanovic, 2001; Cecez-Kecmanovic, 2011; Morrow & Brown, 1994). Philosophical assumptions, or meta-theories, underpin and inform the overall strategy, research design and selection of research methods. By understanding methodological questions researchers become more critical and reflexive about the use and adoption of research methods in their research practice. An understanding of methodology focuses the researcher's attention on meta-theoretical questions, especially those concerned with ontology, epistemology, logic and ethics (Mingers & Walsham, 2010; Morrow & Brown, 1994; Ritzer, 1992). Concerns with the ontological, epistemological, axiological and normative assumptions underpinning an inquiry enable researchers to move beyond a narrow focus on research methods and to adopt a critical and reflective attitude towards method selection and application. These in turn lead to a greater awareness, and understanding, of the strengths and limitations of all methods.

A meta-theory is not aiming to explain any specific natural, social or technological phenomena as such but is concerned with attempts to make sense of different theories that claim to explain these phenomena. In other words, meta-theory is concerned with theories and theorising in a particular disciplinary domain. Meta-theorising examines assumptions behind existing theories in order to achieve a more profound understanding of these theories or different theoretical perspectives (Cecez-Kecmanovic, 2011; Ritzer, 1992).

The brief meta-theoretical discussion in this chapter is designed to draw attention to philosophical assumptions underlying various research paradigms in information systems and knowledge management, and the way they (assumptions) remain implied but often not explicitly recognised in the adoption, and application of, research methods and techniques. Such a meta-theoretical examination is necessary for understanding the relations between a paradigm, affiliated research methods and techniques, and researchers' choices in establishing particular relations. This understanding will help researchers appreciate and reflect on implicit limitations and implications of these choices.

To assist in understanding the methodological landscape, a simplified three-layer presentation of the landscape is depicted in Figure 5.1. At the top is a layer of meta-theoretical assumptions where the different research paradigms can be distinguished and defined. It is of note that in Figure 5.1 we present three widely known paradigms in information systems and knowledge management – the positivist and post-positivist, interpretive, and critical – while indicating that there are other less well-established or emerging paradigms (postmodern, feminist, and sociomaterial). Research methods (survey, experiments, case study, ethnography and many more) are represented in the middle layer. Research methods can be quantitative or qualitative in nature. Research methods are not directly linked to research paradigms but are more or less affiliated with them. While non-deterministic, these affiliations among paradigms and research methods do exist (Crotty, 1998) predominantly due to shared assumptions (to be discussed in the next section). The techniques and tools of data collection and analysis (questionnaire, statistical analysis, interview, thematic analysis and coding, discourse analysis, and others) are presented at the bottom layer suggesting that a method can be applied by choosing one or more of available techniques. For instance, researchers adopting an interpretive case study may use focus groups, interviews and participant observation as data collection techniques and thematic analysis and coding as data analysis techniques (Ezzy, 2002). Grounded theory is an exception as it can be applied as both a method and a data analysis technique (Charmaz, 2006; Strauss & Corbin, 1990).

Figure 5.1 The methodological landscape — from paradigms, to methods to techniques (adapted from Cecez-Kecmanovic, 2011)

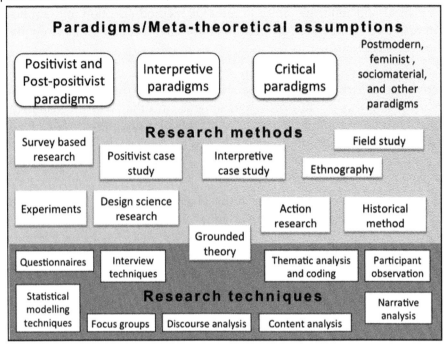

The term research paradigm denotes a broad framework or perspective of a group of theorists who share ontological and epistemological assumptions, adopt a similar logic of scientific explanations and share a common attitude towards ethics and place of values in research. The paradigm "is the broadest unit of consensus within a science and serves to differentiate one scientific community (or sub-community) from another" (Ritzer, 1980, p. 7). By assuming a particular worldview about the nature of the subject matter in their field and how a study should be conducted, researchers adopt a specific paradigm. A paradigm provides a foundation to frame a study and make sense of and acquire knowledge about the subject matter. Research paradigms are generally based on meta-theoretical assumptions in relation to four key aspects:

- *ontology* — the nature and existence of reality
- *epistemology* — the nature of knowledge and the ways of knowing
- the *logic of scientific explanation*
- *ethics* and claims about *values* and normative reasoning concerned with what "ought" to be.

These four sets of assumptions are of central importance for defining research paradigms and understanding research methodologies.

The importance of assumptions in guiding research and determining how reality is seen and studied, what acceptable modes of inquiry are, and what forms of theorising and types of knowledge claims are legitimate, cannot be overstated (Burrell & Morgan, 1979; Neuman, 2014). And yet the assumptions behind paradigms are often taken for granted and rarely questioned or debated within more established paradigm communities. Numerous research studies in information systems and knowledge management, as well as in some other social sciences, do not address, state or problematize assumptions underlying their research and knowledge claims. Such attitudes have detrimental implications for scholarship (Constantinides *et al.*, 2012) and limit our ability to conduct innovative and interesting research (Alvesson & Sandberg, 2011).

In their influential book *Sociological Paradigms and Organisational Analysis*, Burrell and Morgan (1979) brought this issue to the fore and provided a broad framework to examine and debate the meta-theoretical and methodological questions. They argued for a typology of research paradigms in social sciences based on two orthogonal dimensions: "subjectivist vs objectivist" and "order vs radical change" and respective sets of assumptions. The four combinations of these sets of assumptions defined four distinct research paradigms: *functionalism* (positivism), *interpretivism*, *radical humanism* (critical theory) and *radical structuralism*. Burrell and Morgan argued that, consciously or unconsciously, researchers base their work on a series of assumptions that place research in a particular quadrant of their framework.

Orlikowski and Baroudi (1991) argued that the use of these different paradigms, with their different assumptions and methodologies, enables the exploration of phenomena from diverse frames of reference and therefore should be encouraged to provide a richer understanding of the issues under study. The continuing separate use of these different paradigms rests on the belief in "paradigm incommensurability". Paradigm incommensurability is one of the pillars of Burrell and Morgan's (1979) work and refers to the contention that the paradigms are mutually exclusive. Further, it is considered that research methodologies and methods are bound to particular paradigms and are therefore also incommensurate. Some researchers have argued for paradigm integration, but reflect on the drawback that, although the paradigms may blur at the edges, they are based on competing and irreconcilable assumptions. Others have suggested paradigm interplay, which acknowledges differences and similarities by encouraging cross-fertilisation between paradigms (Goles & Hirschheim, 2000, pp. 259–260). Still others consider paradigm incommensurability to be overstated and have argued for a pluralist approach. The pluralist approach suggests that researchers do not have to accept existing paradigms but can develop new ones by drawing on the strengths and weaknesses of the old ones, but have their own assumptions and concerns (Mingers, 2001).

Since the publication of Burrell and Morgan's book, there have been several interesting and worthy attempts to critique and revise paradigm classification and advance debates on dominant versus emerging paradigms. In particular Deetz (1996) argued that the whole nature of the discourse on paradigms in research is too rigid and too strongly grounded in the objective/subjective dichotomy. Instead he proposed that we should be concerned with different *discourses* rather than paradigms, with equally important implications for research methodology. Contrary to the paradigm incommensurability thesis, movement across different discourses is seen as desirable and practically achievable. Other authors extended Burrell and Morgan's framework and provided further arguments for the necessity to distinguish and advance understanding of different paradigms, their assumptions and their importance for methodological decisions (Goles & Hirschheim, 2000; Guba & Lincoln, 1994; Neuman, 2014; Orlikowski & Baroudi, 1991).[2] These authors all agree that there are clear distinctions among positivist, interpretive and critical paradigms based on assumptions about ontology, epistemology, logic of scientific inquiry, and human values and ethics. These assumptions have important methodological implications for research design, selection of methods and techniques, and justification of knowledge claims.

In the next section we focus on positivist, interpretivist, and critical paradigms, as they have been widely accepted as distinct paradigms in the information and knowledge management fields (Chen & Hirschheim, 2004; Klein & Myers, 1999; Myers & Klein, 2011; Orlikowski & Baroudi, 1991; Schultze & Leidner, 2002). Note here an intentional plural form (paradigms) that suggests that these paradigms are not monolithic and that each covers a number of somewhat different but related strands. Other emerging paradigms that require attention include the postmodernist and feminist (Neuman, 2014) and sociomaterial paradigms (Barad, 2007; Orlikowski, 2010). Due to space constraints, they are not discussed in this chapter, but are mentioned to remind the reader that the three paradigms covered here do not present an exhaustive list. Furthermore, we caution the reader that the boundaries among research paradigms are not always clear-cut and the assumptions behind individual paradigms are not always mutually exclusive. For instance, critical social research is emerging in different (sometimes disputed) directions, including post-structuralist, postmodernist, critical feminist and critical realist strands, thus overlapping with other paradigms.

The three major research paradigms

The research approach adopted by researchers underlies the purpose of research, relevant literature and research questions, and affects the research design, selection of methods and what are considered valid research results and

---

[2] In addition, Neuman (2014) for instance discusses postmodernist and feminist paradigms.

contribution to knowledge (Neuman, 2014; Prescott & Conger, 1995). As a result, it is important to note that the assessment of research outcomes and contributions of particular research will be judged differently (according to different criteria) by researchers following different paradigms. The adoption of a research paradigm will depend on the combination of personal knowledge, experience and interests, research training and/or a dominant approach in an affiliated department/school, and the disciplinary culture and tradition as exemplified by highly valued journals or publishing outlets. Despite the fact that the majority of journals proclaim that no preference is given to any research paradigm or type of research, positivist or functionalist research is still dominant in information systems and knowledge management (Chen & Hirschheim, 2004; Orlikowski & Baroudi, 1991; Schultze & Leidner, 2002).

Positivist research is sometimes called traditional or scientific research in that it follows the ideal of the unity of science and is based on the belief that social science research should be conducted according to the same sets of principles and logic as research in the natural sciences (Lee, 1999). Positivist research is based on objectivist or realist ontology – the assumptions that social reality exists out there irrespective of the observer. It is also assumed that social reality is patterned, orderly and stable thus enabling scientists to discover existing regularities and formulate nomothetic explanations or causal laws, underpinned by epistemological realism, which holds that our observations, concepts and theories represent an objectively existing reality (Neuman, 2014; Orlikowski & Baroudi, 1991). The dominant logic of inquiry is hypothetic-deductive that starts with the literature examination of a specific problem in order to assess previous research, identify inconsistencies and tensions, and thereby formulate gaps in the literature. By adopting deductive logic researchers start with theoretical propositions derived from the literature and develop hypotheses that are empirically testable. Hypotheses are tested using quantitative research methods (experiments and surveys) and statistical modelling techniques. Positivist researchers generally aim to answer questions about relationships among well-defined concepts (expressed as measurable variables) with the purpose of explaining, predicting and controlling phenomena. These aims are framed assuming that scientific research is value-free and that research itself is conducted based on "objective" and value-free "facts". Ethical, moral or normative issues are explicitly excluded from empirical research as being of non-scientific nature (except for the ethical conduct of research in relation to subjects involved in research) (Neuman, 2014).

Interpretive researchers question the unity of science ideal and claim that social and natural sciences examine phenomena of a fundamentally different nature, thus necessitating different meta-theoretical assumptions (Mingers & Walsham, 2010; Schwandt, 2000). Instead of objectivist and realist views, interpretive paradigms are based on subjectivist and relativist assumptions: social reality exists as part of human experience and is socially constructed; any characteristics of an object that can be known result from human subjective and intersubjective meaning-making and interpretation. Interpretive paradigms study information and knowledge, strategic information systems, enterprise resource planning systems, decision support systems, expert systems and other knowledge-based systems, *in context*. Interpretive research aims to develop interpretive understanding (*verstehen*) of these complex social phenomena including their meanings, nature, role and effects in social life (Klein & Myers, 1999). It is more likely to describe and understand phenomena from the participants' points of view and always involves interpretation by both researchers and actors (Nandhakumar & Jones, 1997). This includes analysis and understanding of participants' values and feelings in relations to the phenomena studied. Interpretive researchers assume that everything is value-laden and do not believe that value-free social research is possible. They may reflect on their own values but will never judge anybody else's values.

The newer critical approach, or critical social science, advances a humanist perspective in information systems and knowledge management, and argues that social research should be both reflexive and political (Cecez-Kecmanovic, 2001; Neuman, 2014). Critical social science also aims to provide explanation, description and understanding but, unlike positivist and interpretive research, does not consider them sufficient; critical researchers are motivated by a liberating and emancipating purpose and aim at affecting practical affairs, life and working conditions of people. The key distinguishing feature of critical social research is its concern with moral and ethical questions related to (often hidden) forms of domination, control and exploitation through information systems and knowledge management systems (Brooke, 2002; Cecez-Kecmanovic, 2001; Stahl, 2003). In other words, critical research is oriented towards critique and the transformation of the social order (Cecez-Kecmanovic, 2005; Myers & Klein, 2011). Critical researchers believe that any research is a moral-political activity even when researchers do not explicitly take a stance and commit to a value position (Neuman, 2014).

Table 5.1 highlights the key meta-theoretical assumptions underlying the three major research paradigms. (See a more detailed analysis in Neuman, 2014.)

To illustrate how the chosen research paradigm informs and influences the conduct and reporting of research we present three examples.

Positivist, interpretive and critical research paradigms: Examples from the literature

In order to illustrate the distinct nature of the three research paradigms we now analyse three articles that deal with the same research domain (information richness and communication media) but adopt different research paradigms.

Table 5.1 Meta-theoretical assumptions behind the three research paradigms

	Positivist paradigms	Interpretive paradigms	Critical research paradigms
Purpose of research	To discover regularities and causal laws so that people can explain, predict and control events and processes.	To describe and understand phenomena in the social world and their meanings in context.	To empower people to change their conditions by unmasking and exposing hidden forms of oppression, false beliefs and commonly held myths.
Ontology – the nature and existence of social reality	Assumes an ordered and stable reality exists out there waiting to be discovered, irrespective of an observer.	Assumes reality is socially constructed, fluid and fragile, and exists as people experience it and assign meaning to it.	Transcends objective-subjective poles and assumes reality is socially constructed but nevertheless perceived as objectively existing.
Epistemology – the nature of knowledge and the ways of knowing	Takes an instrumental approach to knowledge: knowledge enables people to master and control events. Knowledge represents reality, is stable and additive; statements about reality are true only if they are repeatedly not empirically falsified.	Takes a practical approach to knowledge; aims to include as much evidence about the subject, the research process and context as possible to enable understanding of others' lifeworlds and experiences, and how the researchers came to understand them.	Takes a dialectical approach to knowledge. Knowledge enables people to see hidden forms of control, domination and oppression, which empowers them to seek change and reform existing conditions and social order.
The logic of scientific explanation	The dominant logic of inquiry is hypothetic-deductive: hypothesised relations among variables (logically derived from causal laws or theories) are	The dominant logic of inquiry is inductive and develops idiographic descriptions and explanations based on studies of people and their actions in context; explanations need to	The logic of inquiry can be deductive and inductive but also abductive, seeking creative leaps and revealing hidden forces or structures that help people understand their

	Positivist paradigms	Interpretive paradigms	Critical research paradigms
	empirically tested in a way that can be repeated by others.	make sense to those being studied as well as to the researchers and their community.	circumstances and ways of changing them.
Ethics and claims about values and normative reasoning concerned with what is right or "ought" to be.	Assumes both natural and social sciences are objective and value-free, operating separately from social and power structures; ideally positivist researchers are detached from the topic studied and collect value-free facts.	Questions the possibility of value-neutral science and a value-free research; values are seen as embedded in all human actions (including researchers') and hence are inevitably a part of everything we study, without the judging of one set of values as better than another.	Any research is a moral-political and value-based activity; critical researchers explicitly declare and reflect on their value position(s), and provide arguments for their normative reasoning.

The selected articles – see Box 5.1 – are widely known and highly cited. Box 5.1 provides details of the articles and defines key terms.

The positivist article (Daft *et al.*, 1987) focuses on the proposition that different communication media have different levels of richness. Communication media with high levels of richness (such as face-to-face communication) are best for dealing with highly equivocal situations, whereas media with low levels of richness (such as unaddressed memos) are appropriate for communications with low levels of equivocality. It is assumed that managers will generally behave rationally, thus selecting media appropriately. Successful managers will be those who match a given equivocality of situations with the appropriate communication media (e.g., in highly equivocal situations managers will use the richest available

Box 5.1

Articles for analysis and key terms

Articles for analysis

Positivist: Daft, R. L., Lengel, R. H., & Trevino, L. K. (1987). Message equivocality, media selection and manager performance: implications for information systems. *MIS Quarterly, 11*(3), 355–366.

Interpretive: Markus, M. L. (1994). Electronic mail as the medium of management choice. *Organization Science 5*(4), 502–527. (The study adopts a multi-method approach, our analysis focusses on the interpretive aspects of the analysis.)

Critical: Ngwenyama, O. K., & Lee, A. S. (1997). Communication richness in electronic mail: Critical social theory and the contextuality of meaning. *MIS Quarterly, 21*(2), 145–167.

Key terms in the articles

Equivocality: synonymous with ambiguity – where multiple and conflicting interpretations exist about a situation.

Media richness: communication media are characterised as high or low in richness depending on their ability to facilitate shared meaning. For example, face-to-face communication is classified as having a high degree of communication richness, as it enables instant feedback, multiple cues, language variety, and a personal focus. Conversely, documents, unaddressed reports, fliers, brochures have a low degree of media richness.

medium). Information richness theory predicts that uses and users of media will be similar, independent of environments. The article focuses on the process of communication and not on the individual actors or their context, and therefore assumes that the propositions of media richness theory are context independent, independent of space and time, and can be replicated.

Conversely, Markus (1994) provides rich descriptions to allow the reader to follow her interpretive analysis of data gathered from a wide variety of sources. The results point to the potential usefulness of social definition theory and critical mass theory to understand that use of communication media may depend on the environment and social influences as well as the richness of the media and the equivocality of the communication task. The paper demonstrates that communication richness or leanness emerge from the social context, the interactions between people as well as from communication media. There is a focus on mutual understanding between researcher and actors, and the research is highly context dependent.

Ngwenyama and Lee (1997) reinterpreted Markus's data from the perspective of critical social theory. They proposed that communication is gauged by how people assess communications, how they orient their actions (towards success or understanding) and become subject to, or free themselves from, distorted communications. The study was motivated by the desire to uncover incidences of communication richness that would escape detection in either a positivist or interpretive analysis, and yet shed light on the managerial use of email in companies. The positivist perspective recognises information richness occurring even when the message is distorted. The interpretive perspective recognises richness as occurring when there is mutual understanding, even if that understanding is "incomplete, false, unclear or inappropriate" (Ngwenyama & Lee, 1997 p. 156). Critical research seeks to recognise that actors need to assess the validity of what is being communicated to emancipate themselves from distortion and manipulation. The focus of the paper is on the communication receivers' critique of the validity of what is being communicated and their emancipation from distorted communications. The researchers proposed such critique and emancipation are required for real communication richness to occur.

Table 5.2 draws on these three articles to illustrate how meta-theoretical assumptions provide a fundamentally different way of seeing the world, even when researchers are examining the same phenomena.

Developing research question/s

An examination of a specific problem or phenomenon typically starts with a literature review. Researchers conduct a literature review in order to find out what is known about the problem or phenomenon, what research directions and

Table 5.2 Meta-theoretical assumptions in three research articles

Paradigms	Positivist: (Daft, *et al.,* 1987)	Interpretive: (Markus, 1994) NB: This paper uses several paradigms. The analysis below focuses on Markus's interpretive analysis	Critical: (Ngwenyama & Lee, 1997)
Reason for research	To explain how managers select particular communication media for problem solving and decision-making irrespective of context; the objective is to produce knowledge that will enable organisations to predict and control the implementation of new communication technologies that will contribute to managerial effectiveness and efficiency.	To describe and interpret how and why managers use face-to-face and email communication in a particular organisational context; the objective is to improve understanding of the managers' use of electronic media in communication processes and the implications for effectiveness.	To critically examine and explain managers' use of electronic media in communicative processes beyond the achievement of mutual understanding; the objective is to reveal hidden forms of distorted communication and how participants emancipate themselves from distorted communication.
Ontology – the nature and existence of social reality	Communication medium is conceptualised as a conduit that transports meaning among individuals – as if the meaning were something physical; data are processed into information by technologies and human beings are seen as users of information and passive receivers of the transported meanings.	Communication in an organisation involves meaningful social action, subjective interpretations by managers and others, individual and group consciousness and the lifeworld of people; humans, as intelligent beings in a social context, interpret messages communicated by media in order to understand what a speaker or writer meant.	Approached from a critical theory paradigm, communication in organisations involves people capable of acting and interpreting actions by others, achieving mutual understanding and importantly capable of critically assessing validity claims implied by communicative acts (intelligibility, efficacy and effectiveness, truthfulness, rightness and appropriateness.

Paradigms	Positivist: (Daft, et al., 1987)	Interpretive: (Markus, 1994) NB: This paper uses several paradigms. The analysis below focuses on Markus's interpretive analysis	Critical: (Ngwenyama & Lee, 1997)
	Communication richness is an invariant, objective property of a communication medium and is determined by social cues, capacity for immediate feedback, personalisation and language variety enabled by a medium irrespective of the context; hence media are classified according to level of richness from low (text based) to high (face-to-face).	Communication richness is conceptualised as a function of mutual understanding among people: the extent that one person understands what the other meant by saying or writing; people bring about the richness in their communication.	Communication richness is present when a person engages in communicative processes with an attitude to critique or question validity claims and, if needed, emancipate her/himself from distorted communication.
Epistemology – the nature of knowledge and the ways of knowing	Scientific knowledge explains the appropriate matching of specific communication media (lean vs. rich) with management decision-making situations (equivocal vs. non-equivocal); scientific knowledge accumulates through empirical testing hypothesised relationships between variables – message equivocality and a medium richness.	The nature of knowledge is idiographic and is created by studying social activities mediated via communication media in practice, within lifeworld of actors; knowledge about managers' use of email and other communication media in organisations can be acquired only in context and by investigating meaning construction and sharing.	The nature of knowledge is revelatory and emancipatory; knowledge is acquired by studying the use of communication media to support social actions in situ; the study is sensitive to forms of distorted communication and the ways participants question and critique various validity claims and attempt to emancipate themselves.

Paradigms	Positivist: (Daft, *et al.*, 1987)	Interpretive: (Markus, 1994) NB: This paper uses several paradigms. The analysis below focuses on Markus's interpretive analysis	Critical: (Ngwenyama & Lee, 1997)
The logic of scientific explanation	By depicting the subject matter in terms of dependent variable (media richness) and independent variable (message equivocality) the study empirically tested the hypothesised positive relationship between them; this and two other hypothesis were supported – consistent with observed facts; also no logical inconsistency was found.	The logic of inquiry is inductive and is based on the interpretation of multiple evidentiary types – survey, interview, analysis of archival emails; scientific explanation is developed through idiographic descriptions and explanations based on studies of people, their actions and use of email in a particular context. Markus cross checked her data and analysis with those being studied and found that they resonated with the participants (p. 524).	The logic of inquiry is both inductive and deductive and at times abductive; the study uncovers incidences of communication richness that escaped detection in both a positivist or interpretive analysis, and yet sheds light on the managerial use of email in companies; the authors propose that they are supplying future researchers with better tools to analyse communication richness, namely critical social theory frameworks; they do this by explaining the underlying conditions and previous theories and then analysing Markus's, 1994 data using a critical framework, to produce interesting and useful findings, which were not discovered using other theoretical frameworks.

Paradigms	Positivist: (Daft, *et al.*, 1987)	Interpretive: (Markus, 1994) NB: This paper uses several paradigms. The analysis below focuses on Markus's interpretive analysis	Critical: (Ngwenyama & Lee, 1997)
Ethics and claims about values and normative reasoning concerned with what "ought" to be	Ethics is not considered by the study; the only value addressed is the contribution of the media richness theory to managers' effectiveness; the study does not ask people about their personal values or norms; the researchers do not explicitly discuss values or norms but implicitly assume that objective and value-neutral data were collected and analysed.	The study examines managers' personal values, and the social norms of the organisation, and explicates the norms and values to increase understanding of communication media use; different values or points of view of participants are described but are not judged.	The authors are explicit about their own values as well as those underlying the critical social theory that informed their research; they believe that critical paradigm research is more likely to bring to the surface useful understanding of media and communication richness in organisations than interpretive and positivist paradigms.

paradigms are explored, how the knowledge is acquired and what are the key findings. Moreover, researchers need to critically assess the literature and the state of knowledge related to the chosen problem in order to identify or construct a 'gap' in the literature that motivates their study. Apart from identifying and articulating a gap, researchers also need to argue why it is important to fill the gap, that is, to conduct research that will produce knowledge that fills the identified gap. The articulation of a gap in the literature is an important step towards defining particular research questions that the study intends to answer. We therefore first discuss how a gap is identified or constructed and then examine how it leads to articulation of research questions.

A critique of existing literature often includes claims that literature is incomplete, that certain aspects/phenomena are overlooked, that research results are inconclusive or contradictory, and that knowledge related to the problem of interest is in some ways inadequate (Alvesson & Sandberg, 2011; Barrett & Walsham, 2004). In some cases researchers claim that certain studies, findings, theories or ways of producing knowledge are faulty or inadequate and argue for the need to conduct a new study to correct or address the inadequacies. Such approaches to "gap-spotting" are often adopted for developing research questions from the literature (Alvesson & Sandberg, 2011; Barrett & Walsham, 2004).

Gaps in the literature are rarely obvious or easily identified. Analysis, mapping and critical assessment of literature need to be conducted in creative ways so as to reveal weaknesses, inconsistencies or contradictions in the existing literature on the topic studied (Hart, 2006). Hence gaps are not "found" but are more likely constructed through creative ways of mapping and comparing relevant literature. For instance, the analysis of different papers addressing the same research topic may include classification of results according to some relevant framework or typology. A good example is presented in Schultze and Leidner's (2002) review paper where knowledge management literature is classified according to Deetz's (1996) framework that distinguishes among four discourses: normative, interpretive, dialogical and critical. They classified papers based on their explicit or implicit theoretical assumptions within these four discourses. Such a way of presenting and comparing the literature on knowledge management allowed them to assess the literature from a particular angle: while the normative discourse is overwhelmingly dominant, the dialogical and critical discourses are missing. By doing so they identified and constructed a significant gap in the knowledge management literature open for researchers to explore and thus make contributions to the literature.

Gap-spotting may lead to worthwhile research questions that will enable researchers to make important, but incremental contributions to the literature. However, such contribution by its nature would not challenge assumptions underlying existing literature in any significant way. In Alvesson and Sandberg's (2011) words:

> Whether researchers merely identify or creatively construct gaps in existing literature, they still adhere to the same purpose – namely, "gap-filling" – that is, adding something to existing literature, not identifying and challenging its underlying assumptions, and, based on that, formulate new and original research questions. (p. 249)

Another, and more radical approach to a critical assessment of the literature in a particular domain, named "problematisation" (Alvesson & Sandberg, 2011), aims to identify and challenge the assumptions underlying existing theories and findings. While both approaches require critical scrutiny of the literature in the targeted domain, problematisation goes further in revealing, discussing and challenging assumptions that determine how a research problem is understood and investigated and in that sense limits knowledge that can be gained from research. A researcher can also problematise his or her own assumptions and beliefs as well as commonly held assumptions and beliefs. Importantly researchers problematise and challenge assumptions in order to develop novel and interesting research questions that promise to make a significant contribution to knowledge.

Identifying and/or constructing a gap in the literature, or problematising and challenging assumptions, precede or directly lead to research questions. When done convincingly both provide evidence for formulating research questions. The importance of well-formed research questions cannot be overstated. Research questions not only drive research design and selection of methods but also de facto indicate (delimit) the actual contribution of a research project.

Research questions can be formulated at a more general, abstract level and at a more specific, empirical level. A more general, abstract research question will logically follow from the gap in the literature or problematisation of existing theories but is often theoretical and not suitable for empirical investigations. Such a question is important as it indicates what theoretical contribution the research intends to make. A general or theoretical question needs to be developed further into one or more specific research questions that will be empirically answered. While formulating a general research question or questions is desirable, it is not absolutely necessary and many good papers or theses formulate only empirical research questions.

In order to discuss development of well-formed research questions we need to be more specific about the nature of research undertaken. Namely, for positivist research that uses deductive logic specific research questions need to be precisely defined before empirical research and data collection start. Research questions are formulated using concepts that can be linked to empirical data, also indicating what data need to be collected to answer the questions. If this is not the case, it indicates that research question or questions are not developed enough. In positivist, deductive research a specific research question is often expressed in a form of hypotheses that propose relationship between measurable concepts (variables). When hypotheses are based on or deduced from a theory (or a combination of theories), by testing an hypothesis through empirical research we test the theory.

A good illustration is provided in the paper discussed above by Daft *et al.* (1987). They first aim to answer the questions: "Why do organizations process information?" They then focussed on the use of communication media (including face-to-face and electronic media) in managerial decision-making and problem solving. Their review of the literature led them to formulate a gap: predictions from the literature – that the increasing use of the electronic communications media will decrease the need for face-to-face communications and also increase managerial efficiency and effectiveness – "have not come true" (p. 356). They then formulate the research problem: "why do managers often prefer face-to-face communications for problem solving and decision making?" (p. 356). After developing the concept of media richness as an objective and inherent property of a communication medium (which can be measured on a scale from low to high), and the concept of message equivocality, they formulated three hypotheses:

> **Hypothesis 1**: Managerial information processing will be characterized by a positive relationship between message equivocality and media richness. (p. 359)

> **Hypothesis 2**: Managers will select oral media for communication episodes high in equivocality and written media for communication episodes low in equivocality. (p. 360)

> **Hypothesis 3**: Managers who are sensitive to the relationship between equivocality and media richness are more likely to be rated as high performers. (p. 360)

These hypotheses were tested by studying 60 incidents of managerial communications in a company.

In contrast, in non-positivist and inductive research, formulating very specific research questions before the empirical study does not make much sense. A more general and theoretical question is necessary and often sufficient to determine research design, select research method(s) and initiate the study. More specific questions emerge during the study as the researcher develops deeper understanding of the empirical context and people studied. Even when specific empirical questions are defined in advance (which is typically required for getting ethics approval), it is very likely that they will be changed during the course of the empirical study. Given that in inductive research researchers do not know what they are going to find out in their study, they cannot in advance ask for it. In studying a particular phenomenon they have to be open to new and unexpected events, situations and issues, as well as learn to ask new questions and seek explanations. In other words, researchers seeking discovery cannot formulate their research question/s in advance, as they cannot specify what they are going to discover. As the empirical study progresses research questions become clearer and more specific but it is not until the interpretation of the empirical data that researchers articulate precisely the final research questions. It is only at the point when a research report (a paper or thesis) has to articulate specific research questions, for which the research provides answers, that the questions need to be finally framed. This is what ultimately matters. The struggles and frustrations with various questions during the empirical study are rarely disclosed.

An example of problematisation of existing literature, and especially the numerous studies of managerial communications confirming media richness theory, is provided by Markus (1994) and discussed in Table 5.2. Markus' (1994) study provides a well-structured and comprehensive review of the previous studies of electronic communications and media richness theory and also a well-argued critique based on several social theories. Markus (1994, p. 509) then proposed a number of theoretically-grounded research questions:

> How do managers, especially senior managers, use media, especially electronic mail, and why? More specifically, are empirical observations about managers' use of email consistent or inconsistent with hypothesis derived from information richness theory? Do senior managers make relatively little use for email, compared to low-level managers, and avoid using it for equivocal tasks? Are they more sensitive than lower-level managers to media appropriateness as defined by the theory?

In addition to these Markus (1994, p. 509) proposed the comparison between the predictions based on media richness theory and alternative theoretical explanations:

> Do managers' perceptions of media appropriateness correspond to the information richness scale? Do managers' media uses correspond to the theory's predictions? And do managers' behaviours correspond to their perceptions of media appropriateness? Finally, if the expected pattern of results is not observed, to what extent can alternative explanations — based on a revised information richness scale or on social definitions of media appropriateness — shed light on the findings?

These questions were answered in the empirical study in a selected company using the survey, analysis of emails and interviews (a mixed method).

The examples of research questions provided here are only for illustrative purposes and are not meant to serve as models. It is actually neither typical nor advisable to formulate a large number of research questions, especially for novice researchers. An important lesson from the examples above is that research questions have to be carefully worded, using precisely defined concepts and indicating what kind of data need to be collected.

From research questions to selection of methods

Formulation of research questions determines *what* is being investigated and *what* kinds of answers should be provided by an empirical study. As we have seen above the type of questions and the way questions are formulated are underpinned by a set of meta-theoretical assumptions. It is not so much that researchers consciously think of their meta-theoretical assumptions and then formulate the research question(s). Rather, researchers' more or less consciously-held assumptions shape their understanding of the world and the way they approach a particular problem. The assumptions also affect the attitude towards literature review, the formulation of gaps and research aims as well as research questions. As we discussed above, the form of research question(s) and their fixed or evolving nature is aligned with a nature of research paradigms.

To achieve their aims and answer research questions, researchers conduct an empirical study. In order to argue for and justify their empirical study, researchers need to consider several key methodological issues, including meta-theoretical assumptions, overall research strategy, research design and plan of action that link research aims and questions with the choice of research method(s) and techniques, the adoption of selected methods and techniques, and the way knowledge claims are (will be) made. The process starting from the formulation of research aims and questions, and ending with the selection and adoption of methods and techniques is depicted in Figure 5.2. Importantly the choices made along the way need to be well-argued and should follow logically from the research aims and questions.

First, arguments should be provided for a particular meta-theoretical perspective or paradigm – why is it fruitful or necessary for a specific problem to be studied from, for example, a positivist paradigm? No paradigm is, or should be argued as *a priori*, better than others. Paradigms can be more or less well-suited to study empirically a particular phenomenon and research problem. If for instance the study assumes that media richness is determined by characteristics of a communication medium and aims to develop knowledge about the media richness irrespective of the context, a positivist paradigm can be justified while an interpretive paradigm can be argued to be inappropriate due to mismatch with

Figure 5.2 From formulating research aims and questions to the selection of methods and techniques

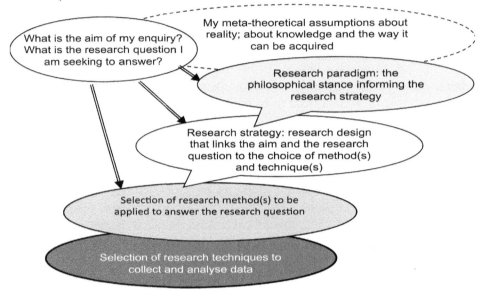

the initial research assumptions. On the other hand, understanding richness in communication emerging from social interaction mediated by communication technologies within a context would justify an interpretive paradigm.

Second, a research strategy (research design and a plan of actions) for the study needs to be developed. The research design and a plan of actions link the aims and research questions to the choice of research methods and techniques. After an empirical study is situated within a specific paradigm (e.g., positivist, interpretive or critical) the number of possible research strategies that can be adopted to answer research questions decreases. When, for instance, a research question about managerial choices of communication media in different situations is examined within a positivist paradigm, research design is practically limited to experiments, survey-based method and positivist case studies. Each of these methods would then use certain data collection techniques (e.g., questionnaire, structured interviews) and data analysis techniques (e.g., statistical modelling, content analysis). In the case of an interpretive study of communication richness in managers' email interactions, research design options would include a field study, ethnography, or an interpretive case study. The adoption of any of these methods would also require certain data collection techniques (e.g., participant observation, field interview, document acquisition, focus groups) and data analysis techniques (e.g., coding and thematic analysis, discourse analysis, narrative analysis). Figure 5.2 illustrates the methodological choices made at each

Figure 5.3 Methodological choices for a positivist empirical study: selection of a path through a methodological landscape

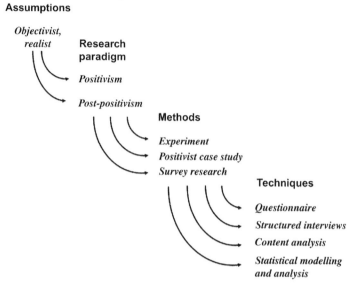

step. The arguments for the methodological choices need to be logically connected and convincing. This is further illustrated in Figure 5.3, which describes the flow of logical reasoning from the meta-theoretical assumptions (objectivist and realist) to paradigms, to methods and techniques.

Third, the detailed research design and a plan of action need to be developed to provide a comprehensive answer to *how* questions such as: How is the survey administered and to whom? How are the subjects for an experiment recruited and selected? How is a field site selected? How is a field study conducted? How are interviewees selected? An important aspect of the detailed research design is the selection strategy. For a positivist survey-based study convincing arguments have to be provided for a selection of a sample that is representative of a population studied. The selection of a site (for example a company, department, project) for a field study may be argued for instance as a typical, critical or extreme case, a purposefully selected or opportunistic case (Miles & Huberman, 1994). A detailed research design and a plan of action should be sufficient and include a comprehensive argument to explain how data analysis will be conducted and knowledge claims made.

Developing a research strategy, that crosses paradigms and uses multi-methods (both quantitative and qualitative) in an empirical study, introduces an additional layer of complexity to the research design. The research strategy in such situations might include a sequence of research phases each of which can adopt a different paradigm; or different segments of a research project going on in parallel can be governed by different sets of assumptions (Mingers, 2003). In both cases the link between the phases or segments of empirical study has to be clearly argued and debated, indicating how the various results will be combined and knowledge claims produced.

Conclusion

This chapter has clearly differentiated methodology (the overall logic of an enquiry) from research methods (the processes, procedures and techniques used to conduct research). Beginning with a meta-theoretical examination of the different paradigms, which made explicit the relations between methodological approach and research methods, we then provided summaries of the ontological, epistemological, axiological and normative assumptions underlying three of the major methodological paradigms – the positivist, interpretive and critical. We illustrated how these sets of underlying theoretical assumptions each provide a fundamentally different way of seeing the world using three seminal articles from the information systems literature. Understanding meta-theoretical foundations enables researchers to adopt a critical attitude towards the literature and knowledge relevant for a research problem of interest. We demonstrated how research questions are formulated by identifying gaps in the literature or through a process of problematising and challenging assumptions, again using examples from the three articles. Finally, we demonstrated how these research questions, carefully formulated and using precisely defined concepts, should logically lead to particular research strategy and methods.

Acknowledgement

The work in Table 5.2 draws on discussion and exploratory writing conducted in 2005 with colleagues Dr Fouad Nagm, Ms Emila Sadrei and Dr Mahmood Chadhar, which we acknowledge with thanks.

References

Alavi, M., & Leidner, D. E. (1999). Knowledge management systems: issues, challenges, and benefits. *Communications of the AIS, 1*(2). Retrieved from http://dl.acm.org/citation.cfm?id=374117.

Alvesson, M., & Sandberg, J. (2011). Generating research questions through problematization. *The Academy of Management Review (AMR), 36*(2), 247–271.

Barad, K. M. (2007). *Meeting the universe halfway: Quantum physics and the entanglement of matter and meaning.* Durham, NC: Duke University Press Books.

Barrett, M., & Walsham, G. (2004). Making contributions from interpretive case studies: examining processes of construction and use. In B. Kaplan, D. Truex, III, D. Wastell, A. Wood-Harper, & J. DeGross (Eds.), *Information systems research: Relevant theory and informed practice* (pp. 293–312). Boston: Kluwer Academic.

Boell, S. K. & Cecez-Kecmanovic, D. (2015). What is an information system? *Proceedings of the 48th Annual Hawaii International Conference on System Sciences HICSS 2015*, Kauai, United States, 8th January 2015.

Brooke, C. (2002). What does it mean to be 'critical' in IS research? *Journal of Information Technology, 17*(2), 49–57.

Burrell, G., & Morgan, G. (1979). *Sociological paradigms and organisational analysis.* London: Heinemann.

Burstein, F., & Linger, H. (2006). Introduction to the special issue: An Australian perspective on organisational issues in knowledge management. *International Journal of Knowledge Management, 2*(1), 1–5.

Cecez-Kecmanovic, D. (2001). Doing critical IS research: The question of methodology. In E. Trauth (Ed.), *Qualitative research in information systems: Issues and trends* (pp. 142–163). Hershey, PA: Idea Group Publishing.

Cecez-Kecmanovic, D. (2005). Basic assumptions of the critical research perspectives in information systems. In D. Howcroft, & E. Trauth (Eds.), *Handbook of critical information systems research: Theory and application* (pp. 19–46). Cheltenham: Edward Elgar.

Cecez-Kecmanovic, D. (2011). On methods, methodologies and how they matter. Paper presented at the European Conference on Information Systems, Helsinki, Finland, 9-11 June 2011. Retrieved from http://aisel.aisnet.org/ecis2011/233.

Cecez-Kecmanovic, D., Kautz, K. H., & Abrahall, R. (2014). Reframing success and failure of information systems—A performative perspective. *MIS Quarterly, 38*(2), 561–588.

Charmaz, K. (2006). *Constructing grounded theory: A practical guide through qualitative analysis.* London: Sage.

Chen, W. S., & Hirschheim, R. (2004). A paradigmatic and methodological examination of information systems research from 1991 to 2001. *Information Systems Journal, 14*(3), 197–235.

Constantinides, P., Chiasson, M. W., & Introna, L. (2012). The ends of information systems research: A pragmatic framework. *Management Information Systems Quarterly, 36*(1), 1–19.

Crotty, M. (1998). *The foundations of social research: Meaning and perspective in the research process.* St Leonards, NSW: Allen & Unwin.

Daft, R. L., Lengel, R. H., & Trevino, L. K. (1987). Message equivocality, media selection, and manager performance: Implications for information systems. *MIS Quarterly, 11*(3), 355–366.

Deetz, S. (1996). Describing differences in approaches to organization science: Rethinking Burrell and Morgan and their legacy. *Organization Science, 7*(2), 191–207.

Ellwey, B. P. W, & Walsham, G. (2015). A doxa-informed practice analysis: Reflexivity and representations, technology and action. *Information Systems Journal, 25*(2), 133–160.

Ezzy, D. (2002). *Qualitative analysis: Practice and innovation*. Crows Nest, NSW: Allen & Unwin.

Goles, T., & Hirschheim, R. (2000). The paradigm is dead, the paradigm is dead... long live the paradigm: The legacy of Burrell and Morgan. *Omega, 28*(3), 249–268.

Guba, E. G., & Lincoln, Y. S. (1994). Competing paradigms in qualitative research. In N. K. Denzin, & Y. S. Lincoln (Eds.), *Handbook of qualitative research* (pp. 105–117). Thousand Oaks, CA: Sage.

Hart, C. (2006). *Doing a literature review: Releasing the social science research imagination*. Thousand Oaks, CA: Sage.

Jasperson, J., Buttler, B. S., Carte, T. A., Croes, H. J. P., Saunders, C. S., & Zheng, W. (2002). Review: Power and information technology research: A metatriangulation review. *MIS Quarterly, 26*(4), 397–459.

Klein, H. K., & Myers, M. D. (1999). A set of principles for conducting and evaluating interpretive field studies in information systems. *MIS Quarterly, 23*(1), 67–93.

Knowledge management. (June 17 2012). *Wikipedia*. Retrieved from http://en.wikipedia.org/wiki/Knowledge_management.

Lee, A. S. (2010). Retrospect and prospect: Information systems research in the last and next 25 years. *Journal of Information Technology, 25*(4), 336–348.

Markus, M. L. (1994). Electronic mail as the medium of managerial choice. *Organization science, 5*(4), 502–527.

Miles, M. B., & Huberman, A. M. (1994). *Qualitative data analysis: An expanded sourcebook* (2nd ed.). Thousand Oaks, CA: Sage.

Mingers, J. (2001). Combining IS research methods: Towards a pluralist methodology. *Information Systems Research, 12*(3), 240–259.

Mingers, J. (2003). The paucity of multimethod research: A review of the information systems literature. *Information Systems Journal, 13*(3), 233–249.

Mingers, J., & Walsham, G. (2010). Toward ethical information systems: The contribution of discourse ethics. *MIS Quarterly, 34*(4), 833–854.

Monteiro, E., Pollock, N., & Williams, R. (2014). Innovation in information infrastructures: Introduction to the special issue. *Journal of the Association for Information Systems, 15*(4). Article 4. Retrieved from http://aisel.aisnet.org/jais/vol15/iss4/4.

Morrow, R., & Brown, D. (1994). *Critical theory and methodology*. London: Sage.

Mumford, E. (2006). The story of socio-technical design: Reflections on its successes, failures and potential. *Information Systems Journal, 16*(4), 317–342.

Myers, M. D., & Klein, H. K. (2011). A set of principles for conducting critical research in information systems. *MIS Quarterly, 35*(1), 17–36.

Nandhakumar, J., & Jones, M. (1997). Too close for comfort? Distance and engagement in interpretive information systems research. *Information Systems Journal, 7*(2), 109–131.

Nandhakumar, J., & Montealegre, R. (2003). Guest editorial. Social and organizational aspects of internet-based information systems. *Information Systems Journal, 13*(2), 109–112.

Neuman, W. L. (2014). *Social research methods: Qualitative and quantitative approaches* (7th ed., International ed.). Boston: Pearson.

Newell, S., & Galliers, R. D. (2006). Facilitating - or inhibiting - knowing in practice. *European Journal of Information Systems, 15*(5), 441–445.

Ngwenyama, O. K., & Lee, A. S. (1997). Communication richness in electronic mail: Critical social theory and the contextuality of meaning. *MIS Quarterly, 21*(2), 145–167.

Orlikowski, W. J. (2010). The sociomateriality of organisational life: Considering technology in management research. *Cambridge Journal of Economics, 34*(1), 125–141.

Orlikowski, W., & Baroudi, J. J. (1991). Studying information technology in organizations: Research approaches and assumptions. *Information Systems Research, 2*(1), 1–28.

Prescott, M. B., & Conger, S. A. (1995). Information technology innovations: A classification by IT locus of impact and research approach. *DATA BASE Advances, 26*(2 & 3), 20–41.

Ritzer, G. (1980). *Sociology: A multiple paradigm science.* Boston: Allyn & Bacon.

Ritzer, G. (Ed.). (1992). *Methatheorizing* London: Sage.

Schultze, U., & Leidner, D. E. (2002). Studying knowledge management in information systems research: Discourses and theoretical assumptions. *MIS Quarterly, 26*(3), 213–242.

Schwandt, T. A. (2000). Three epistemological stances for qualitative inquiry. In N. K. Denzin, & Y. S. Lincoln (Eds.), *Handbook of qualitative research* (pp. 189–213). Thousand Oaks CA: Sage.

Shollo, A., & Galliers, R. D. (2016). Towards an understanding of the role of business intelligence systems in organisational knowing. *Information Systems Journal, 26*(4), 339–367.

Stahl, B. C. (2003). *How we invent what we measure: A constructionist critique of the empiricist bias in IS research.* Paper presented at the Ninth Americas Conference on Information Systems, Tampa, FL., 4–6 August 2003. Retrieved from http://aisel.aisnet.org/cgi/viewcontent.cgi?article=1842&context=amcis2003.

Strauss, A., & Corbin, J. (1990). *Basics of qualitative research: Grounded theory procedures and techniques.* Newbury Park, CA: Sage.

Timbrell, G.T., Delaney, P., Chan, T., Yue, W.A., & Gable, G. (2005). *A structurationist review of knowledge management theories.* Paper presented at the International Conference of Information Systems ICIS, Las Vegas, NV, 11–14 December 2005. Retrieved from http://aisel.aisnet.org/cgi/viewcontent.cgi?article=1226&context=icis2005.

Willcocks, L., & Lee, A. S. (2007). *Major currents in information systems, 2.* London: Sage.

Section II

Research Methods

In this section, Chapters 6–14 examine research methods which are defined as designs for undertaking research, including the theoretical background to these designs. The research methods included are survey, case study, action research, constructivist grounded theory, bibliometric research, design-science research, historical research, ethnographic research and experimental design.

Chapter 6

Survey designs

Kerry Tanner
Monash University, Australia

This chapter explores the major approaches, methods, challenges, designs and modes of survey research. It commences with an outline of the development of surveys as a research method from their early stages to current contexts, and focusses on several fundamental research challenges confronting the survey researcher. These include: sampling and the ability to generalise to the wider population; creating valid and reliable survey instruments; and dealing with potential sources of bias and error in survey research. Subsequent sections outline typical stages in survey research, and differentiate two broad types of survey (descriptive survey and explanatory survey) and several survey modes (postal survey, personal interview-based survey, telephone survey, online survey and mixed-mode survey). The particular types or modes of survey and their associated research designs and administration issues are explained, with examples, and their strengths and limitations are highlighted. It is concluded that, in certain instances, a mixed-mode survey design may be advantageous, in order to capitalise on the strengths and to overcome the limitations of any single mode.

Research Methods: Information, Systems, and Contexts. DOI: http://dx.doi.org/10.1016/B978-0-08-102220-7.00006-6

Introduction

Survey research involves the collection of primary data from all or part of a population, to determine the incidence, distribution, and interrelationships of certain variables within the population (Tanner, 2002, p. 89). Surveys gather data that describe and explain population or sample characteristics, behaviours, attitudes or opinions and may be used to predict future behaviour. They utilise a variety of data collection techniques, including questionnaires (print or online), interviews (face-to-face or telephone), and observation techniques.

Although the basic concepts and methods of survey research have been long established, recent social trends and technological changes have had considerable impact on survey modes and practices. Dillman, Smyth and Christian (2009) traced the historical evolution of social survey research from the 1930s to date. Until the 1960s, they claimed, social surveys were typically conducted by interview at home or work, where an interviewer had the time to build rapport and social conventions encouraged participation and ensured high response rates. Telecommunications developments in the 1970s–1980s led to the rising popularity of telephone surveying, and other technological advances in photocopying, personal computing and sophisticated electronic document design gave impetus to postal surveys. However, from the 1990s a number of new threats (e.g., unlisted phone numbers, call-blocking, 'do-not-call' lists, voice-mail, mobiles and wireless devices, and internet phones) have posed major obstacles to telephone surveying, resulting in plummeting response rates and less representative samples. With postal surveys too, the exponential increase in the number of surveys being circulated by business, community organisations and university students has seen a concomitant decrease in survey response rates. One countervailing force has been the development of the online (email or web-based) survey, which is rapidly disseminated, highly efficient and inexpensive, saving substantial costs in labour, printing, postal or phone charges. The turbulence and complexity of the current situation poses considerable challenges for survey researchers. Dillman, Smyth and Christian (2009) cited research studies which demonstrate that there is no single 'best' mode of survey but that certain survey modes are better for some populations, topics, sponsors and situations, and build the case for a holistic, 'tailored design', approach that may include mixed-mode survey designs. A particular emphasis of their approach, which is supported here, is a social exchange perspective on how to increase motivational factors for survey participation.

Survey research challenges and issues

In order to establish confidence in survey results, researchers need to demonstrate how they have dealt with several fundamental research issues that are outlined in this section. These include issues of sampling and broader generalisation, ensuring that survey instruments are valid and reliable, and dealing with potential sources of bias and error.

Sampling and the ability to generalise in survey research

A sound understanding of sampling is essential for anyone undertaking survey research. As most surveys utilise samples rather than a population census, researchers need to thoroughly understand the constraints that the chosen sampling method and the nature of the 'sampling frame' (i.e., its inclusions and exclusions) impose on their ability to generalise from their sample to the broader population. Valid generalisations can be made only when 'probability' sampling has been used, that is, where samples have been scientifically selected so that the statistical probability of each individual's inclusion in the sample can be specified. With a 'non-probability' sample an individual's chance of inclusion in the sample cannot be specified; consequently assumptions of normality of distribution do not apply and the sample's degree of sampling error cannot be estimated. In selecting samples scientifically, it is important to stress that is the *number* in the sample that is critical, *not* the *proportion* of the total population included in the sample. Survey researchers need to be alert to the relationship between confidence level, the accepted margin of error and required sample size. For instance, at the 95 percent confidence level: an accepted margin of error of $\pm$ 3 percent requires a probability sample of 1,067, while an accepted margin of error of $\pm$ 5 percent requires a sample of 384 (Sue & Ritter, 2007).

In survey research, non-probability samples are typically used for exploratory studies or survey pilot-tests. With these, the researcher cannot legitimately generalise beyond the sample itself. (See Chapter 15: *Populations and samples* for further discussion of sampling.)

Creating valid and reliable survey research instruments

'Validity' relates to how well a survey instrument measures what it purports to measure, that is, its accuracy, whilst 'reliability' concerns the extent to which data from a particular survey instrument is reproducible or stable from one administration to another. To establish the credentials of their research and the degree of confidence that can be placed in their findings, survey researchers need to demonstrate the validity and reliability of their research instruments. This is particularly critical for explanatory surveys.

Validity is generally measured before reliability. As Litwin (1995) explained, there are four broad types of tests for validity of a survey instrument (questionnaire). Two of these (face validity and content validity) involve qualitative assessments. *Face validity* is an informal review of a questionnaire by non-experts, who assess its clarity, comprehensibility, and appropriateness for the target-group, whilst *content validity* involves a formal assessment by subject experts, to determine appropriateness of content and identify any misunderstandings or omissions. The other two types of validity tests (criterion validity and construct validity) entail statistically quantifiable measures (correlation coefficients) between the current survey instrument and other tests, scales or indexes. Tests for *criterion validity* pertain either to *concurrent* validity (comparing results from the survey instrument, and another reputable test, administered to the same respondents) or *predictive* validity (comparing the predictive capacity of the survey instrument with future outcomes, e.g., a scholastic aptitude test prior to university entrance being compared with actual student university results). *Construct validity* of an instrument is assessed retrospectively compared with other tests for the construct; it tests how well the instrument has performed in practice.

Reliability tests provide a statistical measure of how replicable data from a survey instrument with repeated administration amongst the same or similar groups of respondents are. The major tests for reliability include: *test—retest reliability* (correlating results from one survey instrument administered to the same respondents at two different times); *alternate form reliability* (correlating results from two slightly different versions of a survey instrument administered to the same or similar respondents); and *internal consistency reliability* (measuring how well a set of items that combine to form a single scale vary together when administered to a group) (Litwin, 1995).

Careful planning, administration and reporting of tests for validity and reliability of survey instruments increase confidence in survey findings.

Dealing with four potential sources of bias and error

This section examines some further potential sources of bias or error in survey research, which survey researchers need to acknowledge and, insofar as possible, control for.

Coverage error

Coverage error occurs when the selected sampling frame is not fully representative of the chosen population and certain segments of the population are inadvertently excluded or under-represented. An electoral roll, for example, excludes those under voting age. Survey mode is another potential source of coverage error, for example, a telephone directory excluding unlisted numbers and many with mobile devices; or an email list excluding those without an email address. Where identifiable groups within a population are excluded from the chosen sampling frame, the survey researcher needs to source other appropriate lists that can be used to supplement the initial list.

Sampling error

As sampling involves a subset of the larger population, there is an inherent risk of error associated with generalising sample values to the broader population. Samples not accurately representing the main segments of the broader population are biased. Where scientific sampling has been meticulously applied and an adequate-sized sample is selected for an accepted margin of error, the degree of sampling error can be estimated fairly accurately. However, with non-probability samples the degree of sampling error is indeterminate – there is no way of knowing the extent to which the sample is representative of the wider population.

Non-response error

Survey response rate is the ratio between the completed sample and the total sample. It is a useful survey quality indicator. Low response rates are a prevalent concern in survey research: the lower the response rate, the higher the non-response error. The concern here is that those who respond to a survey are likely to differ in material ways from non-respondents, e.g., the less-educated may be less likely to respond than those better-educated. A high response rate is needed for accurate generalisation to a population.

Non-response is attributable to many factors. Broadly, busy lifestyles and proliferating numbers of surveys being circulated are disincentives to participation. More specifically, surveys that seem ill-conceived, poorly designed, unnecessarily long or complex, or requiring data that are difficult to procure are likely to yield low response rates. More focussed target groups generate higher response rates than do less differentiated targets (e.g., the 'general public').

The crucial challenge for survey researchers seeking to minimise non-response error is motivating individuals to respond. Drawing on a social exchange perspective, Dillman, Smyth and Christian (2009) explore factors increasing motivation for survey participation and for decreasing costs of participation. They emphasised that all aspects of survey construction and design and survey implementation procedures must work together effectively to increase motivation to respond.

Measurement error

Measurement error pertains to the difference between obtained survey results and the true values of those particular variables in the population. There are many potential sources of measurement error in survey research. Most surveys are based on self-report data, which can be of questionable accuracy. Individuals will tend to respond to surveys in ways that present themselves in the most positive light, and with responses biased through processes of selective perception, memory and recall. Respondents may provide inaccurate information if they misinterpret a question, do not wish to answer it, or lack the information needed to answer it. With interviews there is a tendency for participants to respond in ways they perceive to be socially acceptable.

However, the major source of measurement error in surveys is poor questionnaire design. Most texts on survey research (e.g., Rea & Parker, 2005; Sue & Ritter, 2007) provide useful guidelines for effective questionnaire design. Such guidelines are given in Chapter 16: *Questionnaires, individual interviews, and focus group interviews*. Particularly insightful is Dillman, Smyth and Christian (2009), which reports on the authors' extensive experiments into the differential impacts on survey respondents of various aspects of questionnaire design, format and layout. Measurement error can be reduced through careful questionnaire design, adequate pre-testing of the survey instrument, and applying tests for validity and reliability.

Typical stages in survey research

Typical stages involved in planning and implementing a survey are outlined below. It must be stressed that these stages are iterative rather than linear and that their order may vary from one type or mode of survey to another.

- The survey topic is identified and its focus refined after reviewing available literature and consulting with stakeholders. Survey objectives, research questions, hypotheses and information sought are clearly articulated.
- The survey population is precisely defined. If the defined population is small, it may be feasible to survey the population, but usually a sample is used.
- The most appropriate survey method and survey mode for gathering the required information is determined. Factors such as research goals, nature of information sought, population characteristics and dispersion, timeline and budget influence this decision.
- Where probability sampling is involved, the sampling frame is procured or compiled from various sources. The required sample size and sampling techniques are determined and the sample is drawn.
- The survey instrument is compiled, paying careful attention to guidelines for effective survey design.
- The survey instrument is pre-tested, and pilot-tested on a number of the intended target audience, to establish its validity and reliability. Any necessary revisions are made.
- An initial letter or email is sent explaining the nature and aims of the survey and enlisting participation.
- The survey is implemented (i.e., questionnaires are mailed/emailed to the sample or interviews are conducted).

- With questionnaires, after the designated due-date for return, follow-up letter(s) or email(s) are sent to non-respondents, to increase the response rate.

- The returned questionnaires, or completed interview schedules, are collected for coding. Respondents' answers to each question are systematically recorded and the data computerised for subsequent analysis. An online questionnaire greatly simplifies this process through automatic downloading of survey data.

- Data are examined for any problems or inconsistencies, and the data file is 'cleansed' prior to running frequencies and other statistical procedures and tests.

- Data are analysed and results recorded and interpreted and conclusions drawn. (See Chapter 18: *Quantitative data analysis*, and Chapter 19: *Qualitative data analysis*.)

- The survey report is prepared and distributed.

Broad types of survey

A long-established categorisation of research is a tripartite division based on research purpose/goals – *exploratory*, *descriptive* and *explanatory* research (e.g., Babbie, 2010; Sekaran, 2010). These categories reflect the relative stage of development or sophistication of knowledge of a research area. Surveys are used mainly for descriptive and explanatory research. *Descriptive* research extends understanding through *describing* characteristics of particular phenomena and elaborating on features of interest, whilst *explanatory* research seeks to analyse and *explain* relationships between variables of interest through testing hypotheses and contributing to the development of theory. This distinction is reflected in the classification of surveys into two broad types – descriptive surveys and explanatory surveys. This section introduces these survey designs, along with examples.

Descriptive (or status) surveys

The main purpose of a descriptive survey is to describe a particular phenomenon: its current situation, its properties and conditions, that is, to answer 'what' as well as 'who', 'when', 'where', 'how much', 'how many', 'how often' questions about it. An alternate term is a *status survey*, or a survey of the *status quo*, a snapshot in time and place.

Descriptive surveys are primarily concerned with fact gathering, enumerating and describing. They use descriptive statistics more than inferential statistics, and rarely involve formal statistical hypothesis testing. Typically, they gather qualitative, 'written-response' data as well as quantitative data, and utilise some qualitative data analysis techniques. Questionnaires (print or electronic) and interviews (face-to-face or telephone) are the primary techniques used in descriptive surveys.

Advantages and limitations of descriptive surveys

Compared with some other research designs, descriptive surveys are relatively straightforward to implement. Their use is appropriate when the primary purpose of the research is to gather facts or information on the incidence and distribution of certain variables within the population. To increase confidence in their survey findings, researchers must be alert to potential sources of error and bias outlined earlier in this chapter and implement measures that address these concerns.

Descriptive surveys provide a snapshot of a situation or phenomenon in one place and at one time. Researchers need to be careful that they do not make invalid claims for their findings by extrapolating them to contexts or time periods outside their range, or by concluding that there are causal links between the factors they have investigated. In natural settings (as opposed to controlled settings such as laboratories), it is difficult to discount rival explanations. Box 6.1 provides an example of a descriptive survey, adapted from Tanner (2002).

Box 6.1

Example of a descriptive survey: Information technology (IT) outsourcing in Australia

Source

Karpathiou, V., & Tanner, K. (1995). *Information technology outsourcing in Australia*. Melbourne: RMIT Department of Business Computing.

The issue under investigation

From the late 1980s, governments and businesses were seriously questioning whether their huge IT investments were delivering value; were looking to business process restructuring and drastic downsizing to maintain competitiveness in an adverse market climate; and saw IT outsourcing as an appealing option. By 1993, IT outsourcing was a pervasive management practice, and federal, state and local governments required their agencies to market-test their IT with a view to outsourcing.

Research questions

In relation to IT outsourcing: What were the motives/influencing factors? What were current Australian trends? Were there differences between practices in the private sector and public sector? Which IT functions and processes were being outsourced? What were the business, structural, technological and staff impacts of IT outsourcing?

The research design

The research comprised a literature review and descriptive survey using a mailed questionnaire. The questionnaire was compiled from literature review insights. There was an initial pilot validation of the questionnaire, and revisions made prior to the mail-out.

The sample

The target population comprised Australian public and private sector organisations with large IT infrastructures. As participants needed IT knowledge and a strategic perspective, IT managers were targeted in each organisation. A suitable sampling frame was identified – MIS 2000 (1993), a directory listing details of Australian and New Zealand public sector (federal, state, local) and private sector organisations with a significant IT infrastructure, and including names of IT managers. All 1,800 Australian organisations listed were included and NZ ones excluded.

Questionnaire design

The first section of the questionnaire profiled the respondent organisation – its sector, industry, size, budget, size and maturity of IT department, degree of alignment between IT function and corporate strategy (variables used for cross-tabulations). Subsequent sections focussed on significant IT outsourcing issues (planning, management, costs, vendor relationships, staff impacts). The final section assessed the organisation's overall evaluation of its outsourcing experience. Most questions included were closed-ended, with some open-ended questions for deeper insights. Although most questions sought objective data, some focussed on personal, subjective evaluations. An early filter question channelled respondents into 'outsourced', 'still considering' and 'rejected outsourcing'.

Response rate

From the initial mail-out of 1,794 questionnaires, 447 responses were received. A single follow-up letter elicited another 51 responses – with a final response rate of 27.8 percent. Further follow-ups were rejected as a significant expense for minimal gain. The generalisability of findings with less than one-third response rate is problematic, as there is no guarantee that non-respondents would have answered in the same way, or would have exhibited the same characteristics as did respondents. Given the low response-rate, care was needed in writing results not to claim more than was justified.

Explanatory (or analytical) surveys

Explanatory (or analytical) surveys attempt to probe further than descriptive surveys, to explain 'how' and 'why', to explore interrelationships of variables and likely causal links between them. Most explanatory surveys are strongly positivist, testing hypotheses and aiming to contribute to the development of theory. They generally use probability sampling, gather quantitative data and apply advanced statistical techniques (inferential statistics).

A caveat is needed concerning the use of surveys to infer causation. In natural settings, it is very difficult to establish causation, as all possible alternative explanations (intervening variables) must be dismissed, for example, if observed data apparently supported the hypothesis 'computer skills decrease with age', the researcher would need to discount rival explanations of 'computer access' and 'computer training' as factors through applying a technique such as elaboration analysis. Where this is done, and major rival explanations are dismissed, confidence can be placed in the survey findings.

The use of surveys to formally validate, test and build theory

One significant application of surveys is in the formal validation, testing and building of theory in a particular discipline. Early on, researchers undertake a comprehensive literature review that reveals the major existing theories pertinent to their topic, for example, the Technology Acceptance Model (Davis, 1989; Davis, Bagozzi & Warshaw, 1989) and its later variants, or Diffusion of Innovations Theory (Rogers, 1962; 2003). Their research focus may be to test an existing theory for its applicability in a different context from the one where the theory was developed (e.g., in a different country or culture, or in a different organisational or business context); to modify an existing theory to account for new insights gained from their literature review or experience; or to test a new theory they have developed. A theory encompasses relevant constructs or variables and their postulated interrelationships (usually presented in diagrammatic format), which are translated into a series of hypotheses that are formally tested with a survey instrument. A typical survey used for this purpose comprises separate sets of items for each construct in the form of statements and associated measurement scales (e.g., 5-point or 7-point scales), along with questions on any relevant demographics and characteristics of respondents (e.g., age, gender, education level, experience with technology) that may be important moderating variables. There is considerable re-use and adaptation of existing validated scales and instruments in such surveys.

Advanced statistical techniques beyond the level of descriptive statistics are applied in the analysis of these data, for example, correlation and regression, analysis of variance, path analysis techniques for model identification and fit, confirmatory factor analysis and structural equation modelling. Rea and Parker (2005) give a clear outline of advanced statistical techniques for survey analysis, while Kline (2005) provides an accessible explanation of structural equation modelling and its constituent elements. (See also Chapter 18.)

Information systems is one discipline that makes extensive use of this form of survey in validating, testing and building theory. Examples can be found by browsing issues of major journals, for example, *MIS Quarterly*. Box 6.2 also provides an example.

Box 6.2

Example of an explanatory survey: Consumer acceptance and use of information technology (IT) online survey

Source

Venkatesh, V., Thong, J. Y. L., & Xu, X. (2012). Consumer acceptance and use of information technology: Extending the Unified Theory of Acceptance and Use of Technology, *MIS Quarterly, 36*(1), 157–178.

Background and purpose of the study

One of the major streams of information systems research has focussed on explaining and predicting individual acceptance and use of IT. Venkatesh, Morris, Davis and Davis (2003) posited a theory that attempted to synthesise insights from eight extant theories/models of technology use; they called this the 'Unified Theory of Acceptance and Use of Technology' (UTAUT). UTAUT identified critical factors in an organisational context/ workplace. The current study sought to extend this theory into the area of consumer technology use and to develop a refined version of the UTAUT model to fit this context, which the authors dubbed 'UTAUT2'.

Modification of the original theory

Adapting a theory to variant contexts is a common approach to extending theory – it helps make the theory more robust and increases its predictive validity. From their literature review on adoption and use of technologies/ consumer adoption and use, the researchers identified an additional three constructs for incorporation into the extended model – hedonic motivation (enjoyment), price value, and habit. They also altered some of the relationships between constructs in the original UTAUT model, and introduced some new relationships. Based on prior literature, they articulated five hypotheses for empirical testing of the revised model.

The population and sample

The survey was undertaken among Hong Kong users of mobile internet technology who access various digital data services. Hong Kong has almost universal penetration of mobile phones, with a 52 percent rate of use of mobile internet in 2011.

Survey method and sample

The population was accessed via an online survey on a popular Hong Kong web-portal that gives residents access to e-government services. The survey involved two stages: with Stage 1 collecting data on exogenous variables and intention to use mobile internet; and Stage 2, four months later, collecting data on previous respondents' mobile internet use. Participants were enlisted by placing a banner advertisement on the web-portal, which remained there for four weeks; a material incentive for participation was also offered (a lucky draw for various prizes). Participants were asked to provide their mobile phone numbers and identity card numbers, so that multiple responses from one person could be eliminated. There were 4,127 valid responses received from Stage 1 of the survey, and 2,220 from Stage 2. However these were reduced to a final sample of 1,512 respondents after removing those with no experience of the mobile internet.

The survey instrument and its measurement scales

The survey instrument included several items (three or four statements) for each of the following model constructs: performance expectancy, effort expectancy, social influence, facilitating conditions, hedonic motivation, price value, habit, and behavioural intention. The original constructs drew on the previous 2003 UTAUT scales, while the three new constructs adapted scales from other researchers. These items utilised 7-point scales ('strongly disagree' to 'strongly agree'). Respondent characteristics captured included age, gender, and experience (in months). Use was measured as a composite index of variety and frequency of six mobile internet applications.

The survey instrument was reviewed for content validity by university staff and information systems academics, and was then pilot-tested on 200 consumers who were not included in the main survey. The instrument scales were assessed as reliable and valid.

Statistical analysis

Partial least squares (PLS) using Smart-PLS software was used to test the model. The measurement model was assessed for reliability and validity and then the various structural models were tested.

Outcomes

The researchers concluded that their extended model, UTAUT2, was broadly supported, and that, compared to the original UTAUT, it "produced a substantial improvement in the variance explained in behavioural intention (56 percent to 74 percent) and technology use (40 percent to 52 percent)" (Venkatesh, Thong & Xu, 2012, p. 157).

Some particular designs used for explanatory surveys

This section outlines three different types of explanatory survey design: static group comparison, longitudinal/panel study and cross-sectional/pseudo-panel designs, and provides examples. These designs involve some type of simulation of an experimental design. However, unlike a formal experiment, there are significant limitations in inferring causality due to the natural setting and associated lack of rigorous controls (e.g., lack of random assignment to different 'conditions').

Static group comparison design

The basic design is given below in Figure 6.1.

Figure 6.1 Basic design for static group comparisons

X = The characteristic under study (i.e., the *independent* variable)
O = An observation or measurement (i.e., of the *dependent* variable)

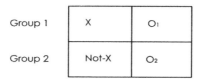

Group 1	X	O_1
Group 2	Not-X	O_2

An example of this design is a study by Williams, Khan and Naumann (2011) into the impacts of dramatic downsizing on business-to-business (B2B) service customers of a large company (see Figure 6.2). The researchers undertook a telephone survey of 534 of the company's B2B customers three months before downsizing and another survey of 994 different B2B customers three months after a dramatic downsizing event.

Figure 6.2 Example of a static group comparison survey design.

X = Impacts of major downsizing on B2B customers of a large company
O = Attitude survey measuring customer satisfaction and likely customer retention

Group 1	X (B2B customers of a large company after a significant downsizing event)	O_1 [Attitude survey (customer satisfaction and likely customer retention)]
Group 2	Not-X (B2B customers of the company before downsizing)	O_2 [Attitude survey (customer satisfaction and likely customer retention)]

Source: Williams, Khan & Naumann 2011.

The static group comparison is a *correlational* design rather than an experiment. There is a lack of random assignment to the two different 'conditions' (which is characteristic of the formal experiment). Rather, subjects are divided into Groups 1 and 2 on the basis of whether or not they possess 'X'. Here, Group 2 ('Not-X') were B2B customers who had not yet experienced downsizing impacts from their major supplier company, while Group 1 ('X') were B2B customers with customer-relationship experience with the company post-downsizing. Both groups participated in a telephone survey on customer attitudes (i.e., their level of satisfaction and likelihood of retention as a company customer). A correlational technique, an *independent samples t-test* was used to compare the means of the two groups for customer satisfaction measures and established that the decrease in customer satisfaction after the downsizing event was significant. Additionally, a direct comparison of the two frequency distributions was undertaken, using a *z-test*, and various other calculations and estimation techniques were applied. The research findings showed "that a significant downsizing event has an immediate and negative impact on customer satisfaction levels and on projected retention rates", and that the losses of customers "substantially offsets the short term labor cost savings from the downsizing" (Williams, Khan & Naumann, 2011, p. 405).

Claiming causation is not possible with this type of design. To infer that X (the independent variable) causes O (the dependent variable), three criteria must be satisfied: X and O must co-vary; X must precede O in time; and there must be no alternative explanations of the group differences in O.

Longitudinal/panel study

A longitudinal study is an extended investigation following changes in certain variables amongst a sample over time. Some longitudinal studies have traced cohorts from birth and followed them up at regular intervals throughout their lives to gather medical/health-related data (e.g., linking diet, smoking and other factors with particular diseases). One popular longitudinal study made into a television documentary series is the British *Seven Up* series (Granada & Apted, 1964–). The sample of 14 children selected from across the socio-economic spectrum was first studied in 1964 at age seven, when they were profiled in terms of their lives, attitudes and aspirations for the future. The cohort has been followed up each seven years since (i.e., *14 Up, 21 Up, 28 Up, 35 Up, 42 Up, 49 Up,* and *56 Up* released in 2012).

The *Longitudinal Surveys of Australian Youth* (LSAY) program (https://www.lsay.edu.au/), which has built on earlier government projects, surveys cohorts of Australian youth annually for ten years to determine trends in their transition from school to higher education, vocational education or employment. The program started in 1995 with a cohort of year nine students, with further cohorts of year nine students (or students aged 15 years) added in 1998, 2003, 2006, 2009 and 2015. Waves of data collection since 2003 have been integrated with the OECD's Programme for International Student Assessment. Each cohort has started with over 10,000 students. Data are collected via computer-assisted telephone interviewing. There are numerous publications derived from the LSAY datasets.

Longitudinal studies like these also do not fully satisfy the criteria for inferring causation. Although there may appear to be some hints of causation, no definite causal links can be established due to potential rival explanations.

Cross-sectional/pseudo-panel design

Cross-sectional designs attempt to achieve what a longitudinal design does, but at one point in time. With this design, the sample is divided into appropriate, mutually exclusive strata (e.g., age); then each stratum is compared with respect to the variable under consideration. This design is widely used in market research and epidemiological, medical and allied health studies. Again, the nature of the design precludes any attribution of causation. Only an identification of possible correlations (relationships) of variables is provided. These studies are often simply descriptive surveys, using stratified samples.

Advantages and limitations of explanatory surveys

Explanatory surveys enable phenomena to be measured in their natural setting rather than in an artificial laboratory setting – and it is impossible to investigate many natural phenomena in a laboratory. They are appropriate when a researcher needs to answer 'how' and 'why' questions about a particular phenomenon or explore interrelationships of variables and possible causal links between them. However, explanatory surveys cannot conclusively establish causal relationships. Rather, they are correlational, identifying interrelationships of variables. These may be interpreted as giving a hint of causality, provided that appropriate statistical techniques are applied to establish that correlations are not spurious relationships.

Survey modes

Survey researchers have several choices of survey mode. This section outlines the major survey modes (i.e., postal, personal interview-based, telephone, online and mixed-mode) and explores their associated administration issues. Selecting an appropriate survey mode requires understanding the features and issues with each mode and their relative strengths and weaknesses. Researchers need to carefully consider these points in relation to their research goals and decide which mode is the most appropriate for their purposes. The final decision may be to select one survey mode or combine the modes in some form. Mixed-mode surveys are useful where the strengths of one mode compensate for the limitations of another.

Some considerations affecting choice of survey mode include: characteristics of the population being surveyed (e.g., degree of literacy, languages spoken, culture, socio-economic status, age-groups, legal status); geographic dispersion of the population; project timeline; cost; required facilities/resources; personnel and their training; nature of the topic and depth of responses sought; length of the survey instrument; whether or not the survey instrument requires graphical representations; anonymity, confidentiality and privacy issues; and typical response rates for the particular survey mode. Table 6.1 compares features of the survey modes along these key dimensions.

Postal (or mail) surveys

A postal (or mail) survey uses a printed questionnaire that is posted out to members of the survey sample, who are asked to complete the survey and then to return it by mail. A cover letter explaining the nature, purpose and sponsorship of the survey and a reply-paid return envelope are usually provided. Postal surveys are relatively easy and straightforward to implement. However, an enduring issue is the typically low associated response rate.

An example of a postal survey is the *IT Outsourcing in Australia Survey* given earlier (see Box 6.1 under 'Descriptive surveys').

Issues with the administration of postal surveys

With prevalent low response rates to postal surveys, the major challenge for the researcher is how to maximise the survey response rate (i.e., increase motivation to respond and make it easy for people to respond). The various procedures reviewed here have this as a primary goal. One major aspect of motivation is the *salience* or importance of the research topic to prospective participants. An interesting questionnaire is a strong motivator to respond, as is the influence of a reputable sponsor identified by company letterhead in conveying a feeling of legitimacy to the survey. In terms of appearance and layout, the questionnaire needs to create a favourable initial impression, as a well-designed document that does not resemble advertising. Appropriate content, a logical sequence, clarity of questions and instructions, ease of completion and brevity are important factors in motivating response (see Chapter 16 for further advice). Adequate pre-testing and piloting testing of the questionnaire are critical.

Table 6.1 Comparison of the features of survey modes along key dimensions

Dimension	Survey mode				
	Postal	Personal interview	Telephone	Online (email)	Online (web)
Population characteristics	Cannot include those with very poor literacy or language skills	Can include all groups, including those with low literacy levels and those difficult to reach (e.g., the homeless)	Can access a reasonable cross-section of the general population but targeting special groups is difficult Can access those with low literacy levels and the housebound	Difficult to access the general population by email Best suited to closed populations that have available email-lists Usually cannot access people with low levels of education, literacy and computer literacy	As for email surveys Some groups lack internet access or have older software or low-speed connections that preclude access to web surveys
Geographic dispersion of the population	Can be geographically dispersed and global. Costs increase with overseas postage	Restricted geographic distribution as dependent on interviewer availability (unless have video-link)	Can be geographically dispersed, but increasing call-cost with distance (unless have internet phones or local interviewers)	Global – no geographic limit to the population that can be accessed	As for email surveys
Sample size	Can accommodate large samples	Small samples	Variable depending on interviewer availability and project funding	Any size of sample can be accommodated easily	As for email surveys
Time taken to implement	Fairly long time-frame	Variable according to number of interviews and interviewers available	Rapid data collection, for example, public opinion or political polls	Rapid data collection	As for email surveys

Dimension	Survey mode				
	Postal	Personal interview	Telephone	Online (email)	Online (web)
Cost	Comparatively inexpensive	Expensive as very labour-intensive	Moderate – labour costs for interviewing, cost of phone calls and telecommunications infrastructure	Generally inexpensive and cost-effective; no costs for distributing the survey	As for email surveys Possibly fees for technical consultants, survey hosting; automatic data capture saving transcription costs
Facilities/ resource requirements	Computer software, printing, postage	Interview room; recording and transcription equipment	Larger-scale projects require sophisticated specialised phone survey equipment and ICT infrastructure	Email address list; email access; survey either within email or an attachment or containing a link to a web-page	Access to web survey software and host website with a secure server (to maintain respondent privacy)
Personnel requirements	Researchers prepare survey and analyse data; support staff assist with survey distribution, returns and data-coding	Interviewers; interviewer training; support staff assist with interview transcription and coding	Telephone interviewers and interviewer training	Researcher for a simple email survey; some may need specialist technical expertise	Usually specialist technical expertise needed for setting up and hosting a web survey
Nature and depth of information sought	Mostly fairly superficial factual, opinion or attitude questions; questionnaire needs to be fairly brief to ensure a reasonable response rate	In-depth probing possible, allowing more complex questions (e.g., 'how' and 'why') and longer responses	Only superficial questions; avoid complex questions and those with many response options. Overall survey length needs to be short	As for postal survey	As for postal survey

Dimension	Survey mode				
	Postal	Personal interview	Telephone	Online (email)	Online (web)
Nature of questions and possible question options	Primarily selecting from pre-defined lists of options; possibly a few open-ended questions	Primarily open-ended questions	Mainly closed-ended questions; questions requiring a brief response or scoring on a standard scale	As for postal survey	As for postal survey. Good for filter questions
Impersonal or personal method	Impersonal	Personal	Less personal than interview but more so than postal or online survey	Fairly impersonal	Impersonal
Ability to have unclear questions explained or queries answered	Nil	Interviewer available to explain and clarify questions	Fairly limited – usually following a standard script, repeating questions more than explaining them	Limited – potentially could email researcher to seek clarification	Nil
Ability to reflect on a response	Have time to consider responses as survey is completed at leisure	Interviewee needs to respond straight away, little time for reflection	As for personal interviews	As for postal survey	Potential for reflection, but survey usually completed in one sitting
Content purely textual or also including visual/ graphic elements	Can accommodate both textual and graphic elements	Interviewer can present graphic representations	Only verbal content, no capacity for graphic representations	Survey within an email – only textual data; graphics possible in survey as email attachment or linked web survey	As for postal survey

Dimension	Survey mode				
	Postal	Personal interview	Telephone	Online (email)	Online (web)
Anonymity and privacy issues	Can maintain anonymity, potentially resulting in more honest answers	Participants can be identified; lack of anonymity can lead to less frank responses	Ability to maintain anonymity varies according to sampling method; lacking visual cues, interviewees may feel less constrained than in a personal interview	With personalised emails, respondents may feel a need to constrain their responses due to their lack of anonymity	As for postal survey Secure server needed for maintaining privacy of respondent data
Response rates	Typically low	Usually high	Low to medium – some variation according to the nature of the survey	Low to medium (higher than web surveys due to personalisation of emails)	Low Prevalence of non-probability samples of self-selected respondents
Options for offering incentives for participation	Can include a material incentive in the mail-out	Can offer incentives at the time of interview	Limited options	More limited than with a postal survey or interview	As for email survey
Likely sources of bias	Non-response bias when the response rate is low Measurement bias when questions are misinterpreted	Interviewer presence may influence responses, for example, answering questions in ways perceived to be socially acceptable	Coverage bias – omitting those without phones or with unlisted numbers (including many mobile phones) Non-response bias with refusals, busy lines or 'no answer' Measurement bias if answer in socially desirable ways	Coverage bias – omitting those without email access, and bias towards the more educated, literate and computer literate Non-response bias when the response rate is low Measurement bias when questions are misinterpreted	Coverage bias – omitting those without internet access Other sources of bias as for email survey

Offering incentives to participate

There is a considerable literature and strong theoretical base underpinning the issue of incentives for survey participation (Dillman, Smyth & Christian, 2009; Sue & Ritter, 2007). Relevant theories are social exchange theory and cognitive dissonance theory. According to social exchange theory, perceived benefits in the form of incentives to participate must outweigh the costs of participation (i.e., the time and effort to complete the survey). Perceived benefits include both material incentives like cash payments, free gifts or prize draws (extrinsic rewards) and intangible ones such as feelings of enjoyment or a sense of social contribution from participating in a worthwhile project (intrinsic rewards). Cognitive dissonance theory helps illuminate social incentives for survey completion. For example, when individuals consider themselves helpful, kind or generous, refusing to participate is incompatible with their self-perception.

Dillman, Smyth and Christian (2009) viewed survey response as a voluntary action within a context of reciprocal social obligations, and showed how survey procedures can build a positive social exchange with prospective survey participants. Their research has demonstrated that a small token incentive given in *advance* of actual participation in a survey (e.g., $5 mailed with a postal survey) is more likely to elicit a survey response than is a much larger amount promised upon submission of a completed survey; the rationale is that this act creates a sense of reciprocal obligation and builds trust, and trust encourages participation.

Involvement in an activity related to the survey, for example, attending a conference, also increases the likelihood of survey participation (Sue & Ritter, 2007).

Correspondence associated with a postal survey

All correspondence associated with a survey needs to adopt a positive, friendly tone and courteous approach that encourages participation. This includes demonstration of positive regard for recipients, providing information, seeking advice and showing appreciation for their contributions, and developing trust through assurances of confidentiality and maintaining security of information.

- *Initial letter.* Before posting the questionnaire, an initial letter is sent to each member of the sample, to invite participation. This letter outlines the research project and its sponsorship, and emphasises the potential value of the study to the participant, the particular target group or the wider society. Reputable sponsorship helps increase the response rate.

- *Cover letter.* A cover letter accompanying the questionnaire is essential — describing the nature of the survey, sponsorship details, incentives for participation, how data will be utilised, and procedural details (e.g., pre-paid return envelope provided, dates for return, how long the survey should take). Although not recommended as a practice, where funding is tight, the initial letter may be combined with the cover letter. In setting the due-date, sufficient time needs to be allowed for questionnaire completion and postal handling in both directions, but any further extension of the due-date is not advised.

- *Follow-up letter(s).* To increase the survey response rate, one or more follow-up letters or postcards are usually sent to those who have not responded by the specified due-date. Most surveys use a system of allocating unique numbers to questionnaires to track responses, so that follow-ups are sent only to non-respondents. Alternately, a letter can be phrased as both a 'thank you' to those who have returned their questionnaires and a reminder for those who have not. There is some disagreement in the literature over the desirable number of follow-ups sent to non-respondents — some authors recommend three or more, while others advocate just one or two. In practice, the number of follow-ups is likely to be constrained by the time schedule for project completion. There is a tendency for the first follow-up letter to encourage a greater percentage of non-respondents to return their surveys, and for each subsequent letter to yield a decreasing percentage (i.e., a manifestation of the law of diminishing returns).

Personal interview-based surveys

A survey can be implemented by an interviewer, in a one-to-one interview. Personal interviews were once a popular survey mode in earlier less-pressured times but are less used today given the constraints facing survey researchers. A personal interview offers greater flexibility than other survey modes, in relation to: the nature of questions that can be asked (e.g., open-ended questions, complex questions that require explanation); the two-way interaction between interviewer and interviewee (i.e., where the interviewer can probe in-depth, ask follow-up questions, offer explanations and clarify any misunderstandings); the ability to access segments of the population that have low rates of literacy or that are difficult to reach; and the ability to make use of graphic representations. Response rates are usually high, partly attributable to direct personal interaction and the rapport the interviewer builds with the participant. However, surveys conducted via personal interview: are costly, time-consuming and resource-intensive to implement; limit the number of participants and their geographic dispersion; allow identification of participants, which may mean that interviewees are less frank in their responses; and may generate responses that are inadvertently biased due to interviewer presence.

One variant of the personal interview-based survey is *the intercept* survey, where respondents passing by a point such as a shopping centre or railway station are interviewed about their behaviour, attitudes or opinions on a pertinent issue, for example, experience and satisfaction with public transport (Rea & Parker, 2005). Interviews conducted in this way are, by necessity, quite short in duration (no more than a few minutes).

Issues with the administration of personal interview-based surveys

Some issues specifically related to administering personal-interview-based surveys include: the recruitment, selection and training of interviewers; resources required; and undertaking the interview. For guidelines on effective interview techniques and developing the interview protocol see Chapter 16.

The recruitment, selection and training of interviewers

If a survey requires multiple interviewers, appropriate recruitment and selection procedures are essential. Poor interviewers can threaten the validity of survey findings. Effective interviewers have sound interpersonal and communication skills, and demonstrate emotional intelligence – they are self-aware, effective managers of their own emotional expression and recognise emotions in others, are enthusiastic and self-motivated, and handle social relationships well (Mayer & Salovey, 1993; Salovey & Mayer, 1990). They quickly develop rapport, are active listeners and sensitive to non-verbal cues. Recruited interviewers require training and practice in interview skills and administration of the interview protocol, and a sound understanding of the research project, its value and sponsorship.

Resources required

Unless interviews are conducted in interviewees' homes, a suitable venue and facilities will need to be arranged. Interviewers need sufficient copies of the interview protocol, and official identification to verify their authenticity. A decision needs to be made about whether or not interviews will be formally recorded and any associated audio- or video-recording equipment arranged.

Undertaking the interviews

Typically, interviewers commence the interview with a concise overview of the research project and approach taken. They stress the voluntary nature of the interviewee's participation, assure confidentiality in the way responses will be handled and reported, and answer any questions. For valid results, questions must be asked as written and in the intended sequence, with further probing as required. In conclusion, interviewers thank the interviewee and outline any arrangements for confirming the interview transcript and distributing the summary of survey findings.

Telephone surveys

Telephone surveys are widely used in market research and political polling, and also in academic research, for example, the aforementioned survey of Williams, Khan and Naumann (2011). With telephone surveys, a geographically dispersed population can be surveyed quickly, saving interviewers' travel costs and time. Also, population segments difficult to reach by other methods (e.g., those with low levels of literacy and the housebound) may be accessible via telephone interview. One appeal of telephone surveying is its capacity for rapid response (e.g., during an election campaign, weekly surveying of political party preferences, voting intentions and preferred leader.) Telephone surveys are less expensive than face-to-face interviews, but more expensive than a postal survey. Long-distance calls, particularly international calls, can be costly, but these costs can be minimised by using internet phones or employing local interviewers.

The researcher considering a telephone survey needs to be aware of limitations of this mode of data collection. The decision on whether a telephone survey is suitable for a particular survey will depend on factors such as: the topic under investigation; whether or not sensitive or complex issues are being explored; the depth of responses sought; the length of the survey; and whether graphic aids are necessary to explain the point. Telephone surveys can also be used as a supplementary mode in a multi-mode survey research design.

In the 1970s–1980s, with telecommunications advances and rising rates of telephone penetration throughout the community, telephone surveys were at their peak. At that time, various writers observed that the response rates for telephone surveys were high in comparison with postal surveys. For instance, in his state-of-the-art review of telephone surveys, Tyebjee (1979) found response rates ranging from 45–95 percent in the studies he examined. However, this situation has changed substantially since the 1990s, with a range of developments having a substantial negative impact on response rates to telephone surveys.

Issues with the administration of telephone surveys

Many issues with the administration of telephone surveys are similar to the personal interview-based survey and other survey modes, but some issues are unique to telephone surveying.

Issues of sampling and non-response bias

Once it was quite straightforward to set up a random sample for a telephone survey from a telephone directory. However, the increasing incidence of people with unlisted phone numbers or on 'do-not-call' lists has made the process of deriving a scientifically-based sample for a telephone survey difficult. Automatic random-digit-dialling is one way to derive a sample for a telephone survey and to access unlisted numbers. It is difficult to target a particular population segment through a telephone directory. Rather, access to a specialised listing/directory that contains the phone numbers of the desired target group is usually required.

With telephone surveys, there are different causes of non-response. The telephone may not be answered because the subject is out, or it may be engaged. In both instances, there needs to be a clear policy for telephone interviewers to follow that specifies how many call-backs should be made before giving up, and whether or not a replacement number is then substituted. The other type of non-response is direct refusal to participate. Refusal rates can be higher at certain times of the day and week. One way to reduce this type of non-response is for the interviewer to ask politely at the outset whether this is a convenient time to speak or whether s/he should call back later at a more suitable time, and then negotiate a time for the call-back. Response rates tend to increase if the respondent is addressed by name, and when the social value of the survey is stressed.

The time of day telephone surveys are conducted is a potential source of bias. If conducted during the day, telephone surveys will yield an over-representation of certain community groups (the retired, parents caring for children, and the unemployed), and conversely an under-representation of others (especially the employed). A strict call-back policy where repeat calls are made in the evenings or on week-ends to numbers that did not answer during the day is essential to ensure a representative final sample.

Selection and training of telephone interviewers

Comments made earlier on the selection and training for personal interview-based surveys are broadly applicable to telephone interviewers. However, the telephone mode that is solely reliant on audio cues does necessitate some special training in telephone interview techniques and etiquette.

Facilities and resources required

Most telephone surveys require sophisticated specialist facilities and technologies to manage the survey process. Professional market research companies utilise the latest technology in telephone surveying. Some examples are: computer-assisted telephone interviewing (CATI), where a telephone interviewer follows an online script and questionnaire form, with the computer automatically filtering and screening questions to be asked based on an earlier response and with the interviewer entering responses into the online form; touchtone data entry, where the respondent records response numbers on keys on their telephone; and interactive voice response, where the computer administers and registers both vocal and keyed responses (Dillman, Smyth & Christian, 2009).

Undertaking the telephone interviews

Because telephone interviews need to be brief (e.g., five to ten minutes), the telephone survey instrument should be short and to-the-point, with a limited number of concise questions. Some types of questions (e.g., complex lists of alternative options) cannot be effectively asked over the telephone. Telephone surveys are unsuited to questions requiring lengthy or involved responses. People are naturally reticent to disclose highly personal information, or information that may be interpreted as an invasion of privacy or risking their personal security, for example, questions pertaining to their income or possessions.

Online surveys

Online surveys are distributed by various electronic means. Data transmitted in electronic form is much more flexible than other modes of survey and greatly facilitates the processes of data collection, data capture and data analysis. The use of online surveys has proliferated over the past decade. Discussion here is limited to two major forms of online survey, the email survey and the web survey.

An email survey may be incorporated into the body of the email, as a separate email attachment, or an email may contain instructions and links for accessing a survey online. Where a survey is incorporated into the body of an email, of necessity it must be: brief, with relatively few questions; straightforward, avoiding branching or other complex question formats; and purely textual, with minimal formatting and no graphics. An email survey included as an attached file provides more formatting options but care must be taken to restrict file-size, as many email systems do not accept attachments over a designated limit. Addressed to named individuals, an email survey can be personalised, which can generate a slightly higher response rate than the more impersonal web survey, but conversely the associated lack of anonymity of respondents may mean they are less frank.

A web survey is mounted on a website and completed online; links to the survey may be made from a website, newsgroup, discussion list, email or other source. There are more options with a web survey than with an email survey — filter questions, complex questions and diverse formats can be accommodated. As respondent anonymity is preserved, responses may be more candid. However, overall response rates for web surveys are relatively low (Dillman, Smyth & Christian, 2009; Sue & Ritter, 2007). Setting up a web survey demands specific technical knowledge and skills. While a researcher may be able to utilise free online survey software (e.g., *Survey Monkey* (http://surveymonkey.com/)) for a small-scale survey, larger or more sophisticated web surveys demand specialist expertise. Web survey design, administration and hosting is a burgeoning field.

Online surveys are more convenient and cost-effective than other survey modes, and ideal for rapid data collection from a widely dispersed population. Automatic data capture of survey responses is a major benefit, saving data entry costs and eliminating transcription errors. Email surveys or email links to web surveys are best suited to closed populations for which email lists are available, for example, university students, or a company's employees, customers or suppliers.

Online surveys are beset by various technological and related issues. An email survey identified as an unsolicited email from an unrecognised source may be relegated to the spam folder. Attached files may be stripped from an email or not opened because of concern for viruses. A web survey can appear very differently on different computers and may not open at all or display as intended with older versions of browser, software or hardware. Also, web surveys may be avoided due to fear of identity theft, phishing scams or privacy breaches. Such factors reduce response rates for online surveys. Box 6.3 provides an example of a web survey.

Box 6.3

Example of a web survey: The information workforce
Online survey of employees who were graduates of LIS programs

Source

Australian Learning and Teaching Council (ALTC) Project. (2010). *Re-conceptualising and re-positioning Australian library and information science education for the 21st Century.*

The research project

The Information Workforce online survey was part of a larger research project, *Re-conceptualising and re-positioning Australian library and information science education for the 21st century*, which aimed to establish a consolidated picture of Australian library and information science (LIS) education, and identify how future education needs could be mediated in a cohesive and sustainable manner. The project, funded by the ALTC and led by Professor Helen Partridge, involved LIS academics from 11 Australian universities. It used a community-based participatory research approach and involved three separate sub-studies: LIS Students, LIS Educators and the LIS Workforce. The online survey reported here was one of the methods used as part of a mixed-method approach by the LIS Workforce Sub-study team (comprising Maureen Henninger, Paul Genoni, Sue Reynolds and Kerry Tanner) to inform its research area. Other methods included an environmental scan, job advertisements analysis and interviews. The online survey targeted information professionals who had been working for at least a year since graduating from a LIS course.

The online survey instrument

The online questionnaire was designed by the four team-members and fine-tuned with feedback from colleagues and the wider project team. The questionnaire was divided into five main sections: education (courses completed), employment (current, past and future plans), industry sector (of current job), work (functions, major tasks, knowledge and skills, and professional development) and demographics.

Survey implementation and responses

After the questionnaire was finalised, a local consulting firm, dataGecko, was employed to convert the questionnaire into online form using its own proprietary software, and to host the survey.

When the web survey was ready, an invitation enlisting participation was circulated widely via professional e-lists of eight different Australian information professional associations and interest groups, to attract as wide a range of information professionals as possible. This approach exemplifies a convenience sample, a form of non-probability sample, characterised by a strong self-selection bias. As the total population was indeterminate, it was not possible to calculate a response rate, or to generalise findings beyond the sample itself. The survey was online for five weeks in late 2010, with 400 total responses – of which 330 were valid completed questionnaires.

Data analysis

After the closure of the survey, dataGecko captured all responses in an Excel file, and ran basic frequencies. The data file and frequencies were passed on to the Workforce Sub-study team for data analysis, with several techniques being used. Basic descriptive statistics for each question were available from the initial spreadsheet. Some of these data were further analysed within Excel; Excel was also used to generate charts for the research report. Selected data were uploaded into the SPSS Statistics to examine relationships between variables, in the form of cross-tabulations. Besides the quantitative data generated from closed response questions, there was a substantial volume of qualitative data captured from open response questions and 'other' options to individual questions. This was manually analysed using content analysis techniques, and various types of categorisations were used to report results.

Issues with the administration of online surveys

This section explores some of the distinctive issues, decisions and processes involved in the administration of online surveys.

Sampling issues

Online surveys are not feasible for accessing the entire population. Their use is limited to those with email and internet access and those lacking such access, compared with those who have access, are likely, for instance, to have lower levels of education and income, lower rates of literacy and computer literacy, to be older and to over-represent certain ethnic groups. This inherent coverage bias is a major disadvantage. It is difficult to derive a scientific sample of the wider population for an online survey because there is no suitable sampling frame available. Sampling frames (e.g., email lists) are typically available only for closed populations or specialised target groups. The limited capacity for deriving a scientific sample of the broader population means that many web-based surveys draw on non-probability samples with their associated problem of self-selection bias. Research reporting can only make valid claims for the particular group of respondents and cannot generalise to the wider population. However, such non-probability samples are acceptable for exploratory research or as part of a multi-method or multi-mode survey approach (i.e., where supplementary means are used to gain access to sections of the population not represented in the sample).

Sue and Ritter (2007) provide a useful overview of sampling techniques for online surveys, identifying the following techniques. *Saturation sampling* is where *all* members on a particular e-list are invited to participate (i.e., a population census approach); here the key issues are minimising non-response bias and ensuring that each person can respond only once. There are some methods that attempt to derive an acceptable probability sample for an online survey, including: contact by telephone, possibly using random digit dialling, and inviting the person to log in to a website; using commercially available *pre-recruited panels* of individuals who have indicated their availability for repeated survey participation; and *intercept sampling*, where randomly or systematically programmed pop-up windows invite a site visitor to participate in a web survey. However, all of these methods have their limitations. Non-probability sampling approaches for an online survey include convenience sampling, volunteer opt-in panels and snowball sampling. *Convenience sampling* occurs where a survey is posted on a website and all visitors to that site are invited to respond, or when an invitation to participate is circulated via, for example, online lists or Twitter. Here respondents self-select, and there is no way to differentiate characteristics of respondents and non-respondents; also it is difficult to prevent multiple responses of one person. *Volunteer opt-in panels* involve the assembling of a group of people who are willing to participate in future online surveys, and collecting relevant demographics about them when they register. Selection of a subset of panel members for a future online survey is based on the desired demographics for the particular survey. *Snowball sampling* or referral sampling can be used in small specialist communities where people are known to each other.

Options for developing and hosting an online survey

After the researcher has developed a questionnaire, it needs to be converted to online form, posted on a website, and responses automatically captured and downloaded to a database. The decision on whether to do this internally or externally is influenced by the availability of requisite technical skills in-house. With the in-house option, access to online survey software is needed. There are many such programs available. One popular example is *Survey Monkey*, which allows researchers to create their own web survey. There are basic and enhanced versions of this software — with a very limited version available free of charge, and a set of enhanced products and services with fees varying according to the nature and extent of the survey and the sophistication of features provided. Programs need to be carefully evaluated in terms of: relative cost for features available; ease of use; number and types of questions and response options; formats available; procedures for distribution, tracking respondents, and capturing responses; and data analysis and reporting options.

With the commercial service option, there are numerous application service providers operating within the online survey market. Charges vary according to services offered, for example, creating the questionnaire, generating a sample, conducting the survey, hosting the survey, analysing data and writing the survey report.

Online survey design, construction and implementation

Designing an online survey requires adherence to general survey design guidelines (see Chapter 16), and additionally considering factors unique to the online environment. Online survey design and survey length are significant contributing factors to response rates — well-designed and shorter questionnaires encourage higher response rates. The email inviting participation in the survey and/or the opening screen for a web survey needs to capture interest and engender motivation to respond.

Current software (e.g., *Survey Monkey*) has made it relatively straightforward to design and create online questionnaires. Some of the available question formats include filter questions that channel respondents according to the way they answer a particular question, lists of options with radio buttons, drop-down lists, check boxes, fill-in-the-blanks, and text-boxes for open-ended questions. Hyperlinks are ideal for providing additional information for respondents, for example, definitions of unfamiliar terms or more detailed instructions, without cluttering the screen and adding length to the questionnaire. Clear and consistent navigation is essential, for example, 'back' and 'next' buttons and a progress bar to inform how much of the questionnaire remains to be answered. Although the web format offers many options for elaborate features and multiple colours, it is generally advisable to keep the design relatively simple. It is important to test the questionnaire in different browsers, screens and operating systems as appearance can change significantly from one system to another. Also, the designer needs to be aware that complex graphics or multi-media formats may not download with outmoded or incompatible software.

Potential participants need to be alerted to the survey. Where a probability sample is involved, this communication is generally by email – an email outlining the purpose, nature and sponsorship of the survey and inviting participation, and if the questionnaire is posted on a website, providing a unique login and link (a unique login avoids the issue of multiple survey submissions by one person). If an email list is not available, sample members can be contacted by post (with the invitation letter containing the URL and login for the survey). An alternate approach is to utilise a randomly or systematically programmed pop-up window aimed at website visitors – the visitor has the choice of either proceeding to the survey or closing the window. With a non-probability sample, a general invitation to participate may be posted on a website for all visitors to see, on related websites, or may be circulated via relevant online lists, discussion forums, Twitter or other social media. After the survey has been submitted, a 'thank you' response is usually automatically generated. A follow-up email can be sent to those who have not responded after a week or two.

Data analysis and reporting

Web survey data will be automatically captured and downloaded into a database, whilst responses to some types of email surveys may need to be manually entered. To maintain respondent privacy, survey response data needs to be stored on a secure server.

Data analysis and preparation of the survey report may be undertaken by the researcher in-house or may be outsourced wholly or in part to an external provider. Some online survey service providers host the survey and provide basic level analysis (e.g., frequencies) but leave the researcher to perform the more advanced statistical analysis and to prepare the final report. Others provide full services.

The survey data file needs to be carefully checked to identify any obvious errors such as responses outside the response range or coding errors and also any incomplete or duplicate responses. The data file needs to be 'cleansed' of such problem data prior to commencing data analysis. (See Chapters 18 and 19.)

Mixed-mode survey designs

The review of survey modes has highlighted the various features, strengths, limitations and challenges of each mode. There is no single 'best' mode – particular modes are better suited to certain populations, research topics and situations than are others. The modes can also be complementary and, in combining two (or more) modes within a research project in a mixed-mode survey design, the strengths of one mode may compensate for the weaknesses in another. However, mixing modes introduces further challenges for the researcher.

One frequently used mixed-mode survey design is the postal survey or web survey combined with personal interviews, which provides a useful blending of the quantitative and qualitative, and the breadth and depth of a topic. This approach was used for the *Information workforce online survey* in Box 6.3 and in the Williamson and Kingsford-Smith study (Williamson, 2008) described in Chapter 2: *The fundamentals of research planning*.

Conclusion

Survey research designs remain pervasive in many fields. Surveys can appear deceptively simple and straightforward to implement. However valid results depend on the researcher having a clear understanding of the circumstances where their use is appropriate and the constraints on inference in interpreting and generalising from survey findings. Initially, the researcher needs to determine whether survey research suits the nature and extent of the research problem being investigated and the type of questions being addressed by the study. The sampling method chosen affects the researcher's ability to generalise from the survey sample to a wider population. Newer electronic survey methods have much to offer, overcoming some of the difficulties of conventional survey administration. Nevertheless, achieving valid representative samples in electronic surveys can be problematic, and particular care needs to be taken in reporting findings to ensure that conclusions drawn from electronic survey data are justified.

For additional guidance on survey research, useful overviews are provided in some general and discipline-specific research methods texts (e.g., Leedy & Ormrod 2016; Mitchell & Jolley 2013; Neuman 2014 on social research; Shaughnessy, Zechmeister & Zechmeister 2009 on research in psychology; and Zikmund 2013 on business research). However, the serious researcher seeking more comprehensive treatment, as well as detailed practical guidance, will find dedicated publications on survey research to have greater utility (e.g., Alreck & Settle 2004; De Vaus 2014; Fowler 2013; and Sage Publications' ten volume *The Survey Kit* (Fink, Bourgie, Fielder, Oishi & Litwin (2003)). Readers with access to Sage's recent interactive databases, *Sage Research Methods Online* (http://methods.sagepub.com) and *Sage Research Methods Cases* (http://methods.sagepub.com/cases), will unearth a wealth of theoretical and practical resources on survey research.

References

Alreck, P., & Settle, R. B. (2004). *The survey research handbook* (3rd ed.). Boston: McGraw-Hill/Irwin.

Australian Learning and Teaching Council (ALTC). (2010). *Re-conceptualising and re-positioning Australian library and information science education for the 21st Century project*. Retrieved from http://www.liseducation.org.au/.

Babbie, E. R. (2010). *The practice of social research* (12th ed.). Belmont, CA: Wadsworth Cengage Learning.

Davis, F. D. (1989). Perceived usefulness, perceived ease of use, and user acceptance of information technology. *MIS Quarterly, 13*(3), 319–340.

Davis, F. D., Bagozzi, R. P., & Warshaw, P. R. (1989). User acceptance of computer technology: A comparison of two theoretical models. *Management Science, 35*(8), 982–1003.

De Vaus, D. A. (2014). *Surveys in social research* (6th ed.). Abingdon, Oxon: Routledge.

Dillman, D. A., Smyth, J. D., & Christian, L. M. (2009). *Internet, mail and mixed-mode surveys: The tailored design method* (3rd ed.). Hoboken, NJ: Wiley.

Fink, A., Bourgie, L. B., Fielder, E. P., Oishi, S. M., & Litwin, M. S. (2003). *The survey kit* (2nd ed.). [10 vols.]. Thousand Oaks, CA: Sage Publications.

Fowler, F. J. (2013). *Survey research methods* (5th ed.). Los Angeles, CA: Sage Publications.

Granada Television International (Producer), & Apted, M. (Director). (1964–). *Seven up series*. [Videodisc set]. New York: First Run Features.

Karpathiou, V., & Tanner, K. (1995). *Information technology outsourcing in Australia*. Melbourne: RMIT Department of Business Computing.

Kline, R. B. (2005). *Principles and practice of structural equation modelling* (2nd ed.). New York: The Guilford Press.

Leedy, P. D., & Ormrod, J. E. (2016). *Practical research: Planning and design* (11th ed.). Boston: Pearson.

Litwin, M. S. (1995). *How to measure survey reliability and validity*. In A. Fink, Bourque, L. B., Fielder, E. P., Frey, J. H., Oishi, S. M., & Litwin, M. S., *The survey kit,* (vol. 7). Thousand Oaks, CA: Sage Publications.

Mayer, J. D., & Salovey, P. (1993). The intelligence of emotional intelligence. *Intelligence, 17*(4), 443–450.

MIS 2000. (1993). Sydney: Strategic Publishing Group.

Mitchell, M. L., & Jolley, J. M. (2013). *Research design explained* (8th ed.). Belmont, CA: Wadsworth Cengage Learning.

Neuman, W. L. (2014). *Social research methods: Qualitative and quantitative approaches* (7th ed., Pearson New International Ed.). Harlow, Essex: Pearson Education.

Rea, L. M., & Parker, R. A. (2005). *Designing and conducting survey research: A comprehensive guide* (3rd ed.). San Francisco, CA: Jossey-Bass.

Rogers, E. M. (1962). *Diffusion of innovations*. New York: Free Press of Glencoe.

Rogers, E. M. (2003). *Diffusion of innovations* (5th ed.). New York: Free Press.

Salovey, P., & Mayer, J. D. (1990). Emotional intelligence. *Imagination, Cognition, and Personality, 9*(3), 185–211.

Sekaran, U. (2010). *Research methods for business: A skill-building approach* (5th ed.). Chichester: Wiley.

Shaughnessy, J. J., Zechmeister, E. B., & Zechmeister, J. S. (2009). *Research methods in psychology* (8th ed.). New York: McGraw-Hill Higher Education.

Sue, V. M., & Ritter, L. A. (2007). *Conducting online surveys*. Thousand Oaks, CA: Sage Publications.

Tanner, K. (2002). Survey research. In K. Williamson (Ed.), *Research methods for students, academics and professionals: Information management and systems* (2nd ed., pp. 89–110). Wagga Wagga, NSW: Charles Sturt University, Centre for Information Studies.

Tyebjee, T. T. (1979). Telephone survey methods: The state of the art. *Journal of Marketing, 43*(Summer), 68–78.

Venkatesh, V., Morris, M. G., Davis, G. B., & Davis, F. D. (2003). User acceptance of information technology: Toward a unified view. *MIS Quarterly, 27*(3), 425–478.

Venkatesh, V., Thong, J. Y. L., & Xu, X. (2012). Consumer acceptance and use of information technology: Extending the Unified Theory of Acceptance and Use of Technology. *MIS Quarterly, 36*(1), 157–178.

Williams, P., Khan, M. S., & Naumann, E. (2011). Customer dissatisfaction and defection: The hidden costs of downsizing. *Industrial Marketing Management, 40* (3), 405–413.

Williamson, K. (2008). Where information is paramount: A mixed methods, multi-disciplinary investigation of Australian online investors. *Information Research: An International Electronic Journal, 13*(4). Retrieved from http://InformationR.net/ir/13-4/isic08.html.

Zikmund, W. G. (2013). *Business research methods* (9th ed.). Mason, OH: South-Western.

Chapter 7

Case study research in information systems

Graeme Shanks[1] and Nargiza Bekmamedova[2]

[1]University of Melbourne, Australia
[2]Embry-Riddle Aeronautical University Asia, Singapore

Case study research is widely used within information systems. This chapter provides an introduction to case study research and discusses a number of issues which have an impact on the successful completion of case study research. We define case study research and highlight its inherent flexibility, discussing the most widely used types of case studies and the different philosophical paradigms within which case study research is conducted. We then provide detailed discussions about the issues that influence the design and conduct of case study research.

Research Methods: Information, Systems, and Contexts. DOI: http://dx.doi.org/10.1016/B978-0-08-102220-7.00007-8

Introduction

The case study research approach is widely used within the information systems discipline. It is well suited to providing an understanding of the interactions between information technology (IT)-related innovations and organisational contexts (Darke, Shanks & Broadbent, 1998). The use of research methods is influenced by the objectives of the research and the specific questions that need to be answered. Research questions about the success and failure of business initiatives related to the development, implementation and use of information systems, associated management practices and interactions of people with the information systems are well suited to case study research (Benbasat, Goldstein & Mead, 1987).

Information systems research is generally interdisciplinary and encompasses the impact of information systems on the behaviour of individuals, groups, and organisations (Ciborra, 2002; Galliers, Markus & Newell, 2006). The case study research approach is appropriate as it enables us to focus on the dynamics of phenomena within single settings (Eisenhardt, 1989). Case study research focusses on contemporary phenomena within real-world settings and includes the experiences of the stakeholders involved.

Case study research is flexible and can be used in different ways within different philosophical paradigms, including positivist, interpretivist and critical theory (Cavaye, 1996). Case studies can be either deductive (theory testing) or inductive (theory building), use qualitative and quantitative data, and investigate one or multiple cases. Due to its flexibility, the case study research approach has been criticised partly because researchers seem to disagree on its purpose and definition. The case study research approach can be considered a design approach, a method, a particular data collection procedure, and an overall research strategy (Shanks, Rouse & Arnott, 1993). While this allows researchers to embrace methodological openness and paradigmatic freedom, it is critical to ensure that the case study is the right strategy based on the purpose of research investigation (Brown, 2008). Designing and scoping a case study research project in order to ensure that the research question(s) are adequately framed and appropriately answered can be challenging, data collection for case study research can be time-consuming and tedious, and often results in the accumulation of large amounts of data (Cavaye, 1996; Yin, 2014). In this chapter, we provide an overview of the case study research as a multi-faceted research approach within the information systems discipline. We highlight its strengths and provide practical advice to researchers undertaking, reporting and evaluating case study research projects.

The chapter is structured as follows. First, we define case study research and explain when it can be used. Next, we provide definitions of key concepts including unit of analysis, single and multiple case study designs, the use of theory and inductive and deductive designs. The pragmatics of conducting case study research are then discussed including designing case study projects, gaining access to organisations, collecting and analysing data and writing case study research reports. Finally, we summarise the key points in the chapter.

What is case study research?

Yin (2003) defines a case study as "an empirical enquiry that investigates a contemporary phenomenon within its real-life context, when the boundaries between phenomenon and context are clearly evident ... and it relies on multiple sources of evidence" (p. 13). In case study research, the emphasis is on contemporary events and contextual conditions, and the experience of the actors is vital. Case study research is useful when phenomena are broad and complex, cannot be studied outside the context in which they occur and require a holistic, in-depth investigation without explicit control or manipulation of variables (Cavaye, 1996; Paré, 2004). 'How' and 'why' research questions are usually investigated in case study research (Yin, 2014). For example, Shanks (1997) investigated how and why strategic data planning was conducted in a large Australian bank. A process-oriented case study was used to discuss the relationships between the actions of those involved in strategic data planning and the outcomes of the initiative. The organisational context was crucial in making sense of the actions and outcomes.

The case study research approach is particularly well-suited to information systems research, since information systems are essentially 'fused' and cannot be separated from the context in which they are implemented and used (Markus & Robey, 1988). This is particularly relevant when examining the implementation and use of complex information systems including enterprise resource planning (ERP) systems and enterprise architectures within complex organisations (Robey, Ross & Boudreau, 2002; Seddon, Calvert & Yang, 2010; Tamm, Seddon, Shanks & Reynolds, 2011). Case studies are particularly suitable for capturing the dynamics of the environment in domains, including system development and implementation (Markus, 1983; Robey & Newman, 1996; Wixom & Watson, 2001), information technology management and outsourcing (Lacity & Willcocks, 1998; Mithas, Ramasubbu & Sambamurthy, 2011; Sambamurthy & Zmud, 1999) and the impact of information systems on organisations and electronic markets (Nevo & Wade, 2010; Xiao & Benbasat, 2007). The case study research approach has a long history of reflection, acceptance and use within the information systems community (Benbasat *et al.*, 1987; Darke *et al.*, 1998; Dubé & Paré, 2003; Lee, 1989).

Case study research involves several data collection techniques including interviews, field observation, questionnaires, and analysis of public and company documents. Both qualitative (i.e., words and extracted meanings) and quantitative (i.e., numbers and measurements) data collection and analysis can be used within case study research.

Theory is very important within case study research. Theory can be defined *a priori* and used to generate propositions for testing. For example, Sarker and Lee (2002) tested three propositions relating to ERP system implementation using a single case study. Theory can also be used as an explanatory lens. For example, Robey and Newman (1996) traced the process of developing and implementing a materials management system in one company over a 15-year period and used several alternative theoretical lenses to interpret the sequential patterns in the data.

Types of case study research

The case study research approach is multi-faceted and may be used in a variety of ways by information systems researchers (Cavaye, 1996). In this section we discuss several different types of case study research and how they are used. These include: research case studies; positivist case study research; interpretivist case study research; and critical case study research.

Research case studies

Research case studies aim to add to the information systems body of knowledge, by addressing important and relevant research questions. They should be designed and conducted following rigorous research processes, including comprehensive data collection and analysis, and be written as stimulating reports that are understandable by peers (Yin, 2014). Research case studies have two main purposes: to describe and develop theory (inductive case studies) or to test theory (deductive case studies).

Case study research has often been associated with description and theory development, where it is used to provide evidence for hypothesis generation and for exploration of areas where existing knowledge is limited (Cavaye, 1996). These case studies are inductive by nature and typically use grounded theory techniques. Eisenhardt (1989) developed a 'roadmap', which describes the process of building theories from case study research. The process starts with the initial formulation of the research question(s). The *a priori* identification of constructs (or concepts) from the literature guides the research process. The emergent themes (from the fieldwork) are then compared and contrasted with the literature. The researcher systematically compares and contrasts theory and data through a number of iterations until the theory accurately reflects the data. A good example of a research case study following this tradition is Orlikowski's (1993) study of CASE tools and organisational change where the author focussed on the actions of important players within several levels of context.

Case study research can be used to test theory, where propositions are derived from an existing theory and then tested (sometimes called hypothetico-deductive case study research). Pattern matching is used to compare empirical data collected from the case study with outcomes predicted by the propositions (Cavaye, 1996). The theory is either validated or else found to be inadequate in some way, and may be further refined (Darke *et al.*, 1998). A good example of a research case study following this tradition is Sarker and Lee's (2002) study of business process redesign in ERP implementation.

Research case studies may be combined with other research approaches. For example, Gable (1994) first uses case study research to define constructs and develop theory which is subsequently tested using survey research. Alternatively, the researcher might choose to use a survey first to understand a particular phenomenon from a wider population and then later conduct in-depth case studies to learn more about the impact of situational and contextual factors. Overall, the choice and sequence of research approaches should be based on a rigorous research design process (Galliers, 1991; Shanks *et al.*, 1993). Research case studies can be conducted within the positivist, interpretivist or critical paradigms, depending upon the underlying philosophical assumptions of the researcher (Cavaye, 1996; Klein & Myers, 1999; Myers & Klein, 2011; Orlikowski & Baroudi, 1991). These paradigms are discussed in Chapter 1: *Research concepts* and, from an information systems perspective, in Chapter 5: *The methodological landscape*.

Positivist case study research

The positivist paradigm is based on an ontology in which an objective physical and social world exists independently of humans' knowledge of it. General laws that are governed by principles of cause-and-effect apply, and human behaviours can be objectively measured. Positivist research is concerned with the development and empirical testing of general theories that govern the natural and social world (Orlikowski & Baroudi, 1991). The researcher remains objective, distant and 'outside' the phenomena being studied. Within this paradigm, case studies are designed based on natural science criteria such as controlled observations, controlled deductions, replication and generalisability (Lee, 1989). Sarker and Lee's (2002) study of 'business process redesign in ERP implementation' is a good example of positivist case study research. Several propositions were generated and then tested using pattern matching of the predictions in the propositions with empirical case study data.

Yin (2003) and Benbasat *et al.* (1987) provide detailed guidelines for positivist case study research. A number of criteria for rigour in positivist case study research have been developed. These include construct validity, internal validity, reliability and external validity. These are introduced by Yin (2003) and discussed in detail by Dubé and Paré (2003). Sarker and Lee (2002) show how the criteria may be used in reporting the rigour of positivist case study research.

Outcomes from positivist case study research may be generalised to theoretical propositions using analytical generalisation, where case studies have been used to develop or test theories. This is very different from statistical generalisation where outcomes are generalised from a sample to a population (Darke *et al.*, 1998).

Interpretivist case study research

The interpretivist paradigm is based on an ontology in which reality is subjective and is constructed and interpreted by individuals as social actors according to their beliefs and value systems. General laws and objective measurement do not make sense within this paradigm, and multiple meanings and realities are constructed by the researcher and participants within the phenomenon under investigation (Darke *et al.*, 1998). The design and use of information systems in organisations is intrinsically embedded in social contexts, including time, location, politics and culture (Orlikowski & Baroudi, 1991). Human individuality and the ability to think and make choices are central in understanding information systems phenomena. Interpretivist research rejects the notion of value-free research and is not concerned with repeatability of an explanation. It aims to explain the meanings attributed to certain behaviours by actors through the use of their language to describe social events and situations, highlighting the subtleties of responses and behaviours within a particular context (Shanks *et al.*, 1993). Shanks' (1997) study of strategic data planning in a large bank is a good example of an interpretivist case study. The study used concepts from structuration theory (Giddens, 1976; Jones & Karsten, 2008) as a theoretical lens and provides a rich description of the activities and context for the strategic data planning initiative as they unfold over time. A number of themes emerged from the data that provide insight into the strategic data planning process.

Walsham (1995) provides detailed guidelines for interpretivist case study research. The criteria for rigour in interpretivist case study research are very different from those for positivist case study research. Criteria for interpretivist case study research include: the hermeneutic cycle, contextualisation, interaction between researcher and participants, abstraction and generalisation of the theories and concepts used, dialogical reasoning, multiple interpretations and the principle of suspicion. Klein and Myers (1999) provide detailed explanations of these seven principles.

Outcomes from interpretivist case study research may be generalised. Walsham (1995) discusses this in detail and identifies four types of generalisation from interpretivist case study research: concept development, theory generation, drawing of specific implications, and contribution of rich insights. These types of generalisation use insights about the studied phenomenon rather than predictions about future events.

Critical case study research

The critical paradigm is based on the belief that "the ability of people to change their material and social circumstances ... is constrained by prevailing systems of economic, political and social authority" (Myers & Klein, 2011, p. 19). In critical research, a critical stance is adopted and the researcher attempts to "critique the *status quo*" (Myers & Klein, 2011, p. 19) through highlighting contradictions within social systems that lead to conflict and inequalities. Critical research aims to transform these social systems and emancipate people. This is different from positivist and interpretivist research, which aim to predict and explain (Orlikowski & Baroudi, 1991). Doolin's (2004) study of the implementation of a large information system in the health sector is a good example of critical case study research. It shows how an information system implemented in a hospital to increase management control over doctors also empowered the doctors to argue for more resources.

Myers and Klein (2011) define three elements of critical research: insight, critique and transformative redefinition. Insight is concerned with developing a broad and detailed understanding of the case study situation. Critique is concerned with revealing "the normative basis of the current situation and the forms of legitimation that justify the current social order" (Myers & Klein, 2011, p. 23). Transformative redefinition is concerned with suggesting improvements to the current situation that may lead to new ways of operating that are mutually beneficial to stakeholders.

Myers and Klein (2011) provide a set of principles for the conduct of critical field research in information systems. These include using core concepts from critical social theorists, taking a value position, revealing and challenging prevailing beliefs and social practices, individual emancipation, improvements in society and improvements in social theories. For further discussion of critical research, see Cecez-Kecmanovic, Klein and Brooke (2008).

Teaching case studies

The case study approach may be used to develop teaching case studies, where the purpose is to illustrate particular situations or phenomena and provide a basis for discussion among students (Yin, 2003). Teaching cases are contextually rich in detail, and students learn by applying and adapting theoretical concepts to business situations described in the case. For example, a teaching case by Butler and Murphy (2008) uses dynamic capability theory to explore and understand the conditions and factors that shape and influence business and information systems capability development and application in a European small-to-medium software enterprise. Teaching cases do not necessarily include complete and accurate descriptions of actual events, as case study details and materials may be changed in order to better illustrate specific points for students (Liang & Wang, 2004) or to be better aligned with learning objectives (Thorogood, Yetton, Vlasic & Spiller, 2004). Teaching case studies provide students with a range of learning outcomes including critical analysis and reasoning skills, knowledge application and synthesis skills in evaluating different options, and complex problem-solving skills where there is no one 'right answer' (Ambrosini, Bowman & Collier, 2010).

Many teaching case studies are written by individuals or teams that are affiliated with the major case study teaching schools (e.g., Harvard Business School, MIT Sloan School of Management). These teaching case studies describe actual business situations, detailing some aspects of organisational life, for example a large ERP implementation or change in senior executive leadership. They include a detailed description of events about a situation, an organisation, an individual, or sometimes even an industry (Ambrosini *et al.*, 2010). They typically include a chronology of significant events, summaries of financial and sales data, statements and opinions of employees in the company, and information about competitors and the industry context. Very often teaching cases illustrate 'best practices' and 'success stories' and can be published in major journals and conferences. (See for example, the *Journal of Information Technology Teaching Cases* (http://www.springer.com/business + %26 + management/journal/41266) and the 'Teaching Cases' Track of the annual European Conference on Information Systems.)

The criteria for developing high-quality teaching cases are very different from those for producing high-quality case study research (Yin, 2003), and include:

- *relevance*: whether the teaching case stimulates student learning and engages students as being a 'hot' topic; whether the case is relevant and captures contemporary real-world situations;

- *value*: whether the teaching case is consistent with learning objectives, believable and understandable by students;

- *preparation*: whether the teaching case is field-based, involves single or multiple units of analysis and is focussed on a single situation; whether the data are confirmed and complete; and

- *presentation*: whether the teaching case is well-written and reflects learning objectives; whether the case is organised by time, topic and analysis is based on decision process (Peterson, 2002).

Teaching case studies are an important resource within the information systems community. They are very useful in stimulating student interest with 'real-world' examples of best practice. They are also useful as complementary materials when conducting research case studies (Ambrosini *et al.*, 2010).

Designing case study research

Case study research needs to be carefully designed and should include: whether the research problem is well suited to case study research; general design and scoping; specification of the unit of analysis; choice of single or multiple case studies including justification for replications; the use of theory within the case study; and techniques for data collection and data analysis.

Research problem suited to case study research

Case study research is an appropriate research strategy where a contemporary phenomenon is studied in its natural setting (Benbasat *et al.*, 1987; Yin, 2014). This type of research is well suited when "research and theory are at their early formative stages" (Benbasat *et al.*, 1987, p. 369), and where the actions of individuals within context are important (Yin, 2014). Case studies are well-suited for investigating 'how' and 'why' research questions.

Situations where case study research may not be appropriate include phenomena that are well understood and mature, where existing theory is well developed, where understanding of how and why the particular phenomenon occurs is not of interest, and where understanding of the contexts of action and the experiences of individuals are not relevant (Darke *et al.*, 1998). In these situations, alternative research approaches, including experiments or surveys are more appropriate. However, they do not produce the rich descriptions and insight that emerge from case study research.

Designing and scoping case study research

Case study research should be interesting, significant and relevant to both researchers and practitioners. The design and scoping of case study research requires completion of a comprehensive literature analysis in order to identify potential knowledge gaps relating to the research questions. This provides a foundation for selection of an appropriate unit of analysis and determination of the number of cases required and the replication strategy (Darke *et al.*, 1998). Other pragmatic issues that impact the design and scope of case study research include the research purpose, the availability of resources and required outcomes (Darke *et al.*, 1998).

Unit of analysis

The unit of analysis is the phenomenon that is being studied, and may be, for example, a group, organisation, project or supply chain. Miles, Huberman and Saldana (2014) define a case as "a phenomenon of some sort occurring in a bounded context ... [and the case is] ... in effect, your unit of analysis" (p. 28). Within information systems, a case may involve a particular technology or system (e.g., a Decision Support System), a potential user or group of users, a management practice (e.g., information systems outsourcing or IT governance), or a particular decision (e.g., adoption of an emerging technology such as cloud computing at the organisational level). The unit of analysis effectively defines what is included in the study and what its context is. Sometimes a case may include a set of subunits of analysis (e.g., a global company with subsidiary companies or a client organisation with multiple outsourcing vendor relationships). Determining the unit of analysis can be a challenging task and should be guided by the research question(s).

Single and multiple case studies

Case study research may be designed using single or multiple cases. A single case is appropriate when it is critical (by meeting all the necessary conditions for testing a theory), unique or revelatory (Yin, 2014). It is frequently used when studying new phenomena with few existing examples. A study of a single case enables the researcher to investigate a phenomenon in-depth, enabling a rich description and revealing its deep structure (Cavaye, 1996). Good examples of single case studies include Marcus (1983) and Sarker and Lee (2002). Single case studies may be used to test existing theories and the outcomes may be generalised (e.g., Sarker & Lee, 2002). Critical appraisal guidelines for single case study research have been established by Atkins and Sampson (2002).

Multiple-case designs allow cross-case comparison and investigation of phenomena in diverse settings. This enables researchers to predict similar outcomes across cases with similar contexts (i.e., literal replication) and therefore strengthen generalisation, or produce contrasting findings based on theoretical conditions (i.e., theoretical replication) to test theory. With literal replication, researchers should continue doing case studies until no new learning occurs, and saturation is achieved (Eisenhardt, 1989). This usually takes at least four and no more than ten cases (Eisenhardt, 1989).

The use of theory

Theory is very important in research case studies. Theory may be built, tested or used as a lens to explain the phenomena under investigation. When theory is used in positivist case study research it should be at sufficient level of detail, with well-defined concepts, relationships and boundary. A good example of the use of theory in positivist case study research may be found in Sarker and Lee (2002), who test three propositions about business process redesign in ERP implementation. Theories used as lenses in interpretivist case study research are usually at a higher level of abstraction. For example, concepts from structuration theory were used by Shanks (1997) to understand strategic data planning in a large bank. Process theories are particularly useful in longitudinal case study research that examines information systems phenomena over time. Different types of process theories may be used in case study research (Markus & Robey, 1988; Van de Ven & Poole, 1995). For example, Arnott (2004) argued for the use of evolutionary process theory in the study of decision support systems development.

Data collection and analysis

Case study research typically includes multiple data collection techniques and data are collected from multiple sources. Data collection techniques include interviews, observations (direct and participant), questionnaires, and relevant documents (Yin, 2014). For detailed discussions of questionnaires, interviews and observation, see Chapter 16: *Questionnaires, individual interviews, and focus group interviews* and Chapter 17: *Observation*. The use of multiple data collection techniques and sources strengthens the credibility of outcomes and enables different interpretations and meanings to be included in data analysis. This is known as triangulation (Flick, 2014).

In case study research, the data collected are usually qualitative (words, meanings, views) but can also be quantitative (descriptive numbers, tables). Qualitative data analysis may be used in theory building and theory testing. Theory building may use the grounded theory approach. Theory testing typically involves pattern matching (Yin, 2014). This is based on the comparison of predicted outcomes with observed data. Qualitative data analysis is usually highly iterative. Visual displays of qualitative data using matrices (classifications of data using two or more dimensions) may be used to discover connections between the coded segments (Crabtree & Miller, 1999; Miles *et al.*, 2014). Data analysis may be undertaken within a case and also between cases in multiple case study research (Eisenhardt, 1989). Quantitative data is typically presented in descriptive, tabular form and used to highlight characteristics of case study organisations and interviewees. See also Chapter 18: *Quantitative data analysis*.

Conducting case study research

Although case study research is flexible and widely used, a number of difficulties are associated with its use by information systems researchers. Darke *et al.* (1998) identify several key issues most often asked about by those contemplating the use of case study research. These issues include gaining access to organisations, collecting data and writing rigorous case study research reports.

Gaining access to organisations

It can be challenging to obtain access to organisations and participants for case study research (Saunders, Lewis & Thornhill, 2015). Research questions need to be interesting and important to organisations to gain their support and participation in case study research. Researchers should reflect on the relevance and significance of the research problem and the potential value that the case study may provide to participating organisations. Researchers need to work with organisations to identify "what's in it for them" (Darke *et al.*, 1998, p. 281). Potential benefits typically include a comprehensive description of the case study within the organisation and a white paper with an executive summary describing insights gained. Researchers should also ensure that participating organisations receive deliverables, including insights identified, within a reasonable timeframe. Finally, researchers should prepare a set of necessary documents, including a cover letter that informs potential organisations about the nature and context of the research project and its objectives, an outline of the research timeframe, the expectations of participants' involvements in the research and the expected research outcomes (Darke *et al.*, 1998).

An important element in case study research is ethical endorsement for the study. Researchers and participating organisations should reach agreement in relation to the confidentiality requirements with regards to the case study data and findings and any limitations on the disclosure of the identities of the case study participants and the organisation itself (Darke *et al.*, 1998).

Efficient and effective collection of data

Effective and efficient data collection for case study research requires careful planning. Collecting case study data from case participants can be difficult and time-consuming (Cavaye, 1996). Prior to visiting case study sites, researchers should collect sufficient background knowledge about participating organisations, including key business information, financial data, organisation charts, and key stakeholder roles within the organisation (including names and positions of all potential case participants). Factual and other straightforward information can be collected from other sources (e.g., annual reports, organisational bulletins). A well-organised and categorised set of case data will facilitate the task of analysing the case study evidence in order to address the research questions (Darke *et al.*, 1998). Also, the case study data must be documented and organised as it is collected in a case study database (Darke *et al.*, 1998; Yin, 2014). Detailed interview protocols should be developed to facilitate efficient and effective data collection from busy case study participants (Yin, 2014).

Writing rigorous case study research reports

Understanding how to write rigorous, convincing and interesting case study reports is crucial for the case study researcher (Darke *et al.*, 1998). In order to establish credibility with readers, researchers must describe in detail how the case study outcomes were arrived at, and present a coherent, persuasively argued point of view (Walsham, 1995). Researchers should provide sufficient evidence for claims made (e.g., quotes from interviews) and explain why alternative interpretations were rejected, to ensure rigour and reliability of the research findings. The overall goal in writing up case studies is to adopt a clear and lucid writing style and to present the critical evidence persuasively and effectively (Van der Blonk, 2003). Walsham (1995) considers that convincing the reader of the validity of case study research is "as much a matter of rhetorical style and flair as it is of accuracy and care in matters of theory and method" (p. 79).

One of the practical difficulties of writing rigorous case study reports is dealing with the large amount and variety of data collected and analysed (Yin, 2014). It is important to explain data collection and analysis techniques used, and justify why they were appropriate for the purpose of the case study (Darke *et al.*, 1998). While examples of case study data as evidence should be included in the main body of the case study report, tables containing further data may be included as appendices. The way a research case study report is structured depends on the philosophical paradigm selected and its design. For positivist, deductive case studies, the report will typically include a detailed description of the case followed by a discussion of the testing of each proposition. For positivist, inductive case studies, the report will typically include a detailed description of the case followed by a discussion of each emergent concept, relationship and the boundary of the theory developed. For interpretivist case studies, the report will typically include a detailed description of the case followed by a discussion of the emergent themes. In all reports it is important to link case study outcomes back to the relevant literature to highlight the contribution to knowledge. Discussions about different types of case study reports may be found in Pettigrew (1990), Van der Blonk (2003) and Van Maanen (2011). There are a number of different ways in which case study research reports may be structured (Pettigrew, 1990; Van der Blonk, 2003; Van Maanen, 2011). Two alternative approaches are thematic and descriptive/thematic (Pettigrew, 1990). In the thematic structure, each section of the report relates to a theme identified within the study. In the descriptive/thematic structure, the report comprises a detailed description of the case followed by a discussion of emergent themes.

Conclusion

Case study research is one of the most widely used research approaches within information systems and is also an important method in library and information studies/science. It is a highly flexible research approach that may be used within different philosophical paradigms, uses theory in several different ways, and must be carefully designed, conducted and written-up. It is particularly suited to investigating the development, implementation and use of information systems within organisations. This chapter has discussed a number of issues that impact the successful completion of case study research, and should help case study researchers to undertake stimulating and valuable case study research.

References

Ambrosini, V., Bowman, C., & Collier, N. (2010). Using teaching case studies for management research. *Strategic Organization, 8*(3), 206–229.

Arnott, D. (2004). Decision support systems evolution: Framework, case study, and research agenda. *European Journal of Information Systems, 13*(4), 247–259.

Atkins, C., & Sampson, J. (2002). Critical appraisal guidelines for single case study research. In S. Wrycza (Ed.), *ECIS 2002: Proceedings of the 10th European Conference on Information Systems: Information systems and the future of the digital economy* (pp. 100–109). Gdansk, Poland: Wydawnictwo Uniwersytetu Gdanskiego.

Benbasat, I., Goldstein, D. K., & Mead, M. (1987). The case research strategy in studies of information systems. *MIS Quarterly, 11*(3), 369–386.

Brown, P. A. (2008). A review of the literature on case study research. *Canadian Journal for New Scholars in Education, 1*(1), 1–13.

Butler, T., & Murphy, C. (2008). An exploratory study on IS capabilities and assets in a small-to-medium software enterprise. *Journal of Information Technology, 23*(4), 330–344.

Cavaye, A. L. M. (1996). Case study research: A multi-faceted research approach for IS. *Information Systems Journal, 6*(3), 227–242.

Cecez-Kecmanovic, D., Klein, H. K., & Brooke, C. (2008). Exploring the critical agenda in information systems research. *Information Systems Journal, 18*(2), 123–135.

Ciborra, C. (2002). *The labyrinths of information: Challenging the wisdom of systems.* Oxford: Oxford University Press.

Crabtree, B. F., & Miller, W. L. (1999). *Doing qualitative research.* Thousand Oaks, CA: Sage Publications.

Darke, P., Shanks, G., & Broadbent, M. (1998). Successfully completing case study research: Combining rigour, relevance and pragmatism. *Information Systems Journal, 8*(4), 273–289.

Doolin, B. (2004). Power and resistance in the implementation of a medical management information system. *Information Systems Journal, 14*(4), 343–362.

Dubé, L., & Paré, G. (2003). Rigor in information systems positivist case research: Current practices, trends, and recommendations. *MIS Quarterly, 27*(4), 597–636.

Eisenhardt, K. M. (1989). Building theories from case study research. *Academy of Management Review, 14*(4), 532–550.

Flick, U. (2014). *An introduction to qualitative research* (5th ed.). London: Sage Publications.

Gable, G. (1994). Integrating case study and survey research methods: An example in information systems. *European Journal of Information Systems, 3*(2), 112–126.

Galliers, R. D. (1991). Choosing appropriate information systems research approaches: A revised taxonomy. In H. E. Nissen, H. K. Klein, & R. Hirschheim (Eds.), *Information systems research: Contemporary approaches and emergent traditions* (pp. 155–173). Amsterdam: Elsevier Science Publishers.

Galliers, R. D., Markus, M. L., & Newell, S. (2006). *Exploring information systems research approaches.* New York: Routledge.

Giddens, A. (1976). *New rules of sociological method.* New York: Basic Books.

Jones, M., & Karsten, H. (2008). Giddens's structuration theory and information systems research. *MIS Quarterly*, *32*(1), 127–157.

Klein, H. K., & Myers, M. D. (1999). A set of principles for conducting and evaluating interpretive field studies in information systems. *MIS Quarterly*, *23*(1), 67–94.

Lacity, M. C., & Willcocks, L. P. (1998). An empirical investigation of information technology sourcing practices: Lessons from experience. *MIS Quarterly*, *22*(3), 363–408.

Lee, A. S. (1989). A scientific methodology for MIS case studies. *MIS Quarterly*, *13*(1), 33–50.

Liang, N., & Wang, J. (2004). Implicit mental models in teaching cases: An empirical study of popular MBA cases in the United States and China. *Academy of Management Learning and Education*, *3*(4), 397–413.

Markus, M. L. (1983). Power, politics, and MIS implementation. *Communications of the ACM*, *26*(6), 430–444.

Markus, M. L., & Robey, D. (1988). IT and organisational change: Causal structure in theory and research. *Management Science*, *34*(5), 583–598.

Miles, M. B., Huberman, A. M., & Saldana, J. (2014). *Qualitative data analysis: A methods sourcebook* (3rd ed.). Thousand Oaks, CA: Sage.

Mithas, S., Ramasubbu, N., & Sambamurthy, V. (2011). How information management capability influences firm performance. *MIS Quarterly*, *35*(1), 237–256.

Myers, M., & Klein, H. K. (2011). A set of principles for conducting critical research in information systems. *MIS Quarterly*, *35*(1), 17–36.

Nevo, S., & Wade, M. (2010). The formation and value of IT-enabled resources: Antecedents and consequences of synergistic relationships. *MIS Quarterly*, *34*(1), 163–183.

Orlikowski, W. J. (1993). CASE tools as organisational change: Investigating incremental and radical changes in systems development. *MIS Quarterly*, *17*(3), 309–340.

Orlikowski, W. J., & Baroudi, J. J. (1991). Studying information technology in organizations: Research approaches and assumptions. *Information Systems Research*, *2*(1), 1–28.

Paré, G. (2004). Investigating information systems with positivist case study research. *Communications of the Association for Information Systems*, *13*(1), 233–264.

Peterson, C. (2002). *Criteria for evaluating the quality of a case study*. Presentation to the Case Studies Workshop at the American Agricultural Economics Association Annual Meeting, Long Beach, CA, July 2002. Retrieved from http://www.farmfoundation.org/news/articlefiles/284-4_peterson.ppt.

Pettigrew, A. M. (1990). Longitudinal field research on change: Theory and practice. *Organization Science*, *1*(3), 267–292.

Robey, D., & Newman, M. (1996). Sequential patterns in information systems development: An application of a social process model. *ACM Transactions on Information Systems*, *14*(1), 30–63.

Robey, D., Ross, J. W., & Boudreau, M. D. (2002). Learning to implement enterprise systems: An exploratory study of the dialectics of change. *Journal of Management Information Systems, 19*(1), 17–46.

Sambamurthy, V., & Zmud, R. (1999). Arrangements for information technology governance: A theory of multiple contingencies. *MIS Quarterly, 23*(2), 261–290.

Sarker, S., & Lee, A. S. (2002). Using a positivist case research methodology to test three competing theories-in-use of business process redesign. *Journal of the Association for Information Systems, 2*(7), 1–72.

Saunders, M. N. K., Lewis, P., & Thornhill, A. (2015). *Research methods for business students* (7th ed.). Harlow: Prentice Hall.

Seddon, P., Calvert, C., & Yang, S. (2010). A multi-project model of key factors affecting organisational benefits from enterprise systems. *MIS Quarterly, 32*(2), 305–328.

Shanks, G. (1997). The challenges of strategic data planning in practice: An interpretive case study. *Journal of Strategic Information Systems, 6*(1), 69–90.

Shanks, G., Rouse, A., & Arnott, D. (1993). A review of approaches to research and scholarship in information systems. In *Proceedings of the 4th Australian Conference on Information Systems* (pp. 29–44). Brisbane, QLD: University of Queensland.

Tamm, T., Seddon, P., Shanks, G., & Reynolds, P. (2011). How does enterprise architecture add value to organisations? *Communications of the AIS, 28*(10), 141–168.

Thorogood, A., Yetton, P., Vlasic, A., & Spiller, J. (2004). Raise your glasses-the water's magic! Strategic IT at SA Water: A case study in alignment, outsourcing and governance. *Journal of Information Technology, 19*(2), 130–139.

Van de Ven, A. H., & Poole, M. S. (1995). Explaining development and change in organisations. *Academy of Management Review, 20*(3), 510–540.

Van der Blonk, H. (2003). Writing case studies in information systems research. *Journal of Information Technology, 18*(1), 45–52.

Van Maanen, J. (2011). *Tales of the field: On writing ethnography* (2nd ed.). Chicago: University of Chicago Press.

Walsham, G. (1995). Interpretive case studies in IS research: Nature and method. *European Journal of Information Systems, 4*(2), 74–81.

Wixom, B. H., & Watson, H. J. (2001). An empirical investigation of the factors affecting data warehousing success. *MIS Quarterly, 25*(1), 17–41.

Xiao, B., & Benbasat, I. (2007). E-commerce product recommendation agents: Use, characteristics, and impact. *MIS Quarterly, 31*(1), 137–209.

Yin, R. K. (2003). *Case study research: Design and methods* (3rd ed.). Thousand Oaks, CA: Sage Publications.

Yin, R. K. (2014). *Case study research: Design and methods* (5th ed.). Thousand Oaks, CA: Sage Publications.

Chapter 8

Action research

Theory and practice

Kirsty Williamson
Monash University and Charles Sturt University, Australia

Action research is explored from a range of perspectives, related to both theory and practice. The complexity of the method, where there is a range of approaches, is emphasised. The chapter defines and positions action research, highlighting the components most commonly emphasised in the literature. It harks back to the original concepts of the founder of action research, Kurt Lewin, and offers a diagrammatic presentation of his action research spiral. The ways in which action research has been used in the information fields provide a highlight. Three different projects are described: one where academic researchers worked with practitioners to assist students to avoid plagiarism; practitioner action research to develop information literacy in the electronic age; and an example from the information systems field, where action research is used to investigate cognitive processes underlying strategy development.

Research Methods: Information, Systems, and Contexts. DOI: http://dx.doi.org/10.1016/B978-0-08-102220-7.00008-X

Introduction

This chapter has the word 'theory' in the title to emphasise the fact that, like all research methods, action research is a design for undertaking research and that, like all research methods, it has theoretical background that underpins that design. This emphasis is necessary with action research because it has tended to be seen as a practical approach which does not offer depth in its design and execution. This has resulted in the method having a lesser status than other methods, except in the field of education where it has been seen as a useful method for improving teaching and learning practices.

In fact, the theory underpinning 'action research method' is complex. The term 'action research' has become an umbrella term for a range of participatory research approaches where one important focus is 'action'. It involves a world view which is "more holistic, pluralist, and egalitarian, that is essentially participative" (Reason, 1998, p. 262). Kemmis and McTaggart (2005), who were part of the prominent Deakin University (Victoria, Australia) group of action research academics (Kemmis & McTaggart, 1988), discuss several different kinds of participatory research. Examples include critical action research, classroom action research, action learning, and action science, all a little different in their theory and practice. However, they gave prominence to participatory action research (PAR) as did others (e.g., Baker, 1999 and Neuman, 2014 although, in both these cases, discussions of action research are brief). Reason (1998), with a more substantial contribution, gave equal treatment to all four kinds of action research: co-operative inquiry; PAR; action science; and action inquiry. According to Schwandt (1997, pp. 112–113), PAR is commonly carried out in communities or groups that are trying to overcome negative or oppressive conditions, that is, it emphasises "political aspects of knowledge production" (Reason, 1998, p. 269). There is therefore considerable complexity, exacerbated by the fact that many authors speak just of 'action research', without qualification.

While there are social science tomes devoted solely to detailed discussion of action research (e.g., Greenwood & Levin, 2007), social research methods books often include relatively short discussions of action research, or omit it altogether, for example, Wildemuth's (2009). The reasons mentioned above have probably been influential. Nevertheless there is no dearth of material, especially in the education field, for example, Carr and Kemmis (2009), Sanguinetti (2000). *The Sage Handbook of Educational Research* (Noffke & Somekh, 2009) provides many examples of educational action research. There is also an international journal, *Educational Action Research* (http://www.tandfonline.com/loi/reac20) which has been published since 1993, supported by the Collaborative Action Research Network. Other professional realms also provide examples: Hart and Bond (1995) from the health and social work fields; Argyris and Schon (1991) and Eden & Huxham (1996) from organisational perspectives. Pickard (2013) provides a chapter on action research from an information perspective. Galliers (1992) includes a chapter on action research from the field of information systems, and Oosthuizen (2002) also provides the perspective of an information systems researcher. Nevertheless, Avison, Lau, Myers and Nielsen (1999), postulated that there is a paucity of action research in the 'information systems' field because the different categories (e.g., action science, PAR, and action learning) bring complexity and "perhaps confusion" (p. 96). They made a strong case for the potential value of action research to the field. Subsequently Myers was a senior editor of a special issue of *MIS Quarterly* (Baskerville & Myers, 2004) that provided six different examples of action research in the information systems field.

Defining and positioning action research

With so many variations of action research, is a general definition possible? According to the 'aims and scope' of the journal *Educational Action Research* (2016), approaches developed in recent years "share the common aim of ending the dislocation of research from practice, an aim which links them with those involved in participatory research and action inquiry". Examples of approaches include: "to promote reflective practice; professional development; individual, institutional and community change; and development of democratic management and administration".

There is no doubt that, in most conceptualisations, action research is participatory research. Participants must feel a sense of ownership over the process, and any "findings and new recommended actions cannot be imposed" (Wadsworth 1991, p. 44). The political element is important: "Who owns the knowledge, and thus who can define the reality?" (Reason, 1998). However, as Hart and Bond (1995) pointed out, action research is more than collaborative research. In their words, "to apply the label to almost any research which involves elements of collaboration or feedback serves to reinforce the criticism that the label is meaningless" (p. 39). Rather, they identify seven criteria of action research, these being that it:

1. is educative;
2. deals with individuals as members of social groups;
3. is problem-focused, context-specific and future-orientated;
4. involves a change intervention;
5. aims at improvement and involvement;
6. involves a cyclic process in which research, action and evaluation are interlinked; and
7. is founded on a research relationship in which those involved are participants in the change process (Hart and Bond 1995, pp. 38–39).

Hart and Bond were aware of the criticisms that have been levelled at action research. It was seen as "partisan" and as "serving particular causes" (Smith, 2007). Questions arose regarding rigour and the expertise of the researchers involved. Smith suggested: "Once we have satisfied ourselves that the collection of information is systematic, and that any interpretations made have a proper regard for satisfying truth claims, then much of the criticism about action research disappears."

The paradigm question

The question of where action research fits in terms of the major paradigms is difficult to address. As Oosthuizen (2002, p. 159) postulated: "Action research can be explained from the perspective of many philosophies." He agreed with Galliers (1992) that action research is a hermeneutical or interpretive approach, "concerned with the study of human actions and social practice" (p. 159). He also acknowledged that "within social sciences, action research could be seen to belong to the critical social sciences stream of philosophies". Williamson, Schauder, Wright and Stockfeld (2002) saw several similarities and differences between interpretivist/constructivist approaches and action research when they discussed their own action research within an interpretivist framework. Similarities were that:

- both commonly see themselves as anti-positivist, rejecting the assertion that a value-free understanding of social relations is either possible or desirable.

- each approach emphasises the viewpoints provided by participants, with action research taking "its cues — its questions, puzzles and problems — from the perceptions of practitioners within particular, local contexts" (Argyris & Schon, 1991, p. 86) and constructivists sharing "the goal of understanding the complex world of lived experiences from the point of view of those who live it" (Schwandt, 1994, p. 118).

- both are open-ended in their approach to research — each premised upon a concern to follow the threads of meaning as they emerge within the research process itself (Williamson et al., 2002, pp. 9–10).

Differences included by Williamson et al. (2002, p. 10) were:

- the significance assigned to different forms of knowledge, with action research seeing the construction of understandings as a collective process undertaken by the participants *as a group* and constructivists often placing emphasis on individual perspectives, even when they are considering how those perspectives reflect the social worlds of those individuals. The risk with the latter approach is that "phenomena such as power or control, which are expressed through relatively durable structures beyond specific situations and face-to-face interactions", can too easily be left out of the picture (Thompson & McHugh, 1995, p. 370).

- the emphasis by constructivists on describing and interpreting the views and meanings of participants rather than working in collaboration with participants to enable them to directly influence, if not determine, the outcomes that affect their lives.

Garrick (2000) saw uncritical approaches, simply describing and interpreting actors' views and feelings, as running the danger of playing a legitimating role rather than achieving change and improvement in the workplace. There is no doubt that key action research theoreticians see critical perspectives as fundamental. For example, Kemmis and McTaggart's (2005) discussion of PAR conceptualised it as 'emancipatory' and 'critical' both aiming "to help people recover, and release themselves from, [firstly], the constraints of irrational, unproductive, unjust, and unsatisfying social structures that limit their self-development and self-determination" and, secondly, "the constraints embedded in the social media through which they interact – their language (discourses), their modes of work, and the social relationships of power" (p. 567). While there are situations requiring this kind of approach, it also needs to be acknowledged that action research can play a role where 'emancipation' from injustice is not required as a focus. Action research can lead to improvements in practices and outcomes in the work place, as examples later on will attest. A key feature, particularly of PAR, is its reflexive nature. Reflecting on processes and outcomes is crucial, as will be seen in Figure 8.1, below.

The orthodox scientific world view has also received criticism from key action research theoreticians. While acknowledging science's role in liberating human society "from the bonds of superstition and Scholasticism", Reason (1998, pp. 261–262), citing Bateson (1972), saw the scientific approach as placing "the researcher firmly outside and separate from the subject of his or her research, reaching for objective knowledge and for one separate truth". At the other end of the spectrum, Sanguinetti (2000) who undertook 'an adventure' in postmodern action research, challenged the elitist affectations of those forms of action research that privilege the role of the professional researcher. This is not a view universally held in the fields of interest to this book, although it is certainly important to critique the role of the professional researcher (Kemmis and McTaggart, 2005). In the fields under discussion, workplace action research sometimes involves experienced researchers (outsiders) working with practitioners (e.g., Oosthuizen, 2002; Williamson, McGregor and Archibald, 2009; Williamson, McGregor & Archibald, 2010; Williamson & McGregor, 2011). At other times, practitioners may lead and conduct the research, and outsiders are not involved (e.g., Visser, 2007). (See examples towards the end of this chapter.)

The role of theory

It is certainly possible to develop or test theory through the processes of action research. Indeed, Avison *et al.* (1999, p. 94) described action research as combining "theory and practice (and researchers and practitioners) through change and reflection in an immediate problematic situation within a mutually acceptable ethical framework". Elliott (2009) used Aristotle's term, phronesis (a kind of wisdom relevant to practical things) in arguing for the need for teachers to build up a body of theory based on action research. He cited Stenhouse (1975) whose view was that "teachers have a central role in generating practically valid research findings that can be cast in the form of an educational theory" (p. 31). There is considerable scope in the education field to use action research to build theories about issues connected with teaching and learning, for example, how young children best learn to read, how curriculum should be developed in specific areas. Such theories can then be further explored or tested.

The action research spiral

Kurt Lewin is generally credited as the person who coined the term 'action research' (Burns, 2000; Smith, 2007). General descriptions of action research approaches almost always contain an account of Lewin's action research spiral (although original Lewin publications are difficult to obtain). They are often accompanied by a diagram (always different as authors construct their own versions). Smith (2007) cited Lewin (1946; reproduced in Lewin, 1948), as describing a spiral of steps which become a 'cycle'. The steps include identifying a problem or creating an idea, planning the action to be taken, implementing that action, reflecting on the processes and outcomes, replanning, implementing, reflecting again and so on.

Figure 8.1 adds another diagrammatic model to the literature, using the many others available for inspiration.

Figure 8.1 The action research spiral

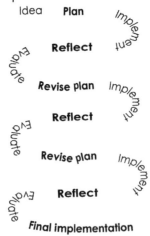

As Kemmis and McTaggart (2005, p. 563) pointed out, the process of these self-contained cycles may not be as 'neat' as diagrams convey. The stages can overlap as a complex piece of action research evolves.

> In reality, the process is likely to be more fluid, open, and responsive. The criterion of success is not whether participants have followed the steps faithfully but rather whether they have a strong and authentic sense of development and evolution in their practices, their understandings of their practices, and the situations [authors' emphases] in which they practice (Kemmis & McTaggart, 2005, p. 563).

At another stage, Kemmis and McTaggart (2005) mentioned being 'frustrated' that people regarded the process of the cycles as the action research method. While following the spiral model should not be seen as comprising *the* 'method' of action research I believe that, in its broader context, action research using the cyclical model can be seen as a method (or approach if this is your preferred term), with dimensions of both theory and practice. Certainly it has produced useful outcomes in the fields of interest to this book. Visser (2007) cogently expressed its contribution when she stated what she saw as the most salient point of action research:

> that it is both a process of change (the action) and a process of learning (the research). Change not only occurs for the situation but also for the researcher. This new knowledge flows from within the action researcher through the change process to the organisation and hopefully, but not necessarily, beyond to contribute to the knowledge of the occupational sector (Visser, 2007, p. 115).

Designing, undertaking and evaluating action research

Action research is very varied in its design and implementation. The circumstances of the research dictate what action is appropriate. This section discusses two different action research project, principally: the *Smart Information Use* project, which comes from my research (with others), the design for which revolved around how to teach high school students to avoid plagiarism; and the *Information Literacy Development in the Electronic Age* project, undertaken by a teacher-librarian as practitioner/researcher using a design which focussed on teaching strategies to achieve the development of critical literacies in a school. The design and action of each of these projects was therefore quite different. Where there is more commonality is in approaches to evaluation.

The evaluation stages of action research usually rely on the kinds of research tools used in other methods. Common tools or techniques include individual and focus group interviews and questionnaires. According to Oosthuizen (2002, p. 170) group feedback analysis "is better than surveys primarily because it involves and encourages feedback from participants." One technique may be used on its own, but commonly more than one will be employed, particularly to ensure triangulation. For example, the *Smart Information Use* project used both individual and focus group interviews, while the *Information Literacy Development in the Electronic Age* project used what were termed pro formas, but which were actually questionnaires with quantitative and qualitative questions. These were administered right through the project, at the end of each spiral. See Chapter 16: *Questionnaires, individual interviews and focus group interviews*, for detailed discussion. Triangulation is mentioned in Chapter 1: *Research concepts*, and discussed in more detail in Chapter 13: *Ethnographic research*.

Smart Information Use project

For the years 2006–2007, Kirsty Williamson, Joy McGregor, John Weckert and Yeslam Al-Saggaf were awarded an Australian Research Council (ARC) Linkage grant in partnership with four secondary schools: an independent boys' college (Melbourne); a Catholic girls' school (semi-rural, Victoria); a co-educational independent college (Melbourne); and a government high school (rural, New South Wales). The problem that had been perceived by teachers and teacher librarians in these schools, as well as by the researchers, was how to teach students to avoid plagiarism by developing their understanding of appropriate and effective information use and, in so doing, learn to generate knowledge themselves. As now, plagiarism was widely seen as a problem in universities, worldwide. The view of the team, when they applied for the ARC grant, was to undertake a project to try to gain common understandings about what plagiarism is, and also to help ameliorate the problem by beginning the education process well before students come to tertiary education.

The approach for the project was not totally action research, although it was a key element. There were three phases. During the first phase, using ethnographic techniques, the academic researchers benchmarked students' information use from the perspective of 'good practice', one criterion of which concerns avoidance of plagiarism. This first phase also explored understandings of what plagiarism is, from the perspectives of students, teachers and teacher librarians. Details of this first phase, including the outcomes, can be found in Williamson, McGregor, Archibald & Sullivan (2007). The findings from Phase 1 were used to inform Phase 2.

During the second phase, the teacher librarians became the researchers and undertook action research to trial strategies/build models for teaching students to avoid plagiarism based on what had been learned in the first phase about students' understandings of what plagiarism is. The approach was to test, reflect, modify, accept or reject ideas, as appropriate. The academic researchers evaluated the strategies either at the end of the action research, or during the action research as well as at the end, as happened in one school. In keeping with a considerable body of action research theory, this evaluation was not undertaken solely by the 'expert' researchers, but as a collaborative appraisal with students, teachers and teacher librarians. (This action research phase is detailed in Box 8.1.) The third phase was the development of an electronic toolkit.

As mentioned above, exploring theory, for example, to suggest possible solutions, can be undertaken using action research. All schools had theoretical views about what might help students to avoid plagiarism. One school in particular was interested in trying to develop students' higher order cognitive processes and to foster their creativity as a way to help students generate knowledge. Teachers and teacher librarians in this school were particularly interested in Ritchhart's (2002) pedagogical approach to developing a classroom where thinking is identified in relation to learning tasks, and where a culture of thinking is developed. Student attributes, which Ritchhart referred to as 'thinking dispositions', include scepticism, open-mindedness, curiosity and truth seeking. In the classroom he advocated, questions are explored from many perspectives, hypotheses are tested, and assumptions are surfaced for deeper examination (Williamson, McGregor & Archibald, 2010). If you are interested in the strategies developed by the schools involved in the project, the approaches of the other three schools are covered in Williamson, McGregor & Archibald (2009) and the approaches of all schools in Williamson and McGregor (2011).

Box 8.1 describes the action research process of the project's second phase.

Box 8.1

Example of action research to devise strategies to help secondary students to avoid plagiarism

At the end of the first phase of the project, a large meeting was held of all the academic researchers, teachers and teacher librarians involved. The objective was to discuss the findings of Phase 1 and the plans schools had in mind for the action research phase. With regard to the latter, ideas were mooted rather than concrete plans laid out. There were to be two action research cycles of planning, implementing change, observing the results, reflecting on outcomes, and considering further modifications. A meeting of the full team was to take place at the end of the first cycle. Time defeated this plan. The following describes the process as it actually occurred.

- Eleven classes, ranging from Year 7 to Year 11 took part across the four schools, with several subject areas being represented and assignments being used as part of the teaching.

- All schools used elements of action research, but differed in the degree of formality and the number of cycles.

- The school particularly focussed on teaching students to think for themselves undertook formal action research using three cycles and their own time frame. Reflection occurred throughout and a moderation meeting of staff evaluated each cycle as it was concluded, discussing the changes and modifications to be made before the next cycle took place.

- At the request of the staff of the school, the university researchers did two rounds of evaluation at this school, the first at the completion of the first cycle, the second at the completion of the third cycle.

- Another school developed their approach and modified it three times, each time conducting trials, reflecting on the outcomes and undertaking their own evaluation (with students, teachers and teacher librarians), although this occurred intuitively rather than in a fully planned way. The final evaluation by the researchers occurred at the end.

- Evaluation by the academic researchers used ethnographic techniques (individual and focus group interviews) to explore the views of students, teachers and teacher librarians.

Examples of the kinds of questions used in the focus groups for this project appear in Chapter 16.

Information Literacy (IL) Development in the Electronic Age project

Karen Visser (2007) was a teacher librarian in a secondary school in Canberra during the early years of the introduction of computers and the internet into Australian schools. She perceived that, while teachers were sometimes at a loss as to how to incorporate new technologies into teaching, learning and assessment strategies:

> the successive and relentless tidal waves of information and communication technologies had sharpened my awareness of how these new learning technologies have created a growing disparity between intended teaching objectives and learning outcomes (p. 113).

She saw teachers as 'digital immigrants' and students as 'digital natives' having vastly different approaches to the role of information technologies in learning and that information professionals were in a unique position to assist in infusing new technologies into the learning process. Her view was that action research could help to bridge the gap. She envisaged three aims for her action research project, where she was both researcher and practitioner.

1. to create a cross-curricular information access program which would develop critical literacies in a variety of information formats for all Year 7 students and their teachers,

2. to develop a set of evaluation measures which would ensure the program remained relevant in successive years, and

3. to provide an opportunity to gather data and reflect on whether equipping teachers with IL skills makes a difference to student learning (Visser, 2007, p. 113).

Box 8.2 describes the action research process used for the project.

Box 8.2

Example of action research to develop information literacy in the electronic age

Three spirals of action research (dubbed the 'triple helix') took place in this long-term project. Multiple stake-holders "represented vertical and horizontal slices of the community (a spiral of spirals)" (Visser, 2007, p. 116). This required a number of sub-projects (single spirals), starting and finishing at different times and lasting different periods of time.

Spiral 1

The first spiral involved the library. Here the original general idea was to "prepare the physical and human resources to have teaching as the core business" (p. 117). After the first action steps (focussed on improving the collection) and the evaluation thereof, the revised plan was developed: improving library staff skills, with the next action step being professional development to improve staff electronic literacy.

Spiral 2

The second spiral focussed on the teachers where the original general idea was to provide a range of information literacy and IT learning incidents. The first action step involved gaining a whole school understanding of information literacy mapping a professional development program against the outcomes, followed by implementation. Evaluation indicated that the revised plan required different levels of training for the wide range of competencies involved. The second action step provided targeted professional development for Year 7 program staff. Visser (2007) provides a detailed analysis of this spiral.

Spiral 3

The students (Year 7) were the subjects of the third spiral, with the beginning idea being to "create a 4-term, 4-subject program of increasing complexity which develops information searching and information management skills for electronic and print sources" (p. 117). The first action step involved technical skills training, along with using tables of contents and indexes in books. Following evaluation, the revised plan was to continue with the program, but allow more time. The second action step included concept mapping and note taking.

Apart from the detailed description of Spiral 2, Visser (2007, pp. 129–130) provides a useful reflection on the 'the core of action research' by reviewing the key terms and discussing how, by the end of the two-year project, "a deep understanding of these core terms led to a new level of awareness, in both the action researcher and the learning community, of how to effectively build an information literate community" (p. 129).

- **Cycle:** The cyclic concept meant that "there was a mechanism to design, implement, evaluate, 'mend or discard' and redesign each phase of the journey before moving on to the next action step … Each spiral took us closer to our goal" (p. 129).

- **Practitioner as researcher:** Strength results from the academic rigour and framework emerging from the researcher role. The practitioner role contributes intimate knowledge of the research setting and the research opportunities therein.

- **Enquiry:** There are two meanings: conducting a formal literature review and questioning the *status quo*. To conduct each spiral, a goal needs to be developed based on questioning of current practice and the outcomes to be attained.

- **Process:** Action research provides an easily accessible and flexible process for researchers.

- **Learning:** Visser (2007) saw this as the most important part. She found it truly enlightening:

  > to reflect on managing priorities and goals, accepting that change was not as fast as I wanted it to be, building on a solid support base for change, calling for help, researching at work while working at research, learning to write in a way which maximised the impact of research findings, asking questions and challenging the norm, and finally celebrating the successes and keeping the disappointments in perspective (p. 130).

- **Reflective:** The repeated opportunities, through evaluation, to reflect deeply at the end of each spiral, enabled the connections amongst the various components to emerge clearly. This Visser (2007) found 'empowering' (p. 130).

Action research to investigate cognitive processes underlying strategy development

A third project is worth including as it used action research in information systems (Box 8.3). The researcher, Majola Oosthuizen, was a Monash University PhD student at the time he undertook the research. Oosthuizen's (2002) chapter in my earlier research methods book, from which this excerpt is taken, is also worth reading for the overview of action research it provides.

Box 8.3

Example of action research to investigate cognitive processes underlying strategy development

The aim of the research was to investigate the nature of strategy development processes within a single large mining company, with the purpose of providing systems to enable effective strategy development. To improve validity of insights, four independents projects were carried out over a period of 18 months (which is quite long for graduate action research projects), to investigate the processes:

Scenario building – investigation of strategy development processes without involvement of computer modelling.

Third party model use – investigation of computer modelling to develop strategy which was originally done by a third party consulting company.

Modelling based on analysis – development of computer models for strategy development, with emphasis on formal analysis.

Modelling based on expert participation - development of computer models for strategy development, with emphasis on expert participation rather than formal analysis.

Each of these projects was concerned with different products and involved different participants. Each also went through multiple cycles, and sometimes cycles within cycles. The researchers participated actively, alongside company participants, in all of these activities. The main tasks of the researcher were to ensure the research process systematically went through cycles which involved critical reflection and to record observations and insights from each cycle.

Source: Reproduced from Oosthuizen (2002, p. 165)

Conclusion

Action research is a flexible method of research, particularly appropriate for initiating, reflecting upon, and evaluating change on an ongoing basis in organisations, such as libraries. A crucial element is collaboration between groups of practitioners or between academic researchers and practitioners. The research needs to be for the benefit of the organisation involved and successful action research will usually bring feelings of 'ownership' of the outcomes within the organisation. Nevertheless, action research needs to be undertaken with rigour and can be used to develop theory. It is advisable, to ensure the best possible outcomes, for novice researchers to team with a more experienced researcher or researchers, or to undertake a study program before embarking on their study.

References

Argyris, C., & Schon, D. (1991). Participatory action research and action science compared: A commentary. In W. Whyte (Ed.), *Participatory action research* (pp. 85–96). Newbury Park, CA: Sage.

Avison, A., Lau, F., Myers, M., & Nielsen, P. A. (1999). Action research. *Communications of the ACM, 42*(1), 94–97.

Baker, T. L. (1999). *Doing social research.* Boston: McGraw-Hill.

Baskerville, R., & Myers, M.D. (Eds.). (2004). Action research in information systems [Special issue]. *MIS Quarterly, 28*(3).

Burns, R. B. (2000). *Introduction to research methods* (4th ed.). Frenchs Forest, NSW: Longman.

Carr, W., & Kemmis, S. (2009). Educational action research: A critical approach. In S. E. Noffke, & B. Somekh (Eds.), *The Sage handbook of educational action research* (pp. 74–84). Los Angeles, CA: Sage.

Eden, C., & Huxham, C. (1996). Action research for the study of organisations. In C. Clegg, C. Hardy, & W. Nord (Eds.), *Handbook of organisational studies* (pp. 526–542). London: Sage.

Elliott, J. (2009). Building educational theory through action research. In S. E. Noffke, & B. Somekh (Eds.), *The Sage handbook of educational action research* (pp. 28–38). Los Angeles, CA: Sage.

Galliers, R. (Ed.). (1992). *Information systems research: Issues, methods and practical guidelines* Oxford: Blackwell Scientific Publications.

Garrick, J. (2000). The construction of 'working knowledge' and (mis)interpretive research. In J. R. Garrick, & C. Rhodes (Eds.), *Research and knowledge at work: Perspectives, case studies and innovative strategies* (pp. 203–216). London: Routledge.

Greenwood, D., & Levin, M. (2007). *Introduction to action research: Social research for social change* (2nd ed.). Thousand Oaks, CA: Sage.

Hart, E., & Bond, M. (1995). *Action research for health and social care: A guide to practice.* Buckingham: Open University Press.

Kemmis, S., & McTaggart, R. (2005). Participatory action research. In N. K. Denzin, & Y. S. Lincoln (Eds.), *The Sage handbook of qualitative research* (3rd ed., pp. 547–603). Thousand Oaks, CA: Sage.

Kemmis, S., & McTaggart, R. (Eds.). (1988). *The action research planner.* Geelong, VIC: Deakin University Press.

Neuman, W. L. (2014). *Social research methods: Qualitative and quantitative approaches* (7th ed.). Harlow, Essex: Pearson New International.

Noffke, S. E., & Somekh, B. (Eds.) (2009). *The Sage handbook of educational action research.* Los Angeles, CA: Sage.

Oosthuizen, M. J. H. (2002). Action research. In K. Williamson (Ed.), *Research methods for students, academics and professionals: Information management and systems* (2nd ed., pp. 159–175). Wagga Wagga, NSW: Centre for Information Studies, Charles Sturt University.

Pickard, A. J. (2013). *Research methods in information* (2nd ed.) Chicago: Neal-Schuman.

Reason, P. (1998). Three approaches to participative inquiry. In N. K. Denzin, & Y. S. Lincoln (Eds.), *Strategies of qualitative inquiry* (pp. 261–291). Thousand Oaks, CA: Sage.

Ritchhart, R. (2002). *Intellectual Character: What is it, why it matters, and how to get it.* San Francisco, CA: Jossey-Bass.

Sanguinetti, J. (2000). An adventure in 'postmodern' action research: Performativity, professionalism and power. In J. Garrick, & C. Rhodes (Eds.), *Research and knowledge at work: Perspectives, case studies and innovative strategies* (pp. 232–249). London: Routledge.

Schwandt, T. (1994). Constructivist, interpretivist approaches to human inquiry. In N. K. Denzin, & Y. S. Lincoln (Eds.), *Handbook of qualitative research* (pp. 118–137). Thousand Oaks, CA: Sage.

Schwandt, T. A. (1997). *Qualitative inquiry: A dictionary of terms*. Thousand Oaks, CA: Sage.

Smith, M. K. (2007). Action research. *The encyclopedia of informal education*. Retrieved from http://www.infed.org/research/b-actres.htm.

Thompson, P., & McHugh, D. (1995). *Work organisations: A critical introduction* (2nd ed.). London: Macmillan.

Visser, K. (2007). Action research. In S. Lipu, K. Williamson, & A. Lloyd (Eds.), *Exploring methods in information literacy research* (pp. 111–132). Wagga Wagga, NSW: Centre for Information Studies, Charles Sturt University.

Wadsworth, Y. (1991). *Do it yourself social research*. Sydney: VCOSS/Allen & Unwin.

Wildemuth, B. M. (2009). *Applications of social research methods to questions in information and library science*. Westport, CT: Libraries Unlimited.

Williamson, K., & McGregor, J. (2011). Generating knowledge and avoiding plagiarism: Smart information use by high school students. *School Library Research, 14*. Retrieved from http://www.ala.org/aasl/sites/ala.org.aasl/files/content/aaslpubsandjournals/slr/vol14/SLR_GeneratingKnowledge_V14.pdf

Williamson, K., McGregor, J., & Archibald, A. (2009). Assisting students to avoid plagiarism. Part 1: The instructional practice approach. *ACCESS, 23*(3), 19–25.

Williamson, K., McGregor, J., & Archibald, A. (2010). Assisting students to avoid plagiarism. Part 2: The inquiry learning approach. *ACCESS, 24*(2), 21–25.

Williamson, K., McGregor, J., Archibald, A., & Sullivan, J. (2007). Information seeking and use by secondary students: The link between good practice and the avoidance of plagiarism. *School Library Media Research, 10*. Retrieved from http://www.ala.org/aasl/aaslpubsandjournals/slmrb/slmrcontents/volume10/williamson_informationseeking

Williamson, K., Schauder, D., Wright, S., & Stockfeld, L. (2002). Oxymoron or a successful mixed marriage? A discussion of the use of action research within an interpretivist framework. *Qualitative Research Journal, 2*(1), 7–17. Retrieved from http://www.stiy.com/qualitative/1AQR2002.pdf#page=7

Chapter 9

Constructivist grounded theory
A 21st century research methodology

James E. Herring
Charles Sturt University, Australia

The application of constructivist grounded theory is critically examined and the distinguishing features of a grounded theory approach are evaluated. The value and limitations of constructivist grounded theory are discussed in relation to other approaches to grounded theory. Aspects of different types of coding are examined, and key elements of constructivist grounded theory, including the development of categories, theoretical sampling, and the development of a grounded theory, are evaluated, with examples from the author's research on information literacy and transfer being used to illustrate the use of constructivist grounded theory.

Research Methods: Information, Systems, and Contexts. DOI: http://dx.doi.org/10.1016/B978-0-08-102220-7.00009-1

Introduction

This chapter will present a critical review of the development and use of constructivist grounded theory, supported with examples of the use of this method in this author's research. The chapter will outline the developments in grounded theory, and present a case for a constructivist approach. It will then critically examine, with research examples, aspects of the application of constructivist grounded theory, including the formation of areas of exploration, and grounded theory techniques of memo writing, coding, category development, theoretical sampling, theory development, and evaluation. A concept map of the chapter is shown in Figure 9.1 below.

Figure 9.1 Concept map of this chapter

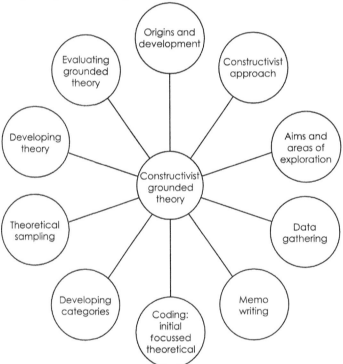

Note: This diagram should be read clockwise from 'Origins and development' to gain an overall view of the chapter.

The development of grounded theory

According to Dey (2004, p. 80), "there is no such thing as 'grounded theory', if we mean by that a single, unified methodology, tightly defined and clearly specified". This quotation demonstrates that there is a wide range of views on grounded theory.

Glaser and Strauss (1967) were the originators of grounded theory, and their book *The Discovery of Grounded Theory*, engendered a move away from the focus on quantitative research, which was prevalent at the time in many disciplines. Glaser and Strauss' (1967) work presented a series of techniques which would allow social science researchers to derive theory from detailed analysis of data gathered in a range of social settings. Pidgeon and Henwood (2004) and Charmaz (2014) argued that Glaser and Strauss' (1967) view was an objectivist one, implying that there were social relationships which objectively existed, and which would emerge from the data using the grounded theory method.

Most research methodologies are subject to reinterpretation over time by researchers from different standpoints, and this is the case with grounded theory. In the 1980s and 1990s, Strauss (1987) and Strauss and Corbin (1998) presented alternative versions of grounded theory, in which new approaches were introduced, differing from the original version. The debate over what should constitute grounded theory has continued into the 21st century, with Glaser opposing changes from the core elements of grounded theory, as suggested by Strauss and Corbin (1998). Glaser (2002) also vehemently rejected the view that grounded theory could be constructivist. According to Charmaz (2014, p. 8) Glaser argued that Strauss and Corbin's techniques "force data and analysis into preconceived categories and, thus, contradict fundamental tenets of grounded theory".

One of the key differences between the approaches of Glaser, Strauss and Corbin, and many 21st century grounded theorists, is that all of the former adopted an objectivist view of the researcher's role. Bryant (2003) argued that, in the objectivist view, researchers are viewed as being totally objective, that is, they believe that they analyse gathered data free from any influences, such as previous research experience or knowledge of the literature. In the view of Bryant (2003, p. 2), no researcher can be completely objective, and the notion of the objective researcher who gathered data "from which theories somehow emerge is now so severely discredited". Since the 1990s, researchers such as Bryant (2002 & 2003), Charmaz (2005 & 2014), and Bryant and Charmaz (2010) have argued for the development of constructivist grounded theory. Charmaz (2014, p. 17) identified key differences in the approach of constructivist grounded theorists, arguing that:

> Glaser and Strauss talk about discovering theory as emerging from data separate from the scientific observer. Unlike their position, I assume that neither data nor theories are discovered. Rather, we are part of the world we study and the data we collect. We *construct* [Charmaz's emphasis] our grounded theories through our past and present involvements and interactions with people, perspectives and research practices.

Pidgeon and Henwood (2004) took a similar view, arguing that, while constructivist grounded theorists stressed the systematic analysis of data in the same manner as objectivist researchers, they themselves took an interpretivist approach when analyzing data and developing theory. (Interpretivist/ constructivist approaches are discussed in Chapter 1: *Research concepts*.)

Despite the differences in the views of constructivist and objectivist grounded theorists when debating the role of the researcher, or the development of theory, there remains a core set of techniques which are used by all grounded theorists. Birks and Mills (2011, p. 9) stated that these include "initial coding and categorization of data; concurrent data collection and analysis; writing memos; theoretical sampling; constant comparative analysis … ; theoretical saturation; and theoretical integration". These techniques will be discussed below.

Aims and areas of exploration

One of the key characteristics of a grounded theory approach is that the researcher does not set out to prove a particular hypothesis. Also, while the researcher will identify key areas to be researched, a grounded theory approach implies that some aspects of the research may change as the research develops. One implication of this potential change is that, instead of constructing concrete objectives for a study, within a set of clear aims, a researcher may want to outline areas of exploration. The advantage of having areas of exploration is that researchers are less restricted than they might be if specific objectives were developed. In this author's own research (Herring, 2010), which aimed to examine and interpret the view of year seven students in relation to information literacy and transfer, the areas of exploration included:

- the views of year seven students on information literacy practices and on transfer,
- the views of teachers and teacher librarians on information literacy practices and on transfer,
- the extent to which year seven students viewed themselves as transferrers of information literacy practices, and
- what teachers and teacher librarians considered to be the key factors in increasing the transfer of information literacy practices amongst year seven students (Herring 2010, p. 15).

In this research, transfer related to the ability and willingness of students to transfer information literacy practices across time and across the curriculum. When these areas of exploration were pursued, the researcher was able to identify previously unidentified aspects of information literacy and transfer in the schools where the research was carried out. While these aspects may have been identified within specific objectives, areas of exploration allow the researcher to have a more open mind about the direction of the research study, and this is a key advantage.

The process of constructivist grounded theory

The process of constructivist grounded theory includes data gathering, memo writing, coding, developing categories, theoretical sampling, developing theory and evaluation, as discussed below.

Data gathering

Adopting a constructivist grounded theory approach to research does not restrict the researcher to particular techniques or tools of data collection. Charmaz (2014, p. 26) argued: "Methods *are* [Charmaz's italics] merely tools. However, some tools are more useful than others." A researcher adopting constructivist grounded theory has a choice of data gathering tools. In most cases, the researcher will be seeking to gather data which is rich in meaning, and this will tend to favour qualitative data collection tools, although a combination of qualitative and quantitative tools may be used. The most important aspect of using grounded theory is the researcher's recognition that, whatever data collection approaches are used, each tool will inform the content of the next one used.

In this author's research (Herring 2010), the data were collected via a student diary, a student questionnaire, interviews with students, and interviews with teacher librarians and teachers in three state high schools in rural Australia. In each school, students from year seven (first year in high school) participated. An important difference between a grounded theory approach and the use of other research methods was that only data from the first tool were completed in advance. In the author's study of information literacy and transfer, the student diary was constructed and then completed by students. The questionnaire contents were constructed *after* an analysis of the data from the student diary. This analysis identified the key topics to be included in the questionnaire. For example, in their diary, most students expressed enthusiasm for formulating their own questions when undertaking a history assignment. The questionnaire sought to discover whether this enthusiasm would continue when students completed a different assignment in the following term, and thus the questionnaire content was heavily influenced by the analysis of the diary. The subsequent interviews with students and staff were based around key issues identified by the researcher in further analysis of both the diary and the questionnaire.

Memo writing

Charmaz (2014, p. 162) referred to memo writing as "conversing with yourself". The use of memo writing by grounded theorists enables the researcher to note down thoughts, ideas and concepts throughout the period of research. Memos are personal notes and are often written in a shorthand that perhaps only the researcher will be able to fully interpret. This author (Herring, 2010) used memo writing in all stages of the research into information literacy and transfer, that is, during observation, analysis of the diary and the questionnaire, as well as in the periods between interviews with students and staff. Memo writing allows the researcher to instantly note down reactions to what has been read or heard. For example, in analyzing the questionnaires completed by students, this author noted in a memo that: "Some students use puzzling phrases. They say that they did not have time to develop a concept map. But this takes no time at all. What do they really mean by not having enough time? Need to follow this up in the interviews."

Holton (2010, p. 267) argued that "memo writing is a continual process that helps to raise the data to a conceptual level, and develops the properties of each category". When researchers are involved in coding and category formulation, which are discussed below, memos enable them to constantly ask the questions: 'What does this mean?' and 'What does this imply?' For example, when Herring (2010) discovered that, while almost all students believed that transfer of information literacy practices, such as question formulation, was beneficial, most students did not willingly transfer practices, he noted in a memo that:

> This is really odd. These students say [in the questionnaires] that next year's year seven students should transfer practices BUT the same students don't seem willing to transfer. Why this contradiction? What is influencing these students who believe one thing but do something different?

Although memos written by the researcher often display immediate reactions and may not form the basis of meaningful interpretation, they allow the researcher to explore codes and categories from different angles, and can be very valuable in developing theoretical aspects of grounded theory research. Memos written when constructing theory are often directly useful to the researcher.

Coding

The coding of data is central to constructivist grounded theory. Data are gathered using techniques suitable to the study. The data are then analysed by identifying codes which are attached to sections of the data. Charmaz (2014) noted that codes were the researcher's means of *interpreting* what was happening in the data, rather than describing what the main topics of the data might be. Thus coding in constructivist grounded theory differs from other types of analysis. In some data analysis (e.g., of questionnaires), researchers will seek to identify particular keywords which different participants use, and attach significance to these keywords (a form of content analysis, discussed in Chapter 19: *Qualitative data analysis*). Using grounded theory techniques, the researcher reads the data, asks *what is happening* in the data, and writes down codes, in the form of phrases, which denote the actions, attitudes or opinions of the research participants. It should be noted that Marshall (2002, pp. 56–57) refers to the "messy realities of technique" and argues that, for many researchers, analysing data is often "full of muddle and confusion".

Table 9.1 demonstrates an example of coding from this author's (Herring, 2010) research. The codes demonstrate how the researcher *interprets* what the students were doing when they commented on brainstorming – thus the use of the words *valuing* and *linking*. This is demonstrably a different approach from identifying keywords, for example, the word *help* occurs in two out of the four diary entries, but is not viewed as the most important aspect of the entries.

Table 9.1 Examples of codes developed from student diaries

Student diary entry on mind mapping and question formulation	Code
It will help me judge who is the cruellest tyrant because it will make me think about this in different ways.	Valuing mind mapping as an aid to understanding the topic
Because it's got the things that I want to find out on the internet or in books.	Valuing mind mapping as an aid to information retrieval
Because you need to find information and those questions will help you because you can find answers to these questions.	Valuing question formulation as an aid to information retrieval
You can go back to your questions when it's time to write up the assignment.	Valuing mind mapping as an aid to structuring the assignment

The above is an example of initial coding, which helped the researcher to form the content of the next stage of data collection – student questionnaires. Once further data have been gathered, the researcher can then undertake focussed coding, which Glaser (2004) referred to as selective coding. Focussed coding allows the researcher to identify patterns in the research, and is the first step in the establishment of categories, which in turn will form the grounded theory developed for the research topic. Table 9.2 shows examples of focussed coding from this author's research, leading to possible categories. This focussed coding took place after initial analysis of the student questionnaires, and further analysis of both the diaries and the questionnaires. Further focussed coding was done following analysis and interpretation of the data from interviews with students and school staff.

Corbin and Strauss (2008, p. 160) argued that coding "means putting aside preconceived notions about what the researcher expects to find in the research, and letting the data, and the interpretation of it, guide analysis". This is an important point. While constructivist researchers cannot be free of the influence of their own knowledge (e.g., from the literature review) and experience, it is vital that they accept the evidence that the data present, and do not try to fit the data to any preconceived notions. Birks and Mills (2011, p. 62) advised researchers to "wave the red flag", if they are tempted to allow their own beliefs to influence the interpretation of the data. Patton (2002) acknowledged that this can be difficult, and stressed the need for researchers to be reflexive.

The final stage is theoretical coding, in which the researcher goes back over both the initial and focussed coding, and identifies theoretical codes, which are based on abstract concepts, rather than empirical statements made by participants. These theoretical codes are likely to become aspects of the categories which the researcher develops.

Table 9.2 Examples of focussed coding

Possible category	Focussed coding	Initial codes
Thinking and making connections	<ul><li>Valuing the links between mind mapping/question formulation with later stages</li><li>Learning from experience, for example, of question formulation</li><li>Thinking about the task holistically</li></ul>	Valuing question formulation as an aid to exploring the topic Valuing mind maps in relation to selection for inclusion in the assignment Valuing questions as an aid to thinking
Engaging with the topic	<ul><li>Being influenced by motivation</li><li>Engaging because of understanding or ability</li></ul>	Being engaged after developing the mind map Being engaged after formulating questions Being engaged through understanding

Table 9.3 Examples of theoretical coding

Theoretical code	Focussed codes from which the theoretical code was developed
Thinking and making connections	Being aware of prior learning; valuing learning about mind maps and question formulation; thinking about the task holistically.
Being engaged	Viewing confidence as being based on motivation or interest; thinking about their own learning; relating subject knowledge to information literacy practices.
Being aware of the information environment	Evaluating different sources of information; valuing other students' views as an information source; valuing the written mind map as an individual information source.
Not valuing/understanding information literacy concepts and practices	Not valuing question formulation as a precursor to information retrieval; not valuing information retrieval or information evaluation; lacking the ability to judge criteria for including information or concepts in the assignment.

Table 9.3 continues examples from research on information literacy and transfer (Herring, 2010). The examples show that, when a researcher develops theoretical codes in constructivist grounded theory, the codes are wide ranging, and are the result of the researcher interpreting a number of focussed codes, and identifying an encompassing title for these codes. The researcher examines, compares and interprets all previous codes, and produces a number of theoretical codes, until no more theoretical codes can be found. This process is referred to as 'theoretical saturation' by some grounded theorists (Glaser, 2004), but Dey (2010) views theoretical saturation as not being possible. One of the criticisms of grounded theory, including constructivist grounded theory, is that there can appear to be no end to the researcher's attempts to identify theoretical codes. In reality, the researcher must judge the quality of the theoretical codes developed and move on to the development of key categories and a grounded theory.

Developing categories

Dey (2010, p. 170) argued that "categories are theoretically informed" and create "a conceptual space for the sensitizing role of categories". This implies that researchers should create categories which can be seen as concepts, for example, 'being engaged', and that researchers have the depth of empirical evidence from a study to justify the creation of these categories. Categories are at the heart of grounded theory research. Birks and Mills (2011, p. 89) stated: "Overall, grounded theory analysis is categorical in its intent." There has been much debate amongst leading grounded theorists, such as Glaser (2004), Strauss and Corbin (1998), and Charmaz (2014) about how categories can or should be formed. In constructivist grounded theory, categories are developed from initial, focussed and theoretical coding. The responsibility for category development lies with the researcher, whose analysis, detailed comparison and interpretation of the data leads to the creation of categories which are meaningful in the context of the research, and are conceptual in nature. Dey (2010, p. 169) pointed out that in the classical grounded theory view "a well-defined category will have attributes that are jointly sufficient and singly necessary to identify the category". In contrast, constructivist grounded theorists take a different view and argue that categories are "approximate and provisional" (Dey, 2010, p. 169). The category 'being engaged', an example from Herring's (2010) research, has many facets and attributes, such as students reflecting on their own learning, or identifying their individual motivation to seek information and ideas about a particular topic, but is likely to have further attributes which were not identified in the research under consideration. Thus categories exist within the context of each research study, and *may* be relevant in other contexts.

When grounded theorists develop categories from their research data, they may be faced with a large number of *potential* categories. It is the researcher's task to identify which categories are the most important from the range of categories developed. In this author's research (Herring, 2010), two major categories were eventually presented, as these represented the major findings of the research. The two major categories were *valuing information literacy practices* and *culture of transfer*. Given that the original aim of the research was to explore students' and school staff's views on information literacy and transfer, the two major categories may not appear surprising. What is most relevant to the application of the constructivist grounded theory method here is that neither of these concepts had been considered by the researcher prior to the study. That is, the major categories were constructed from, and grounded in, the data gathered from the research participants.

There is no single way to identify one or more major categories in a study, but the researcher must seek to develop these categories by attempting to explain, via these categories, the vital aspects of the study. Thus, in relation to information literacy and transfer, the two most important elements identified by this author were that students valued information literacy practices, and that there had to be a culture of transfer in these students' schools if students were to progress from valuing the transfer of information literacy practices, to putting transfer into practice. Constructivist grounded theorists examine a list of categories and then how these categories might be brought together as a major category. For example, *valuing information literacy* was developed from existing categories, which related to students being engaged with their learning, and recognising value in particular information literacy practices, and teachers' assumptions and beliefs about information literacy.

The development of categories is one of the most intense aspects of constructivist grounded theory research, as researchers need to engage in thinking theoretically about the interpretation they place on the gathered data. For this author, mind mapping was a useful tool to tease out which categories could be ranked higher than others, and also whether existing categories could be grouped under a more general and conceptual category. When the major categories have been developed, the researcher then needs to test the categories using theoretical sampling.

Theoretical sampling

In grounded theory research, theoretical sampling can be viewed in two ways. Birks and Mills (2011, p. 69) argued that "through theory directed sampling, you are able to examine concepts from various angles, and question their meaning for your developing theory". These authors believe that theoretical sampling should be employed throughout the research, as a grounded theory researcher will be developing aspects of theory from the early stages of research. Constructivist grounded theorists (Charmaz, 2014; Dey, 2010) tend to have a more restricted view of theoretical sampling, viewing it as a tool employed by the researcher to test the categories created, by going back to the participants in the field of study. This author agrees with the latter view, and employed theoretical sampling by presenting the categories to both students and staff in the three schools involved in the study.

Both views of theoretical sampling can be regarded as valid, and Birks and Mills (2011) would view this author's research as reflecting both views. These authors argue that a researcher starts with purposeful sampling of a particular population (e.g., year seven students) and then identifies areas to pursue in the next step (e.g., students' ability to evaluate information), by examining results from the purposeful sampling. This process continues with each technique used (e.g., interviews), the key aspect being that the research focus is not pre-ordained by the researcher, but is dictated by aspects of the developing theory.

In this author's constructivist grounded theory approach, theoretical sampling was seen as a way of testing the final categories identified by the researcher. This author returned to the three schools and conducted interviews with groups of school staff (teachers and teacher librarians) and year seven students. These interviews highlighted aspects of each of the two major categories – valuing information literacy practices, and culture of transfer – and asked whether the groups agreed with the researcher's interpretation of the data gathered from diaries, questionnaires and interviews. This is a very important step in constructivist grounded theory, as it determines the validity of the categories from the viewpoint of the participants of the research, that is, not from the researcher's viewpoint or that of the researcher's colleagues and/or supervisors. It is also important because, if the participants do not agree with the categories, the researcher needs to take a step backwards and revise the categories. In fact, the categories were confirmed via the interviews, but this process also enabled further development of the grounded theory. An example of this development was that, in the theoretical sampling interviews with students, the researcher discovered more detail about staff and student beliefs about the need for a culture of transfer in the schools.

Developing theory

The development of a grounded theory is the end point for grounded theory researchers, and can be seen as the summit towards which the researcher climbs during the research study. Bryant and Charmaz (2010, p. 1) argued that grounded theory is "a systematic, inductive and comparative approach for conducting enquiry for the purpose of constructing theory". As noted above, while classical grounded theorists view theory as emerging from collected data, constructivist grounded theorists view their theories as being constructed by the researcher. For inexperienced researchers, developing a theory can be a difficult concept, particularly as there are different views about what exactly constitutes a theory. Theories are also often seen by new researchers as being highly complex, and related to fundamental themes in society, for example, Marx's theory of class struggles. In some cases, novice researchers will only realise what a theory might look like after they have constructed a grounded theory themselves.

Birks and Mills (2011, pp. 112–113) defined theory as "an explanatory theme comprising of a set of concepts related to each other through logical patterns of connectivity". Dey (1999, p. 242) argued that "A theory is not just a haphazard collection of concepts – the ideas in a theory are related in a systematic way. To be well-grounded conceptually, the relationships between concepts used in a theory must be set out systematically." A *grounded* theory, as the name implies, is constructed from the application of grounded theory techniques, in particular theoretical sampling. Once the grounded researcher has finally tested the major categories, there is an opportunity for the researcher to ask what the categories' content might imply for the world of the research participants, and to construct (as recommended by Charmaz, 2006) a series of theoretical statements. A key aspect of constructivist grounded theory development is that a grounded theory is not viewed as generalisable, but relates to the context of the research study. Thus, this author's grounded theory can be seen as applicable to the schools involved in the study, and while it *might* be applicable in other schools in Australia or in other countries, that is for further research to discover.

Theoretical statements, the combination of which constitutes the researcher's grounded theory, are an interpretation by the researcher of what happened in the empirical context of a study, but are expressed in a more theoretical manner. Corbin and Strauss (2008, p. 89) argued that within a grounded theory study, there are 'conditions' which relate to what happens within a context, 'interactions' which relate to why research participants act in certain ways or have certain opinions, and 'consequences' which relate to the results of research participants taking certain actions or having certain views. These elements can be seen in theoretical statements, and are expressed not as examples from the data, but as more abstract statements. For example, in this author's research which focussed on year seven students, information literacy practices and transfer, the following two theoretical statements were constructed.

> Some students take a metacognitive view of their use of information literacy practices, and are capable of making connections across a range of practices. These students are proactive and take a more personal and reflective approach. Other students take a more received practice and passive approach and, while they make short-term connections between practices, are unlikely to be reflective without prompting from the teacher or teacher librarian. A small minority of students do not understand the concepts behind information literacy practices, do not make connections, and make little use of information literacy practices.

> Students' beliefs about transfer are important as these beliefs are one factor in determining whether students will transfer information literacy practices. If students value transfer and are encouraged to value transfer by teachers and teacher librarians, they are more likely to transfer. Most students will need to be prompted to transfer practices and a minority of students will not transfer as they lack understanding of transfer as a concept.

In both of these statements, which are selected from the nine statements which constitute the grounded theory, the researcher refers to conditions (e.g., students taking a proactive or passive approach), interactions (e.g., students take this approach because they take a metacognitive or received practice view), and consequences (e.g., most students will not transfer unless prompted to do so by teachers). It is important that theoretical statements are taken as a whole and not singly, as the statements build up a wide-ranging grounded theory, and the reader can see clear links between the statements. Writing theory is perhaps the most intellectually demanding (but also the most satisfying) part of conducting a constructivist grounded theory study. Researchers should not expect to construct a theory without having a number of drafts, which can be examined by colleagues and/or supervisors.

Evaluation

Charmaz (2014, p. 337) cited four criteria for evaluating grounded theory research:

- *credibility*, which includes the extent to which there is a close correlation between sufficiency of data collected and convincing development of categories and theory
- *originality*, which includes the extent to which the grounded theory might challenge or extend current beliefs about the studied world
- *resonance*, which includes the extent to which the categories presented provide an in-depth view of the studied world
- *usefulness*, which includes the extent to which the research findings and developed theory might contribute to the wider world.

When a researcher has completed the first draft of a constructivist grounded theory report, it is important to consider whether the study stands up to the criteria cited above. By definition, grounded theory research should not be superficial and in many cases will involve the use of more than one approach to data collection. The research should be original, in that the researcher should try to identify an area — a particular area in a particular context — that has not been subject to in-depth research. For example, this author's research topic on information literacy and transfer, has been the subject of many widely held assumptions in schools and, while anecdotal evidence existed, there was no existing study to be found by the researcher. Charmaz's (2014) term 'usefulness' implies that the grounded theory might be discussed in the wider context of the study, and that others (e.g., teachers and teacher librarians in a range of countries) might use the theory as a guide to future practice. However, constructivist grounded theorists do not *assume* that their theory will have practical application. Rather, they hope that their theory will inform future practice.

Conclusion

Grounded theory has developed greatly in the almost 50 years since its original version was published and further developments can be expected in the next 50 years. For the present, this chapter has sought to raise the key issues in taking a constructivist grounded theory approach. For this author, the development of a constructivist grounded theory implies that the researcher will take an iterative approach to data collection and analysis (see Figure 9.2 below for this author's research journey); will constantly question codes and categories which are developed; will engage in theoretical sampling in order to test categories from the research participants' viewpoints; and will construct a theory by means of a series of interlinked theoretical statements. Constructivist grounded theory in practice is intellectually demanding, energy sapping, and intermittently frustrating but, for the persistent researcher, it can be a great source of insight and satisfaction. Practitioners who are presented with a constructivist grounded theory, can use the theory to question existing practice and develop new practices, which may lead to significant improvements in their working environments.

Figure 9.2 A constructivist grounded theory journey

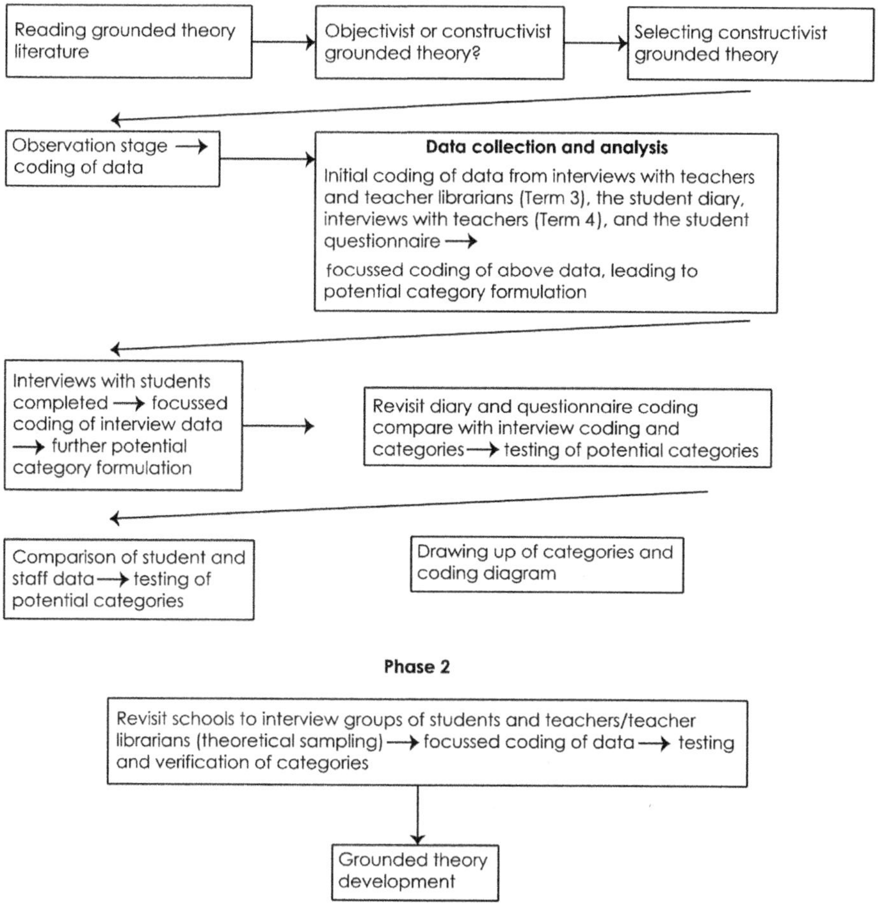

References

Birks, M., & Mills, J. (2011). *Grounded theory: A practical guide*. London: Sage.

Bryant, A. (2002). Regrounding grounded theory. *The Journal of Information Technology Theory and Application*, 4, 25–42.

Bryant, A. (2003). A constructive/ist response to Glaser. *Forum Qualitative Sozialforschung/Forum: Qualitative Social Research*, 4(1). Retrieved from http://www.qualitative-research.net/index.php/fqs/article/view/757

Bryant, A., & Charmaz, K. (2010). (Eds.). *The Sage handbook of grounded theory*. London: Sage.

Charmaz, K. (2005). Grounded theory in the 21st century: Applications for advancing social justice studies. In N. Denzin, & Y. Lincoln (Eds.), *The Sage handbook of qualitative research* (3rd ed., pp. 507–535). Thousand Oaks, CA: Sage Publications.

Charmaz, K. (2014). *Constructing grounded theory: A practical guide through qualitative analysis* (2nd ed.). London: Sage.

Corbin, J., & Strauss, A. (2008). *Basics of qualitative research: Techniques and procedures for developing grounded theory*. London: Sage Publications.

Dey, I. (1999). *Grounding grounded theory: Guidelines for qualitative inquiry*. San Diego: Academic Press.

Dey, I. (2004). Grounded theory. In C. Seale, G. Gobo, J. Gubrum, & D. Silverman (Eds.), *Qualitative research practice* (pp. 80–93). London: Sage Publications.

Dey, I. (2010). Grounding categories. In A. Bryant, & K. Charmaz (Eds.), *The Sage handbook of grounded theory* (pp. 167–190). London: Sage.

Glaser, B. (2002). Constructivist grounded theory? *Forum Qualitative Sozialforschung/ Forum: Qualitative Social Research*, 3(2). Retrieved from http://www.qualitative-research.net/index.php/fqs/article/view/825/1792

Glaser, B. (2004). Remodeling grounded theory. *Forum Qualitative Sozialforschung/ Forum: Qualitative Social Research*, 5(1). Retrieved from http://www.qualitative-research.net/index.php/fqs/article/view/607/1315

Glaser, B., & Strauss, A. (1967). *The discovery of grounded theory: Strategies for qualitative research*. Chicago: Aldine.

Herring, J. (2010). Year seven students, information literacy and transfer: A grounded theory. Retrieved from http://researchoutput.csu.edu.au/R/-?func=dbin-jump-full&object_id=13144&local_base=GEN01-CSU0

Holton, J. (2010). The coding process and its challenges. In A. Bryant, & K. Charmaz (Eds.), *The Sage handbook of grounded theory* (pp. 265–290). London: Sage.

Marshall, H. (2002). What do we do when we code data? *Qualitative Research Journal*, 2(1), 56–70.

Patton, M. (2002). *Qualitative research and evaluation methods* (3rd ed.). Thousand Oaks, CA: Sage Publications.

Pidgeon, N., & Henwood, K. (2004). Grounded theory. In M. Hardy, & A. Bryman (Eds.), *Handbook of data analysis* (pp. 625–648). London: Sage.

Strauss, A. (1987). *Qualitative analysis for social scientists*. Cambridge: Cambridge University Press.

Strauss, A., & Corbin, J. (1998). *Basics of qualitative research* (2nd ed.). London: Sage.

Chapter 10

Bibliometric research

Gaby Haddow
Curtin University, Australia

Bibliometric research is concerned with aspects of communication, such as citations, journal articles and content. It applies quantitative methods to a body of literature to explore the communication patterns, trends and networks occurring in that literature. Originating in positivist sociology, bibliometrics has developed its own laws and measurement techniques. The impact factor and the h-index are examples of key indicators that are applied in many bibliometric studies. An understanding of important indicators and how to design bibliometric studies will provide those new to the field with the knowledge and skills to undertake this type of research. In doing so, the researcher must be aware of important challenges, assumptions and limitations associated with bibliometric research.

Research Methods: Information, Systems, and Contexts. DOI: http://dx.doi.org/10.1016/B978-0-08-102220-7.00010-8

Introduction

Bibliometric research examines authorship, publication, citation, and content by applying quantitative measures to a body of literature. In this chapter, the collective term 'literature' refers to a body of articles, journals, conference proceedings, books, or indeed, any form of recorded information. An important feature of bibliometric research is the quantification of patterns and trends. It is this that differentiates bibliometric research methods from other forms of analysis applied to a body of literature, such as textual analysis and historical research.

With strong links to professional practice in areas such as collection management and research support, a sound understanding of bibliometric research methods enables the researcher to work across all subject areas. A skilled bibliometrician can accomplish this because the underlying assumptions and techniques of bibliometric research apply to all fields.

This chapter opens with a brief history and clarification of the terminology used in bibliometric research, followed by an overview of the laws and indicators applied in the field. The study design and examples for three types of bibliometric research, citation analysis, authorship and affiliation, and content analysis, form the main body of the chapter. It concludes with an outline of the assumptions and limitations involved in bibliometric research.

Background and terminology

Bibliometric research or 'bibliometrics', the term coined by Alan Pritchard in 1969 (Nicholas & Ritchie, 1978), has antecedents in the 19th century. Influential philosophers such as Auguste Comte (credited as the founder of positivism as mentioned in Chapter 1: *Research concepts*) believed that scientific activity, particularly activity that indicated esteem, could be measured. The first systematic investigation of factors associated with scientific prominence was by De Candolle, published in 1885 (De Bellis, 2009). This early work aimed to identify and measure scientific productivity in order to describe, in quantitative terms, the mechanisms of science and its contribution to human progress. A focus on counting remains central to bibliometric research today, but in the intervening years the field has developed increasingly sophisticated methods and a deeper understanding of the constraints inherent in bibliometric research. Box 10.1 discusses the terms 'scientific' and 'science' in relation to bibliometric research.

Box 10.1

The terms 'scientific' and 'science' in relation to bibliometric research

Scientific activity or science is used by many bibliometric researchers to mean any academic pursuit from which new knowledge emerges, regardless of the discipline area. Early forms of bibliometric research focussed on the publications and activities of scientific societies and generally these societies were concerned with the hard sciences. Membership and publishing in the societies' journals was a measure of esteem and provided an ideal sample for analysing the progress of science and the productivity of scientists. The continued use of the term is seen in databases, such as *Web of Science* and *ScienceDirect*, which index scholarly work from the full range of disciplines.

Using the term bibliometrics for the first time in 1969, Pritchard described its purpose:

> to shed light on the process of written communications and of the nature and course of a discipline (in so far as this is displayed through written communication) by means of counting and analysing the various facets of written communication (cited by Nicholas & Ritchie, 1978, p. 9).

Pritchard's definition reflects its period, which was before the widespread use of computer technologies and electronic forms of communication. As information has moved from the published page to digital formats, so too has bibliometric research. De Bellis (2009, p. 3) accounts for these advances, stating: the aim of bibliometrics is "to analyze, quantify, and measure communication phenomena to build accurate formal representations of their behavior for explanatory, evaluative, and administrative purposes".

Terminology

The terminology associated with bibliometrics is complicated by different approaches to the field and the emergence of digital information. Early terms include: *scientometrics* (coined by Russian researchers, Nalimov and Mulchenko, in the same year as Pritchard described bibliometrics), and *informetrics*, which was first used in the 1990s (Wilson, 1999). Digital formats gave rise to the terms *cybermetrics*, *netometrics* and *webometrics*. More recently, the term *altmetrics* has entered the lexicon. *Altmetrics* draws on metrics, such as reads, downloads and views, generated by social media and has rapidly attracted the attention of bibliometricians and researchers (Priem, 2014).

The distinction between many of these terms is not always clear, although some are evident. Webometrics and cybermetrics, which are not discussed in this chapter, are concerned with examining web links between entities, while scientometrics and bibliometrics, frequently used interchangeably, tend to refer to investigations involving more traditional communication channels, such as journals and conference proceedings (in print or electronic formats).

In addition to the terminological imprecision of the field, key elements of bibliometric research can create confusion. The *citation* is an important unit of analysis in bibliometric studies. It is the acknowledgement given by one work (the citing work) to another work (the cited work). Citations are sometimes described as references, readings, bibliographic references and footnotes. In this chapter, citing and cited will be used to describe the relationship between the giving and receiving works. A further level of complexity arises when citation patterns are tracked over time. As Figure 10.1 illustrates, a citing work (B) of documents C to G may become a cited work (by A).

Figure 10.1 Cited and citing works, co-citation and bibliometric coupling

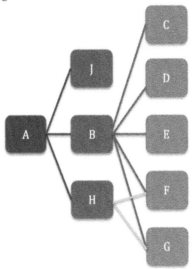

Figure 10.1 is also useful to explain terms that are frequently used in citation analysis: *co-citation* and *bibliometric coupling*. The documents C to G are co-cited works (by B), just as the three documents in the centre column are co-cited works (by A). When two or more works give citations to the same works, illustrated in the figure by B and H each citing F and G, then those citing works (B and H) are said to demonstrate bibliometric coupling. Bibliometric coupling suggests that a

relationship exists between works, and is based on the assumption that if the same documents are being cited by a number of works, then those works are discussing similar topics. *Web of Science* uses bibliometric coupling to compute 'related records' for indexed items.

Another term used in bibliometric research is *self-citation*. Although it usually refers to authors citing their own work, self-citation can also relate to journals or affiliations, for example, when a journal article cites an article published in the same journal or an author cites a work by authors with the same affiliation (such as the same department, institution, country).

Eugene Garfield

A chapter about bibliometric research would be incomplete without discussing the immense contribution of Eugene Garfield, the "undisputed patriarch of citation indexing" (Cronin & Barsky Atkins, 2000, p. 1). For over forty years Garfield's citation indexes were the only sources of citation data. The indexes not only facilitated bibliometric research, they also encouraged its development and, at times, questionable application; to the extent that their creator wrote: "... in the hands of uninformed users, unfortunately, there is the definite potential for abuse" (Garfield, 1998, p. 68). The *Science Citation Index* (*SCI*) was first published in 1963 by Garfield's company the Institute for Scientific Information (ISI), and was followed by the *Social Sciences Citation Index* (*SSCI*), and the *Arts and Humanities Citation Index* (*AHCI*). Originally in print, the three indexes now form the core content of *Web of Science*.

Garfield and a colleague created a tool for selecting journals for the *SCI* that has become the best-known measure of journal influence, the impact factor (De Bellis, 2009). Published in the *Journal Citation Reports* (*JCR*), impact factors have achieved a level of notoriety that Garfield could never have envisaged (Monastersky, 2005). Regardless of the criticisms that have been directed at the impact factor, and the use of citations generally, Garfield's influence in bibliometric research is undeniable. It is evident in the vast amount of research that has drawn data from the citation indexes and in the language of the field. Even now, many years since the indexes were acquired by the Thomson Corporation, researchers and practitioners still speak of ISI when referring to the *Web of Science* indexes.

The role of scholarly communication patterns and disciplinary differences

Another important figure in bibliometrics was Derek de Solla Price, an historian of science who made a significant contribution to our understanding of the scholarly communication patterns of different fields (Price, 1965, 1970). Price examined the growth of science, including the time that literature remained cited. He used citation frequencies and age to identify differences in literature use to define "hard science, soft science, technology, and nonscience" (Price, 1970, p. 3). This work indicated that cutting-edge research is likely to cite more papers and more recent papers than research in the softer sciences.

Scholarly communication patterns reflect the nature of scholarship in a field. For example, humanities researchers are more likely to write books or book chapters, medical researchers will tend to publish journals articles, and conference papers are preferred by engineers. In the humanities, citations are generally to older publications, while science fields cite more recent works. Even within fields there will be different scholarly communication patterns. In education, for example, there are science-focussed areas like educational psychology, and social sciences areas such as curriculum design. These differences will influence the numeric value of bibliometric indicators calculated for fields.

Bibliometric laws and indicators

A framework of laws and indicators provides the key components for bibliometric research. While the laws are the theoretical foundation developed to explain how different aspects of recorded communication behave, the indicators are the tools used to undertake bibliometric research. There are many indicators available to the researcher and a good understanding of them is vital to ensure that a bibliometric study produces meaningful results.

Bibliometric laws

Three important laws of bibliometrics illustrate how the field sought to develop theories relating to the quantification of 'communication phenomena'. Each law is based on the distribution of entities: publications by authors, articles in journals, and terms in text. They are described here without formulae. (See Andres, 2009; De Bellis, 2009.)

Lotka's law of scientific productivity (1926)

Lotka's law is concerned with the productivity of authors, measured by publications. It provides a method of calculating the contribution of authors to a body of literature stating that: within a specific scientific field, a small number of authors produce high numbers of publications, while approximately 60 percent of authors produce only one publication. If the number of authors contributing one publication to a field is known, Lotka's formula can predict the number of authors contributing two, three or more publications.

Bradford's law of scattering (1934)

Bradford's law focusses on the scatter of relevant articles in journals in a field and is a method of ranking journals by productivity. According to Bradford's law, journals can be grouped into three zones, each containing the same number of articles. The most productive journals publish the most relevant articles in a field and form the 'core' journals. In the next zone, more journals are responsible for the same number of articles, and the least productive journals are in the outer zone. In practice, Bradford's law can support collection development decisions by identifying core journals in a field.

Zipf's law of word frequency in long texts (1935)

Zipf's law states that if words in a long text are ranked in order of decreasing frequency, then a word's frequency multiplied by its rank will result in a constant. The example provided by most sources to illustrate Zipf's law is his examination of *Ulysses* by James Joyce. For this work he found "the tenth most frequent word in the novel was mentioned 2,653 times, the one hundredth most frequent word occurred 265 times, and the five thousandth most frequent word occurred 5 times" (De Bellis, 2009, p. 107). Zipf's law has applications in the areas of indexing and ontology development.

The laws of Lotka, Bradford, and Zipf furnished a platform from which researchers could examine facets of communication. In reality, this work has generally remained at the theoretical end of the research spectrum, and it is the bibliometric indicators, developed to measure productivity and influence, that have emerged as central tools in bibliometric research and practice.

Bibliometric indicators: Measures of productivity and influence

Until the end of the 20th century, the *impact factor* dominated as a method of ranking journals. While the impact factor remains widely used as a measure of journal influence, new citation databases and a raft of new indicators were added to the bibliometrics toolkit in the early 2000s. In 2004, the first competitors to Thomson Reuters' citation indexes, *Scopus* (published by Elsevier) and *Google Scholar*, were launched. Around the same period, the *h*-index (Hirsch, 2005), Eigenfactor, Article Influence, SCImago Journal Rank and others entered the field (Bar-Ilan, 2008a; Jacso, 2010; Järvelin & Persson, 2008; Leydesdorff, 2009; West, Bergstrom, & Bergstrom, 2010).

While a bibliometric indicator can be as simple as calculating citations per paper, the measures described below were developed to produce more sophisticated indicators of productivity or influence. These measures, and variations on them, often feature as automatic calculations in citation databases and in numerous bibliometric studies. A useful source of information about a number of indicators is the Centre for Science and Technology Studies (CWTS, http://www. journalindicators.com/methodology).

The impact factor

The impact factor is a method of ranking journals. Due to its virtual monopoly for many years, the impact factor has been used extensively in research and practice, forming the basis of research into core journals of a field, creating lists of quality journals, and in research assessment of individuals, groups and institutions (Altmann & Gorman, 1998; Glanzel & Moed, 2002; Mathiesen, Perry, Sellers, & Smith, 2004; Nisonger, 2000; Schloegl & Stock, 2004; Smith, 2008).

Impact factors are calculated annually and published in *JCR* around June of each year. Originally calculated for a two-year publishing window for journals in the *SCI* and the *SSCI*, the *JCR* now includes a five-year impact factor. Using the traditional two-year impact factor as an example, the formula for a 2015 impact factor is:

$$\text{Journal} \times \text{impact factor}$$
$$= \frac{\text{Cites in 2015 to articles published by journal} \times \text{in } 2013 + 2014}{\text{Number of articles published by journal} \times \text{in } 2013 + 2014}$$

Essentially, an impact factor is the average number of citations received by a typical article in a journal. A journal impact factor of one means that, on average, every article published in that journal is cited once within the specified period. Logically, this suggests an article in a journal with a high impact factor is likely to receive more citations than an article in a journal with a low impact factor. As noted below, many subsequent indicators have used the same basic formula with variations.

Much of the criticism levelled against the impact factor revolves around the calculation. It does not account for differences in scholarly communication between fields and therefore comparing journal impact factors across fields is not advisable. A notable feature of *JCR* is that impact factors are not calculated for the *AHCI* journals. The scholarly communication practices in these fields would result in impact factors so low to render them meaningless. Table 10.1 illustrates the vast differences between impact factors for six subject categories, three from the Science and three from the Social Sciences editions of *JCR*.

Table 10.1 Journal impact factors: Ranges for six fields

JCR subject category	Number of journals	Range of impact factors (two year)	
		Highest	Lowest
Medicine, General & Internal	154	59.588−0.014	
Physics, Applied	145	38.891−0.200	
Statistics & Probability	123	4.634−0.270	
Business	119	7.288−0.028	
Geography	77	5.679−0.086	
International Relations	86	3.275−0.014	

Source: Data from the 2015 edition of Journal Citation Reports.

Another criticism of impact factors relates to the coverage of journals by the indexes, the majority of which are English-language journals from North America and Europe. Thomson argues the selective inclusion of journals (only 12,000) is vital to maintaining the quality of the indexes, with Bradford's law invoked to support the selection of core journals. However, as a result, many journals are not represented in *JCR*, and this selectivity lends itself to the perception that inclusion in the indexes equates with higher quality and status.

Of all the concerns about the misuse of impact factors, evaluating an article or the author of an article on the basis of this indicator is possibly the most important to address (Cameron, 2005; Leydesdorff, 2008; Moed, 2002; Monastersky, 2005). An impact factor is a journal measure, and an average at that. An individual article within a journal may be excellent or poor, and may attract many or few citations. Assessing an article as lower quality because it is published in a journal with a low impact factor is flawed and potentially unjust.

The *h*-index

Hirsch (2005) proposed the *h*-index as a measure of a scientist's productivity. Using article and citation numbers, the calculation is simple and can be performed manually. To arrive at an *h*-value, a scientist's publications list and citations to those publications are required. The publications are ordered from highest to lowest citations and the *h*-value is calculated at the point where the number of citations is equal to the number of papers. For example, if a scientist has 15 publications and 6 of these have been cited 6 or more times, the *h*-value is 6. As in:

Publication	1	2	3	4	5	**6**	7	8	9	10	11	12	13	14	15
Citations	18	11	10	9	7	**6**	5	5	4	4	4	2	2	1	0

The *h*-index has become widely known and used by researchers to indicate their influence. It is calculated and listed in *Web of Science, Scopus* and *Google Scholar*. Like the impact factor, the *h*-index does not allow for different scholarly communication patterns and therefore comparisons across fields may lead to erroneous conclusions. The *h*-index advantages scientists with longer publishing careers and because it does not rely on averages, it never drops; it can only increase as citations and papers increase. This means a scientist with an established *h*-index could subsequently publish numerous papers that were never cited, with no negative effect. Although the *h*-index was developed to measure scientists' productivity, the index can be applied to other research subjects, such as a group of scientists or journals, and it has been widely adopted in bibliometric research. Examples include studies by Jacso (2008), Nixon (2014), Norris and Oppenheim (2010), Oppenheim (2007), and Vanclay (2008).

SCImago Journal Rank, CiteScore and SNIP

With the launch of the *Scopus* database, two new measures of influence were introduced to bibliometrics. The SCImago Journal Rank (SJR) is a direct competitor with *JCR*'s impact factor and is published freely online and in *Scopus*. Based on a two-year publishing period, a calculation akin to the impact factor is performed, then an algorithm similar to that used by Google PageRank to assign a prestige value to citations is applied. This value varies according to disciplinary field and the citing journal. It is argued that the SJR results in ranking which "best reflect the citation relationships between scientific sources" (Gonzalez-Pereira, Guerrero-Bote, & Moya-Anegon, 2009, p. 18). The SJR also excludes journal self-citations, addressing a criticism of the impact factor that does not. While the SJR has not been subject to the same long-term scrutiny as the impact factor, a number of studies have compared the SJR with other measures (e.g., Ahlgren & Waltman, 2014; Falagas, Kouranos, Arencibia-Jorge & Karageorgopoulos, 2008; Jacso, 2010).

In 2016, Elsevier introduced CiteScore as a new indicator. CiteScore uses the same calculation method as the impact factor, but over a three year publishing period.

Source Normalized Impact per Paper (SNIP), developed by Henk Moed (2010) and revised in 2012 (Waltman, van Eck, van Leeuwen & Visser, 2013), is published in *Scopus*, using a three-year period in its calculation. An important feature of SNIP, like SJR, is that it adjusts for different fields' citation behaviour by weighting citations in fields that typically have lower citation numbers.

The Eigenfactor™ and Article Influence

Researchers at the University of Washington first launched the Eigenfactor website in 2007 (Eigenfactor.org, 2017). Based on a five year publishing period and using the same basic formula as the impact factor, the Eigenfactor score calculation excludes a journal's self-citations and adjusts for a journal's citing behaviour. That is, the Eigenfactor score is based on the likelihood of a journal being consulted by someone tracking a citation trail and applies weighting accordingly (West *et al.*, 2010), therefore reflecting the influence of citing journals. The related Article Influence score is calculated by dividing the Eigenfactor score for a journal by the number of articles published in the journal over the specified period. Eigenfactor and Article Influence scores are published in the *JCR*, from which citation data are sourced.

Citation analysis, authorship and content analysis: Study design

While citations are the primary data source for the indicators discussed above, researchers new to bibliometrics should also be familiar with authorship and affiliation studies – the subject of increasingly sophisticated methods – as well as content analysis. In many bibliometric studies two or more of these methods are combined.

Sampling for bibliometric research

In most cases, a bibliometric research sample will be selected using non-probability sampling methods, particularly purposive sampling. (See Chapter 15: *Populations and samples*.) The sample will be a defined body of literature, usually limited by subject area, format and time, or restricted to a defined set of authors. Some studies examine several subject areas for comparative purposes, but many will focus on a single field. The field of interest is important because it is likely to influence the selection of sampled literature, as discussed above. Frequently sampled formats are: journals, journal articles, books, Web pages, newspapers, conference papers and theses.

Examples of defined samples are:
- citation analysis:
  - articles in Australian geography journals published over six years;
  - doctoral theses by genetics researchers from the UK and USA, 2005–2009;
  - 2015 citations to biotechnology researchers at ten European institutions;
- author and affiliation studies:
  - North American nursing journals from 1990–2000;
  - papers delivered at five international engineering conferences between 2007 and 2016;
  - chapters in anthropology books published over a 20-year period;

- content analysis:
  - five major Australian newspapers from June–December 2016;
  - websites of the first 20 results from a *Google* search for diabetes treatment;
  - history journals published by UK university presses between 2000–2010.

Time is a parameter in most of these samples. It is an important consideration to ensure that a study is manageable, and to justify and link results to research objectives. For example, a comparison of international news content of newspapers would benefit from aligning the time period with a significant international event, and citation analysis of Australian geography journal articles over the period of a research assessment exercise will provide a framework and context for the results. The main citation databases are frequently used to define a journal sample and *UlrichWeb: Global Serials Directory* provides information to determine parameters for a sample.

While data for bibliometric studies are relatively easy to collect, researchers should not underestimate the time it may take to ensure their data are clean. That is, the names of authors, publications, and institutions will not always be presented in the same way. Acronyms, name variations and spelling errors are highly likely in any large sample and the researcher will need to work through the data to correct these and create consistency across the dataset.

Data analysis in bibliometric research

Although data analysis for bibliometric research can involve advanced mathematical skills, these are not essential. With the assistance of suitable software and an understanding of descriptive statistics (see Chapter 18: *Quantitative data analysis*), the researcher can conduct a range of bibliometric studies. Even some of the more sophisticated approaches, such as network analysis and science mapping, are available to researchers with the time and inclination to acquire the skills to learn the software functions needed for these studies.

The main citation databases automatically calculate several of the indicators discussed above and generate reports for a citation search. Citation analysis using data from other sources, for example, manual calculations for the impact factor and *h*-index require only general mathematical skills.

Perhaps the most important aspect of data analysis for the new researcher is an excellent understanding of what their data mean. The citation indexes are particularly challenging in this regard, but careful planning and systematic data collection will overcome most of the issues that can arise. Bibliometric research findings are often presented as percentages, and in frequency tables and graphs.

Citation analysis

Citation analysis is the study of relationships associated with citing and cited works. Much of the research relies upon the notion "that citation counts correlate with a variety of subjective and objective performance measures" (Cronin, 1984, p. 27). Citation analysis has a special attribute: it can examine scholarly communication patterns, looking back and forwards (through citing and cited works) from one point in time. Its ability to describe a body of literature and trace influence from a variety of approaches, as well as the ready availability of citation data, has resulted in a profusion of published citation studies (a fraction of which are Batterham, 2011; Becker & Chiware, 2015; Harter, 1996; Mathiesen, *et al.*, 2004; Narin & Carpenter, 1975; Oppenheim & Summers, 2008; Peritz, 1981; Smith, 2008; Via & Schmidle, 2007). Some examples of citation analyses include:

- identifying citation characteristics in a body of literature, by examining format, age, place of publication, and language of cited works to describe the nature of scholarly communication and information use in a field;

- calculating number of citations per paper to an author's work, to identify impact; analysing citations to works outside a field to observe knowledge transfer and interdisciplinary activities;

- determining the proportion of citations given by a nation's authors to works from the same nation to assess whether citing bias is occurring;

- ranking journals using bibliometric indicators to identify key journals in a field; and

- analysing co-citation and bibliographic coupling in a body of literature to identify networks of scientific activity.

As well as contributing to the scholarly communication literature, citation studies have applications in practice. An understanding of the importance of different sources to a field's researchers can assist in the development of indexing tools and databases; identifying core journals is useful in collection development; and citations per paper and the impact of journals in which researchers publish are used in some research assessment exercises.

Citation data

Citation indexes are the main data source for citation analysis. *Web of Science*, *Scopus* and *Google Scholar*, directly or through the *Publish or Perish* software (Harzing, 2016), enable researchers to rapidly identify citations to a sample of literature. They also generate automated calculations for bibliometric indicators, reducing the manual analysis required. In general, the citations in these sources are from journal articles and conference proceedings, and their extent and coverage of fields differ. Box 10.2 sets out comparisons amongst the three key data sources.

Box 10.2

Comparisons between *Web of Science, Scopus* and *Google Scholar*

- *Scopus* indexes more titles and includes more records than *Web of Science*.

- *Web of Science* indexes fewer titles, as a raw number and proportionally, in social sciences and arts and humanities than *Scopus*.

- *Scopus* indexes more conference proceedings than *Web of Science*.

- *Google Scholar* has excellent coverage of conference papers and non-English language journals, while *Web of Science* and *Scopus* are weak in their coverage of non-English language journals.

- *Google Scholar* is a useful source of citation data for some social sciences and arts and humanities fields.

- *Web of Science* includes the 'cited reference search' function which identifies citations from non-indexed sources, such as books, reports and theses. Books and conference proceedings are also indexed by *Scopus*, making these types of publications a potential subject of study.

- *Google Scholar* includes citations to non-scholarly materials, such as pre-prints and technical reports, and might over-report citations due to duplication of records (Bar-Ilan, 2008b; Falagas, Pitsouni, Malietzis & Pappas, 2008; Jacso, 2008; Mongeon & Paul-Hus, 2016; Norris & Oppenheim, 2007; Prins, Costas, van Leeuwen & Wouters, 2016; Vaughan & Shaw, 2008).

- Google Book Search has also been found to be a useful citation source for social sciences and humanities books (Kousha & Thelwall, 2009).

For subject fields and formats that are not adequately covered by the major citation sources, citation data can be collected from the body of literature being studied. In this case, access to the full-text of the sample is required to record the citations listed; a labor-intensive approach that, for the sole researcher, would necessitate drawing on a limited sample for analysis.

An example of citation study design is presented in Box 10.3.

Box 10.3

Example of citation analysis study design

Research question

Who is citing Australian and Canadian educational research journals?

Objective

To compare the influence of these journals.

Defining the sample of journals

Several parameters for inclusion are important to consider. For example:

- If the study is intending to use the main citation databases for data collection, then the journals must be indexed in these sources.
- What is the definition of 'research' and 'education'? Published journal lists are useful tools.
- How many journals and how are they selected? Indicators, such as impact factors can provide rankings to define cut-off points.
- How are Australia and Canada defined as places of publication? Many journals commence publishing in a country and are later taken up by international publishers.
- What is the publication period (time parameter)?

Identifying the units of analysis

Which aspects of citing behaviour will be examined? They may include:

- number of citations received (citations per paper)
- citing author affiliation
- format and age of citations
- most frequently citing journals
- citing journal place of publication.

Data collection

Education journals are reasonably well indexed by the major citation databases, but the researcher must decide whether one or more citation source will be used, and justify the decision. While a number of the units of analysis can be collected using the database's functions, additional data will be needed to identify citing author affiliation and journal place of publication.

Data analysis

Data analysis will usually take the form of descriptive statistics, such as frequency tables and graphs.

Challenges

The major citation databases will locate only those citations given by works indexed in the database.

Authorship and affiliation

Authorship and affiliation studies are concerned with 'ownership' relationships that exist in a body of literature. This method can range from investigating very simple phenomena, such as the contribution of authors affiliated with a defined set of institutions, to highly sophisticated studies of networks of authors (Abramo, D'Angelo, Di Costa, & Solazzi, 2009; Hoekman, Frenken, & Tijssen, 2010; Mularski, 1991; Narin & Carpenter, 1975; Ossenblok, Verleysen, & Engels, 2014; Park, 2008). Authorship and affiliation methods are frequently combined with citation analysis to perform a deeper examination of productivity. Some examples include:

- counting the number of papers by authors in a field to compare productivity;
- identifying contribution by authors from sectors within a field to establish who (practitioners/researchers, institutions, nation) are participating in the field; and
- analysing co-authorship to describe collaboration patterns.

In recent years, author and affiliation studies have increasingly focussed on collaboration patterns (either between different sectors such as industry and academia, or different nations) as indicators of science and innovation activity, and knowledge transfer. One argument posed is that developing nations are more likely to seek international collaborators to improve the perceived status of their publications, while researchers from developed nations are confident to collaborate within their own country. Collaboration research has applied sophisticated software tools in data analysis to produce maps depicting the nature and extent of collaborations.

Author and affiliation data

Author and affiliation data are frequently readily available in the literature under examination, although further searches for names and places may be required.

Units of analysis can relate to gender, position type (for example, practitioner or academic), institution type (such as a special or public library), institution name, and nationality. The researcher should be aware of potential sources of author or affiliation data prior to data analysis. For example, a study exploring the gender of authors will need to identify gender for ambiguous or unfamiliar names. Inconsistency in the data, as noted above, can also create additional work and the researcher must devise a method to identify all name variants. While many of the large databases have introduced functions that co-locate an author's works under a specified institution name, these are not always reliable and further research to establish affiliation may be required. Box 10.4 provides an example of author and affiliation study design.

Box 10.4

Example of author and affiliation study design

Research question

Who are the authors in Australian geography journals?

Objective

To describe the contribution of different sectors and institutions to the literature.

Defining the sample

- How many and what type of journals? This could be based on target audience of journal or type of publisher (commercial, university), defined using published lists.
- Access to full text if required. (for additional affiliation information)
- Types of articles included. (editorials, regular features)
- Period of publication. (time parameter)

Identifying the units of analysis

- sector (academic or professional) of authors
- role (position) of author
- institutional affiliation
- country of affiliation.

Data collection

Appropriate sources are required to ensure consistency in the collection of additional author and affiliation data. A list of categories for units of analysis can be drawn from an initial scan of the sample. Units of analysis should be recorded in a systematic way. For example, if an author is listed as a 'director' is this equivalent to a 'manager'?

Data analysis

Although some qualitative data will be collected, such as category terms, these would be analysed using quantitative methods to report frequencies in the findings.

Challenges

How will multi-authored articles be treated — as whole or fractional counts?

Content analysis

Content analysis is the examination of the content of a body of literature, in this case using quantitative methods. (For a qualitative approach to content analysis, see Chapter 19: *Qualitative data analysis*.) The examination may be for specific terms (such as the incidence of a word) or concepts (such as phrases that suggest a particular perspective). It should be a systematic examination guided by clearly defined categories with which to code the content. (For a description of data coding, see Chapter 18.) Objectivity is an important aspect of content analysis and the researcher must attend to issues that may introduce bias in the results. Content analysis of word use has applications in thesaurus creation, and taxonomy and ontology development, as in Zipf's law. A combination of content and citation analysis can provide an indication of the context in which a citation is made. In our field, extensive research into the research content of journals has been conducted in order to determine the commitment of the LIS profession to developing a research base; combining author and affiliation with content analysis (Clark, 2016; Enger, Quirk, & Stewart, 1988; Tuomaala, Järvelin & Vakkari, 2014; Peritz, 1980; Shema, Bar-Ilan & Thelwall, 2015). Examples of content analysis are:

- examining journals to measure the extent of research being published in a field;
- identifying the main research methods and/or subject areas in a field; and
- examining newspaper content to determine the way in which an issue is portrayed.

The sample and subject of interest in content analysis is limited only by the imagination and skills of the researcher. However, content analysis does require particular attention to the coding of categories being examined. For example, a study of research article content must begin with a definition of research and clear guidelines about how to categorise different research approaches. This is especially important if the researcher is seeking to make judgements on content, such as positive, negative or neutral portrayal of a subject. Although software programs are available to undertake automated content analysis, the researcher must still be aware of how the program determines and analyses content.

Content data

The most important data consideration for content analysis is access to the sample required by the study's inclusion criteria and for the full term of the study. Older materials may be difficult to access in their original form and literature uploaded during the early years of the internet is often presented in a manner that will add hours of work to the analysis. Box 10.5 provides an example of content analysis study design.

Box 10.5

Example of content analysis study design

Research question

How do Australian newspapers report health research findings?

Objective

To describe the type and nature of health research reporting.

Defining the sample

Parameters for inclusion may involve:
- target audience of newspaper (broadsheets or tabloids)
- access to full text
- how much content and over what period (daily, weekly, health sections only)
- publisher (representing a range of perspectives)
- place of publication (state-based, national).

Identifying the units of analysis

Unambiguous categories for units of analysis might be:

- health topic
- subjects of research (children, women, aged)
- type and size of study (clinical trial, survey)
- nature of reporting (positive, negative, neutral)
- researchers/institution/country responsible for research.

Data collection

Access to the content sample is critical. A pilot study will enable the researcher to create unambiguous categories for the units of analysis prior to data collection. The context in which data are reported in the sample can be important; therefore the data collection tools should allow entry of extracts of text.

Data analysis

Ideally, content analysis coding involves two or more researchers to reduce the potential for bias in the data analysis stage. Because in many cases this is not feasible, the researcher must ensure that the guidelines for coding data into categories are transparent. A coding sheet that lists all categories and their potential data elements (with scope notes for additional explanatory information) should be developed for this purpose. The findings will be reported in quantitative terms, generally as descriptive statistics such as frequencies and cross-tabulations.

Challenges

Developing categories and ensuring coding is systematic and unbiased.

Challenges in bibliometric research

There are a number of challenges in bibliometric research which include defining a body of literature, gaining access to data, defining units of analysis, counting citations and authors, and the problems of comparing across fields.

- *Defining a sample:* This requires systematic and defendable criteria. While probability sampling is an option, content type, place of publication, and field form the parameters in many studies and each can present demarcation difficulties.

- *Access to data:* The number of citations retrieved from different data sources may vary and there will be overlaps as well as unique citations in each. If the body of literature being sampled is not indexed adequately in a major source, then extensive manual effort may be required for data collection. Additional sources of data may be required for author and affiliation studies.

- *Defining units of analysis:* A systematic and consistent approach to assigning categories, such as affiliation and content types, is critical. Careful planning and coding sheets should reduce the potential for bias and ill-defined categories.

- *Counting citations:* Self-citations are usually included in citation data, but this presents problems because some fields have extremely high self-citation rates. Thus self-citations should be considered when comparing fields. Manual citation analysis requires additional definitional decisions, such as whether references in footnotes are included in the citation count?

- *Counting authors:* An author in multi-authored works can be counted as one or as a fraction of the total authors. This decision has implications for the final results. Previous research can be used to justify the decision and to compare findings.

- *Comparisons across fields:* Different scholarly communication patterns must be considered when making comparisons across fields in order to reach valid conclusions.

Assumptions and limitations of bibliometric research

Bibliometric research is bound by a number of assumptions and is limited by the quantitative methods it applies to a body of literature. While it can be argued that bibliometric research provides objective measures of communication phenomena, the counter-argument is that "publication counts, citation scores, and impact factors do not necessarily tell the whole story" (Cronin, 2014, p. 14). For example, the findings of bibliometric studies do not tell us anything about the reasons these phenomena occur; reasons which could originate in social, political or psychological conditions. Citations may not be made because of lack of access to information rather than an oversight in acknowledging the most relevant work. Co-authorship might be related to geographical proximity, and the range of possible motivations behind content is vast.

Citation analysis has attracted extensive discussion about the meaning of citing and the use of citation-based indicators to evaluate research and researchers (Cameron, 2005; Cole, 2000; Cronin, 1984; De Bellis, 2009; Garfield, 1979; Kaplan, 1965; Lawrence, 2008; Leydesdorff, 2008; Moed, 2005; Smith, 1981; Steele, Butler, & Kingsley, 2006). The recurring question in this debate is: what does a citation measure? Is it impact, influence, quality, a combination, or none of these?

A researcher undertaking citation analysis makes a number of assumptions, the most important being: (a) a relationship of some kind exists between a cited and citing work; (b) all cited documents have been read; (c) citations are made to the most relevant work; and (d) all citations are equal.

In reality, these assumptions are flawed. Research has found that not all citations are equal and citations might be given for less than honourable reasons. These include: diplomatic citing of a colleague or non-citing of a competitor; adding citations to make a paper look more scholarly; self-citing to increase citation numbers; citing to avoid taking responsibility for an argument; and incorrect citations, either accidental or as a result of using an existing incorrectly recorded citation (Cronin, 1984; Kaplan, 1965; Smith, 1981).

Conclusion

Bibliometric research ranges from relatively simple descriptions of a body of literature to highly sophisticated modelling of social networks. The subjects of bibliometric research can be discrete groups of items or samples comprising thousands of records, across all disciplinary fields. By applying the quantitative measures of bibliometric research, problems relating to participation and response rates do not arise. Nevertheless, bibliometric approaches raise concerns regarding conclusions about phenomena that cannot always be explained by a number. As well as establishing a sound understanding of the tools and measures used in bibliometric research, researchers need to acknowledge the field's limitations and familiarise themselves with the debate that surrounds the use of bibliometric measures

Recently, bibliometrics has gained a much wider audience in the higher education sector as governments apply bibliometric indicators to the assessment of research performance. A good grounding in bibliometric research will significantly benefit practitioners and researchers in this sector. It will enable them to judge the meaning and implications of chosen measures and to undertake bibliometric research that challenges and tests these measures.

References

Abramo, G., D'Angelo, C. A., Di Costa, F., & Solazzi, M. (2009). University-industry collaboration in Italy: A bibliometric examination. *Technovation, 29*(6−7), 498−507.

Ahlgren, P., & Waltman, L. (2014). The correlation between citation-based and expert-based assessments of publication channels: SNIP and SJR vs. Norwegian quality assessments. *Journal of Informetrics, 8*(4), 985−996.

Altmann, K. G., & Gorman, G. E. (1998). The usefulness of impact factor in serial selection: A rank and mean analysis using ecology journals. *Library Acquisitions: Practice and Theory, 22*(2), 147−159.

Andres, A. (2009). *Measuring academic research: How to undertake a bibliometric study.* Oxford: Chandos.

Bar-Ilan, J. (2008a). Informetrics at the beginning of the 21st century: A review. *Journal of Informetrics, 2*(1), 1–52.

Bar-Ilan, J. (2008b). Which h-index? A comparison of WoS, Scopus and Google Scholar. *Scientometrics, 74*(2), 257–271.

Batterham, R. J. (2011). A ten year citation analysis of major Australian research institutions. *Australian Universities' Review, 53*(1), 35–41.

Becker, D. A., & Chiware, E. R. T. (2015). Citation analysis of Masters' theses and Doctoral dissertations: Balancing library collections with students' research information needs. *Journal of Academic Librarianship, 41*(5), 613–620.

Cameron, B. D. (2005). Trends in the usage of ISI bibliometric data: Uses, abuses, and implications. *Portal-Libraries and the Academy, 5*(1), 105–125.

Clark, K. W. (2016). Reference Services Review: Content analysis, 2012–2014. *Reference Services Review, 44*(1), 61–75.

Cole, J. R. (2000). A short history of the use of citations as a measure of the impact of scientific and scholarly work. In B. Cronin, & H. Barsky Atkins (Eds.), *The web of knowledge: A festschrift in honor of Eugene Garfield* (pp. 281–300). Medford, NJ: Information Today.

Cronin, B. (1984). *The citation process: The role and significance of citations in scientific communication.* London: Taylor Graham.

Cronin, B. (2014). Scholars and scripts, spoors and scores. In B. Cronin, & C. R. Sugimoto (Eds.), *Beyond bibliometrics: Harnessing multidimensional indicators of scholarly impact* (pp. 1–21). Cambridge, MA: The MIT Press.

Cronin, B., & Barsky Atkins, H. (2000). The scholar's spoor. In B. Cronin, & H. Barsky Atkins (Eds.), *The web of knowledge: A festschrift in honor of Eugene Garfield* (pp. 1–7). Medford, NJ: Information Today.

De Bellis, N. (2009). *Bibliometrics and citation analysis: From the Science Citation Index to cybermetrics.* Lanham, Maryland: The Scarecrow Press.

Eigenfactor.org. (2017). Journal ranking. Retrieved from http://www.eigenfactor.org/projects/journalRank/

Enger, K. B., Quirk, G., & Stewart, J. A. (1988). Statistical methods used by authors of library and information science journal articles. *Library & Information Science Research, 11*, 37–46.

Falagas, M. E., Kouranos, V. D., Arencibia-Jorge, R., & Karageorgopoulos, D. E. (2008). Comparison of SCImago journal rank indicator with journal impact factor. *Faseb Journal, 22*(8), 2623–2628.

Falagas, M. E., Pitsouni, E. I., Malietzis, G. A., & Pappas, G. (2008). Comparison of PubMed, Scopus, Web of Science, and Google Scholar: Strengths and weaknesses. *Faseb Journal, 22*(2), 338–342.

Garfield, E. (1979). *Citation indexing: Its theory and application in science, technology, and humanities.* New York: John Wiley & Sons.

Garfield, E. (1998). From citation indexes to informetrics: Is the tail now wagging the dog? *Libri, 48*(2), 67–80.

Glanzel, W., & Moed, H. F. (2002). Journal impact measures in bibliometric research. *Scientometrics, 53*(2), 171–193.

Gonzalez-Pereira, B., Guerrero-Bote, V. P., & Moya-Anegon, F. (2009). The SJR indicator: A new indicator of journals' scientific prestige. Retrieved from https://arxiv.org/abs/0912.4141

Harter, S. P. (1996). The impact of electronic journals on scholarly communication: A citation analysis. *The Public-Access Computer Systems Review, 7*(5), 5–34. Retrieved from http://journals.tdl.org/pacsr/article/viewFile/6007/5636

Harzing, A. W. (2016). Publish or perish. Retrieved from http://www.harzing.com/resources/publish-or-perish

Hirsch, J. E. (2005). An index to quantify an individual's scientific research output. *Proceedings of the National Academy of Sciences, 102,* 16569–16572.

Hoekman, J., Frenken, K., & Tijssen, R. J. W. (2010). Research collaboration at a distance: Changing spatial patterns of scientific collaboration in Europe. *Research Policy, 39,* 662–673.

Jacso, P. (2008). The pros and cons of computing the h-index using Google Scholar. *Online Information Review, 32*(3), 437–452.

Jacso, P. (2010). Comparison of journal impact rankings in the SCImago Journal & Country Rank and the Journal Citation Reports databases. *Online Information Review, 34*(4), 642–657.

Järvelin, K., & Persson, O. (2008). The DCI index: Discounted cumulated impact-based research evaluation. *Journal of the American Society for Information Science and Technology, 59*(9), 1433–1440.

Kaplan, N. (1965). The norms of citation behavior: Prolegomena to the footnote. *American Documentation, 16*(3), 179–184.

Kousha, K., & Thelwall, M. (2009). Google book search: Citation analysis for social science and humanities. *Journal of the American Society for Information Science and Technology, 60*(8), 1537–1549.

Lawrence, P. A. (2008). Lost in publication: How measurement harms science. *Ethics in Science and Environmental Politics, 8*(1), 9–11.

Leydesdorff, L. (2008). Caveats for the use of citation indicators in research and journal evaluations. *Journal of the American Society for Information Science and Technology, 59*(2), 278–287.

Leydesdorff, L. (2009). How are new citation-based journal indicators adding to the bibliometric toolbox? *Journal of the American Society for Information Science and Technology, 60*(7), 1327–1336.

Mathiesen, S. G., Perry, R., Sellers, S. L., & Smith, T. (2004). Evaluation of social work journal quality: Citation versus reputation approaches. *Journal of Social Work Education, 40*(1), 143–160.

Moed, H. F. (2002). The impact factor debate: The ISI's uses and limits. *Nature, 415* (6873), 731–732.

Moed, H. F. (2005). *Citation analysis in research evaluation.* Dordrecht, The Netherlands: Springer.

Moed, H. F. (2010). Measuring contextual citation impact of scientific journals. *Journal of Informetrics, 4*(3), 265–277.

Monastersky, R. (2005). The number that's devouring science. *The Chronicle of Higher Education, 52*(8), A12.

Mongeon, P., & Paul-Hus, A. (2016). The journal coverage of Web of Science and Scopus: A comparative analysis. *Scientometrics, 106*(1), 213–228.

Mularski, C. A. (1991). Institutional affiliations of authors of research articles in library and information science: Update. *Journal of Education for Library and Information Science, 31*(3), 179–186.

Narin, F., & Carpenter, M. P. (1975). National publication and citation comparisons. *Journal of the American Society for Information Science, 26*(2), 80–93.

Nicholas, D., & Ritchie, M. (1978). *Literature and bibliometrics.* London: Clive Bingley.

Nisonger, T. E. (2000). Use of the Journal Citation Reports for serials management in research libraries: An investigation of the effect of self-citation on journal rankings in library and information science and genetics. *College & Research Libraries, 61*(3), 263–275.

Nixon, J. M. (2014). Core journals in library and information science: Developing a methodology for ranking LIS journals. *College & Research Libraries, 75*(1), 66–90.

Norris, M., & Oppenheim, C. (2007). Comparing alternatives to the Web of Science for coverage of the social sciences' literature. *Journal of Informetrics, 1*(2), 161–169.

Norris, M., & Oppenheim, C. (2010). Peer review and the h-index: Two studies. *Journal of Informetrics, 4*(3), 221–232.

Oppenheim, C. (2007). Using the h-index to rank influential British researchers in information science and librarianship. *Journal of the American Society for Information Science and Technology, 58*(2), 297–301.

Oppenheim, C., & Summers, M. A. C. (2008). Citation counts and the Research Assessment Exercise, part IV: Unit of assessment 67 (music). *Information Research: An International Electronic Journal, 13*(2). Retrieved from http://informationr.net/ir/13-2/paper342.html

Ossenblok, T. L. B., Verleysen, F. T., & Engels, T. C. E. (2014). Co-authorship of journal articles and book chapters in the social sciences and humanities (2000–2010). *Journal of the Association for Information Science and Technology, 65*(5), 882–897.

Park, T. K. (2008). Asian and Pacific region authorship characteristics in leading library and information science journals. *Serials Review, 34*(4), 243–251.

Peritz, B. C. (1980). The methods of library science research: Some results from a bibliometric study. *Library Research, 2,* 251–268.

Peritz, B. C. (1981). Citation characteristics in library science: Some further results from a bibliometric survey. *Library Research, 3*, 47–65.

Price, D. J. de Solla (1965). Networks of scientific papers. *Science, 149*(3683), 510–515.

Price, D. J. de Solla (1970). Citation measures of hard science, soft science, technology, and nonscience. In C. E. Nelson, & D. K. Pollock (Eds.), *Communication among scientists and engineers* (pp. 3–22). Lexington, MA: Heath Lexington Books.

Priem, J. (2014). Altmetrics. In B. Cronin, & C. R. Sugimoto (Eds.), *Beyond bibliometrics: Harnessing multidimensional indicators of scholarly impact* (pp. 263–287). Cambridge, MA: The MIT Press.

Prins, A. A. M., Costas, R., van Leeuwen, T. N., & Wouters, P. F. (2016). Using Google Scholar in research evaluation of humanities and social science programs: A comparison with Web of Science data. *Research Evaluation, 25*(3), 264–270.

Schloegl, C., & Stock, W. G. (2004). Impact and relevance of LIS journals: A scientometric analysis of international and German-language LIS journals: Citation analysis versus reader survey. *Journal of the American Society for Information Science and Technology, 55*(13), 1155–1168.

Shema, H., Bar-Ilan, J., & Thelwall, M. (2015). How is research blogged? A content analysis approach. *Journal of the Association for Information Science and Technology, 66*(6), 1136–1149.

Smith, D. R. (2008). Citation analysis and impact factor trends of 5 core journals in occupational medicine, 1985–2006. *Archives of Environmental & Occupational Health, 63*(3), 114–122.

Smith, L. C. (1981). Citation analyses. *Library Trends, 30*, 83–106.

Steele, C., Butler, L., & Kingsley, D. (2006). The publishing imperative: The pervasive influence of publication metrics. *Learned Publishing, 19*(4), 277–290.

Tuomaala, O., Järvelin, K., & Vakkari, P. (2014). Evolution of library and information science 1965-2005: Content analysis of journal articles. *Journal of the Association for Information Science and Technology, 65*(7), 1446–1462.

Vanclay, J. K. (2008). Ranking forestry journals using the h-index. *Journal of Informetrics, 2*(4), 326–334.

Vaughan, L., & Shaw, D. (2008). A new look at evidence of scholarly citation in citation indexes and from web sources. *Scientometrics, 74*(2), 317–330.

Via, B. J., & Schmidle, D. J. (2007). Investing wisely: Citation rankings as a measure of quality in library and information science journals. *Portal: Libraries and the Academy, 7*(3), 333–373.

Waltman, L., van Eck, N. J., van Leeuwen, T., & Visser, M. S. (2013). Some modifications to the SNIP journal imp act indicator. *Journal of Informetrics, 7*(2), 272–285.

West, J. D., Bergstrom, T. C., & Bergstrom, C. T. (2010). The Eigenfactor Metrics (TM): A network approach to assessing scholarly journals. *College & Research Libraries, 71*(3), 236–244.

Wilson, C. S. (1999). Informetrics. *Annual Review of Information Science and Technology, 34*, 107–247.

Chapter 11

Design-science research

Ron Weber

Monash University and University of Queensland, Australia

This chapter explains the nature of design-science research and indicates the contexts in which it is likely to be an appropriate research method to use. It also examines various approaches to design-science research that have been proposed in prior literature, points out their similarities and differences, and evaluates their strengths and weaknesses. Finally, it articulates an alternative approach to design-science research (which nonetheless is based on earlier approaches) that is aimed at (a) helping researchers undertake higher-quality design-science research, and (b) better evaluating the strengths and weaknesses of design-science research that has been done already.

Research Methods: Information, Systems, and Contexts. DOI: http://dx.doi.org/10.1016/B978-0-08-102220-7.00011-X

Introduction

Historically, two types of research have been undertaken within the information systems discipline. The first type reflects a classical scientific tradition (Figure 11.1(a)). Researchers focus on building and testing theories, or they seek to obtain a deep understanding of the phenomena that are their focus using various kinds of generalisations and abstractions that they create (such as frameworks or models). For instance, they might develop a theory (either through deduction or induction) to account for why some individuals in an organisation resist the implementation of an information system even though *prima facie* it appears beneficial for them (e.g., Markus, 1983). They then might test their theory using a case study research method, a survey research method, or an experimental research method.

The second type of research reflects an engineering research tradition (Figure 11.1(b)). Researchers focus on building some kind of artefact they believe will be useful to a particular stakeholder community. They then evaluate the merits of the artefact in various ways. For instance, they might build software that has features that they believe will facilitate group decision-making. They might then evaluate this software using an experiment to determine the extent to which it improves the effectiveness and efficiency of the decision makers who use it. This latter type of research has come to be called 'design-science research' (March & Smith, 1995).

This chapter focuses on developing a deeper understanding of this second type of research — namely, design-science research. We will explore its nature, the ways it might be conducted rigorously, and its strengths and weaknesses. As you study the chapter, you will see the design-science research paradigm is still evolving. A number of outstanding issues that bear on the conduct of high-quality design-science research remain unresolved. Nonetheless, after studying the chapter, hopefully you will be better placed to undertake and evaluate design-science research.

Figure 11.1 Types of research

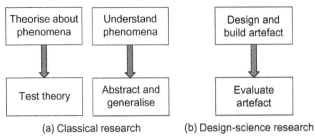

(a) Classical research   (b) Design-science research

Goals of design-science research

Researchers who undertake design-science research have the goal of producing artefacts (human-made objects) that are useful. There is some disagreement within the literature, however, about the nature of the artefacts that are the products of design-science research. Moreover, researchers who undertake classical research also have the goal of producing an artefact – specifically, a theory, model, abstraction, or generalisation that assists them to understand the real world. In this light, the boundaries between classical research and design-science research are unclear.

An early, seminal paper on design-science research is Hevner, March, Park, and Ram (2004). The authors argue the artefacts produced by design-science research can take four forms (Hevner *et al.*, 2004, p. 77):

- *Constructs*: A construct is a conceptual object that researchers create as a means of describing and representing some type of phenomena in the world, such as classes of things (e.g., businesses), subclasses of things (e.g., small businesses), components of things (e.g., employees of a business), properties of things (e.g., the level of profitability of businesses), states of things (e.g., a business is either liquid or bankrupt), events that occur to things (e.g., a business makes a sale), and processes that things undergo (e.g., a business receives, fills, and despatches an order). For instance, Barney (1991) proposed the construct of a strategic resource, which is a resource (thing) that is rare, valuable, and difficult to imitate or substitute. This construct has motivated and underpinned much research about the kinds of information systems that enable organisations to have a sustainable, competitive advantage in a marketplace (Wade & Hulland, 2004).

- *Models*: A model is a conceptual object that comprises constructs and associations among these constructs as a way to describe and represent some subset of real-world phenomena. Depending on the nature of the constructs linked by an association, the association can have different types of meanings. For instance, database researchers sometimes model a database system as a three-level architecture comprising (a) an internal schema, which describes the physical storage structure of a database, (b) a conceptual schema, which provides a user-oriented (logical) view of an entire database, and (c) an external schema, which describes only that part of a database that interests a particular user (or group of users) (Elmasri & Navathe, 2016, pp. 36–37) This model shows major components of a database system. It also shows that the properties of each component depend on the properties of the other components. By representing database systems using this three-level architecture, database researchers have been able to set useful boundaries on the problems that are the focus of their work. For instance, some researchers focus on how to build better conceptual schemas (e.g., Parsons & Wand, 2008), while others focus on how to better map a conceptual schema to an internal schema (e.g., Flynn & Laender, 1985).

- *Methods*: A method is a set of actions (the actions are often ordered) that is used to achieve some outcome (a product or service). For instance, the 'prototyping' system development method was developed as a means of building effective information systems (a *product*) in environments where users have substantial uncertainty about their information requirements (Naumann & Jenkins, 1982). This method subsequently proved useful with the development of other types of systems, such as business intelligence systems (e.g., Arnott, 2006). A method might also be used to achieve a *service* outcome, such as the identification of an information systems strategy for an organisation (e.g., Ives & Learmonth, 1984).

- *Instantiations*: An instantiation is a hardware/software system that researchers produce using some method to implement a construct or model. For instance, in the early days of group decision support systems, researchers at the University of Arizona and University of Minnesota constructed hardware/software instantiations of group support systems that they designed (Dennis, George, Jessup, Nunamaker, & Vogel, 1988; Gallupe, DeSanctis, & Dickson, 1988). These instantiations allowed them to investigate how feasible it was to build these systems and to assess their strengths and limitations.

A subsequent, seminal paper on design-science research by Gregor and Jones (2007) takes a somewhat different stance on the product of design-science research. These authors argue (p. 322) that the product of design-science research is a *design-science theory*. This theory "can apply to either a generalized product architecture or to a generalized method". Such a theory "shows the principles inherent in the design of an IS artefact that accomplishes some end, based on knowledge of both IT and human behaviour" (p. 322).

In other words, for Gregor and Jones (2007), the artefact of interest to design-science researchers is some type of *generic* hardware/software system or some type of *generic* method for building a hardware/software system. The generic system or generic method is a precursor to building a theory to account for the system's or method's structure, behaviour, and effects on its environment. In short, design-science research produces a two-piece 'bundle' that comprises (a) a generic system architecture and/or a generic method, and (b) a theory that applies to the system and/or method. Unlike Hevner *et al.* (2004), therefore, Gregor and

Jones (2007) do *not* see *constructs* and *models* as potentially being the artefactual products of design-science research. Instead, they are components of a design-science theory. (See also Gregor, 2006.)

In a similar vein, Kuechler and Vaishnavi (2012) argue that design-science research should produce a theory. They believe two types are needed. The first is a directive-prescriptive design-science theory (as per Gregor and Jones). The second is an explanatory-predictive theory that accounts for the artefact's effects on its environment. This latter theory mirrors the traditional type of theory found in the natural and behavioural sciences. Its constructs, associations, and boundaries often are derived from higher-level 'kernel' theories. For instance, a design-science researcher might use a kernel theory of judgment and decision making proposed in the behavioural sciences to explain and predict why certain features of a decision support system will lead to less biased decision making (Kuechler & Vaishnavi, 2012, pp. 411–414).

Undertaking high-quality design-science research

As the nature of design-science research has become better understood, a significant concern has been to articulate ways in which design-science research can be undertaken so it is deemed *rigorous* (e.g., Walls, Widmeyer, & El Sawy, 1992). A related concern has been to formulate criteria that might be used to assess the *quality* of work done under the rubric of design-science research (Peffers, Tuunanen, Rothenberger, & Chatterjee, 2007).

The subsections below discuss three approaches that have been proposed to assist researchers to undertake high-quality design-science research. Each provides a somewhat different perspective on how such research should be done.

Guidelines approach

Hevner *et al.* (2004, p. 82) see design-science as "inherently a problem solving process". It involves activities that are done to produce an innovative, useful artefact. They propose seven *guidelines* "to assist researchers, reviewers, editors, and readers to understand the requirements for effective design-science research" (p. 82). They do not intend the guidelines be used in 'mandatory or rote' ways; rather, the guidelines should be employed thoughtfully and adapted to the requirements of a particular design-science research project. Nonetheless, they argue (p. 82) that "each of these guidelines should be addressed in some manner for design-science research to be complete". Table 11.1 summarises their seven guidelines.

Table 11.1 Hevner *et al.*'s (2004) guidelines for design-science research

No.	Guidelines	Explanation
1	Produce a viable artefact	Design-science research must produce a workable, practical artefact in the form of a construct, model, method, or instantiation.
2	Ensure that the artefact produced is relevant and important	The artefact produced must assist with the resolution of a problem that is deemed relevant and important to some stakeholder community.
3	Rigorously evaluate the artefact produced	The effectiveness and efficiency of the artefact must be evaluated using rigorous methods. For instance, it might be evaluated analytically using a mathematical model or empirically using a field study or experiment. The evaluation of an artefact should also include 'an element of style', which reflects 'human perception and taste'.
4	Produce an artefact that makes a research contribution	The artefact produced must make a significant contribution to knowledge via the artefact itself, or the methods used to construct the artefact, or the methods used to evaluate the artefact. For this outcome to occur, the contribution to knowledge must be novel. Moreover, it will be easier to demonstrate a contribution to knowledge if the artefact provides a solution to a previously unsolved problem, or it is uncertain whether a working artefact can even be constructed, or the artefact's ability to perform 'appropriately' is unclear.
5	Follow rigorous construction methods	The artefact must be constructed in a rigorous way. In particular, construction methods must be sufficiently well specified and formalised for other researchers to be able to replicate the way it is constructed. Appropriate levels of rigour should be chosen, however, because excessive rigour can result in the relevance of the artefact being undermined (its usefulness to stakeholders is decreased).

No.	Guidelines	Explanation
6	Show the artefact is the outcome of a search process	The artefact should reflect the outcome of a search process whereby available means (actions and resources) are used to reach a desired end under the constraint of 'laws' that apply (natural or social laws). The current state of a system (e.g., the artefact being designed) is compared against a goal state. Actions are then taken (sometimes based on heuristics) to reduce the differences between the current and the goal states. The search for actions to reduce differences is iterative until an optimal or a satisfactory solution (match between the current and goal states) is found. To achieve tractable design solutions, the search process often involves simplification and abstraction of the means, ends, and laws and decomposition of the overall problem into simpler sub-problems.
7	Clearly communicate the research process and outcome	The research process and outcome must be communicated clearly to stakeholders (both researchers and practitioners). Sufficient detail must be provided to enable (a) the artefact to be constructed and used effectively, and (b) the resources needed to build and use the artefact to be determined.

Hevner *et al.*'s (2004) guidelines provide a useful, high-level perspective on the way in which high-quality design-science research should be done. The guidelines have two limitations, however.

First, the guidelines apply to other types of research beside design-science research. For instance, suppose researchers develop a theory and test it via an experiment. The domain of their theory must be specified clearly (Guideline 1). They should also show why the domain, covered by the theory, is important and relevant (Guideline 2). The experiment they conduct to test their theory (Guideline 3) should be designed to mitigate threats to validity (Guideline 3). They should show why their theory and experimental results make an important, novel contribution to knowledge (Guideline 4). In light of their statistical results, they might show how they modified their theory and perhaps undertook further tests of the refined theory (Guideline 6). They must communicate their research effectively to other researchers and practitioners (Guideline 7). In short, the guidelines do not tease out the unique nature of design-science research – indeed, based on these guidelines, the distinction between design-science research and other kinds of research is unclear.

Second, while Hevner *et al.* (2004) describe the *nature* of their guidelines, the criteria that might be used to assess how well researchers conform to each guideline are not always clear. For example: What criteria should be used to assess whether the artefact is *viable*? What criteria should be used to assess whether the artefact has been *evaluated rigorously*? What criteria should be used to assess whether *rigorous construction methods* have been followed? What criteria should be used to assess whether the research process and outcomes have been *communicated effectively* to stakeholders? In the absence of clear, explicit criteria that can be used to assess how well each guideline has been followed, researchers can easily craft a narrative contending that they have done design-science research. Whether they have conducted *high-quality* design-science research, however, is another matter.

Design-theory approach

In seeking to articulate the fundamental nature of design-science research, Gregor and Jones (2007) take a somewhat different tack from Hevner *et al.* (2004). Their focus is the fundamental *components* of a design-science *theory* rather than guidelines to be followed when undertaking design-science research. In this regard, Gregor and Jones (2007) argue all high-quality design-science theories have six *mandatory* components; moreover, some have a further two (*optional*) components. These appear to be *necessary* rather than *sufficient* components of a high-quality design theory. In other words, the fact that a design-science theory possesses the components gives no guarantee the theory provides a significant contribution to knowledge. Table 11.2 below provides an overview of the components that Gregor and Jones (2007) describe.

Table 11.2 Gregor and Jones's (2007) components of a design-science theory

No.	Guidelines	Explanation
Mandatory (core) components		
1	Purpose and scope	The purpose and scope of the generic artefact must be articulated. The environment in which the artefact will be used must also be specified, because the same artefact can be used for different purposes in different environments. In essence, the purpose and scope of the artefact circumscribe the boundary of the design theory.
2	Constructs	Constructs provide representations of 'entities of interest'. These entities may correspond to phenomena in the real world (e.g., a software fault) or components of the artefact (e.g., a relational table). In some cases, constructs can be decomposed into sub-constructs. Such constructs might be part of another design theory.

No.	Guidelines	Explanation
3	Form and function	The structure and function of the components that make up a method or instantiation must be described. In essence, a blueprint that describes the artefact's overall architecture must be provided.
4	Mutability	The feasible ways in which an artefact will accommodate changing user requirements or can be modified to meet changing requirements should be articulated.
5	Testable propositions	It must be possible to state testable propositions about the artefact that can be used as a basis for evaluating whether it achieves its intended purposes. These propositions make take the general form that a product artefact, if instantiated, will work and serve its intended purposes or a method artefact, if followed properly, will lead to an outcome that achieves its intended purposes. Such general-form propositions can be made more specific by framing particular outcomes for specific types of environments in which the artefact will be used.
6	Justificatory knowledge	The reasons why an artefact takes its particular form and function and the reasons why it will achieve its intended purposes should be explained and justified. This justificatory knowledge is often based upon other theories (sometimes called 'kernel' theories). For instance, justificatory knowledge might rely on natural-science theories about the physical capabilities and limitations of hardware and software or social-science theories about the ways humans are likely to behave when they engage with the artefact in particular environments and with particular objectives in mind.
	Optional components	
7	Implementation principles	The principles to be used in implementing an instance of the artefact should be specified. For instance, alternative ways to build a product artefact might be described, or guidelines for implementing a process artefact can be provided.
8	Instantiation	An example instance of the artefact can be used to illustrate it is viable to build or possible to use and that the artefact achieves its intended purposes. An example instance can also serve as a 'representation or exposition' of the design theory (a way of making its abstract nature more concrete and understandable).

Gregor and Jones's (2007) components provide a useful basis for evaluating the quality of a design-science *theory* – a theory that has the purpose of accounting for the behaviour of some artefact. Their components provide only minimal guidance, however, in terms of the processes that researchers might use to *produce* high-quality artefacts. Moreover, their 'framework' for a design-science theory is intended to cover only 'a method' or 'a product' (Gregor & Jones, 2007, p. 320). It does not cover 'constructs' or 'models', which are the focus of many design-science researchers.

Design-science research methodology approach

Peffers *et al.* (2007) argue information systems researchers need a research methodology that produces design-science research that is deemed "valuable, rigorous, publishable" (p. 49). Accordingly, they propose a six-step, iterative process for conducting design-science research:

1. Identify, define, and motivate the focal problem.
2. Define objectives that a solution (possibly partial) to the focal problem must achieve.
3. Design and develop the artefact.
4. Demonstrate the artefact can be used to help solve the focal problem.
5. Evaluate how well the artefact solves the focal problem.
6. Communicate the outcomes of the research.

Other design-science research methodologies have been proposed (Holmström, Ketokivi, & Hameri, 2009; Iivari, 2015; Mandviwalla, 2015; Pries-Heje & Baskerville, 2008). All have some level of overlap, and all have strengths and weaknesses (e.g., they highlight or provide only a superficial account of different aspects of the design-science research process). Perhaps the best approach to choosing a methodology is to evaluate which one seems best suited to addressing the focal problem. The chosen methodology should then be executed rigorously.

An alternative approach to evaluating design-science research

One way we might evaluate the quality of design-science research is to decompose our evaluation task into two components: (a) evaluating the quality of the *process* used; and (b) evaluating the quality of the *outcomes* obtained (Figure 11.2). The motivation for framing and decomposing the evaluation task in this way is a belief that design-science researchers have a greater chance of producing high-quality research outcomes if they employ a high-quality research process.

Figure 11.2 Evaluating quality of design-science research

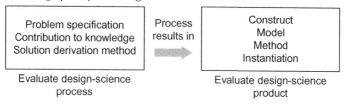

Problem specification Contribution to knowledge Solution derivation method	Process results in	Construct Model Method Instantiation
Evaluate design-science process		Evaluate design-science product

If we use this approach, however, an important *caveat* exists. Unfortunately, through experience we know that having a high-quality research *process* is neither a necessary nor sufficient condition for achieving a high-quality research *outcome*. Other factors beside the process used can affect the quality of the outcome – for instance, the design-science researcher's creativity in dealing with a particular design problem. Similarly, good design-science research outcomes can be achieved even when a poor design-science research process has been used. For instance, even with a poor process, researchers might serendipitously identify an innovative and profound solution to an important design problem. Nonetheless, often the quality of the design-science research process is likely to be a good predictor of the quality of the design-science research outcomes.

In this light, the two subsections below examine some criteria we might use to evaluate how well each task has been performed. As you study these subsections, recall that the problem addressed by design-science researchers, in the information technology (IT) domain, must somehow involve IT.

Evaluating a design-science research process

When we evaluate the *process* used to produce a design-science research outcome, we use criteria that apply to a *generic* design-science research process. We then evaluate how well a specific instance of a design-science research process conforms to the quality standards manifested in these criteria.

To understand the stance we are adopting, consider how we would evaluate the process used to conduct an experiment. We would assess the ways in which the experiment has been planned and executed to determine how well it mitigates threats to internal validity, construct validity, statistical conclusion validity, and external validity (Cook & Campbell, 1979). These types of threats to the validity of any specific experiment we design apply generically – that is, they apply to all types of experiments. We evaluate how well an instance of an experiment mitigates these threats.

In a similar vein, when we evaluate a design-science research *process*, we evaluate how well it has been planned and executed. Our approach involves *three* major steps:

- evaluate how well the design-science research problem has been specified;
- evaluate whether a solution to the design-science research problem constitutes a contribution to knowledge; and
- evaluate how a solution to the problem was obtained.

Executing each step involves our making *judgements*. No hard-and-fast rules are available; no rote process exists on which we can rely. Moreover, we might conclude the successful completion of just one of these steps constitutes a significant contribution to design-science knowledge. For instance, a rigorous, creative specification of a research problem may represent a major breakthrough in solving a longstanding, difficult design problem.

Evaluating the problem specification

As a first step in evaluating the design-science research process that design-science researchers have used, we should consider how well they have specified the problem they are seeking to resolve via their research. In this regard, three issues should be our focus.

First, we should evaluate the extent to which design-science researchers have *clearly specified* the problem that is their focus. From experience with problem solving, we know that poorly specified problems often lead to poorly specified solutions. We should look for evidence, therefore, that indicates design-science researchers have succumbed to a temptation to jump to solutions without first having a good understanding of the problem they are seeking to solve. In particular, we should be alert to design-science research that manifests a 'solution looking for a problem'.

In describing the problem, design-science researchers should discuss the following issues:

- *Who*? Who is experiencing the problem? The 'who' is a thing in the real world. It might be animate — for instance, a person or a group of people who have a particular need or some type of wildlife whose existence is under threat. It might also be inanimate — for instance, a machine or system that humans have created that is not performing properly.
- *What*? What is the nature of the problem? What is the desired end state (the 'ends') of the thing (the animate or inanimate 'who') that the design-science researcher is seeking to achieve or satisfy (e.g., easier access to information for a manager or greater output from a computer-controlled machine on a production line)?

- *Why?* Why can't the desired end state of the thing be achieved with existing means? What is the cause of the problem? Why is it difficult to proceed from a state that the thing currently experiences to the desired end state?

- *When?* When does the thing experience the problem? Is it ongoing? Or does it occur only at certain times or under certain circumstances?

- *Where?* Does the thing experience the problem in all places? Or does the problem occur only in certain locations?

- *Stakeholders?* Beside the thing that experiences the problem directly, are other things affected by the problem?

In a nutshell, the problem description should enable interested parties to understand two characteristics of the problem that is a design-science researcher's focus: (a) the *nature* of the problem, and (b) the *boundary* of the problem.

Second, we should evaluate whether design-science researchers have specified the problem they are seeking to address at an appropriate *level of abstraction or generality*. Here our concern is with whether the problem has been specified too narrowly or too broadly. If it has been specified too narrowly, it is unlikely to be deemed interesting. Moreover, any solution to a narrowly defined problem that a design-science researcher proposes is unlikely to be deemed a substantive contribution to knowledge. If the problem has been specified too broadly, however, its practical usefulness is likely to be questioned. It may be difficult to map any solution to the problem or to the actions one needs to undertake in practice to bring about a resolution to a particular instance of the problem.

Third, we should evaluate whether design-science researchers have *framed* the problem they are seeking to address in a *rich, creative way*. In particular, they should reflect carefully about whether the problem that is their focus is analogous to other types of problems that have commanded the attention of design-science researchers. If analogous problems exist, solutions to these problems might inform solutions to the particular problem that the design-science researcher is seeking to address. It is often through analogy that creative insights occur and solutions to design-science problems are discovered (e.g., Floyd, 1979).

Evaluating the likely contribution to knowledge

Design-science researchers must provide a compelling justification for why obtaining a solution for the problem they are seeking to address will provide a contribution to knowledge. In this regard, contributions to knowledge that are deemed to be 'revelatory' or 'transformative' are likely to be valued more highly than contributions to knowledge that are deemed to be 'incremental' (Corley & Gioia, 2011).

To assist design-science researchers evaluate whether their research is likely to make a contribution to knowledge, Gregor and Hevner (2013) provide a framework that has two dimensions: (a) the extent to which problems in the application domain are well known; and (b) the extent to which solutions to problems in the application domain are well known. They identify four situations a design-science researcher might encounter:

1. *Routine Design*: The researcher is applying known solutions to known problems.

2. *Improvement*: The researcher is developing novel solutions to known problems.

3. *Exaptation*: The researcher is adapting known solutions to new problems.

4. *Invention*: The researcher is developing new solutions for new problems.

Only design-science research that provides improvement, exaptation, and invention is likely to be deemed as providing a contribution to knowledge, with invention likely to be deemed the highest contribution.

Another way that design-science researchers might seek to show why their suggested solution to a problem is an important contribution to knowledge is by arguing that the solution will provide important *practical* benefits — for instance, an organisation that deploys the solution might be able to provide a service that it currently sells to its customers much more effectively and efficiently. Alternatively, they might argue that a solution to the problem will provide an important contribution to *science* — for instance, the solution provides a way of structuring a generic type of problem that is encountered often in research or practice, decomposing the problem into its component parts, and identifying potential solutions for the component problems.

Because science is a social process, the extent to which design-science researchers will be able to convince others of the importance of the problem they are addressing will to some extent depend on the quality of the *rhetoric* they use. In this regard, based on a study of journal articles published in the organisation studies field, Locke and Golden-Biddle (1997) argued that successful researchers who have their work published in high-quality journals use *two* fundamental processes to show the importance of their work. First, the researchers 'construct intertextual coherence'. They organise the existing literature in some way to enable them to show how their research fits in with this literature. Second, the researchers 'problematize the existing literature'. They 'subvert' this literature to show how their own research makes a contribution to knowledge.

We can use Locke and Golden-Biddle's (1997) model to evaluate how well design-science researchers have framed their arguments to support the contribution to knowledge their research is intended to make. Did they show how the problem they were addressing was anchored in prior literature (either scientific or practitioner literature)? Did they show how this literature was problematic either in its conceptualisation of the problem or the solutions that had been proposed?

Evaluating how the solution was derived

Deriving a solution to a design-science research problem involves exercising creativity, knowledge, and insight. It often requires multiple iterations of a trial-and-error search process. Nonetheless, when evaluating how design-science researchers obtained a solution to the problem that was their focus, we should consider *four* issues associated with the possible state space and the transition paths that exist between the initial state and the end (goal) state (Figure 11.3).

First, we should evaluate the extent to which the desired *end state* (goal state) was articulated formally (and thus clearly and precisely). The end state is associated with something in the world (for some problems, multiple end states of a thing may constitute acceptable solutions or the solution to the problem may involve end states of multiple things). To specify the end state, the relevant attributes of the thing must be identified. Values that these attributes must assume in the end state then must be described (the end state is represented by the vector of values for these attributes). In essence, the end state gives important criteria that can be used to judge whether the design-science research outcome can be deemed successful.

Second, we should evaluate the extent to which the *initial state* was articulated formally. The initial state of the focal thing must be transformed to the end state via a set of intermediate states. In some cases, a *set* of initial states of the thing may have to be considered. In some cases, also, the initial states of multiple things may bear on the solution to the problem (the solution may involve end states of multiple things, or the states of several things may affect which states are traversed by the thing or things that somehow must be transformed to an end state).

Figure 11.3 Evaluation of solution derivation

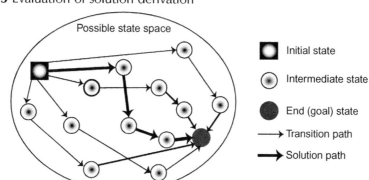

Third, we should evaluate the extent to which possible *transition paths* between the initial state and the desired end state (sequences of intermediate states) were well specified. Some questions we might address are the following:

- Is the set of possible transition paths between the initial state and end state that were specified by the design-science researcher complete?

- If the number of possible transition paths between the initial state and end state was too large to specify, what transition paths were chosen for consideration, and how were they chosen?

- Have the resources needed to traverse particular transition paths been specified accurately and completely?

- Have any critical constraints on transition paths that need to be considered by the design-science researcher been articulated clearly.

Fourth, we should evaluate how design-science researchers chose the transition path they eventually deemed to be the *solution transition path*. In particular, we should examine the nature and appropriateness of the search process undertaken and the criteria used to choose the best (or satisfactory) transition path. In some cases, the design-science researcher might have been able to use some type of mathematical optimisation or constrained optimisation procedure. In other cases, some kind of heuristic search process might have been the only possible way to determine a satisfactory solution path. In still other cases, prior research or experience might indicate that a particular solution path (e.g., a certain type of system development method) is likely to be effective. Whatever the approach taken by the design-science researcher in choosing a solution path, it should be clear and well justified.

Evaluating design-science research outcomes

Recall that Hevner *et al.* (2004) argue a design-science research project can produce four types of outcomes: constructs, models, methods, and instantiations. What criteria might we use, therefore, to evaluate the quality of these outcomes? Note that our focus is squarely on the *outcomes* of the design-science research project and not the *process* used to produce them.

As an analogy, again consider an experiment. When we examine the process used to conduct the experiment, we might conclude that all reasonable steps have been undertaken to mitigate threats to the validity of the experiment. In other words, a high-quality *process* has been used to conduct the experiment. This does not guarantee, however, that we will conclude we have high-quality *results*. For instance, we might conclude the results provide us with no new insights into the phenomena we are studying or that the results confuse rather than illuminate our understanding of the phenomena. In short, unfortunately we have a rigorously planned and executed experiment that has produced results we deem to have little value. For this reason, both the *results* (the outcomes) and the *process* need to be considered.

Evaluating constructs

Recall that a construct is a conceptual object that researchers create as a means of describing and representing some type of phenomena in the world – for instance, classes of things, subclasses of things, components of things, properties of things, states of things, events that occur to things, and processes that things undergo. If a *construct* is the outcome of design-science research, *two* criteria might be used to evaluate its quality.

First, we can evaluate whether the construct has been defined rigorously. For instance, if the construct has been proposed as a representation of some class of things in the real world (e.g., personalised business intelligence systems), we ought to be able to determine clearly which things are covered by the construct and which things are *not*. Similarly, if the construct has been proposed as a representation of some property of things in the world (e.g., level of virtualness of a project team), we ought to be able to determine clearly what the property means and what types of things in the real world are likely to possess the property.

Second, we can evaluate whether the construct is novel, revelatory, and important. Perhaps the construct allows us to 'see' phenomena that previously we did not 'see' or clarify our perceptions of phenomena that previously were obtuse. For instance, by articulating the characteristics of strategic information systems, Ives and Learmonth (1984) helped managers 'see' which systems in their organisation's portfolio of systems could be used to provide competitive advantage in the marketplace. Moreover, managers were then better able to plan the kinds of information systems they needed to develop to assist their organisation to survive and prosper over the long run.

Evaluating models

Recall that a model is a conceptual object that comprises constructs and associations among these constructs as a way to describe and represent some subset of real-world phenomena. If a *model* is the outcome of design-science research, *four* criteria might be used to evaluate its quality.

First, we can evaluate the extent to which the *constructs* in the model have been defined rigorously. The nature and meaning of each construct must be clear such that we can easily identify those phenomena in the world that are *instances* of the construct.

Second, we can evaluate the extent to which the *associations* in the model have been defined rigorously. The associations show how the constructs in the model are related to one another. The meaning of the associations will vary depending on the meaning of the constructs. For instance, if two constructs represent properties of two different things, an association between the constructs might mean changes in the value of one property occur subsequent to changes in the value of the other property. If the two constructs represent two different processes that a thing undergoes, an association between the two constructs might mean the thing first undergoes one process and then undergoes the other process. If the two constructs represent different things, an association between them might mean one thing is a component of the other thing. Whatever the nature of the association, its meaning must be clear. Moreover, arguments in support of its existence and importance (or materiality) must be compelling.

Third, we can evaluate whether the *boundaries* of the model are clear. We must be able to determine what phenomena the model covers and what phenomena the model does *not* cover. For instance, Sambamurthy, Bharadwaj, and Grover (2003) provide a model that they argued (p. 238) shows how:

> information technology investments and capabilities influence firm performance through a nomological network of three significant organizational capabilities (agility, digital options, and entrepreneurial alertness) and strategic processes (capability-building, entrepreneurial action, and coevolutionary adaptation).

They pointed out (p. 241), however, that their model applies only to "firms operating in moderate to rapidly changing business environments, such as the high-tech, retailing, and business-services sectors". In short, they did not believe their model provided a good account of how IT investments and capabilities influence firm performance in *stable* business environments. In such environments, another model is needed (or their model will have to be modified in some way).

Fourth, we can evaluate whether the model is *novel, revelatory,* and *important.* As with constructs, the model may allow us to 'see' phenomena that previously we had not 'seen' or to obtain a deeper understanding of phenomena that previously we had understood only partially or superficially. Sometimes, design-science researchers also will have been able to use the model that they have formulated to generate mathematical outcomes or to undertake simulations. The analyses undertaken or simulation results obtained can be evaluated to determine the extent to which they provide important insights and significant contributions to knowledge about the phenomena the model is intended to represent.

Evaluating methods

There are *three* approaches we might use to evaluate any *methods* produced as the outcome of design-science research. First, we can assess whether the method is *novel, interesting,* and *important.* By using the method, it must be possible to provide a service or make a product that some group of stakeholders deem important. Moreover, the method must not be a replication of or a minor enhancement of an existing method. It must add substantively to knowledge about how to provide some service or make some product.

Second, in some cases, design-science researchers might have provided a *theory* or *model* (or at least the rudiments of a theory or model) as a justification for why they believe use of their method will lead to high-quality outcomes. For instance, they might have sketched out a theory that associates certain characteristics of their method with certain characteristics of the service their method will provide or certain characteristics of the product their service will bring into existence (Figure 11.4). If such a theory or model is provided (or we have sufficient information to construct such a theory or model ourselves), we can evaluate the quality of the theory or model (e.g., see Weber, 2012). For instance, we can evaluate how rigorously its constructs have been defined, whether its associations are clear and well justified, and whether ways of falsifying the theory or testing the robustness of the model are apparent.

Figure 11.4 Theory accounts for method characteristics and service or product characteristics

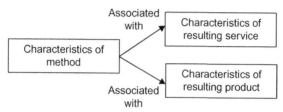

Third, we can use the method for its *intended purpose* and evaluate the outcome. For instance, if the method has been developed to provide a service, we can execute the method and conduct an evaluation of the service provided. Similarly, if the method has been developed to make a product, we can execute the method and conduct an evaluation of the resulting product. In essence, we *instantiate* the method and appraise the instantiation (see the subsection below).

Evaluating instantiations

Recall that design-science researchers may provide an *instantiation* of a method they have devised or product they have designed. Our approach to evaluating instantiations will depend on whether (a) we are dealing with *method* instantiations or *product* instantiations, and (b) design-science researchers themselves have undertaken some type of evaluation of their instantiation.

If we are evaluating an instantiation of a *method*, we should first check to see whether the design-science researcher has provided a *theory* to account for why their method achieves some type of desired outcome (an improved IT-based service or high-quality IT-based product). The researcher should provide a rationale that relates characteristics of their method to characteristics of the desired outcome. Weber (2012) provides a framework that can then be used to evaluate the quality of any theory that design-science researchers have proposed. For instance, the theory should have rigorously defined constructs, provide compelling arguments to support any hypothesised associations among its constructs, and articulate clearly the states and events that it covers.

Next, we should evaluate the instantiation to determine whether it provides *evidence* in support of the merits of the method. To the extent a design-science researcher has provided high-quality theories to account for why their method will lead to a desired outcome, we are better placed to pinpoint those characteristics of the method and the resulting outcome that we should scrutinise.

In some cases, design-science researchers themselves might have undertaken some type of formal evaluation of the method they have developed. For instance, they might have done an experiment or engaged in action research to evaluate their method. In such cases, we can use published criteria to assess how well the research approach used to evaluate the method has been designed and executed (e.g., criteria for the conduct of high-quality experiments, such as those given by Cook & Campbell (1979), or criteria for the conduct of high-quality action research, such as those given by Davison, Martinsons, & Kock (2004)).

If we are evaluating an instantiation of a *product*, we should follow the same three steps. First, we should assess the quality of any *theory* proposed by the design-science researcher to account for why their product will possess desirable characteristics or lead to desirable outcomes. Second, we should assess the *instantiation* to determine whether it possesses these characteristics or has led to these outcomes. Third, to the extent design-science researchers have themselves undertaken a formal evaluation of their product, we can assess the *design and execution* of their research method against published criteria.

When evaluating a *product* instantiation, one matter we should consider is whether we are assessing the product as a *closed system* or an *open system* (or both). For instance, a design-science researcher might have developed a computational model to study the outcomes of different evolutionary patterns in an artificial life form (Watson, Mills, & Buckley, 2011). The computational model is a *closed* system. It does not interact with its environment; rather, the phenomena of interest are changes in certain characteristics of the artificial life form under different patterns of evolution. In the evaluation of a closed-system instantiation, our focus is squarely on the artefact.

Alternatively, design-science researchers might have developed software that they claim is new and innovative and that purportedly improves the effectiveness and efficiency of its users. Here we are dealing with an *open* system. We must assess the impact of the software on its users as they interact with the software over time. Unlike the evaluation of a closed-system instantiation, therefore, we must take into account both the behaviour of the artefact and the behaviour of the artefact's environment (which include the software's users) as patterns of interaction between the two unfold.

Conclusion

This chapter has studied the research method that has come to be called design science. Unlike traditional research that focusses on building and testing theory or providing interpretations of real-world phenomena, design-science research focusses on building and evaluating useful artefacts. While some debate exists within the design-science literature about the types of artefact that might be produced via design-science research, many scholars argue they include constructs, models, methods, and instantiations.

An examination of criteria by which the quality of design-science research might be evaluated has been central to the chapter. Specifically considered have been some early seminal works on how design-science research should be done. Because of the limitations of these works, a framework has been used to organise quality-evaluation criteria around the design-science *process* and the design-science *product*. As greater experience with and knowledge about the design-science research process continues to be acquired, our understanding of the criteria we should use to evaluate design-science research will be enhanced.

References

Arnott, D. (2006). Cognitive biases and decision support systems development: A design science approach. *Information Systems Journal, 16*(1), 55–78.

Barney, J. (1991). Firm resources and sustained competitive advantage. *Journal of Management, 17*(1), 99–120.

Cook, T. D., & Campbell, D. T. (1979). *Quasi-experimentation: Design & analysis issues for field settings.* Chicago: Rand McNally College Publishing Company.

Corley, K. G., & Gioia, D. A. (2011). Building theory about theory: What constitutes a theoretical contribution. *Academy of Management Review, 36*(1), 12–32.

Davison, R. M., Martinsons, M. G., & Kock, N. (2004). Principles of canonical action research. *Information Systems Journal, 14*(1), 65–86.

Dennis, A. R., George, J. F., Jessup, L. M., Nunamaker, J. F., Jr., & Vogel, D. R. (1988). Information technology to support electronic meetings. *MIS Quarterly, 12*(4), 591–624.

Elmasri, R., & Navathe, S. B. (2016). *Fundamentals of database systems* (7th ed.). Boston: Pearson.

Floyd, R. W. (1979). The paradigms of programming. *Communications of the ACM, 22*(8), 455–460.

Flynn, D. J., & Laender, A. H. F. (1985). Mapping from a conceptual schema to a target internal schema. *The Computer Journal, 28*(5), 508–517.

Gallupe, R. B., DeSanctis, G., & Dickson, G. W. (1988). Computer-based support for group problem-finding: An experimental investigation. *MIS Quarterly, 12*(2), 277–296.

Gregor, S. (2006). The nature of theory in information systems. *MIS Quarterly, 30*(3), 611–642.

Gregor, S., & Hevner, A. R. (2013). Positioning and presenting design science research for maximum impact. *MIS Quarterly, 37*(2), 337–355.

Gregor, S., & Jones, D. (2007). The anatomy of a design theory. *Journal of the Association for Information Systems, 8*(5), 312–335.

Hevner, A. R., March, S. T., Park, J., & Ram, S. (2004). Design science in information systems research. *MIS Quarterly, 28*(1), 75–105.

Holmström, J., Ketokivi, M., & Hameri, A.-P. (2009). Bridging practice and theory: A design science approach. *Decision Sciences, 40*(1), 65–87.

Iivari, J. (2015). Distinguishing and contrasting two strategies for design science research. *European Journal of Information Systems, 24*(1), 107–115.

Ives, B., & Learmonth, G. P. (1984). The information system as a competitive weapon. *Communications of the ACM, 27*(12), 1193–1201.

Kuechler, W., & Vaishnavi, V. (2012). A framework for theory development in design science research: Multiple perspectives. *Journal of the Association for Information Systems, 13*(6), 395–423.

Locke, K., & Golden-Biddle, K. (1997). Constructing opportunities for contribution: Structuring intertextual coherence and "problematizing" in organization studies. *Academy of Management Journal, 40*(5), 1023–1062.

Mandviwalla, M. (2015). Generating and justifying design theory. *Journal of the Association for Information Systems, 16*(5), 314–344.

March, S., & Smith, G. F. (1995). Design and natural science research on information technology. *Decision Support Systems, 15*(4), 251–266.

Markus, M. L. (1983). Power, politics, and MIS implementation. *Communications of the ACM, 26*(6), 430–444.

Naumann, J. D., & Jenkins, A. M. (1982). Prototyping: The new paradigm for systems development. *MIS Quarterly, 6*(3), 29–44.

Parsons, J., & Wand, Y. (2008). Using cognitive principles to guide classification in information systems modeling. *MIS Quarterly, 32*(4), 839–868.

Peffers, K., Tuunanen, T., Rothenberger, M. A., & Chatterjee, S. (2007). A design science research methodology for information systems research. *Journal of Management Information Systems, 24*(3), 45–77.

Pries-Heje, J., & Baskerville, R. (2008). The design theory nexus. *MIS Quarterly, 32*(4), 731–755.

Sambamurthy, V., Bharadwaj, A., & Grover, V. (2003). Shaping agility through digital options: Reconceptualizing the role of information technology in contemporary firms. *MIS Quarterly, 27*(2), 237–263.

Wade, M., & Hulland, J. (2004). Review: The resource-based view and information systems research: Review, extension, and suggestions for future research. *MIS Quarterly, 28*(1), 107–142.

Walls, J. G., Widmeyer, G. R., & El Sawy, O. A. (1992). Building an information system design theory for vigilant EIS. *Information Systems Research, 3*(1), 36–59.

Watson, R. A., Mills, R., & Buckley, C. L. (2011). Global adaptation in networks of selfish components: Emergent associative memory at the system scale. *Artificial Life, 17*(3), 147–166.

Weber, R. (2012). Evaluating and developing theories in the information systems discipline. *Journal of the Association for Information Systems, 13*(1), 323–346.

Chapter 12

Researching history

Graeme Johanson
Monash University, Australia

Researchers tend to focus excessively on the future and neglect the relevance of the past. Yet the study of history provides deep understanding of individuals, societies, organisations, and global structures in the hope of enlightening and improving the present. At its best, history is an entertaining and informative reconstruction of probable causes of habits, trends and events, and it explores human motives, experiences, behaviours, fears and hopes. The fundamental resource of the historian is evidence from the past. Evidence can be difficult to analyse for comprehensive meaning, but five evaluative techniques are recommended to help to manage the task: detection, scepticism, attribution and disentanglement, verification and clarification, storytelling and explanation. Many examples are given to show how the techniques are deployed by historians.

Research Methods: Information, Systems, and Contexts. DOI: http://dx.doi.org/10.1016/B978-0-08-102220-7.00012-1

Introduction

This chapter brings together three main themes. It analyses what history is today, and what it feeds on (evidence in the past). Historians are scouring bottom feeders, but they also thrive at the top of the evidentiary food chain; they can adopt a worm's-eye and eagle's-eye view equally. Evidence provides elementary sustenance and refined delicacies for the historian's hunger for truth, but at the same time it is imbued with unavoidable surprises, and the interpretation of some obscure evidence demands specialist knowledge. As a second theme, the chapter cites many examples of histories that showcase historical skills in the fields of information research, in narrow and broad guises, sometimes requiring interdisciplinarity, and there are numerous references to inspire further research. Examples of written histories proffer deep understanding of people, organisations, and experiences in the past, they present aesthetic narratives, and they put forward wisdom for potential future practice. This chapter embraces digital developments, outlining both their strengths and traps for historians. Finally, the chapter shows how historians 'do' research by describing and illustrating the use of five key intellectual techniques. If the suggested toolkit is used well, it will lead to history that is much more than introverted nostalgia or popular storytelling. History provides strengths of broad social benefit; it is important for calibrating our future orientations; and it encourages attitudes of mental acuity, critical self-awareness, and well-articulated restraint on irrational actions. Some of these themes have been explored before (Johanson, 2002).

The future is not what it used to be

The title of this section of the chapter highlights a tendency for much research to rush towards the new and the innovative, with little thought devoted to reflection on the past. The roles of memory and intent in historical research are explored here, because history would not exist without them.

History deals with the past, whereas much research into computer and information systems focuses on a compelling future – on technological change, global efficiencies, new applications, breakthrough inventions, even computopias (Masuda, 1980). One historian speculated that the

> relentless fixation with the future may have something to do with the inherent 'forwardness' of computers, powered as they are by logics of linear progression and lateral sequencing. The computer creates a teleology of forward progress (Wright, 2007, p. 3).

Yet, as *Google Scholar* acknowledges in its logo, today we 'stand on the shoulders of giants'. The saying itself – used for centuries by scholars to pay tribute to prior thinkers – originated in Europe before the twelfth century (Merton, 1993). The inexorable progression of time requires that history deals with what was – with our past (McGarry, 1988).

For better or worse, we create history as well as being shaped by it (Giddens, 1984). Some historians depict human actors as mere conduits for passing on valuable factual information (Vreeken, 2005); others see them as inextricably involved in the actual shaping of events, and reacting to them in imaginative ways (Capurro & Hjørland, 2003). Whichever view is adopted, humans are both the actors and purveyors of history. Whether (from a philosophical perspective) humans act freely and independently, or simply in reaction to relentless external influences on them, or a mixture of both, they are all enmeshed in history, and it is normal for them to show a keen interest in having some control over it (White, 1995). By extension, some historians view the future as more or less predetermined. Thus a philosophical approach known as 'Whig history' perceives in events an inevitable development towards human liberty and enlightenment, working towards a liberal democracy and a liberal economy (Fukuyama, 1992). A Marxist historian tends to identify historical stages which inevitably lead towards classlessness and egalitarianism (Parker, 2000). Many other panoptic world views are debated by historians. Typically they are self-critical.

For most purposes in the study of history, it has to be assumed that humans normally act with intent. We assume that they have aims, purposes, or plans. Negligent and irrational behaviour is more difficult to evidence. Intent affects our behaviour in our daily lives all the time (Searle, 2010). The belief that humans act with intent is fundamental to the writing of history (Evans, 2002).

Our curiosity with our personal past, and our obsession with observing and understanding the lives of others, bolsters our concerns for our own history. We like to be remembered. The many common uses of the word 'memory' demonstrate our preoccupations with our proximate past. Computing has borrowed the word 'memory' to allude to actual chips capable of holding past data over time, and data storage, which may be external to a given machine. Memory in daily use means a capacity for reviving a thought of things past, acts of remembrance, processes for memorialising, and objects serving as mementos.

Memory is fundamental to thinking and acting – and thus historical research. Memory is transmitted by structured institutions, oral traditions, published records, images, the commemoration of actions and events, and historical places (Clark, 2016). Organisational memory relies on records of information or tacit knowledge of past events, which are shared and communicated within an organisational group. Its current uses are researched in their own right as 'knowledge management' (Nonaka, 1995).

Various filters control which memories survive and which memories have influence. The reverse side of the memory coin is social amnesia — important acts of collective forgetting — which the novelist Kundera reminds us of: "the struggle against power is the struggle of memory against forgetting" (Kundera, 1980, p. 3). Much research energy has been devoted to recounting the deliberate, sad destruction of cultural memory, often in the form of iconic artefacts or edifices (Bevan, 2006). The sublimation of the past affirms an inclination within authorities to destroy relevant evidence (Australia. Human Rights and Equal Opportunity Commission, 1997). In reality, memory guides our assumptions about the nature of our identity and future, about what we believe we are, about what is probable, and what we desire (Halbwachs, 1992).

What is history?

Historians are purposeful researchers who concentrate their energies on human motives, experiences, behaviours, fears and hopes more than most researchers. They hold a mental magnifying glass over individuals, societies, organisations, and global structures, and specialise in recording and passing on what they observe upon close examination. History is a continually updated, methodical description and recording, a well-qualified reconstruction of the probable causes of trends and events. This section defines the core characteristics of scholarly history.

History attempts to tell what happened in the past with the aim of enlightening and improving the present (McCrank, 2002). Buckland saw special virtue in scrutiny of the past:

> We understand objects, individuals, and institutions better if we know about their past experiences, and we understand the ideas and theories better if we know how they developed and what has already been said and done with them (Buckland, 2003, p. 679).

History can be both instructive and entertaining. As Huizinga wrote: "No other discipline has its portals so wide open to the general public as history" (Huizinga, 1984, p. 39). Participants and their descendants feel entitled to assert a right of ownership over their past (Evans, 2002).

Popularly it is assumed that anyone can tell a story. Some assert that "history is nothing but a series of stories, whether it be world history or family history" (Holt & Mooney, 1996, p. 9). To write good history, a scholarly historian requires a set of skills which demand significant capabilities, based on thorough training. An historian must be able to: identify the source of historical documents and assess their credibility; contrast the differing values, behaviours and institutions involved; differentiate between historical facts and interpretations; consider the multiple perspectives of various people; where possible, analyse cause-and-effect relationships and multiple causes; challenge arguments of historical inevitability; compare and evaluate competing historical narratives; differentiate those interpretations of history which are tentative, and those which are more firmly conclusive; evaluate major debates among historians; and hypothesise the influence of the past (McCrank, 2002).

Methods of research described in other chapters of this book are often adopted by historians. Other types of research adopt history methods too. An example is the use of Cultural Historical Activity Theory in the discipline of information systems, to identify past practices in order to help solve current system problems by refining understandings of usage (Igira & Gregory, 2009). Another is in geographical information systems, where the use of historical data is commonplace (Doorn, 2005).

On a broader level, a crucial example of borrowing from others is the formulation of a hypothesis, to guide the historian's thinking, analysis, and findings. It is said that the idea of a hypothesis really belongs to science. Some hypotheses are more complex or less factual than others; all of them imply some study of cause and effect (McCrank, 2002). Any link between cause and effect partly depends on how precisely and comprehensively the separate terms in the hypothesis, and the links between the terms, can be spelt out. Thus a precise hypothesis may be: The American experience of 9/11 caused the national government in the USA to pass powerful new surveillance laws to gather information secretly about its citizens and visitors. Whereas an example of a loose hypothesis may be: in times of national crisis, governments tend to watch over threatening political behaviours and pry into citizens' privacy more closely than in peaceful times. The potential link between cause and effect in the former (it being more precise) is much easier to demonstrate than in the latter (which is more vague).

Journals with historical articles are numerous; many thousands of volumes of history have been written in book form too. A host of history reference tools are available online. There is a steady interest in history in the disciplines of librarianship, archives and records, partly because many practitioners in those fields are steeped in the traditions of the humanities and the social sciences. Recent published history topics of interest include biographies of key figures, and the history of: reading, publishing, social and organisational memory, cultural artefacts (books, newspapers, magazines, journals), intellectual life, technologies, important institutions (including businesses), repository functions (whether electronic or print), records and recordkeeping, the maintenance of the heritage of science, social sciences, and humanities, the products of popular culture, links between cultural institutions and education, government regulation of speech and print, and forms of expression of issues about gender, race, power, politics, and religion in relation to information repositories (Buchanan & Hérubel, 2011; Rayward, 1996).

A recent bibliography of 340 pages gives another impression of the breadth of historical publications, by including the following topics: autobiography, automatic indexing, collecting, database development, electronic archives, feminism, forgeries, genres, language use, literary canons, memory, misinformation, mythography, palimpsests, professionalisation, telecommunications, and virtuality (McCrank, 2002). It is important to remember that many topics span more than one disciplinary locus. Thus the history of print connects with libraries, printing, technological change, authorship, editing, publishing, reading, literacy, journalism, book and mass media businesses, intellectual property law, fiction, entertainment, telecommunications, cultural transmission, and political imperialism. To illustrate this list, all of these themes are addressed in *A Study of Colonial Editions in Australia, 1843–1972* (Johanson, 2000). Australian-born Professor Boyd Rayward has gone the furthest in extending the hand of scholarly friendship to 'sister' disciplines (Rayward, 1996). He has researched in Sydney, Chicago and Champaign, Illinois. Rayward has an eclectic history research record. He writes the history of the international organisation of knowledge, of utopian schemes of knowledge organisation, of Paul Otlet's early twentieth-century ideas about hypertext and the origins of information science, and of digitisation and networking (Rayward, 1996).

Australia has a strong foundation in published academic history in information research. For 13 years – under the guidance of Professor Jean Whyte – the Graduate School of Librarianship, Archives and Records at Monash University strongly promoted historical research (Jenkin, 2010). The first Australian PhD thesis in the field, completed in 1985, was a history of *The Library Association of Australasia, 1896–1902* (Talbot, 1985). Professor Boyd Rayward at the School of Information, Library and Archive Studies, at the University of New South Wales from 1986 to 1999, showed a similar passion. Whyte's and Rayward's colleagues and graduates are still active, dispersed around the globe. Much Australian publishing activity has revolved around library history forums. The first was held in 1984, the most recent in 2016. Most of the 12 forum proceedings have been published.

Evidence is rarely self-evident

The advent of automatic data monitors and computer storage has increased enormously the quantity of information available to the historian: "The voice of history must be heard, but this is not easy in a world of information overload, mass communication, and general din" (McCrank, 2002, p. 20).

The historian uses data like every other researcher, but calls them collectively 'evidence', which dictates and directs the success of an enquiry. This section explores special features of evidence, and how they affect historians' uses of it. Examples from the history of information research are given to illustrate assertions about the importance of the inextricable nexus between evidence and the historian.

Although it is an exaggeration to assert that 'the evidence speaks for itself', as people often do, it is the basic ingredient of historical analysis. Where it is missing, only surmising can occasionally suggest substitutions. The historian must spend a lot more time than other researchers on identifying and unearthing useful evidence (Shep, 2006). The historian engages with unique data. Historical writing is the product of a struggle between imagination and evidence (Dening, 2009). Evidence cannot be created afresh, because it is past. In the early phases of a history project, the researcher looks broadly at what sorts of evidence are available, where evidence is located, and whether the likely skills for analysis are in the professional toolkit. Preliminary discoveries will indicate whether further steps can be taken.

For instance, study of the 30,000 clay tablets in the British Museum in London from the Library of Ashurbarnipal in Nineveh from 700 BC requires highly specialised in-situ handling skills and knowledge. The writing on the tablets is cuneiform (Polastron, 2007) and it records administrative trivia, history, geography, medicine, religion, magic, omens, rituals, astronomy, diplomatic secrets, and epic stories. But more recent history calls for a quite different set of skills. Making sense of the habits behind 'social grooming' messages (created since 2006), archived in the collection of billions of tweets in the Library of Congress in Washington, requires other expertise altogether (Raymond, 2010). The amount of professional effort required to sift the useful from the useless is similar in both examples (Byrne, 2011). Getting close to the evidence may require years of preparatory learning. It is not surprising that career historians specialise.

The research focus of the historian narrows later on, as discrete slabs of evidence are chosen carefully for analysis. It can be hard to tell where it will lead. The evidence may defy all existing understandings, and require decades of analysis for re-creation and use, as did the words on the famous Rosetta Stone. Why is it important? In 196 BC the priests of King Ptolemy V of Egypt issued a decree of honour, on a black basalt slab in three languages – hieroglyphic, demotic, and Greek – for preservation. The stone became lost, as well as some of the language. French soldiers in Egypt resurrected the stone in 1799 – the French leader, Napoleon, sent scientists with his conquering armies to take advantage of such eventualities. The Greek language was understood at the time, only fragments of demotic were known, and the meaning of all hieroglyphics had been lost completely. There were three texts in three languages on the stone – correctly assumed to contain the same message. They were finally decoded by French and British linguists in 1822 (Clayton, 2006). The British captured the Stone when they overthrew Napoleon, and deposited and preserved it in a public repository for all to admire. It is the most viewed artefact in the British Museum in London.

Imagination in interpreting evidence is essential, and how effective it is will depend somewhat on the historian's personal experiences and empathy. How did participants in past experiences think and feel? How were they *likely* to think and feel? Did they set out to deceive future observers? The intense interest of the historian in human motives and behaviours makes history overlap with the principles that lie behind researching biography (Curthoys & McGrath, 2009).

Not all the evidence can be examined sometimes, often for very practical reasons. Some evidence will have disappeared, or will be secret, as mentioned. As family members we know well how different members give different accounts of past events, or obfuscate (Griffiths 2016). As journalists and detectives can relate, one eyewitness may see quite different things from another eyewitness. Yet the historian tries to make sense of the whole puzzle of first-hand accounts, that is, of 'primary' evidence. Participants' thoughts may have to be deduced from what others observed about behaviours at an event, such as at a calamity like an eruption or earthquake. Knowledge of the psychology of perception and observation should assist the historian in this instance. Pliny the Younger (as historian) struggled to rationalise several handwritten eyewitness accounts of the eruption of Mount Vesuvius in 79 AD with his own on-the-ground observations. Many details of his summary of the burial of Pompeii have been used by modern volcanologists, providing another example of interdisciplinarity (Wallace-Hadrill, 1994).

In some situations, it will be unnecessary for an historian to provide all the evidence about long-established facts. Repetitive confirmation of a piece of common knowledge is unnecessary. For instance, few students of computer science have not heard of the innovations of Alan Turing, the brilliant mathematician, who helped to unravel the German Enigma code in World War Two, and to develop machine intelligence. His genius is very well known in the history of computing (Hodges, 1992).

Other evidence will be overlooked inadvertently upon a cursory examination, but will be reintegrated into mainstream historical commentary after considered reflection. Some evidence is mulled over many times. Evidence provided by modern DNA tests on old, organic samples are an example of re-examining old data with new tools. The historian and librarian Kevin Morgan is well-known for having achieved the official posthumous pardon of a so-called Melbourne murderer, hung in 1922, after being falsely convicted of killing a schoolgirl. In state archives in 1995 Morgan discovered samples of the girl's hair. The 1922 murder conviction had depended on matching her hair with some hair on a rug. Recent scientific analysis – orchestrated by Morgan – showed that they were not connected. He claimed to have identified the real murderer (Morgan, 2005).

The urges to nurture or to destroy evidence suggest an intrinsic power in the evidence itself. As a society we delegate to groups and organisations the responsibility for keeping or destroying evidence; only a small proportion of all historical records remain extant. Collecting and caring for evidence, and weeding it, are part of the professional duties of curators, custodians, librarians, archivists, recordkeepers, and others (Johanson, Schauder & Lim, 1997). Many publicly-funded collecting institutions are under a statutory obligation to keep specified publications and records – as an element of their *raison d'etre* – because of their national significance and long-term value to scholars in future (Legal Deposit Libraries Act, 2003). Conditions of access to evidence are often spelt out in legislation. A reason for recent widespread hostility to Wikileaks is that it flouts century-old conventions on secrecy surrounding national security topics, and effectively invents a separate subversive archive of politically-sensitive evidence (Lidberg, 2013).

The value of evidence changes over time, in unpredictable ways, as do the purposes for collecting and using it. Since the 1830s in Europe tidal gauges have measured the oceans' edges for local purposes. Much of this old data is now very useful for determining the effects globally of climate change (Steele, Thorpe & Turekian, 2009).

This section has described the nature of evidence and how the historian manages it. It is hard to imagine many limits to the variety of evidence that may attract the attention of the historian, yet the multitude of sources can make it hard to filter out useful evidence from extraneous trivia. The process of identification of evidence takes place in phases, from the broad to the particular. Esoteric evidence is so obscure that specialised background knowledge is needed to extract its meaning. Evidence is resurrected and reviewed by a historian at a time well past its creation, and new interpretations and discoveries become possible as time passes. It is not uncommon for a historian to have to reconcile different 'eyewitness' accounts. The use of evidence can reveal unexpected scandals, and some of it harbours such potential for harm that access to it is strictly controlled by laws.

Evaluating the evidence

With the endless proliferation of potential evidence there is more and more need to sift the wheat from the chaff. What are the expert's tools for doing it? The previous section identified some complications arising from the nature of evidence itself. Today digital ephemerality is an additional burden. There is a threat to the life expectancy of evidence; digital data are too easily destroyed. Again, McCrank sounds the alarm:

> The history of one of the most dramatic communications revolutions in history … may eventually become the largest black hole of historical knowledge yet known … because modern Western culture has become so self-destructive and mutable (McCrank, 2002, p. 27).

For the sake of argument, this section assumes that all the relevant evidence from the past is to hand. This section identifies five evaluative techniques that historians use when researching, namely that of: the detective, the sceptic and verifier, the attributor and disentangler, the clarifier, and the storyteller and explainer. They sum up historical methodology. The evidence is subjected to a thorough grilling, to a series of intellectual assessments that lie at the heart of historical method. The historian has a 'conversation' with the evidence. Although the five points are isolated and described separately here, in fact they are deployed interactively, and they overlap to some extent. Remarkable texts that enlarge on the brief treatment here can be found in any one of the six editions of *The Modern Researcher* by Barzun and Graff (Barzun & Graff, 2004) or in *The Art of Time Travel* by Tom Griffiths (2016). To show how the intellectual techniques work in practice, summary examples of up-to-date historical writings are presented here. Others have been presented before (Johanson, 2002).

Detective

Early in the research process, the historian aims to connect contexts of the evidence, and then to explore possible links between them. Initially the explanatory options are large. Evidence may need to be held up to the light for closer inspection. Historians have a mental check-list of questions. They might ask: what evidence is left after the event? If some evidence is not available, how much information is required to indicate a change of circumstances? A process of identification begins any search, then a tentative reconstruction of activity, events, structures, sequences. Where is the key evidence likely to be found? How complete is it? What gaps are there? Are the gaps accidental or intentional? What form was the evidence in before? What form is it in now? How can it be laid out carefully today for reinterpretation? Who should be entrusted with testing it? Are appropriate experts available?

Some examples in this chapter have already shown evaluation by use of detective skills and many more exist. As another example, a historian may be faced with a large collection of unsorted and undated personal letters in antiquated handwriting to arrange in chronological order (Gugliotta, 2011).

With the advent of *Google Books*, unprecedented scope for historical detective work has been opened up. Twenty-five million books have been digitised, and can be read and scanned electronically, in individual titles or as an entire corpus (Michel *et al.*, 2011). *Google* copied the books in major libraries in 100 countries with the aim of permitting use of a 'web crawler' to index the books' content and analyse the connections between them (Google, 2007).

An estimated total of 129 million books have been produced by 10,000 different publishers. Most of them are in English (Howard, 2012). *Google* has decided to cease its digitisation program (Grimmelmann, 2016), but physicists have taken an interest in what the collective content of the books can identify about historical trends, in a way that could never be undertaken manually. As detective historians we can learn about the lifespan of words, the evolution of grammar, the adoption of technology, censorship, historical epidemiology, and other gradual and sudden changes (Petersen, Tenenbaum, Havlin, & Stanley, 2012).

The newly-named discipline of 'culturomics' thus derives from a combination of physics and history. The neologism 'culturomics' refers to the statistical study of culture over time by analysis of words and phrases in a very large corpus of digitised texts. It is not unlike content analysis, described in other parts of this book (TFC, 2012). It allows the historian to scour millions of published words and concepts to determine meaningful patterns which can then be matched up against other sources of evidence. Changes over time in the information disciplines could be tracked using culturomics. There are key ideas that wax and wane in usage in professional and research literature: 'physical bibliography', 'shelf reading', 'microfiche', 'diplomatics', 'document life cycle', 'business process re-engineering', 'information enterprise', 'competitive intelligence', and 'disintermediation' are a few. Culturomics may be used to determine when these terms were in vogue, where, and why. There has been a large recent increase in words describing information and communications technologies and medical developments, and the time gap between their invention and widespread adoption in publications is much less than with older innovations.

As well as providing openings for new research, obviously there are methodological and other limitations to culturomics, yet to be explored (Leetaru, 2011). Nevertheless the detection of the content of a vast reservoir of 25 million books, published in the past, provides enormous potential for many future hypotheses and investigations on many historical topics. The data are publicly available (Michel *et al.*, 2011). Similar analysis is being applied to other big data repositories (Correia, Jepson, Malhado & Ladle, 2016).

Sceptic and verifier

After finding relevant evidence, the historian is led to ask how reliable the evidence is. Once found, can it be depended on? How credible were the producers of the data, and the distributors of it? Is evidence internally consistent? Is the evidence genuine and typical of the evidence emanating usually from the scrutinised source? Was the creator of the evidence regarded as reliable at the time by contemporaries? Are there other witnesses who agree with the accounts recorded via the primary source? How extensively was it distributed? Have the curators of the evidence selected it for storage with care? Have the data been corrupted over time? In what ways? By whom? Who had a vested interest in ensuring its survival or disappearance? What parts of it have gone missing, and why?

The importance of the role of sceptic and verifier is shown by the demonstrably false anecdotes spread about Ida Leeson, Sydney librarian. She was fondly remembered by hundreds of researchers whom she assisted in the Mitchell Library, Sydney, and she encouraged many writer-friends as their personal advocate and informal adviser (Berzins, 1986). She worked in the Mitchell Library in Sydney, from 1909 to 1944, rising to the top job as the first female Mitchell Librarian; then during World War Two worked in an Australian military intelligence think-tank, and afterwards in various administrative, library and research jobs connected with the south Pacific. She lived with a female friend for much of her adult life, and attracted misogynist stereotyping as a result. Being an assertive, successful, female librarian was sufficient to attract narrow-minded prejudice in itself (Kirkland, 1997), but adding lesbianism to her lifestyle just compounded the opprobrium. At her death in 1964, her family destroyed all of her personal papers.

Her historian-biographer, Sylvia Martin, was obliged to rely heavily on interviews with those who knew Ida Leeson. (Oral history is a domain of specialisation in its own right) (Clark 2016). An entire chapter of the biography (Martin, 2006) is devoted to rumours about Leeson. Their main protagonist was the renowned and respected Australian historian, Manning Clark, who wrote late in his life in his autobiography (Clark, 1993) that young researchers like himself would play a game; they would ask Leeson to fetch books from high shelves on a ladder, and then they would peep at Leeson's coloured garters tied at the bottom of her bloomers, which showed under her skirt. At first sight, motives for recording such an anecdote are impossible to determine. Clearly Clark felt a need to poke fun at Leeson, but why? Strangely, he also acknowledged that he absorbed much of human value from a warm relationship with her (Clark, 1993). Yet Clark admired clever raconteurs (McKenna, 2011), and he used the same yarn several times in public speeches. He could be loose with the facts in order to dramatise an event, (Bridge, 1994) to aggrandise his own role, (McKenna, 2007) and his acquaintances indulged in similar chauvinism. In perpetuating this trivial anecdote, his behaviour was not that of a careful, detached historian.

The Clark myth is easily refuted by reference to a few basic facts. Leeson did not work at the Mitchell Library when Clark said that he researched there and observed her (in 1947). As chief Librarian, her job did not involve fetching books for readers, even of the calibre of Manning Clark! There were no ladders in the reading room. She did not wear fancy or colourful clothes. Leeson's biographer concluded that although "this rather silly and decidedly non-sexy story of the bloomers might have been affectionate, it was also condescending, even with a whiff of prurience" (Martin, 2006, p. 188).

The story would be hardly worth noting if such a public figure as Clark had not attempted to capitalise on it, and had not done so in a generation when full respect for women, human rights and historical veracity were at a high pitch. Broadcasting it on several occasions — as Clark did — for 20 years was more than an indiscretion, but his real motives are hard to determine. Yet they highlight the need for verification.

Attributor and disentangler

The next set of history questions relate to the true overall meaning of the evidence. Who created the evidence, and why? To whom is it attributed? What did the data mean to its creator, and its original audience? To whom should it have meaning? Is the meaning still complete? Does the evidence require language translation? If it were presented to an audience today, would it be understood and believed fully? Who has copied it, used it, and for what purposes? What does it tell about the relevance of the evidence to different generations? Can the evidence be disentangled sensibly?

As an example, any historian focused on the extensive history of 'the book' must try to disentangle the roles played by millions of printed and bound texts in all languages over many centuries. Book functions are complex (Manguel, 1996) and have been interpreted and re-interpreted many times. Many scholars claim an interest in them: "... an international network of sociologists, anthropologists, economists, art historians, librarians, and bibliographers as well as literary critics and theorists" (Birch, 2009, p. 143). Although countless books have disappeared altogether (Kelly, 2005), the book reflects very significant values of the culture of its creators. Its fate has been determined by wavering costs of production, extent of sales, and success with its readership.

China is credited with the first known printed book in 868 AD. It was very much in demand, one of a number of early Zen Buddhist texts (Winchester, 2008). It contained a 'verbatim' conversation between Buddha and a follower, and was one in a genre that began transferring oral stories to print (Mäll, 2003). New books quickly resulted from its publication; by the start of the new century (907 AD) devout scholars had written 800 commentaries on it. Little wonder that entirely fresh interpretations of its 'true' meaning soon emerged. Remarkably the 868 *Diamond Sutra* can be read in its entirety today online in original Sanskrit or in translation (Needham, 1969). At the time, only a handful of male priests could read it (Hansen, 1990).

Over centuries religious institutions continued to limit the creation and use of serious books to their own elites, to maintain control over dogma and theological interpretation. 'Vernacular' books, that is, popular and entertaining scripts in local dialects, were treated with disdain by power-brokers (Green, 1994).

Transmission of the content of books through centuries is demonstrated by a fresh example, *Concerning Military Matters,* a prized Roman manual written in 450 AD but still in use in Europe 1,100 years later (Allmand, 2011). The author advocated reform of the declining Roman imperial army. The life of this book was much longer than it is for books today. It was produced as a bound handwritten manuscript, known as *incunabulum,* and was based on plagiarism from diverse Roman sources of the time (by the author's own admission) (Watson, 1969). Later it took on machine-printed form. The little that is known of its author is what the author reveals about himself. The original of this text can be read online by military historians, even those behind modern movies and TV series.

In Europe in the 1440s, a German blacksmith and goldsmith (Johannes Gutenberg) connected several pre-existing technologies together to create a printing press for books containing religious propaganda. His primary aim was to stay afloat financially (Pettegree, 2000). Although often implied with hindsight, in fact Gutenberg had no altruistic motives about popularising knowledge (Harlow, 1999). He struggled with deep debt all his life.

Reading of books for leisure grew alongside a massive increase in journals and newspapers (Briggs & Burke, 2010, p 108). Popular novels awaited the wider spread of literacy and affluence during the 19th century, and the creation of global publishing companies, economical manufacture of paper, rapid printing technologies, cheap editions, distribution by local booksellers, and the creation of free public libraries (Birch, 2009). Dutifully, readers in European colonies consumed huge quantities of imperial books for more than 200 years (Crane, Stafford & Williams, 2016), struggling to impress with the quality of their own small literatures (Trainor, 1997).

The drawn-out development of the book as a functional social artefact, and the content and manufacture of books as historical information in their own right, highlight the many forms and uses of evidence. The book is pervasive in countless essential human activities and is the foundation of multiple historical perspectives. Yet as well as serving as evidence in itself, it has disseminated knowledge and entertainment very widely, and is sustained digitally (Birch, 2009, p. 143). Over time evidence inevitably becomes neglected and needs reinterpretation by an historian. It is resurrected and disentangled to remove mystery, distortion and misuse. Time-honoured historical skills and new technological methods assist with the disentanglement.

Clarifier

On a nitty-gritty level, clarifying involves systematic internal checking by the historian. Several questions may need to be answered. Has the evidence been reviewed by anyone since its creation? Is it confirmed by outside sources? Does one piece of evidence corroborate others? Have people twisted the evidence over time to their own ends? Have exaggerations, distortions, or legends grown up around it, which had no place in the original context? Have the later glosses destroyed the meaning or impact intended by the original creator?

The history of mechanics' institutes highlights some of the challenges of clarification. There is a very large quantity of evidence about them. The original evidence — personal anecdotes, testimonials, published library catalogues, membership lists, financial ledgers, official meeting records, government reports – has been used for different purposes over time; there are several variants of their history. Which is correct? This section shows briefly how they can be clarified.

What were their aims? Mechanics' institutes emerged in the early 19th century in the United Kingdom (UK) with the following ideals: to encourage "the humbler classes … assisted by a few of the leading and wealthy inhabitants" to collect small amounts of funds to provide instruction in "science, literature and the arts, to the exclusion of controversial divinity, party politics, and subjects of local dispute, by means of a library of circulation, lectures, evening or day classes, and a reading room" (Anonymous, 1844). The multiple motivations behind the 'movement', as it soon became known, were not the same in every time or place. They were designed for many reasons – to enable labourers who wanted a basic education to improve themselves, to promote basic literacy, to abolish superstition by encouraging wholesome reading and 'rational' thinking, to help mechanics to enjoy their leisure time without alcohol, to provide their own social support in small towns, to encourage workers with middle class aspirations, to teach the scientific principles which increasingly lay behind urban factory jobs, and to promote utilitarian moral and social reform generally. It is doubtful that any single institute alone would be capable of satisfying all of these ambitions. The official injunction to avoid political controversy was ignored in practice by the many institutes which aimed to actively encourage a full agenda of politicking.

1823 is nominated as the year in which mechanics' institutes were 'founded' in Glasgow and Edinburgh. Yet the evidence shows that there were many precursors to mechanics' institutes, dating back to as early as 1717 – the Spitalfields Mathematical Society consisted of volunteer weavers, braziers, bakers, and bricklayers (Rose, 2002). A professor at Glasgow University, George Birkbeck, provided free lectures to mechanics 22 years before a mechanics' institute was formally established there. He then moved to London where he was involved (with the help of political philosophers) in the creation of the London Mechanics' Institute in 1824. His early biographer idolised the heroic 'great man' as the creator of mechanics' institutes (Godard, 1888; Kelly, 1952). From a historiographical perspective, a single starting-date is impossible to establish precisely. There is no doubt that the number of British institutes grew rapidly, to 702 in 1850, but their origins went back more than a century and they were not the fulfilment of the dreams of one man, nor even of just a handful of philanthropic men (Altick, 1967). At first there was clear demand from the mechanics themselves.

In Australia, the mechanics institutes evolved differently from the British model. Here, from the beginning, the institutes functioned primarily as small subscription libraries of popular books and newspapers for middle-class men (Barker, 2007). It was not until the 1960s in Australia that they were superseded fully by public library systems (Biskup & Goodman, 1995). In most parts of Australia, the mechanics' institutes continued to provide book collections of variable quality until state governments took full responsibility for the provision of comprehensive library services (Lyons & Taksa, 1992).

In England, the emergence of public libraries was different. They began to arrive by virtue of an act of parliament in 1850. In contrast to the British colonies, where mechanics' institutes assisted with the development of fully-fledged adult education and eventually public libraries, within a few years of their foundation in the UK many mechanics' institutes were said to have failed. The veracity of such judgement depends to some extent on the criteria used to determine failure. The position of the institutes was complicated by the fact that working class men formed hundreds of informal self-instruction groups in small British towns, not named institutes, but named 'mutual improvement societies' (by historians), which were supposedly of lesser merit. Evidence of the relationship between the institutes and the societies has not been plotted, and neither are clearly defined. Over time some of the societies actually grew into mechanics' institutes, suggesting a fluidity of membership and pseudo-organisational progress that is bound to undermine the possibility of any clear-cut historical conclusions anyway (Altick, 1967; Rose, 2002). Following this line of argument, the only assured conclusion may well be that the evidence cannot be fully clarified.

Storyteller, explainer

The culmination of historical research is often the resolution of a hypothesis, as mentioned earlier. Towards the end of the evaluative process, the researcher asks whether the original hypothesis can be accepted, or whether it should be reviewed or rejected. Uncertainty about drawing a conclusion may comprise a sort of 'conclusion' in fact, a tentative resolution.

The historian has a duty to describe and explain the past as accurately as possible in the present, to show why we are, what we are, where we are. The evidence should be selected and connected as a story which appeals in its telling – stimulating excitement, fear, respect, understanding and awe. Whether it is presented in the form of the spoken word, film, printed text, music, picture, multimedia, or by other means, it should be both entertaining and instructive.

The story should synthesise the best of the evaluated evidence to demonstrate authenticity in the links in the chain of causation. The historian presents cause and effect in the form of 'most likely' explanations – not as absolute truths. Universally-valid generalisations from historical research across time and space rarely hold water. Deduction – moving logically from a generalisation about the past to a particular instance in the present – is usually not attempted extensively by historians. It is too foolhardy. Chance plays too great a part. The level of 'proof' in history is on the balance of probabilities, as in fact it is in most disciplines.

An illustration of the importance of hypothesis, synthesis of evidence, level of proof, and storytelling is found in a study of the records created and kept by British and Australian prime ministers. Graeme Powell (1994) reviewed the size and content of the personal and public archives of prime ministers in both countries, to determine what they had in common, how they differed, and whether there are noticeable recordkeeping traditions shared across nations.

Powell noted that British prime ministers only began to publish memoirs after World War Two. Since then every British prime minister has published an autobiography, with variable levels of "honesty and humility" (Powell, 1994, p. 97). In contrast, few Australian prime ministers have bothered.

Initially Powell stated that "a great deal of evidence has been lost forever" because of official and personal neglect (Powell, 1994, p. 93). Each prime minister regarded his or her records as owned personally, and they were not intended for public scrutiny. Powell pursued this research question: what guided prime ministerial attitudes to their legacies?

With regard to levels of proof, Powell was cautious enough to point out that his "explanations can only be expressed tentatively, for at present they must rely for evidence largely on the personal papers that happen to have survived and that are now mostly preserved in public archives and libraries" (Powell, 1994, p. 93).

Powell deduced that a parallel study of prime ministers' particular background experiences would complement his general study of their regard for records *per se*, and may in fact confirm his conclusions. He found that their recordkeeping customs are linked not so much to different political traditions, nor to legislation about record retention, but to complex personal characteristics, how widespread their communication networks were, breadth of interests outside of politics, the nature of their educational and literary backgrounds, occurrence of a regular home life, private wealth, a respect for history, the employment of private secretaries to assist with recordkeeping, and a supportive public service.

Conclusion

This chapter described how historical research is done. It began with an account of the nature of history, and by examples aimed at showing how history is relevant to information research. It described the many permutations of evidence and how to manage them. The five techniques for determining the reliable meaning of evidence – detection, scepticism, attribution and disentanglement, verification and clarification, and storytelling and explanation – equip the historian with a uniquely-powerful intellectual toolkit. Perhaps they compensate somewhat for the inability of the historian to make definitive conclusions about causation. Remember that the history of information is central to all human activity:

> Managing information has a long and interesting history ... It is intimately and intricately bound up with the cultural imperatives, the modes of thought, belief and investigation, the interrelated economic, social, political, administrative, recreational and educational systems that are characteristic of different times and places (Rayward, 1996).

References

Allmand, C. (2011). *The 'De Re Military' of Vegetius. The reception, transmission and legacy of a Roman text in the Middle Ages.* Cambridge: University Press.

Altick, R. D. (1967). *The English common reader: A social history of the mass reading public 1800–1900.* Chicago: University of Chicago Press.

Anonymous. (1844). *Westminster Review, 41,* 417–418.

Australia. Human Rights and Equal Opportunity Commission. (1997). *Bringing them home: Report of the national inquiry into the separation of Aboriginal and Torres Strait Islander children from their families.* Canberra: Commonwealth of Australia. Human Rights and Equal Opportunity Commission.

Barker, D. (2007). *From mechanics' institutes to free libraries: Aspects of public policy, community culture, and library provision in Victoria, 1839–1946.* (PhD thesis). Monash University, Melbourne, Australia.

Barzun, J., & Graff, H. (2004). *The modern researcher.* Belmont, CA: Thomson/ Wadsworth.

Berzins, B. (1986). Ida Leeson. *Australian dictionary of biography.* Canberra: National Centre of Biography, Australian National University.

Bevan, R. (2006). *The destruction of memory: Architecture at war.* London: Reaktion Books.

Birch, D. (Ed.). (2009). *The Oxford companion to English literature* (7th ed.). Oxford: Oxford University Press.

Biskup, P., & Goodman, D. M. (1995). *Australian libraries.* Wagga Wagga, NSW: Centre for Information Studies, Charles Sturt University.

Bridge, C. (1994). *Manning Clark: Essays on his place in history.* Melbourne: Melbourne University Press.

Briggs, A., & Burke, P. (2010). *A social history of the media: From Gutenberg to the Internet.* Cambridge: Polity.

Buchanan, A. L., & Hérubel, J.-P. V. M. (2011). Subject and historiographic characteristics of library history: Disciplinary considerations and scholarship. *Journal of Scholarly Publishing, 42*(4), 514–533.

Buckland, M. K. (2003). The grand challenges for library research. *Library Trends, 51* (4), 675–686.

Byrne, A. (2011). Wikileaks and Web 2.0: Privacy, security and other things that keep me awake at night. *Archives and Manuscripts, 39*(1), 49–66.

Capurro, R., & Hjørland, B. (2003). The concept of information. *Annual Review of Information Science and Technology, 37*(1), 343–411.

Clark, A. (2016). *Private lives, public history*. Carlton, VIC: Melbourne University Press.

Clark, M. (1993). *Quest for grace*. Melbourne: Penguin.

Clayton, P. A. (2006). *Chronicle of the pharaohs: The reign-by-reign record of the rulers and dynasties of ancient Egypt*. London: Thames & Hudson.

Correia, R. A., Jepson, P. R., Malhado, A. C., & Ladle, R. J. (2016). Familiarity breeds content: Assessing bird species popularity with culturomics. *PeerJ, 4*. Retrieved from https://peerj.com/articles/1728.pdf

Crane, R., Stafford, J., & Williams, M. (Eds.). (2016). *The world novel in English to 1950*. Oxford University Press.

Curthoys, A., & McGrath, A. (2009). *How to write history that people want to read*. Sydney: University of New South Wales Press.

Dening, G. (2009). Writing: Praxis and performance. In A. Curthoys, & A. McGrath (Eds.), *Writing histories: Imagination and narration* (pp. 6.1.–6.10). Melbourne: Monash University.

Doorn, P. (2005). A spatial turn in history. *Geographical Information Management International, 19*(4). Retrieved from http://www.gim-international.com/issues/articles/id453-A_Spatial_Turn_in_History.html

Evans, R. J. (2002). Prologue: What is history? – Now. In D. Cannadine (Ed.), *What is history now?* (pp. 1–18). Houndmills, UK: Palgrave.

Fukuyama, F. (1992). *The end of history and the last man*. New York: Avon Books.

Giddens, A. (1984). *The constitution of society: Outline of the theory of structuration*. Berkeley, CA: University of California Press.

Godard, J. G. (1888). *George Birkbeck, the pioneer of popular education: A memoir and a review*. London: Bemrose.

Google Inc. (2007). *Google Books history*. Retrieved from https://www.google.com/googlebooks/about/history.html

Green, D. H. (1994). *Medieval listening and reading: The primary reception of German literature, 800–1300*. Cambridge, UK: Cambridge University Press.

Griffiths, T. (2016). *The art of time travel: Historians and their craft*. Carlton, VIC: Black Inc.

Grimmelmann, J. (2016, 11 May). Hail and farewell to the Google Books case. *Publishers Weekly*. Retrieved from http://www.publishersweekly.com/pw/by-topic/digital/copyright/article/70326-hail-and-farewell-to-the-google-books-case.html

Gugliotta, G. (2011, 28 March). Deciphering old texts, one woozy, one curvy word at a time. *New York Times*. Retrieved from http://www.nytimes.com/2011/03/29/science/29recaptcha.html

Halbwachs, M. (1992). *On collective memory*. (L. A. Coser, Trans.). Chicago: University of Chicago Press.

Hansen, V. (1990). *Changing gods in medieval China, 1127–1276*. Princeton, NJ: Princeton University Press.

Harlow, J. (1999, 28 November). Gutenberg is man of the millennium. *Sunday Times*, London. Retrieved from http://cool.conservation-us.org/byform/mailing-lists/bookarts/1999/11/msg00246.html

Hodges, A. (1992). *Alan Turing: The enigma*. London: Vintage.

Holt, D., & Mooney, B. (1996). *The storyteller's guide*. Little Rock, AR: August House.

Howard, J. (2012, 9 March). Google begins to scale back its scanning of books from university libraries. *The Chronicle of Higher Education*. Retrieved from http://chronicle.com/article/Google-Begins-to-Scale-Back/131109/

Huizinga, J. (1984). *Men and ideas: History, the Middle Ages, the Renaissance: Essays*. Princeton, NJ: Princeton University Press.

Igira, F. T., & Gregory, J. (2009). Cultural historical activity theory. In Y. K. Dwivedi, B. Lal, M. D. Williams, S. L. Schneberger, & M. Wade (Eds.), *Handbook of research on contemporary theoretical models in information systems* (pp. 434–454). Hershey, PA: IGI Global.

Jenkin, C. E. J. (2010). *Jean Primrose Whyte: A professional biography*. Melbourne: Monash University Publishing.

Johanson, G. (2000). *A study of colonial editions in Australia, 1843–1972*. Wellington, NZ: Elibank Press.

Johanson, G. (2002). Historical research. In K. Williamson (Ed.), *Research methods for students, academics and professionals: Information management and systems* (2nd ed., pp. 195–208). Wagga Wagga, NSW: Centre for Information Studies, Charles Sturt University.

Johanson, G., Schauder, D., & Lim, E. (1997). The virtual library and the humanities: A report. *Australian Humanities Review*. Retrieved from http://www.australianhumanitiesreview.org/emuse/library/johanson.html

Kelly, S. (2005). *The book of lost books*. London: Penguin.

Kelly, T. (1952). The origins of mechanics' institutes. *British Journal of Educational Studies, 1*(1), 17–27.

Kirkland, J. J. (1997). The missing women library directors: Deprivation versus mentoring. *College & Research Libraries, 58*(4), 375–383.

Kundera, M. (1980). *The book of laughter and forgetting*. New York: A. A. Knopf.

Leetaru, K. H. (2011). Culturnomics 2.0: Forecasting large-scale human behavior using global news media tone in time and space. *First Monday, 16*(9). Retrieved from http://firstmonday.org/ojs/index.php/fm/article/view/3663/3040

Legal Deposit Libraries Act (2003). Retrieved from http://www.legislation.gov.uk/ukpga/2003/28/pdfs/ukpga_20030028_en.pdf

Lidberg, J. (2013). From freedom to right – where will freedom of information go in the age of WikiLeaks? *Australian Journalism Review, 35*(2), 73–85.

Lyons, M., & Taksa, L. (1992). *Australian readers remember: An oral history of reading 1890–1930*. Melbourne: Oxford University Press.

Mäll, L. (2003). *Studies in the Astasahasrika Prajnaparamita and other essays*. Tartu: Centre for Oriental Studies, University of Tartu, Estonia.

Manguel, A. (1996). *A history of reading*. London: HarperCollins.

Martin, S. (2006). *Ida Leeson: A life*. Crows Nest, NSW: Allen & Unwin.

Masuda, Y. (1980). Computopia: Rebirth of theological synergism. In Y. Masuda (Ed.), *The information society as post-industrial society* (pp. 146–154). Tokyo: Institute for the Information Society.

McCrank, L. J. (2002). *Historical information science: An emerging unidiscipline*. Medford, NJ: Information Today.

McGarry, K. (1988). *The changing context of information: An introductory analysis*. London: Library Association Publishing.

McKenna, M. (2007). Being there: The strange history of Manning Clark. *The Monthly*. March.

McKenna, M. (2011). *An eye for eternity: The life of Manning Clark*. Melbourne: Miegunyah Press.

Merton, R. K. (1993). *On the shoulders of giants: A Shandean postscript*. Chicago: University of Chicago.

Michel, J.-B., Shen, Y. K., Aiden, A. P., Veres, A., Gray, M. K., Google Books Team, . . . Aiden, E. L. (2011). Quantitative analysis of culture using millions of digitized books. *Science, 331*(6014), 176–182.

Morgan, K. J. (2005). *Gun alley: Murder, lies and failure of justice*. Pymble, NSW: Simon & Schuster.

Needham, J. (1969). *Within the four seas: The dialogue of East and West*. London: Allen & Unwin.

Nonaka, I. (1995). *The knowledge-creating company: How Japanese companies create the dynamics of innovation*. New York: Oxford University Press.

Parker, D. (2000). *Revolutions: The revolutionary tradition in the west, 1560–1991*. London: Routledge.

Petersen, A. M., Tenenbaum, J., Havlin, A., & Stanley, H. E. (2012). Statistical laws governing fluctuations in word use from word birth to word death. *Scientific Reports, 2*, 313. Retrieved from http://arxiv.org/abs/1107.3707

Pettegree, A. (Ed.). (2000). *The Reformation world*. London: Routledge.

Polastron, L. X. (2007). *Books on fire: The tumultuous story of the world's great libraries*. London: Thames & Hudson.

Powell, G. (1994). Prime ministers as recordkeepers: British models and Australian practice. In S. McKemmish & M. Piggott (Eds.), *The records continuum; Ian Maclean and Australian Archives: First fifty years* (pp. 93–109). Melbourne: Ancora Press, Monash University.

Raymond, M. (2010). How Tweet it is!: Library acquires entire Twitter archive. Retrieved from http://blogs.loc.gov/loc/2010/04/how-tweet-it-is-library-acquires-entire-twitter-archive/

Rayward, W. B. (1996). The history and historiography of information science: Some reflections. *Information Processing and Management, 32*(1), 3–17.

Rose, J. (2002). *The intellectual life of the British working classes.* New Haven, CT: Yale University Press.

Searle, J. R. (2010). *Making the social world: The structure of human civilization.* Oxford: Oxford University Press.

Shep, S. J. (2006). Historical investigation. In G. E. Gorman, & P. Clayton (Eds.), *Qualitative research for the information professional* (pp. 160–181). London: Facet.

Steele, J. H., Thorpe, S. A., & Turekian, K. K. (2009). *Measurement techniques, platforms and sensors.* London: Academic Press.

Talbot, M. (1985). *The Library Association of Australasia, 1896–1902.* (PhD thesis, Monash University, Melbourne, Australia.)

TFC. (2012). Culturomics and the Google book project. Retrieved from http://www.technologyreview.com/blog/arxiv/27608/

Trainor, L. (1997). Colonial editions. In P. Griffith, R. Harvey, & K. Maslen (Eds.), *Book and print in New Zealand: A guide to print culture in Aotearoa* (pp. 113–117). Wellington: Victoria University Press.

Vreeken, A. (2005). The history of information: Lessons for information management. *Sprouts: Working Papers on Information Systems, 5*(2), Retrieved from aisel.aisnet.org/cgi/viewcontent.cgi?article = 1087&context = sprouts_all

Wallace-Hadrill, A. (1994). *Houses and society in Pompeii and Herculaneum.* Princeton, NJ: Princeton University Press.

Watson, G. R. (1969). *The Roman soldier.* Ithaca, NY: Cornell University Press.

White, E. (1995). *The burning library: Writings on art, literature and sexuality, 1969–1993.* London: Picador.

Winchester, S. (2008). *Bomb, book and compass: Joseph Needham and the great secrets of China.* Camberwell, VIC: Penguin.

Wright, A. (2007). *Glut: Mastering information through the ages.* Washington: Joseph Henry.

Chapter 13

Ethnographic research

Kirsty Williamson
Monash University and Charles Sturt University, Australia

This chapter introduces the complexity of ethnographic research and the multiplicity of ways of undertaking and labelling it. The almost interchangeable use of the labels, participant observation and ethnography, is particularly emphasised. The focus of the chapter is on the various kinds of ethnography; their similarities and differences, rather than on a description of the major tools, interviews and observation, which are the subjects of other chapters. Positivist, constructivist, critical and postmodern approaches are discussed and compared, along with a range of contemporary approaches, for example, visual and online. Recent uses of autoethnography in information research are documented. Ways of ensuring the trustworthiness of ethnographic research are explored. A number of examples of the use of ethnography in the information field are provided, including a virtual example focussed on online communities in Saudi Arabia.

Research Methods: Information, Systems, and Contexts. DOI: http://dx.doi.org/10.1016/B978-0-08-102220-7.00013-3

Introduction

The term 'ethnography' derives from the Greek word, 'ethnos', meaning a people or a cultural group. When 'ethno' is combined with 'graphic' to form the word 'ethnographic' it denotes the study and description of humankind. The word 'ethnography' means, specifically, 'writing about people' (Burns, 2000, p. 393). It is a widely used method because it provides a way of exploring, in-depth, people's beliefs, values and behaviours (Gottlieb, 2006). It is also a research method with a long and complex history. Originally an anthropological method, "early ethnography grew out of the interests of westerners in the origin of culture and civilization" (Vidich & Lyman, 2003, p. 60), which early ethnographers believed would be understood through study of contemporary 'primitive' people. In other words, early ethnography was an attempt to account for the origins, histories and multiplicities of races, cultures and civilizations. Ethnography is still regarded as a way of understanding someone else's experience and translating that in comprehensible form for others who have not had that experience (Prus, 1997). Vidich and Lyman (2003) provide a fascinating historical account of the development of ethnography, from the 15th and 16th century to the postmodern era.

The complexities associated with ethnographic method are immediately evident when you come to realise the associated diversity of terminology. A broad term, of which ethnography is part, is 'fieldwork' (Baker, 1999; Neuman, 2014) which means that sometimes this broader term is applied. Keesing and Strathern (1998, p. 7) described fieldwork as "intimate participation in a community and observation of modes of behavior and the organisation of social life". This definition is interesting in that it describes 'participant observation', often used almost synonymously with the term 'ethnography'. Participant observation, "better known among anthropologists as advanced hanging out" (Gottlieb, 2006, p. 49), specifically describes the fieldwork method used by ethnographers. Through participant observation, ethnographers have aimed to immerse themselves in their settings, to become participants in the scenarios they are studying. An early ethnographer, Malinkowski (1922), did this in foreign parts, as did Mead (1960). There is thus a close relationship between ethnography and participant observation, although modern approaches to ethnography do not necessarily require observers to be full participants in their settings. While it can be argued that participant observation describes the fieldwork component, and ethnography the writing part,

> anthropologists themselves tend to confuse the two, if only because they are constantly writing descriptive and analytical notes about their daily interaction with people whom they have chosen to study and with whom they are sharing their lives. In other words, the writing process is never entirely separate from the fieldwork process (Moeran, 2007, p. 3).

Thus, if you are pursuing the term ethnography in the literature, you should be aware that you need to search for participant observation as well as ethnography. For example, Wildemuth (2009) discussed participant observation from a library and information science/studies (LIS) perspective and Taylor, Bogdan & DeVault (2015) devoted a chapter of their *Introduction to Qualitative Research Methods* to detailed description for the undertaking of participant observation. There is much literature about ethnography/participant observation from which to choose. Two seminal authors, who are still widely cited, are Geertz (1973) and Spradley (1979; 1980). There are many references from a general social science or qualitative research perspective, for example, Atkinson and Hammersely (1998), both prolific writers in the field of qualitative research; Delamont (2004); Fielding (2001); Gottlieb (2006); Hammersley (1990); Hammersley and Atkinson (1995); Neuman (2014); Patton (2015); Prus (1997); Silverman (2005); Tedlock (2005); Thwaites, Davis & Mules (1994); Van Maanen (1988); and Vidich and Lyman (2003). There is also a *Handbook of Ethnography* (Atkinson, Coffey, Delamont, Lofland & Lofland, 2001), published by Sage, as well as the Sage handbooks of qualitative research cited in Chapter 1. Other writers present specific arguments or perspectives, or discussion of specific types of ethnography, for example, Chang (2008) about authoethnography. Some of these will be discussed below.

Although this chapter draws on the social science and qualitative research literature, there are also publications tailored to specific fields. For LIS, in addition to Wildemuth (2009), examples are Bow (2002); Grover & Glazier (1992); Mellon (1990) and Pickard (2013). Myers (1999) wrote eloquently about his perception that ethnographic research "is well suited to providing information systems researchers with rich insights into the human, social and organizational aspects of information systems" (p. 2). Sayago and Blat (2010) are advocates of ethnography in human-computer interaction (HCI) research. Other information systems researchers, interested in virtual communities, have used ethnography and discussed its attributes for their purposes (e.g., Dodge & Kitchin, 2001). Burns (2000) discussed ethnography from an education perspective while Moeran (2007) and Van Maanen (2002) have focussed on organisational ethnography. Although some of the references, cited above, are not recent according to their publication dates, they are still very valuable, in keeping with many older publications in the research methods field.

This chapter provides a discussion of the various kinds of ethnography, their similarities and differences. It does not describe, in detail, the tools for undertaking ethnography/participant observation since they are the topics of other chapters: Chapter 16: *Questionnaires, individual interviews, and focus group interviews*, and Chapter 17: *Observation*. Nevertheless, two examples, employing those tools, are included towards the end of this chapter and should provide the reader with some guidance about the design and implementation of ethnographic method. While mostly the term 'ethnography' is used, the approach of this chapter is that ethnographic techniques can often be equated with participant observation.

Ethnography: Frameworks and approaches

While the origins of ethnography were anthropological, early in the 20th century a different discipline group, viz., functionalist sociologists, particularly at the University of Chicago, entered the field and began to employ ethnographic methods to study cultural issues closer to home. Examples are immigration, vice, racial discrimination, homelessness, suicide and mental disorders (Van Maanen, 1988, pp. 17–22). The so-called 'Chicago School' dominated the intellectual and professional landscape of sociology from 1892 until 1942. According to Deegan (2001), by 1930 it was said to have trained over half of all the sociologists in the world. As time went by, anthropologists, sociologists, and other academic disciplines undertaking ethnography borrowed extensively from each other, and a range of tools or techniques, such as interviews, focus groups and questionnaires began to be used (Bow, 2002). This increased the flexibility of modern ethnography by enabling the use of multiple tools and approaches thus allowing researchers to "validate their eyewitness accounts through other forms of documentation" (Angrosino & Pérez, 2000, p. 676). Such a snap-shot version of the history of ethnography, however, takes little account of the different approaches and phases of development of the use of the method over more than a century. The following discusses the various frameworks[1] that have been used by ethnographers. They include positivist, constructivist, critical theorist and postmodern approaches.

Positivist framework

Positivist approaches to research in general are detailed in Chapter 1: *Research concepts*. In keeping with other researchers of the early 20th Century, ethnographers were initially positivist in outlook, adopting a realist framework. These ethnographers believed there was a single reality to be discovered "that was free of the influences of time and context, subjective interpretations of reality and human agency" (Saule, 2002, p. 179). Thus early positivist ethnographers saw themselves as scientists seeking to illuminate the truths behind human activity and behaviour. The background of researchers and their subjectivities were not considered important or influential in their analyses of other, often quite different, cultures. Ethnographers normally spent a long period of time in a society (usually

---

[1] The term 'frameworks' in the case of sciences and the humanities signifies assumptions, norms, values and traditions that create, perpetuate and institutionalise particular forms of knowledge within a particular field of study (Stanfield, 1998, p. 346).

a small homogeneous culture), participated in daily life of members and carefully observed "their joys and sufferings as a way of obtaining material for social scientific study. This method was widely believed to produce documentary information that not only was 'true' but also reflected the native's own point of view about reality" (Tedlock, 2005, p. 467). Apart from Malinowski (1922) and Mead (1960), Bateson (1972) is an example of this positivist approach. "In these texts, the ethnographers portray themselves as objective and distant observers of the culture. Data are presented as indisputable reality" (Saule, 2002, p. 160).

Just as research, in general, was affected by the emergence of post-positivists, so too was ethnography. Post-positivists began to assert that, while there is a single reality, it is difficult to discern, meaning that a universalist approach to the study of cultures and people was flawed. This opened the way to the development of different, interpretivist approaches to ethnographic study of which constructivist ethnography is the most prominent; to critical ethnography; and then postmodern approaches.

Constructivist framework

Interpretivist/constructivist approaches to research, in general, are detailed in Chapter 1. Ethnographers, associated with the constructivist paradigm, set out to explore a particular cultural setting, believing that:

> human beings do not find or discover knowledge so much as we construct or make it. We invent concepts, models, and schemes to make sense of experience, and we continually test and modify these constructions in the light of new experience. Furthermore, there is an inevitable historical and sociocultural dimension to this construction. We do not construct our interpretations in isolation but against a backdrop of shared understandings, practices, language, and so forth (Schwandt, 2003, p. 305).

Thus ethnographic interpretations are likely to be multiple and can be conflicting, even when a particular culture is shared. In other words, because reality within a cultural group "exists only in the minds of each individual, and each individual's perception of what is real will differ from others, reality itself is pluralist and relativist" (Saule, 2002, p. 182). It is interesting that, although he is most famous for coining the term 'thick description' as applied to ethnography, Clifford Geertz (1973) stressed "multiple perspectives or interpretive frameworks, that is, multiple motivational frames that inform social events and actions" (Atkinson & Delamont, 2005, p. 832).

Constructivists also recognise that researchers construct their own meanings and cannot be objective. It is therefore important for researchers to be aware of their likely influence on interpretations made in their ethnographies and to make explicit their backgrounds and interests. Because ethnography is the result of the interactions of researchers and those being studied, an inductive approach is required. Researchers need to listen to the perspectives of participants and build analysis and theory from those (Saule, 2002, p. 182), as do grounded theorists. In other words, constructivists work with the people being studied through a dialectic of analysis, critique, and reanalysis (Schwandt, 1998, p. 243).

The multiple perspectives, which are the outcome of constructivist ethnography, are seen as relativist, or not providing an absolute truth, and have been criticised in the literature for this, for example, by Hammersley (2002) whose views are discussed, below, in relation to validity in ethnography.

Critical ethnography

Critical theorists, like constructivists, believe that reality is constructed by individuals or within social groupings, but see historical realism as a key influencing factor. For example, a history of repression, determined by social stratification systems such as those determined by patriarchy, ethnocentricity or ageism, influence the ways in which people choose, and are able to construct their own realities. The Denzin and Lincoln books, especially the handbooks, are very strong on critical theory and emancipatory approaches. For example, *The Sage Handbook of Qualitative Research*, third edition (2005) includes a chapter on emancipatory cultural politics (Denzin, 2005) and another touches on emancipatory feminism (Olesen, 2005). Several other chapters discuss critical ethnography from a range of perspectives (e.g., Fine & Weis, 2005; Foley & Valenzuela, 2005; Kincheloe & McLaren, 2005; Tedlock, 2005). Madison (2005) writes about critical ethnography as street performance in Ghana. If you have access to volumes of *The Handbook*, other than the third edition, you are likely to find other chapters by the same authors on similar topics, given that the same authors usually appear in more than one edition.

Critical ethnography has been defined simply by Thomas (1993) as "a type of reflection that examines culture, knowledge, and action ... [and opens] to scrutiny otherwise hidden agendas, power centers, and assumptions that inhibit, repress, and constrain" (pp. 2–3). The use of critical ethnography by Cecez-Kecmanovic (2001) fits this definition, as discussed in Chapter 2: *The fundamentals of research planning*. A more political definition of critical theory, which is broad but applicable to critical ethnography, is provided by Kincheloe and McLaren (2005) and reproduced in part here.

> We are defining a criticalist as a researcher or theorist who attempts to use her or his work as a form of social or cultural criticism and who accepts certain basic assumptions; that all thought is fundamentally mediated by power relations that are socially and historically constituted; that facts can never be isolated from the

domain of values or removed from some form of ideological inscription ... that language is central to the formation of subjectivity (conscious and unconscious awareness); that certain groups in any society and particular societies are privileged over others ... [Oppression] ... is most forcefully reproduced when subordinates accept their social status as natural, necessary, or inevitable (p. 304).

The sentiments in this quotation are quite typical of most critical emancipists. Certainly, as Cecez-Kecmanovic (2001) found, there are situations where researchers in the information field will confront issues of power relations affecting studies they are undertaking. There needs to be awareness of power as a factor. However, the value-laden texts of critical ethnography, where notions of impartiality and objectivity are entirely absent, are mostly not required in our field, as perhaps is indicated by the few critical ethnographies undertaken by information researchers. I must emphasise that there are topics where the approach is entirely appropriate, indeed required, such as in the case of the research of Lipu (2010) whose work focussed on the role of information literacy for Papua New Guinean women, particularly in terms of empowerment in a predominantly male society where women are often oppressed.

There is also criticism of critical theory/ethnography in the literature. Hammersley (1990) postulated that the emancipatory model of critical theory is too narrow in its approach, in terms of the topics considered important and in the "conception of the appropriate audience for research" (pp. 67−69). Only those who can be described as 'oppressed' are deemed worthy of study. Researchers may also ignore "the complexities and contradictions that exist in any social grouping" in order to write "a 'good' emancipatory ethnographic text" (Saule, 2002, p. 184). In a later publication, Hammersley (1992) discussed the difficulty of distinguishing between "political insight and political prejudice" (p. 15). Saule (2002) elaborated upon this by asking: "At what point within critical theory does an ethnographic text become a diatribe for a political movement and/or ideal, rather than a scholarly look into the culture of a social grouping?" (p. 184).

Another vulnerable point is that many critical theorists believe that knowledge about a particular social group, for example, an African-American community, can only be realised and expressed by that community (hooks [sic], 1988; Omolade, 1994; Spivak, 1988). It can be argued that, with this approach, "the need for validity and rigour of analysis becomes lost and the possibility of qualified individuals who are removed from a social grouping contributing to ethnographic analysis is no longer possible" (Saule, 2002, p. 184).

Linked to this criticism has been a concern about the potential for the maintenance of stereotypes in critical theory and the study of groups in isolation from broader structures of society (Fine, 1998; Fine & Weis, 2005). Fine and Weis (2005) proposed 'compositional studies' as providing a broader ethnographic context.

Compositional studies are undertaken in relation to key social and economic structures, that is, involving 'oscillation' from the local to the structural. Fine and Weis' argument was that "*no* one group can be understood as if outside the relational and structural aspects of identity formation" (p. 66). In other words, each group must be seen in relation to "other 'groups' and to larger sociopolitical formations".

As the views of Fine and Weis (2005) indicate, some critical ethnographers are changing as communities evolve and change, and responses are made to the arguments regarding the limitations of the critical approach.

Postmodern ethnography

In some ways, the constructivist approach to ethnography is also postmodern at least from the perspective of some writers. According to Vidich and Lyman (2003), Norman Denzin is a leader of postmodern approaches to ethnography. His advice to ethnographers was that they should:

> immerse themselves in the lives of their subjects and, after achieving a deep understanding of these through rigorous effort, produce a contextualized reproduction and interpretation of the stories told by the subjects. Ultimately, an ethnographic report will present an integrated synthesis of experience and theory (Vidich & Lyman, 2003, p. 94).

This is also the constructivist approach. Moreover, Clifford Geertz, whose views on multiple perspectives are stated above, is mentioned by Vidich and Lyman (2003, pp. 92−93) in a postmodern context. It seems that the abandonment by contemporary ethnographers of the earlier positivist frameworks is seen as marking the beginning of postmodernism. Constructivists and postmodern ethnographers also share the view that the boundaries between researchers and the researched are blurred (Guba, 1981, 1990). Giddens' (1984) view, quoted in Chapter 1, reflects this: "There is no clear dividing line between informed sociological reflection carried on by lay actors and similar endeavours on the part of specialists" (pp. xxxii−xxxiii).

The true postmodernist ethnographer also embraces other aspects of the post-modern movement: the sense of detachment and displacement (Vidich & Lyman, 2003, p. 91), and an acceptance of deconstruction, where authors lose all authority. In some of these postmodern forms, the distinctions between the researcher and the researched completely disappear (Van Maanen, 1995).

New, experimental approaches to ethnography have become part of this movement. They include confessional ethnography "where researchers narrate stories in which they play the central protagonists" (Saule, 2002, p. 188). Self or autoethnographies are another example.

Autoethnography

Autoethnography is "research, writing, and method that connect the autobiographical and personal to the cultural and social" (Ellis, 2004, p. xix). Chang (2008) emphasised that autoethnography is about understanding the relationship between the self and others. The role of 'culture' is fundamental, as is clear from Ellis' quotation. Moreover, while accepting the notion of 'individual culture', Chang stated her "nonnegotiable premise: the concept of culture is inherently group-oriented, because culture results from human interactions with each other" (pp. 16–17).

Examples of autoethnography are starting to appear in the information research literature. Gorichanaz's (2015) research was mentioned in Chapter 1's discussion of 'phenomenology'. This was because it drew on interpretative phenomenological analysis. However autoethnography also provided a methodological underpinning for his exploration of his information experience as an 'ultrarunner' during his first one hundred mile race. Drawing on Smith, Harré and van Langenhove (1995), Gorichanaz argued that wider applicability of single cases can emerge from a meta-analysis of single studies. As Yin (2012) postulated, even a single case study can make a single theoretical contribution.

Another example of autoethnographic research, this time from the field of information behaviour, is a work in progress being undertaken by two researchers working together, one in Australia and one in South Africa (Anderson & Fourie, 2015).

Further comments on contemporary ethnography

Returning to the point made in the introduction to this major section: flexible approaches to ethnography are now acceptable and frequently encountered. Even quantitative data, though used less than qualitative data, "are frequently employed to some degree or other in ethnographic work" (Atkinson & Hammersley, 1998, p. 117).

The problem with traditional approaches to ethnography is the large amount of time required for fieldwork, analysis and writing up results – to the point that Myers (1999) implied that the length of time involved has been a deterrent to the use of ethnography in information systems research. Because the detailed insights of ethnographic inquiry are still desirable in many situations, "researchers have developed lightweight or rapid forms of ethnography to gain useful insight in less time" (Wildemuth, 2009, p. 66). She provides an example where a researcher, in designing a new information retrieval system, wishes to investigate the ways in which people use documents in their current work. In other words, the study is not investigating the whole of a culture, but a highly specific aspect. Another example, where the traditional approach was curtailed, was provided in Bow (2002, p. 271) and is included again in Box 13.1, with slight amendment.

Box 13.1

Example of ethnography/participant observation:
Telephone use at home

Gillard, Wale and Bow (1994) undertook an ethnography of telephone use at home without participating or observing. To participate and observe over a period of time within a setting usually requires the researcher to become a member of the group being studied, or at least to be present in the setting for a period of time. When the setting of the study is the home, this becomes difficult as it is usually a private space in which couples, families and friends carry out personal relationships and routines, which they do not necessarily want to share with strangers. Whilst observing in the home may be possible (and does occasionally occur in research within short spaces of time), participating as a family member is impossible. The researcher can never be a member of the family, and is sure to change the dynamics of the family they are studying. The solution to this problem is to interview respondents in a way which will reveal data similar to those which might be collected if the researcher were actually participating in, and observing, the activities of the participants. This means that researchers need to ask questions about attitudes and opinions, and also questions about what people do. They need to learn as much as possible about the context of participants' lives and preferably to interview them in their home or work environment.

The above would not be regarded as examples of ethnography by all researchers. I have used similar approaches but, rather than claiming to have undertaken 'ethnographies', have couched my research as using ethnographic techniques in a constructivist framework (Williamson, 2006).

Visual and virtual ethnography

Other contemporary developments are the use of visual ethnography and online or virtual ethnography. As an example of the former, video-taping is now sometimes part of ethnographic method, requiring specialised analysis. "The development of digital technology in both still and video modes makes it increasingly appealing for ethnographers to explore these technologies as they become both more affordable and user friendly" (Gottlieb, 2006, p. 57).

Pink (2007) provides a good introduction to visual ethnography, while Iedema and his colleagues contribute examples from the health field (e.g., Carroll, Iedema & Kerridge, 2008; Iedema, Long, Forsyth & Lee, 2006). A journal dedicated to visual ethnography, titled *Visual Anthropology*, is focussed "on the study of human behavior through visual means" (http://www.tandfonline.com/toc/gvan20/current). A deep exploration of the 'visual' in ethnography is provided by Harper (2005). Gottlieb (2006, p. 57) also pointed out that some ethnographers have begun to use body-based techniques, for example, to chart bodily movements in dance. She mentioned the possibilities this opens for the study of infants. "Developing means of analysing body-based communications affords us new theoretical insights into important domains of human experience that Western scholarship often ignores" (Gottlieb, 2006, p. 57).

Virtual or online ethnography has growing importance in the information field because of the interest of researchers in online communities and other kinds of internet and social media (e.g., Facebook, Twitter and YouTube) use. An example of an online ethnography is provided below, and there is reference to another. Hine's (2000) *Virtual Ethnography*, is a frequently cited reference. She made the point that: "ethnography can … be used to develop an enriched sense of the meanings of the technology and the cultures which enable it and are enabled by it" (p. 8). Nevertheless, there are particular issues to consider with virtual ethnography, particularly because of the lack of visual cues. "Therefore, it is necessary to develop a critical sense to evaluate virtual sources carefully, and to avoid making claims of certainty that cannot be backed up by other means" (Angrosino, 2005, p. 743). Miller and Slater (2000) examine the internet from an ethnographic perspective; Jones is a prolific author who explores the nature of online communities (e.g., Jones, 1997; Jones & Kucker, 2001); and Markham (2005) explores the methods, politics and ethics of representation in online ethnography.

Ethics require attention in all ethnographic research and there are particular issues in online ethnography, as discussed by Angrosino (2005). Ethics associated with ethnography/ participant observation are also discussed briefly below, in the example of Al-Saggaf's work and in Chapter 17. Ethics, from an overall research perspective, are discussed in Chapter 20: *Ethical research practices*.

Trustworthiness in ethnographic studies

As with all research, trustworthiness, which positivist label 'validity' is an important consideration. The issue of rigour with regard to interpretivist research is discussed in Chapter 1, and the points made there need not be repeated here.

Concerns about, and approaches to, validity in ethnography

The issue of the validity of ethnography, where multiple perspectives prevail, continues to concern some writers. Hammersley is one such author who admitted that ethnographic texts are often criticised for not being scientific enough. In 1990, he commented: "We can never be absolutely certain about the validity of any knowledge claim" (Hammersley, 1990, p. 73). In 2002, he made an effort to address what he saw as one of "the central ambiguities in ethnography: between a commitment to a methodology based on naïve realism and a theoretical approach based on constructivism that is often taken to imply relativism" (Hammersley, 2002, p. 76). His solution is to draw on both approaches to engage in what he calls 'subtle realism'. This is a complicated notion which involves collecting all the various constructions of reality which participants provide but assessing them "based on judgements about plausibility and credibility: on the compatibility of the claim, or the evidence for it, with the assumptions about the world that we take to be beyond reasonable doubt" (2002, p. 73). If you are interested in this argument, I urge you to read Hammersley (2002) for yourself, as it is impossible to encapsulate his views adequately in a couple of sentences.

Schwandt (1998) seemed to be indicating a similar approach to Hammersley's (2002) view when he stated: "Truth is a matter of the best-informed and most sophisticated construction on which there is consensus at any time", although it begs the question of who should decide this. My own approach, based on several broadly ethnographic projects, is to search for the consensus and dissonance in participants' multiple views. I have found that the meanings that were shared, and those that were not, emerged clearly in studies of particular groups, for example, women with breast cancer (Williamson, 2005) or online investors (Williamson & Kingsford Smith, 2010). That is not to say that the dissonance can necessarily be disregarded: it may provide valuable insights.

The difficulties associated with multiple perspectives in ethnography are further exacerbated by the ever-broadening audience (Armstrong, 2008), some of whom are undisciplined in the sense of not being constrained by knowledge of the scientific approach to research:

> We are faced, therefore, with the situation where we collect data from a variety of people who themselves, have a variety of interests, and publish our analyses in a variety of sites for a variety of readers, each of whom brings his or her own interests to the text. The text always escapes the author. The work produced will not be read conclusively; it will be read by its relevance to readers who assign meaning to it according to their own valuations (Armstrong, 2008, pp. 64–65).

Ways of ensuring trustworthiness

There is some discussion of ways of ensuring trustworthiness in Chapter 1, but only a brief mention of triangulation — which is an important approach.

Triangulation

Triangulation emphasises the use of multiple methods and theoretical constructs (Guba, 1990, p. 23), thus adding rigour, breadth, and depth to a study (Denzin & Lincoln, 1998, p. 4). There are four common forms of triangulation: (1) data triangulation means that the ethnographer uses a variety of data sources for the study, for example, a range of different informants; (2) method triangulation means the use of multiple methods in the same project (Janesick, 1998), for example, interviews and observation (called tools or techniques in this book); (3) if possible, the ethnographer uses or consults several different researchers (interviewers/observers) to provide multiple perspectives; and (4) the ethnographer uses multiple theories and/or perspectives to interpret a single set of data.

While triangulation may not establish trustworthiness beyond question, it will show to the text's readers and the researcher's peers that rigour has been applied to the collection and analysis of the data, and the writing up of the text. Writing persuasively is important, rather than relying on 'scientific proof' (Denzin & Lincoln, 1998). As well as providing evidence of triangulation, it is also important that ethnographers explain in the text the effects they believe that their own backgrounds may have played on the undertaking of the ethnography or at least to acknowledge that there will be some degree of effect. As Charmaz (2003) noted, in discussing constructivist grounded theory, "the viewer creates the data and ensuing analysis through interaction with the viewed" and therefore the data do not provide a window on an objective reality (p. 273). This means that, although there is every effort made to present the viewpoint of participants, there is acceptance that "we shape the data collection and redirect our analysis as new issues emerge" (p. 271).

Generalisability

Chapter 15: *Populations and samples*, provides a discussion of generalisability related to qualitative and quantitative research and most of the points made there need not be repeated here. However, the point about 'naturalistic generalisations' (Stake, 2003), implying parallels and comparisons as a form of generalisation, is reinforced by Armstrong (2008, p. 55): "No good ethnography is self-contained. Implicitly or explicitly ethnography is an act of comparison."

Speaking specifically of ethnography, Myers (1999) made the following point with regard to the information systems field: "Over time, as more ethnographies are completed, it might be possible to develop more general models of the meaningful contexts of various aspects of information systems development and application." He added that, in the meantime: "Just as it is possible to generalize from one case study to theory, so it is possible to generalize from one ethnography to theory" (Myers, 1999, p. 7).

The points made about the wider applicability of single case studies, in the 'autoethnography' section, above, are also relevant here.

Designing and undertaking ethnographic research

In deciding whether to choose to use ethnography/participant observation, you should consider whether your topic and research questions are appropriate. Chapter 2 attempts to assist with that decision. As Bow (2002, p. 271) stated: "If your interest is to learn about certain characteristics, behaviours, or opinions of your research participants in depth, then ethnography may be a good choice." Ethnography is not the only qualitative approach, however. You should also consider case study, for example (Chapter 7) or action research (Chapter 8). For example, case study may be best suited to a research project where an organisation is the key research focus, rather than the individual actors. Action research may work better where the research focusses on change within a workplace, requiring acceptance and ownership by those affected. A strength of ethnography is that it emphasises human perceptions and beliefs in particular contexts.

Once having chosen ethnography/participant observation, there is a range of ways in which the research can be designed. Decisions will be contingent on your topic, your questions, the setting and participants. Potentially you can combine:

> a number of techniques, such as interviewing, focus groups, observation, and questionnaires, but also [there is] ... the flexibility to emphasise some techniques over others, and to leave some techniques out altogether − depending on the requirements and constraints of the research itself, such as the time, money and resources which are available (Bow, 2002, p. 267).

Two different examples, illustrating how ethnographic designs have been used in information research, are included below. Gaining permission to enter the field is an important step, which is discussed in Chapter 17 and also in Chapter 7, in relation to case study research.

Uses of ethnography in information research

The purpose of this section is to provide some examples of how ethnography/ participant observation has been used in the information field. The first example comes from my own research (with others) and has the title: *Older people: Overcoming barriers to public internet access*. The piece here is adapted from Bow (2002). The second project was PhD research, which took place between 2000 and 2002 and is an example of online ethnography. This study could have been as easily undertaken by a researcher in the LIS field, as by someone from the information systems field. In fact the researcher is at present an Associate Professor in the School of Computing and Mathematics at Charles Sturt University. With a LIS background, I was one of his supervisors. His thesis, now published as a book (Al-Saggaf, 2012), is entitled *Online communities in Saudi Arabia: An ethnographic study*. Al-Saggaf was an outstanding PhD student who completed his PhD studies in two and a half years, full-time, published widely based on his research, and was renowned for a talk he gave to other PhD students entitled 'How to manage your supervisors'!

Another of my PhD students, Oliver Burmeister, also at present an Associate Professor in the School of Computing and Mathematics at Charles Sturt University, undertook an online ethnography within constructivist and HCI frameworks. His thesis, completed in 2010, is entitled 'What seniors value about online social interaction: The case of an online community' (Burmeister, 2010). This study explored values which were important to seniors in their interactions in the Australian GreyPath online community for seniors. Burmeister, Weckert & Williamson (2011) presented some of the results from this study.

Older people: Overcoming barriers to public internet access

Williamson and her colleagues (Bow, Williamson & Wale, 1996; Williamson, Bow & Wale, 1996; and Williamson, Bow & Wale, 1997) were interested in the barriers faced by older adults in using the internet in public libraries. These were the early days of public internet access and older adults were reluctant users. The researchers used ethnographic method as described in Box 13.2. They saw their role as observers primarily, but also as participants, positioning their research as 'observer as participant' on the Glesne and Peshkin (1992) scale, described in Chapter 17.

Box 13.2

Older people: Overcoming barriers to public internet access

In 1996, the researchers recruited 120 participants, aged 60 and older, in three public libraries in Victoria, Australia, with the aim of exploring the barriers to the use of the internet in public settings by older adults. The participants filled in questionnaires exploring the relationships between how they felt about computers, their current experience of computers and the internet, their current knowledge of the internet and other demographic factors. Sixty of the participants were further invited to participate in an observation study. This involved participants being observed while they attempted to use the internet (most for the first time). The observers only intervened when participants were unable to proceed alone. They systematically recorded their observations about problems the participants experienced as they attempted to use the internet. While the research could have been described as a 'usability study', the researchers did not use that label.

Observers interacted with participants as guides and interviewers, but they attempted to take the role of empathetic peers, which was appropriate given that the observers were, themselves, not young. The researchers also spent some time familiarising themselves with the libraries and internet access in each of the settings. There is an element of participation within the familiarisation process itself, because the researchers were participating in something participants were also to use. The researchers could not do traditional participant observation, given that there was no established behaviour involving internet use by seniors at the time. Instead, they recruited participants from their natural setting (the library) to participate in an activity they did not normally do, in order to understand the barriers to undertaking that activity.

The study revealed a number of problems for older people in using the internet. For example, some of the internet functions did not make immediate sense to new users, some of the fonts were too small or too faint for people with vision impairments to see properly (Williamson, Bow and Wale, 1996). It appeared that unfamiliarity and fear of the internet were the main reasons for older adults not using it. After the study, 85 percent of the respondents indicated they would use the internet again.

Adapted from Bow, 2002, p. 270.

Online communities in Saudi Arabia: An ethnographic study

Yeslam Al-Saggaf, was interested in the impact on the lives of Saudi Arabians of the introduction of the internet to their country in 1999. In a country "where Islam acts as a main force in determining social norms, values and practices" (Al-Saggaf, 2012, p. 1), he particularly wanted to explore the impact of the opening up of cross-gender communication (not sanctioned in the off-line world). Apart from his thesis, now published as a book (Al-Saggaf, 2012), he has a number of other publications, some with his supervisors (e.g., Al-Saggaf & Williamson, 2004; Al-Saggaf & Williamson, 2006; Al-Saggaf, Weckert & Williamson, 2002; and Al-Saggaf, Williamson & Weckert, 2002). The first two of these four references are methodological: Al-Saggaf and Williamson (2006) discusses the constructivist paradigm chosen for the research; Al-Saggaf and Williamson (2004) focusses on the findings from the use of one of the chosen techniques, semi-structured interviews. Box 13.3 describes Al-Saggaf's research.

Box 13.3

Online communities in Saudi Arabia:
An ethnographic study

Research questions

Because Al-Saggaf (2012) wanted to learn as much as possible about his topic, he did not want to start with specific questions. Since this was interpretivist research, it was an acceptable approach. After the data collection began, the following research questions emerged and remained to guide the study:

- What are the characteristics of participation in online communities?
- What is the influence of the communication medium on participation online?
- What is the influence of the individuals' offline culture on participation online?
- What are the effects of participation in online communities on individuals' offline lives?
- What are the advantages and disadvantages of participation in online communities? (Al-Saggaf, 2012, p. 8)

Definition of an online community

While Al-Saggaf (2012) presented a complex discussion of what constitutes an online community, he used Rheingold's definition in most of the papers (as cited above), after the thesis was completed:

> *Virtual communities are social aggregations that emerge from the Net when enough people carry on those public discussions long enough, with sufficient human feeling, to form webs of personal relationships in cyberspace (Rheingold, 2000, p. xx).*

Research methodology

The research methodology combined the constructivist paradigm, with ethnographic method. The major data collection tools were observation and semi-structured interviews, but there were four stages involved: (1) unobtrusive observation of a virtual community; (2) a participant observation in another similar virtual community; (3) online semi-structured interviews with regular participants; and (4) face-to-face semi-structured interviews with key informants. Findings obtained through these techniques were triangulated to assist in establishing the trustworthiness of the research results (Al-Saggaf & Williamson, 2006). Al-Saggaf's use of observation will be outlined in Chapter 17.

Entry to the research sites and ethical issues

Informed consent was obtained for the online and face-to-face interviews, in accordance with the requirements of the Ethics in Human Research Committee at Charles Sturt University. The ethical issues involved in the observation components were more complicated. The observation involved use of two different online forums, public spaces open to all and requiring only a nickname and password for the posting of contributions. Al-Saggaf investigated extensively the ethical issues involved. He found a general consensus that research on the internet "is exempt from 'human subjects' classification if there is no intervention with the persons doing the activities being observed and the collection of data does not involve these persons' identities" (Personal communication from John Weckert, a computer ethics specialist, 10 September 2001). Others, including Eysenbach and Till (2001), provided further support.

Findings

Key findings relate to cross-gender communication, not permitted in Saudi Arabia before. Participants learned a great deal from their interaction with each other, became more sociable and more open-minded. "In a country where freedom to verbalise one's ideas and views is limited, participants found in the online community a gateway or 'an opening' to express their ideas and views" (Al-Saggaf, Weckert & Williamson, 2002).

Conclusion

Part of the conclusion relates to the advantages of using ethnography to undertake this study: "Doing ethnography from within a constructivist paradigm enabled the conduct of unobtrusive observation and participation in ways which yielded results that are deep, meaningful and rich in nature."

Source: Al-Saggaf & Williamson, 2004.

Conclusion

Modern ethnography/participant observation offers a cornucopia of options for understanding the world of others and is underpinned by a rich literature, which needs to be explored prior to your making a decision about using the method. I must emphasise that the researcher should carefully consider the suitability of a topic for this kind of research, the amount of time and maybe expense, and the other choices available, for example, case study or action research, where ethnographic tools are also used. Consider, too, the broad, methodological framework, involving choices, for example, of paradigm and data collection tools. Questions of validity/trustworthiness need to be carefully considered, along with the ethics requirements that should be met, including those that may be specific to online ethnography. Please do not be deterred by these requirements. I am an enthusiast with regard to the value of ethnography as a research method. If you have limitations which do not enable a full ethnography, the use of ethnographic techniques, within your chosen framework, will be worthwhile.

References

Al-Saggaf, Y. (2012). *Online communities in Saudi Arabia: An ethnographic study.* Saarbrücken: LAMBERT Academic Publishing.

Al-Saggaf, Y., Weckert, J., & Williamson, K. (2002). What individuals in Saudi Arabia say about their participation in online communities. In P. Isaias (Ed.), *Proceedings of the WWW/Internet 2002 International Conference, Lisbon Portugal, 13–15 November 2002* (pp. 363–371). [s.l]: IADIS.

Al-Saggaf, Y., & Williamson, K. (2004). Online communities in Saudi Arabia: Evaluating the impact on culture through online semi-structured interviews. *Forum Qualitative Sozialforschung/Forum: Qualitative Social Research, 5*(3). Retrieved from http://www.qualitative-research.net/fqs-texte/3-04/04-3-24-e.htm

Al-Saggaf, Y., & Williamson, K. (2006). Doing ethnography from within a constructivist paradigm to explore virtual communities in Saudi Arabia. *Qualitative Sociology Review, 11*(2). Retrieved from http://www.qualitativesociologyreview.org/ENG/volume4.php

Al-Saggaf, Y., Williamson, K., & Weckert, J. (2002). Online communities in Saudi Arabia: an ethnographic study. Paper presented at the Australasian Conference on Information Systems, Melbourne, 4–6 December, 2002. *ACIS 2002 Proceedings*, Paper 62. Retrieved from http://aisel.aisnet.org/cgi/viewcontent.cgi?article=1162&context=acis2002

Anderson, T., & Fourie, I. (2015). Collaborative autoethnography as a way of seeing the experience of care giving as an information practice. *Information Research: An International Electronic Journal, 20*(1). Retrieved from http://www.informationr.net/ir/20-1/isic2/isic33.html#.WIHhrXrzJnk

Angrosino, M. V. (2005). Recontextualizing observation: Ethnography, pedagogy, and the prospects for a progressive political agenda. In N. K. Denzin, & Y. S. Lincoln (Eds.), *The Sage handbook of qualitative research* (3rd ed., pp. 729–746). Thousand Oaks, CA: Sage.

Angrosino, M. V., & Pérez, K. (2000). Rethinking observation: From method to context. In N. K. Denzin, & Y. S. Lincoln (Eds.), *Handbook of qualitative research* (2nd ed., pp. 673–702). Thousand Oaks, CA: Sage.

Armstrong, K. (2008). Ethnography and audience. In P. Alasuutari, L. Bickman, & J. Brannen (Eds.), *The Sage handbook of social research methods* (pp. 54–67). Los Angeles: Sage.

Atkinson, P., Coffey, A., Delamont, S., Lofland, J., & Lofland, L. (2001). *Handbook of Ethnography*. London: Sage Publications.

Atkinson, P., & Delamont, S. (2005). Analytic perspectives. In N. K. Denzin, & Y. S. Lincoln (Eds.), *The Sage handbook of qualitative research* (3rd ed., pp. 821–840). Thousand Oaks, CA: Sage.

Atkinson, P., & Hammersley, M. (1998). Ethnography and participant observation. In N. K. Denzin, & Y. S. Lincoln (Eds.), *Strategies of qualitative inquiry* (pp. 110–136). Thousand Oaks, CA: Sage.

Baker, T. L. (1999). *Doing social research*. Boston: McGraw-Hill.

Bateson, G. (1972). *Steps to an ecology of mind*. New York: Ballantine.

Bow, A. (2002). Ethnographic techniques. In K. Williamson (Ed.), *Research methods for students, academics and professionals: Information management and systems* (2nd ed., pp. 265–279). Wagga Wagga, NSW: Centre for Information Studies, Charles Sturt University.

Bow, A., Williamson, K., & Wale, K. (1996). *Barriers to public internet access.* Paper presented at the communications research forum 1996, Monash University, Melbourne. Canberra: Bureau of Transport and Communications Economics.

Burmeister, O. (2010). *What seniors value about online social interaction: The case of an online community.* (Ph.D. Thesis). Charles Sturt University, Wagga Wagga, NSW, Australia.

Burmeister, O., Weckert, J., & Williamson, K. (2011). Seniors extend understanding of what constitutes universal values. *Journal of Information, Communication & Ethics in Society, 9*(4), 238–252.

Burns, R. B. (2000). *Introduction to research methods* (4th ed.). Frenchs Forest, NSW: Longman.

Carroll, K., Iedema, R., & Kerridge, R. (2008). Reshaping ICU ward round practices using video-reflexive ethnography. *Qualitative Health Research, 18*(3), 380–390.

Cecez-Kecmanovic, D. (2001). Doing critical IS research: The question of methodology. In E. Trauth (Ed.), *Qualitative research in information systems: Issues and trends* (pp. 142–163). Hershey, PA: Idea Group Publishing.

Chang, H. (2008). *Autoethnography method.* Walnut Creek, CA: Left Coast Press.

Charmaz, K. (2003). Grounded theory: Objectivist and constructivist methods. In N. K. Denzin, & Y. S. Lincoln (Eds.), *Strategies of qualitative inquiry* (2nd ed., pp. 249–291). Thousand Oaks, CA: Sage.

Deegan, M. J. (2001). The Chicago school of ethnography. In P. Atkinson, A. Coffey, S. Delamont, & J. Lofland (Eds.), *The handbook of ethnography* (pp. 12–24). London: Sage.

Delamont, S. (2004). Ethnography and participant observation. In C. Seale, G. Gobo, J. F. Gubrium, & D. Silverman (Eds.), *Qualitative research practice* (pp. 217–229). London: Sage.

Denzin, N. K. (2005). Emancipatory discourses and the ethics and politics of interpretation. In N. K. Denzin, & Y. S. Lincoln (Eds.), *The Sage handbook of qualitative research* (3rd ed., pp. 933–958). Thousand Oaks, CA: Sage.

Denzin, N. K., & Lincoln, Y. S. (1998). Introduction: Entering the field of qualitative research. In N. K. Denzin, & Y. S. Lincoln (Eds.), *The landscape of qualitative research: Theories and issues* (pp. 1–34). London: Sage.

Dodge, M., & Kitchin, R. (2001). *Mapping cyberspace.* New York: Routledge.

Ellis, C. (2004). *The ethnographic I: A methodological novel about teaching and doing autoethnography.* Walnut Creek, CA: AltaMira.

Eysenbach, G., & Till, J. E. (2001). Ethical issues in qualitative research on internet communities. *British Medical Journal, 323*(7321), 1103–1105.

Fielding, N. (2001). Ethnography. In N. Gilbert (Ed.), *Researching social life* (2nd ed., pp. 145–163). London: Sage.

Fine, M. (1998). Working the hyphens: Reinventing self and other in qualitative research. In N. K. Denzin, & Y. S. Lincoln (Eds.), *The landscape of qualitative research: Theories and issues* (pp. 130–155). London: Sage.

Fine, M., & Weis, L. (2005). Compositional studies, in two parts: Critical theorising and analysis on social (in)justice. In N. K. Denzin, & Y. S. Lincoln (Eds.), *The Sage handbook of qualitative research* (3rd ed., pp. 65–84). Thousand Oaks, CA: Sage.

Foley, D., & Valenzuela, A. (2005). Critical ethnography: The politics of collaboration. In N. K. Denzin, & Y. S. Lincoln (Eds.), *The Sage handbook of qualitative research* (3rd ed., pp. 217–234). Thousand Oaks, CA: Sage.

Geertz, C. (1973). *The interpretation of cultures*. New York: Basic.

Giddens, A. (1984). *The constitution of society: Outline of the theory of structuration*. Berkeley, CA: University of California Press.

Gillard, P., Wale, K., & Bow, A. (1994). *A major line to the outside world: Defining the significance of telecommunications within their social contexts*. Melbourne: RMIT Telecommunications Needs Research Group.

Glesne, C., & Peshkin, A. (1992). *Becoming qualitative researchers: An introduction*. White Plains, NY: Longmans Publishing Group.

Gorichanaz, T. (2015). Information on the run: Experiencing information during an ultramarathon. *Information Research: An International Electronic Journal*, 20(4). Retrieved from http://www.informationr.net/ir/20-4/paper697.html#.WHf6uXrzJnk

Gottlieb, A. (2006). Ethnography: Theory and methods. In E. Perecman, & S. R. Curran (Eds.), *A handbook for social science field research: Essays & bibliographic sources on research design and methods* (pp. 47–68). Thousand Oaks, CA: Sage.

Grover, R., & Glazier, J. D. (1992). Structured participant observation. In J. D. Glazier, & R. R. Powell (Eds.), *Qualitative research in information management* (pp. 61–84). Englewood, CO: Libraries Unlimited.

Guba, E. G. (1981). Criteria for assessing the trustworthiness of naturalistic inquiries. *Educational Communication and Technology*, 29(2), 75–91.

Guba, E. G. (1990). The alternative paradigm dialog. In E. G. Guba (Ed.), *The paradigm dialog* (pp. 17–27). London: Sage.

Hammersley, M. (1990). *Reading ethnographic research: A critical guide*. London: Longman.

Hammersley, M. (1992). *What's wrong with ethnography? Methodological explorations*. London: Routledge Press.

Hammersley, M. (2002). Ethnography and realism. In A. M. Huberman, & M. B. Miles (Eds.), *The qualitative researcher's companion* (pp. 65–80). Thousand Oaks, CA: Sage.

Hammersley, M., & Atkinson, P. (1995). *Ethnography: Principles in practice* (2nd ed.). London: Routledge.

Harper, D. (2005). What's new visually. In N. K. Denzin, & Y. S. Lincoln (Eds.), *The Sage handbook of qualitative research* (3rd ed., pp. 747–762). Thousand Oaks, CA: Sage.

Hine, C. (2000). *Virtual ethnography*. London: Sage Publications.

hooks, B. [sic] (1988). *Talking back: Thinking feminist, thinking black*. Toronto: Between the Lines.

Iedema, R., Long, D., Forsyth, R., & Lee, B. (2006). Visibilising clinical work: Video ethnography in the contemporary hospital. *Health Sociology Review, 15,* 156–168.

Janesick, V. H. (1998). The dance of qualitative research design: Metaphor, methodolatory and meaning. In N. K. Denzin, & Y. S. Lincoln (Eds.), *Strategies of qualitative inquiry* (pp. 35–55). London: Sage.

Jones, S. G. (1997). The internet and its social landscape. In S. G. Jones (Ed.), *Virtual culture: Identity & communication in cybersociety* (pp. 7–35). London: Sage.

Jones, S. G., & Kucker, S. (2001). Computers, the internet and virtual cultures. In J. Lull (Ed.), *Culture in the communication age* (pp. 212–225). London: Routledge.

Keesing, R., & Strathern, A. (1998). *Cultural anthropology: A contemporary perspective* (3rd ed.). Fort Worth, TX: Harcourt Brace.

Kincheloe, J. L., & McLaren, P. (2005). Rethinking critical theory and qualitative research. In N. K. Denzin, & Y. S. Lincoln (Eds.), *The Sage handbook of qualitative research* (3rd ed., pp. 303–342). Thousand Oaks, CA: Sage.

Lipu, S. (2010). Feminist perspectives of information literacy: conceptualising a new sphere for IL research. In A. Lloyd, & S. Talja (Eds.), *Practising information literacy: Bringing theories of learning, practice and information literacy together* (pp. 331–356). Wagga Wagga, NSW: Centre for Information Studies, Charles Sturt University.

Madison, D. S. (2005). Critical ethnography as street performance: Reflections of home, race, murder, and justice. In N. K. Denzin, & Y. S. Lincoln (Eds.), *The Sage handbook of qualitative research* (3rd ed., pp. 537–546). Thousand Oaks, CA: Sage.

Malinowski, B. (1922). *Argonauts of the western Pacific*. London: Routledge & Keegan Paul.

Markham, A. N. (2005). The methods, politics, and ethics of representation in online ethnography. In N. K. Denzin, & Y. S. Lincoln (Eds.), *The Sage handbook of qualitative research* (3rd ed., pp. 793–820). Thousand Oaks, CA: Sage.

Mead, M. (1960). *Coming of age in Samoa: A psychological study of primitive youth for western civilization*. New York: Mentor.

Mellon, C. (1990). *Naturalistic inquiry for library science: Methods and applications for research, evaluation and teaching*. New York: Greenwood Press.

Miller, D., & Slater, D. (2000). *The internet: An ethnographic approach*. New York: Berg.

Moeran, B. (2007). From participant observation to observant participation: Anthropology, fieldwork and organisational ethnography. *Creative encounters working papers*. Retrieved from www.cbs.dk/creativeencounters

Myers, M. (1999). Investigating information systems with ethnographic research. *Communications of the Association for Information Systems, 2*(Article 23), 1–19. Retrieved from http://aisel.aisnet.org/cais/vol2/iss1/23/.

Neuman, W. L. (2014). *Social research methods: Qualitative and quantitative approaches* (7th ed.). Harlow, Essex: Pearson New International.

Olesen, V. (2005). Early millennial feminist qualitative research: Challenges and contours. In N. K. Denzin, & Y. S. Lincoln (Eds.), *The Sage handbook of qualitative research* (3rd ed., pp. 235–278). Thousand Oaks, CA: Sage.

Omolade, B. (1994). *The rising song of African American women*. New York: Routledge Press.

Patton, M. Q. (2015). *Qualitative evaluation and research methods* (4th ed.). Los Angeles, CA: Sage Publications.

Pickard, A. J. (2013). *Research methods in information* (2nd ed.). Chicago: Neal-Schuman.

Pink, S. (2007). *Doing visual ethnography* (2nd ed.). London: Sage.

Prus, R. (1997). *Subcultural mosaics and intersubjective realities: An ethnographic research agenda for pragmatising the social sciences*. New York: State University of New York.

Rheingold, H. (2000). *The virtual community: Homesteading on the electronic frontier* (Rev. ed.). Cambridge, MA: MIT Press.

Saule, S. (2002). Ethnography. In K. Williamson (Ed.), *Research methods for students, academics and professionals: Information management and systems* (2nd ed., pp. 177–193). Wagga Wagga, NSW: Centre for Information Studies, Charles Sturt University.

Sayago, S., & Blat, J. (2010). Telling the story of older people e-mailing: An ethnographical study. *International Journal of Human-Computer Studies, 68*(1–2), 105–120.

Schwandt, T. A. (1998). Constructivist, interpretivist approaches to human inquiry. In N. K. Denzin, & Y. S. Lincoln (Eds.), *The landscape of qualitative research: Theories and issues* (pp. 221–259). London: Sage.

Schwandt, T. A. (2003). Three epistemological stances for qualitative inquiry: Interpretivism, hermenuetics, and social contructionism. In N. K. Denzin, & Y. S. Lincoln (Eds.), *The landscape of qualitative research: Theories and issues* (2nd ed., pp. 292–331). Thousand Oaks, CA: Sage.

Silverman, D. (2005). *Doing qualitative research* (2nd ed.). London: Sage.

Spivak, G. C. (1988). Can the subaltern speak? In C. Nelson, & L. Grossberg (Eds.), *Marxism and the interpretations of cultures* (pp. 271–313). Chicago: University of Illinois Press.

Spradley, J. P. (1979). *The ethnographic interview*. New York: Holt, Rhinehart & Winston.

Spradley, J. P. (1980). *Participant observation*. New York: Holt, Rhinehart & Winston.

Stake, R. (2003). Case studies. In N. K. Denzin, & Y. S. Lincoln (Eds.), *Strategies of qualitative inquiry* (2nd ed., pp. 134–164). Thousand Oaks, CA: Sage.

Stanfield, J. (1998). Ethnic modelling in qualitative research. In N. K. Denzin, & Y. S. Lincoln (Eds.), *The landscape of qualitative research: Theories and issues* (pp. 333–358). London: Sage.

Taylor, S. J., Bogdan, R., & DeVault, M. (2015). *Introduction to qualitative research methods: A guidebook and resource* (4th ed.). New York: John Wiley & Sons.

Tedlock, B. (2005). The observation of participation and the emergence of public ethnography. In N. K. Denzin, & Y. S. Lincoln (Eds.), *The Sage handbook of qualitative research* (3rd ed., pp. 467–481). Thousand Oaks, CA: Sage.

Thomas, J. (1993). *Doing critical ethnography*. Newbury Park, CA: Sage.

Thwaites, T., Davis, L., & Mules, W. (1994). *Tools for cultural studies: An introduction*. Melbourne: MacMillan.

Van Maanen, J. (1988). *Tales of the field: On writing ethnography*. Chicago, IL: The University of Chicago Press.

Van Maanen, J. (1995). An end to innocence. In J. Van Maanen (Ed.), *Representation in ethnography* (pp. 1–35). London: Sage.

Van Maanen, J. (2002). The fact of fiction in organizational ethnography. In A. M. Huberman, & M. B. Miles (Eds.), *The qualitative researcher's companion* (pp. 101–118). Thousand Oaks, CA: Sage.

Vidich, A. J., & Lyman, S. M. (2003). Qualitative methods: Their history in sociology and anthropology. In N. K. Denzin, & Y. S. Lincoln (Eds.), *The landscape of qualitative research: Theories and issues* (2nd ed., pp. 55–129). Thousand Oaks, CA: Sage.

Wildemuth, B. M. (2009). *Applications of social research methods to questions in information and library science*. Westport, CT: Libraries Unlimited.

Williamson, K. (2005). Where one size does not fit all: Understanding the needs of potential users of a portal to breast cancer knowledge online. *Journal of Health Communication*, 10(6), 567–580. Retrieved from http://www2.gwu.edu/~cih/journal/index.htm

Williamson, K. (2006). Research in constructivist frameworks using ethnographic techniques. *Library Trends*, 55(1), 83–101.

Williamson, K., Bow, A., & Wale, K. (1996). Older people, new technology and public libraries. In *Reading the future: Proceedings of the Australian Library and Information Association, Melbourne Australia, 9–11 October 1996*, (pp. 161–170). Canberra, ACT: ALIA.

Williamson, K., Bow, A., & Wale, K. (1997). Encouraging public internet use by older people: A comparative study of city and rural areas. *Journal of Rural Social Research*, 7(3/4), 3–11.

Williamson, K., & Kingsford Smith, D. (2010). Empowered or vulnerable? The role of information for Australian online investors. *Canadian Journal of Information and Library Science*, 34(1), 39–81.

Yin, R. K. (2012). *Applications of case study research* (3rd ed.). Thousand Oaks, CA: Sage.

Chapter 14

Experimental research

Kerry Tanner
Monash University, Australia

This chapter reviews the major aims, concepts, issues and designs used in experimental research. It differentiates laboratory experiments (true experiments) from field experiments undertaken in natural settings (pre-experimental and quasi-experimental designs), and outlines the most commonly encountered research designs of each approach, along with examples. It considers the relative strengths and weaknesses of each design in terms of the trade-offs that must be made between establishing causation and enabling generalisation of findings beyond the immediate research setting.

Research Methods: Information, Systems, and Contexts. DOI: http://dx.doi.org/10.1016/B978-0-08-102220-7.00014-5

Introduction

Experimental research is undertaken when a researcher wishes to trace cause-and-effect relationships between defined variables. However, there are major constraints on causal inference in experimental research, and the type of experimental design chosen has a significant influence on the inferences that can be validly drawn from experimental results. Within the information field, experimental designs are much more common in information systems research than in library and information management research.

This chapter builds on earlier work of the author (Tanner, 2002). It provides an introduction to experimental research and reviews the most frequently encountered types of experimental designs. Statistical analysis techniques used in experiments are beyond the scope of the chapter. (See Chapter 18: *Quantitative data analysis* for an overview of this area. For a more exhaustive treatment, see sources such as Clarke and Kempson (1997), and Shadish, Cook and Campbell (2002).)

The chapter begins with a discussion of the philosophical paradigms and underpinning concepts of experimental research, highlighting differences between laboratory experiments and field experiments undertaken in natural settings. Within the broad categories of laboratory experiments (true experiments) and field experiments (pre-experimental and quasi-experimental designs), it then outlines the most popular forms of experimental research design and provides examples. It considers the relative strengths and weaknesses of each research design in terms of the trade-offs that must be made between establishing causation and enabling generalisation of findings beyond the immediate research setting. Important considerations in determining the most appropriate form of experimental design for a research project include: the type of research questions being addressed by the study; the degree of control that the researcher has over conditions under investigation; and whether or not the phenomenon of interest can be studied outside its natural setting. These factors are considered in relation to the major types of experimental design explored.

Philosophical paradigms and underpinning concepts

Experimental research is typically construed as strongly positivist. Laboratory-based experiments are often presented as the classic example of the traditional positivist paradigm. However, some types of field experiments may be regarded more as post-positivist in nature (Guba & Lincoln, 1994; Heron & Reason, 1997), whilst action research (see Chapter 8: *Action research*) is often considered as a recent development of experimental design in the participatory paradigm (Baskerville & Wood-Harper, 1996).

Laboratory experiments exemplify classic scientific method. This research tradition is based on a *hypothesis-testing* research approach, on a *deductive* process of logical inference, where reasoning proceeds from general principles to particular instances, as presented in Figure 14.1.

Figure 14.1 Deductive reasoning process

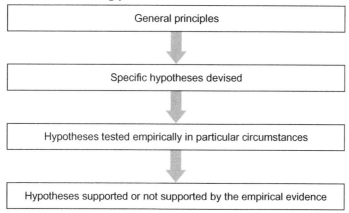

Core concepts

The following sub-sections introduce and explain the process and core concepts associated with experimental research.

Hypotheses and statistical probability testing

A hypothesis is a statement or proposition about a predicted relationship between two or more variables, which is empirically testable. For example, a researcher may start with a hypothesis: *(H_1) Participants using a decision support system (DSS) show greater decision accuracy than those using printed documents.* To empirically test this hypothesis, it is conventionally stated in its *null* form, that is, *(H_0) There is no difference in decision accuracy between participants using a DSS and those using printed documents.* Null hypotheses are designed for statistical probability-testing purposes and are based on the assumption of 'no difference' between experimental and control groups. The researcher hopes that statistical tests will show that there is a statistically significant difference between experimental and control groups (i.e., a difference not explained by chance), and thus support their hypothesis (e.g., H_1 above), establishing a likely causal link between the variables under study. (See Chapter 18 for further discussion of statistical hypothesis testing of experimental designs.)

Variables

A *variable* is an element, or factor, which is under investigation. In an experiment, the following types of variables need to be identified:

- The *independent* or *causal* variable is the factor manipulated by the researcher to see what impact it has on another variable(s). It is the presumed cause. For example, in the hypothesis above, the independent variable is *type of decision support*, with two conditions – *use of a decision support system* and *use of printed documents*. In the experiment, participants in the experimental groups would be assigned either to a group provided with a DSS or to one provided with only printed documents.

- The *dependent* or *effect* variable is the factor that is measured to determine how it has responded to a particular treatment or cause. In the example above, the dependent variable is *decision accuracy*. The experiment would present scenarios and tasks to participants in each group and then measure their decision accuracy on the allocated tasks.

- An *extraneous* or *confounding* or *intervening* variable is an unknown element, which is not the focus of the study, but that is assumed to account for some of the effects observed, for example, unexpected loud music from a concert next to the venue of the experiment may interrupt participants' thought processes and affect their decision accuracy. Generally field experiments are more prone to the presence of confounding variables than are laboratory experiments.

- A *moderating* variable in some way moderates the impact of another variable under study. For instance, decision accuracy may be affected not only by the use of a DSS versus printed documents, but also by participants' education or numeracy skills.

Reliability

Reliability refers to the consistency of results produced by a measuring instrument when it is applied more than once in a similar situation; or the stability, consistency and dependability of measures. Most experiments involve a series of tests, and it is important to ensure reliability in subsequent administrations of the experimental treatment.

Validity

Validity is the capacity of an instrument to measure what it purports to measure, or to predict what it was designed to predict; or the accuracy of observations. Experimental research focusses on two major types of validity:

- *Internal* validity – the conclusiveness of results, that is, confidence that observed results are attributable to the impact of the independent variable, and not caused by other unknown factors.

- *External* validity – the generalisability of research findings, that is, the extent to which they can be generalised to other populations, settings or treatments.

Experiments conducted in laboratory settings are high in internal validity, as the researcher can control and manipulate the independent variable and accurately measure its effects on the dependent variable and ensure that confounding variables do not influence results. However, laboratory experiments are widely criticised on the basis that their artificial, contrived settings do not enable generalisation of findings to 'the real world' (i.e., they are low in external validity).

Conversely, field experiments, in reflecting the 'richness' of a real-world setting, rate high on external validity but low on internal validity. Although researchers attempt to control variables under study in field experiments, many elements are outside their control; hence it is difficult to verify that the effects observed were attributable to the independent variable.

Experimental and control groups

Experimental research involves the differentiation of two basic conditions: exposure and non-exposure to the treatment condition of the independent variable. The *experimental group* is the group exposed to the treatment condition, while the *control group* is not subjected to treatment. There can be multiple experimental and control conditions in an experiment. Observations are recorded for each group, and the groups are then compared, with differences in the experimental group presumed to be attributable to the application of the treatment.

Randomisation (random assignment)

Randomisation ensures that experimental and control groups are equivalent in composition; it is an integral feature of a valid experimental design. A necessary pre-condition for applying statistical testing procedures in experiments is that initially subjects must be *randomly assigned* to experimental and control groups.

Another means of controlling for potential confounding variables in an experiment is by a process of *deliberate matching* of experimental and control groups for equivalence. However, in practice only a few confounding variables (e.g., gender, age and experience) will be identified; it is not possible to match groups on all possible confounding variables. Hence, wherever possible, randomisation is the preferred practice for achieving equivalence of experimental and control groups.

Experimental design notations

In describing experimental designs, 'X' is a shorthand form used to indicate the application of a treatment condition of the independent variable, and 'not-X' the lack of such a treatment. 'O' is the abbreviation for an observation or measurement (the dependent variable). Multiple measurements are indicated as O_1, O_2, O_3, etc. The abbreviation 'R' is used in diagrams of experimental design to indicate 'randomisation' in assigning subjects to experimental or control conditions. These abbreviations are used in diagrams describing different experimental designs in this chapter.

Inferring causation in experimental research

While it is difficult to establish cause-and-effect relationships conclusively with any research design, laboratory experiments offer the greatest potential for inferring causal relationships. This is due to their careful control of experimental conditions, and to the practice of randomisation ensuring that groups are equivalent in composition. To infer causation, a researcher needs to be able to eliminate alternative explanations. In experimental research, some of the main alternative explanations are:

- *Selection effect.* If participants can select their own treatment condition (experimental or control), groups will not be equivalent. Randomisation addresses this alternative explanation.

- *Maturation.* Any naturally occurring process within persons that could account for the observed change.

- *History.* Any event to which subjects are exposed around the time of the experiment, which could account for observed differences between subjects.

- *Instrumentation.* Any change in measurement instrument or procedures from one application of a treatment to another.

- *Mortality.* Participants dropping out from a study.

The laboratory experiment (or true experiment)

The laboratory experiment, as the classic example of 'scientific method', is the most suitable of any method for testing hypotheses involving cause-and-effect relationships, due to rigorously controlled conditions, including the isolation of the independent and dependent variables from other confounding variables. Eliminating potential confounding variables is much easier in a laboratory situation than in a naturalistic setting (e.g., participants' own work environments).

The basic true experimental design model involves subjects (who have been randomly assigned to groups) experiencing some condition of the independent variable (experimental groups), or lack of such a condition (control groups), and then being measured on the dependent variable. For instance, with the independent variable *type of decision support* example, separate experimental groups would be formed for the two conditions of the variable, *DSS* and *printed documents*, whilst groups provided with no type of decision support would be control groups. The same scenarios and tasks would be assigned to all experimental and control groups, with results assessed for *decision accuracy* (dependent variable) and analysed statistically. Conclusions would then be drawn on the impact of the different types of decision support.

Particular laboratory experiment research designs

The following notations are used in the models illustrated in Figures 14.2 to 14.12:

Notation	Description
R	Randomisation or random assignment
X	The application of a treatment; the independent or experimental variable; a cause
O	An observation or measurement; the dependent variable; an effect
$O_1, O_2 \ldots$	The first, second [etc.] measurement.

Simple experiment, or randomised two-group design

This is the simplest valid experimental design. Subjects are randomly assigned to either the experimental group or the control group; the treatment is administered to the experimental group; then measurements are taken and outcomes analysed statistically. A familiar example is with medical experiments, where a new drug is administered to the experimental group, and a placebo to the control group. Another example is an experiment on the impact of noise on task performance, where the experimental group completes a task in a noisy situation while the control undertakes the same task in a quiet environment. Outcomes for each group (O_1, and O_2) are then compared statistically and conclusions drawn.

Figure 14.2 presents the basic model, along with an example.

Figure 14.2 Randomised two-group design

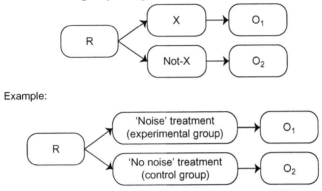

Example:

Variations on the basic model include two or more experimental conditions *and* a control group, or two or more alternative treatments *instead of* a control group. See Figure 14.3.

Figure 14.3 Variation on the basic two-group design

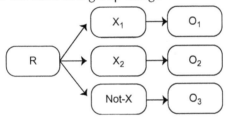

An example of this type of experimental design is Huang and Windsor's (1998) experiment on the effectiveness of multimedia executive support systems (ESS) compared with purely text-based ESS. In this experiment, the older purely text-based form of ESS was the control (not-X), and two multimedia ESS prototypes, one that used purely visual multimedia (X_1), and another that used both audio and visual multimedia (X_2) were the experimental groups. All groups were given the same task, analysing a business proposal and identifying potential threats and opportunities based on the information provided, and their results (O_1, O_2 and O_3) were then compared statistically.

Pre-test/post-test control group design (or four-cell experimental design, or before-and-after two-group design)

The pre-test/post-test control group design is another 'classic' experimental design. See Figure 14.4. It involves experimental and control groups, selected through randomisation. Both groups are initially tested, and measured on the variable under consideration. Then the experimental group is subjected to the treatment and subsequently re-tested. The control group is isolated from the experimental treatment and is also re-tested. In analysing results, comparisons are made between pre-test and post-test scores for each group (i.e., within-group scores: O_1 and O_2; O_3 and O_4), and also the between-group scores (i.e., O_1 and O_3; O_2 and O_4), with any observed differences presumed to be attributable to the experimental treatment.

Figure 14.4 Basic model for the pre-test/post-test control group design

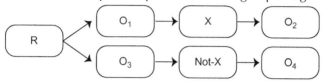

An example of a pre-test/post-test control group design is an experiment testing the efficacy of a new training program for enhancing information retrieval skills. Here participants would be randomly assigned to either the experimental or control condition and all given the same initial information retrieval test (i.e., O_1 and $O_{3)}$. After the experimental group has undertaken the information retrieval skills training program, both experimental and control groups would be re-tested (i.e., O_2 and O_4). Both *within-group* scores (i.e., O_1 and $O_{2;}$ and O_3 and O_4) and *between-group* scores (i.e., O_1 and O_3; and O_2 and O_4) would be included in the statistical analysis of results. Besides analysing the effectiveness of the training program, researchers may also be interested in assessing the impact on results of moderating variables such as age and prior experience.

One potential problem with a pre-test preceding a post-test is that subjects may be sensitised to the purpose of the experiment, and hence bias their post-test scores (i.e., a *maturation* effect).

Again, there are variations on this basic design, such as where there are multiple experimental groups and a control, or multiple experimental groups instead of a control.

Factorial designs

A factorial design involves two or more independent variables under study (designated X, Y, etc.). Both the *independent* effects and the *interactive* effects of these variables on the dependent variable are studied. These designs can be very complex methodologically, especially where more than two variables are involved.

The basic model for a two-by-two factorial design is shown in Figure 14.5, whilst Figure 14.6 following presents an example (Arnott & O'Donnell, 2008).

Figure 14.5 Basic model for a 2x2 factorial design

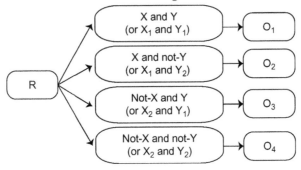

Figure 14.6 Example of a 2x2 factorial design

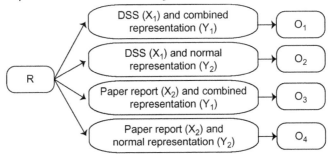

Source: Arnott & O'Donnell 2008.

Box 14.1 presents an example of a laboratory experiment with a 2x2 factorial design, conducted by Arnott and O'Donnell (2008).

Box 14.1

Arnott and O'Donnell's laboratory experiment (2x2 factorial design)

Arnott and O'Donnell's (2008) research focussed on the use of a DSS for forecasting exponential growth. Their independent variables were: (1) form of decision support (X), with two conditions – DSS (X_1) and paper-based report (X_2); and (2) nature of the representation (Y), again with two conditions – combined (Y_1) and normal (Y_2). The dependent variable was

346

forecast accuracy. Hypotheses were that there would be greater forecast accuracy amongst: participants using a DSS rather than a paper-based report (H_1); participants given a combined representation rather than a normal representation (H_2); participants using a DSS with a combined representation rather than a normal representation (H_3); and participants using a paper-based report with a combined representation rather than a normal representation (H_4).

The 178 graduate information systems students who volunteered to participate in the experiment were randomly assigned to one of the four groups shown in Figure 14.6. Randomisation ensured that the groups were similar in terms of age, mathematics skills and relevant work experience. The 90 students assigned to a DSS group undertook the experiment in a computer laboratory, whilst the 88 using a paper-based report performed the task in a classroom.

In the allocated decision task, participants were provided with a dataset of unit sales figures for iPods over a three-year period and asked to forecast iPod unit sales for an upcoming quarter. The 'normal' representation of the dataset comprised a table and a normal graph of quarterly unit sales over the period, whilst the 'combined' representation included the former plus an additional graph of the data presented on a logarithmic scale. Forecast accuracy was determined by calculating the absolute difference between a participant's forecast figure and the actual unit sales figure for that quarter.

Statistical analysis and hypothesis testing were performed with analysis of variance (ANOVA). Only the first hypothesis was supported, that is, that using a DSS significantly improved decision performance, regardless of the type of representation used.

Source: Arnott and O'Donnell 2008.

Strengths and limitations of the laboratory experiment

Due to the rigorous controls exercised and the ability to rule out rival explanations, laboratory experiments have a much higher *internal validity* than other research designs. Hence findings may be interpreted as having greater integrity. Also, the laboratory experiment is the most suitable of any of the research designs for testing hypotheses involving causal relationships.

The major weakness of laboratory experimental designs is their *external validity*. When an experiment is conducted in rigidly controlled laboratory conditions, its generalisability to other populations and settings lacking those controls is questionable. Interpretivists criticise experimental designs for the highly artificial environments they create, for divorcing a phenomenon from its natural setting where it cannot be observed in its totality. To help to overcome this limitation, some researchers will follow up an initial laboratory investigation with a field experiment.

Several other fundamental issues have been raised with the application of laboratory experiments in information systems research (Fjermestad & Hiltz 1999; Introna & Whitley 2000). Too often experiments are crafted with the convenience of the researcher in mind (e.g., ease of access to 'captive' populations) more than developing designs that have the potential to yield worthwhile research outcomes. A case in point is the disappointing result from a substantial body of experimental research into the performance of Group Support Systems (GSS) compared with that of face-to-face groups. Fjermestad and Hiltz (1999), in their excellent review article on approximately 200 controlled experiments into GSS reported in the information systems literature between 1982 and 1998, highlighted some of these concerns. GSS combine computer, communication and decision technologies to support problem formulation and problem solution in group settings. It has been repeatedly demonstrated that GSS work best in situations with: established groups having appropriate leadership (such as work teams with project leaders) rather than *ad hoc* groups; medium-to-large-sized groups rather than small ones; heterogeneous groups rather than homogeneous ones; multiple sessions rather than a single session; and complex rather than simple tasks. However, in the overwhelming majority of the experiments, researchers ignored these insights. Only 5.5 percent of the experiments which were investigated used established groups (94.5 percent used *ad hoc* groups); 94 percent lacked group leaders; and over 90 percent used students, predominantly undergraduates, as subjects. Most experiments involved groups of only two to five members; 73 percent of them used a single problem-solving session; and very few used complex tasks. Fjermestad and Hiltz opined that such practices limit the value of much experimental research in the field, and offer useful advice for improving the design of future experiments.

A more recent analysis in similar vein is Lee and Dennis's (2012) dissection of a failed controlled laboratory experiment into decision-making with a GSS. In their 'hermeneutic interpretation' of what went wrong, they identified a major disparity between the researchers' perspective on how subjects would use the GSS and the actual perspective of their research subjects. The researchers imputed "to the human subjects, the 'conduit model' of communication and the 'calculator model' of human information processing" whilst their student subjects imported "into the laboratory, their socially constructed world of personal friends, their histories and ... popular culture" (p. 3), and appropriated "the experimental task in ways unanticipated by the experimenters" (p. 25). Lee and Dennis stressed that experimental researchers, insofar as possible, should draw their participants from the population to whom their theories refer (e.g., managers) and consider much more carefully how they design experimental tasks.

Field experiments (pre-experimental and quasi-experimental research designs)

A field experiment is conducted in a natural setting rather than in a laboratory. It has the advantage of reflecting a real-world setting. However, while the researcher attempts to control variables under study in a field experiment, many elements are outside the researcher's control, so that it is more difficult to verify that the effects observed were attributable to the independent variable.

Due to considerable differences in the types of research design that can be labelled a field experiment, there is great variation in the rigour of different field experiments (and hence the ability to infer causation and to generalise from them). Some field experiments can fairly closely match a laboratory environment, but many do not. Experiments conducted in the field are often loosely categorised as either pre-experimental or quasi-experimental research designs. These designs are outlined in this section.

Pre-experimental research designs

Pre-experimental designs, as the term suggests, are rudimentary in nature, bearing some similarities to a laboratory experiment but lacking many of the controls, which makes them methodologically weak. These designs utilise neither experimental and control conditions, nor randomisation; hence there is no meaningful comparison. Also, they are unable to overcome the problem of rival explanations. Pre-experimental designs are better avoided where there are alternatives – but often there are none. Examples of some particular pre-experimental research designs are provided below.

One-shot case study

This is the simplest type of pre-experimental design (see Figure 14.7).

Figure 14.7 Basic model for one-shot case study

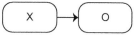

A person, group, organisation or object is exposed to some event, situation or intervention (treatment), the effects are observed, and interpretations made. For example, suppose that a law firm, which had previously provided in-house library and information services, decides to outsource these services to an external legal services provider. A researcher traces the changes within the law firm throughout the duration of the outsourcing process and then draws conclusions about the impacts of legal services outsourcing on law firms. Although this approach is typical of everyday reasoning, it is very limited as an experimental design, with little 'scientific' validity. There are no meaningful comparisons, and many possible sources of rival explanations (e.g., selection, history). Nevertheless, a single case study can be a valid research method if the researcher does not aim to generalise findings beyond the individual case. Single case studies are widely used in information systems and information management research. They are particularly useful for exploratory studies designed to identify areas worthy of further investigation. For guidance on circumstances where a single case study is appropriate, see Chapter 7: *Case study research in information systems.*

One-group pre-test/post-test design

The basic model for the one-group pre-test/post-test design is shown in Figure 14.8.

Figure 14.8 Basic model for one-group pre-test/post-test design

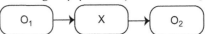

Here a group is observed or tested both before and after a particular event, situation or intervention (treatment). For instance, a library conducting information skills training for students may test students on their information skills before and after the training course and presume any changes in outcomes are due to the training. In introducing a pre-test before the treatment as well as the post-test after it, the design is a slight improvement on the one-shot case study. However, without a control-group comparison, it is difficult to assess whether or not observed changes are attributable to the training; many rival explanations remain.

Static group comparison

A static group comparison design is a correlational design used in field studies. See Figure 14.9. Subjects are divided into groups on the basis of whether or not they possess X, the characteristic under study, and observations are subsequently recorded. Randomisation is not used.

Figure 14.9 Basic model for static group comparison design

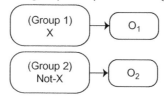

The static group comparison is also considered as a type of explanatory survey design. See Chapter 6: *Survey designs* for further discussion and an information systems example (Williams, Khan & Naumann, 2011).

Strengths and limitations of pre-experimental research designs

As pre-experimental designs are weak methodologically, they should be avoided when there are alternatives. However, they may constitute the only option open to the researcher. They are acceptable for an exploratory study, where the researcher wishes to gain insights or gather ideas, but not to generalise to the wider population. Lacking the controls of a laboratory experiment (i.e., randomisation and experimental and control conditions), there are serious threats to internal validity with pre-experimental designs. They provide no meaningful comparison, and are unable to overcome the problem of rival explanations. Also, external validity (generalisability) may be suspect as samples are not representative.

Quasi-experimental research designs

Quasi-experimental research designs are a compromise between a laboratory experiment and pre-experimental designs. Although it is preferable to use a laboratory experiment where possible, in natural settings that is rarely an option. Quasi-experimental designs are a considerable improvement methodologically on pre-experimental designs. Here groups are formed by deliberate selection, not by random assignment.

Through the use of quasi-experimental designs in field research, it is possible to infer or hint what might be likely causal links, but not to *prove* causality. This is because techniques used are *correlational* in nature: correlation demonstrates that two factors are in some way related, but does not enable inference that A caused B (for instance, B could have caused A, or both A and B may have been caused by another external factor). To claim a causal link between an independent variable (X) and a dependent variable (O), three criteria must be satisfied: X and O must co-vary; X must precede O in time; and there must be no alternative explanations of the group differences in O. In the quasi-experimental designs described in this section, it is evident that no single design fulfils all three criteria for demonstrating causation. Particular types of quasi-experimental research designs follow.

Pre-test/post-test non-equivalent control group design

This design is a combination of the static group comparison design and a one-group pre-test/post-test pre-experimental design. Incorporating features of both significantly enhances the strength and rigour of the design. The pre-test/post-test non-equivalent control group design includes pre-test information of baseline levels (enabling selection to be ruled out as a rival explanation), and a comparison group. However, like other quasi-experimental designs, the groups are not formed by random assignment, but rather by deliberate selection. This type design is most frequently encountered in medical, nursing and allied health fields. The basic model is shown in Figure 14.10:

Figure 14.10 Basic model for pre-test/post-test non-equivalent control group design

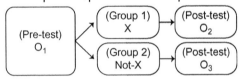

For example, a company may wish to investigate job satisfaction amongst its employees before and after the introduction of its new enterprise system. The new system will bring about major changes in the nature of existing work processes and tasks, and it is anticipated that these changes could impact on the job satisfaction of employees. (Note here that the introduction of the new enterprise system is the independent variable, and changes in job satisfaction, the dependent variable.) As the system is to be 'rolled out' over time, division by division, it is decided to include two divisions of the company, Division A and Division B, in the research. All employees from both divisions take an initial job satisfaction survey (i.e., pre-test O_1) prior to the initial introduction of the enterprise system. The system is first rolled out in Division A; it will not be implemented in Division B for another year. After Division A has implemented the enterprise system, it serves as the experimental condition, whilst Division B, which is still operating under the previous work structures, acts as the control. Some months after the system implementation in Division A and before the enterprise system is rolled out in Division B, employees from both divisions take another job satisfaction survey (i.e., post-tests O_2 and O_3). Changes both *within* groups and *between* groups are traced, and conclusions drawn. This design can also be described as an explanatory survey (see Chapter 6).

Interrupted time-series design

Interrupted time-series designs are an extension of the pre-experimental one-group pre-test/post-test design, using a *series* of observations/measurements both before and after the treatment condition. Conducted over an extended period (i.e., a longitudinal design), the time-series design enables the elimination of maturation and testing as threats to internal validity. With this design, trends in data can be examined before, during and after an intervention or treatment. The basic model for this design is shown in Figure 14.11:

Figure 14.11 Basic model for interrupted time series design

$$O_1, O_2, O_3, O_4 \quad \rightarrow \quad X \quad \rightarrow \quad O_5, O_6, O_7, O_8$$

For example, a state government is introducing a sophisticated new automated ticketing system for use on all types of public transport within the state. It plans to undertake an extensive investigation into many aspects of performance and usage of the new system. To enable it to have an effective baseline for comparison purposes, it applies (to the existing/old system) a set of tests/measurements at three-monthly intervals commencing a year before the 'go live' date for the new ticketing system (i.e., tests O_1, O_2, O_3 and O_4). After the launch of the new ticketing system (i.e., intervention X), the same set of tests/measurements is applied (to the new system) at three-monthly intervals during the first year of its operation (i.e., tests O_5, O_6, O_7 and O_8). Comparisons are drawn between the time-series data pertaining to the operation of the old system and the new system. A variation is the introduction of a second group as a control, which is tested at the same intervals as the treatment group, but is not exposed to the treatment condition.

Regression-discontinuity design

The regression-discontinuity design builds on the pre-experimental static group comparison design by introducing a series of comparison groups, addressing the issue of selection as a potential rival explanation. It is a cross-sectional design. The basic model is depicted in Figure 14.12:

Figure 14.12 Basic model for regression-discontinuity design

Regression-discontinuity designs draw on a set of continuous numeric data, such as scores on a scholastic aptitude test or an index of some form of social disadvantage. The treatment or intervention (X), for example, a compensatory program designed to enhance life skills and confidence, or educational potential, is targeted at those within a designated range of the numeric scale in a particular disadvantaged group. With a scholastic aptitude test, it may be those who scored between 40 percent and 49 percent on the test. The experimental groups experience the intervention, whilst those outside the designated scale range constitute control groups that are not exposed to the intervention. Both experimental and control groups are then retested to determine the effectiveness of the intervention (e.g., in redressing the disadvantage). These designs are more typically encountered in educational and social research than in information systems research.

Advantages and limitations of quasi-experimental research designs

In field research where it is not possible to use a true experimental design, a quasi-experiment is an option that does permit some hints of causality to be made, but not conclusively proven. While internal validity remains an issue with quasi-experimental designs, their external validity is greater than the laboratory experiment. Eliminating particular types of rival explanations enhances the strength and rigour of quasi-experimental designs in comparison with pre-experimental designs.

Conclusion

Researchers use experimental designs when they wish to explore possible causal links between variables. There are major constraints on causal inference in research, and there is a trade-off between a researcher's ability to establish definite causal links and to generalise findings to real-life settings. This is the classic conflict between internal and external validity in research design. The laboratory experiment is the design best suited to establishing causation, but it suffers from limited generalisability to natural settings. On the other hand, the field experiment enables greater generalisation to an external population, but sacrifices the ability to establish causation with any degree of confidence. While it is theoretically possible to maximise both internal validity and external validity by first undertaking laboratory research followed by a field experiment, cost is likely to be a major deterrent factor for most researchers.

For additional guidance on experimental research, most research methods texts provide brief overviews (e.g., Leedy & Ormrod 2016; Neuman 2014). For more extended treatment, see Bickman and Rog, (2009), Christensen (2007), Gravetter and Forzano (2012), Mitchell and Jolley (2013), and Shaughnessy, Zechmeister and Zechmeister (2009).

References

Arnott, D., & O'Donnell, P. (2008). A note on an experimental study of DSS and forecasting exponential growth. *Decision Support Systems, 4*(1), 180–186.

Baskerville, R. L., & Wood-Harper, A. T. (1996). A critical perspective on action research as a method for information systems research. *Journal of Information Technology, 11*(3), 235–246.

Bickman, L., & Rog, D. J. (Eds.). (2009). *The SAGE handbook of applied social research methods* (2nd ed.). Los Angeles, CA: SAGE.

Christensen, L. B. (2007). *Experimental methodology* (10th ed.). Boston: Pearson/Allyn & Bacon.

Clarke, G. M., & Kempson, R. E. (1997). *Introduction to the design and analysis of experiments*. London: Wiley.

Fjermestad, J., & Hiltz, S. R. (1999). An assessment of group support systems experimental research: Methodology and results. *Journal of Management Information Systems, 15*(3), 7–149.

Gravetter, F. J., & Forzano, L. B. (2012). *Research methods for the behavioral sciences* (4th ed.). Belmont, CA: Wadsworth Cengage Learning.

Guba, E. G., & Lincoln, Y. S. (1994). Competing paradigms in qualitative research. In *Handbook of qualitative research*. Thousand Oaks, CA: Sage.

Heron, J., & Reason, P. (1997). A participatory inquiry paradigm. *Qualitative Inquiry, 3*(3), 274–294.

Huang, A. H., & Windsor, J. C. (1998). An empirical assessment of a multimedia executive support system. *Information & Management, 33*(5), 251–262.

Introna, L. D., & Whitley, E. A. (2000). About experiments and style: A critique of laboratory research in information systems. *Information Technology & People, 13*(3), 161–173.

Lee, A. S., & Dennis, A. R. (2012). A hermeneutic interpretation of a controlled laboratory experiment: A case study of decision-making with a group support system. *Information Systems Journal, 22*(1), 3–27.

Leedy, P. D., & Ormrod, J. E. (2016). *Practical research: Planning and design* (11th ed.). Boston, MA: Pearson.

Mitchell, M. L., & Jolley, J. M. (2013). *Research design explained* (8th ed.). Belmont, CA: Wadsworth Cengage Learning.

Neuman, W. L. (2014). *Social research methods: Qualitative and quantitative approaches* (7th ed., Pearson New International Ed.). Harlow, Essex: Pearson Education.

Shadish, W. R., Cook, T. D., & Campbell, D. T. (2002). *Experimental and quasi-experimental designs for generalized causal inference*. Belmont, CA: Wadsworth Cengage Learning.

Shaughnessy, J. J., Zechmeister, E. B., & Zechmeister, J. S. (2009). *Research methods in psychology* (8th ed.). New York: McGraw-Hill Higher Education.

Tanner, K. (2002). Experimental research designs. In K. Williamson (Ed.), *Research methods for students, academics and professionals: Information management and systems* (2nd ed., pp. 125–146). Wagga Wagga, NSW: Centre for Information Studies, Charles Sturt University.

Williams, P., Khan, M. S., & Naumann, E. (2011). Customer dissatisfaction and defection: The hidden costs of downsizing. *Industrial Marketing Management, 40*(3), 405–413.

Section III

Research Techniques

In this section, Chapters 15—19 explore the techniques or tools used for sample selection, data collection and data analysis. Although selected techniques are part of research method (design), they are discussed separately here, given that specific techniques (such as individual interviews) can be used with a number of different methods. The techniques discussed are sampling, questionnaire design, individual interviews, focus group interviews, observation, quantitative data analysis, and qualitative data analysis, including qualitative content analysis and discourse analysis.

Chapter 15

Populations and samples

Kirsty Williamson

Monash University and Charles Sturt University, Australia

This chapter provides a discussion of populations and the samples which are selected to represent them. The terms are introduced and defined, followed by the two major types of sampling: probability and non-probability. The concept of random sampling is explained, in relation to the former, and the types of probability sampling described: simple random sampling; systematic sampling; stratified random sampling; and cluster sampling. The major types of non-probability sampling are also described: accidental or convenience sampling; snowball sampling; quota sampling; and purposeful/purposive sampling. Issues of sample size and generalisability are discussed in relation to both probability and non-probability samples.

Research Methods: Information, Systems, and Contexts. DOI: http://dx.doi.org/10.1016/B978-0-08-102220-7.00015-7

Introduction

This chapter is the first in a series aiming to introduce different tools used in research. The reason that data gathering and analysis tools are presented separately from methods is that mostly the former can be used in more than one method. For example, sampling is relevant to almost all research methods.

Because it is usually impossible to include the whole of the research population (defined below) in a research project, researchers mostly need to select a sample, or a portion of the population. Nevertheless, there are occasions when this is not necessary because it is possible to use the 'population', for example, all the academic librarians in a particular university. Williamson (1986) used a population to carry out research based in a Citizens' Advice Bureau (CAB), where the aim was to survey all users during a two-month period. In a way, these CAB respondents could have been regarded as a sample, since not all potential CAB users took part. However, there was no sample selection involved, and it was legitimate to regard the users of the CAB for the two-month period as a population. Generalisations could be made for the particular period involved, especially as the response rate was high.

The type of sampling adopted by the researcher is very much related to the purpose of the research, which is also reflected in the types of research questions and the methodology selected. For example, if a broad picture is desired, a large sample is required in order to be able to generalise to the chosen population. In contrast a qualitative, in-depth study needs a smaller sample.

It is important to note that the term 'random sampling' is frequently misused. For a sample to be correctly designated as 'random' each element of the population must have as much chance of being selected as any other element (discussed below).

It is also important to note that the term 'representative', as applied to a sample, does not necessarily mean that the sample has been randomly selected. Payne (1990, p. 23) postulated that positivist and interpretivist research "may have very different ideological roots but there is a common concern in ensuring that respondents are *representative*". Interpretivists do not usually select random samples, but they often try to represent the main types of people who are part of their population in their sample (e.g., different age groups or ethnic groups). This does not make these samples representative in the way that random samples are. Nevertheless, sampling is important in all types of research.

Most research methods books include information on sampling. Examples are Alreck and Settle (2004); Babbie (2008); Baker (1999); Connaway and Powell (2010); Fowler (2009); Neuman (2014); Patton (2015); Pickard (2013) and Savin-Baden and Major (2013). There are several references specific to sampling for qualitative research, which will be detailed in the non-probability sampling section, below.

Definition of terms

The following, based on Williamson (2002, p. 226), defines some of the terms relevant to sampling. Further explanation can be found in the texts listed above.

- *Population.* A complete set of all those elements (e.g., people, institutions) which have at least one characteristic in common. An example would be all New South Wales academic librarians or all New South Wales academic libraries. In the selection of a population for a study, considerations include: size, costs in time and money to the researcher, and accessibility.

- *Population stratum.* A subdivision of a population based on one or more specification, for example, all New South Wales academic librarians under the age of thirty.

- *Element.* An individual member or unit of a population. Each academic librarian would be an element of the population of academic librarians. Especially where a researcher focusses on an individual element, the term 'case' may be used.

- *Sample.* A selection of elements from the total population to be studied. A sample is any part of the population, whether it is representative or not. (A sample is usually drawn because it is less costly and less time consuming to survey than the population, or it may be impractical or impossible to survey the population as a whole.)

- *Sampling frame.* The list of elements from which a sample is selected. Sampling frames are discussed below.

- *Population parameter.* A population mean which is a characteristic of the population, for example, its mean age.

- *Sample statistic.* A measure descriptive of a sample characteristic.

- *Sampling error.* In probability sampling, sampling error is the degree to which the sample characteristics approximate the characteristics of the population. The difference between, for example, the sample mean age (the sample statistic) and the population mean (or the population parameter) is called the sampling error (Baker, 1999, p. 143).

Types of sampling

There are two basic types of samples: probability and non-probability. The former is most associated with positivist research; the latter with interpretivist approaches. Each has its own set of rules and conventions.

Probability sampling

Probably all readers of this book have been selected in a random sample as polling companies use probability sampling for their surveys, for example, of voting intentions before elections.

Some kind of random selection is required for probability sampling. With this type of sampling, the probability or likelihood of the inclusion of each element of the population can be specified. More specifically, each element of the population (or strata or cluster, if stratified or cluster sampling is used) must have an *equal* and *independent* chance of being included in the sample. The first step in achieving this is to know the parameters of the population. For example, if the population is 1,000 Australian academic librarians, then each element must have a 1/1,000 chance of being drawn. It must be possible, also, to be able to locate and list each of those librarians. It is only when probability sampling is used that it is possible to consider the sample as definitely representative and to generalise to the population from which the sample was drawn. In evaluating research, it is important to note whether a researcher makes broad generalisations from research findings where a random sample has not been selected or where the response rate has been so low as to undermine the validity of the chosen sample. There is a tendency of some qualitative researchers to generalise inappropriately – where the findings are only applicable to their specific participants – although theoretical generalisations may be possible (Myers, 1999). Moreover, some authors have argued that there are some grounds for generalisation in interpretive research, as discussed below.

Sample size in probability sampling

With probability sampling, used in positivist, quantitative research, the prevailing view is that the larger the sample the better (Connaway & Powell, 2010, p. 128; Park, 2006, pp. 126–127). I would agree with Park's point that, in his experience, "sample sizes of fewer than 200 observations often make it challenging to employ appropriate empirical methods or to produce results that are statistically significant" (p. 127). Although Connaway and Powell also see small samples as placing "significant limitations on the types of statistical analyses that can be employed" (p. 129), they propose that it is pointless to select a larger sample than necessary. They offered four criteria, as summarised below, to help determine the necessary sample size:

1. The less accuracy that is required between the sample and the population, the smaller the sample needs to be.

2. The greater the variability within the population, the larger the sample needed to achieve accuracy or representativeness. In other words, a homogeneous population is likely to require a smaller sample size than a heterogeneous one.

3. The method of sampling can affect the required size. For example, stratified sampling, discussed below, requires fewer cases for accuracy than simple or systematic sampling.

4. Sample size decisions should be made in relation to the kinds of statistical analyses to be used (because of the statistical limitations posed by small samples). Complex analyses with a larger number of variables may require a larger sample. (Adapted from Connaway & Powell, 2010, p. 129.)

Baker (1999) added another criterion: a smaller sample relative to the size of the population may work well if the population is very large. In other words, the sampling ratio can be calculated by dividing the sample size by the population size.

> If a population is under 1,000, it is generally thought that a sampling ratio of 30 percent is good. For populations of 10,000 or more, a sampling ratio of 10 percent may be adequate. For large populations of over 150,000, a 1 percent ratio may suffice, and for very large populations of over 10 million ... sampling ratios of 0.025 percent, or 2,500 may work for most purposes (Baker, 1999, p. 152).

As defined above, *sampling error* indicates the degree to which sample characteristics approximate the characteristics of the population. Formulae are available for calculating sampling error or 'the standard error of the mean', which represents how much the average of the means of an infinite number of samples drawn from a population deviates from the actual mean of that same population" (Connaway & Powell, 2010, p. 132). The calculation of sampling error is complex and requires careful study if you are undertaking a study for which sampling error needs to be known. Connaway and Powell (pp. 132–134), provide details. Nevertheless, it should be borne in mind that, "in general, the smaller the sample, the greater the sampling error; conversely, the larger the sample, the smaller the sampling error. That is why larger samples are considered preferable" (Williamson, 2002, p. 227).

Baker (1999) emphasised that sampling error "is *not* the result of mistakes made in the sampling procedures; instead it represents the variability of the sample from the population" (p. 143). In discussing nonsampling errors, Baker saw nonresponse as a major source of this, whereas Connaway and Powell (2010, p. 148) stated that "nonresponses reduce the sample size and introduce sampling error by eliminating a subset of the population", an opinion endorsed by Burkell (2003). Undoubtedly nonresponse introduces bias in survey research. Gobo (2008, p. 194) cited Groves and Lyberg (2008) in stating that "nonresponse error threatens the characteristic which makes the survey technique unique among research methods: its statistical inference from sample to population". Burkell spoke of an entire conference in 1999, the International Conference on Survey Nonresponse in Portland, Oregon, as being devoted to nonresponse and of the widely held opinion that "75% to 90% is sufficient to support generalizations from the surveyed sample to the population of interest" (p. 241). A response rate of 75 percent plus is difficult to obtain, although easier in telephone surveys than where mailed questionnaires are used (Williamson, 2002, p. 101). Connaway and Powell acknowledged that the received wisdom is that the minimum acceptable response rate is 75 percent and stated that many surveys have gathered reliable data with lower response rates: "The critical issue is how much the nonrespondents differ from those who did respond. An acceptable response rate can be lower for a homogeneous population than for a heterogeneous one" (Connaway & Powell, 2010, p. 166).

It is important to note that researchers should state the limits on generalisation where the response rate is low. Chapter 6: *Survey designs* provides further discussion on this issue. It is also important to note that there are companies that provide statistical advice regarding sample size choices.

Types of probability sampling

There are several types of probability sampling. Included here are simple random sampling, stratified random sampling, systematic sampling, and cluster sampling.

(1) Simple random sampling

Simple random sampling gives each element in the population an equal and independent chance of being included in the sample. The chance of the selection of every possible combination of elements must also be equal. If we take the sampling frame of 1,000 academic librarians, mentioned above, then the next stage is to number each element of this population, from one to 1,000. If you want to draw a simple random sample of 100 from that population, you need to be sure that you are as likely to include academic librarians numbered 500 and 1,000 as those numbered 1 and 3 or 56 and 120. A simple 'fishbowl draw' could be used to achieve this, that is, you could number 1,000 slips of paper and mix them up in a large container. However this is unwieldy, requiring the numbers to be thoroughly mixed and, in order to keep constant the chance of each element and combination thereof being selected, each slip of paper would need to be replaced in the container after it has been retrieved and noted. For example, if 82 of your sample of 100 have been selected, but you have not been replacing the slips representing those 82 librarians, then the eighty-third element has a one in 918 chance of being selected and not a one in 1,000 as was the case with the first selected element.

Alternatively, random number tables can be used. These are continuous row/column sequences of numbers (in our case including the numbers from one to 1,000) which are listed randomly and where no number appears more frequently than another. By choosing a random starting point, you can work across or down to select the required sample. Computer-generated random sampling is by far the easiest way to do this selection these days. To begin, you need to have the elements in your sampling frame listed on your computer. Trochim (2006b) provides a good explanation of the process for one of the many computer programs that can generate a series of random numbers. The result is a list of elements in random order from which, in our case, the first one hundred can be selected. Other electronic resources that can provide random number sets include Random.org and Microsoft Excel.

Case, Johnson, Andrews, Allard and Kelly (2004) provide an example of a computer-assisted survey which used Waksberg random-digit dialling procedures to contact a total of 2,454 potential respondents. Given that only 41 percent of eligible households (882 Kentucky residents, of whom only four percent were African American) agreed to be polled, the issues of possible bias come into play, as discussed above. Nevertheless the approach of Case *et al.* was thorough. They calculated their sampling error as $+/-$ 3.3 percent at the 95 percent confidence level, also stating that: "Compared to the actual population of the state, the sample under-represents both African Americans (8.5% of the state population) and males, although it is otherwise a fair representation of Kentucky adults" (p. 663).

(2) Systematic sampling

It is generally believed that, except in some circumstances, detailed below, systematic sampling is as effective as simple random sampling – and easier to achieve (Babbie, 2008; Connaway & Powell, 2010; Trochim, 2006b; Wildemuth, 2009). To undertake systematic sampling the researcher must have a set of random numbers or a random number table and a list of the population, preferably numbered but a complete alphabetical, non-hierarchical list is acceptable. A random starting point must be chosen, from which every nth element is selected. In the case of our sampling frame (population) of 1,000 academic librarians, n would equal 10 if the sample size was to be 100 (1,000/10). Thus a sampling interval of 10 would be used, with a random starting point between one and 10. So that each random number has an equal and independent chance of being selected, "the list should be considered circular in that the researcher would select every nth name, beginning with a randomly chosen starting point and ending with the first name of the interval immediately preceding the starting point" (Connaway & Powell, 2010, p. 123). Examples of sets of random numbers, along with further information on the processes of systematic sampling, are readily available in the literature (e.g., Babbie, 2008; Connaway & Powell, 2010; Wildemuth, 2009).

There is a strong caveat with regard to lists that researchers might want to use for selecting a systematic sample. The list itself must be comprehensive and randomly arranged. Should a list be hierarchically arranged, for example, if our list of academic librarians was arranged by job description, perhaps from chief librarians through to clerical assistants, then a biased sample would be produced by using that list. It is surprising that Connaway and Powell mentioned systematically selecting from a telephone directory in a seemingly approving way. As Guthrie (2010, p. 60) stated, not all telephone books or electoral rolls list every city resident, even less so now with the prevalence of mobile (cell) phones.

(3) Stratified random sampling

This form of sampling is useful for reducing "the number of cases needed to achieve a given degree of accuracy or representativeness" (Connaway & Powell, 2010, p. 123) or to gain stronger data where demographic or social characteristics, such as sex or region, may have an important influence (Baker, 1999, p. 157). Bloom (2008) wrote of stratifying by some baseline characteristics which included "geographic location, organizational units, demographic characteristics, and past outcomes" (p. 124).

The process involves listing the population (which of course needs to be known) into groups or strata where each element can appear in only one stratum. From these strata, random samples are drawn either by simple random sampling or systematic sampling, which can vary from stratum to stratum (Connaway & Powell, 2010, p. 123). An example, again focussed on our population of 1,000 academic librarians and based on Williamson (2002, pp. 228–229), involves dividing our population according to gender and age. For example:

Males aged 20–45	Females aged 20–45
Males aged 46–69	Females aged 46–69

There are two kinds of stratified random sampling that can be used, based on these strata: proportionate random sampling and disproportionate random sampling.

(a) *Proportionate stratified random sampling* is used where the researcher wants to represent a specific characteristic in the sample in exact proportion to the distribution of those characteristics in the population. Table 15.1 shows a putative distribution for our example, above. Here the sample size is still 100.

Table 15.1 Distribution using proportionate random sampling

Academic librarians	No. in population	No. in sample
Males aged 20–45	60	6 (10%)
Males aged 46–69	200	20 (10%)
Females aged 20–45	340	34 (10%)
Females aged 46–69	400	40 (10%)
Totals	**1,000**	**100**

For each of the strata, for example, females aged 20–45, a separate random sample is selected by either simple random sampling or systematic sampling. While representativeness is enhanced by this process, and sampling error is reduced, there is little point in going to these lengths if your population is reasonably homogeneous and your sample is likely to be representative anyway.

(b) *Disproportionate stratified random sampling* is used when there is a need to weight or over-represent a particular stratum or particular strata in the sample. It might be because strata, important to the research, are so small that they are likely to be barely represented if they are not given extra weight in the sample. In the example above males, aged 20–45, make up a small group and the group of males, aged 46–69, is also considerably smaller than either of the female groups. It could be that the researcher is keen to ensure that the views of these strata should emerge strongly during a research project and decides to weight those groups disproportionately. Indeed, the decision could be to vary the sampling ratio across strata so that samples of the same size are selected from each stratum. Table 15.2 illustrates how the ratios would need to change to achieve this weighting.

Table 15.2 Distribution using disproportionate random sampling

Academic librarians	No. in population	No. in sample
Males aged 20–45	60	25 (41.6%)
Males aged 46–69	200	25 (12.5%)
Females aged 20–45	340	25 (7.3%)
Females aged 46–69	400	25 (6.25%)
Totals	**1,000**	**100**

If you use disproportionate stratified random sampling, you need to be aware that statistical analysis must be undertaken with care. Wildemuth (2009) recommended that a statistician be consulted before making a final decision on weightings "to ensure that the sample size from each stratum will support the analyses you are planning" (p. 119). In warning about potential statistical problems with disproportionate stratified random samples, Connaway and Powell (2010) stated:

> It should be recognized that, in theory, one cannot make legitimate use of various nonparametric statistical tests, tests for the significance of correlation, analysis of covariance, and so on, without substantial modifications. Unfortunately, statistical textbooks seldom address this issue (p. 125).

(4) Cluster sampling

"Cluster sampling may be used when it's either impossible or impractical to compile an exhaustive list of the elements composing the target population" (Babbie, 2008, p. 231). In this case, "the sampling units are clusters of elements, rather than individuals" (Wildemuth, 2009, p. 119). If we take our example of academic librarians: on the one hand, it may be deemed difficult to request, and obtain, complete lists of all library staff in all 40 Australian public universities (the number in 2016); on the other hand, it would be possible to randomly sample say six academic libraries, one from each Australian state. All library staff in the selected universities could then be surveyed.

Multistage cluster sampling can also be used. The first stage in our example could be as described above. To focus the survey even further, we might decide, as a second stage, to randomly select a sample of specific campus libraries, rather than to survey every librarian in each of the university library systems selected. (Most Australian universities have multiple campuses.) This approach is particularly useful where survey by interview, rather than by self-administered questionnaire, is planned. It maximises efficiency and minimises the expense and effort involved in undertaking interviews in many different locations. It is also possible to use a combination of stratified and simple random sampling, "to achieve a rich variety of probabilistic sampling methods that can be used in a wide range of social research contexts" (Trochim, 2006b). However, as Connaway and Powell (2010) warned:

> Multistage cluster sampling does sacrifice accuracy, because sampling error can occur at each stage. In a two-stage sampling design, the initial selection of clusters is subject to sampling error, and the sampling of elements within each cluster is subject to error (pp. 126–127).

Because of the complications that are introduced through multistage cluster sampling, it would be advisable to seek statistical advice prior to undertaking multistage cluster sampling.

Non-probability sampling

Some writers (e.g., Trochim, 2006a and Wildemuth, 2009) appear to have believed that non-probability sample will only be used if it is not feasible or practical to use probability sampling or for pre-testing prior to undertaking research with a probability sample. In fact, grounded theorists and other interpretivists, requiring small samples for their research, whether for personal or focus group interviews, do not aspire to using probability sampling and do not see their sampling approaches as second best. In fact, in discussing 'case study in social research', Mabry (2008) stated:

> Development of deep understanding does indeed take time, so few cases can usually be selected even for multi-case studies. The basis for making selections of cases and human subjects is consequently purposeful or purposive, since random selection might easily fail to yield the most informative sites or samples of human subjects, skewing findings because of sampling bias (p. 223).

Sampling in qualitative research, almost invariably of the non-probability type, is widely discussed in the literature. (See qualitative research methods books listed in this chapter and elsewhere in the book.)

The issue of generalisability

Generalisability is one of the most crucial issue related to sampling. My view is that, even with probability sampling, generalisability has its limitations. Contexts are never fixed and unchanging so that, even if a sample is randomly selected, the response rate is high, and generalisations are appropriate, these generalisations will only pertain as long as circumstances are not significantly altered.

Nevertheless, "the difference between nonprobability and probability sampling is that nonprobability sampling does not involve *random* selection and probability sampling does" (Trochim, 2006a). As discussed above, this does not necessarily mean that a non-probability sample is not representative; it just means that the rationale of probability sampling does not underpin this kind of sample selection. Some writers therefore have stated that generalisability from non-probability samples is inappropriate as there has not been a definable, wider population from which the sample has been selected (e.g., Babbie, 2008; Connaway & Powell, 2010; Wildemuth, 2009). The issue of generalisability with non-probability samples is, however, not as clear-cut as these writers have stated. Indeed, the value of generalisations, even using probability sampling, has been called into question. Patton (2015) expressed the view that there are deep philosophical and epistemological issues related to all generalisations. He cited the following from Cronbach (1975), whom he described as a major figure in psychometrics and methodology: "Generalizations decay. At one time a conclusion describes the existing situation well, at a later time it accounts for rather little variance, and ultimately it is valid only as history" (p. 711). Patton saw Cronbach's (1980) notion of 'extrapolation' as useful:

> Extrapolations are modest speculations on the likely applicability of findings to other situations under similar, but not identical conditions.
> … Extrapolations can be particularly useful when based on information-rich samples and designs (Patton, 2015, p. 713).

There are also those who have argued that the particular necessarily bears traces of the universal, for example, Denzin and Lincoln (1998) who cited Sartre's (1981) views about this issue. They postulated that each individual or case "must be studied as a single instance of more universal social experiences and social processes" (Denzin & Lincoln, 1998, p. xiv). Stake (2003) made a similar point in talking about 'naturalistic generalization' as providing parallels to actual experience. Mabry (2008) suggested that case studies can convey 'vicarious experience' and also the 'evidentiary base': "These *readerly* or *open texts* invite readers to construct individual interpretations and empower them to generalize to cases of interest to them" (p. 223). Gobo (2008, pp. 193–213) argued a strong case for why "qualitative researchers do not need to throw away the baby generalization with the bathwater of probability sampling, because we can have generalizations without probability" (p. 194).

If you do want to make explicit generalisations, whether from interpretive research, or even where you have a random sample but with a low response rate or where tests of significance have not been carried out, you should be aware of the need for a good understanding of the issues involved. The discussion of 'trustworthiness of research' in Chapter 1: *Research concepts*, and especially the issue of 'transferability', is also related to the present discussion. Generalisability with non-probability samples is also discussed in Chapter 13: *Ethnographic research.*

One strategy that can sometimes be employed, to indicate how closely the sample represents the population for key variables, is to point out the differences between the proportions of key groups (such as age groups) in each. This can be done whether a sample is randomly selected or not. Box 15.1 provides an example of a comparison between proportions of key groups in a sample and population.

Box 15.1

Example of a comparison between proportions of key groups in a sample and a population

In a study of the information, communication and telecommunications needs of older adults, Williamson (1995) built a purposive sample of 202 older Victorians. It was important to indicate how closely the sample reflected the Victorian population of older people, with regard to key variables such as 'sex' and 'age'. It was reported that:

The sample consisted of 202 people, aged sixty and over, of whom 87 (43.1 percent) were males and 115 (56.9 percent) were females. At the time of the 1991 Census, 44 percent of the Victorian population aged sixty and over were males and 56 percent were females – very close indeed to the sample proportions (Williamson, 1995, p. 100).

With regard to age, the following table was included:

Sample respondents by age

Age group	No. of respondents	% of respondents	1991 VIC census %
60 to 74 (young aged)	146	72.3	70.1
75 to 84 (old old)	44	21.8	23.5
85 + (very old)	12	5.9	6.4
Total	**202**	**100.0**	**100.0**

In comparison with the 1991 Census, the 'young aged' was slightly over-represented in the sample and the other two groups slightly under-represented.

Adapted from Williamson (2002, p. 230).

Sample size in non-probability sampling

As intimated above, non-probability samples are small. Given the in-depth nature of the interviews undertaken in the kind of research involved, this is a necessary requirement.

How should sample size be determined? Morse (1994) recommended 30 to 50 interviews and/or observations for grounded theory and ethnographic studies involving interviews. By 2000, she was concerned to modify this statement having found that some researchers were using the guideline in a literal fashion:

> Estimating the number of participants in a study required to reach saturation depends on a number of factors, including the quality of the data, the scope of the study, the nature of the topic, the amount of useful information obtained from each participant, the use of shadowed data [the extent to which participants talk about the experiences of others vis-à-vis their own experiences], and the qualitative method and study design used (Morse, 2000, p. 3).

The sample size that is used for planning purposes may not be the size at the end of a project. Indeed, it is wise to overestimate the sample size so that there are sufficient funds available for the study (Morse, 2000, p. 3).

'Saturation' is one term used in relation to sample size. It "theoretically occurs when the researcher is no longer seeing or hearing new information" (Savin-Baden & Major, 2013, p. 317). Another term is 'redundancy', which also means new information is not forthcoming. Savin-Baden and Major postulated that the notion of saturation (or redundancy) is misplaced, especially in constructivist/constructionist studies, as there is always more to learn.

In grounded theory, *saturation* refers to 'saturation of categories', that is, of the categories developed from the data (Charmaz, 2006) which is different from meaning that no new information is forthcoming, discussed further in Chapter 9: *Constructivist grounded theory*.

By far the best rule of thumb, if you use a non-probability sample, is to ensure that you continue sampling until you have deep, rich data sets which take "into account cultural complexity and multiple interpretations of life" (Charmaz, 2005, p. 538). The consensus seems to be that sample size in non-probability research should be determined towards the end of the study, with an optimistic estimate made at the beginning.

Types of non-probability sampling

There are a number of different types of non-probability sampling, of which purposeful and theoretical sampling have the greatest credibility. Others to be briefly outlined here are accidental/convenience sampling, snowball sampling, and quota sampling.

(1) Accidental/convenience sampling

As the label implies, an accidental or convenience sample "is merely an available sample which appears able to offer answers of interest to your study" (Baker, 1999, p. 138). Researchers select people who are at hand until they believe that they have sufficient data to meet the aims of the study. For example, if you wanted to investigate student perceptions of their academic library, it should be possible to select a convenience sample by standing at the library door and requesting interviews with students as they leave the library. Another approach is to call for volunteers, perhaps offering a reward for agreeing to an interview.

The main problem is that there can be no assurance that samples, selected in these ways, will be representative of the population being investigated (Babbie, 2008; Connaway & Powell, 2010; Trochim, 2006a). For example, the researcher may have chosen a quiet period of low library use. Generalisation to the population is definitely not advised.

(2) Snowball sampling

With snowball sampling you begin with a few individuals who are appropriate interviewees according to the aims of your study. You then ask them to identify other individuals who could also be interviewees. This method is used when eligible people are difficult to identify and locate. A number of writers used the example of homeless people (Babbie, 2008; Connaway & Powell, 2010; Trochim, 2006a) while Wildemuth's (2009) example was prostitutes. Again, there is no certainty of a representative sample using this method and generalisation is not advised. Indeed, Biernacki and Waldorf (1981) offer a useful discussion of the problems associated with snowball sampling. They urged the need for the researcher to "actively and deliberately develop and control the sample's initiation, progress, and termination" because good snowball sampling "does not magically proceed on its own" (p. 143). It taps into pre-existing social networks, which may render the sample too homogeneous. Snowball sampling can also be used in developing a purposive sample and is mentioned, below, in that section.

(3) Quota sampling

Although a type of non-probability sampling, quota sampling has some similarities to stratified random sampling, to the extent that there are proportional and non-proportional options (Trochim, 2006a). To undertake quota sampling, you need to know the characteristics of the population you aim to investigate. You then set a quota for each characteristic of interest. With proportional quota sampling, each characteristic must be represented in proportion to its occurrence in the population. For example, again you might want to investigate views of academic librarians and believe that age will be an important variable. While you need to know the numbers in each of the age groups involved, you can select a quota sample for each group without needing to list the population. You can then interview the most convenient people in each group until your quota for each is filled. This is why some writers see quota sampling as the same as accidental sampling, except that steps are taken to ensure that certain elements of the population are represented proportionally (e.g., Connaway & Powell, 2010).

If you want to give more emphasis to some age groups over others, you can use non-proportional quota sampling. You might particularly want to do this if you think that the views of the youngest groups, for example, need to be disproportionally represented.

There are problems of possible biases arising from this type of sampling and caution should be exercised with generalisations. As Babbie (2008, p. 206) stated: "You should treat quota sampling warily if your purpose is statistical description."

(4) Purposeful or purposive sampling

> The logic and power of qualitative purposeful sampling derives [sic] from the emphasis on in-depth understanding of specific cases: *information-rich cases*. Information-rich cases are those from which one can learn a great deal about issues of central importance to the purpose of the research (Patton, 2015, p. 53).

In the previous edition of his book Patton (2002) outlined 15 different types of purposive sampling that included 'snowball or chain sampling', as described above. One of the more frequently used is 'criterion sampling' where all the cases included "meet some predetermined criterion of importance" (Patton, 2002, p. 281). For example, it might be important to the research questions to include only chief librarians in your purposeful sample and you might want them all to have had at least five years in that role. These, then, would be two criteria for sample inclusion.

In the latest edition of his book, Patton (2015) has expanded to 40 options of purposeful sampling, grouped into eight categories, one of which is "concept or theoretical sampling" (Patton, 2015, p. 264), which is very important in grounded theory. 'Theoretical sampling' was first developed by Glaser and Strauss (1967) on the basis that cases should be chosen for theoretical, not statistical reasons. As mentioned in Chapter 1 and detailed in Chapter 9, the emphasis of grounded theory is on inductive theoretical development. Thus in theoretical sampling, cases may be chosen to attempt "to replicate or extend the emergent theory" (Eisenhardt, 2002, p. 13).

Conclusion

This chapter provides a brief introduction to the research concepts of populations and sampling. The sampling vocabulary is important to master. 'Random sample' is one of the most misused terms in the research lexicon (Williamson, 2002, p. 232). Random samples need to be selected according to probability sampling which has given each element of the population an equal and independent chance of being selected. Standing on a street corner and interviewing people, at random, will not achieve the purpose. The response rate also must be sufficiently high to ensure that the sample is valid.

Having a random sample is not mandatory in order to undertake quality research. Indeed, a random sample is not appropriate for interpretivist (qualitative) methods. Particularly theoretical or other forms of purposive sampling are completely acceptable.

The issue of generalisability, raised here, is complex and should be carefully considered whatever method is employed. This chapter has provided many references to published material to enable researchers to explore the issue further and to understand it well.

References

Alreck, P. L., & Settle, R. B. (2004). *The survey research handbook* (3rd ed.). Boston: McGraw-Hill.

Babbie, E. (2008). *The basics of social research* (4th ed.). Belmont, CA: Thomson Wadsworth.

Baker, T. L. (1999). *Doing social research.* Boston: McGraw-Hill.

Biernacki, P., & Waldorf, D. (1981). Snowball sampling: Problems and techniques of chain referral sampling. *Sociological Methods & Research, 10*(2), 141–163.

Bloom, H. S. (2008). The core analytics of randomized experiments for social research. In P. Alasuutari, L. Bickman, & J. Brannen (Eds.), *The Sage handbook of social research methods* (pp. 115–133). Los Angeles: Sage.

Burkell, J. (2003). The dilemma of survey nonresponse. *Library & Information Science Research, 25*(3), 239–263.

Case, D. O., Johnson, J. D., Andrews, J. E., Allard, S. L., & Kelly, K. M. (2004). From two-step flow to the internet: The changing array of sources for genetics information seeking. *Journal for the American Society for Information Science, 55*(8), 660–669.

Charmaz, K. (2005). Grounded theory in the 21st century: Applications for advancing social justice studies. In N. K. Denzin, & Y. S. Lincoln (Eds.), *The Sage handbook of qualitative research* (3rd ed., pp. 507–536). Thousand Oaks, CA: Sage.

Charmaz, K. (2006). *Constructing grounded theory: A practical guide through qualitative analysis.* London: Sage.

Connaway, L. S., & Powell, R. (2010). *Basic research methods for librarians* (5th ed.). Santa Barbara, CA: Libraries Unlimited.

Denzin, N. K., & Lincoln, Y. S. (1998). Introduction to this volume. In N. K. Denzin, & Y. S. Lincoln (Eds.), *Strategies of qualitative inquiry* (pp. xi–xxii). Thousand Oaks, CA: Sage.

Eisenhardt, K. M. (2002). Building theories of case study research. In A. M. Huberman, & M. B. Miles (Eds.), *The qualitative research companion* (pp. 5–35). Thousand Oaks, CA: Sage.

Fowler, F. J. (2009). *Survey research methods* (4th ed.). Thousand Oaks, CA: Sage.

Glaser, B. G., & Strauss, A. L. (1967). *The discovery of grounded theory: Strategies of qualitative research*. Chicago: Aldine.

Gobo, G. (2008). Re-conceptualizing generalization: Old issues in a new frame. In P. Alasuutari, L. Bickman, & J. Brannen (Eds.), *The Sage handbook of social research methods* (pp. 193–213). Los Angeles: Sage Publications.

Guthrie, G. (2010). *Basic research methods: An entry to social science research*. New Delhi: Sage.

Mabry, L. (2008). Case study in social research. In P. Alasuutari, L. Bickman, & J. Brannen (Eds.), *The Sage handbook of social research methods* (pp. 214–227). Los Angeles: Sage.

Morse, J. M. (1994). Qualitative data: Fact or fantasy? In J. M. Morse (Ed.), *Critical issues in qualitative research methods* (pp. 1–7). Thousand Oaks, CA: Sage.

Morse, J. M. (2000). Determining sample size. *Qualitative Health Research*, 10(1), 3–5.

Myers, M. (1999). Investigating information systems with ethnographic research. *Communications of the Association for Information Systems*, 2(Article 23), 1–19. Retrieved from http://aisel.aisnet.org/cais/vol2/iss1/23/

Neuman, W. L. (2014). *Social research methods: Qualitative and quantitative approaches* (7th ed.). Harlow, Essex: Pearson New International.

Park, A. (2006). Using survey data in social science research in developing countries. In E. Perecman, & S. R. Curran (Eds.), *A handbook of social science field research: Essays and bibliographic sources on research design and methods*. Thousand Oaks, CA: Sage Publications.

Patton, M. Q. (2002). *Qualitative evaluation and research methods* (3rd ed.). Newbury Park, CA: Sage Publications.

Patton, M. Q. (2015). *Qualitative evaluation and research methods* (4th ed.). Los Angeles, CA: Sage Publications.

Payne, P. (1990). Sampling and recruiting respondents. In M. Slater (Ed.), *Research methods in library and information studies* (pp. 23–43). London: Library Association.

Pickard, A. J. (2013). *Research methods in information* (2nd ed.). Chicago: Neal-Schuman.

Savin-Baden, M., & Major, C. H. (2013). *Qualitative research: The essential guide to theory and practice*. London: Routledge.

Stake, R. (2003). Case studies. In N. K. Denzin, & Y. S. Lincoln (Eds.), *Strategies of qualitative inquiry* (2nd ed., pp. 134–164). Thousand Oaks, CA: Sage.

Trochim, W. M. K. (2006a). Nonprobability sampling. *Electronic resources for research methods: Qualitative research methods*. Retrieved from http://www.socialresearchmethods.net/kb/sampnon.php

Trochim, W. M. K. (2006b). Probability sampling. *Electronic resources for research methods: Qualitative research methods.* Retrieved from http://www.socialresearchmethods.net/kb/sampprob.php

Wildemuth, B. M. (2009). *Applications of social research methods to questions in information and library science.* Westport, CT: Libraries Unlimited.

Williamson, K. (1986). Information seeking by users of a Citizens Advice Bureau. *The Australian Library Journal, 35*(4), 87–195.

Williamson, K. (1995). *Older adults: Information, communication and telecommunications.* (Doctoral thesis). RMIT, Melbourne, Australia.

Williamson, K. (Ed.). (2002). *Research methods for students, academics and professionals: Information management and systems* (2nd ed.). Wagga Wagga, NSW: Centre for Information Studies, Charles Sturt University.

Chapter 16

Questionnaires, individual interviews and focus group interviews

Kirsty Williamson
Monash University and Charles Sturt University, Australia

This chapter considers three types of very popular data collection techniques: questionnaires, individual interviews, and focus group interviews. Beginning with questionnaires, the discussion focusses on their uses, advantages, disadvantages, as well as their design. The section on individual interviews covers structured, semi-structured and unstructured interviews; the uses of each type; their advantages and disadvantages; and the roles of the interviewer. An example of questions and prompts, used in a semi-structured interview, completes the discussion. The section on focus groups covers similar territory — of uses, advantages and disadvantages — and concludes with examples of how focus groups have been used in research projects: the first emphasising the process of setting up and management of focus groups; the second an example of questions and prompts.

Research Methods: Information, Systems, and Contexts. DOI: http://dx.doi.org/10.1016/B978-0-08-102220-7.00016-9

Introduction

Questionnaires, of the self-administered kind, are the most prevalent type of data research instrument in the social sciences, being most closely associated with survey method, to the point that many people call the instrument a 'survey', rather than a 'questionnaire'. Yet a questionnaire can be used in a range of different ways, in a number of different research designs, and can also be administered by interview. A questionnaire might be used for some of the data collection in experimental design or in a case study, or as one of the techniques in an ethnographic study. Individual and focus group interviews are very widely used in interpretivist studies, also in a variety of ways. Individual interviews are the key instrument in grounded theory studies.

Questionnaires

Questionnaires have been frequently used in the information management/library and information studies (LIS) field, especially in user studies aimed at establishing the needs of users or evaluating libraries from user perspectives. They have also been used in the information systems field, for example, during development and implementation phases. Where there are large numbers of potential users of a new system, especially across a number of sites, questionnaires can be helpful in identifying information and processing requirements. They can also help gather information about the types of use made of systems and of user satisfaction with systems (Williamson, 2002, p. 236). In this chapter the emphasis is on self-administered questionnaires, although questionnaires can also be used in structured interviews (discussed below). Circumstances where self-administered questionnaires are appropriate include:

- where you want to target a large and geographically dispersed population at relatively low cost and in a relatively short time;
- when the purpose of the study is easily explained in print, and when instructions and questions can be couched in easily understood language;
- when you require broad, rather than in-depth data and you want to be able to generalise, without qualms, to your population (remembering that your response rate needs to be adequate);
- when you are investigating a topic of a personal nature, where the anonymity of a self-administered questionnaire can encourage respondents to provide frank, truthful answers;
- where you want to afford privacy to participants, or where efficiency will be enhanced, demographic information can be provided via a questionnaire prior to interviews; and
- when you want to provide feedback during an experiment.

Advantages of questionnaires

Some of the advantages of self-administered questionnaires are at least implied by some of the points above, for example, the low cost involved in collecting large amounts of data, compared with undertaking interviews, and the anonymity offered to respondents which can encourage frank answers. Others are that:

- they can be answered at a time convenient to the respondent and are less intrusive than interviews;

- interviewer bias is avoided, at least in the sense that there are no variations in the ways in which questions are asked of respondents and no visual cues to influence responses; and

- data from the responses are relatively easy to collect and analyse, especially if attention is paid to designing the questionnaire with the analysis in mind.

Disadvantages of questionnaires

There are also disadvantages to using self-administered questionnaires, especially for major surveys (rather than for other uses such as the collection of demographic data prior to interviews or as part of experimental design).

- *Adequate response rate is difficult to obtain.* Response rates from mailed questionnaires can be very low. (See discussion of acceptable response rates in Chapter 15: *Populations and samples.*) Hand-delivered questionnaires are likely to fare better but increase costs and inconvenience, and are impractical in a wide geographic area. Attention to questionnaire design and follow-up mailings can result in higher response rates.

- *Representative responses from all groups in the population are difficult to obtain.* Certain groups are more likely to respond: women, the better educated, older rather than younger people, people who are more opinionated about the topic (Connaway and Powell, 2010). This means that there is lesser representation of other groups, which would also include people with disabilities and those for whom English is a second language.

- *Respondents are unable to qualify answers or seek clarification.* This is particularly important where respondents find questions to be ambiguous or where they feel they do not fit neatly into any of the categories offered. There is also no opportunity for reviewers to elaborate so that questions are better understood, or to seek further information through use of prompts as are used in semi-structured interviews. Allowing plenty of space for written comments on the questionnaire can help to a certain extent.

- *Complex questions cannot be asked.* Questions need to be simple and straight-forward. Even then misinterpretations can occur. Pilot testing can assist with this.

- *Supplementary observational data are not available.* Interviews will often provide this but, with self-administered questionnaires, there is usually no personal contact between researcher and respondent.

- *Lack of control over how and when the questionnaire is answered.* While flexibility about how and when they complete the questionnaire may be an advantage for respondents, researchers cannot be sure that respondents have taken the task seriously.

Questionnaire design

Questionnaires are ubiquitous in our world; filling them in is a common experience. Many people have felt frustration with poorly designed questionnaires, for example, asking ambiguous questions or not providing adequate response options. This is because it is often not realised that expert knowledge is required to develop a good questionnaire. Although online questionnaires are now common, the fundamentals of questionnaire design are perennial. The topic of questionnaire design is well covered in the social sciences research literature, either as a separate topic or as part of a discussion of survey method. References include Alreck and Settle (2004); Babbie (2008); Baker (1999); Connaway and Powell (2010); de Leeuw (2008); Guthrie (2010); Neuman (2014); Oppenheim (2000); Pew Research Centre (http://www.pewresearch.org/methodology/u-s-survey-research/questionnaire-design/); Pickard (2013); StatPac (2014); and Wildemuth (2009). The Web has a wealth of resources but care about quality needs to be exercised. One reliable site, which leads to references for a range of research methods topics, is Electronic Resources for Research Methods (http://informationr.net/rm/). Chapter 6: *Survey designs*, discusses online questionnaires (email and web-based).

The first step, if the questionnaire is to be used in a major survey, is to decide on the kinds of data you need to answer your research questions. Even if you believe you have an understanding of the issues to be investigated and the population to be targeted, it is still a good idea to undertake some exploratory interviews with typical prospective respondents. Doing this will help you frame questions and to develop response categories for specific questions.

The appearance of the questionnaire is vital. It is much better to adequately space the questions and the response boxes to check, or the code numbers to circle, than to try to make your questionnaire look shorter by squeezing questions into the smallest space possible. "An improperly laid out questionnaire can lead respondents to miss questions, confuse them about the nature of the data desired and even lead them to throw the questionnaire away" (Babbie, 2008, p. 278).

There are two major types of questions asked on questionnaires: *closed* and *open* questions. The more commonly asked are the former, where respondents are presented with different categories from which to choose. Because they provide frames of reference and make clear the kinds of answers sought, they guide respondents' replies, thus making it easier and quicker for respondents to answer. They are also easier to code.

Closed questions

These can be classified as either *factual* or *opinion*. The examples that follow are based on Williamson (2002, pp. 237–238). In this example, assume that those asked to complete the questionnaires are recruited within the Lamington Public Library and have therefore used the library at least once.

Factual questions

Factual questions are straightforward questions which give respondents categories from which to choose answers that are correct for them.

Example 1

Are you a member of the Lamington Public Library?   YES ☐
                                                      NO ☐

If the answer to this question is 'no', you can direct the respondent to miss questions that are relevant to members only or, if you have just one additional question that applies only to members, you could use what Babbie (2008) called a 'contingency question'. The following is an example.

Are you a member of the Lamington Public Library?
              YES   NO
If yes:
How long have you been a member?
    Less than six months   ☐
    Six to twelve months   ☐
    More than one year and up to two years   ☐
    More than two years and up to five years   ☐
    More than five years and up to ten years   ☐
    More than twenty years   ☐

You might think that, in the example above, the categories could be expressed more simply, for example, 'one to two years' rather than 'more than one year and up to two years'. However, one of the basic lessons to learn is that categories need to be mutually exclusive. If the simpler form is used, how will the respondent, who has been a member for one year exactly, choose between the categories 'six to twelve months' and 'one to two years'?

Example 2

In this example, you need to be sure that you have an 'other' category. Many closed questions require this.

Why do you use the Lamington Public Library? Tick as many boxes (categories) as applicable.

1.	To borrow books.	☐	1	2	0[*]
2.	To borrow other material (e.g., DVDs).	☐	1	2	0
	Please specify all other materials borrowed, including DVDs if applicable.				

_____

_____

3.	To read newspapers or other materials in the library.	☐	1	2	0
4.	To use the online databases.	☐	1	2	0
5.	To use the internet.	☐	1	2	0
6.	To bring your children.	☐	1	2	0
7.	To attend classes or other library meeting or functions.	☐	1	2	0
8.	To use the photocopying facilities.	☐	1	2	0
9.	Other. Please specify all your other uses.	☐	1	2	0

_____

_____

[*]The numbers on the right of the boxes are pre-coding options to enable easier analysis. For example, if the first box has been ticked, 1 would be circled; if the first box is not ticked, 2 would be circled. If the respondent has ticked no boxes for the whole of that particular question, then 0 = no response is circled.

If it you want to know the relative importance of the various reasons why people use the public library, then you can ask respondents to number the boxes, above, in the order of importance for those categories that are applicable to them, omitting those that are not applicable. You need to take care with requests for ranking. StatPac (2014) warned that ranking becomes increasingly difficult as the number of items increases and recommended that a maximum of five items should be ranked.

Opinion questions

Opinion questions are often measured on a Likert scale. For example:

Are you satisfied with the Lamington Public Library?' Circle only one number on the scale:

1	2	3	4	5
Very satisfied	Satisfied	Undecided	Unsatisfied	Very unsatisfied

The numbers, used above, provide easy pre-coding. (See Chapter 18: *Quantitative data analysis* for a discussion of coding for data analysis.) You need either to use 'numbers' or 'boxes' consistently. To use numbers in the second example of a factual question, you could ask respondents to circle 1 if a reason for use applies to them and 2 if it does not. However, this is not as straightforward as ticking a box – or not ticking the box if the reason does not apply.

Open questions

The advantage of open questions, which allow respondents to express their answers freely, is that they do not attempt to force respondents to choose amongst categories which they feel do not entirely fit their situations or views. If respondents do not understand the question, the response categories, or even the topic (always a danger with a self-administered questionnaire), it will become clear in an open response. An example of an open question follows:

> In your own words describe your level of satisfaction with the Lamington
> Public Library.

Other tips for good questionnaire design

A number of suggestions to ensure good questionnaire design have already been made. Particularly important is the presentation of your questionnaire, with careful attention to be paid particularly to spacing and lay out. It is essential to ensure that the response categories you offer are mutually exclusive, as in the first factual example, and that you provide all possible alternative options, plus an 'other, please specify' category. As already pointed out, it is good practice to undertake some exploratory interviews beforehand, to ensure that you ask appropriate questions and develop a full range of response options.

There is a range of considerations that will assist in ensuring accurately completed questionnaires and in obtaining a high response rate. (1) Place the questionnaire on letterhead and include an introductory letter explaining your research, personally addressed if possible. (2) Place response boxes or numbers close to the questions or categories to which they relate so that there is no confusion. (3) Clearly number questions and pages, and place the word 'over' at the bottom of the front side of each double-sided page. (4) Give a date by which the questionnaire should be returned. (5) Even if a stamped addressed envelope is included to facilitate return of the questionnaire, include the name and address on the questionnaire itself in case the original envelope is lost. (6) Thank the respondent for filling in the questionnaire and offer to provide a short report of the findings. (7) Use polite follow-up cards, letters, or emails to remind respondents of the importance of returning the questionnaire. (Phoning will be particularly effective, if possible.)

Other more major tips include the following.

- Select only the questions that are essential to accomplish the objectives of your study, with a view to making the questionnaire just as long as it needs to be – and no longer.

- Instructions need to be crystal clear at the beginning and wherever required throughout the questionnaire, especially if some questions are not applicable to all respondents. You should avoid the latter situation if possible.

- Organising questions into related groups, with a smooth transition from one group to another, will assist respondents. Sensitive questions, including demographic ones, should be asked towards the end of the questionnaire. Use consistent response options, for example, boxes to tick or numbers to circle.

- Questions should be clearly and simply worded. Check carefully for any ambiguities and avoid jargon. There are several types of questions to avoid:

  - Questions which use imprecise words that might be defined differently by different respondents, for example, 'Do you use the Lamington Public Library regularly?' 'Do you think that most people are satisfied with the LPL?' (It is hard to know how respondents would define 'regularly' and 'most'. The second example also uses an abbreviation which should be avoided.)

  - Leading (or loaded) questions which indicate to respondents what the expected answer would be. 'Wouldn't you like to be a member of the Lamington Public Library?' suggests that the required answer is 'yes'.

  - Questions beyond respondents' capabilities, for example, asking them to compare the present Lamington Public Library with the same library of ten years ago.

  - Statements with negatives, to which respondents have to agree or disagree. For example, respondents are likely to be confused if asked to agree or disagree with the statement 'I do not think that service at the Lamington Public Library is satisfactory'. Think about the way you would respond to this statement.

  - Double-barrelled questions, each part of which may require a different answer. For example, with the question: 'Do you borrow books from the Lamington Public Library and from other libraries as well?' might draw a 'yes' response to the first part and a 'no' to the second, with no option for respondents to make their more complex answer clear.

  - Hypothetical questions, where respondents have not actually experienced particular situations or needs, are known to elicit unreliable responses. For example, 'If the Lamington Public Library were to install self-service for the issuing of library books, would you use it?'

Piloting the questionnaire

It is mandatory to test the questionnaire with typical respondents who can alert you to ambiguities and other problems, and perhaps suggest improved wording. It is especially useful to discuss the interpretations of questions that such respondents have made. They may not be the same as your own. The respondents used in this process should be excluded from the survey proper.

Individual interviews

According to Fontana & Frey (2005, p. 698), interviews have become so prevalent in the developed world that "a number of scholars have referred to the United States as 'the interview society'". Regardless of purpose, they continued: Both qualitative and quantitative researchers tend to rely on the interview as the basic method of data gathering (p. 698).

Interviews are widely used in research in both information management/LIS and information systems, with the former including topics about information-seeking behaviour, library use, and the effects of the introduction of new technology into libraries. In the information systems field, information about user requirements for a proposed new system is often gathered by interviews, both unstructured and structured. "Unstructured interviews allow users to articulate their specific concerns and needs while structured interviews are useful for detailed or specific information about current operations and requirements" (Williamson, 2002, p. 243). Myers and Newman (2007) discussed the potential difficulties, pitfalls and problems, associated with the qualitative interview in information systems research, and suggested guidelines for their conduct.

Interviews come in a range of types and with diverse purposes. They can be used in surveys to ask pre-determined questions, especially in the case of telephone interviews. The personal contact necessary to do this may mean a higher response rate although the present-day frequency of use of the telephone for soliciting support of all kinds is likely to have made it more difficult to recruit respondents this way. These interviews will be highly structured, with questions and probably answer categories predetermined.

Interviews of a different kind are frequently used in qualitative research. Post-positivists use interviews to discover the elusive 'truth' which they believe exists, but which is difficult to identify. Their interviews are likely to be carefully structured and different from those of ethnographers or researchers undertaking case studies. Ethnographers are likely to be interviewing in an interpretivist or naturalistic context, with the aim of eliciting the meanings of participants or to understand them from their own points of view. Fidel (1993, p. 219) used terms such as 'nonmanipulative', 'noncontrolling', 'open' and 'flexible'. Exploratory interviews, appropriate to the early stages of most research projects, are also flexible and may be completely unstructured. They are used to understand the types of participants likely to be involved in a study, and the kinds of questions which are appropriate for the topic.

Interviews can also be used in experimental design or to supplement findings from a self-administered questionnaire (i.e., as part of a 'mixed methods' approach).

Be aware that, if it is important to discuss the philosophical/paradigmatic framework for your research, you should give close consideration to the issues involved while selecting your methods and techniques. In other words, make sure that you understand the paradigmatic implications of your choice of methods.

Interviewing for surveys is covered in most social science research methods books, for example, Babbie (2008), de Leeuw (2008); Guthrie (2010); and Neuman (2014). Qualitative interviews, mostly semi-structured or unstructured and taking place in interpretivist frameworks, though not necessarily labelled as such, are discussed in Baker (1999); Brinkmann and Kvale (2015); Doucet and Mauthner (2008), Fontana and Frey (1998; 2005); Patton (2015); Punch (2014); Rubin and Rubin (2011); Savin-Baden and Major (2013); Spradley (1979); Taylor, Bogdan & DeVault (2015); and Wildemuth (2009). These interviews are sometimes called 'ethnographic', for example, by Spradley (1979), given that interviews are an important technique in ethnography. Although published as long ago as 1979, Spradley's book is still quite frequently cited and is worth trying to locate. Focus group interviews are also 'qualitative' but are covered in a separate section, below.

Types of interviews

The major types of interviews are (1) structured; (2) semi-structured; and (3) unstructured. Focus group interviews are another type again. Because many of the same principles apply to both semi-structured and unstructured interviews, these are discussed together.

Structured interviews

Structured interviews are also sometimes labelled standardised or scheduled. As indicated above, this type of interview is principally a questionnaire administered by interview. Each of the respondents is asked exactly the same questions in the same, fixed order, although there may be an 'open comments' section similar to that in a self-administered questionnaire. Standardised interviews make it easy to compare respondents' answers. It might be deemed necessary to have this kind of comparability in a single or multi-site case study, or to elicit answers in experimental design. The schedule used for the interview should be pilot-tested in the same way as for a self-administered questionnaire.

The advantages of using structured interviews rather than self-administered questionnaires, include: (1) higher response rates, mentioned above, as well as the greater motivations for respondents to provide higher quality responses, especially because of the opportunity for interviewers to establish a rapport through personal interaction; (2) the ability to ask more complex questions with fewer 'don't knows' and non-responses because clarification and explanation can be provided to respondents; (3) the opportunity to obtain extra information through chatting to respondents before and after the interview, observing them and perhaps their living conditions; (4) the control interviewers can exercise on the interview context to ensure that respondents give careful attention to their responses; and (5) the opportunity to obtain responses from people who are unable to fill in questionnaires, for example, the aged, young children, the illiterate, and some groups with disabilities.

The disadvantages include: (1) the much greater expense in time and money, compared with self-administered questionnaires; (2) interviewer and inter-interviewer variability which, even with training, is difficult to avoid. "Even the same interviewer may vary in the tone of voice used to ask questions, in responses to answers, and in the use of probes" (Williamson, 2002, p. 245); (3) the inclination of respondents to answer in ways they consider acceptable to the interviewer, perhaps influenced by personal interviewer qualities, for example, age, gender, or social class, or their opinions and expectations revealed either consciously or unconsciously. The cartoon in Figure 16.1 illustrates the problems of cultural and attitude differences between interviewers and interviewees, as well as the need for clear questions.

Figure 16.1 How not to conduct interviews

'Next question: I believe that life is a constant striving for balance, requiring frequent tradeoffs between morality and necessity, within a cyclic pattern of joy and sadness, forging a trail of bittersweet memories until one slips, inevitably, into the jaws of death. Agree or disagree?'

Source: © The New Yorker Collection 1989 George Price from cartoonbank.com. All Rights Reserved.

It is for these reasons that the role of interviewers, and the kinds of qualities they require, are widely discussed in the literature, for example, Baker (1999); Neuman (2014); Wildemuth (2009). Certainly interviewers need to be personable, engaging, and ready to listen; even with structured interviews, there is now less emphasis on interviewers remaining distant, objective and 'faceless' (Fontana & Frey, 1998, p. 73).

Neuman (2014) traced the evolution of survey interviewing from the 1960s and 1970s, when interviewers were trained to obtain complete and accurate answers.

> By the 1980s–1990s, improving interviews shifted to standardizing interviewer behaviour. We carefully trained interviewers to read each survey question as exactly written, to use neutral probes, to record respondent answers verbatim, and to be very non-judgmental. We emphasized making each interview situation an identical experience (Neuman, 2014, p. 349).

The most recent state of the art, according to Neuman (2014), sees split approaches, with the dominant group adhering to the need for 'standardized interviewer behaviour' and a minority group advocating that the interview should be flexible, collaborative and conversational (influenced by interpretivist approaches according to Neuman). The idea behind the *conversational interview* is that there is a need for interviewers to use wording for questions which is appropriate to each interviewee so that the intent of the researcher is properly conveyed. However, as Neuman cogently pointed out, "only a highly trained, socially adept interviewer who has a deep understanding of the researcher's intent in each survey question may be able to reach a shared understanding of that intent with many diverse respondents" (p. 350). Regardless of the choice made between conversational and standardised interviews, interviewers need careful training – unless the researcher acts as the sole interviewer.

With regard to the printed schedule, setting out the questions and providing response options: there should be written instructions, in all cases, which should be at the beginning and as necessary throughout. Whether the interviews are face-to-face, by telephone or internet enabled, for example, by Skype, the form should be carefully laid out, as in a self-administered questionnaire, with spaces for date and time of interview. Early questions should enable decisions about whether respondents meet the criteria of the survey (e.g., that they are users of the Lamington Public Library). Response categories need to include a 'don't know', a category offered only if no other response is forthcoming.

To facilitate smooth interview process, conversational-style transition phrases, not necessary in a self-administered questionnaire, are often used, for example, 'Could you now please tell me...' (Baker, 1999). Otherwise the schedule for a structured interview is not much different from a self-administered questionnaire. Again sensitive questions, including demographic ones, should be asked towards the end of the interview. Apart from the requirement for careful consistency in structured interviewing, desirable or essential attributes of interviewers are largely applicable to all types of interviews.

Semi-structured and unstructured interviews

Although a scheduled list of questions, and often prompts as well, are used in semi-structured interviews, they are usually flexibly administered in order to capture the perspectives of participants as far as possible while ensuring that interviewees focus on issues relevant to the study. A key characteristic of this kind of interview is the opportunity offered to follow up on leads offered by participants. Unstructured interviews provide the same opportunity but without a scheduled list of questions. Each participant answer basically generates the next question.

An unstructured interview would be appropriate in a phenomenological study of one person's experience of phenomena (see Chapter 1: *Research concepts*). It might also be used in a case study to collect extensive data from key informants. Patton (2015) saw unstructured interviews as occurring naturally as part of participant observation. An unstructured interview could also be useful when a systems developer cannot predict user reactions to a prototype of a new design feature, and has no preconceptions about its effect. The developer may want to elicit as many free-flowing thoughts as possible about a first-time contact with the feature, in order to incorporate fresh ideas into the system. Another purpose could be to gain an understanding of a topic, in-depth, before compiling a structured or semi-structured interview schedule or self-administered questionnaire.

The semi-structured interview has more in common with the unstructured, in-depth interview, than with the standardised, structured interview. Indeed, semi-structured interviews can also be regarded as being 'in-depth'. Some of the literature does not make a difference between the two, referring simply to 'qualitative interviewing' (e.g., Baker, 1999; Brinkmann and Kvale 2015). Baker (1999, p. 247; citing Schwandt, 1997) postulated that "in a qualitative interview, the interview is constructed more as a discourse between two or more people which is not so fully controlled by the interviewer's questions but is in fact constructed by both the interviewer and the respondent over the course of the discussion". This resonates with Charmaz's (2003) opinion that "the viewer creates the data and ensuing analysis through interaction with the viewed" (p. 271). It means that interviewers will almost certainly receive multiple and often contradictory views from interviewees, as is consistent with key precepts of the interpretivist approach. Williamson and Kingsford Smith (2010) spoke of looking for 'consensus and dissonance' in their interview data.

One of the advantages of semi-structured and unstructured interviews is the opportunity they provide to support research findings with direct quotations from participants. It is therefore important to record both semi-structured and unstructured interviews so that researchers can support their findings by correctly reporting what participants have said. This means that the "... audience is at least partially able to project themselves into the point of view of the people depicted" (Patton, 2015, p. 33, citing Lofland, 1971, p. 4). However, recording must be done only with the permission of the interviewee. Before the interview begins, informed consent needs to be obtained from the interviewee and permission to record the interviewee can be obtained as part of this. (See Chapter 20: *Ethical research practices*, for further discussion of informed consent.)

For the kinds of research I have undertaken in the field of LIS, I have found that the semi-structured interview has worked very well. I have often started with unstructured interviews with key informants, as a way of understanding the topic, particularly if my partners and I have insufficient knowledge of the topic involved. For example, before we undertook a study with the Australian Plants Society Victoria, about data and information management and sharing in environmental voluntary groups (Kennan, Williamson & Johanson, 2012), we conducted two very long interviews with key members of the organisation to gain understanding of the types of questions and prompts we should use with other participants.

Chapter 2: *The fundamentals of research planning* discusses an ARC Discovery project (Williamson & Kingsford Smith, 2010) in which Kingsford Smith and I investigated, inter alia, the role of information in online investment. Box 16.1 returns to that project and provides a list of questions and prompts that Kingsford Smith and I used to explore one of the research questions outlined in Chapter 2.

Box 16.1

Example of the use of questions and prompts in a semi-structured interview: Information seeking by online investors

Research question

What are the key sources of information used by investors and the reasons for their importance?

The following were the questions and prompts developed to answer that research question. Please note that questions asked of interviewees should be primarily geared to answering your research questions. Very important is the point that we only used the prompts if participants did not spontaneously mention each of the listed characteristics. Obtaining spontaneous responses is ideal, but the prompts ensure that issues important to the research are not overlooked because a participant has not thought to mention them. A semi-structured interview schedule thus enables participants to freely provide their perspectives but also ensures that issues that are of key significance to the research are discussed.

Questions and prompts

1. Do you have a preferred or key source of information? If so, could you please tell me why it is your preferred source?

Prompts: Ease of access, speed of access, currency, type of content, reliability/accuracy, format, cost effectiveness

2. What are the other sources of information that are important to you and why?

Prompts: Ease of access, speed of access, currency, type of content, reliability/accuracy, format, cost effectiveness

As indicated in Chapter 2, the online investment project used mixed methods. The initial online survey was followed by the qualitative (interpretive) component, which provided the theoretical drive (Morse 2003). The theoretical drive is determined by the component (usually positivist/quantitative or interpretivist/qualitative) which will play the more important part in answering the research questions. Because the interviewees were purposively selected from the almost 200 survey respondents who offered to be interviewed (from a sample of 520), we did not need to collect demographic data; it had already been provided in the questionnaire responses. Had we not had this survey data, we would have used a demographic, self-administered questionnaire at the beginning of the interview. Unless your interviewees are very old, very young, or disabled, a good way to collect demographic data about interviewees is by self-administered questionnaire at the beginning of an interview or focus group. This approach saves time and affords privacy to interviewees.

While there is not the same need for consistency in questioning for in-depth interviewing as there is for structured interviewing, interviewers for all types of interviews should be "flexible, objective, empathetic, persuasive, a good listener" (Fontana and Frey, 1998, p. 55). It is mandatory for interviewers to seek the views of participants, rather than to express their own. High levels of concentration are required so that the most appropriate follow-up questions can be asked and so that all required areas are covered in the level of depth necessary to answer the research questions. Analysis of structured interviews will mostly be similar to that of self-administered questionnaires, discussed in Chapter 18. Analysis of semi-structured and unstructured interviews is discussed in Chapter 19: *Qualitative data analysis.*

Focus group interviews

The contemporary focus group interview generally involves 8 to 12 individuals who discuss a particular topic under the direction of a moderator who promotes interaction and assures that the discussion remains on the topic of interest (Stewart & Shamdasani, 1990, p. 10).

The quotation, above, provides a pithy definition of a focus group. While eight to ten people is mostly the recommended number, Krueger (2002), considered an authority on focus groups, preferred focus groups of six to eight (slightly different from the seven to ten which he proposed in 1994). Wildemuth (2009, p. 246) cited Langer (2001) as pointing out "that some studies may need to use smaller groups", which the latter labelled as 'minigroups'. Having myself used smaller groups (of four or five people) on occasions, I can say that these groups will work very well if your participants are well informed on the topic, that is, are 'information-rich' participants (Krueger & Casey, 2009). My experience has been that more than ten participants can be difficult to manage, particularly if they are highly involved and anxious to contribute. Greater skills on the part of the interviewer or moderator are required for bigger groups, although focus groups of all sizes require skilled and experienced handling.

Other key defining characteristics of focus groups are: (1) participants should be reasonably homogeneous; (2) as with individual interviews, they collect qualitative data regarding perceptions, feelings and opinions, in participants' own terms and frameworks of understanding; (3) the data are produced through group interaction in an interview process; and (4) they discuss a limited number of questions on the topic because soliciting many opinions, and giving each focus group member enough opportunity to speak, tends to be time consuming.

As with individual interviews, demographic information can be collected by each participant filling out a form before the discussion starts.

Advantages and disadvantages of focus groups

On the one hand, interesting ideas can be stimulated through group interaction, meaning that good quality data may result. Different opinions amongst participants are likely to emerge within the same dataset, rather than needing to be inferred from individual interviews. For this reason, the discussion in a focus group has often been found to reveal "a more nuanced perspective on a topic than could have been discovered through individual interviews" (Wildemuth, 2009, p. 242). On the other hand, even if the focus group is carefully controlled, minority views may dominate and the full range of views, which would be forthcoming from individuals, might not emerge. Ensuring commonality of background and anonymity, as far as possible, will assist in encouraging contribution.

Focus groups are an efficient way of collecting data at less cost in time and money, compared with individual interviews; "a small number of focus groups may generate as many different ideas about the topic as a dozen or more individual interviews" (Wildemuth, 2009, p. 243). On the negative side, these ideas may not be as well developed as through individual interviews, as focus group participants must take turns in voicing their opinions. Also, the logistics of assembling appropriate focus groups in suitable locations (without too many participants failing to turn up) may not be as easy as at first appears. The advent of the online focus group obviates logistical problems of finding a central venue for conducting a focus group interview. See Wildemuth (2009, pp. 248–249) for a discussion of conducting focus groups online. Krueger and Casey (2015) provide 'cutting edge' coverage of telephone and internet focus group interviewing as well as conducting international and cross-cultural focus groups.

As with individual interviews (semi-structured and unstructured), there is an opportunity to provide clarification, to follow-up on leads and to observe body language. The open responses of focus groups particularly often result in large and rich amounts of data in participants' own words. However, because there can be considerable diversity of opinion, the analysis is usually more difficult than for individual interviews. The categories and themes, identified during the analysis, can be more widely dispersed within the discussion and therefore within the typed transcript. The role of the moderator is therefore especially important for keeping participants on track in a focus group. The task is more difficult than it is for individual interviews. As Krueger (1994, p. 16) pointed out: "The open-ending questioning, the use of techniques such as pauses and probes, and knowing when and how to move into new topic areas requires a degree of expertise typically not possessed by untrained interviewers." Krueger (2002) offers useful assistance to focus group moderators.

In addition to the authors already cited, other authors who discuss the advantages and disadvantages of focus groups include Barbour (2007) and Morgan (1997).

Uses of focus groups

Focus groups have been particularly used in market research, to understand the thinking of consumers and also by political parties to gauge the responses of their electors to policy ideas. They are also used in many other areas of endeavour, including in information management, LIS and information systems. Focus groups could be used for evaluating the effectiveness of a library service or a website; or for understanding community information and library needs. Glitz (1998) provides detailed discussion in relation to libraries and librarians and Weare (2013) explores focus group research in academic libraries. An example of how focus groups were used to explore the impact on the public library of the retirement of the baby boomers is outlined in Box 16.2. In information systems research, Shanks and O'Donnell (1997) used focus groups to identify key issues related to the development of a data warehouse. A review article, focussed on the use of focus groups in industrial product design (Bruseberg & McDonagh-Philp, 2002), may be useful for information systems researchers.

Both focus groups and individual interviews are suited to exploring topics in depth and therefore have many points in common. The choice of one over the other will depend on a number of factors including whether it is important to gain in-depth understandings of each person's opinions or experiences, in which case individual interviews will be chosen. Clearly the topic needs to be suitable for focus group interviews. The simplest test, according to Morgan (1997, p. 17), is to consider "how actively and easily the participants would discuss the topic of interest". It is also important to consider whether other approaches are more appropriate or whether focus groups should be used as part of a suite of techniques in ethnography/participant observation. (See Chapter 13: *Ethnographic research*.)

The variety of ways in which focus groups can be used include:

- as a self-contained technique, the results of which can stand on their own;
- as an exploratory technique prior to undertaking a survey with a self-administered questionnaire or structured interview;
- as a follow-up technique to explore, and expand on, information obtained through a survey;
- as part of mixed methods research which includes a survey and complementary focus group interviews; and
- as part of a suite of techniques, for example, questionnaires, individual interviews and/or focus groups, used for ethnography/participant observation, action research, or case study.

Examples of the use of focus groups

The following are two examples of how focus groups have been used in my own research. The first, including Box 16.2, presents an example of where focus groups were used in combination with individual interviews. The method was described as "ethnographic within a constructivist framework, with qualitative techniques (focus groups and individual interviews) being principally used" (Williamson, Bannister & Sullivan, 2010, p. 183). The emphasis in Box 16.2 is on how the focus groups were set up and managed. The example in Box 16.3 is of the use of focus groups as part of an action research study. The emphasis in this second example is on the interview schedule used for one of the focus groups.

(1) *The impact on the public library of the retirement of the baby boomers*

With funding and support from Upper Murray Regional Libraries, Public Libraries Australia and the State Library of NSW, my research group, Information and Telecommunications Needs Research (ITNR), conducted research on this topic over a period of years. Publications from this project apart from Williamson, Bannister and Sullivan (2010), cited above, include Williamson *et al.* (2006). The need for the research was based on the very large numbers of baby boomers who had already retired or were likely to do so in the near future. Their retirement would present a challenge to the public library to meet their needs as well as an opportunity to entice them to be volunteers in, and therefore contributors to, their public library. Baby boomers were defined as those born between 1946 and 1965, the definition used by the Australian Bureau of Statistics. The individual interviews were with gatekeepers, defined as visionary leaders in the baby boomer age range, who had a broad knowledge of the needs of their communities. Nine gatekeepers were library managers and eight were prominent community members.

For the ITNR baby boomer project, the researchers considered that focus groups, selected from the membership of different Australian library services, would be a good way to explore the relevant issues from the perspective of both librarians and library users who were part of the baby boomer cohort. A series of seven focus groups was conducted including two that were undertaken as part of a pilot study in 2005. It was decided to add five more during the study proper in 2007–2008, despite Morgan's (1997) view that the number in a focus group series should be three to five because normally, within that range, "data collection no longer generates new understanding" (p. 43). Because it was important to represent capital city, regional and rural libraries across the whole of Australia, seven focus groups were considered to be justified. Many of the same questions were asked in both the pilot project and in the study proper and so the findings emerged from all seven focus groups. The following was the process used to set up and organise the focus groups.

Box 16.2

Example of the process of setting up and conducting focus groups

1. The team, including representatives from the funding partners, brainstormed ideas about which library services should be targeted for the project. From the pilot study in 2005, we had representation from one city library service (Melbourne) and one regional city library service (Newcastle). In 2007, we added three capital city library services (in Sydney, Perth and Brisbane), another regional city (Darwin) and rural service (Mildura). There was over-representation of capital city library services and under-representation of rural ones but, as is usually the case, practical issues such as access and cost came into play.

2. Our partners, closely involved as they were in the library world, helped us through contacts they had with the library services involved. We then communicated with the person nominated to be our liaison representative from each library service, outlining our requirements for a mutually convenient date, a suitable venue to hold the focus group, and for focus group participants. We had clear guidelines for the recruitment of participants, suited to the goals of the project. In each case, we wanted a purposeful sample, of the 'criterion' kind (discussed in Chapter 15), that particularly balanced the numbers of males and females, as well as the numbers of 'leading edge' boomers (born between 1946 and 1955) and 'trailing edge' boomers (born between 1956 and 1965). The latter requirement was very important to obtaining a mix of older boomers (possibly already retired) and younger boomers (many of whom would be still in the workforce). As often happens, the recruitment did not fully meet the criteria we set up. Since we were dependent on the libraries involved to recruit participants (and there was no other way we could do this), we did not have control over the final focus group samples. There was almost twice the number of leading edge boomers, compared with trailing edge boomers, in the sample and well over twice as many females as males. Since public library users are more often female than male, the predominance of females in the sample was appropriate. While there is no hard evidence, it is also likely that there were more leading edge than trailing edge boomers who were library users. It is interesting to note that the best-balanced sample was in Sydney where the State Library of NSW paid for a recruiting firm to find participants, the latter of whom were also paid.

3. In some cases, participants were given the 'information statement', approved by Charles Sturt University Ethics in Human Research Committee at the time of recruitment; in other cases they needed to read it at the beginning of the focus group. All participants needed to sign an 'informed consent' form. Participants also filled in a demographic questionnaire prior to the commencement of the focus groups.

4. Two experienced interviewers were used to conduct all of the focus groups, which were recorded with the permission of the participants. One took responsibility for the audio equipment, some note taking, and followed up on leads if missed by the principal interviewer. Patton (2015) concurred with this necessity. To aid transcription, difficult for the typist, given the multiple voices involved, participants were asked (and reminded if they forgot) to state their names the first two or three times that they spoke.

(2) Generating knowledge and avoiding plagiarism: Smart information use by secondary students

Joy McGregor and I, with two other colleagues, were awarded an Australian Research Council (ARC) Linkage grant with four secondary schools on the above topic for the years 2006–2007. ARC Linkage grants are for academic/industry research collaborations. The research took place in three phases: (1) Researchers benchmarked student and staff understandings of plagiarism and its corollary, appropriate and effective information use. (2) Teachers and teacher librarians used action research to develop strategies to teach students to use information to generate new knowledge and avoid plagiarism; and (3) Researchers evaluated the success of the strategies. Publications from the project include Williamson, McGregor, Archibald and Sullivan (2007) and Williamson and McGregor (2011). This project is discussed further in Chapter 8: *Action research.*

The action research, used in the second phase, was evaluated by focus group interviews with students and staff (teachers and teacher librarians), although occasionally staff were interviewed individually or in pairs. Box 16.3 gives an example of the questions and prompts used with one of the staff focus groups. Once again, the questions were geared to answering the research questions for that component of the research. Again we only used the prompts (though more sparingly than in the example for the semi-structured interview) if participants did not spontaneously mention the issues of interest. Thus, as with the semi-structured interview schedule discussed above, participants could freely provide their perspectives at the same time as we ensured that issues of significance to the research were covered.

Box 16.3

Example of questions and prompts used in a focus group interview of teachers and teacher librarians: Smart information use by secondary students

Background

The school, where this particular list of questions and prompts was used, had developed a model aimed at teaching students to think for themselves. Both teachers and teacher librarians took part in the focus group. The aims of the questions were to compare previous approaches to teaching with the new model; to explore whether teachers and teacher librarians had shared the same focus in their teaching of the new approach; to ascertain which elements of the new model were the most and least productive; and to ascertain the effect on plagiarism which was the focus of the project.

Research question

To gauge, through an evaluation process, the extent to which the new teaching models (developed through the action research) influence students' understandings of plagiarism and the extent to which it occurs in their assignments.

Questions and prompts

1. Was this way of teaching a topic different? If so, how?
2. Do you think you shared the same focus as each other?
3. Which elements seemed to be most productive in terms of student learning?
4. Which elements seemed to be least productive in terms of student learning?
5. Do you think the students will change their practice (i.e., to avoid plagiarism)?
6. (If yes) In what way? (If no) Why not?
7. Do you think the teachers will change their practice? (If yes) In what way? (If no) Why not?
8. Do you think the students gained any metacognitive awareness of the processes they used?

9. Prompts: Metacognition: Thinking about their own thinking – being aware of how they think about and plan their practice.

10. Do you think you will incorporate anything from this project into your teaching and/or collaborative practice?

Do you have any advice you would give other teachers or teacher librarians, after being involved with this project?

Conclusion

This chapter has discussed a range of techniques for collecting quantitative and qualitative data from people. It is important to consider the research questions, research philosophy and methods, that is, the methodology for the research, before deciding on which technique or techniques are appropriate. Regardless of the choice or choices made, detailed understanding and careful thought are required. In all cases, considerable care, forethought and planning are needed for the collection of good quality data. Piloting questions is an essential precursor.

References

Alreck, P. L., & Settle, R. B. (2004). *The survey research handbook* (3rd ed.). Boston: McGraw-Hill.

Babbie, E. (2008). *The basics of social research* (4th ed.). Belmont, CA: Thomson Wadsworth.

Baker, T. L. (1999). *Doing social research*. Boston: McGraw-Hill.

Barbour, R. (2007). *Doing focus groups*. London: Sage.

Brinkmann, S., & Kvale, S. (2015). *InterViews: Learning the craft of qualitative research interviewing* (3rd ed.). Los Angeles: Sage.

Bruseberg, A., & McDonagh-Philp, D. (2002). Focus groups to support the industrial/ product designer: A review based on current literature and designers' feedback. *Applied Ergonomics, 33*(1), 27–38.

Charmaz, K. (2003). Grounded theory: Objectivist and constructivist methods. In N. K. Denzin, & Y. S. Lincoln (Eds.), *Strategies of qualitative inquiry* (2nd ed., pp. 249–291). Thousand Oaks, CA: Sage.

Connaway, L. S., & Powell, R. (2010). *Basic research methods for librarians* (5th ed.). Santa Barbara, CA: Libraries Unlimited.

de Leeuw, E. (2008). Self-administerd questionnaires and standardized interviews. In P. Alasuutari, L. Bickman, & J. Brannen (Eds.), *The Sage handbook of social research methods* (pp. 313–327). Los Angeles: Sage.

Doucet, A., & Mauthner, N. (2008). Qualitative interviewing and feminist research. In P. Alasuutari, L. Bickman, & J. Brannen (Eds.), *The Sage handbook of social research methods* (pp. 328–343). Los Angeles: Sage.

Fidel, R. (1993). Qualitative methods in information retrieval. *Library and Information Science Research, 15*(3), 219–247.

Fontana, A., & Frey, J. H. (1998). Interviewing: The art of science. In N. K. Denzin, & Y. S. Lincoln (Eds.), *Collecting and interpreting qualitative materials* (pp. 47–78). Thousand Oaks: Sage.

Fontana, A. F., & Frey, J. H. (2005). From neutral stance to political involvement. In N. K. Denzin, & Y. S. Lincoln (Eds.), *The Sage handbook of qualitative research* (3rd ed., pp. 695–728). Thousand Oaks, CA: Sage.

Glitz, B. (1998). *Focus groups for libraries and librarians.* New York: Forbes.

Guthrie, G. (2010). *Basic research methods – An entry to social science research.* New Delhi: Sage.

Kennan, M., Williamson, K., & Johanson, G. (2012). Wild data: Collaborative e-research and university libraries. *Australian Academic & Research Libraries, 43* (1), 55–78.

Krueger, R. A. (1994). *Focus groups: A practical guide for applied research* (2nd ed.). Thousand Oaks, CA: Sage.

Krueger, R.A. (2002). Designing and conducting focus group interviews. Retrieved from http://www.eiu.edu/~ihec/Krueger-FocusGroupInterviews.pdf

Krueger, R. A., & Casey, M. A. (2009). *Focus groups: A practical guide for applied research* (4th ed.). Thousand Oaks, CA: Sage.

Krueger, R. A., & Casey, M. A. (2015). *Focus groups: A practical guide for applied research* (5th ed.). Thousand Oaks, CA: Sage.

Morgan, D. L. (1997). *Focus groups as qualitative research* (2nd ed.). Newbury Park, CA: Sage.

Morse, J. M. (2003). Principles of mixed methods and multimethod research design. In A. Tashakkori, & C. Teddlie (Eds.), *Handbook of mixed methods in social and behavioral research* (pp. 189–208). Thousand Oaks, CA: Sage.

Myers, M., & Newman, M. (2007). The qualitative interview in IS research: Examining the craft. *Information and Organization, 17*(1), 2–26.

Neuman, W. L. (2014). *Social research methods: Qualitative and quantitative approaches* (7th ed.). Harlow, Essex: Pearson New International.

Oppenheim, A. N. (2000). *Questionnaire design, interviewing and attitude measurement* (2nd ed.). New York: Continuum International Publishing Group.

Patton, M. Q. (2015). *Qualitative evaluation and research methods* (4th ed.). Los Angeles, CA: Sage Publications.

Pickard, A. J. (2013). *Research methods in information* (2nd ed.). Chicago: Neal-Schuman.

Punch, K. F. (2014). *Introduction to social research: Quantitative and qualitative approaches* (3rd ed.). London: Sage.

Rubin, H. J., & Rubin, I. S. (2011). *Qualitative interviewing: The art of hearing data* (3rd ed). Thousand Oaks, CA: Sage.

Savin-Baden, M., & Major, C. H. (2013). *Qualitative research: The essential guide to theory and practice.* London: Routledge.

Shanks, G., & O'Donnell, P. (1997). *Focus group on data warehousing.* Melbourne: Department of Information Systems, Monash University.

Spradley, J. P. (1979). *The ethnographic interview.* New York: Holt, Rhinehart & Winston.

StatPac. (2014). Qualities of a good question. Retrieved from http://www.statpac.com/surveys/question-qualities.htm

Stewart, D. W., & Shamdasani, P. N. (1990). *Focus groups: Theory and practice.* Newbury Park, CA: Sage.

Taylor, S. J., Bogdan, R., & DeVault, M. (2015). *Introduction to qualitative research methods: A guidebook and resource* (4th ed.). New York: John Wiley & Sons.

Weare, W. H., Jr. (2013). Focus group research in the academic library: An overview of the methodology. *Qualitative and Quantitative Methods in Libraries (QQML), 1,* 47–58.

Wildemuth, B. M. (2009). *Applications of social research methods to questions in information and library science.* Westport, CT: Libraries Unlimited.

Williamson, K. (Ed.). (2002). *Research methods for students, academics and professionals: Information management and systems* (2nd ed.). Wagga Wagga, NSW: Centre for Information Studies, Charles Sturt University.

Williamson, K., Bannister, M., Makin, L., Johanson, G., Schauder, D., & Sullivan, J. (2006). 'Wanting it now': Baby boomers and the public library of the future. *The Australian Library Journal, 55*(1), 54–72.

Williamson, K., Bannister, M., & Sullivan, J. (2010). The crossover generation: Baby boomers and the role of the public library. *Journal of Librarianship and Information Science, 42*(3), 179–190.

Williamson, K., & Kingsford Smith, D. (2010). Empowered or vulnerable? The role of information for Australian online investors. *Canadian Journal of Information and Library Science, 34*(1), 39–81.

Williamson, K., & McGregor, J. (2011). Generating knowledge and avoiding plagiarism: Smart information use by high school students. *School Library Media Research, 14.* Retrieved from http://www.ala.org/aasl/sites/ala.org.aasl/files/content/aaslpubsandjournals/slr/vol14/SLR_GeneratingKnowledge_V14.pdf

Williamson, K., McGregor, J., Archibald, A., & Sullivan, J. (2007). Information seeking and use by secondary students: The link between good practice and the avoidance of plagiarism. *School Library Media Research, 10.* Retrieved from https://www.ala.org/ala/mgrps/divs/aasl/aaslpubsandjournals/slmrb/slmrcontents/volume10/williamson_informationseeking.cfm

Chapter 17

Observation

Kirsty Williamson
Monash University and Charles Sturt University, Australia

This chapter focusses on the rich and varied approaches to observation as a technique or tool available to researchers. The flexibility of observation enables it to be used in a range of different research methods, often in combination with other techniques such as interviews. There is also a variety of kinds of observation, including structured or unstructured forms The chapter discusses the various ways in which 'participation' has been conceptualised, focussing on different observer roles as well as levels of participation, from non-participation to complete participation. Examples provide illustration. Ways of undertaking observation are also discussed, for example, gaining entry to a setting, selecting a sample and data collection techniques which includes note taking. Validity and reliability, together with ethical issues, specifically focussed on observation, are also within the scope of the chapter.

Research Methods: Information, Systems, and Contexts. DOI: http://dx.doi.org/10.1016/B978-0-08-102220-7.00017-0

Introduction

Observation is a widely used technique or tool, regarded by many as fundamental to research. For example Adler and Adler (1998),[1] who are widely cited in the literature, described observation as "the bedrock source of human knowledge" (pp. 79-80) and referred to early classicists' use of observation, for example, Aristotle's botanical observations on the Island of Lesbos. The founder of sociology, Comte, regarded observation as one of the four core research methods, along with comparison, historical analysis, and experimentation (Adler & Adler, 1998, p. 80). I prefer to use the labels, 'technique' or 'tool', rather than 'method' as observation is rarely used as a sole approach to research (Adler & Adler, 1998). Rather it is used in a number of different research methods, such as case study, grounded theory, action research, and ethnography/participant observation. Indeed, Adler and Adler described observation as "stepchild to its more widely recognised offshoot: participant observation" (p. 80). Apart from titling their chapter, *Observational Techniques*, they postulated that: "Where the future of observation shines more brightly is in the use of this technique as an integrated rather than a primary method" (p. 105). The labelling becomes particularly complicated with regard to participant observation which, as described in Chapter 13: *Ethnographic research*, is often considered as synonymous with, or an alternative label for, ethnography. I believe that participant observation, as a *form* of observation, can also be regarded as a technique or data collection tool.

As one of the techniques or tools used in methods such as ethnography or case study, observation is very often combined with interviews. There is a clear advantage in this approach as it enables the researcher to triangulate data from two different sources. Sometimes short interviews may be conducted spontaneously during participant observation when opportunities arise but often they are formally organised and conducted as in the example of Terry Asla's research, documented below.

The advantages of observation include that it permits researchers to study people in their natural environments in order to understand them and their context more deeply than it is possible to gauge through interview, where interviewees may be unaware of important nuances or unwilling to disclose certain information (Patton, 2015). Nevertheless, there are issues to consider, including the intermittent and unpredictable nature of certain behaviours and the difficulty of always having an observer on hand when a spontaneous, but critical event occurs (Connaway & Powell, 2010; Wildemuth, 2009). There is also the fact that people do not like being watched. Wildemuth discussed this and other issues, with specific reference to observation in libraries.

---

[1] The 1998 chapter is a reprint of Adler and Adler's frequently cited original work published in Denzin, N. K., & Lincoln, Y. S. (1994). *The handbook of qualitative research* (2nd ed.). Thousand Oaks, CA: Sage.

There is a variety of ways in which observational techniques are classified and described. One such categorisation is "structured versus unstructured observation" (Connaway & Powell, 2010; Punch, 1998). Another is diversely described around the concept of participation, with the discussion frequently focussing on observer roles (Adler & Adler, 1998; Angrosino, 2005; Baker, 2006; Chatman, 1984; Chatman, 1991; Chatman, 1992; Lofland, Snow, Anderson & Lofland, 2006; Patton, 2015; Spradley, 1980 (a still highly regarded book); Wildemuth, 2009). Both of these approaches are described below. Savin-Baden and Major (2013) discuss observation, in general, as a data-collection technique.

Types of observation

There are various ways in which observational techniques are described, indicating a range of types of observation available to researchers. There can be some similarities in approaches, although described by different terminology or labels.

Structured versus unstructured observation

Structured observation is more often associated with quantitative research approaches and unstructured observation is mainly linked to qualitative research. "Quantitative observations, conducted in situations deliberately designed to ensure standardization and control, differ markedly from observations framed by the qualitative paradigm" (Adler & Adler, 1998, p. 81).

Structured observation

Quantitative approaches to observation tend to be highly structured, requiring detailed, pre-developed observation schedules (Punch, 1998), which might include dichotomous categories to record whether a specific behaviour is present or not, or rating scales to record the level of an activity or degree to which a particular behaviour is present. An example is provided by Baker (1999) who discussed Travis Hirschi's Index of Delinquency, designed to record the incidence of delinquent behaviour. Sometimes a pre-existing observation schedule may be available. For example, Burns (2000, pp. 409-410) provides two pro-forma suggestions for observing groups when holding meetings. Researchers sometimes use audiovisual equipment to improve accuracy and aid analysis. This helps to avoid overloading the observer, "which is one of the most serious threats to observational accuracy" (Connaway & Powell, 2010, p. 182). Connaway and Powell also provide the following steps to increase the reliability of structured – and sometimes unstructured observations:

1. Developing adequate definition of the kinds of behavior that are to be recorded, and being certain that they correspond to the specific concepts to be studied.

2.   Carefully training the observers to ensure that they are adequately prepared and that they have confidence in their ability or judgement to check the appropriate categories.

3.   Avoiding observer bias. Generally the observer should take behaviors at their face value and not attempt to interpret their 'real' meaning, at least not at the time the observations are made (Connaway & Powell, 2010, p. 183).

Usability testing

Usability testing measures "observation and analysis of users' behavior while they interact with a system or prototype" (Prasse & Connaway, 2008, p. 215). Structured observation schedules are common in usability testing, which is used particularly for evaluating technological applications by trying them out on potential users. Prasse and Connaway (2008) provide a detailed discussion.

Unstructured observation

'Unstructured observation' is associated with qualitative research. While qualitative researchers will have a general research question they want to answer, specific research questions are usually developed during the observation process.

As Adler and Adler proposed:

> Qualitative observation is fundamentally naturalistic in its essence ... [It draws the observer into the]...complexity of the world where connections, correlations, and causes can be witnessed as and how they unfold. Qualitative observers are not bound, thus, by predetermined categories of measurement or response, but are free to search for concepts or categories that appear meaningful to subjects (Adler & Adler, 1998, p. 81).

With unstructured observation, careful note taking is essential – unobtrusively, on the spot, and certainly in detail following the observation session (discussed below). The use of recording equipment is not recommended because people are often wary when they are being recorded, with the effect that the situation moves from the naturalistic to the artificial. While observers usually start out with a broad approach, observations narrow and become more focussed as the research progresses – a funnelling effect as Spradley (1980) called it. Examples of how observers become immersed in their settings and progressively narrow their focus come from two of my former PhD students, who undertook ethnographic research in online communities, the first in Saudi Arabia, the second within GreyPath, an Australian online community for seniors.

Observation of Saudi Arabian online communities

Yeslam Al-Saggaf, who focussed on online communities in Saudi Arabia, began his research with unobtrusive observation of a virtual community, followed by participant observation in another similar virtual community (Al-Saggaf, 2012; Al-Saggaf & Williamson, 2006; and Al-Saggaf, Williamson & Weckert, 2002). In the first stage, which lasted four months (between mid-March 2001 and mid-July 2001), he became familiar with the online culture of the first community, its vocabulary, history, and people. He also became aware of the nature of the activities, the key features of participation and the general behaviour of the participants of the community. In the field notes, the researcher identified the patterns and the key features of participation and made a checklist of observational categories for use in the second stage. Table 17.1 sets out these categories. Order is not important.

Table 17.1 Observational categories developed in first stage of observation

Observational categories				
grouping	meeting offline	information sharing	religion	friendship
history	flaming	complimenting	disclosure	status
trivia	offline culture	humour	obscenity	love
religious influence	shyness	defending	withdrawal	intimacy
respect	intellectual	emotional support	commitments	family atmosphere
reputation	language	misunderstanding	name known	attention

Source: Al-Saggaf & Williamson, 2006, p. 11.

In the second stage of the observation, field notes were made daily, mainly focussed on these categories and recording information about the discussion and messages related to them. "During this process, the researcher always asked himself: Why was the instance interesting? And: Why was he interested in it?" (Al-Saggaf, Williamson & Weckert, 2002). Simultaneously, he recorded his own reactions, reflections and interpretations of his observations. Since the researcher was concerned about the subjectivity of a single observer, he compensated at a later stage of the research by using triangulation with data from other techniques such as interviewing. Thus issues of validity (discussed in Chapter 13, and also below) were considered by Al-Saggaf. (Al-Saggaf's research is discussed further in Chapter 13.)

Observation of GreyPath, an online community for seniors

Oliver Burmeister's focus was an Australian online community for seniors, called GreyPath, where he explored what members most valued about their online social interaction, along with implications for improving technological design (Burmeister, 2010; Burmeister, Weckert, & Williamson, 2011). His method was ethnographic within constructivist and human-computer interaction (HCI) frameworks. Burmeister combined, in two stages, observation with interviews – as Al-Saggaf had done. The purpose of the first stage (the observation) was to inform the researcher about the nature of GreyPath members and their activities, and to begin the process of identifying values that could subsequently be explored with participants during individual interviews. Burmeister (2010, p. 128) described himself as a 'complete observer' on the continuum of participant observation, given that the Charles Sturt University Ethics in Human Research Committee would not allow him to enter the private areas of GreyPath (e.g., the chat rooms) without the impossible task of gaining permission of every participant. His observation was therefore unobtrusive and confined to public spaces for which permission from the administrator, alone, was required. Public spaces are the places on the site where anyone can go, members and non-members, for example, the coffee shop forum.

Burmeister (2010) observed GreyPath real-time online activity every Monday for 11 months, with each observation session typically lasting at least three hours. He also reviewed archival information for the past week, thus giving him access to online activities for the whole of each week. The observation involved all contributors – management and members – and a wide range of activities, including forums (threaded emails on various topics, including jokes), online learning initiatives and information on jobs for seniors.

Burmeister (2010), as he acknowledged, followed the pattern of his colleague, Al-Saggaf, in conducting unstructured observation during the first three months, looking specifically "for how social interaction values were expressed in the GreyPath community". In this time, he developed a list of categories (values) which he refined and clustered during the more structured observation which followed. He used the same data analysis approach for both the observation and interview stages, as Figure 17.1 indicates.

Figure 17.1 Four-step analytic process

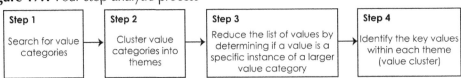

Source: Burmeister, 2010, p. 127.

In the observation stage, seven key values emerged from three themes (value clusters): peer values; online behaviour values; and relationship values. Table 17.2 presents the values in those themes with the 'key values' asterisked.

Table 17.2 Five key values from unobtrusive observation

Theme (value clusters)	Value categories (key values asterisked)
Peer values	<ul><li>Belonging to a community of peers*</li><li>Cooperation</li><li>Corporate identity (management)</li><li>Enriching others' lives*</li><li>Health (mental and physical)</li></ul>
Online behaviour values	<ul><li>Art</li><li>Computer literacy</li><li>Freedom of expression*</li><li>Innovation (management)</li><li>International reach (management)</li><li>Keeping informed</li><li>Life-long learning</li><li>Meeting legal requirements (management)</li><li>Money</li><li>Profitability (management)</li><li>Protecting others from harm</li><li>Pursuing hobbies</li><li>Recency (management)</li><li>Respect*</li><li>Technical leadership (management)</li><li>Travel</li><li>Usability</li></ul>
Relationship values	<ul><li>Fairness*</li><li>Friendship and avoiding loneliness*</li><li>Human well being</li><li>Not getting embarrassed</li><li>Online identity</li><li>Trust*</li></ul>

While the interview stage added considerable depth and much more diversity to the outcomes of the observation, the observation stage of the study provided an important overview for Burmeister and assisted him in developing his interview questions.

From non-participation to complete participation

As mentioned above, 'participation' has been variously conceptualised, with Atkinson and Hammersley (1998) mooting that participant observation is not easy to 'pin down' (p. 111). These authors were also critical of the distinction often drawn between participant and non-participant observation, believing that "this simple dichotomy is not very useful", apart from the fact that "in a sense *all* social research is a form of participant observation, because we cannot study the social world without being part of it" (p. 111). They saw the fourfold typology, widely discussed in the literature – complete observer, observer as participant, participant as observer, and complete participant – as more subtle but still problematic because of offering only discrete options. The fourfold typology is widely attributed to Gold (1958) but, as Gold himself admitted, it was Buford Junker (1952) who first "suggested four theoretically possible roles for sociologists conducting field work" (Gold, 1958, p. 217). Gold, however, was part of Junker's team, shared in Junker's conceptualisations and, in his PhD thesis completed in 1954, "explored the dimensions of Junker's role conceptions and their controlling effects on the product of field study" (p. 217).

Chatman (1984, p. 429) defined roles in participant observation as "the characteristic posture(s) researchers assume in their relationship" with the people whom they are studying. In the introduction to her major study of the information world of retired women (Chatman, 1992), she identified only three roles: (1) the researcher as an objective recorder of events; (2) the researcher as participant, engaging in activities to gather data; and (3) the researcher as total participant, becoming integrally involved in the daily lives of the study participants (1992, p. 3). As widely noted, the last approach is usually called 'going native'. Chatman's view was that the first and third approaches are problematical, the first because the researcher who attempts to be an objective observer will not be "privy to motivational factors or to subtle influences affecting behaviour" and the third because the researcher "has given up an important measure of objectivity in which to report data free of bias" (p. 3). She therefore chose the role of participant observer for her two-year study of the use of information by women in a retirement community, visiting frequently, eating with the residents and taking part in activities, for example, poker games, if she felt they would assist her data gathering. In other words she used outsider/insider roles as appropriate.

Insider/outsider roles

A different set of role labels, again, was proposed by Adler and Adler (1998) who built on their earlier work (Adler & Adler, 1987). They mooted that, since the Junker/Gold fourfold typology was proposed, there had been a shift to greater involvement, even membership roles, by researchers, with three types seeming to predominate: "the complete-member-researcher, the active-member-researcher, and the peripheral-member-researcher" (Adler & Adler, 1998, p. 84). They postulated that even researchers in peripheral membership roles feel that an insider's perspective is vital to gaining an accurate understanding of participants in the setting and that therefore they interact closely enough to gain this perspective. Both outsider/insider roles are possible with this typology. The active-member-researcher becomes more involved again in group activities, perhaps assuming responsibilities within the group and becoming more of an 'insider' than 'outsider' through forging closer bonds with members. Complete-member-researchers are often already members of a group they decide to study or become 'genuine' members or 'insiders' as the research proceeds. Their goal is "complete depth of the subjectively lived experience" (p. 85). Auto-observation, enabling researchers' observations of others to be augmented with their own thoughts and feelings (p. 97), would be included here.

The conceptualisation of outsider/insider perspectives is a focus of discussion in the literature (e.g., Lofland *et al.*, 2006; Spradley, 1980). Lofland *et al.* concluded that there is a necessary tension between insider/outsider roles for researchers and that, whatever their relationship to the setting, "it is simultaneously an advantage and a drawback" (p. 23). Spradley postulated that simultaneous insider/outsider experiences occur from time-to-time but can be disrupted. For example, researchers may suddenly realise that they are acting as full participants, without observing as an outsider; at other times they can stand apart and become more detached. In Spradley's view: "Doing fieldwork involves alternating between the insider and outsider experience and having both simultaneously" (p. 57).

Participant observation continua

Spradley (1980) promoted the view that flexibility in roles is necessary in participant observation. He offered five types of participation focussed on a researcher's degree of involvement both with people and the activities observed. In the examples that he provided, it is clear that a researcher might begin as one type of participant and move to become another. It therefore seemed appropriate to place Spradley's five roles on a continuum which Figure 17.2 is *my* attempt to do. The definitions he gave to each of the points are below the figure.

Spradley's pioneering work is still highly pertinent. It is a fluid, flexible approach as is that of Glesne and Peshkin (1992) who took the Junker/Gold fourfold typology but, rather than focussing on just four categories, placed them on a continuum, ranging from mostly observation to mostly participation. They emphasised that the researcher's role may fall at any point along the continuum and is likely to shift to "different points at different times in the data collection process" (p. 40). While Glesne and Peshkin did not provide a figure, Figure 17.3 illustrates the continuum as they described it. The definitions Glesne and Peshkin gave to each of the points are below the figure.

Figure 17.2 Spradley's participation categories, placed on a continuum — where passive participation denotes low involvement and complete participation denotes high involvement

Spradley's participation categories				
Non-participation (no involvement)	Passive participation	Moderate participation	Active participation	Complete participation
⟶	⟶	⟶	⟶	⟶

Non-participation: Researcher has no involvement with the people or activities studied. Spradley gave examples of ethnographic studies of television programs but modern examples could involve technologies such as video-taping. An example of this type of observation is included below.

Passive participation: Researcher is present but does not participate or interact to any great extent.

Moderate participation: Researcher seeks a balance between being an insider and outsider, between participation and observation.

Active participation: Researcher seeks to do what other people are doing, not merely to gain acceptance, but to more fully learn the cultural rules of behaviour.

Complete participation: The researcher studies a situation in which they are already ordinary participants (Spradley, 1980, pp. 58-62).

Source: Spradley, 1980.

Figure 17.3 Glesne and Peshkin's participant observation continuum

Glesne and Peshkin's participant observation continuum			
Complete observer	Observer as participant	Participant as observer	Full participant
⟶	⟶	⟶	⟶

Complete observer: The observer is as unobtrusive as possible and has little or no interaction with those being studied.

Observer as participant: Researcher is primarily an observer but has some interaction.

Participant as observer: Researcher becomes more of a participant than observer.

Full participant: Researcher is simultaneously a functioning member of the group and an investigator (Glesne & Peshkin, 1992, p. 40).

Source: Bow, 2002, p. 268; Glesne & Peshkin, 1992.

Again, it should be emphasised that this is a continuum which allows flexibility for the researcher's roles to change during the course of a study. Other authors have also emphasised the need for a flexible approach. For example, Patton (2015) postulated that: "The extent of participation is a continuum that varies from complete immersion in the setting as full participant to complete separation from the setting as a spectator, with a great deal of variation along the continuum between these two end points" (p. 336).

Undertaking observation

This section describes and discusses the crucial steps and issues involved in undertaking observation. The focus is particularly on choosing and gaining entry to a setting; deciding on the sample; data collection, particularly note taking; validity and reliability; and ethical issues. Data analysis is covered in Chapter 19: *Qualitative data analysis*.

Gaining entry to a setting and selecting a sample

Observers/ethnographers need a setting or settings in which to undertake their research. The decision about what is an appropriate site or sites relates to the goal of the research. In the examples of virtual ethnographies, discussed above, the researchers chose online communities of various kinds. Oliver Burmeister chose the online community for seniors, GreyPath, because his goal was to explore what seniors value about online social interaction. Both Burmeister and I, his principal supervisor, had met the CEO of GreyPath through an Australian listserv called NEAT (Network for Education, Ageing and Technology), to which we both belonged. As Lofland *et al.* (2006) stated:

> There is a great deal of wisdom in the old saying, "It's not what you know but who you know that counts." Gaining entrée to a setting or getting permission ... is not only greatly expedited if you have 'connections', but oftentimes access is well-nigh impossible without them (p. 42).

In Burmeister's case, he was able to make use of an existing professional link. If you do not have a link, you will need to identify key gatekeepers and develop the connection, a more difficult position to be in. For example, Chatman (1992, pp. 3-8) discusses her problems in gaining entry to the various sites (and participants within them) for her research focussed on the information worlds of specialised populations, particularly those of lower socio-economic status. Her accounts are entertaining but the frustrations were huge – extending from her being labelled a 'spy' (p. 4) during her study of university janitors to facing 'closed doors' during her study of the information world of retired women.

Sometimes one is lucky enough to gain entry through project partners as Joy McGregor and I were able to do in the case of the four high schools which provided sites for us for our partly ethnographic and partly action research study of smart information use by secondary school students (Williamson, McGregor, Archibald & Sullivan, 2007). In each case, permission from the school principal was required to enable the participation of the school in the Australian Research Council Linkage project – and entrée to the sites followed suit. (The project is discussed at greater length in Chapter 8: *Action research*.)

In some cases, researchers are already part of a community where they see an opportunity to undertake research of interest to them. This was the case with Karen Visser (2007), whose study took place in an Australian high school where she was employed as a teacher librarian (discussed in Chapter 8). Although hers was action research, there were elements of participant observation involved. Another example is presented below – of Terry Asla's participant observation in a retirement community where he had been employed for many years prior to his decision to undertake PhD research focussed on the role of information in successful ageing. He chose a contrasting second retirement community in the same neighbourhood where he also had connections and therefore gained easy entry.

A common setting for library and information science (LIS) researchers is a library. Given and Leckie (2003), whose research is discussed below, undertook observation in central public libraries in two large Canadian cities. As reported by Wildemuth (2009), McKechnie (1996; 2000) chose a public library system in an urban setting and then four individual libraries from within that system in order to explore the role of the public library in opening the door to learning for preschool girls. As also reported by Wildemuth (2009), Westbrook (1995; 1998) undertook observations partly in her role as a librarian at a mid-western university, but more particularly in the offices of her participants (their work settings) as part of her exploration of the information-seeking experiences of women's studies faculty. In all cases, permission would have needed from the library directors and Westbrook required the agreement and assistance of the Women's Studies Program Office to recruit participants. The parents and children in McKechnie's study were recruited by various methods, with parents needing to give their permission for their children to be involved.

The sample to be the focus of the observation will be identified sometimes before, sometimes after, and sometimes simultaneously with the selection of the setting. For example, McKechnie (1996; 2000) knew that her sample would be preschool girls before she sought settings for her research. She therefore needed libraries that met certain criteria regarding preschoolers (Wildemuth, 2009, pp. 206-207). In the case of the *Smart Information Use Project* (Williamson *et al.*, 2007), the first phase of which used ethnographic method, the year levels of the students to be involved were determined after the schools became part of the project – through discussions of the research team, the teacher librarians, and the teachers who were willing to have their classes take part.

Data collection

Some aspects of data collection have been mentioned above, especially in the section on structured and unstructured observation. Here the focus is on the note taking needed in unstructured observation used by qualitative researchers, including participant observers. These researchers, while they might record formal interviews that might be part of their ethnographic research, will not usually introduce technology for their observation so as not to change the natural setting. Their early aim will be to develop rapport with participants in the setting by chatting, helping out, taking part in activities and generally immersing themselves in the culture (taking into account the perspectives on insider/outsider roles, discussed above).

Some writers, for example, Patton (2015) have emphasised that training is essential for good observation. We are all familiar with the stories of the widely varying accounts that observers of exactly the same situations, can give. "The fact that a person is equipped with functioning senses does not make that person a skilled observer" (Patton, 2002, p. 260). Patton proposed that trained and prepared observers can report "with accuracy, authenticity, and reliability" (p. 260) and provides brief guidelines (pp. 260-261).

Note taking

Almost all publications which discuss observation provide advice on note taking, described as memo writing by constructivist grounded theorists – what Charmaz (2006) referred to as "conversing with oneself" (p. 72). Those who provide extensive discussion include Baker (1999); Chatman (1992); Lofland *et al.* (2006) who have a whole chapter on logging data; Spradley (1980) who has a whole section on making an ethnographic record; and Taylor, Bogdan and DeVault (2015). Chapter 9: *Constructivist grounded theory* discusses memo writing.

A key rationale for the use of observation is the fact that so much can be learnt from apparently trivial happenings and remarks. Observers therefore need to pay careful attention to the accurate recording of their observations (Lofland *et al.*, 2006). "Notes can include observations, impressions, feelings hunches, and questions which emerge" (Myers, 1999, p. 9). Some observers start out with a notebook and are meticulous about having it to hand at all times. Others, perhaps while they are observing in communities where they also have a working role, tend to lapse and find themselves making notes on scrap of paper, whatever is available. For example, Terry Asla, whose work is discussed below, bought a handsome Moleskine brand notebook, just as Hemmingway used. Nevertheless, since he was employed at one of the retirement homes where he collected data, he more often found himself writing on paper napkins or programs and retreating quickly to his office to type up his notes (Asla, personal communication, 10 July, 2012). Even complete observers find it difficult to take notes inconspicuously, as related below in the example of the observation of Given and Leckie (2003). Thus detailed field notes need to be written after observers leave the field (Baker, 1999, p. 260).

Because "forgetting begins as soon as the experience ends" (Ely, 1991, p. 79), the consensus in the literature is that notes should be written up as soon as possible after observations are made and always within 24 hours. Baker (1999),

Guthrie (2010) and Taylor, Bogdan and DeVault (2015) are some of the writers emphasising the need for the self-discipline required for timely recording of detailed field notes.

The data from field notes must be stored efficiently so that there is easy access for analysis which should start early in the process. Lofland *et al.* (2006) give some good advice for handling "what at times can feel like overwhelming mountains of information" (p. 95). While analysis issues will be discussed in Chapter 19, their five basic requirements for effective data management need to be considered at the recording stage:

1. You must be able to log or record data promptly.
2. Data must be available for duplication.
3. Data must be available for coding.
4. Coded categories must be easily accessible for examination and analysis, including tabulations of specific kinds of activities, characteristics, etc.
5. Since coding categories tend to emerge and be revised over time, data must be accessible for revised coding (Lofland *et al.*, 2006, p. 95).

There is no uniform system for recording data available in the literature, as confirmed by Lofland *et al.*, but as they pointed out, some system is necessary (p. 95). For example, Chatman (1992, pp. 15-17) organised her field notes into observation notes, method notes and theory notes. You need to work out your own system, remembering the advice, above. It is best to have electronic files, which *must* be backed. If you have interview data, it is a good idea to treat these in the same way. Other related documents should be stored in the same folder. I would advise you to print hard copies of your data as well, especially as the volume expands.

Validity and reliability

Issues of validity, reliability and generalisability are discussed in the chapter related to this one, Chapter 13, but some extra points are noted here, specifically regarding observational studies. Chatman (1992) discusses three kinds of validity needing to be considered so that a 'true picture' (p. 12) is obtained. Face validity concerns whether observations "make sense because they fit into an unexpected or plausible frame of reference" (p. 12). Criterion validity "occurs when the research establishes the accuracy of the findings by employing an additional method of inquiry" (p. 13). Often the latter will be interviews. Construct validity relates to whether the findings have meaning "in light of the conceptual framework guiding the study" (p. 14).

Reliability, or the concern with obtaining consistent reliable research results with replication, is linked to the generalisability of findings. As Adler and Adler, (1998, p. 88) suggested: "Like many qualitative methods, naturalistic observation yields insights that are likely to be accurate for the group under study and unverified for extension to a larger population." One answer, according to these authors, is to conduct observations repeatedly and systematically over varying times and conditions, with credibility being enhanced by consistency of findings. Given and Leckie (2003), whose observation is discussed below, did this and found some differences across various times of the day and evening. To my mind, the differences, as well as the similarities, enhanced the credibility of their study.

Ethical issues

Ethical issues with observation, as with ethnographic research generally, are complex and there is widespread discussion in the literature. (See, for example, Adler & Adler, 1998; Angrosino, 2005; Baker, 2006; Glesne & Peshkin, 1992; Lofland *et al.*, 2006; Spradley, 1980; Taylor, Bogdan and DeVault, 2015, as well as Chapter 20: *Ethical research practices*.)

These days, university and government ethics committees, referred to as institutional review boards in the USA, provide ethical frameworks for researchers. In the USA, institutional review boards "grew out of federal regulations beginning in the 1960s, that mandated informed consent for all those participating in federally funded research" (Angrosino, 2005, p. 735). They have, at times, been controversial with researchers. While Australia, for example, has a uniform set of guidelines for ethical research, there can be variations in ways university committees apply them. In my experience, approval for the complete observer role is more straightforward to obtain than for more participative roles. The issue is often discussed as covert versus overt research in the literature (e.g., Lofland *et al.*, 2006). Usually for overt, participative research, the permission of all participants is required. Thus for the observation stage of his research, Burmeister was restricted to the public areas of GreyPath by the Charles Sturt University's Ethics in Human Research Committee. Although he was not required to obtain permission from participants (indeed it would have been impossible to do this), it could be argued that this was 'covert' or 'disguised' research. According to Adler and Adler (1998), disguised research has been outlawed by institutional review boards in the USA. They expressed concern over the limitations and referred to 'moral hair-splitting' over some ethical issues related to observation.

> We must admit to the view that the more adamant calls for the pristine purity of openness are just a touch naïve in several ways. First the distinction between covert and overt research is often blurred and clouded in actual practice. ... In some situations fieldworkers may well be able to develop viable and accepted open roles as researchers over time, but to announce one's research interests upon first entering the setting would lead to being rejected forthright (Lofland *et al.*, 2006, pp. 38-39).

Nevertheless, observers need to be very much aware of the ethical issues involved in observation which, as Adler and Adler (1998, p. 101) pointed out, is "liable to abuse in the invasion of privacy". They urged that researchers must consider "the relative harm and benefits to both private persons in society and the advancement of scientific knowledge" (Adler & Adler, 1998, p. 102). Most of the principles outlined by the American Anthropological Association in 1971 are still applicable. They include the following:

1. Consider informants (i.e., research participants) first.
2. Safeguard informants' rights, interests and sensitivities.
3. Protect the privacy of informants.
4. Don't exploit informants (Spradley, 1980, pp. 20-25).

Examples of observation in the information field

Chatman's (1992) study of the information world of retired women is a key example of the use of participant observation/ethnography in the information fields. The examples from the PhD virtual ethnographies, discussed above, are others. Wildemuth (2009, pp. 203-208) provides two examples which are worth pursuing: one (Westbrook, 1995) focussed on the use of periodicals by faculty in women's studies in two United States universities; the other (McKechnie, 1996) involved the researcher in a 'student' role observing the use of the public library by preschool girls. Both researchers produced dissertations which are cited in the reference list of this chapter, but another publication on each piece of research (Westbrook, 1998 and McKechnie, 2000) are also included in the references.

Two other examples are presented here in some detail. The first is the observation undertaken by Given and Leckie (2003) as part of a larger Canadian study aimed at mapping the social activity space of the public library; the second Terry Asla's observation within a PhD ethnographic study of the role of information in successful ageing in the Fourth Age.

A recent example of self-observation concludes this section.

Mapping the social activity space of the public library

Given and Leckie's (2003) observation could be described as 'non-participant', unobtrusive, or that of the complete observer. The authors, themselves, described it as the "'sweeping seats' observational method" (p. 366). 'Sweeping seats' referred to the regular observation walks undertaken by the researchers. They used this method as part of a suite of methods to examine "central public libraries and the roles they play in promoting and sustaining a vibrant public culture in today's large cities" (Given & Leckie, 2003, p. 366). Box 17.1 describes their observation.

Box 17.1

Given and Leckie (2003) 'sweeping seats' observational research

Research aim

To use the 'seating sweeps' observational method to study individuals' use of public libraries in two large Canadian cities.

Research question

What uses do individuals actually make of the public space of central libraries?

Method[2]

- In two Canadian libraries, the researchers undertook observational walks (or sweeps) through the public areas and their immediate external seating areas: five floors in one library; seven in the other.

- The research team initially mapped and photographed the visual space on all floors.

- Data were gathered on a 'seating sweeps checklist' created in advance of formal data collection at each site. Data included who was using the library, activities taking place and their locations, and belongings accompanying users.

- Each member of the research team was assigned one to two floors for data collection at designated times of day.

- Data collection lasted one full week. Sweeps were conducted three times per day at different intervals.

- The checklist was continually monitored and revised throughout the first few sessions of formal data collection.

When one of the researchers noticed that regular library users were aware of being watched, the team adjusted their behaviour, making their notes

---

[2] The label 'method' is used here because it is the term used by the authors, although conceptualised in this book as 'observational technique'. In contrast 'research methodology' is the label used in the description of Asla's study and for that of Al-Saggaf's research in Chapter 13: *Ethnographic research*. 'Methodology' is appropriate in the latter two cases because paradigm choice, as well as the method and tools or techniques used for exploring the research questions, are all included in the description. For further elaboration, see Chapter 1: *Research concepts*, and Chapter 5: *The methodological landscape*.

behind protective barriers such as stacks and filing cabinets, the aim being to document unobtrusively events happening in the space. "The goal in using these approaches was not to deceive patrons, or to manipulate their behaviors in any way, but to have the observers blend in with the library surroundings and unobtrusively document events happening in the space" (Given & Leckie, 2003, p. 377).

Findings

1. Contrary to expectations from the literature, the majority of users were men and younger than 60 years of age, as far as could be ascertained.

2. The busiest time of day in the libraries was mid-afternoon and Saturday was one of the slower days of the week.

3. Most patrons sat at study carrels or at work tables; far fewer library users were located at computer workstations (library catalogue, database, and internet access).

4. Reading was the most common activity across all age groups and at all times of the day — pointing to the need to highlight the importance of books and reading within library spaces.

Conclusion

"The seating sweeps method points to the inherent value of observational studies: the opportunity to see what people really do within the library space" (Given & Leckie, 2003, p. 383). The authors summarised the advantages but pointed out that, "although observation studies can provide an insightful glimpse of 'what' is happening in libraries, they do not indicate 'why' patrons do what they do" (p. 383), for which other techniques are required. (It should be pointed out, however, that Given and Leckie were referring only to the observational approach used in their study — the complete observer approach. Other approaches on the participant observation continuum do enable the investigation of 'why' questions.)

The role of information for people in the fourth age

My PhD student, Terry Asla, graduated in 2013. His thesis is available online (Asla, 2013). His research focussed on people in the Fourth Age, or people in the very last stage of life, and the role that information plays in whether or not they are ageing successfully. Observation played a major part in the study as described in Box 17.2. Publications about this study, although not highlighting the role of observation, include Asla and Williamson (2015) and Williamson and Asla (2009).

Box 17.2

Terry Asla's observation of the role of information for people in the Fourth Age

Research questions

1. What roles do information and technology play in the daily lives of people in the Fourth Age, residing in US retirement communities?
2. What is the relationship between their human information behaviour (HIB) and whether or not they perceive themselves to be ageing successfully?

Research methodology

Within an interpretivist/constructivist framework, Asla used ethnographic method to explore his research questions. His 25 participants were residents in two retirement communities – which he called The Midlands and Plaza Towers – in Kansas, USA. His two principal techniques were interviews (separate HIB and backgrounder schedules) and participant observation.

Participant observation

Asla chose to place himself on the Glesne and Peshkin (1992) continuum but noted that his position was not constant. This is in keeping with the view of Glesne and Peshkin, as well as of Spradley (1980): that the researcher's role may fall at any point along the continuum and is likely to shift to "different points at different times in the data collection process" (Glesne & Peshkin, 1992, p. 40). Although he noted that his participation was as a staff member and PhD student and not as a resident, Asla was well integrated into the community at Midlands. Thus he saw himself as towards the full participant end of the continuum (participant as observer). Later, at Plaza Towers, where he visited frequently and took part in community life before beginning his interviews, he was less well integrated and saw himself more as 'observer as participant'.

Asla's role at the Midlands, where he was present in the lives of participants during the two years of the data collection, offered him an 'insider' role which he saw as a singular advantage. He already had strong rapport with his participants through his years of work in this retirement community. He had the opportunity to chat with participants, hear them chatting to each other, and observe their activities. His role as a staff member also gave him an opportunity, at times, to stand back and be detached, thus enabling him to alternate between insider and outsider roles, as Spradley (1980) and others have discussed. At Plaza Towers, his observation was more limited but still yielded valuable data.

The observation data in Asla's study was crucial, given that the age and state of health of his participants resulted in less rich interview data than one would expect with most populations.

Self-observation of an ultrarunner

Gorichanaz (2015) undertook self-observation as part of a project focussed on his 'information' experience during an ultramarathon. He drew on principles from three different approaches: interpretative phenomenological analysis, autoethnography and systematic self-observation. His use of the former two approaches are discussed in earlier chapters.

In relation to the self-observation component, Gorichanz drew on Rodriguez and Ryave (2002) to emphasise that "many phenomena are observable only by the person having the experience" and that "many aspects of any experience are taken for granted and thus go unnoticed and unremembered". Gorichanaz thus used *systematic* self-observation, using time-based, interval recording and free-format narrative recording. Both these methods aim at more immediacy and therefore greater accuracy by reducing 'faulty memory' problems due to time lapses. In practice, his use of voice memos, at intervals on the run, was imperfect partly because of heavy rain for the first ten hours of the event, which sometimes made it impossible to use his smart phone.

Conclusion

Observation is an important research technique or tool, which is mainly combined with other techniques in a range of methods. Before embarking on its use, I urge wide reading about the different ways in which the technique has been conceptualised and used. In considering a form of participant observation, there is much to consider with regard to the role or roles which would be best to adopt. It is important to think flexibly about the options. Other considerations are choosing a site or sites, gaining entry and establishing rapport with participants if participant observation is intended. If observation is, at any stage, unstructured, being rigorous about note taking is important and there should be forward thinking with regard to analysis, which should begin during the data collection period – and as early as possible within it. As with ethnography, where observation is often a tool, issues of validity/trustworthiness and of behaving ethically are crucial. As I said in regard to ethnography, researchers should not be deterred by these considerations which are important, but should not be seen as barriers to using a technique which can bring many rewards.

References

Adler, P. A., & Adler, P. (1987). *Membership roles in field research*. Newbury Park, CA: Sage.

Adler, P. A., & Adler, P. (1998). Observational techniques. In N. K. Denzin, & Y. A. Lincoln (Eds.), *Collecting and interpreting qualitative materials* (pp. 79–109). Thousand Oaks, CA: Sage Publications.

Al-Saggaf, Y. (2012). *Online communities in Saudi Arabia: An ethnographic study*. Saarbrücken: LAMBERT Academic Publishing.

Al-Saggaf, Y., & Williamson, K. (2006). Doing ethnography from within a constructivist paradigm to explore virtual communities in Saudi Arabia. *Qualitative Sociology Review, 11*(2). Retrieved from http://www.qualitativesociologyreview.org/ENG/volume4.php

Al-Saggaf, Y., Williamson, K., & Weckert, J. (2002). Online communities in Saudi Arabia: An ethnographic study. Paper presented at the Proceedings of Australasian Conference on Information Systems, Melbourne, 4–6 December, 2002. *ACIS 2002 Proceedings*, Paper 62. Retrieved from http://aisel.aisnet.org/cgi/viewcontent.cgi?article=1162&context=acis2002

Angrosino, M. V. (2005). Recontextualizing observation: Ethnography, pedagogy, and the prospects for a progressive political agenda. In N. K. Denzin, & Y. S. Lincoln (Eds.), *The Sage handbook of qualitative research* (3rd ed., pp. 729–746). Thousand Oaks, CA: Sage.

Asla, T. (2013). *The Fourth Age: human information behavior and successful aging* (Unpublished doctoral dissertation). Charles Sturt University, Wagga Wagga, NSW. Retrieved from http://www.openthesis.org/documents/Fourth-Age-Human-Information-Behavior-601676.html

Asla, T., & Williamson, K. (2015). Unexplored territory: Information behaviour in the Fourth Age. *Information Research: An International Electronic Journal, 20*(1). Retrieved from http://www.informationr.net/ir/20-1/isic2/isic32.html#.VVvK7GOc6M0

Atkinson, P., & Hammersley, M. (1998). Ethnography and participant observation. In N. K. Denzin, & Y. S. Lincoln (Eds.), *Strategies of qualitative inquiry* (pp. 110–136). Thousand Oaks, CA: Sage.

Baker, L. M. (2006). Observation: A complex research method. *Library Trends, 55*(1), 171–189.

Baker, T. L. (1999). *Doing social research*. Boston: McGraw-Hill.

Bow, A. (2002). Ethnographic techniques. In K. Williamson (Ed.), *Research methods for students, academics and professionals: Information management and systems*

(2nd ed., pp. 265–279). Wagga Wagga, NSW: Centre for Information Studies, Charles Sturt University.

Burmeister, O. (2010). *What seniors value about online social interaction: The case of an online community* (PhD thesis). Charles Sturt University, Wagga Wagga, NSW.

Burmeister, O., Weckert, J., & Williamson, K. (2011). Seniors extend understanding of what constitutes universal values. *Journal of Information, Communication & Ethics in Society, 9*(4), 238–252.

Burns, R. B. (2000). *Introduction to research methods* (4th ed.). Frenchs Forest, NSW: Longman.

Charmaz, K. (2006). *Constructing grounded theory: A practical guide through qualitative analysis.* London: Sage.

Chatman, E. A. (1984). Field research: Methodological themes. *Library & Information Science Research, 6*(4), 425–438.

Chatman, E. A. (1991). Channels to a larger social world: Older women staying in contact with the great society. *Library & Information Science Research, 13,* 281–300.

Chatman, E. A. (1992). *The information world of retired women.* Westport, CT: Greenwood Pr.

Connaway, L. S., & Powell, R. (2010). *Basic research methods for librarians* (5th ed.). Santa Barbara, CA: Libraries Unlimited.

Ely, M. (1991). *Doing qualitative research: Circles in circles.* Philadelphia: Falmer Press.

Given, L., & Leckie, G. (2003). 'Sweeping' the library: Mapping the social activity space of the public library. *Library & Information Science Research, 25,* 365–385.

Glesne, C., & Peshkin, A. (1992). *Becoming qualitative researchers: An introduction.* White Plains, NY: Longman Publishing Group.

Gold, R. L. (1958). Roles in sociological field observations. *Social Forces, 36*(3), 217–223.

Gorichanaz, T. (2015). Information on the run: Experiencing information during an ultramarathon. *Information Research: An International Electronic Journal, 20*(4). Retrieved from http://www.informationr.net/ir/20-4/paper697.html#.WHf6uXrzJnk

Guthrie, G. (2010). *Basic research methods: An entry to social science research.* New Delhi: Sage.

Lofland, J., Snow, D. A., Anderson, L., & Lofland, L. H. (2006). *Analyzing social settings: A guide to qualitative observation and analysis* (4th ed.). Belmont, CA: Wadsworth/Thomson.

McKechnie, L. E. F. (1996). *Opening the "preschoolers' door to learning." An ethnographic study of the use of public libraries by preschool girls* (Doctoral dissertation, University of Western Ontario, Canada). Ottawa: National Library of Canada.

McKechnie, L. E. F. (2000). Ethnographic observation of preschool children. *Library & Information Science Research, 22*(1), 61–76.

Myers, M. (1999). Investigating information systems with ethnographic research. *Communications of the Association for Information Systems*, 2(Article 23), 1–19. Retrieved from http://aisel.aisnet.org/cais/vol2/iss1/23/

Patton, M. Q. (2015). *Qualitative evaluation and research methods* (4th ed.). Los Angeles, CA: Sage Publications.

Prasse, M. J., & Connaway, L. S. (2008). Usability testing: Method and research. In M. L. Radford, & P. Snelson (Eds.), *Academic library research: Perspectives and current trends* (pp. 214–252). Chicago: Association of College and Research Libraries.

Punch, K. F. (1998). *Introduction to social research: Quantitative and qualitative approaches.* London: Sage.

Savin-Baden, M., & Major, C. H. (2013). *Qualitative research: The essential guide to theory and practice.* London: Routledge.

Spradley, J. P. (1980). *Participant observation.* New York: Holt, Rhinehart & Winston.

Taylor, S. J., Bogdan, R., & DeVault, M. (2015). *Introduction to qualitative research methods: A guidebook and resource* (4th ed.). New York: John Wiley & Sons.

Visser, K. (2007). Action research. In S. Lipu, K. Williamson, & A. Lloyd (Eds.), *Exploring methods in information literacy research* (pp. 111–132). Wagga Wagga, NSW: Centre for Information Studies, Charles Sturt University.

Westbrook, L. (1995). *The information seeking experiences of women's studies* (Unpublished Doctoral dissertation). University of Michigan, Michigan.

Westbrook, L. (1998). Using periodicals in women's studies: The faculty experience. *The Serials Librarian*, 35(1/2), 9–27.

Wildemuth, B. M. (2009). *Applications of social research methods to questions in information and library science.* Westport, CT: Libraries Unlimited.

Williamson, K., & Asla, T. (2009). Information behavior of people in the fourth age: Implications for the conceptualization of information literacy. *Library & Information Science Research*, 31(2), 76–83.

Williamson, K., McGregor, J., Archibald, A., & Sullivan, J. (2007). Information seeking and use by secondary students: The link between good practice and the avoidance of plagiarism. *School Library Media Research*, 10. Retrieved from http://www.ala.org/aasl/sites/ala.org.aasl/files/content/aaslpubsandjournals/slr/vol10/SLMR_InformationSeeking_V10.pdf

Chapter 18

Quantitative data analysis

Judithe Sheard

Monash University, Australia

This chapter provides a brief introduction to quantitative data analysis, explaining processes for the preparation of quantitative data and common techniques for data description and analysis. The context for the examples used in the chapter is a project management website, used by information technology (IT) students in the third year of their undergraduate degree. The description of data preparation includes data cleaning, as well as data transformation and integration. Statistics, used to investigate numerical data, include descriptive statistics for describing distributions and relationships between variables, and inferential statistics. The latter cover testing for differences between distributions using parametric and nonparametric tests (according to the type of data involved). Examples of different types of tests are provided, using the project management website dataset which is the focus of the chapter.

Research Methods: Information, Systems, and Contexts. DOI: http://dx.doi.org/10.1016/B978-0-08-102220-7.00018-2

Introduction

Quantitative research, in contrast to qualitative research, deals with data that are numerical or that can be converted into numbers. The basic methods used to investigate numerical data are called 'statistics'. Statistical techniques are concerned with the organisation, analysis, interpretation and presentation of numerical data. Statistics is a huge area of study with wide application across many disciplines, including information systems and other areas of information research. With the advent of computers, and particularly personal computers, the statistical processes to handle and analyse data have become more accessible. However, there is a danger that analysis may be performed on data without an understanding of the appropriate statistical tests to use and how they should be applied. The aim of this chapter is to provide a basis for decisions about data preparation and analysis and how the results of analysis should be interpreted and reported.

The chapter explains processes and methods used in data preparation and analysis of data, using descriptive and inferential statistics. A dataset containing data of student usage of a project management website is used to illustrate the concepts covered. A number of the most common statistical tests are introduced and applied to the dataset. The techniques presented can be applied in Excel or a standard statistical software package, for example, SAS (https://www.sas.com/en_us/insights/analytics/statistical-analysis.html), R (https://www.r-project.org) or Statistical Package for the Social Sciences, IBM SPSS software (http://www-01.ibm.com/software/analytics/spss/). There are many other techniques used in data analysis, for example, exploratory data analysis techniques of regression, factor analysis, classification and clustering, but they are beyond the scope of this chapter.

Context for discussion: Project management website usage dataset

The dataset used to illustrate various concepts and analysis techniques contains data on student usage of a project management website. The website was used by IT students undertaking a capstone project in the third year of their undergraduate degree. All capstone project students were required to use the project management website to record details of their capstone project activities and times spent on those activities. The website also contained facilities for file management, event scheduling, and communication. Details of the website can be found elsewhere (Ceddia & Sheard, 2002).

The dataset contains a summary of student usage of the website over 42 weeks of their project. Each record in the dataset holds information about one student's use of the project management website over the course of the project, including the total time spent using the website and the total number of sessions (website accesses). An activity level of Low, Medium or High was determined from the average number of sessions per week as follows: Low — up to two sessions per week, Medium — more than two and up to four sessions per week, and High — more than four sessions per week. Each record also includes the student gender and final project mark. The specific information fields in each record are as follows:

1. *Gender* — male or female
2. *Project mark* — 0 to 100 inclusive
3. *Session count* — total number of accesses to the project management website during the project
4. *Activity level* — Low, Medium, High
5. *Total access time* — total minutes spent accessing the website during the project

The following questions were formulated to frame an analysis of the students' usage of the project management website. Broadly, the aims of the analysis were to investigate student work patterns, determine any differences in usage based on gender, and determine any relationship between usage and final project results. The specific questions to be addressed are:

1. How often did students use the project management website over the course of the project?
2. How long did students spend using the project management website?
3. Was there any difference in project marks between the male and female students?
4. Was there any difference in project marks based on level of activity?
5. Was there any difference in level of activity on the website between the male and female students?
6. Was there any difference in the time spent on the website by the male and female students?
7. Was there any relationship between time spent on the website and final project marks?

In the remainder of this chapter these questions will be investigated using techniques for descriptive and inferential statistical analysis.

Data preparation

Quantitative data can come from a variety of sources. A common source is questionnaires administered in either paper or electronic (online) form. Quantitative data can also be gathered from other sources such as interviews, observations, or automatic processes such as web server log files. Regardless of the source, the data typically take the form of a set of records with each record containing data about one case or participant in the study. To analyse the data, using computer software such as Excel or SPSS, it is necessary to transcribe the data into tabular form with each row representing one case and each column representing one data item. Each cell contains a value of a particular data item (the column it is in) for an individual case (the row it is in).

Before any analysis is performed on the dataset it is important to ensure that the data are error free and are in a form that is suitable for analysis. This involves various tasks to clean the data, recode or transform the data and integrate data from other sources. Data preparation is typically a time-consuming process. It should be conducted systematically and thoughtfully as this will help ensure the trustworthiness and meaningfulness of future analysis results.

Data cleaning

Cleaning of data involves tasks to ensure that the data are relevant and accurate. This process may involve removing or changing erroneous data, removing unnecessary data, replacing missing data, and eliminating outlying data (i.e., data outside expected ranges). It is important to note that the data cleaning must exclude unwanted data without impoverishing the dataset or introducing bias.

Erroneous or unwanted data can be present in a dataset for a variety of reasons. Problems may occur at the data collection stage. For example, a survey questionnaire may contain irrelevant, ambiguous or confusing questions leading to uninterpretable responses. Survey respondents may not have finished a questionnaire that they found too long or may not have responded co-operatively due to questions that they perceived to be intrusive. Errors can be introduced during data entry. For example, due to human error, values may be miskeyed, questionnaire forms may be lost or may be entered twice resulting in duplicate records. Data collected via automatic processes can also contain errors. For example, data collected from web server log files may have missing data due to system failure. Another issue with web log files is that they may contain multiple records for each user interaction because a request for a web page might involve downloading separate files for content and graphics. Including all such entries in an analysis would result in an inaccurate picture of user accesses (Cooley, Mobasher, & Srivastava, 1999).

To clean a dataset, problems must first be identified and then, where possible, rectified. If an error has occurred during data entry then it is often possible to correct the error by checking the original source document. However, if the problem has occurred during data collection then it is usually not possible to be corrected. For example, if a survey respondent has not entered a value for date of birth, or has entered an impossible date, then that item is typically flagged as a missing value in the dataset. An important point to note here is that missing values are not zero values. If a response critical to the analysis is missing or in error, then the whole record may have little value and a decision may be made to remove it from the dataset. In the case of the multiple records for user accesses on web server files, the cleaning process would involve removing specific records from the dataset prior to analysis.

Datasets can sometimes contain data which have values beyond the range of what would be reasonably expected. These outliers may be genuine values that highlight an unusual situation or might be erroneous data values that could distort the analysis. Outliers should be examined carefully before keeping or discarding. Often the decision about including an outlier depends on the context and the analysis to be conducted. For example, in the collection of data for the project management website dataset there were a couple of sessions with very long durations, for example, more than 24 hours. After consideration, it was decided that these session times were erroneous, and to include them would have given misleading results when calculating time spent at the website; it was therefore decided to filter these out before calculating the total usage time. Further explanation of this process is provided elsewhere (Sheard, 2006; Sheard, Ceddia, Hurst, & Tuovinen, 2003).

There are a number of techniques which are useful to employ in a data cleaning process. Firstly, it is a good idea to reconcile the number of data collection forms with records in the dataset. Secondly, an eye scan over the dataset may pick up problems, for example, a block of missing data, a partially completed record, or an unusual value. Thirdly, statistical software is invaluable for cleaning a dataset, particularly large datasets. A simple check to identify duplicate records is to sort the records and scan the dataset. Generating a set of descriptive values for each variable can highlight errors. For numerical data, examining the minimum and maximum values of a variable can readily show illegal or unusual values. For example, in the project management website dataset, the project marks should have values between zero and 100 inclusive, so any values outside this range are invalid. For non-numeric (nominal) variables, generating frequencies of values will highlight any invalid values. It is also useful to cross check values across variables. For example, it would be useful to check that the ages of vehicle licence holders are not less than the legal driving age.

Data transformation and integration

Before a dataset is analysed it may be necessary to transform data items so that they are in a form that is suitable for meaningful analysis. Individual data items can be recoded, or new data items derived from one or more existing data items.

The creation of a dataset for analysis involves transferring data from the data collection instrument (e.g., questionnaire, log file) to a format which can be read by the data analysis tool. Often the data are transcribed without change. However, the transfer may involve coding of the data into a form that will facilitate analysis. For example, if a question on a survey form has a fixed number of possible responses then it is often simpler and sometimes necessary for analysis to establish numerical codes for possible responses. Using an example from the project management website dataset, the gender variable response 'male' was coded as 1 and 'female' was coded as 2. Recoding may be necessary to create *ordinal* variables (values with a known order) from *nominal* variables (values with no specific order) so as to use the order of the values in analysis. For example, the names of the days of the week (nominal values) may be given the numerical values 1-7. If a survey question contains options such as 'not applicable' or 'don't know' then these may be allocated special codes or coded as 'missing data'. Note that it is usually not sensible to set these to the value zero. A complication occurs if the respondent is able to choose more than one response for a particular question; for example, if checkboxes are used on a form. In this case separate columns are typically created for each possible response.

Data from one variable may be grouped or recoded into a different variable. The data transformations will depend on the aims of the analysis and are specific to each application. For example, in the project management website dataset the activity levels of Low, Medium and High were calculated from the session counts. This was necessary to provide a grouping variable for comparison of project marks across the activity levels.

Data from different sources may be integrated to enable more extensive or meaningful analysis. In the project management website dataset, demographic data of gender and project mark, which were taken from class records, were combined with data collected from the project management website.

Statistical analysis

Data in quantitative form often result in large complex datasets, and quantitative analysis is required in order to derive meaningful information from the data. This section provides only a brief overview of statistical techniques that may be used in analysis of quantitative data. More details of these techniques may be found in books which cover quantitative methods, for example, Burns (2000); Punch (2013); Wiersma and Jurs (2009); or introductory books on statistics, for example, Kranzler, Moursand and Kranzler (2010) or Salkind (2016). Reporting of common statistical tests is explained in Mitchell, Jolley and O'Shea (2013). Details of how to apply the statistical tests in the software package SPSS may be found in Brace, Snelgar, and Kemp (2012) and Coakes, Steed and Ong (2012).

A range of statistical techniques can be applied in the analysis of data. Broadly, these may be grouped into *descriptive* statistics, which are used to describe the data, and *inferential* statistics, which are used to analyse the data in order to draw inferences. Data may be analysed in many different ways. The analysis conducted will be determined both by the objectives of the study and by the characteristics of the data items.

The first consideration in data analysis is to determine the *measurement* scale of each data item to be analysed. There are four levels, as follows:

- *Nominal* (or categorical) – measures without order. Data items may be categorised or grouped. For example, *gender*.

- *Ordinal* – measures with order. Measures may be represented by categories that can be ordered or ranked. The categories may be numeric but equal intervals between measurement scores on the scale are not established. For example, *activity level*.

- *Interval* – measures with order and with equal intervals on a scale. For example, *project mark*.

- *Ratio* – measures with order, equal intervals on a scale, and a true zero point (a point at which the trait being measured is totally absent). For example, *total access time*. With a true zero point it is possible to say, for example, that one student spent twice as much time using the website as another student.

These levels form a hierarchy of increasing information held in items at each level of measurement. For each level there are different descriptive and inferential statistical techniques that can be applied to the data. In the following sections, all the tests presented for interval scale data items will also apply to ratio scale data; therefore only interval scale data tests will be mentioned and the application to ratio scale data tests is implied.

The next section provides an overview of the most common descriptive and inferential statistical analysis techniques that can be applied at each level of measurement. The questions formulated for the investigation of student usage of the project management website are used to demonstrate the analysis and reporting.

Descriptive statistics

Descriptive statistics are used to describe aspects of sets of quantitative data to enable interpretation and comparison. A descriptive statistic could be the value of an individual data item (variable) or a summary of a single variable or group of variables. Using examples from our project management website dataset, an individual variable value could be the maximum session count and a summary could be the total session count for all students over the course of the project.

Values of individual variables or summaries can be presented in text, tabular or graphical form.

Descriptive statistics often involve *distributions* of data. In the project management website dataset, a distribution could be the project marks for all students. Descriptive statistics can be used to show relationships between variables. For example, a descriptive statistic could show the relationship between the project mark and the time spent on online project activities over the course of the semester.

The particular techniques used for each description will depend on the scale of measurement of the item.

Describing distributions

There are three main ways a distribution can be described for ordinal and interval data: firstly, the *measure of central tendency* (where the distribution is located on the scale of measurement), secondly, its *dispersion* (the degree of spread), and, thirdly, its *shape*. For nominal data, only the measure of central tendency is applicable. Measures are used to describe each characteristic of a distribution and it is often useful to show the distributions graphically.

Measure of central tendency

The measure of central tendency gives an average of the values of the distribution. The most commonly used measures of central tendency are the *mean*, *median* and *mode*.

- *Mean* — the arithmetic mean is determined by the sum of the values in the distribution divided by the number of values. The mean is used for interval scale data. However, if the distribution is asymmetrical or has outlying points, the mean may not give a good measure of the average of the values of the distribution. In this case, a median should be used as the measure of central tendency.

- *Median* — the point on the scale below which half of the values lie. This is used for ordinal data and for interval data which have an *asymmetrical* distribution or where the distribution contains *outlying* points.

- *Mode* — the value with the most frequent occurrence. Note that a distribution may contain more than one mode. This is the only measure of central tendency that can be applied to nominal data.

Dispersion

The measure of dispersion indicates the degree of spread or distribution of the data. This is only used for ordinal and interval scale data. There are several measures which may be used.

- *Range* – the difference between the maximum and minimum values on the scale of measurement. This gives a measure of the spread of values but no indication of how they are distributed.

- *Interquartile range (IQR)* – the data values are divided into four equal sections, called *quartiles,* and the interquartile range is the range of the two middle quartiles, that is, the middle half of the dataset. This is a useful measure if the dataset contains outlier values.

- *Variance* – the average of the squared deviations from the mean of the distribution, where the deviation is the difference between the mean of the distribution and a value in the distribution. This is used for interval scale data.

- *Standard deviation* – the average deviation from the mean of the distribution. This is the positive square root of the variance. This is used for interval scale data.

Note that the variance and the standard deviation both show the dispersion of the values around the mean; however, the standard deviation uses the same unit of measurement as the original values.

Shape

The shape of the distribution is important for determining the type of analysis that can be performed on the data. An important shape for interval scale data is the *normal distribution* or 'bell curve'. Normal distributions are special distributions with certain characteristics which are a requirement for statistical tests on interval scale variables.

The main considerations for shape are:

- *Skewness* – the extent to which the distribution is asymmetrical. A symmetrical distribution has a value of zero for the measure of skewness. The sign of the value indicates whether the distribution is positively skewed (peak to the left) or negatively skewed (peak to the right). A value of skewness within the range $+2$ to -2 is considered acceptable for common statistical tests. A normal distribution has a skewness of zero.

- *Kurtosis* – the extent to which the distribution is flat or peaked. A value of zero for kurtosis indicates that the shape is close to that found in a normal distribution. The sign of the value indicates whether the distribution is more peaked (positive) or flatter (negative) than a normal distribution. A value of kurtosis within the range $+2$ to -2 is considered acceptable for common statistical tests.

- *Modality* – the number of peaks in the distribution. For example, a bimodal distribution has two distinct peaks.

Relationships between variables

In analysis of data, we are often interested in the relationship between variables. For example, a question of interest might be: 'Is an increase in the number of interactions with learning material associated with an increase in exam performance?' The degree of relationship is called a correlation and is measured by a correlation coefficient (r), which can take a value from $+1.0$ to -1.0. The absolute value indicates the strength of the relationship and the sign indicates whether it is a positive or negative relationship. A value of zero indicates no linear relationship. Table 18.1 shows general 'rule of thumb' interpretations for correlation coefficients. Using this scale, a correlation of 0.75 between exam performance and interaction with learning material would indicate a strong relationship.

Table 18.1 Interpretation of correlation coefficients

Coefficient value	Interpretation
0.8 to 1.0	Very strong relationship
0.6 to 0.8	Strong relationship
0.4 to 0.6	Moderate relationship
0.2 to 0.4	Weak relationship
0 to 0.2	Very weak to no relationship

The relationship between two variables as measured by a correlation test is an indication of shared variability. To determine the proportion of variance in one variable that is accounted for by variance in the other variable, the square of the correlation coefficient (r^2) is computed. This is called the *coefficient of determination*. For example, a correlation coefficient of 0.75 for the relationship between exam performance and interaction with learning materials would give a coefficient of determination of 0.56. Using the coefficient of determination we can now report that 'the proportion of exam performance that is explained by the interactions with the learning material is 56 percent'.

Graphical descriptions of data

Datasets can be described graphically in a variety of ways. Graphical displays can readily show the shapes of distributions, indicate where differences or relationships might be present and highlight any outliers. They can enable comparisons to be made between different distributions. Graphical displays are useful for data cleaning and exploratory analysis. It is often helpful to display graphs of data in order to become familiar with a dataset before analysis.

One of the most common graphical forms used to show a distribution is the *bar graph*. On a bar graph the horizontal axis has a point for each data value and the vertical axis represents the frequency of each value. For interval data, which can usually take many values, a *histogram* is typically used. On a histogram, each point on the horizontal axis represents a range of values. It is important to note that the size of the range should be chosen carefully. If the range is too wide then patterns in the distribution may be hidden; if the range is too narrow then it may be hard to discern any patterns.

Other types of graph suitable for displaying interval scale data are the *box plot* (see Figure 18.4) and *stem and leaf plot* (see Figure 18.1. These show the main features of a distribution in an easily interpretable form and are often used in exploratory data analysis. The box plot shows the median, upper and lower quartiles, outliers, and minimum and maximum values. A stem and leaf plot is similar to a histogram but shows more information about the distribution. A limitation of stem and leaf plots is that they are only suitable for small datasets ($<$ 100 data items).

A commonly used graph for showing the relationship between two variables is a *scatterplot*. This is a two-dimensional graph displaying the value of one variable plotted against the value of another variable, for each case in a dataset. The scatterplot pattern aids interpretation of the type and strength of the relationship between the two variables and is useful for highlighting outliers.

Reporting descriptive statistics

When reporting an analysis of a dataset, descriptive statistics should be used to provide an overall description of the dataset and descriptions of variables within the dataset. Descriptive statistics should include the size of the dataset (e.g., number of records), characteristics of the sample or population that the data were collected from (e.g., gender distribution) and descriptions of variables related to the key questions in the study (e.g., project mark, session count, activity level, total access time).

Examples of descriptive data from the project management website dataset

To illustrate how descriptive statistics may be used and reported, examples of descriptive statistics for the study of student activity in the project management website are presented below. Note that the descriptive statistics are used to answer the first two questions in the investigation.

Overall description of the dataset

Summary data of student use of an online project management website were collected over 42 weeks of the capstone project. There were 251 students in the cohort comprising 176 (70 percent) males and 75 (30 percent) females. The mean project mark of the cohort was 68.8 with a standard deviation of 14.1. The minimum mark was 27 and the maximum was 96. The distribution of marks for the female students is shown using a stem and leaf plot (see Figure 18.1). This shows that most marks were between 52 and 88, inclusive, but there were three extremely low marks. In the column labelled Stem & Leaf, the numbers on the left give the tens value and the leaves, on the right, indicate the unit value for each number. So, for example, there were nine values in the 80s: two values of 80, one of 82, three of 84, two of 85, and one of 88. The shape of the leaves forms something like a histogram on its side.

Figure 18.1 Female students: Distribution of project marks shown using a stem and leaf plot

```
            Project mark stem and leaf plot
    Frequency      Stem & Leaf
      3.00         Extremes  (=≤37)
      1.00         4 . 5
     14.00         5 . 23555667777889
     24.00         6 . 003334455777778888999999
     23.00         7 . 000012233333334667888889
      9.00         8 . 002444558
      1.00         9 . 4
                   Stem width: 10 cases
                   Each leaf: 1 case
```

For each student, data about the total time and number of sessions spent at the project management website were collected. Analysis of this data was used to address questions 1 and 2, as follows.

Question 1

How often did students use the project management website over the course of the project?

The total number of sessions recorded for each student ranged from 27 to 604. The median number of sessions was 117 and the mean was 135. A histogram of session counts is shown in Figure 18.2. Examination of the distribution of the session counts showed that they were positively skewed (2.18) and had a peaked distribution as indicated by the high kurtosis value (8.04). There were a number of outlying values, with four students recording more than 400 sessions for the project duration.

The proportions of students in each activity level were: 27 percent Low (zero to two sessions per week), 48 percent Medium (> two and up to four sessions per week), and 25 percent High (> four sessions per week).

Figure 18.2 Frequency of sessions per student

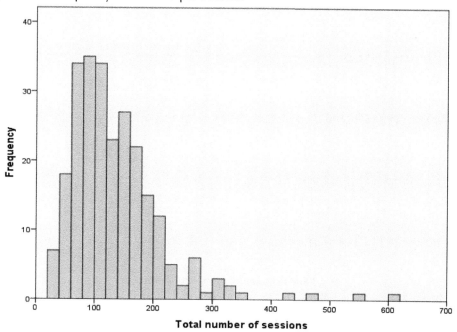

Question 2

How long did students spend using the project management website?

The total amount of time spent by students over the course of the project varied from 194 to 4,369 minutes (3 hrs 14 mins to 72 hrs 49 mins). The median time was 841 minutes (14 hrs 1 min) and the mean was 955 minutes (15 hrs 55 min). Examination of the distribution of the session times showed that they were positively skewed (2.04) and had a peaked distribution as indicated by the high kurtosis value (7.48). A histogram of times is shown in Figure 18.3. There was one noticeable outlying time with a student spending more than 72 hours at the website during the semester.

Exploring the data further, a pair of box plots enables a comparison between the total times spent at the website by the female and male students (Figure 18.4). The median values, as indicated by the lines bisecting the boxes, show that the median time spent was higher for the female students; however, the males showed a wider distribution in scores, more *extreme* values (defined as 3 or more IQRs above the box) and *outlier* values (defined as between 1.5-3 IQRs above the box). Each extreme value (shown by the symbol '*') and outlier (shown by the symbol 'o') is tagged with a value indicating the project mark for that student. Another

Figure 18.3 Total time spent at website per student

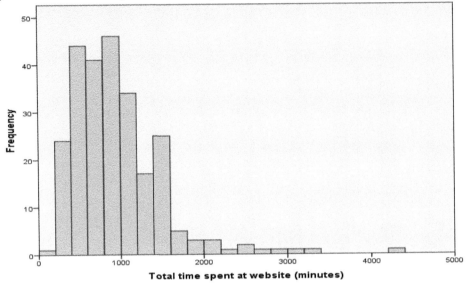

Figure 18.4 Total time spent at website for female and male students

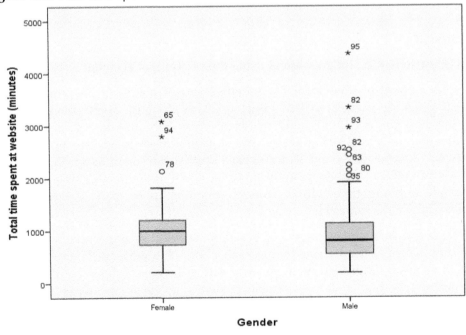

interesting aspect is that all but one of the students with an extreme or outlier time also achieved a high project mark of 75 or more.

Inferential statistics

From the descriptions of data it is possible to observe differences in values of variables, patterns in distributions and relationships between variables. However, to draw conclusions about the data we need a basis upon which to decide whether what we observe has occurred due to differences in the particular variable we are exploring or due to some other factor. To do this we need to move beyond descriptive to inferential statistics.

Inferential statistics are used to make decisions about a population under study from samples of that population, commonly through hypothesis testing. The role of hypothesis testing is to make a judgement as to whether the result obtained from analysis could have occurred by chance. The *null hypothesis*, which is the hypothesis of no difference or no relationship, is tested through these statistical tests. A *level of significance* is used to establish whether the null hypothesis should be accepted or not. The level of significance is the point which the researcher uses to determine whether the observed difference or relationship is too large to be attributed to chance. A measure called the p value assesses the probability that any differences found are due to factors other than the hypothesised reason. A commonly used level of significance is 0.05. A p value less than 0.05 indicates a probability of less than 5 percent that the observed difference is due to chance, and is generally considered sufficient basis for rejecting the null hypothesis.

The level of significance recognises that there is always the possibility of errors which are beyond the control of the researcher. The level chosen by the researchers indicates the type and level of risk they are prepared to take. Increasing the p value increases the risk of rejecting the null hypothesis when there is no difference (this is called a Type I error). Reducing the p value increases the risk of accepting the null hypothesis when there is actually a difference (this is a Type II error).

For example, a question of interest from our project website data might be, 'Was there any difference in final results between the male and female students?' To test this we would propose a null hypothesis: 'There was no difference between the final results of the male and female students.' From our test and the level of significance chosen we would determine whether there is sufficient support for rejecting the null hypothesis.

As a cautionary note, when a significant difference or relationship is found as the result of a test it is also important to consider the practical significance of the finding. For example, if a test of the effectiveness of a new reading program found that students' reading levels increased from 73 percent to 76 percent then this small difference, even assuming it is significant, may not be enough to justify the cost of implementing the new program.

There are many inferential statistical tests, which can be grouped into two broad categories of:

- *Parametric analyses* – used for data on the interval scale which meet specific assumptions;
- *Nonparametric analyses* – typically used for nominal or ordinal scale data but also used for interval data that fail to meet the assumptions for parametric tests.

The next section provides an overview of analysis techniques for testing for differences and testing for relationships.

Testing for differences between distributions using parametric tests

In testing for differences between two or more distributions on the interval scale we are testing for a difference between the means of these distributions. This is a simplification of what is actually happening and for more explanation see Burns (2000), Wiersma (2009) and Kranzler *et al.* (2010). There are different tests that may be used depending on the number of distributions we are testing and whether they are related. In related distributions, each element of one distribution matches a specific element of the other, for example, one distribution contains the pre-test scores of a group of students and the other contains the post-test scores of the same students. In unrelated distributions, such as the project marks for the male students and for the female students, there is no such matching.

For parametric tests, the data and distributions we are testing should meet the following conditions:

1. Data are measured on the interval scale.
2. Data values are independent. This is not applicable for *paired-samples t-tests* (see Table 18.2).
3. Data values are selected from a normally distributed population. A normal distribution will have one peak, not be too highly skewed and have normal kurtosis. Tests which may be used to test for normality are the Kolmogorov-Smirnov or Shapiro-Wilk tests (Brace, *et al.*, 2012; Coakes, *et al.*, 2012).
4. There is a homogeneity of variance between the distributions, that is, no difference between the variance across two or more distributions. This may be tested with Levene's test (Brace, *et al.*, 2012; Coakes, *et al.*, 2012).

Table 18.2 provides a summary of the most common parametric tests used to test for differences between distributions. For each test, a statistic is calculated, which is used to determine a value for *p*. To determine the value of *p* it is also necessary to determine the number of *degrees of freedom* for the test. The 'degrees of freedom' is defined as the number of values in the final calculation of a statistic that are free to vary. This value is a little less than the sample size. For specific details on how to calculate the degrees of freedom see Wiersma and Jurs (2009).

Table 18.2 Parametric tests for difference

Statistical test	Statistic	Interpretation
t-test (independent-samples)	*t*	There is no difference in the mean values of two distributions.
t-test (paired-samples)	*t*	There is no difference in the mean values for matched pairs of subjects or responses from subjects on two separate occasions. The requirement for independent data values does not apply for related measures.
ANOVA (one-way)	*F*	There is no difference in the mean values of two or more distributions. Single independent variable (factor).
ANOVA (two-way)	*F*	There is no difference in the means of values of two or more distributions. Two independent variables (factors) are included and also a hypothesis for their interaction.

Examples of parametric tests from the project management website dataset

The following are examples of the use of inferential statistics on parametric data through investigations of questions 3 and 4, outlined earlier in the chapter. For each test, an example is given of the way the results of the test could be reported. Typically, the value of p is not reported: just the level that was used to determine significance. Also, the value of the statistic resulting from a test is only reported if significance is found. For all tests in these examples, the level of significance used is 0.05.

Question 3

Was there any difference in project marks between the male and female students?

The hypothesis is: 'There was no difference in project marks between the male and female students.'

The project mark variable is on the interval scale and we are testing the difference in means between two independent groups (male and female). This indicates that the appropriate test to use is the independent samples *t*-test. As this is a parametric test, it is important to check the four conditions explained previously. In this case these are all met. Firstly, the data are measured on the interval scale. Secondly, the values are independent as the marks were gained individually by each student. Thirdly, the measures for skewness (-0.783) and kurtosis (0.463) were within acceptable ranges and a Kolmogorov-Smirnov test (Brace, *et al.*, 2012; Coakes, *et al.*, 2012) indicated a normally distributed sample. Fourthly, there was no difference in variance across the distributions of male and female marks as indicated by Levene's Test for Equality of Variance.

The independent samples *t*-test returned a value of 0.812 for the *t* statistic. The number of degrees of freedom was 249 (number of cases minus number of groups). The *p* value was 0.418, which was greater than the 0.05 limit for significance. On the basis of this test we would not reject the null hypothesis. The result of this test could be reported as:

> The mean mark of the female students was 67.69 with a standard deviation of 11.56 and the mean mark of the male students was 69.27 with a standard deviation of 15.06. The mean marks were compared using an independent samples *t*-test and no difference was found at a level of significance of 0.05.

Note that if a significant result was found then we would also report the t statistic and the degrees of freedom. The format for reporting the result of a *t*-test if a significant difference is found is:

> t (degrees of freedom) $= t$ statistic, $p <$ level of significance

Question 4

> Was there any difference in project marks based on level of activity?

The hypothesis is: 'There is no difference in project marks based on level of activity.'

As determined in the description for question 3, the project mark variable is on the interval scale and satisfies the conditions for a parametric test. In this case as we are testing for the difference between the means of the project marks across three groups (Low, Medium and High activity levels), the appropriate test to use is the One-way Analysis of Variance (ANOVA) test.

The ANOVA test returned a value of 4.528 for the F statistic. The p value was 0.012 which was less than 0.05. On the basis of this test we would reject the null hypothesis. The test could be reported as follows:

> The High activity students attained higher project marks ($M = 72.79$, $SD = 16.59$), than the Medium activity students ($M = 68.64$, $SD = 13.53$), who in turn gained higher project marks than the Low

activity students ($M = 65.46$, $SD = 11.74$). A one-way ANOVA found that these differences were significant ($F(2, 248) = 4.528$, $p < 0.05$).

The standard format for reporting the ANOVA test includes two degrees of freedom values. The first value (2) is calculated as the number of groups minus 1. The second value (248) is calculated similarly to the t-test. This is the number of cases across all groups minus the number of groups.

Testing for differences between distributions using nonparametric tests

Nonparametric tests are used to test for differences between distributions of nominal and ordinal scale data. They are also used for interval scale data which do not meet the conditions necessary for parametric tests. See Table 18.3 for a summary of the most common nonparametric tests. Note that the first test is used for nominal data and the other three are used for ordinal (or sometimes interval) data. For each test a statistic is calculated, which is used to determine a value for p.

In testing for differences in distributions of nominal variables we are testing that the relative proportions of values of one variable are independent of the relative proportions of values of the other variable. For example, 'Are the proportions of male and female accesses to a website the same for each day of the week?'

In testing for differences between two or more distributions on the ordinal (or interval) scales, we are actually testing for a difference between the medians of these distributions. Once again, this is a simplification of what is actually happening and for more explanation see Burns (2000), Wiersma and Jurs (2009) and Kranzler *et al.* (2010). There are different tests that may be used depending on the number of distributions being tested and whether they are related.

Table 18.3 Nonparametric tests for difference

Statistical test	Statistic	Hypothesis tested
Chi-square (χ^2) test for independence	χ^2	Two variables are independent.
Mann-Whitney U	U	There is no difference in the median values from two distributions.
Wilcoxon matched-pairs signed rank test	W	There is no difference in median values for matched pairs of subjects or responses from subjects on two separate occasions.
Kruskal-Wallis	K	There is no difference in the median values from three or more distributions.

Examples of nonparametric tests from the project management website dataset

The following are examples of the use of inferential statistics on nonparametric data through investigations of questions 5 and 6. For each test, an example is given of the way the results of the test could be reported. As for parametric tests, typically, the value of p is not reported: just the level that was used to determine significance. Also, the value of the statistic resulting from a test is only reported if significance is found. For all tests in the examples the level of significance used is 0.05.

Question 5

Was there any difference in level of activity on the website between the male and female students?

The hypothesis is: 'There was no difference in level of activity on the website between the male and female students.'

What we are testing for here is whether there are differences in the proportions of male and females in each activity level. As the gender variable is nominal data, the appropriate test to use is the chi-square test.

The chi-square test returned a value of 0.278 for the χ^2 statistic. The number of degrees of freedom was 249. The p value was 0.870 which was greater than the 0.05 limit for significance. On the basis of this test we would not reject the null hypothesis. The result of this test could be reported as:

The proportions of male and female students in the Low, Medium and High activity groups were compared using a chi-square test and no difference was found at $p < 0.05$.

Note that if a significant result were found then we would also report the χ^2 statistic, degrees of freedom and sample size. The format for reporting the result of a chi-square test if a significant difference is found is:

χ^2 (degrees of freedom, sample size) $= \chi^2$ statistic, $p <$ level of significance

Question 6

Was there any difference in the time spent on the website by the male and female students?

The hypothesis is: 'There was no difference in the time the male and female students spent on the project website.'

The access time variable was on the interval scale indicating that a parametric test would be appropriate. However, the distribution of data was outside the acceptable range for skewness (2.04) and had high kurtosis (7.48), indicating that the data were not normally distributed. A nonparametric test was therefore deemed more appropriate. As we are testing for difference in the median values between two distributions a Mann-Whitney U test is appropriate.

The Mann-Whitney U test returned a value of 5196 for the U statistic. The p value was 0.008 which was less than the 0.05 limit for significance. On the basis of this test we would reject the null hypothesis. The result of this test could be reported as follows:

> The median time spent at the project management website by the female students was 999 minutes and the median time spent by the male students was 803 minutes. A Mann-Whitney U test indicated that this difference was significant ($U = 5196$, $p < 0.05$).

Note that sometimes the sample size is included in the reporting of the results.

Testing for relationships

Measuring a relationship between two variables using a correlation test was previously presented as a descriptive statistical technique. However, correlations can also be conducted in the context of inferential statistics. There are different correlation tests, depending on the measurement scale of the data variables to be tested. See Table 18.4 for a summary of the most common tests. Note that if there is a difference in the level of measurement, then the test appropriate for the lower measure should be used. For example, if one variable was on the interval scale and the other was on the ordinal scale then a Spearman rank order correlation test should be used.

Table 18.4 Tests for relationship

Correlation test	Level of measurement
Pearson product-moment	Both distributions on the interval scale
Spearman rank order	Both distributions on the ordinal scale
Contingency coefficient	Both distributions on the nominal scale

For a Pearson product-moment correlation test, the data should meet the following conditions:

1. Data variables are measured on the interval scale.
2. Data values are selected from a normally distributed population.
3. The relationship between the two variables is linear. It is useful to examine this with a scatterplot.
4. There is homoscedasticity: the variability in values for one variable is similar at all values of the other variable. Again it is useful to use a scatterplot to examine this.

For a Spearman rank order correlation test there are fewer conditions:

1. Data variables are measured on the ordinal scale.

2. The relationship between the two variables is *monotonic* (values of one variable tend to increase when the values of the other variable increase), but not necessarily linear.

Note that the degrees of freedom for a correlation is the number of cases minus two.

Example of a relationship test from the project management website dataset

The following is an example of the use of inferential statistics from the project management website dataset.

Question 7

Was there any relationship between time spent on the website and final project marks?

The hypothesis is: 'There was no relationship between the time spent on the project management website and final project marks.'

The project marks and access time variables were on the interval scale indicating that a parametric test would be appropriate. However, as previously determined, the access time data were not normally distributed. This indicated that the most appropriate test for relationship was Spearman's rank order.

The Spearman rank order test returned an r_s value of 0.237. The number of degrees of freedom was 249. The p value was 0.000 which was less than the 0.05 limit for significance. Therefore, on the basis of this test we would reject the null hypothesis. The result of this test could be reported as:

A Spearman correlation test showed there was a weak relationship (r_s (249) = 0.237) between the time spent at the project management website and the project mark. This relationship was found to be significant at $p < 0.05$.

Note that a correlation shows a relationship that is associative, but tells us nothing about causality. That is, the correlation coefficient does not necessarily show that one variable is causing an effect on the other.

Summary of results of analyses

Although the investigation of the student usage of the project management website found no difference in access rates between the male and female students, the female students spent more time using the website than the male students.

Despite the extra time spent by the female students, no difference was found between the final project marks achieved by the male and female students. Overall, only a weak relationship was found between the time spent using the website and final project results.

Conclusion

This chapter has outlined the common techniques for descriptive and inferential statistical analysis and explained the processes necessary for preparing data for analysis using standard statistical software. Gaining meaningful information from analysis of quantitative data is not just an exercise in using statistical tests: it involves decisions about what data are to be used, how the data should be prepared, what tests are appropriate, and how they should be applied. It is important that these activities are conducted as an integrated and systematic set of processes where the researcher gains a thorough understanding of the nature and limitations of the dataset, ensuring that the analysis produces results that are valid and relevant to the aims of the research.

References

Brace, N., Snelgar, R., & Kemp, R. (2012). *SPSS for psychologists* (5th ed.). London, UK: Palgrave Macmillan.

Burns, R. (2000). *Introduction to research methods* (4th ed.). London: Sage Publications.

Ceddia, J., & Sheard, J. (2002). *Evaluation of WIER – A capstone project management tool*. Paper presented at the International Conference on Computers in Education (ICCE 2002). Auckland, New Zealand.

Coakes, S. J., Steed, L., & Ong, C. (2012). *SPSS version 20.0 for Windows: Analysis without Anguish*. Milton, QLD: John Wiley & Sons.

Cooley, R., Mobasher, B., & Srivastava, J. (1999). Data preparation for mining World Wide Web browsing patterns. *Knowledge and Information Systems, 1*(1), 1–27.

Kranzler, J. H., Moursund, J., & Kranzler, J. (2010). *Statistics for the terrified* (5th ed.). Upper Saddle River, NJ: Pearson College Div.

Mitchell, M., Jolley, J., & O'Shea, R. (2013). *Writing for psychology* (4th ed.). Belmont, CA: Wadsworth.

Punch, K. F. (2013). *Introduction to social research: Quantitative and qualitative approaches* (3rd ed.). London: SAGE Publications.

Salkind, N. J. (2016). *Statistics for people who (think they) hate statistics* (6th ed.). Thousand Oaks, CA: Sage Publications.

Sheard, J. (2006). *An investigation of student behaviour in web-based learning environments*. (Doctoral Dissertation, Monash University, Melbourne, VIC.)

Sheard, J., Ceddia, J., Hurst, J., & Tuovinen, J. (2003). Determining website usage time from interactions: Data preparation and analysis. *Journal of Educational Technology Systems, 32*(1), 101–121.

Wiersma, W., & Jurs, S. (2009). *Research methods in education* (9th ed.). Boston, MA: Pearson Education.

Chapter 19

Qualitative data analysis

Kirsty Williamson[1], Lisa M. Given[2] and Paul Scifleet[2]

[1]Monash University and Charles Sturt University, Australia [2]Swinburne University of Technology, Australia

Qualitative data analysis, used by researchers to make sense of their data, comes in a variety of approaches which tend to be aligned with particular conceptual frameworks and methods. This chapter focusses on three approaches: thematic analysis and category coding, qualitative content analysis, and discourse analysis. With thematic analysis and category coding, which can be considered a foundational inductive approach, the researcher looks for connections within data, often collected in the field, and identifies thematic patterns. The approach is demonstrated with suggested steps that a researcher might follow. The emergence of qualitative content analysis from quantitative content analysis introduces the second approach, which focusses on a wide range of media, is inductive and deductive, highly systematic, and starts with an initial framework. Steps for undertaking this type of analysis are also included. The last approach, discourse analysis, is also used for a wide range of media. Its focus is on exploring the underlying meaning of phenomena, including their social implications. Three types are discussed: linguistic, psychosocial and critical discourse analysis. The uses of discourse analysis in information studies are explored. A brief comparison of the three approaches concludes the chapter.

Research Methods: Information, Systems, and Contexts. DOI: http://dx.doi.org/10.1016/B978-0-08-102220-7.00019-4

Introduction

Qualitative data analysis involves sorting and categorising field notes and interview transcripts in a systematic way. The goal is to transform raw data into findings or results. In other words, qualitative data analysis is the way that researchers make sense of the data they have collected in order to communicate their findings to others. Yet another way of explaining the process is that it is essentially about detection, with the tasks being "defining, categorising, theorising, explaining, exploring and mapping" (Ritchie & Spencer, 2002). Usually researchers using qualitative data analysis 'work up' from data (Richards & Richards, 1998). Also known as the 'bottom up' approach, the idea is that researchers begin their analysis with the data, immersing themselves until patterns emerge and theories develop. Although most commonly associated with grounded theory, it is also the approach of many other types of qualitative data analysis (Williamson & Bow, 2002).

Lofland, Snow, Anderson & Lofland (2006, pp. 195—196) outlined four defining features of qualitative data analysis.

1. The results or findings arise through an analysis process that is skewed in the direction of induction rather than deduction.

2. The primary analytic agents are the researchers themselves.

3. Because of the inductive and agent-driven character of qualitative analysis, it is a highly interactive process between the researcher and the data.

4. It follows that the process is labour intensive and time consuming.

Many writers about qualitative data analysis encourage researchers to analyse data as they collect them. Not only does this include grounded theorists such as Charmaz (2014), Glaser and Strauss (1967), and Strauss and Corbin (1998), but also many others such as Lofland *et al.* (2006) and Miles, Huberman and Saldana (2014). Indeed, a mantra of most writings on qualitative data analysis is that analysis must not be left until all the data are collected: "Overlapping data analysis with data collection not only gives the researcher a head start in analysis but, more importantly, allows researchers to take advantage of flexible data collection" (Eisenhardt, 2002, p. 16). This is the approach of qualitative theorists who believe that the freedom to make adjustments during data collection aids in the development of theory for the reason that flexibility allows for promising hunches to be pursued through additional questions or sources of data. Simultaneous collection and analysis of data allow for both to "mutually shape each other" (Sandelowski, 2000, p. 338). Such dialectic by historians with the 'evidence' is described in Chapter 12: *Historical research.*

The issue of using specialist software for manipulation and analysis of qualitative data brings a greater difference of opinion than the issue of when analysis should begin, although few would disagree with the view that "the hard work of coding data is intellectual, not mechanical" (Dohan & Sanchez-Jankowski, 1998, p. 482).

The use of computer-based analysis is widely discussed in the literature, including by Coffey and Atkinson (1996); Dohan & Sanchez-Jankowski (1998); Kelle (1995); Lofland *et al.* (2006); Mayring (2000); Miles *et al.* (2014) and Richards and Richards (1995; 1998). Although some of these references are from the 1990s, they are still relevant and useful. Some researchers have embraced computer-aided qualitative data analysis as faster and more efficient; others are sceptical. Each researcher needs to explore and understand the issues, in consultation with colleagues if relevant, and make a decision which may vary from project to project.

As noted in Chapter 17: *Observation*, data from interviews and field notes must be stored efficiently so that there is easy access for analysis. There is no uniform system available for recording data but, as Lofland *et al.* (2006) pointed out, some system is necessary. It is best to have electronic files of transcribed interviews, observation data and memos, which should always be backed up on external disc drives or CDs. Other related documents should be stored in the same folder. It is a good idea to print hard copies of your data as well, especially as researchers often find it is easier to immerse themselves in their data using printed rather than electronic copies.

There are many different types of qualitative data analysis which tend to be aligned with particular conceptual frameworks and methods. They include grounded theory analysis, textual analysis, content analysis, discourse analysis, network analysis, sociolinguistic analysis, semiotic analysis, dramaturgical analysis, and sense-making analysis. This chapter begins with what might be considered the foundational approach to qualitative data analysis: category coding and thematic analysis. The second major section discusses qualitative content analysis, which organises the content of mostly text-based communications into categories of substantive meaning. Finally discourse analysis, which explores the underlying meaning of the phenomenon under study, including its social implications, is introduced and discussed. Grounded theory analysis is included in Chapter 9: *Constructivist grounded theory*.

Thematic analysis and category coding: An overview

In this section, we focus on the process of thematic analysis and category coding which is widely used by qualitative researchers, such as ethnographers, for the analysis of interviews and unstructured observation data. In at least one respect it is similar to qualitative content analysis in that the aim is to analyse the content of data (Burnard, 1991; Sandelowski, 2000). However, the kinds of analysis discussed in this section are very much the result of interaction between the researcher and the data, "between the observer and the observed" (Denzin and Lincoln, 1998, p. 40). The frameworks which underpin research from which these kinds of data emerge are often constructivist/constructionist or critical theory perspectives. The kinds of analysis used by post-positivists, such as Miles and Huberman (1994) and the earlier grounded theorists, for example, Glaser and Strauss (1967) — who believe in an objective reality, or a "transcendental realism" (Denzin & Lincoln, 1998, p. 40) — are somewhat different. Their emphasis is on developing "some system for categorizing the various chunks [of data] so the researcher can quickly find, pull out and cluster the segments relating to a particular research question, hypothesis, construct or theme" (Miles & Huberman, 1994, p. 57).[1] The analysis, discussed below, although not specifically constructivist grounded theory analysis, is more closely related to that approach, which "shreds notions of a neutral observer and a value-free expert" (Charmaz, 2014, p. 13). This means that, although there is every effort made to present the viewpoint of participants, there is acceptance that "researchers must examine rather than erase how their privileges and preconceptions may shape the analysis" (Charmaz 2014, p. 13).

Themes, categories and coding

The aim of data analysis is to enable outcomes that "make connections, identify patterns and contribute to greater understanding" (Glesne and Peshkin, 1992, p. 146). On the one hand, a pattern emerging from the data can be viewed as a theme: a more general insight that is apparent from the whole of the data (Bradley, Curry & Devers, 2007, p. 1760) or a "meaningful 'essence' that runs through the data" (Morse, 2008, p. 727) — or part thereof. On the other hand, connections are important to category identification for which coding plays a key role. Different segments or instances within the data are linked by coding to a particular idea or concept. The codes, providing the links, are frequently referred to as 'data categories'. Sometimes researchers will split data categories into sub-categories.

As Coffey and Atkinson (1996, p. 27) postulated: "The important analytic work lies in establishing and thinking about such linkages, not in the mundane processes of coding." The process of developing codes, promotes reflection and ideas, as the researcher interacts with the data. Coding (labels which can be concise or more descriptive) is a way of developing new thinking about data, as bits are identified and connected. It is not necessarily a process of data reduction but can be used "to expand, transform, and reconceptualize data" (Coffey & Atkinson, 1996, p. 29). In other words, coding can be about going "beyond the data, thinking creatively with the data, asking the data questions, and generating

---

[1] There is now a third edition of the methods source book (Miles *et al.*, 2014). SAGE publications charged Johnny Saldana with updating the late Miles and Huberman (1994) methods source book while maintaining "the general spirit and integrity of the original" (Miles *et al.*, 2014, p. xvii). According to Saldana, "I have smoothed down the second edition's semiquantitative edges to align and harmonize the original authors' approach with that of current qualitative inquirers." (p. xviii).

theories and frameworks" (Coffey & Atkinson, 1996, p. 30). The most important characteristic of codes is that they are

> heuristic devices for discovery ... [Codes in interpretivist research] must not restrict the scope of the investigation in advance by determining precise categories, since the goal is not to recover certain already known phenomena in the empirical field but to discover new ones (Seidel & Kelle, 1995, p. 58).

Coding can be undertaken at different levels – from general, inclusive codes (where the number of codes will be small), to a large number of codes with fairly exclusive meanings (Coffey & Atkinson, 1996). Including codes of different degrees of generality means that data retrieval can be undertaken at different levels. Coffey and Atkinson (1996) provide good examples of different kinds and levels of coding – from succinct one-word labels producing "a very thin and flat set of categories ... only the bare bones" (p. 40) to categories that reflect informants' views more closely. Their examples are extended and informative – including a description of how to move from coding to interpretation. Miles *et al.* (2104) discuss coding extensively, making a distinction between first and second cycle codes and coding. They particularly emphasised the stage, 'data condensation', leading to 'data display' and then to 'drawing and verifying conclusions'.

Identification of themes and categories involves different processes (Morse, 2008). The experience of one of this chapter's authors is that the identification of the smaller concepts (categories) is the earlier part of the process, and the more general insights, or themes, often emerge later. It is a good idea to start with physically marking up printed interview transcripts or observational notes – always with margin notes and sometimes with different highlighting colours to link ideas. Sometimes analysis is done alone; sometimes a researcher works with a research assistant or a PhD student beginning his or her data analysis; or a researcher works in a team where individual analysis is followed by a comparison of analyses amongst team members. The steps are, to some degree, flexible and similar to those outlined in the literature, especially by Burnard (1991).

Steps in identification of categories and themes

On the one hand, it is important to be systematic in your data analysis and 'true' to the viewpoints of your participants in analysing interview transcripts. On the other hand, there is a role for deep and creative thinking on the part of the researcher. Similarities, differences, consensus and dissonance within the data all play a role and researchers should try to engage with these, thinking about their implications. It is important to be aware that the process is not smooth and unproblematic: especially in the beginning there is likely to be confusion and indecision. That is not to say that it is not possible to work one's way through the process and achieve a satisfactory outcome.

The following are the steps which one of this chapter's authors has followed in her analysis of interview transcripts. A similar approach can be used for memos, recommended for recording ideas and theories throughout the project – or for observation notes. It is important to try to immerse yourself in the data right through the process, attempting to hear the voices of participants and to relate to their perspectives. It is also important to keep the research questions close at hand to guide the analysis process (Given and Olson, 2003).

Step 1

The researcher (along with other team members, if others are involved) reads the first batch of transcribed interviews. It is a good idea to begin with four or five transcripts so that comparisons can commence, making margin notes from the beginning, usually descriptive and not necessarily succinct.

Step 2

Having made copious margin notes on a few transcripts, the researchers re-read those initial transcripts and begin to develop a set of categories that appear to work across them. The categories are recorded in a list, which can be referred to as a coding manual. At this stage, the set of categories is fluid and far from complete.

Step 3

The remaining transcripts are coded, using the listed categories but adding to them and refining them as needed. Some smaller categories may be collapsed into broader, more inclusive categories during this process or we might decide to develop sub-categories in some cases. At all times, 'context' is crucial.

Step 4

Categories and sub-categories are re-listed. If others are involved, this is the time for comparisons and adjustments to the coding manual to be made. Major themes should now be clear and ready to be listed.

Step 5

By this stage the transcripts, especially the ones on which the analysis was begun, are usually quite messy. Starting with a clean set of print copies, each transcript needs to be coded according to the finalised list of codes. Coloured highlighting pens can be used for major categories or themes.

Step 6

At this stage, specialist software, for example, NVivo or ATLAS.ti can be used. Another approach is to develop 'voice sheets' for themes, and for categories within themes. Voice sheets are so named as they record the quotations (and therefore voices) of participants. While writing an article, or other project report, voice sheets facilitate the telling of a 'story' from the perspective of participants, while the researcher makes the connections and linkages, and identifies consensus and dissonance amongst those voices. Developing the voice sheets is essentially a cut and paste computer task. The process and examples are included in Williamson and Kingsford Smith (2010). Computer programs such as NVivo automate this process – and enhance it through enabling hierarchical networks of coded categories – although it is a major task to input the data into these programs and there are dangers and pitfalls which Richards and Richards (1995) attempted to address so that a 'conceptual structure' (p. 81) is developed. New versions of NVivo permit analysis of video content.

Information seeking by online investors: An example of analysis

Below is an example of the analysis from an Australian Research Council Discovery project, part of which focussed on the role of information in online investment (Williamson, 2008; Williamson & Kingsford Smith, 2010). The methodology for this project, although not specifically the data analysis, is discussed at some length in Chapter 2: *The fundamentals of research planning*. This was a study using mixed methods: a survey, with 520 responses provided frequency counts about investment activity and information seeking; individual interviews with 26 participants, purposively selected to represent the survey respondents, added in-depth perspectives. The interview questions, related to one of the research questions, are outlined in Chapter 16: *Questionnaires, individual interviews and focus group interviews*. Box 19.1 sets out the first stage of the coding, using five interview transcripts. Limited space in this chapter precludes an example of more detailed analysis. Good examples for the kind of analysis under discussion here are included in Coffey and Atkinson (1996).

Box 19.1

Example of the first stage of coding:
Information seeking by online investors

Research question

As outlined in Chapter 16, the research question is: What are the *key* sources of information used by investors and the reasons for their importance?

The responses and beginning coding are for the question: Do you have a preferred or key source of information? If so, could you please tell me why it is your preferred source?

Responses	Initial descriptive code
1. Oh definitely, the Australian Stock Exchange because you always have to go back to the raw source … rather than reading other people's interpretation. … It's available instantly.	▪ Key source: Aust. Stock Exchange ▪ Raw source best ▪ Sceptical of others' interpretations ▪ Instant timing
2. I regard all [sources of information] with a certain amount of scepticism. You've got to be sceptical of what people are saying to some extent. I mean experience shows that they don't always project the right thing.	▪ Key source: none ▪ Sceptical of others' interpretations
3. Yea, only Commsec [major online broker]. … It's easy to utilise. I think because it's got a lot of different tools with it as well that I find easy to use, with Commsec. Reliability with their information.	▪ Key source: online broker ▪ Availability of different tools ▪ Ease of use ▪ Reliable information
4. Just things like visiting a shopping mall gives me the most valuable information … being able to predict things like recessions by just seeing how purchasing behaviour is being changed, whether people are visiting more discount stores or whether they're going to higher-end retailers.	▪ Key source: personal observation in market place ▪ Economic predictors
5. Well I can't say I have any key source, no … would always turn to, besides the obvious things, direct company information, I will always read that. But other than that, I use a variety of sources.	▪ Key source: direct company information ▪ Variety of source use

Note: Before the question was answered, each participant was reminded about their responses to the survey questions about information seeking. Depending on the answer to the open questions, a series of follow-up prompts was used. The aim was for spontaneous, unprompted answers, if possible, but prompts ensured that issues important to the research were not overlooked. Their use also enabled counts of the numbers who used each key resource – establishing the strength of support and thus the more – and less – important sources of information for online investing. Counting is sometimes appropriate. This is not "a quasi-statistical rendering of the data, but rather a description of the patterns or regularities in the data that have, in part, been discovered and then confirmed by counting" (Sandelowski, 2000, p. 338).

Qualitative content analysis: An overview

Qualitative content analysis is a method for studying the meaning that is contained in the body of a message. It is done by classifying and organising the content of a communication systematically into categories that describe the topics, themes and context of that message. Although it is most often applied to text, qualitative content analysis can be applied to any type of media – textual, verbal or visual. It has been used in domains as varied as the analysis of political speeches, foreign policy documents, newspapers and television shows. The focus is on documents rather than on responses to stimuli, questions directly asked of people, or as a result of actively engaging with people. It is an unobtrusive method where the only requirement is that the communications have been made by people (Krippendorf, 2004; Prasad, 2008). This is one of the key features that distinguish it from other qualitative approaches to research data analysis where similar coding techniques are employed. Yet, like other methods that apply qualitative coding techniques, such as discourse analysis and genre analysis, qualitative content analysis accepts that the meaning of communication is not immutable but that it is constructed in the context of the questions asked of it. Qualitative content analysis is thus mainly an interpretive approach that allows a researcher to describe the topics and themes that are most meaningful to the research objectives of the study.

Foundations of content analysis

The roots of qualitative content analysis reside in a quantitative approach to measuring the frequency of topics with word counts and statistics (described in Chapter 10: *Bibliometric research*). The adoption and growth of quantitative approaches to analysing content paralleled changes in mass communication and the rise of the mass media. In the mass media environment, the advantages – and value for understanding society – of being able to identify and measure the occurrence of the topics reported in the news, was quickly recognised. Stempel (1989) pointed out that drawing conclusions and formulating opinions on the basis of what we read and hear about is what we all do; analysing the content of media is simply a logical extension of that. One of the first studies to apply quantitative content analysis formally occurred in 1893, when an analysis of New York newspapers, published between 1881 and 1893, demonstrated a change in news coverage from religious, scientific and political matters, to gossip, sport and scandals (Krippendorf, 2004). By identifying and tabulating the themes of news, the study set a trend for gauging social issues prevalent in media. Importantly, researchers realised that, if the findings from studies like the 1893 newspaper study are to be accepted, then the approach taken to content analysis needs to be systematic and reliable.

Quantitative approaches for establishing reliability in content analysis grew significantly during World War II when it was used as technique for understanding the content of wartime propaganda. Working from the Library of Congress, Laswell (1952) described content analysis as an actuarial method for documenting the language of politics. Among other cold war topics, he was interested in the symbolic expressions of hostility between the USA and the USSR. He found that, by measuring the relative frequency of the symbols of hostility in communications, and their relationship to changes in the intensity of hostility between the two geo-political powers, a meaningful indicator of the state of the relationship could be established. Content analysis was seen as a deliberate, statistical simplification designed to discover "uniformities in the mass" (Laswell, 1952, p. 52). Isolating explicit symbols of communication, however, is not without complications. Deciding the right categories of representation, tendencies to multiply categories, coding errors and difficulties in resolving agreement between coders have been perennial problems in content analysis that Laswell aimed to address. Methods for categorisation, sampling and measurement established during this time resulted in the now widely used definition of quantitative content analysis as "a research technique for the objective, systematic and quantitative description of the manifest content of communication" (Berelson, 1952, p. 18).

Berelson's definition set the standard for understanding content analysis as an objective method for quantifying the *manifest* (i.e., explicit and apparent) topics that occur in texts. In its strictest sense, this stance is closely associated with post-positivism. It preferences a methodology with *a priori* research design, hypothesis testing and strict rules for investigation. Objectivity and reliability reside in predetermining the categories that will be used for measuring the occurrence of topics in texts. The most evident units of content are assigned to categories designed to test the research hypothesis. A systematic approach allows different people to apply the same categories and statistical models to corresponding data consistently, supporting the reliability, replication and validity of the study. Laswell (1952), Neuendorf (2002) and Stempel (1989) present exemplary quantitative studies. Importantly, focussing on the manifest content "means that content must be coded as it appears rather than as the content analyst feels it is intended" (Stempel, 1989, p. 126). Any inferences, other than those evident in the surface of the communication, are excluded from quantitative studies.

Qualitative content analysis

The methodological distinctions between quantitative and qualitative content analysis come down to the scope of inferences that can be made through analysis. Both approaches accept that, at a minimum, any predetermination of the categories that will be used, requires *a priori* understanding of the universe in which the communication takes place; categories do not determine themselves (Krippendorf 2004; Laswell 1952). Even so, quantitative analysis restricts itself to those categories of interpretation that verify and confirm relationships quantified and tested by hypothesis, while qualitative content analysis is less constrained. It accepts that human communications are not always apparent and extends an interpretivist methodology to allow for subjective interaction between the researcher and the communications that will allow new understandings of the content to emerge. That texts are socially constructed and open to interpretation is widely acknowledged in the methodological approach of most analysts, including Altheide (1996), Groeben and Rustemeyer (1994), Kracauer (1952), Macnamara (2005), Mayring (2000), Prasad (2008), Schreier (2012), and Weber (1990). Qualitative content analysts accept that counting the frequency of categories can be a very effective indicator of importance and often work with summary statistics that support the description of contents. However a reliance on quantifying only the most apparent topics in communication is avoided. For the qualitative analyst, simply because a topic occurs fewer times in a communication does not mean that it is a lesser topic and, more importantly, the meaning of a communication is not always evident on the surface. As human communications typically need to be understood holistically within their context, qualitative content analysis is premised on an understanding that interpretation is required to account for the intricacies of latency and the rhetorical intent a topic attains. An investigation of *obesity* in news media may indicate the rise to prominence of a major health issue but interpretation, beyond the frequency of a term, is required to understand the comedic, political and socio-cultural dimensions that load the topic. Rather than disregarding erroneous expression, innuendo, irony, metaphor and double entendre, as statistically negligible (Laswell, 1952), qualitative content analysis is at liberty to explore their intent within communications.

Comparison with quantitative content analysis

The widespread and increasing availability of digital media, proliferated through desktop computerisation and the internet, has seen an increasing number of both quantitative and qualitative approaches to categorising the contents of communication under the rubric of content analysis. Both methods share common features: they emphasise a systematic and ordered approach to research; they prioritise the research problem or hypothesis from the outset; they have formal steps for selecting the unit of analysis, and for developing and applying categories to content; and they analyse and report the findings of the research.

Although qualitative content analysis is a systematic method, it acknowledges the central role of the investigator in a research process that is designed to support reflexivity and interaction. Most commonly applied to documents and textual data, it is closely aligned with hermeneutic traditions of induction and interpretation where the goal is not only to understand what any given unit of content may represent but to understand the characteristics, dialogue and process of the social context in which meaning is created, that is, to understand the sociality of the communication: "Documents which are not simply agglomerations of fact participate in the process of living, and every word in them vibrates with the intentions in which they originate and simultaneously foreshadows the indefinite effect they may produce" (Kracauer, 1952. p. 641).

Steps in qualitative content analysis

Qualitative content analysis is an approach to analysis that focusses on interpreting and describing, meaningfully, the topics and themes that are evident in the contents of communications when framed against the research objectives of the study. While different analysts vary in their approaches (for a discussion of major differences see Hsieh & Shannon, 2005) the following steps, based on Altheide (1996), Mayring (2000), and Schreier (2012), outline the conventions of qualitative content analysis.

Step 1. Focussing research objectives on communications

Qualitative content analysis needs to pursue a research objective that can be answered from the content of communications (Altheide, 1996; Mayring, 2000). It is, in this sense, communications-centric. The research problem should be specific enough to inform the type of communication appropriate to the investigation (e.g., a particular set of speeches by a political leader, printed news media in general or, comparisons across different media) as well as the appropriate unit for analysis within the chosen media (e.g., particular sections of a speech, entire newspaper edition, advertisements, segments of TV news). In other words, the research problem needs to be defined sufficiently to allow the researcher to locate suitable sources of communication. The researchers need to familiarise themselves with the determinate universe, including both context and process for the creation of the communications (Altheide, 1996).

Step 2. Establishing the frame for the research

The research frame can be considered as very similar to a 'picture frame', shaping the view in which the analysis takes place (Altheide, 1996). In qualitative content analysis, the emphasis a researcher places on one frame over another will influence category development and analysis. For example, the objective of research may be to understand 'how obesity is being represented in news media', but whether the research is framed as 'obesity as a public health issue' or 'obesity as a social stigma' will affect issues ranging from selection of the unit of analysis through to the themes and categories of analysis (Altheide, 1996). In this example, 'treatment' and 'health policy' are likely to be important themes when analysing 'obesity as a public health issue' but they may not be as significant within the frame of 'obesity as a social stigma'.

Step 3. Selecting the unit of analysis, sampling and coding

The unit of analysis refers to the level of communication that a researcher decides to analyse, that is, whether it is to be individual documents, a collection of documents or, in the case of social media research, a collection of messages (Altheide, 1996; Schreier, 2012). The appropriate unit of analysis should emerge through the process of developing the research objectives and framing the study. When selecting the materials for analysis, both statistical and purposeful sampling techniques can be used. For a study of short message communications in social media, sampling messages statistically, with techniques ranging from random sampling through to stratified sampling, might be the best approach for dealing with the sheer mass of communications. More often, where a researcher has a detailed understanding of the study's objectives, purposefully selecting communications that will inform the conceptual and theoretical issues is often the best approach (Altheide, 1996; Schreier, 2012). The researcher can also make distinctions between individual communications and parts of communications through using different approaches to coding within, and across, communications. Determining the depth and level of granularity for coding content is dependent on research objectives. When coding, the convention is to include the immediate context of the surrounding text that is assigned to a category so that the meaning of the segment is maintained (as illustrated in Box 19.1).

Step 4. Developing content categories

A researcher's conceptual understanding of a research problem and frame develops from the outset and many of the themes and categories emerge inductively very early on. The process of category development should start from the moment the research commences by listing key concepts and categories emerging from the research problem (Altheide, 1996; Mayring, 2000). The researcher should establish criteria for category use by recording definitions and descriptions of categories. By documenting the key concepts as they emerge and applying these during analysis, the researcher develops a sequence of categories that can grow. Mayring (2000) described the process of category development as a 'feedback loop' with categories derived inductively from the theoretical background of the research, formalised and applied from the top-down, while the researcher remains open to adjusting and modifying categories. Although there is no definitive number of categories best suited to qualitative content analysis, analysts often report using about 20 categories (Altheide, 1996). Altheide (1996) and Schreier (2012) present useful accounts of category development in their work.

Step 5. Protocols for analysis

Researchers using qualitative content analysis cannot assert, with certainty, that either the original sender or the recipient of the message share their understanding. Even so, providing the categories used for coding and analysis are an adequate representation of the research objective and, if they have been applied consistently, researchers can support the reliability of the research (Schreier, 2012). Reliability is established by placing emphasis on the process of category definition and the procedures that will be used for assigning codes to content. This means that the protocols developed (e.g., for coding content) need to be treated as part of the research process (Altheide, 1996). Category definition should involve procedures for agreement about the meaning of categories, and their use, to be evaluated by an independent party. This can be achieved by involving a second researcher as a conversant in category and content definition to confirm suitability of the categories and their use. Reliability can be evaluated by checking consistency in the application of the categories to the content either, over time for a single coder, or by checking the agreement of multiple coders in the use of categories to the same content, that is, to determine inter-coder reliability.

Step 6. Performing data analysis and preparing the findings

There is no one single technique for assigning content to categories (Hsieh & Shannon, 2005). While some researchers continue to work with pen and paper to code content and develop reports, there are also sophisticated software packages available (e.g., ATLAS.ti, NVivo) that support the same processes and add many advanced features to assist analysis, including the automatic generation of word counts and keyword lists, matching and sorting facilities, audio and video tagging. Even when aided by technology, the process of qualitative content analysis remains one of constant iteration and verification. It is important to compare and contrast key differences and extreme cases as the analysis is undertaken (Altheide, 1996). Developing analytical notes is essential. The analyst usually develops a narrative including descriptive summaries, illustrative examples and overviews of each category that may include both quotations from the content and frequency counts of category occurrence.

Examples of the use of qualitative content analysis

'What is the Australian news media saying about obesity? How is obesity portrayed in social media? Is it a social stigma? Or public health issue?' Qualitative content analysis rests on an assumption that questions like these can be answered by comparing, contrasting and describing the contents of communication (Schreier, 2012). It does so without any strong theoretical commitment of its own and this is one criticism that has been levelled at it

(Weber, 1990). Nevertheless, while some researchers have seen qualitative content analysis's apparent 'neutrality' as an issue, others have seen it as an advantage (Macnamara, 2005). Qualitative content analysis offers a set of procedures to support whichever theoretical lens a researcher brings to it and because of this it is often used as the supporting method for other qualitative approaches including ethnomethodology, semiotics, genre analysis and discourse analysis (Macnamara, 2005). Riemer, Overfeld, Scifleet and Richter's (2012) categorisation of short message communications is an example of using qualitative content analysis to support a genre analysis of the types of communication taking place on the enterprise social network of the international consultancy firm, Capgemini. The study used both summary statistics and the description of messages communicated within the network to demonstrate how the appropriation of technology is being socially constructed in the workplace. The research demonstrated an important shift in emphasis in the organisational use of social media, from top-down models of adopting technology to bottom-up models of appropriation.

Discourse analysis: An overview

> Perhaps the only thing all commentators are agreed on in [the area of discourse analysis] is that terminological confusions abound (Potter & Wetherell, 1987, p. 6).

The challenges in naming and defining discourse analysis have not lessened in the 30 years since Potter and Wetherell published their 1987 text *Discourse and Social Psychology: Beyond Attitudes and Behaviour*. Discourse analysis takes many forms across disciplines (e.g., sociology, philosophy, linguistics, nursing), which can confuse and confound researchers who are new to this methodological approach and its various methods. Further, Potter (2008) noted that "[discourse analysis] has developed as a contested terrain where different books with 'discourse' in their titles can exist with no overlap in content" (p. 217). Rather, given this research context, discourse analysis

> is best seen as a cluster of related methods for studying language use and its role in social life. Some of these methods study language use with a particular interest in its coherence over sentences or turns, its role in constructing the world, and its relationship to context. Others take discourses to be objects in their own right that can be described and counted (Potter, 2008, p. 217).

Discourse analysis offers a unique approach to the qualitative analysis of social texts; this approach acknowledges that our world is shaped by social interactions and by the range of texts available to us (e.g., magazines, movies, newspapers, advertisements, websites, video games, political speeches, scholarly articles, drawings). The approach goes beyond counting instances of a phenomenon (e.g., the number of times women are shown using technology in advertisements) to explore the underlying meaning of that phenomenon, including its social implications. A text derives meaning from its situated use and can be spoken, written or delivered as a non-linguistic sign; texts interact and combine in various contexts to form discourses (Georgakopoulou & Goutsos, 2004, p. 3). As Burr (2015) noted:

> A discourse refers to a set of meanings, metaphors, representations, images, stories, statements and so on that in some way together produce a particular version of events. It refers to a particular picture that is painted of an event, person or class of persons, a particular way of representing it in a certain light (pp. 74-75).

Discourse analysis can be used on its own or may be part of a larger mixed- or multi-methods study. The findings may also set the contextual stage for other qualitative methods and analyses (e.g., a discourse analysis of policy documents can inform the design of an interview guide, to be used with policy makers). By using discourse analysis, researchers can enhance the scope of inquiry by exploring how discourses inform social context. This aids in the interpretation of data, allows researchers to explore research questions that are socially, temporally and culturally grounded, and helps scholars to uncover the assumptions they bring to their projects. Discourse analysis functions in similar ways to other qualitative analyses of textual material; audio and video data can be analysed for themes and patterns, and discourse analysis can also be used alongside other modes of inquiry (e.g., grounded theory of interview data). In addition, a theoretical framework (e.g., feminist deconstructionism; social positioning theory) may be used as an analytic lens to examine the discourses at play in the social scenes being investigated.

Varied approaches to discourse analysis

There are two main understandings of discourse that direct analysis: 1) a communicative discourse, which focuses on the exchange of texts that communicate messages; and 2) a representational discourse, which examines the combination of texts that construct a version of reality. These two conceptions of discourse are intertwined; communicative discourse produces and reinforces (or changes and undermines) representational discourse, while representational discourse impinges upon and shapes communicative discourse (Georgakopoulou & Goutsos, 2004, p. 3).

Within these two broad categories there are many different (but related) ways to analyse data using discourse analysis. Although researchers may disagree on the specific labels used for these approaches, or where best to draw lines between them, discourse analysis can be separated into three over-arching groups that share a specific point of focus: linguistic discourse analysis; psychosocial discourse analysis; and critical discourse analysis. By first understanding the basic tenet of linguistic discourse analysis (i.e., that language only signifies in context), we can proceed into psychosocial discourse analysis (i.e., which holds that people's subjective realities – being constituted largely by language and textual experiences – are also context-bound). From there, we can move into the critical discourse analysis dimension, which argues that the discursive matrices that constitute identity are products of hegemony and ideology (i.e., dominant versus subordinate discourses). The following sections explore these three areas, in brief, and discuss projects in information studies that use these approaches.

Linguistic discourse analysis

This type of communicative discourse analysis explores "all forms of [linguistic] interaction, formal and informal" (Potter & Wetherell, 1987, p. 7). The analysis may explore the tone or subtlety of voice, eye contact, body language and other signs that are used in conveying a message, alongside the structure of the text itself. For example, a researcher might explore patterns in pause length in an interviewee's responses when particular topics are raised. These approaches to discourse analysis are grounded in the notion that language is only signified in context. Barton (2004) defined linguistic discourse analysis as "a method for analysing the ways that specific features of language contribute to the interpretation of texts in their various contexts" (p. 57). She also identified two key points of focus for linguistic discourse analysis: structure, or a unit of language (sound, syllable, word, phrase, clause, sentence); and function, or a use of language for a particular purpose (informational, expressive, social) (p. 57). A key principle here is that meaning is not inherent in the text; the same text may signify differently depending on its context and how the text is delivered (Georgakopoulou & Goutsos, 2004, pp. 1-2).

Psychosocial discourse analysis

Psychosocial discourse analysis explores the role of discourse in creating subjective, social reality. This approach acknowledges that individuals experience texts in many different ways and that a person's understanding of reality is largely constituted by language. As Potter and Wetherell (1987) noted:

> Language is so central to all social activities it is easy to take for granted. Its very familiarity makes it transparent to us ... [When] raising issues of culture, on the one hand, and nature of the self, on the other, it is virtually impossible to disentangle them from questions about language and its role in human affairs (p. 9).

Language comes to us through dialogue (e.g., discussions with friends, supervisors, family), absorption (e.g., reading a book, listening to a lecture, watching television) and expression (e.g., writing, delivering a presentation). These texts are always contextual (i.e., discursive) as they exist in a social framework. Mumby (1988) noted that to understand the meaning within social interactions an individual must first understand how that interaction is organised; whether people were playing a game, engaged in a conversation, making a trip across town, or sitting in a board meeting, those individuals had to understand how that social context 'worked' (i.e., how it was discursively determined) to fully engage in and understand the experience.

Critical discourse analysis

Critical discourse analysis takes linguistic and psychosocial approaches one step further by analysing the data from a decidedly critical stance. These analyses examine the discourse – the social 'story' at play in the investigation – but also ask why that particular person is relating that particular tale. Critical discourse analysis examines the dominant and subordinate discourses on offer in society and explores notions of resistance and appropriation of discourses among various social actors. In doing so

> discourse analysis not only captures something important about the social world, but also plays a key ethical and political role in showing how social phenomena are discursively constituted: it demonstrates how things come to be as they are, that they could be different, and thereby that they can be changed (Hammersley, 2003, p. 758).

Critical discourse analysis encourages researchers to ask questions like:

- If we are determined by social discourse, what determines the discourse?
- What rules, codes, and ideologies dictate the way we engage in discourse – that is, how we speak, behave, interact, and perceive?
- If discourse refers to a particular view of an event, who creates that view?

The work of Michel Foucault, for example, has been particularly influential in critical discourse analysis (in what is typically called 'Foucauldian discourse analysis'). In *The Archaeology of Knowledge*, Foucault posited that for words and concepts that we assume have real, distinct referents, we must relate "them to the body of rules that enable them to form as objects of a discourse and thus constitute the conditions of their historical appearance" (Foucault, 2000, p. 427). This 'body of rules' leads to the formation of dominant discourses, or texts whose authority permits their passing as knowledge, truth, immutable law, or 'common sense'. Critical discourse analysis emphasises that ideas, facts and knowledge are not static, but change as the discourse(s) change.

Discourse analysis in information studies: A brief overview

In information studies there are many calls for, and uses of, discourse analysis to explore understandings of situated language use within information contexts. Frohmann (1992) conducted what is arguably the first discourse analysis study in the field, followed by an exploration of discourse analysis as a research method (Frohmann, 1994). Tuominen and Savolainen (1996) were among the first to identify social constructionism as a way to examine information use as discursive action, followed by Tuominen's (1997) own work in this area. Budd and Raber (1996), Olsson (1999) and Talja (1999) also explored the usefulness of discourse analysis to the field of information studies during this period. Chelton (1997). Given (2000), Jacobs (2001), McKenzie and Carey (2000), Stevenson (2001), and other scholars soon followed with projects that used discourse analysis approaches. Given (2002) published an overview of discourse analysis and its use with social positioning theory, as a result of her work exploring mature university students' academic information behaviours.

The usefulness and reach of discourse analysis as a research methodology in information studies has gained strength in the past two decades. Budd's (2006) review of discourse analysis as it applies to the study of communication in the field focussed on two key areas: linguistic discourse analysis and critical discourse analysis. In a special issue on discursive approaches to studying information seeking, editors Talja and McKenzie (2007) took a decidedly more inclusive approach; the resulting collection "represents the first gathering together of discursively inspired research into information needs, seeking, and use" (p. 105) and includes work by Olsson (2007), Savolainen (2007), Veinot (2007), among others. These papers, and other recent publications by Hicks (2014), O'Connor and Rapchak (2012), and Oliphant (2015), demonstrate that discourse analysis will continue to hold a strong place in research approaches in information studies in the years to come.

Conclusion

What are the similarities and differences amongst the three types of data analysis discussed in this chapter? All three approaches identify topics and themes, are principally interpretive, analyse language, and regard context as important. In contrast to thematic analysis and category coding, which particularly focus on data collected in the field, a wide range of media sources may be analysed with the other two approaches. In comparison to themes and category coding which is inductive, qualitative content analysis is inductive and deductive, more specifically systematic, and starts with an initial framework. Discourse analysis emphasises meaning in the narrative – the whole picture – and more explicitly examines dialogue and social contexts than the other two approaches. The most appropriate approach to use will depend on consideration of the needs of the research, the methodology, and the kinds of outcomes which are important to the project.

References

Altheide, D. L. (1996). *Qualitative media analysis*. Thousand Oaks, CA: Sage Publications.

Barton, E. (2004). Linguistic discourse analysis: How the language in texts works. In C. Bazerman (Ed.), *What writing does and how it does it: An introduction to analyzing texts and textual practices* (pp. 57–82). Mahwah, NJ: Lawrence Erlbaum Associates.

Berelson, B. (1952). *Content analysis in communication research*. New York: Free Press.

Bradley, E. H., Curry, L., & Devers, K. J. (2007). Qualitative data analysis for health services research: Developing taxonomy, themes and theory. *Health Services Research, 42*(2), 1758–1772.

Budd, J. M. (2006). Discourse analysis and the study of communication in LIS. *Library Trends, 55*(1), 65–82.

Budd, J. M., & Raber, D. (1996). Discourse analysis: Method and application in the study of information. *Information Processing and Management, 32*(2), 217–226.

Burnard, P. (1991). A method of analysing interview transcripts in qualitative research. *Nurse Education Today, 11*(6), 461–466.

Burr, V. (2015). *Social constructionism* (3rd ed.). London: Routledge.

Charmaz, K. (2014). *Constructing grounded theory: A practical guide through qualitative analysis* (2nd ed.). London: Sage.

Chelton, M. K. (1997). *Adult-adolescent service encounters: The library context*. (Doctoral Dissertation, Rutgers University, New Brunswick, NJ.)

Coffey, A., & Atkinson, P. (1996). *Making sense of qualitative data*. Thousand Oaks, CA: Sage Publications.

Denzin, N. K., & Lincoln, Y. S. (1998). Part 1: Methods of collecting and analysing empirical materials. In N. K. Denzin, & Y. S. Lincoln (Eds.), *Collecting and interpreting qualitative materials* (pp. 35–45). Thousand Oaks, CA: Sage.

Dohan, D., & Sanchez-Jankowski, M. (1998). Using computers to analyse field data: Theoretical and practical considerations. *Annual Review of Sociology, 24*, 477–498.

Eisenhardt, K. M. (2002). Building theories of case study research. In A. M. Huberman, & M. B. Miles (Eds.), *The qualitative research companion* (pp. 5–35). Thousand Oaks, CA: Sage.

Foucault, M. (2000). *The archaeology of knowledge*. In J. Rivkin, & M. Ryan (Eds.), *Literary theory: An anthology*. Malden, MA: Blackwell. (Originally published in 1969 as *Archéologie du savoir*.)

Frohmann, B. (1992). The power of images: A discourse analysis of the cognitive viewpoint. *Journal of Documentation, 48*(4), 365–386.

Frohmann, B. (1994). Discourse analysis as a research method in library and information science. *Library & Information Science Research, 16*(2), 119–138.

Georgakopoulou, A., & Goutsos, D. (2004). *Discourse analysis: An introduction* (2nd ed.). Edinburgh: Edinburgh University Press.

Given, L. M. (2000). The social construction of the 'mature student' identity: Effects and implications for academic information behaviours. (Doctoral Dissertation, University of Western Ontario, London, ON.)

Given, L. M. (2002). Discursive constructions in the university context: Social positioning theory and mature undergraduates' information behaviours. *The New Review of Information Behaviour Research, 3,* 127–141.

Given, L. M., & Olson, H. A. (2003). Knowledge organization in research: A conceptual model for organizing data. *Library & Information Science Research, 25*(2), 157–176.

Glaser, B. G., & Strauss, A. L. (1967). *The discovery of grounded theory: Strategies of qualitative research.* Chicago: Aldine.

Glesne, C., & Peshkin, A. (1992). *Becoming qualitative researchers: An introduction.* White Plains, NY: Longman Publishing Group.

Groeben, D., & Rustemeyer, R. (1994). On the integration of quantitative and qualitative methodological paradigms. In I. Borge, & P. Mohler (Eds.), *Trends and perspectives in empirical social research* (pp. 308–326). Berlin: De Guyter.

Hammersley, M. (2003). Conversation analysis and discourse analysis: Methods or paradigms? *Discourse and Society, 14*(6), 751–781.

Hicks, D. (2014). The construction of librarians' identities: A discourse analysis. *Canadian Journal of Information and Library Science, 38*(4), 251–270.

Hsieh, H. F., & Shannon, S. E. (2005). Three approaches to qualitative content analysis. *Qualitative Health Research, 15*(9), 1277–1288.

Jacobs, N. (2001). Information technology interests in scholarly communication: A discourse analysis. *Journal of the American Society for Information Science and Technology, 52*(13), 1122–1133.

Kelle, U. (1995). Using hierarchical categories in qualitative data analysis. In U. Kelle (Ed.), *Computer-aided qualitative data analysis* (pp. 80–95). London: Sage.

Kracauer, S. (1952). The challenge of qualitative content analysis. *Public Opinion Quarterly, 16*(4), 631–642.

Krippendorf, K. (2004). *Content analysis. An introduction to its methodology.* Thousand Oaks, CA: Sage Publications.

Laswell, H. D. (1952). *The comparative study of symbols. An introduction.* Stanford, CA: Stanford University Press.

Lofland, J., Snow, D. A., Anderson, L., & Lofland, L. H. (2006). *Analyzing social settings: A guide to qualitative observation and analysis* (4th ed.). Belmont, CA: Wadsworth/Thomson.

Macnamara, J. (2005). Media content analysis: Its uses, benefits and best practice methodology. *Asia Pacific Public Relations Journal, 6*(1), 1–34.

Mayring, P. (2000). Qualitative content analysis. *Forum Qualitative Sozialforschung / Forum: Qualitative Social Research, 1*(2). Retrieved from http://www.qualitative-research.net/index.php/fqs/article/viewArticle/1089/2385

McKenzie, P. J., & Carey, R. (2000). What's wrong with that woman?" – Positioning theory and information-seeking behaviour. In A. Kublik (Ed.), *CAIS 2000: Dimensions of a global information science: Proceedings of the 28th annual conference of the Canadian Association for Information Science, Edmonton, Alberta.* Edmonton: University of Alberta. Retrieved from https://journals.library.ualberta.ca/ojs.cais-acsi.ca/index.php/cais-asci/article/view/20/16

Miles, M. B., & Huberman, A. M. (1994). *Qualitative data analysis: An expanded source book* (2nd ed.). Thousand Oaks, CA: Sage.

Miles, M. B., Huberman, A. M., & Saldana, J. (2014). *Qualitative data analysis: A methods sourcebook* (3rd ed.). Los Angeles: Sage.

Morse, J. M. (2008). Confusing categories and themes. *Qualitative Health Research, 18*(6), 727–728.

Mumby, D. K. (1988). *Communication and power in organizations: Discourse, ideology, and domination.* Norwood, NJ: Ablex Publishing.

Neuendorf, K. A. (2002). *The content analysis guidebook.* Thousand Oaks, CA: Sage Publications.

O'Connor, L., & Rapchak, M. (2012). Information use in online civic discourse: A study of health care reform debate. *Library Trends, 60*(3), 497–521.

Oliphant, T. (2015). Social justice research in library and information sciences: A case for discourse analysis. *Library Trends, 64*(2), 226–245.

Olsson, M. (1999). Discourse: A new theoretical framework for examining information behaviour in its social context. In T. D. Wilson, & D. K. Allen (Eds.), *Exploring the contexts of information behaviour: Proceedings of the 2nd information seeking in context conference, Sheffield, UK* (pp. 136–149). London: Taylor Graham.

Olsson, M. (2007). Power/knowledge: The discursive construction of an author. *Library Quarterly, 77*(2), 219–240.

Potter, J. (2008). Discourse analysis. In L. M. Given (Ed.), *The Sage encyclopedia of qualitative research methods* (pp. 217–220). Thousand Oaks, CA: Sage.

Potter, J., & Wetherell, M. (1987). *Discourse and social psychology: Beyond attitudes and behaviour.* London: Sage.

Prasad, D. B. (2008). Content analysis. A method for social science research. In D. K. Lal Das, & V. Bhaskaran (Eds.), *Research methods for social work* (pp. 173–193). New Delhi: Rawat.

Richards, T., & Richards, L. (1995). Using hierarchical categories in qualitative data analysis. In U. Kelle (Ed.), *Computer-aided qualitative data analysis: Theory, methods and practice* (pp. 80–95). London: Sage.

Richards, T., & Richards, L. (1998). Using computers in qualitative research. In N. K. Denzin, & Y. S. Lincoln (Eds.), *Collecting and interpreting qualitative materials* (pp. 211–245). London: Sage.

Riemer, K., Overfeld P., Scifleet, P., & Richter, A. (2012). Eliciting the anatomy of technology appropriation processes: A case study in enterprise social media. *Proceedings of the 20th European conference on information systems, ECIS 2012*, Barcelona, Spain, 13th June 2012.

Ritchie, J., & Spencer, L. (2002). Qualitative data analysis for applied policy research. In A. M. Miles, & M. B. Huberman (Eds.), *The qualitative research companion* (pp. 305–329). Thousand Oaks, CA: Sage.

Sandelowski, M. (2000). Whatever happened to qualitative description. *Research in Nursing and Health, 23*(5), 334–340.

Savolainen, R. (2007). Information behaviour and information practice: Reviewing the 'umbrella concepts' of information-seeking studies. *Library Quarterly, 77*(2), 109–132.

Schreier, M. (2012). *Qualitative content analysis in practice*. Thousand Oaks, CA: Sage Publications.

Seidel, J., & Kelle, U. (1995). Different functions of coding in the analysis of textual data. In U. Kelle (Ed.), *Computer-aided qualitative data analysis: Theory, methods and practice* (pp. 52–61). London: Sage.

Stempel, G. H., III (1989). Content analysis. In G. H. Stempel, III. & B. H. Westely (Eds.), *Research methods in mass communication* (2nd ed., pp. 124–136). Englewood Cliffs, NJ: Prentice Hall.

Stevenson, S. (2001). The rise and decline of state-funded community information centres: A textually oriented discourse analysis. *Canadian Journal of Information and Library Science, 26*(2–3), 51–75.

Strauss, A., & Corbin, J. (1998). *Basics of qualitative research: Grounded theory procedures and techniques* (2nd ed.). Newbury Park, CA: Sage.

Talja, S. (1999). Analyzing qualitative interview data: The discourse analytic method. *Library & Information Science Research, 21*(4), 459–477.

Talja, S., & McKenzie, P. J. (2007). Editors' introduction: Special issue on discursive approaches to information seeking in context. *Library Quarterly, 77*(2), 97–108.

Tuominen, K. (1997). User-centered discourse: An analysis of the subject positions of the user and the librarian. *Library Quarterly, 67*(4), 350–371.

Tuominen, K., & Savolainen, R. (1996). A social constructionist approach to the study of information use as discursive action. In P. Vakkari, R. Savolainen, & B. Dervin (Eds.), *Information seeking in context: Proceedings of an international conference on research in information needs, seeking and use in different contexts, 14–16 August, 1996, Tampere, Finland* (pp. 81–96). London: Taylor Graham.

Veinot, T. (2007). 'The eyes of the power company': Workplace information practices of a vault inspector. *Library Quarterly, 77*(2), 157–179.

Weber, R. P. (1990). *Basic content analysis* (2nd ed.). Thousand Oaks, CA: Sage Publications.

Williamson, K. (2008). Where information is paramount: A mixed methods, multi-disciplinary investigation of Australian online investors. *Information Research: An International Electronic Journal, 13*(4). Retrieved http://www.informationr.net/ir/13-4/paper365.html

Williamson, K., & Bow, A. (2002). Analysis of quantitative and qualitative data. In K. Williamson (Ed.), *Research methods for students, academics and professionals: Information management and Systems* (2nd ed., pp. 285–303). Wagga Wagga, NSW: Centre for Information Studies, Charles Sturt University.

Williamson, K., & Kingsford Smith, D. (2010). Empowered or vulnerable? The role of information for Australian online investors. *Canadian Journal of Information and Library Science, 34*(1), 39–81.

Section IV

Research Practice and Communication

In this section, Chapters 20–22 examine a range of issues concerned with research practice and the communication or dissemination of research. Ethical research practices are the focus at the beginning of the section, followed by research data management and, finally, issues associated with the publication and dissemination of research findings.

Chapter 20

Ethical research practices

Graeme Johanson
Monash University, Australia

There are many reasons why ethics are essential to good information research, and why all research demands ethical stances. The chapter encourages self-reflection by the researcher on different types of ethical problems which need to be resolved from the point of planning research through to its final dissemination. A tendency to discuss ethics in terms of hard-and-fast rules is tempered by a call for nuance in specific contexts. The chapter summarises the philosophical bases of research ethics, providing illustrations, and discusses many arguments for and against research ethics codes, committees, and practices. Reasons for supporting the increasing attention dedicated to information ethics and intercultural research ethics are provided.

Research Methods: Information, Systems, and Contexts. DOI: http://dx.doi.org/10.1016/B978-0-08-102220-7.00020-0

Introduction

This chapter gives an account of why information researchers need to devote special attention to ethics. If there is one aspect of human activities globally that is more affected by challenges to moral principles than any other, it is with respect to uses of information and communications technologies. Imagine a world in which every person can collect data continually by means of a wearable camera which is permanently switched on. What would happen to privacy, confidentiality, free consent, data storage and deletion, or attitudes of participants towards research? (Mok, Cornish, & Tarr, 2015).

The relationship between the researcher and ethics is well researched in its own right, and many examples from the literature are cited in this chapter to support the general propositions that are put forward. Researcher responsibilities have become more onerous (Ferguson, Thornley, & Gibb, 2016). The advent of information and communications technologies has caused many occasional ethics concerns to leapfrog to the forefront of debate about research practices. As a result, 'information ethics' have become the basis of several research associations, journals, conferences, and discussion forums, and they raise issues which are widely broadcast — in addition to academic publications — in social media and the mass media.

It is common for people to believe that they exercise appropriate ethical insights to cope with daily life and that they behave ethically. They are not always so sure why they believe this is the case. Therefore the philosophical underpinnings of good ethical research behaviour are outlined in brief. It is argued that developing a constructive attitude to a duty of care among researchers is as important as the guidelines that emanate from ethics codes and committees. To affirm effective implementation of research ethics, a right to subtle contextual decision-making is to be upheld. No ethical strictures should remove the moral capacities of experienced researchers themselves to resolve a specific dilemma in consultation with colleagues (Lucivero, 2016).

The chapter also emphasises the need to pay attention to alternative ethical paradigms in other cultures. There are three levels of intercultural ethics: relating to differing cultural concepts, to national interests, and to ever-expanding devotion to universal human rights.

To show that research ethics are diffused through all research phases, the chapter provides practical examples which link to research planning and design, data collection, data management, authorship and ownership, research publication, and peer review. The chapter concludes that extra intensive effort is required in order to undertake research more ethically.

Research as an ethical hot-house

Research by its nature is ethically-intensive. Research can take many forms, from a naive matter-of-fact enquiry about a daily activity to revolutionary discoveries with universal impact. Each involves ethics – moral decisions about the effects of the act of enquiring. For the moment let us define serious research as a close examination of phenomena in order to improve knowledge, or an investigation of solutions to human problems (NHMRC, 2007; Williamson, Burstein, & McKemmish, 2002). Systematic research consistently throws up many more ethical challenges than most other activities. Why so? Because research threatens the *status quo*; it stirs people up; it involves probing scrutiny, sometimes uncomfortable surveillance; it makes disruptive discoveries; it requires fixed ways of thinking about problems; at times it proposes universal panaceas which contradict longstanding adherence to local or minority beliefs; it can recommend reform, restructure, improvement and create world-changing innovations; it imposes value judgements; it rewards elite forms of special expertise; and it consumes huge resources (Ess, 2002; Macfarlane, 2009; Redclift, 2005). This long (yet incomplete) set of reasons intuitively suggests that many important issues arise which require considered consensus – issues such as transparent data management; open debate about radical discoveries; effective communication to decision-makers of the complexity of serious research findings; manipulation of our basic humanness; rights of access to knowledge; profiting personally from knowledge; selective disclosure of information; accountability; conflicts of interest; the separation of the public from the private spheres; respect for cultural difference; and long-term protection of data (Hauptman, 2008; Johanson, 2002; Redclift, 2005).

In view of the many ethical dilemmas posed by research, a researcher needs to adopt a self-reflective attitude to manage them. If you put yourself in the shoes of a person or activity being researched, you will quickly understand how many ethical questions arise. How would you want a researcher to handle you, evaluate you, examine you, report on you, or your intimate surroundings? (Bouma, 2004). Thus, while research does not require ethical solutions which are entirely different from those thrown up by daily situations, it attracts more potential challenges.

What are research ethics and who advocates them? Research ethics are a system or theory of moral principles, about the rules and standards which guide human conduct in research, expressed in deliberate motives and actions, affirmed by an individual or a particular group (Weber, 1949). Relevantly, 'information ethics' focus on the many moral issues attached to information and communications technologies (ICTs). They are applied especially to groups of professionals which deal with information, such as librarians, archivists, recordkeepers (Hauptman, 2008), systems developers, computer scientists, lawyers, journalists, authors, publishers, media managers (Zimmer, 2010), business analysts, communications engineers (Carbo & Smith, 2008) – and (a little perversely one could add) spies.

A flurry of research activity about ethics has marked the last two decades, instigated largely by the ubiquity of powerful ICTs which enable the tackling of large-scale global problems, increasingly using multi-disciplinary research approaches (Ess, 2002). It is hard to imagine any scientific research being undertaken without computing – or other research for that matter. Contemporaneously the internet and networks have become standard research tools and popular objects of study in their own right.

In 1992 a dedicated journal began, *The Journal of Information Ethics*. In 1995 the Centre for Computing and Social Responsibility was formed in the United Kingdom (Froehlich, 2004). The global Association of Internet Researchers launched gracefully between 1998 and 1999 (McLemee, 2001) and soon produced an ethics guide for researchers (Ess, 2002). In 1999 the International Centre for Information Ethics was established in Germany, with its own journal, *The International Review of Information Ethics*, and another journal *Ethics and Information Technology* began in the Netherlands. In 2011 UNESCO committed to global, generic principles:

> Ethical principles for knowledge societies derive from the Universal Declaration of Human Rights [Article 19] and include the right to freedom of expression, universal access to information, particularly that which is in the public domain, the right to education, the right to privacy, and the right to participate in cultural life. One of the most challenging ethical issues is the inequity of access to ICTs between countries, and between urban and rural communities within countries. Along with the benefits of a digitally connected world come the threats of misuse and abuse ... [such as] the safety of children on the internet (UNESCO, 2011).

Increasing concern for human rights and values has paralleled the growth of information technologies and activity around ethical research. The World Summits on the Information Society (in 2002 and 2005) have sustained it (Carbo & Smith, 2008). The psychologist Professor Steven Pinker has plotted them:

> What's true of technological progress may also be true of moral progress. Individuals or civilizations that are situated in a vast informational catchment area can compile a moral know-how that is more sustainable and expandable than even the most righteous prophet could devise in isolation (Pinker, 2011, p. 479).

Ethical research involves and uses humans respectfully and equitably without changing them or their surroundings involuntarily in any way. Data are collected with informed consent and are kept confidential by researchers, who destroy them after use within a reasonable time, if this is part of their agreement with the ethics committee through which their application was approved. Researchers (without extraneous pressures) are allowed to choose freely the subject of research, the manner of conduct of the research, and the process of dissemination of the results of the research. The research participants can opt out at any time. Human interactions in research are motivated by moral intentions. Ethics cannot be evaded (MacIntyre, 1998). Ethical research is practised within accepted moral systems and is based on broad human duties, as have been described before (Johanson, 2002).

The basis of ethical practice

Interest in ethics is as old as philosophy, and ethics is a major branch of that discipline. Why should researchers bother with the philosophy behind ethics? There are two fundamental reasons. Firstly, it is impossible to understand ethical behaviour properly without consideration of its origins. Secondly, because researchers from different cultures function with different philosophical rationales, it may be necessary for one researcher to understand and respect the perspectives of another (Australian Institute of Aboriginal and Torres Strait Islander Studies, 2012). They may need to work together in multicultural teams or in one another's milieu (Ess, 2002).

From an entirely pragmatic point of view, there are widely-accepted values that lie behind ethical research behaviour, and by revealing their preconceptions and research values, researchers enable others to comprehend the bases of and motives behind their work, and to make better judgements about the quality and relevance of their research (Macfarlane, 2009). A few examples of desirable research values are described as courage, respectfulness, fairness, resoluteness, sincerity, humility, reflexivity, access, tolerance, liberty, justice, beneficence, protection, objectivity, open-ness, honesty, and responsible behaviour (Hauptman, 2008; Macfarlane, 2009; Neazor, 2007; NHMRC, 2007). These terms may seem as emotive as they are abstract, but they can be justified on close analysis by using appropriate case studies which can be found in multiple texts (Spinello, 2003; Tavani, 2016).

Respectful understanding of alternative philosophies is necessary. An example of an influential value system which dictates an overly-prescriptive approach to research (to the unfortunate exclusion of other rationalities) is found in the discipline of development informatics (Johanson, 2011). In the developed West it is a common but misguided assumption that information systems can assist in most activities around the globe and that the mere provision of ICTs to poor countries will inevitably lead to desirable liberal economic and democratic outcomes (Mansell, 2010). The World Bank subscribed to these notions for years (Chan, 2002). Researchers now accept the different values of developing areas and understand why the effects of hegemonic systems and networks are not always positive (Steyn, 2011).

Philosophical underpinnings

Many philosophical theories are put forward as the basis for ethics. Just three are mentioned here: deontology, teleology, and discourse ethics. Sometimes they are called 'meta-ethics', large bundles of ideas about why researchers should be ethical (Singer, 1986; Tavani, 2016).

1. 'Deontology', or 'rule-based ethics', focuses on duty, and the ethical principles derived from generally-accepted rules which guide actions. Using this perspective, researchers are said to be autonomous agents adopting positive values which give rise to a sense of moral duty (Spinello, 2003).

2. 'Teleology', 'consequentialism', or 'utilitarianism' is the second meta-ethic. Here the justification for research action is based on ends and purposes; the goals and purposes of acts are paramount, and ethics are based on the consequences of action. The main question behind this meta-ethic is whether a research action causes social good for the majority, or harm? (Tavani, 2016).

3. 'Discourse ethics', 'argumentation ethics', or 'ethical collectivism' uncover normative or ethical truths by examining the preoccupations of discourse. The validity of a moral norm cannot be justified in the mind of an isolated individual reflecting on the world, it is said. The norm is justified only in processes of argumentation between individuals in dialectic. The underlying ideal is that conversations among researchers on moral issues allow understandings of ethical norms to be developed and shared best, whether in organisations or in society generally. This third meta-ethic can be said to derive from deontology (Tavani, 2016).

Confusingly, it is sometimes hard to differentiate the separate areas of meta-ethics, and in fact a mixture of them can be deployed (Iacovino, 2002).

The use of ethics codes and policies

In order to make research ethics easily accessible and effective, many ethics principles have been codified and published, and most prestigious research universities and institutions have a research ethics committee to set guidelines and monitor the practices of staff and higher degree students. Universities set out rights and responsibilities of research students in various policies, handbooks and websites. Researchers are required to follow their lead. Some professional associations and businesses subscribe to codes of ethics also, some with regard to research.

The old Hippocratic Oath for medical doctors is an early example of a code, especially in relation to patient confidentiality:

> I will use regimens for the benefit of the ill in accordance with my ability. ... Into as many houses as I may enter, I will go for the benefit of the ill. ... And about whatever I may see or hear in treatment, or even without treatment, in the life of human beings – things that should not ever be blurted out outside – I will remain silent, holding such things to be unutterable (Von Staden, 1996, p. 701).

Privacy is singled out for respect in this code, but sad to say, the Oath did not stop Dr Josef Mengele and 350 other Nazi doctors from forcing prisoners in concentration camps to undergo horrific physical 'experiments' in Germany in the 1940s, then at trial from trying to justify their murders by arguing that the Hippocratic Oath made no mention of the sort of torture 'research' which they perpetrated on helpless victims. The Nazis tried eugenics (population manipulation) in the form of 'racial hygiene' and the mass extermination of 'undesired' groups (Macfarlane, 2009). Enforcement of ethical behaviour is more difficult than codification. The need to standardise rules surrounding medical research in Australia led to the evolution of a general *National Statement on Ethical Conduct in Human Research* which is widely followed (NHMRC, 2015). Thankfully under the Australian scheme the Nazi 'defence' would fail.

Another significant code emanates from the Australian Institute of Aboriginal and Torres Strait Islander Studies, called *Guidelines for Ethical Research in Australian Indigenous Studies* (Australian Institute of Aboriginal and Torres Strait Islander Studies, 2012), acknowledging special features of Indigenous culture, including unique local knowledge and sacred spiritual dimensions of everyday life. Such guidelines are found among other indigenes, or 'First Nations', also. In the past governments controlled every feature of Aboriginal life, including who and what was 'researched'. Rather than just being scrutinised as inanimate objects of curiosity, Aborigines are now full partners in and drivers of rich research agendas (Gammadge, 2011; Russell, 2006).

The Australian Library and Information Association has concise ethics policies, as do the Australian Computer Society and the Records Management Association of Australia, and in the USA the Association for Information Science and Technology (ASIS&T) the Association of Computing Machinery and the Computer Ethics Institute, to mention a few. It is hard to understand why the last-mentioned group feels a need to present itself as 'hip' and 'cool' by using language which trivialises: for example, 'Commandment 3' states: "Thou Shalt Not Snoop Around In Other People's Computer Files" (Fairweather, 2004). Ethics deserve more professional and considered treatment.

Universities and research institutions set up ethics committees which have been inspired by the national medical statement, and they advise on, approve, and monitor ethical research in all disciplines (Ess, 2002). An element of dissatisfaction with the imposition of medical values on social science research is emerging (Dodson & Sterling, 2012). Nevertheless the *National Statement* espouses five accepted practical guidelines:

1. Researchers must treat with dignity and respect the persons, groups and organisations which participate in their research.

2. Research must refer to the work of others who have researched in the area before, and it must be conducted and/or supervised by persons qualified to do the work who have the necessary facilities to ensure the safety of the participants.

3. The potential benefits of the research project must substantially outweigh any potential harm to participants, or users of the research output.

4. Participants in the research must be able to make a voluntary, informed decision to participate.

5. Research is a public activity, conducted openly and accountably to both the researcher's community and to participants in the research (Bouma, 2004).

Responsibility for research ethics implementation

Macfarlane (2009) complained that codification of ethics leads to an over-dependence on enforcement and compliance, rather than on a positive approach to helping to solve ethical problems that a researcher encounters in projects:

> Education and training offered to researchers in universities ... tend to reflect an agenda dominated by a concern for the rights of (mainly) human subjects and the costs and benefits of undertaking research. Sets of principles are written down to which researchers are expected to adhere. These principles ... frequently consist of little more than an explanation of an operating code of conduct. Contradictions between principles are left unexplained and unexplored. ... Few regulatory committees ... take an interest in ethical dilemmas. ... They act as gatekeepers to the research process rather than ethical mentors or guides (Macfarlane, 2009, p. 3).

A research institution fears fall-out (and litigation) because of research mistakes, argued Macfarlane, but the ethical dilemmas faced by the bulk of researchers are usually small and subtle, and are not major disasters (as was the badly-researched drug Thalidomide which caused thousands of birth deformities) (Mills, 2007).

As an example of the need for subtle treatment, for mature guidance, rather than remote hard-and-fast controls, consider the delicate issue posed by the requirement for maintaining the anonymity of a research subject when the subject is part of a small group where all the members are well known to each other. Such a dilemma could arise where a group of librarians, archivists, recordkeepers, or system developers were the subject of research. That is, deductive disclosure of participants to other participants arises as an ethical research dilemma for the researcher; members can easily identify other members because they know them and their environment so well (Johanson, Williamson, & Schauder, 2007). In one research report, two researchers solved this dilemma by emphasising the virtue of 'care' in dealing with the teacher-participants who were known to each other. Voluntary consent was obtained, the subjects benefited from the research, trust was engendered, and ostentatious power-play was avoided (Costley & Gibbs, 2006). Another ethnographer dealt with a similar issue in other practical ways. Her project required that she interview migrants in one country, then visit family members in another country, to evaluate the impact of migration on their long-term emotional bonds. Her research required honesty in her own reflections (as researcher) about the sincerity and harmony of the family relationships, careful self-management in order to separate her own emotional reactions to her up-close observations, from the sincerely-held (but separate) emotions of the interviewees, and post-project contact with subjects to pass on symbolic family messages and gifts (Baldassar, 2008). In this study, complete emotional disengagement and non-communication between participants would have defeated the purpose of the project entirely. In cases of deductive or essential disclosure a narrow code does not assist; the researchers themselves need ethical breathing space to act responsibly and constructively, and for the researchers to build trust with all of the participants, and vice versa (Vannini & Gladue, 2008; Williams, 2012).

There are other limitations associated with codes of ethics. Cynics say that there is rarely agreement about moral solutions to ethical problems, meaning that consensus in ethical code form is impossible; that no-one has the right to 'judge' others; or that ethics are a private and subjective matter. The counter-arguments are fairly obvious. Disagreement is nuanced commonly in real life, and is rarely black-and-white, and does not obviate a need for accepted guidelines to harmonise our social interactions. A process of making judgements about good behaviour or misbehaviour is widely accepted and does not require condemnation or punishment of others automatically or absolutely. Humans congregate and function in groups, not as independent moral actors; in any group harm can arise for minorities in the absence of agreed protocols, where only a majority ethic dominates. The arguments for the benefits of adopting ethics standards are strong. They bolster good behaviour because they reflect group values; they mean that norms of behaviour are more likely to be understood in that they provide an educational and communication tool; they are a useful channel for public advocacy; they provide a base-line of values against which progress of ethical decision-making can be measured; they already control many aspects of life anyway (as with our mutually-agreed laws); they help guide those to whom we delegate responsibility for the effective management of our practical ethics; and they provide assistance when ethical crises arise (Tavani, 2016).

How can research ethics mistakes be handled? Standard problem-solving techniques are recommended. These are: specify the facts of the problem situation; define the moral dilemma posed; identify the concerned constituencies and their interests; clarify and prioritise the values and principles at stake; formulate options for action by the researcher (and managing supervisor); and identify the potential consequences of acting on the problem, or failing to act (Ferguson *et al.*, 2016).

Intercultural research ethics

Intercultural ethics present very complex problems. In this section the term 'culture' includes behaviours, beliefs, and symbols of a particular group based on values, ways of thinking and living, social relationships, and ethnicity. Giving due respect to relations between cultures presents challenges for the researcher.

Sub-cultures can be found within a nation. They are not a new development. Long ago (in the 1850s) the differences within one nation between different cultural groups — religious faith, new medical practice, radical scientific theories, and fresh political ideology — were demonstrated starkly in London.

The Church of England believed that pain in child-birth was God-sent. Queen Victoria, about to give birth to her eighth child, had other ideas. She used innovative anaesthesia for the first time and alerted the bulk of the British public to the advantages of the use of recently-researched ether for the relief of pain (Mills, 2007). Around the same time, another clash of cultures occurred on a wider scale. Charles Darwin was completing his scientific research and finalising the publication of his revolutionary theories of evolution, in contradiction of the Christian theory that placed God at the centre of the universe of creation of all life. Public uproar resulted. Darwin's friend, Charles Babbage, the inventor of the programmable computer, backed creationism, asserting that God was a divine designer, making laws for the invention of all species (Babbage, 1837; Macfarlane, 2009), while many renowned geological and botanical researchers of the time felt obliged to support Darwin (Lennox, 2010). Public defence of the ethical consequences of challenging entrenched cultures was expected of the researchers. In the same decade, the socialist Karl Marx — exiled from Germany — spent many months researching in the British Library, and writing up his novel political theories which were to revolutionise modes of government in many countries for more than a century to come. Marx used an open repository of publicly-funded knowledge (the Library) to develop his restrictive ideology. He challenged the underlying system of values which lay behind his host country's faith in an emerging system of parliamentary democracy (Diamond, 2012).

International intercultural ethics confront us today on a large scale. Without good understanding of the cultural core of our own ethics, much confusion can arise. A growing literature deals with three aspects of intercultural ethics. Firstly, some commentators note words for some ethics concepts that do not exist in other languages, and deduce that those cultures do not countenance the concepts at all. The second focus of literature concentrates on traditional, national, cultural norms which affect research and which vary from place to place. The third topic deals with universal human rights, advocating them as a means to help improve the poor quality of life of the world's bulk of disadvantaged people. There is much more to cultural awareness than requesting that research participants sign a consent form (Marshall & Rossman, 2016). A few examples illustrate these three overlapping intercultural ethics topics.

Language and ethics

Language is integral to culture. In Thailand there is no word for 'privacy', and in Japan there is no term for 'human dignity': both terms are rooted in Western tradition. Privacy refers to the right of individuals to keep information about themselves to themselves, and to reveal it at their bidding alone. It becomes an ethical issue when a researcher wants to quiz individuals about personal characteristics. In China, privacy is interpreted traditionally as a 'shameful secret', although the narrow meaning is being eroded by adoption of modern Western thinking about an entitlement to personal space (Capurro, 2008; 2010). Analysis can be taken to a deeper level, as in the observation that in Buddhist philosophy in Thailand the individual self does not exist, but only in relation to a person's family (Capurro, 2008). 'Being private' applies to the group only; unlike attitudes in the West, the self is denied (Redclift, 2005). Research interviews in Thailand or China about an individual right to privacy are unlikely to succeed. Intercultural ethics produce strange bedfellows. In China, filtering software (a firewall) researched and developed in Silicon Valley, is used to limit and monitor citizen access to the internet (Hauptman, 2008). It is not possible to research censorship or online confidentiality in China.

Variations in cultural norms and ethical practice

The second discussion of intercultural ethics relates to variations in ethical practice, based on traditions, from country to country. Some variations have serious consequences. Take intellectual property, and discussion about the extended 'right' of an author of an original creative expression to maintain control over and profit from a personal invention or creation, perhaps based on prior research. In the West, intellectual property laws have been in operation for centuries, but in Asia the concept of intellectual property is new. Globalisation creates a need for standardisation and co-ordination. Individual endeavour is strongly rewarded in Western culture.

There has been much debate about conflicting cultural perceptions of ownership of research knowledge and plagiarism as a result. Many people believe that stealing online content is inoffensive, arguing that it is in the public domain, although they are less inclined to plagiarise printed material (Baruchson-Arbib & Yaari, 2004). Intellectual property is being imposed on Asian countries by means of Western legal, political and economic hegemonies. Whether the underlying reasons for the lack of an intellectual property tradition in Asia are due to different value systems, or to pragmatic economic development, or to other local inhibitors, is hotly debated (Yu, 2012). Is it ethical not to restrict unauthorised uses of published research?

Another national variation occurs in Japan, where medical researchers do not tell a patient with cancer or a serious mental condition about their illnesses, but out of respect for the role of the close family, *they* are informed instead of the patient, in the hope that sharing bad news with the group as a whole will provide a broad support network to the sick individual (Macfarlane, 2009).

Another difference in national tradition relates to the philosophies behind ethical behaviour; the USA favours utilitarian ethics, while Europe tends towards deontology (Ess, 2002; Iacovino, 2002). Europe advocates much more strongly for online privacy than does the USA (Ess, 2002). Within Europe, the British tend to act pragmatically with ethics and research, while the French focus on broad ethical principles (Neazor, 2007). France promotes a constitutional right to oblivion, to allow citizens to destroy online data about themselves (Rosen, 2010). National cultural scars affect what research is acceptable. Still in the shadow of the horror of eugenics and Nazism, Germany will not permit stem cell research today (Macfarlane, 2009). Many such national ethical differences affect research.

Human rights, ethics and research

The third area of interest — human rights, ethics and research — has been growing rapidly in recent years. The huge cultural gap between rich and poor nations is seen as unethical *per se* (Hauptman, 2008), and any research which promotes better well-being, reduced poverty, and digital inclusion is lauded as moral. The donors of overseas aid frequently require research as a precursor to funding (Steyn, 2011). Researchers defer to utilitarianism, and fear that the spread of the Western info-sphere may overwhelm and destroy local Indigenous culture, especially oral culture. Such a risk is seen as unethical (Capurro, 2008). Searching its conscience, pondering its effects as a fortifier of the propagation of one global language (English), *Google* aims to help to preserve 3,054 threatened languages with a special research project (Angotti, 2012). Whilst some linguists label the *Google* effort as tokenistic research, others praise it for encouraging cultural plurality (Kamrani, 2012). In addition to the Universal Declaration of Human Rights, already mentioned, the more recent Charter of the World Summit on the Information Society (2005) has affirmed the need for Western researchers to remain vigilant (Carbo & Smith, 2008) about access to knowledge, freedom of expression, privacy, transparency, accountability, and research to assist social inclusion (Capurro, 2010). Applying deontology, or a set of ethical duties, researchers are expected to accept the view that no culture is regarded as superior to another (Australian Institute of Aboriginal and Torres Strait Islander Studies, 2012).

Research phases requiring ethical behaviour

There are at least six phases in research where ethics are relevant. They are in planning and design, collecting data, management and storage of the data, publication, ownership and authorship, and peer review.

Research planning and design

Research should not be undertaken unless at the start it promises to be viable, manageable and responsible. The first step in any research is to prepare a plan which (*inter alia*) avoids problems raised by ethical pitfalls or unethical topics. There are a number of examples. The first refers to groups which are over-researched, and which resent being asked too frequently to satiate researcher hunger for information via survey or interview. After more than a decade of excessive observation, a community of harassed Chinese migrants in Prato, Italy, resented being interviewed or photographed (Johanson & Fladrich, 2015).

Some commercial companies show scant regard for ethical planning. Today, under the guise of market research, Amazon, Barnes & Noble, and Apple consistently collect precise, personal information about their e-readers who are using Kindles, Nooks and iPads. The companies have collected more data than they can hope to process meaningfully, and it is all done without obtaining formal consent of any purchaser of e-books. What they have learnt in the space of the past few years provides more information than has ever been available before to a researcher interested in reading habits. For example, their research reveals that:

> non-fiction books tend to be read in fits and starts, while novels are generally read straight through, and ... nonfiction books, particularly long ones, tend to get dropped earlier. Science-fiction, romance and crime-fiction fans often read more books more quickly than readers of literary fiction do, and finish most of the books [which] they start. Readers of literary fiction quit books more often and tend [to] skip around between books (Alter, 2012).

The consequences of this type of monitoring for future authors and researchers are great. Publishers can narrow research and creativity by prescribing content and limiting it to what they know will sell.

Another example of 'research' which should never begin involves online forums or communities and secret observation (or manipulating) of discussions of personal problems by vulnerable participants, or others. It is a very unethical practice. Online communities are far more accessible to any snooper than physical communities (McLemee, 2001). There is a danger, for example, that friends of a sick member of a 'confidential' online support group may find out about the member's illness before he tells them directly himself, by means of an unidentified 'researcher' who posts the sufferer's name and details online without permission (Stevens, O'Donnell, & Williams, 2015). Observers have been known to invent anonymous personas in order to conceal their unethical surveillance of groups online (Geetha & Sheriff, 2013; Rosen, 2010). Large governments have been checking sensitive personal data for decades (Sula, 2016).

Another example shows that planning of research can be influenced by a desire to control outcomes. Consider organisations (including businesses, libraries and archives) which attempt to control the impacts of research that affects their status or image. Image management pervades research just as much as any other organised activity (Bolino, Long, & Turnley, 2016). Weaknesses or failures revealed by research can embarrass. A library researcher showed how libraries failed badly in providing quality service, and the research report was perceived as threatening when released. Michael Ramsden (1978) undertook a study covertly. He used research assistants to impersonate members of the public, and arranged for them to ask for answers to preconceived questions in a random sample of Melbourne's public libraries. Half of the questions were answered incorrectly by staff. This poor result was a major shock to librarians.

The Ramsden study is still quoted in current literature, partly because it broke new ground, and partly because the project could now be regarded as an unethical mode of research, and not undertaken. There is energetic discussion among sociologists about the ethics of researching 'under cover', in effect, of deceiving participants. There are many arguments for and against deception, even if it causes no obvious harm, and they all lead to the dilemma of the need for subtle approaches:

> The ethics of social research must inevitably be situation ethics; even social scientists who proclaim absolutes betray them in actual practice. Exceptions and contingencies abound, and often derail even the most reasonable-sounding general formulations. … The ethics of disguised observation [should] be evaluated on a situational, case-by-case basis, and … the ethics of a particular strategy cannot be determined in a blanket fashion (Goode, 1996, p. 14).

Goode's arguments (which are well worth studying) beg the question as to whether there can be any ultimate, objective basis for ethical research practice.

At the time of the release of the Ramsden findings, in the memory of the author of this chapter, there was much consternation among the library profession about the consequences of making the findings too widely available. The research methodology was examined closely and affirmed. Because of the novelty of its design and findings, the study was widely cited at the time, and it has never been replicated in its entirety (Ramsden, 1978).

Collecting data

The second phase of research ethics relates to aspects of collecting data. In this phase, obtaining informed consent to participation in research can raise many ethical questions. We may ask if participants truly understand the impact of the research (Daniels, 2008). Can they change their minds and withdraw after all of the data are collected, and analysis is under way? Does the researcher only use the data for the purpose for which the original consent was obtained, or is the researcher permitted to extend or alter the use *ex post facto*? Surveys suggest that about 90 percent of Britons believe that they should be told which researchers use their data, that they should be allowed to correct factual errors about them on databases, and that they should be asked if third parties want access to their data (Rosen, 2010; Thomas & Walport, 2008).

There are other data collection issues, such as whether interviewees will try to please an interviewer-researcher with the sort of answers that they think the interviewer expects, especially if the interviewees feel in any way intimidated (Carlin, 2006; Williams, 2012). Is it ethical to use such data? Other problems can be that some topics should never be raised in questions (e.g., culturally secret knowledge) (McCoy, 2008), or that the questions can never be answered honestly. For example, lying is notoriously difficult to research, because dishonesty is the stock-in-trade of fraudsters who cannot provide reliable data (Vrij, 2000).

The management and storage of data

This third phase covers three inter-related activities of future research: long-term custodial preservation to ensure the use of data in perpetuity (if this is agreed to by stakeholders), security to prevent unauthorised tampering with data, and consideration of the viability of appending raw data to research publications. Ethics apply in each case. If research data cannot be preserved for later researchers, then over time its validity and usefulness may be jeopardised. Secondly, the data should not be altered or tampered with, or its integrity will be open to question. Thus secure storage is required and an undertaking made that data will be effectively destroyed (e.g., by shredding) after at least five years of storage (the usual agreement made between ethics committees and researchers). Thirdly, if raw data is not provided to future researchers, in publication or by a hot link, then it is difficult for future researchers to react to and to add to the earlier findings. The ethical principle in operation here is that future research pursuit relies heavily on the publically-accessible data of constructive researchers from the past, and that data should be protected sustainably.

In practice, e-research data repositories are difficult to differentiate from digital libraries, archives, records repositories, or research data collections, and indeed e-repositories may include all of the named functions. Their advantages are clear. They offer online access to masses of data resources on any topic, new modes of publication and peer review, corporate information management (records management and content management systems), re-use of research data, and centralised long-term preservation of research data (NHMRC, 2015). In the USA and Europe enormous amounts of money are spent to develop them inter-operably with common services. They are labour-intensive, for example, raising the question as to who should be responsible for stripping records of personal data when they are deposited? They are also complex: how can cultural sensitivities be tracked fairly as they change over time? (University of Texas, 2011). In addition, 'future proofing' against technology obsolescence is a major research challenge (Heery, 2005).

Institutions (including libraries, archives, research repositories) which manage large volumes of 'big data' have developed clear policies to help to keep data secure and unaltered (Hauptman, 2008; University of Texas, 2011). The advent of 'big data' does not introduce completely fresh ethical issues, but it magnifies and 'complicates' them (Sula, 2016). The policies should be standardised to ensure future usefulness. Forthcoming impacts of big data are discussed in Chapter 23: *The future of information research.*

Publication of research data and findings

Many researchers regard full publication of research data as an asset for checking the credibility of prior research. In the context of problems arising from the drug, Vioxx, the editor of the *Medical Journal of Australia* said:

> I think [that] if you're [editing] a journal which publishes major randomized controlled trials that are practice-changing, there is a strong argument to publish the raw data. If you look at the Vioxx scandal, for example, when the data was re-analysed, very different conclusions were drawn. ... It is very hard (Medew, 2011).

The drug Vioxx was meant to be just a painkiller but it doubled the risk of heart attack when taken, and the producer agreed to pay $US950 million in compensation and damages to victims in the USA (Feeley & Voreacos, 2011).

The process of publishing full data is messy and inconsistent:

> Scientists are failing to make raw data publicly available, even when prompted to do so by journals ... [A] study of 500 papers from the 50 highest-impact journals reveals wide variation in data-sharing policies [in science] and in researchers' adherence to them. The findings come amid a growing push for sharing raw research data — both to facilitate further research and to better prevent fraud or error. ... Looking at the first ten papers published in each journal in 2009, the researchers found that, of the 351 papers covered by some data-sharing policy, only 143 fully adhered to that policy (Corbyn, 2011).

Nevertheless the trend to open-ness is strong, scientists asserting that data needs to be re-examinable by anyone in order to be reliable (Hernon & Altman, 1995). It is as well to be reminded, as we are by Hauptman, of the reason for the assertion, that is, that "research in all areas is carried out by human beings who are sometimes lazy, inefficient, ambitious, greedy, agenda-ridden, or in a hurry" (Hauptman, 2008, p. 242).

Ethical issues arise with research publication because this is the stage in the research process where research is subjected to widespread scrutiny. There is a strong public interest in fraud, and its consequences, which can take many forms: fabrication, falsification, plagiarism, and deception (NHMRC, 2015). A new method for personal researcher identification is available to help to reduce impersonation (Butler, 2012). Where genuine mistakes are published accidentally, public retractions can be expected. Retractions are not always published. They place knowledge repositories (e.g., libraries) in a difficult ethical quandary. Who should track errors, especially in view of the fact that they are perpetuated *ad infinitum* online? (Hauptman, 2008).

Some research results are strictly censored for political expediency, and their leaking leads to dire crises. A destructive case in 2003 concerned Dr D. C. Kelly, a biological warfare researcher, employed by the British government, who disagreed with the government as to the potency of so-called 'weapons of mass destruction' in Iraq. The government was intent on going to war to reveal them; Kelly did not believe that they existed. His views were leaked to the mass media. After the media exposure, Kelly was grilled by a parliamentary enquiry. He died two days later (Macfarlane, 2009). The government claimed that the cause of death was suicide; an enquiry has withheld access to the post-mortem findings for 70 years; and his friends and research colleagues cried foul play (Vallely, 2012). The ethics of the release of Kelly's research knowledge highlights the delicacy of some publication processes. Evidence in the case is still contested.

Ownership and authorship

The fifth phase relates to contentious ownership of research and findings, and proper acknowledgement of authorial contributions (NHMRC, 2015). There are many challenging situations. Research which uses data created by deceased authors can create further ethical dilemmas about ownership. For example, the Jewish fiction writer Franz Kafka wanted all his papers burnt at his death in 1924. A friend did not respect his wishes. The extant collection contains unpublished manuscripts. In Tel Aviv a friend of the friend of Kafka 'owns' the extant writings now; the state of Israel asserts that they are of national significance and should be donated to the National Library of Israel for future researchers. Israel did not exist when Kafka died (Frenkel, 2012).

When a research project is undertaken collaboratively, it can be hard to determine who 'owns' which outcomes, and who is responsible for them (Bell, Hill, & Lehming, 2007). When the collaboration involves community ownership, for instance, individual contributions can pale into insignificance (Australian Institute of Aboriginal and Torres Strait Islander Studies, 2012). When a new researcher is coached to publication by an experienced writer, or team of writers, it is ethical to ask where the authorial responsibility lies (Keen, 2007).

It is common for the names of senior researchers to appear in a publication byline because they have supervised the research but not actually undertaken laboratory or field work for the project themselves. Is the practice ethical? On occasion deference to experience leads to disagreement. Sometimes a 'name' is added just for prestige, even if that 'author' has contributed nothing else (Game & West, 2002), and "institutional pressures may dictate that the most senior researcher or colleague is listed as the first author regardless of contribution" by that person (Keen, 2007, p. 387). The precedence implied by the order of the published names of co-authors is ethically fraught. The potential problems cited here are compounded by the fact that there are no published multi-disciplinary guidelines on the ethics of authorship (Game & West, 2002).

Another ethical issue is raised by publishers who normally require an author to sign a contract, often claiming ownership of all intellectual property; author-researchers then may have very little control over how their work is used (Ibanez, Kositsky, Mao, & Moussaoui, 2006).

Peer review

The final phase of research ethics concerns the assumption that authoritative publications will be thoroughly and impartially peer reviewed (NHMRC, 2015). It is often said that mistakes in scientific research are no impediment to the emergence of reliable, ethical knowledge because "science is self-correcting"

(Hauptman, 2008, p. 240). That is, because science is cumulative, later scientists test the validity of previous research to confirm or disavow it. There are problems with this argument, in that replication rarely uncovers all errors, and in that there is little motivation for a second scientist to prove a first scientist wrong; moving forwards with new work is usually more effective and prestigious (Hernon & Altman, 1995). One survey of scientists showed that one-third of them admit to research misconduct in one form or another; this is hardly an ethical way to behave (Hauptman, 2008). There are no guidelines about the ethical behaviour expected of a repository (e.g., library) that happens to be a storehouse of incorrect publications or data (Johnson, 2016). In the past publishers have been sued for publishing errors which cause harm.

Another significant consideration about peer review is the potential for conflict of interest, where the research is supported by an organisation with a vested interest in publishing narrow opinions, and ignoring others. Good ethics demand that competing interests be separated in research decision-making. Many research scientists work for commercial enterprises. Drug companies are a major influence on published medical research, with 15 percent of health scientists admitting to allowing drug sponsors to suppress research results (Macfarlane, 2009). Under pressure from lobby groups, authors and editors withdraw papers on the verge of publication (Hauptman, 2008). Many professors own patents on their own inventions, and are likely to promote them above competitors, as well as shares in specific medical companies (Hauptman, 2008; Medew, 2011).

Conclusion

The cases mentioned in this chapter give a clear indication that improved understanding of ethical research practice must be encouraged. It is not just in the field of information ethics that dynamic change is occurring. There are many reasons as to why researchers generally must be keen to make ethical decisions. Every research situation has its own unique characteristics, and hence researchers must exercise personal judgements in solving unusual, unexpected, and subtle dilemmas.

Multi-cultural research teams increase in number, and are likely to continue to grow, driven by the need for financial efficiencies and the need for international solutions to large problems. Respect for cultural diversity (whether inside a country or across countries) is a *sine qua non*. The ability to subvert information and knowledge systems increases as rapidly as the research and ethical practices which aim to stop the deterioration or falsification of research data. Powerful governments, and business and private industry, take greater control of much research, corralling it for security or for profit. Secrecy raises many ethical questions about the nature of the 'public good'. Partly as a counterbalance, the growth of globalising and democratising effects of communications networks on research is exploited universally. More public scrutiny of ethical behaviour in research stimulates a wide, healthy discussion of public values. Years ago Johanson (2002) pointed out that that there was much more published research about ethical research practices than there had been ten years before. The magnification, diversification and extension of discussion continues to lead to improved ethical research practices.

References

Alter, A. (2012, June 29). Your e-book is reading you. *Wall Street Journal*. Retrieved from https://www.wsj.com/articles/SB10001424052702304870304577490950051438304

Angotti, D. (2012, June 21). Google's Endangered Languages Project fights to save 3,054 languages. *Search Engine Journal*. Retrieved from http://www.searchenginejournal.com/google-endangered-languages-project/45284/.

Australian Institute of Aboriginal and Torres Strait Islander Studies (2012). *Guidelines for ethical research in Australian indigenous studies* (pp. 1–15). Canberra: Australian Institute of Aboriginal and Torres Strait Islander Studies.

Babbage, C. (1837). *The ninth Bridgewater treatise: A fragment*. London: John Murray. Retrieved from http://archive.org/stream/ninthbridgewater00babbiala#page/n23/mode/2up

Baldassar, L. (2008). Missing kin and longing to be together: Emotions and the construction of co-presence in transnational relationships. *Journal of Intercultural Studies*, 29(3), 247–266.

Baruchson-Arbib, S., & Yaari, E. (2004). Printed versus internet plagiarism: A study of students' perception. *International Journal of Information Ethics*, 1(6), 1–7.

Bell, R. K., Hill, D., & Lehming, R. F. (2007). The changing research and publication environment in American research universities. In National Science Foundation (Ed.), *Working paper SRS 07-204* (p. 46). Arlington, VA: National Science Foundation.

Bolino, M., Long, D., & Turnley, W. (2016). Impression management in organizations: critical questions, answers, and areas for future research. *Annual Review of Organizational Psychology and Organizational Behavior*, 3, 377–406.

Bouma, G. (2004). *The research process*. Melbourne: Oxford University Press.

Butler, D. (2012). Scientists: Your number is up. *Nature News*, 485(7400), 564.

Capurro, R. (2008). Intercultural information ethics. *Journal of Information, Communication & Ethics in Society*, 6(2), 116–126.

Capurro, R. (2010). *Global intercultural information ethics from an African perspective*. Paper presented at the Second African Information Ethics Conference 6–7 September 2010, Gaborone, Botswana.

Carbo, T., & Smith, M. M. (2008). Global information ethics: intercultural perspectives on past and future research. *Journal of the American Society for Information Science and Technology, 59*(7), 1111–1123.

Carlin, A. (2006). "Rose's gloss": Considerations of natural sociology and ethnography in practice. *Qualitative Sociology Review, 2*(3), 65–77.

Chan, S. (2002). *Liberalism, democracy and development.* Cambridge: Cambridge University Press.

Corbyn, Z. (2011, September 14). Researchers failing to make raw data public; Adherence to data-sharing policies is as inconsistent as the policies themselves. *Nature.* Retrieved from http://www.nature.com/news/2011/110914/full/news.2011.536.html.

Costley, C., & Gibbs, P. (2006). Researching others: Caring as an ethic for practitioner researchers. *Studies in Higher Education, 31*(1), 27–54.

Daniels, D. (2008). Exploring ethical issues when using visual tools in educational research. In P. Liamputtong (Ed.), *Doing cross-cultural research: Ethical and methodological perspectives* (pp. 119–133). Dordrecht: Springer.

Diamond, M. E. (2012). The British Library, and why I love librarians [Blog post]. Retrieved from https://learnearnandreturn.wordpress.com/2012/04/12/the-british-library-and-why-i-love-librarians/.

Dodson, L., & Sterling, S. R. (2012). Ethics of participation: Research or reporting? *Electronic Journal on Information Systems in Developing Countries, 50*(6), 1–14.

Ess, C. (2002). *Ethical decision-making and internet research: Recommendations from the Association of Internet Research ethics working committee.* Irvine, CA: Humanities Research Institute, University of California.

Fairweather, N.B. (2004). Commentary on the 'Ten Commandments for computer ethics'. Retrieved from http://courses.cs.vt.edu/professionalism/WorldCodes/10.Commandments.html.

Feeley, J., & Voreacos, D. (2011, December 5). Merck to plead guilty, pay $950 million in U.S. Vioxx probe. *Bloomberg Businessweek.* Retrieved from http://marc-lemenestrel.net/IMG/pdf/merck_to_plead_guilty_pay_950m_in_u.s._vioxx_probe_-_bloomberg.pdf.

Ferguson, S., Thornley, C., & Gibb, F. (2016). Beyond codes of ethics: How library and information professionals navigate ethical dilemmas in a complex and dynamic information environment. *International Journal of Information Management, 36*(4), 543–556.

Frenkel, S. (2012, May 30). Kafka's final absurdist tale plays out in Tel Aviv [Audio podcast]. NPR. Retrieved from http://www.npr.org/2012/05/30/153985994/kafkas-final-absurdist-tale-plays-out-in-tel-aviv.

Froehlich, T. (2004). A brief history of information ethics. *Textos universitaris de biblioteconomia i documentacio, 13.* Retrieved from www.ub.edu/bid/13froel2.htm.

Game, A., & West, A. W. (2002). Principles of publishing. *The Psychologist, 15*(3), 126–129.

Gammadge, B. (2011). *The biggest estate on earth: How Aborigines made Australia.* Crows Nest, NSW: Allen & Unwin.

Geetha, R., & Sheriff, A. M. (2012). The techniques and rationale of e-surveillance practices in organizations. *International Journal of Multidisciplinary Research, 2*(2). Retrieved from https://ssrn.com/abstract=2480083.

Goode, E. (1996). The ethics of deception in social research: A case study. *Qualitative Sociology, 19*(1), 11–33.

Hauptman, R. (2008). Intermezzo: ethics and information. *Business Information Review, 25*(4), 238–252.

Heery, R. (2005). *Digital repositories review.* Bath, UK: University of Bath.

Hernon, P., & Altman, E. (1995). Misconduct in academic research: its implications for the service quality provided by university libraries. *Journal of Academic Librarianship, 21*(1), 27–37.

Iacovino, L. (2002). Ethical principles and information professionals: theory, practice and education. *Australian Academic & Research Libraries, 33*(2), 57–74.

Ibanez, M.S., Kositsky, A., Mao, J., & Moussaoui, Y. (2006). *A new publishing paradigm: Returning journal proceeds to scholarly institutions.* Retrieved from http://www.mcafee.cc/Classes/BEM106/Papers/2006/Library.pdf.

Johanson, G. (2002). Ethics in research. In K. Williamson (Ed.), *Research methods for students, academics and professionals: Information management and systems* (pp. 67–83). Wagga Wagga, NSW: Centre for Information Studies, Charles Sturt University.

Johanson, G. (2011). Delineating the meaning and value of Development Informatics. In J. Steyn, & G. Johanson (Eds.), *ICTs and sustainable solutions for the digital divide: theory and perspectives* (pp. 1–18). Hershey PA: Information Science Reference.

Johanson, G., & Fladrich, A. M. (2015). Ties that bond: Mobile phones and the Chinese in Prato. In L. Baldassar, G. Johanson, N. McAuliffe, & M. Bressan (Eds.), *Chinese migration to Europe; Prato, Italy, and beyond* (pp. 177–194). Houndmills, UK: Palgrave: Macmillan.

Johanson, G., Williamson, K., & Schauder, D. (2007). Recording oral memory: Views of indigenous Victorians. In A. Williamson, & R. de Souza (Eds.), *Researching communities with community participation: Grounded perspectives on engaging communities in research* (pp. 219–242). Auckland: Muddy Creek Press.

Johnson, H. R. (2016). Foucault, the "facts" and the fiction of neutrality: Neutrality in librarianship and peer review. *Canadian Journal of Academic Librarianship, 1*(1), 24–41.

Kamrani, K. (2012, June 21). Google supports the endangered languages project [Blog post]. Retrieved from https://anthropology.net/2012/06/21/google-supports-the-endangered-languages-project/.

Keen, A. (2007). Writing for publication: pressures, barriers and support strategies. *Nurse Education Today*, 27(5), 382–388.

Lennox, J. (2010). Darwinism. In E. N. Zalta (Ed.), *Stanford encyclopedia of philosophy*. Stanford, CA: Stanford University. Retrieved from http://plato.stanford.edu/entries/darwinism/.

Lucivero, F. (2016). *Ethical assessments of emerging technologies*. (The International Library of Ethics, Law and technology, 15). Switzerland: Springer.

Macfarlane, B. (2009). *Researching with integrity: The ethics of academic enquiry*. New York: Routledge.

MacIntyre, A. C. (1998). *A short history of ethics: A history of moral philosophy from the Homeric age to the twentieth century*. London: Routledge.

Mansell, R. (2010). The information society and ICT policy: A critique of the mainstream vision and an alternative research framework. *Journal of Information, Communication and Ethics in Society*, 8(1), 22–41.

Marshall, C., & Rossman, G. B. (2016). *Designing qualitative research*. Los Angeles: Sage.

McCoy, B. F. (2008). Researching with aboriginal men: A desert experience. In P. Liamputtong (Ed.), *Doing cross-cultural research: Ethical and methodological perspectives* (pp. 175–191). Dordrecht: Springer.

McLemee, S. (2001). Internet studies 1.0: A discipline is born. *Chronicle of Higher Education*, 47(29), A24.

Medew, J. (2011). Bad medicine. *The Age*. Retrieved from http://www.theage.com.au/national/bad-medicine-20110511-1eiql.html

Mills, J. (2007). *Ethically challenged: Big questions for science*. Carlton, VIC: Melbourne University Publishing.

Mok, T. M., Cornish, F., & Tarr, J. (2015). Too much information: visual research ethics in the age of wearable cameras. *Integrative Psychological and Behavioral Science*, 49, 309–322.

National Health and Medical Research Council (NHMRC). (2007). *Australian code for the responsible conduct of research*. Canberra, ACT: National Health and Medical Research Council.

National Health and Medical Research Council (NHMRC). (2015). *National statement on ethical conduct in human research*. Canberra, ACT: National Health and Medical Research Council.

Neazor, M. (2007). Recordkeeping professional ethics and their application. *Archivaria*, 64(Fall), 47–87.

Pinker, S. (2011). *The better angels of our nature; the decline of violence in history and its causes*. London: Penguin.

Ramsden, M. J. (1978). *Performance measurement of some Melbourne public libraries: A report to the Library Council of Victoria*. Melbourne: Library Council of Victoria.

Redclift, N. (2005). Introduction: Fighting for the high ground: Anthropological perspectives on moral conflict. In N. Redclift (Ed.), *Contesting moralities; science, identity and conflict* (pp. 1–20). London: UCL Press.

Rosen, J. (2010, July 19). The web means the end of forgetting. *New York Times Magazine*. Retrieved from http://www.nytimes.com/2010/07/25/magazine/25privacy-t2.html?pagewanted=all&_r=0

Russell, L. (2006). Indigenous records and archives: mutual obligations and building trust. *Archives and Manuscripts*, 34(1), 32–43.

Singer, P. (1986). *Practical ethics*. Cambridge: Cambridge University Press.

Spinello, R. A. (2003). *Case studies in information technology ethics*. Upper Saddle River, NJ: Prentice Hall.

Stevens, G., O'Donnell, V. L., & Williams, L. (2015). Public domain or private data? Developing an ethical approach to social media research in an inter-disciplinary project. *Educational Research and Evaluation*, 21(2), 154–167.

Steyn, J. (2011). Paradigm shift required for ICT4D. In J. Steyn, & G. Johanson (Eds.), *ICTs and sustainable solutions for the digital divide: theory and perspectives* (pp. 19–44). Hershey, PA: Information Science Reference.

Sula, C. A. (2016). Research ethics in an age of big data. *Bulletin of the Association for Information Science and Technology*, 42(2), 17–21.

Tavani, H. T. (2016). *Ethics and technology: Controversies, questions, and strategies for ethical computing*. Hoboken, NJ: Wiley.

Thomas, R., & Walport, M. (2008). *Data sharing review report*. London: Information Commissioner, Department of Justice.

UNESCO. (2011). Information for All Programme (IFAP). Retrieved from http://www.unesco.org/new/en/communication-and-information/intergovernmental-programmes/information-for-all-programme-ifap/about-ifap/history/.

University of Texas at Dallas Information Security (2007). *Data classification standards* (pp. 1–4). Dallas, Texas: University of Texas at Dallas.

Vallely, P. (2012). The Kelly affair: Anatomy of a conspiracy theory. *Independent*. Retrieved from http://www.independent.co.uk/news/uk/home-news/the-kelly-affair-anatomy-of-a-conspiracy-theory-2058065.html

Vannini, A., & Gladue, C. (2008). Decolonised methodologies in cross-cultural research. In P. Liamputtong (Ed.), *Doing cross-cultural research: Ethical and methodological perspectives* (pp. 137–159). Dordrecht: Springer.

Von Staden, H. (1996). 'In a pure and holy way': Personal and professional conduct in the Hippocratic Oath. *Journal of the History of Medicine and Allied Sciences*, 51(4), 404–437.

Vrij, A. (2000). *Detecting lies and deceit: The psychology of lying and the implications for professional practice*. Chichester, UK: Wiley.

Weber, M. (1949). *The methodology of the social sciences*. New York: The Free Press.

Williams, R. (2012). *The responsibility of the researcher – An unfolding theme*. Paper presented at the Australian Housing and Urban Research Institute Emerging Scholars Symposium, Melbourne, Australia.

Williamson, K., Burstein, F., & McKemmish, S. (2002). Introduction to research in relation to professional practice. In K. Williamson (Ed.), *Research methods for students, academics and professionals: Information management and systems* (pp. 5–23). Wagga Wagga, NSW: Centre for Information Studies, Charles Sturt University.

Yu, P. K. (2012). Intellectual property and Asian values. *Marquette Intellectual Property Law Review, 16*(2), 329–399.

Zimmer, M. (2010). Innovations and challenges in teaching information ethics across educational contexts. *International Review of Information Ethics, 14*(12), 17–22.

Chapter 21

Managing research data

Mary Anne Kennan

Charles Sturt University, Australia

This chapter describes the various forms and sources of research data and the importance of planning to appropriately manage data throughout their life cycle. The many reasons that data should be managed within research projects and programs (and beyond to enable future use) are discussed. Legal, ethical and policy reasons for planning are introduced, as are practical and pragmatic reasons, along with the role of researchers in data management processes. Ten important components of a data management plan are addressed and a checklist for researchers in the early stages of constructing a data management plan is provided. The chapter concludes by providing references to useful data management tools and resources.

Research Methods: Information, Systems, and Contexts. DOI: http://dx.doi.org/10.1016/B978-0-08-102220-7.00021-2

Introduction

Researchers, research funders and research institutions such as universities place increasing importance on data management planning as a way of improving the access to, and the longevity, sharing and reuse of research data. Formal research data management is a developing area and best practice is emerging. Data management has traditionally been an 'orphan' activity expected to be carried out, but not explicitly taught, supported or funded (Donnelly, 2012, p. 94). As Donnelly pointed out, neglecting data management is risky for institutions and funders as activities which do not attract attention such as funding, reward or recognition are the first to suffer when time or money get tight. Thus it is important for data management plans to have associated policies, infrastructures, staffing and systems to support researchers in their implementation.

Research data are heterogeneous and can take many forms depending on the research problem being addressed and the discipline of the researcher. Thus different types of data in different disciplines require different treatment in the data management process. In disciplines where data may be impossible to reproduce and is important over time (such as the data in longitudinal studies in the social sciences or climate data in the environmental sciences), stress may be placed on preservation, but in fields where fast and easy sharing of data is desirable (such as medicine and the biological sciences) the planning and management emphasis may be on discovery and reuse. A plan must be fit for purpose for the particular types of research and data. Once a plan is written, the plan and its operationalisation must move forward together as a living document, and be in the minds of researchers and data managers/curators across the life cycle of a research project, as well as the generally longer life of the data.

Research data: Forms and sources

There is a wealth of information on the complexities of research data, defined as data "collected, observed or created for the purposes of analysing to produce original research results" (Rice, 2009, p. 16). Data sources are varied. In the life and physical sciences, data are generally gathered or produced by researchers through observations, experiments or by computer modelling. Borgman (2007, p. 182) provides some examples from different scientific disciplines: X-rays in medicine, protein structures in chemistry, spectral surveys in astronomy, specimens in biology, events and objects in physics. In the social sciences researchers may gather or produce their own data from, e.g., interviews, surveys, and observations, or obtain it from third parties such as the Australian Bureau of Statistics or the Organisation for Economic Co-operation and Development. Humanities data often come from cultural records, archives and objects, both published and unpublished (Borgman, 2007).

Digital data

Researchers have always collected data as evidence for their findings and claims. These data are now increasingly becoming digital. For example, scientific research used to be based in the laboratory. In the past, scientists kept meticulous notebooks, recording and detailing data and all stages of research. Now much research, even research conducted in a laboratory, uses computers in some way and produces digital data. Similarly much humanities and social science research data, which may have been textual data, recorded in notebooks, are now in a digital format in word processing documents, databases and spreadsheets. Digital research can often be complex and heterogeneous, meaning that the issues in data management and curation are similarly complex. Issues include: technology obsolescence; technology fragility (e.g., corruption of files); lack of guidelines on good practice; inadequate financial and human resources to manage data well; and, lack of evidence about best infrastructures (Oliver & Harvey, 2016).

Why research data need to be managed

Until recently data have rarely been seen by people beyond the initial research team. Data are usually analysed, summarised and published as a summary, often theorised, in articles, books and other publications. Analysed and published data are generally selective representations of a small amount of the raw data originally collected by the researchers (Latour, 1987). The analysis and summary of data in publications inevitably incorporate methodological and pragmatic choices made by the researchers at different stages of the research and limit subsequent interrogation of the data. Data that are abstracted and prepared for publishing in these ways do not necessarily provide sufficient information for future users (Markauskaite, 2010). These considerations have led to the rise of the open data movement. 'Open data' is an emerging term in the process of defining how scientific data may be published and re-used without price or permission barriers. It is related, but not completely analogous, to open access to publications (Murray-Rust, 2008). For discussion of 'open access' issues, see Chapter 22: *Research dissemination*.

There are several reasons for managing data, whether or not they are made open, within research programs, to enable sharing and future use. The characteristics of data that are particularly relevant here include that data:

1. are expensive to collect and therefore publicly funded research should be publicly available (Murray-Rust 2008);

2. may be unique, e.g., represent a snapshot in time or space (Henty, Weaver, Bradbury & Porter, 2008);

3. can be re-used to reproduce and validate original findings, to advance the original research or to open another line of enquiry (Witt, 2009);

4. can also contribute to answering questions which may require inter-disciplinary problem solving (Cragin, Palmer, Carlson & Witt, 2010);

5. may be used to examine a phenomenon from different epistemic or social perspectives (Markauskaite, 2010); and

6. may need to be collected from a variety of sources, beyond the scope of one research team, time or location (Borgman, 2007).

Several of the points, above, imply the need for data sharing, which is a key element of collaboration (Borgman, 2006; Williamson, Kennan, Johanson, & Weckert, 2016). Altruism, citation and the potential for new collaboration opportunities may motivate some researchers to share their data, but currently there are no explicit and tangible rewards for doing so and researchers report it as low on the list of their priorities (Henty, Weaver, Bradbury and Porter, 2008; Markauskaite, Kennan, Richardson, Aditomo & Hellmers, 2012).

Data come in sets — the collation of many individual datum. In most research, researchers create or use a number of datasets or databases. These sets of data are referred to as data collections. Data collections are defined by the infrastructure, organisations, and individuals needed to provide persistent access to them. Research data collections can refer to the output of a single researcher, collaborative teams or laboratories, be produced during the course of a specific research project, and beyond that if they are stored, created and preserved into the future.

The useful life of data and data collections is referred to as the data life cycle. Decisions made at each stage of the data life cycle determine what data are available at the next stage, how they are handled, and the purposes for which they are useful (Wallis, Borgman, Mayernik, & Pepe, 2008). The life cycle of data will be different in different disciplines or research traditions within those broad headings. At different stages in the life cycle, different people will be responsible for the data. There are many different data life cycle models: including that of the Digital Curation Centre (DCC) in the United Kingdom, which focusses on data curation and preservation issues (DCC, n.d.; Higgins, 2008; Higgins, 2012) and that of the Data Documentation Initiative (DDI) (2012) both of which elaborate researcher and curator roles in data conceptualisation, collection, processing, distribution, discovery, analysis, repurposing, and archiving.

Data management planning and processes

Reasons for the need to plan for data management were mooted in the introduction to this chapter. This section examines legal, ethical and policy requirements for planning, as well as discussing pragmatic and practical reasons to plan. The role of researchers in the planning process and the influences of organisations and associated actors on planning are also discussed, along with the processes involved in data management.

Legal, ethical and policy requirements for planning

Decisions made in relation to the management of research data should be informed by relevantlegislation and codes; national and institutional policy; and procedures and guidelines that the research project must adhere to. These will vary in different countries and states. The examples given here are largely Australian, but similar ones will inform research practice in many other countries.

In Australia, the *Australian Code for Responsible Conduct of Research* guides institutions and researchers in responsible research practice. The Code has been jointly developed by the National Health and Medical Research Council (NHMRC), the Australian Research Council (ARC) and Universities Australia. Compliance with the Code is a pre-requisite for NHMRC and ARC funding (NHMRC/ARC/Universities Australia, 2007). Other related national codes exist for the ethical conduct of research (e.g., NHMRC/ARC/AVCC, 2007). A central aim of the Australian Code for the Responsible Conduct of Research is that sufficient data and materials are retained to justify the outcomes of research and to defend such outcomes should they be challenged. The Code also makes recommendations about what research data and associated information should be kept (NHMRC/ARC/Universities Australia, 2007). Similarly, national ethical codes make recommendations about the ethical considerations that should be considered by researchers regarding their data. (See Chapter 20: *Ethical research practices*.) A data management plan enables processes and checks to be put in place to ensure these requirements are met.

In addition there are legislative requirements in different jurisdictions that need to be taken into consideration by researchers. A plan enables compliance issues to be visible and achievable. For example, in New South Wales, institutions and researchers will be guided by the provisions of the *State Records Act 1998* regarding the retention and disposal of research data. Various copyright acts may also apply to data, including digital forms of text and images, packaged variously as videos or DVDs, for example. The code of computer programs (both the human readable source code and the machine readable object code) is protected by copyright as a literary work. Data compilations such as datasets and databases can also be protected by copyright. Although, as a general rule of copyright, ownership resides with the author or creator, copyright can belong to a person's employer or via contract to others, depending on conditions of employment or via contracts in multi-institutional collaborations. If researchers wish to share their data online, deposit into a database, repository or archive, or allow others to access and use their data in any way, they will need to build appropriate permissions and licenses into their ethical approval processes and their data management plan and metadata.

Finally, there will be an array of institutional polices that will have a bearing on any research data management plan. Taking my own institution as an example, these may include policies on intellectual property, research data management, authorship, and ethics policies.

Pragmatic and practical reasons to plan

Good research data management practices ensure that researchers and institutions are able to meet their obligations to funders, improve the efficiency of research, and make data available for sharing, validation and re-use. Without proper management, data, or the media on which they are stored, may quickly become outdated or obsolete. Data may be misinterpreted through poor or inadequate description, or can sometimes go missing entirely, especially if files are not maintained and backed up on a regular basis. Without a data management strategy and skills, data can become lost or rendered useless, or be unable to provide their optimal usefulness. Many research funding bodies recognise this and now, around the world, are requiring data management plans to be attached to applications for funding. The plans go through peer review, along with the rest of the application.

The role of researchers

When many researchers think about data management, they may be thinking about common research processes involving data in an active research project or program rather than the management of data through its entire life cycle. For example, quantitative researchers may be talking about processes they already undertake in preparing their data for statistical analysis, for example cleansing, coding, documenting, variable creation, checking and digitising (e.g., the processes described in Chapter 18: *Quantitative data analysis*). Qualitative researchers might consider the work they do with their data, for example documenting, coding, describing, sorting, summarising, and iterative analysing (e.g., the processes described in Chapter 19: *Qualitative data analysis*). Data management planning includes these processes within the research process, but also can include longer-term concerns such as storage, curation, preservation, and description. These processes are better performed by or in conjunction with data librarians, curators and managers within researchers' institutions.

Unmanaged data present financial and opportunity loss, and yet the description, long-term storage and preservation of data are not necessarily key concerns of researchers who create and use data. Nevertheless, effective data management must begin with the researcher or research team (Pryor, 2012). Because data management is a part of digital preservation which is a part of data curation, generally a data management plan will fit into a suite of policies and procedures. Good data management requires input from a team of stakeholders: from the research team, to university policy makers, information technology and information management staff, and librarians or information managers.

Many researchers will regard the full cycle of data management planning as an additional and unwelcome burden. Some researchers question why data need to be kept after the results of the research have been published and statutory requirements met. However, there are a range of reasons that data need to be maintained before, during and after the research results have been published. Key issues to be considered are:

- *Risk minimisation.* Many researchers have had an experience of data loss or corruption. Many research data are kept on degradable, portable (and therefore easily lost) media such as external disk drives, CD-ROMs, DVDs, USB flash drives and memory sticks.

- *Funder and institutional policies and requirements, legislation (such as the State Records Acts).* These require data management planning.

- *Not all data management plans are the same.* Some will be complex and require that data are preserved and archived. Others may simply require that data are stored for a period of time and then destroyed. Researchers need to know into which category their data fall.

- *Contribution to future research.* Some data will contribute to future research and there are good arguments for their retention with open access. For other data there are strong ethical reasons which constrain sharing and reuse.

- *Planning and curation from the creation stage.* It is far cheaper and less time consuming to plan and appropriately curate data from the creation stage, than it is to correct mistakes or attempt to recover data later from obsolete storage media or after corruption has occurred (Donnelly, 2012).

Influences of organisations and other actors

Every data management plan will need to be different, reflecting the particular research involved; the disciplinary backgrounds of the researchers and the influences on them; national, funder and institutional policies; whether the data are ethically sharable; and whether they are unique or reproducible. Donnelly (2012, p. 88) lists the influences and actors as: funder requirements; deposit requirements, e.g., data and metadata formats; organisational and project requirements; research group and laboratory requirements and constraints; disciplinary, social and personal influences; publisher requirements; and legal requirements.

A number of people and groups may need to be involved in the planning and implementation stages, from the researchers, to data librarians, to repository or archive managers. Other people who may need to be involved include research policy staff and grants officers and, where appropriate, technical and laboratory staff. It is not realistic to expect all stakeholders to become experts in all the aspects of data management, but the planning process and policy should enable clear identification of roles and responsibilities at each stage of the process.

The processes involved

The Digital Curation Centre (DCC, n.d.) in the UK recommends three stages in data management planning. The first is at the grant application or project conceptualisation stage. This plan is relatively short and promissory. Once funding is achieved and/or the project definite, the core plan should be developed. Towards the end of the project, the full plan is finalised and includes long-term management and preservation plans often developed in consultation with people with relevant expertise such as archivists and information managers, curation and preservation specialists, and repository managers (Kennan, 2016).

There are no hard and fast rules abou t what should be included in a data management plan, as each plan depends on the nature of the research and data. However, some guidance is necessary. Donnelly (2012) lists ten important components of a data management plan:

1. *Introduction and context*: addresses the aims of the project and the data management plan, the intended audience of each, and relates the plan to relevant policies and procedures.

2. *Data types, formats, standards and capture methods*: describes the data and the metadata which will make the data (re)usable.

3. *Ethics and intellectual property*: includes legal obligations, licensing, sharing, embargo periods and release schedules.

4. *Access, sharing and re-use*: expands on the above, by addressing who are the likely re-users, and when and how the data might be accessed.

5. *Short-term storage and data management*: provides specifics during the research project lifetime, e.g., when data are likely to be only available to team members, or if there are likely to be large resource requirements, and specifying data volumes and formats.

6. *Deposit and long-term preservation:* need to be addressed where the usefulness of a dataset is likely to outlive the interest or career of the original researcher/s. Aspects to consider include selection, appraisal, and future discovery, access and preservation.

7. *Resourcing:* the human, financial and infrastructure resources that are required for the short- and long-term management of the data.

8. *Adherence and review:* how the plan will be adhered to, how often it will be reviewed, and who will be responsible for these activities.

9. *Statement of agreement:* formalises the plan, especially in the case of multi-partner projects.

10. *Annexes:* may be included, e.g., contact details and expertise of nominated data managers, glossary of technical terms, references to previous versions of the plan (if appropriate) (Donnelly, 2012, pp. 93–94).

Each of the components above has multiple parts.

Data management planning tools and resources

There are many tools and resources created to assist researchers with data management planning. Researchers beginning data management planning need to first consult with research collaborators (or supervisors in the case of research higher degree students), consider disciplinary norms, and check the data management and reporting requirements of their institutions, collaborators and research fund granting bodies. Many of these people and bodies may have quite explicit requirements and guidelines. If not, Box 21.1. contains examples of some useful tools and resources for beginning research data planners.

Box 21.1

Data management planning tools and resources

Tools for reference. Book mark for referral in your research practice.

Australian National Data Service (ANDS) data management planning resources
http://ands.org.au/datamanagement/index.html

Australian National Data Service (ANDS) data management plans
http://ands.org.au/guides/data-management-planning-awareness.html

Digital Curation Centre checklist, and online planning tool and other resources
http://www.dcc.ac.uk/resources/data-management-plans

Purdue University data management plan (DMP) self-assessment tool
http://purr.purdue.edu/resources/14/download/DMP_Self_Assessment.pdf

Queensland University of Technology data management planning tools
https://dmp.qut.edu.au/

UK Data Archive. Create and Manage Data
http://www.data-archive.ac.uk/create-manage

University of California, DMP Tool
https://dmp.cdlib.org/

Conclusion

This chapter has explored the reasons researchers, institutions and information managers need to plan for the management of research data. It has also examined the processes involved and the basic components of a data management plan. Different management processes and plans are required for different types of research and data. For example, when small amounts of data are collected or the data are simple transcriptions of interviews or small surveys, data management plans may only need to be minimal and adaptable to the immediate research. As the scale of the project or the data collection increases, where the number of people involved is large, or where the data may have a use beyond its original purpose (i.e., be suitable for re-use or sharing), then data management plans need to become more explicit and complete (Borgman, 2007). This chapter provides the basic foundational concepts and reasons for researchers to plan and manage their data and concludes with the links to some tools and resources useful for data management planning.

References

Borgman, C. L. (2006). What can studies of e-learning teach us about collaboration in e-research? Some findings from digital library studies. *Computer Supported Cooperative Work, 15*(4), 359–383.

Borgman, C. L. (2007). *Scholarship in the digital age: Information, infrastructure, and the Internet*. Boston: MIT Press.

Cragin, M. H., Palmer, C. L., Carlson, J. R., & Witt, M. (2010). Data sharing, small science and institutional repositories. *Philosophical Transactions of the Royal Society A: Mathematical, Physical and Engineering Sciences, 368*(1926), 4023–4038.

Data Documentation Initiative (DDI). (2012). *Why use DDI?* Retrieved from http://www.ddialliance.org/training/why-use-ddi.

Digital Curation Centre (DCC). (n.d.). *DMP Online*. Retrieved from https://dmponline.dcc.ac.uk/.

Donnelly, M. (2012). Data management plans and planning. In G. Pryor (Ed.), *Managing research data*. London: Facet.

Henty, M., Weaver, B., Bradbury, S. J., & Porter, S. (2008). *Investigating data management practices in Australian universities.* Canberra: Australian Partnership for Sustainable Repositories. Retrieved from http://apsr.anu.edu.au/orca/investigating_data_management.pdf

Higgins, S. (2008). The DCC curation lifecycle model. *International Journal of Digital Curation, 3*(1), 134–145.

Higgins, S. (2012). The lifecycle of data management. In G. Pryor (Ed.), *Managing research data* (pp. 17–45). London: Facet.

Kennan, M. A. (2016). *Data management: Knowledge and skills required in research, scientific and technical organisations.* Paper presented at IFLA World Library and Information Congress, 82nd IFLA General Conference and Assembly 13–19 August, Columbus, OH. Retrieved from http://library.ifla.org/1466/1/221-kennan-en.pdf.

Latour, B. (1987). *Science in action.* Cambridge, MA: Harvard University Press.

Markauskaite, L. (2010). Digital media, technologies and scholarship: Some shapes of eResearch in educational inquiry. *Australian Educational Researcher, 37*(4), 79–101.

Markauskaite, L., Kennan, M. A., Richardson, J., Aditomo, A., & Hellmers, L. (2012). Investigating eResearch: Collaboration practices and future challenges. In A. Juan, T. Daradoumis, M. Roca, S. Grasman, & J. Faulin (Eds.), *Collaborative and distributed e-research: Innovations in technologies, strategies and applications* (pp. 1–33). Hershey, PA: IGI Books.

Murray-Rust, P. (2008). Open data in science. *Serials Review, 34*(1), 52–64.

NHMRC/ARC/Universities Australia. (2007). *Australian code for the responsible conduct of research.* Canberra: Australian Government. Retrieved from https://www.nhmrc.gov.au/guidelines-publications/r39

NHMRC/ARC/AVCC. (2007, updated 2015). *National statement on ethical conduct in human research.* Canberra, Australian Government. Retrieved from https://www.nhmrc.gov.au/guidelines-publications/e72.

Oliver, G., & Harvey, R. (2016). *Digital curation* (2nd ed.). London: Facet.

Pryor, G. (Ed.) (2012). *Managing research data.* London: Facet.

Rice, R. (2009). *DISC-UK datashare project: Final report.* Bristol: JISC. Retrieved from http://repository.jisc.ac.uk/336/1/DataSharefinalreport.pdf.

Wallis, J., Borgman, C., Mayernik, M., & Pepe, A. (2008). Moving archival practices upstream: An exploration of the life cycle of ecological sensing data in collaborative field research. *International Journal of Digital Curation, 1*(3), 114–126.

Williamson, K., Kennan, M. A., Johanson, G., & Weckert, J. (2016). Data sharing for the advancement of science: Overcoming barriers for citizen scientists. *Journal of the Association of Information Science and Technology, 67*(10), 2392–2403.

Witt, M. (2009). Institutional repositories and research data curation in a distributed environment. *Library Trends, 57*(2), 191–201.

Chapter 22

Research writing and dissemination

Mary Anne Kennan and Kim M. Thompson
Charles Sturt University, Australia

This chapter begins by reinforcing the integral role of writing and dissemination in the research process, while acknowledging that writing and dissemination practices vary from discipline to discipline, field to field. Despite these differences, there are characteristics and processes that most research writing and dissemination have in common, and these are discussed here. From the general structure of a research report to the importance of writing throughout the research process, key aspects of research writing are addressed after which dissemination and publishing are defined and major and emerging forms of publication are described. The chapter concludes with a discussion of peer review and the ethics of authorship.

Research Methods: Information, Systems, and Contexts. DOI: http://dx.doi.org/10.1016/B978-0-08-102220-7.00022-4

Introduction

An archaeologist who uncovers the remains of an ancient civilization, extracts the mummies, skeletons, artworks and other objects, puts them in a warehouse, studies them, and then locks the door and never shares insights or analyses with peers, the profession, or the public, could be said to be engaging in grave robbing, not research. Research is incomplete until it is communicated, used, disseminated and further developed within a community (Borgman, 2007). Research is used to inform policy, drive practice, expand understandings of related phenomena, and advance theory in order to further research. Decision-makers should be able to access and use your research to make decisions, improve services, understand the community and user needs, and to know of advances in the field.

Research is published and disseminated in many formats, for example: journal articles, conference papers, book chapters, research monographs, reports, and grey literature. Writing up research, whether for examination or for dissemination through publication, is different from essay or general report writing and the writing style, length, structure and format depends on the outlet. Conference papers are often shorter than full journal articles; dissertations or theses usually are much more detailed than monographs; a research website may include only general information about the project or findings. Each type of publication is written for a different audience. Knowing your audience and the expectations for research dissemination in your field is imperative because every field is different.

Some research writing is disseminated to a very specific audience. This applies to research proposals, discussed below; other research reports and papers may also be written for a very limited audience (such as proprietary or corporate studies). Although proposals and proprietary reports will typically have explicit structure and formatting instructions to which the writer must adhere, most research writing is unguided and so understanding general research writing and dissemination principles and practices will help beginning researchers confidently navigate the research dissemination process. This chapter provides an introduction to the research writing process, research dissemination and publication, and related ethical issues.

Where to start

It is important to become familiar with the key influential works in your field. Sometimes books are the resources that contain the seminal definitions, theories, and broad-brush overviews you will need to know, but journal articles may be where you can find the latest advances related to your area of study. When considering whether to publish your study findings as a book or as a series of journal articles, think about which venue would allow you to have a greater impact on the field. In academe, it is thought to be important for researchers to try to disseminate findings to as wide a population as possible. However, some journals and book publishers are considered to have more credibility and/or esteem than others and so the ranking or reviewing of books, journals, or articles is not uncommon. Journals can be ranked based on number of subscriptions: a journal that has 5000 subscribers is likely to have a greater impact than the journal that has 50 subscribers. Citation counts can also be used to assess impact: if a book or article is cited in 150 other publications, the work is noted as having a higher impact than one that is seldom cited or not cited at all. (See Chapter 10: *Bibliometric research*, for a discussion of these issues.) Another way to assess the value of a manuscript is through peer assessment, where scholars in the field evaluate the overall quality of the work. When deciding where to publish your research, start by reading journals and books that you have found useful in the literature review of your research project, and discuss potential publication outlets with supervisors, colleagues and mentors.

When you decide to submit an article to a journal, read the guidelines for authors and the journal's aims and scope, read through the journal's tables of contents, and read some articles published over the last couple of years before deciding upon it as a publication outlet for your research. Look for journal trends: What has occupied the pages of the journal over the past few years? Is there a call for papers in which your research fits? Has the journal published other works that relate to the main themes or topics you research? Are there editorial pieces in past issues indicating an interest in your research topics? Finally, check whether the journal's style is a fit with your own style and that of your research. Are the articles written in plain language, highly theoretical, or somewhere in between? Is there a balance of theoretical work, literature review, and empirical research including case studies, or does the journal focus on one type of article, or one narrow domain? Does the journal have a particular methodological slant?

It is also important to have an audience in mind when selecting a venue for publication. Some book publishers focus only on textbooks or only publish works related to particular topics or themes. With regard to journals, some have a deeply scholarly approach and require rigorous research methods, with deep description and often challenging applications of theory. These journals target experienced researchers and are generally best avoided by the novice researcher and those writing about practice-based research.

Book and journal publishers have different lengths of time from submission to publication. These time frames can vary from a couple of months to a couple of years. In summary, given that there are many issues to consider that can minimise the prospect of rejection, it is important to spend a bit of time on deciding where and how you will disseminate your results well before you reach the final writing up stages.

The research writing process

Research writing, as all writing, needs to be readable. Key terms need to be defined, theories and contexts clearly explained, the scope of the project delineated, and the significance and purpose of the study stated.

Research often commences with writing a proposal directed to faculty committees for dissertations/theses or to funding bodies for research grants. Research proposals are a specific form of writing and are not typically published or widely distributed. A research proposal is essentially a plan written to a specific audience of readers, so it is important to know how much your readers will know about your topic and how much to include and exclude. Proposals are intended to persuade the reader to support, fund, or approve a research idea or project. All research proposals must describe the topic to be researched, the specific research questions or problems, and why the research needs to be done. Proposals also explain exactly how the research will be conducted, including the methodology (which includes paradigm, method/s and technique/s), and outline in detail the resources that will be required and the estimated time each aspect of the research will take. Universities, the faculties within them, as well as grant funding bodies will each have their own guidelines and requirements for layout and content of proposals, which must be closely followed to increase the chances for the acceptance of proposals. The audience for the proposal therefore determines the approach to be taken.

In relation to the reporting of research, there are some normative structures and guidelines that can help new researchers navigate the research writing process, as discussed below.

Structure

Research outputs tend to have a standard structure. The most basic outline for research reporting is:

- introduction and background;
- literature review;
- methodology (which includes paradigm/s, research method/s and technique/s);
- analysis (which, in some fields, may be considered as part of 'methodology');
- findings and discussion; and
- conclusion.

The introduction will state the research problem and the purpose of the research, the scope and significance of the study, and provide a thesis statement or central argument, including assumptions that guide the rest of the report. The literature review is a focussed summary of relevant publications and research that informed and guided the study. The methodology encompasses a critical analysis of the paradigm, the strategy for linking research problems and questions with a particular approach, and the particular research methods and techniques used to answer the research questions or understand the phenomena. Not every research report discusses its full theoretical framework. Some journals expect a detailed methodology, and others prefer just a methods section. The analysis section includes how the data were analysed, clearly specifying what statistics were used, if any, and, how theories or frameworks helped in understanding the data. Findings are what were discovered through the research process, and the conclusion is a wrap-up of findings and discussion, a restatement of the thesis, and sometimes a statement of where you think the next step in the research process should go.

Not all research writing must conform to the above writing structure. More creative representations can be found in such resources as Marvasti's (2008) chapter 'Writing and presenting social research' and Creswell's (2014) *Research Design*. New researchers will also see a variety of ways to formally present research as they read the literature of their field and work on their literature review.

Reviewing the literature

As the famed scientist-researcher Sir Isaac Newton (Feb 5, 1676) wrote to his colleague Robert Hooke, "If I have seen further it is only by standing on the shoulders of giants." In other words, by reviewing what others have contributed to the field already, the researcher can bring the research to a new and higher level. A literature review will be developed from books, journal articles, dissertations/theses, websites and, as available, reports, white papers and any other relevant material. It is important to remember that not everything about a given topic is retrievable using a *Google* or even a *Google Scholar* search. Academic library databases and catalogues should be used, and academic librarians, who are trained as experts with particular databases, can be called upon to ensure that the literature search is exhaustive. While it may not be possible to find or read everything on a particular topic, it is important to make your searching of the literature as comprehensive as possible and to continue to monitor the literature on the topic throughout your research project (Boell & Cecez-Kecmanovic, 2010; McKibbon, 2006).

A review of the literature not only provides you with knowledge of what research has previously been done so that you do not unintentionally repeat work that has already been completed, but it also sets up a basis for the importance of your study. You will note deficiencies in the current body of literature. No research project answers all possible questions about a particular topic. Often these limitations will be identified by the author or authors in the 'suggestions for future research' or 'limitations of the study' sections. Your research should clearly state how your study fills the gaps left by others. When writing up your research, you will likely read many more works than you actually cite in your literature review. This is normal. Your literature review is not a reading log, but rather it should succinctly review that which is relevant to the actual piece that you are writing. Detailed instructions for writing literature reviews can be found in texts such as Hart (2014) and Bates (1992). Chapter 2: *The fundamentals of research planning* and Chapter 5: *The methodological landscape* (in this book) also discuss the preparation and writing of literature reviews.

Writing as you research

Rather than waiting until the research project is complete, writing about your research as you go will help you make certain that you are fair and accurate in your write-up, that you include all the relevant steps you have taken in your study, and ensure that your analysis is completely represented and has a logical flow. Writing as you go serves other purposes too. Latour (2005, p. 127) suggested that writing textual accounts are the social scientist's laboratory, that the writing up of research not only prepares the research for others to read, but also is a part of the research process. You should expect to revise sections of the report as your analyses unfold, rewriting your introduction or literature review to include more background or deleting some as the focus of your research evolves and changes. You may need to add more detail to your methodology section to support your findings and analyses as the writing progresses. This is part of the research writing process and should be expected; give yourself enough time to draft and redraft as required. Writing well can take weeks or months of time and requires many revisions and a piece of written work may have many iterations before it is 'finished'.

Study significance

Research writing needs to clearly delineate what is learned from the research and answer the 'so what?' question. So what if 90 out of 100 users can find the needed document from the database? So what if a reference interviewer asks leading or biased questions? So what if the software crashes 0.01 percent of the time? Be explicit in your discussion of how these findings can and should be interpreted and why they are important. What effect might the research have on users? While it is important to be aware that not all research is generalisable *per se*, how might your research affect general practices? Be conscious and clear about who benefits from the research. Do the findings imply changes to services and practice? Do they contribute to better theoretical understanding? Can policy be affected or practice improved by what you have discovered from your research? What further research questions arise from these findings?

Guides for authors

At some point during the research process you will need to decide where you will send your paper for review and publication. The review process will be discussed further below, but at this point it is important to note that each journal or conference and each book publisher has a different scope, different audience, and could have different submission and review processes. Guides for authors are usually found on the front or back inside covers of journals and on conference and publisher websites. You will want to be familiar with the publisher's guidelines for author rights and copyright, structure and citation guidelines, how tables and graphs should be presented, and other ethical and formatting issues.

Formatting, style, and citation

Editors of books and journals usually have standardised formatting and style guidelines. Common guidelines include the American Psychological Association (APA), Chicago, Turabian, Harvard and Modern Language Association (MLA). Handbooks for each of these well-known styles are available in libraries and some very basic formatting instructions can be found online, for example via university learning centres. Publishers and editors will specify the citation style in the guide for authors.

Citation is the way we demonstrate that we are familiar with relevant literature and acknowledge the intellectual parentage of, and relationships between, our research and the research of others. It also provides a method of supporting our arguments with the work of others who have done research in a similar area. Tracking the use of seminal works in the field is another purpose. Discovering whom key authors have cited and who has cited key authors will lead you to other, related literature.

You will need to be sure you do not plagiarise others or yourself in your different outputs. Cutting and pasting large chunks of text (even if it is from your own work) to use in multiple publications is not generally acceptable. When you refer to or use your own and other published works, you must provide a formal citation (AIS, 2015; NHMRC, 2007).

Revising, editing and proofing

Interviewer: How much rewriting do you do?

Hemingway: It depends. I rewrote the ending of Farewell to Arms, *the last page of it, thirty-nine times before I was satisfied.*

Interviewer: Was there some technical problem there? What was it that had stumped you?

Hemingway: Getting the words right. (Plimpton, 1958)

It is not just writers of fiction who have to revise their work. All authors need to examine their work over and over again until it accurately communicates the message the text is intended to impart to the reader. Revision may involve changing the order of the content, including more or less information, or otherwise making the writing better able to convey the intended message and more understandable to the intended reader.

Once the revision is completed, the next task for the author is editing, that is, preparing the written work for publication. Editing involves the correction of spelling, punctuation, and grammar. Through self-editing, you may also find additional revisions are required. At this stage you will want to check your work against the publishers' guide for authors to ensure your work meets all the requirements in terms of style, format, length, and citations. This is not a quick process and so sufficient time should be allowed for these formatting and other self-editorial revisions.

The final step in this process is proofreading. This is where you give the work a final close read to correct any typographical errors or mistakes. It is important to do this before you submit your work for review or examination. Journal editors and reviewers do their work on a voluntary basis, so offer them the courtesy of making it less of an onerous task. Furthermore, a well written, revised, and edited work is easier to read and its message is clearer. Authors may go through many iterations of revision, editing, and proofing before they are satisfied with their work. It is also valuable at these stages to ask peers and mentors to provide feedback, to offer what is in essence a 'friendly review'.

Dissemination and publishing

To disseminate in the research context means to communicate, share or spread information or knowledge widely. This is referred to as scholarly communication. Scholarly communication can occur through formal and informal channels. Graham (2000) characterised scholarly communication as flowing through three channels: 1) informal networks, such as through conversations and seminars; 2) initial public dissemination, for example, via conferences, preprints or working papers; and 3) formal publishing through journals, books, and other similar outlets. Publishing has many meanings, the simplest is to make public. Usually, however, the term publishing refers to the process of the production and dissemination of literature or information. Sometimes it can also refer more specifically to the activity of preparing and issuing books, journals, and other written material for sale.

Types of formats

As mentioned earlier, research is disseminated in many formats. The different formats and dissemination methods serve different purposes and address different audiences. The most common ways to disseminate research in the information field include:

1. research reports
2. dissertations or theses
3. monographs or books
4. journal articles
5. conference presentations and papers.

Each of these types of dissemination routes has a different purpose and different audience and so needs to be approached in different ways. A single research study may result in multiple publications. You may end up with a conference presentation based on your literature review, one article focussing on methodology, and one or more additional articles arguing how your findings might influence policy, practice, future research, or theory. Journals, dissertations/theses, and other publications usually have a word count specified. A dissertation may run to 100,000 words, but a full journal article reporting findings from the dissertation could have a limit of 6,000 to 8,000 words. Rather than try to encapsulate your entire dissertation in one journal article, consider which audiences might be interested in different aspects of your findings or theories and plan to disseminate those particular pieces in appropriate outlets.

Research reports

Organisations providing grants, fellowships, scholarships, and other financial or data support will expect to receive reports of the research and results. Research partners external to your organisation may also request research reports as the study progresses. Reports can be written periodically throughout the research process. For example, quarterly reports may be written to keep associates informed about how the research is progressing and to let them know of interim findings and analyses; annual reports may be required for multi-year studies to demonstrate to funders that the research is on target and progressing at a reasonable rate and that the monies are being used wisely. These research reports are usually written for internal readers, those who have interest in how the money or data they have contributed is being used. The audience may consist of experts in the field, other researchers who have little or no knowledge of the field of your study or the methods you are using, or the reader could have no background in research whatsoever. It is important to know your potential reader and write at a level that will satisfy that group of individuals.

Dissertations/theses

A research dissertation or thesis will be expected to cover every aspect of the research process. Every university will have their own guidelines about how a dissertation or thesis should be structured and presented; when writing it is important to consult these guidelines in addition to consulting the members of your supervisory team. It is also very useful to read a selection of theses or dissertations in your field from your own institution and also from other universities. Dissertations and theses are available in academic libraries and online databases. Some universities ensure that electronic versions of new theses and dissertations are on open access.

The audience for a dissertation or thesis is primarily a committee or selection of expert examiners. Some of these readers may be experts in fields related to yours but not particularly familiar with exactly the same literature or topics you are reviewing and addressing with your research. Because of this, even dissertations and theses should be written in a readable fashion, defining all key terms and concepts and clearly explaining methods used, statistics presented, and all figures, charts, and graphs. The copyright of a dissertation or thesis is usually retained by the graduating doctoral or master's student.

Monographs

Research monographs can be reformatted editions of dissertations, theses, or other significant research reports. Monographs are published by university presses and commercial scholarly publishers. A point of difference is that authors may get a royalty payment for monographs, whereas for most other research dissemination, such as journal articles and conference papers, authors do not receive direct payment. As a commercial work, a monograph will typically be edited to be readable to a more general or specific audience, depending on to whom the publisher will be marketing the book. The readership of a research monograph will likely be individuals with varying levels of expertise in the field, ranging from students to academics, practitioners to lay people. When writing, you can assume the reader will have some interest in the topic, but he or she may not have much background in the field. Research monographs are usually peer-reviewed.

Edited books and chapters

Research can also be published as chapters in edited books, a compilation of articles or other material on the same subject but by different authors collected together in one book by an editor or editors. Edited books may be compilations of seminal articles previously published or can consist of previously unpublished chapters about new research findings. Editors may invite researchers to write one or more chapters about specific research findings or methodologies based on the invitee's expertise. Editors may also send out a general 'call for chapter proposals', on a topic around which a book is to be focussed. In this case, any researcher can submit a brief proposal. These proposals are then reviewed by the editor/s or peer-reviewed and, if accepted, the chapter is written by the researcher and then re-reviewed before publication.

Journal articles

Journals are aimed at a particular audience and may have specific topic or subject coverage, target explicit types of methodologies, and may even have a distinct tone. Each journal has different submission and acceptance rates, reviewing procedures, and editorial boards. Prestige is related to these factors. The articles in journals categorised as scholarly are peer-reviewed and relate to a particular academic discipline, field, or sub-field. Professional journals or magazines take articles that may not be peer-reviewed and may not always be research-based. Researchers can be very strategic about selecting journals in which to publish their work based on carefully considered criteria. Established authors understand that there are complex relationships between journals in their field and differentiations in rankings and reputations. Beginning researchers are advised to research these relationships in their field. In many fields there are articles discussing and ranking different journals, and often research evaluation exercises such as the Research Excellence Framework (REF) in the United Kingdom and the Excellence in Research for Australia (ERA) list or rank journals in different fields (c.f., ABDC, 2016; Nisonger & Davis, 2005; Haddow, 2008; Pember & Cowan, 2009).

Conference presentations and papers

Many researchers present their findings at regional, national, and international conferences. There are many different types of conferences – some professional, some scholarly, some combining research and practice. For conferences with a scholarly bent, full research papers are submitted and peer-reviewed, whereas at other conferences a paper is accepted after receipt of a proposal or abstract, and is more of a presentation than a paper. Most professional associations hold conferences which, among other things, disseminate research associated with that profession. Large international conferences are worthwhile dissemination venues. For library and information science, for example, the International Federation of Library Associations and Institutions (IFLA) is aimed at practising librarians, the Association for Information Science and Technology (ASIS&T) annual meetings are where practitioners and scholars come together, and then there are more academic conferences like Conceptions of Library & Information Science (COLIS).

Key information systems conferences are those affiliated with the Association of Information Systems (AIS) and can be international (The International Conference on Information Systems), regional (Pacific Asia Conference on Information Systems), or focussed on particular sub-fields. The archives field disseminates research at the Research Forum associated with the Annual Meeting of the Society of American Archivists, at the annual conferences of the various national societies of archivists, and at the International Conference on the History of Records and Archives (I-CHORA) every two years and the International Council on Archives Congress every four years.

In general, a good way to find out about appropriate conferences at which to disseminate your research is to talk to other people researching in your area of interest and to note which ones produce articles on your topic of interest. Note that, as with journals, conferences can vary in audience, approach, and quality. Even if your conference paper has a formal written component (which would generally be similar to a journal article), you need to think of the oral presentation component as being related but separate, concerned with keeping the audience's attention and fitting the time frame, as well as presenting the research.

Open access

Open access is a term that refers to using the internet and other technologies to deliver research publications freely to potential readers, not all of whom will have access to subscription-charging journals, books, or conference proceedings. There are two general types of open access publishing: gold and green. Gold open access or open access publishing is when authors deliberately select an online open access journal, conference or book publisher. There are many examples of open access journals listed in *The Directory of Open Access Journals* (DOAJ) supported by the Lund University Library. DOAJ (http://www.doaj.org) covers free, full text, quality-controlled scientific and scholarly journals.

Another route to open access is called green open access or self-archiving (Kennan & Wilson, 2006). Authors publish their work in traditional (subscription) access journals, but then also make a version of their work freely available through an open access repository. Repositories manage and disseminate digital works. Publications can be self-archived at either the pre- or post-peer review stage depending on the copyright agreement authors have with a publisher. You can check Sherpa RoMEO (http://www.sherpa.ac.uk/romeo/) for publisher policies on copyright and self-archiving. On doing so you will find a good proportion of publishers permit self-archiving. Alternatively when you sign the copyright or distribution agreement with a publisher you may negotiate for self-archiving rights. The focus of green open access is to provide access, not to provide all the functions provided by a journal. For example, the journal will still coordinate peer review.

Many institutions have their own open access repositories, often called institutional repositories. If yours does not, then disciplinary repositories cater for specific fields, for example: *E-LIS: E-prints in Library and Information Science* (http://eprints.rclis.org/) run by an international group of volunteers and supported by various organisations, and the Social Science Research Network (http://www.ssrn.com) co-hosted by a number of universities and other organisations, which has an information systems network.

Emerging forms of dissemination

Other internet-based online developments, such as e-lists, blogs, wikis, RSS Feeds, chat technologies and other Web 2.0 tools, also enable wide dissemination. Works published using these informal research communication and dissemination platforms do not undergo traditional peer review or other institutionalised certification, and so there is debate about their value. However, as their use matures, new forms of more informal, dynamic peer review may emerge (Hey & Trefethen, 2008). These tools can do more than just disseminate or make available the full text of research papers. With these new tools, research data can be integrated with books and journal articles to create a world that allows researchers and readers to see the whole knowledge production cycle (Fink, Kushch, Williams, & Bourne, 2008; Hey, Tansley, & Tolle, 2009). For example, readers of publications can not only see and use the original data, but also redo the analysis or combine the data with other data for other purposes. Moving images and visualisations could report research in ways other than textual formats. New ways to disseminate or make research public are constantly emerging and being evaluated by the research community (Markauskaite, Kennan, Richardson, Aditomo, & Hellmers, 2012).

Peer review and ethical writing

In any field of research, peer review is an important part of the research process, as it is used to uphold standards and offer credibility. The idea is that peers familiar with the literature, methodology, and the area of study of your paper can read for quality assurance. When a paper is submitted to a journal or conference, the editor generally sends it to two or three expert reviewers or referees. Multiple reviewers may give similar or contrasting reviews. For example, one reviewer may note that the publication needs more exploration of the literature, while another reviewer may consider the research to be sufficiently rigorous and well written for publication. In this case, the editor often makes the final decision, and a good editor will guide authors with regard to which of divergent paths suggested may be the most appropriate.

Before any research article or paper is accepted by a journal or conference, it will need to go through a peer review process. There are different kinds of review, for example:

Editorial review is when the editor or editorial board read and review the work, deciding whether or not to accept the paper, sometimes suggesting changes before the work will be accepted.

Blind review is when the author does not know who the reviewers are, but the reviewer is allowed to know whose work is being reviewed. The idea is that this allows the reviewer to be candid with recommendations.

The standard reviewing process among high quality journals and conferences is to use the *double blind review*. The author does not know who will be reviewing his or her work and the reviewer does not know whose work is under review. In this, an anonymised version of your submission is sent to at least two outside reviewers whom the editors regard as having appropriate expertise in the area of your research. The reviewers then assess the submission, providing detailed feedback, and make a recommendation as to whether it should be accepted or not and what changes, if any, are needed before publication.

Revisions post-review

It is rare for any submission, even those from experienced authors, to be accepted without change. The majority of articles require *some* amendments before they are ready to be published. Most reviewers work very hard to provide constructive feedback and authors should try not to take the critique personally. When you receive your referees' reports, you should go through them in detail and use them to develop a plan for revising your manuscript. You do not necessarily have to follow all the reviewers' instructions. As intimated above, sometimes reviewers' advice may be contradictory, or sometimes there may be compelling reasons not to make a suggested change. After you have completed your revisions, you should respond to the editors saying which changes you have made and where, and which changes you have not made and why you have not made them. They will then let you know whether they find this acceptable, require you to revise further, or find the article not acceptable for the particular outlet.

Inevitably some submissions are rejected. Read the referees' and editor's reasons for rejection carefully — it may simply been an indicator that you have not chosen the appropriate journal for your work, and you may need to search elsewhere for the right audience. After considering the reasons for rejection, think about whether another journal or conference might be a suitable alternative and if so, revise the manuscript accordingly and resubmit.

A dissertation or thesis does not go through peer review in the same sense that journal articles do; however, it is examined by experts in the field. Examiners are given specific instructions that may vary slightly institution by institution, and the process of examination is related to that of peer review.

The ethics of authorship

As an author writing up research you take responsibility for the research and how it was conducted. Authorship also confers ownership of the written work. Therefore it is important to exhibit honesty and integrity in all your research communications. It is important that new researchers make themselves aware of the particular ethical requirements that surround the dissemination and publication of research. A brief discussion of some of the issues follows. A plethora of ethics statements and codes of conduct with substantial sections on dissemination, publication and authorship (c.f. NHMRC, 2007; ICMJE, 2016) reflect the importance of the issue.

Examples of practices generally considered to be unethical include:

- publishing the same data in different forms in different journals unless it is acknowledged, as in the case of a research program where research is ongoing and later work builds on earlier work, or where the data is published in different ways for different audiences;

- submitting the same paper simultaneously to more than one journal in the hope of having at least one journal accept it or with the intent of withdrawing it from the journal that responds last;

- submitting works without all authors giving their active consent to being authors and approving both the submitted and published versions; and

- not acknowledging people who, and organisations which, contribute in substantial ways to the work, without actually being authors.

Sometimes determining who should be listed as an author and in what order authors should be listed can be difficult, especially where there are power relationships between the authors or where the research is conducted by teams comprising members from difficult disciplines with different research cultures. The first author gets the most credit and so they should also do most of the work.

Conflicts can arise over authorship, so it is best if the order and role of each author is discussed openly and agreed upon early in a research project. As conflicts can arise, the *Australian Code for the Responsible Conduct of Research* (NHMRC, 2007) has a section on dissemination and authorship based on the earlier Vancouver Convention (ICMJE, 2016). The most important sub-section is as follows:

> Attribution of authorship depends to some extent on the discipline, but in all cases, authorship must be based on substantial contributions in a combination of:
>
> - conception and design of the project,
> - analysis and interpretation of research data, and
> - drafting significant parts of the work or critically revising it so as to contribute to the interpretation.
>
> The right to authorship is not tied to position or profession and does not depend on whether the contribution was paid for or voluntary. It is not enough to have provided materials or routine technical support, or to have made the measurements on which the publication is based. Substantial intellectual involvement is required (NHMRC, 2007, section 5.1).

Conclusion

Writing up and disseminating research is a key component of the research process. This chapter has discussed the importance of dissemination, the research writing process, and the essential components of a research report. The practicalities of writing and dissemination were also addressed, including selecting the right publication outlet, the writing itself, reviewing, and the ethics of authorship. Writing may not be an easy task for beginners, and even seasoned researchers may find it difficult at times, but the importance of disseminating the insights, findings, methodologies, new and modified methods, theories, and analyses that result from our studies makes it a necessary part of the research process.

References

Association of Information Systems (AIS). (2015). AIS code of research conduct. *AIS Administrative Bulletin, 2014.0224.01*. Retrieved from https://c.ymcdn.com/sites/aisnet.org/resource/resmgr/Admin_Bulletin/AIS_Code_of_Research_Conduct.pdf.

Australian Business Deans Council (ABDC). (2016). *ABDC journal quality list*. Retrieved from http://www.abdc.edu.au/pages/abdc-journal-quality-list-2013.html.

Bates, M. J. (1992). Rigorous systematic bibliography. In H. D. White, M. J. Bates, & P. Wilson (Eds.), *For information specialists: Interpretations of reference and bibliographic work* (pp. 117–130). Norwood, NJ: Ablex Publishing.

Boell, S. K., & Cecez-Kecmanovic, D. (2010). Literature reviews and the hermeneutic circle. *Australian Academic & Research Libraries, 41*(2), 129–144.

Borgman, C. L. (2007). *Scholarship in the digital age: Information, infrastructure, and the Internet.* Cambridge, MA: MIT Press.

Creswell, J. W. (2014). *Research design: Qualitative, quantitative, and mixed methods approaches* (4th ed.). Los Angeles, CA: Sage.

Fink, J. L., Kushch, S., Williams, P. R., & Bourne, P. E. (2008). Biolit: Integrating biological literature with databases. *Nucleic Acids Research, 36*(supplement 2), W385–W389. Retrieved from http://nar.oxfordjournals.org/content/36/suppl_2/W385.full.

Graham, T. W. (2000). Scholarly communication. *Serials: The Journal for the Serials Community, 13*(1), 3–11.

Haddow, G. (2008). Quality Australian journals in the humanities and social sciences. *Australian Academic & Research Libraries, 39*(2), 13.

Hart, C. (2014). *Doing a literature review: Releasing the social science research imagination.* London: Sage Publications.

Hey, A. J. G., Tansley, S., & Tolle, K. M. (2009). *The fourth paradigm: Data-intensive scientific discovery.* Redmond, WA: Microsoft Research.

Hey, T., & Trefethen, A. (2008). E-science, cyberinfrastructure, and scholarly communication. In G. M. Olson, A. Zimmerman, & N. Bos (Eds.), *Scientific Collaboration on the Internet* (pp. 15–31). Cambridge, MA: MIT Press.

International Committee of Medical Journal Editors (ICMJE). (2016). *Recommendations for the conduct, reporting, editing, and publication of scholarly work in medical journals.* Retrieved from http://www.icmje.org/icmje-recommendations.pdf.

Kennan, M. A., & Wilson, C. S. (2006). Institutional repositories: Review and an information systems perspective. *Library Management, 27*(4/5), 236–248.

Latour, B. (2005). *Reassembling the social: An introduction to Actor-network-theory.* Oxford: Oxford University Press.

Markauskaite, L., Kennan, M. A., Richardson, J., Aditomo, A., & Hellmers, L. (2012). Investigating eResearch: Collaboration practices and future challenges. In A. Juan, T. Daradoumis, M. Roca, S. Grasman, & J. Faulin (Eds.), *Collaborative and distributed e-research: Innovations in technologies, strategies and applications* (pp. 1–33). Hershey, PA: IGI Books.

Marvasti, A. (2008). Writing and presenting social research. In P. Alasuutari, L. Bickman, & J. Brannen (Eds.), *The Sage handbook of social research methods* (pp. 602–616). Los Angeles: Sage.

McKibbon, K. A. (2006). Systematic reviews and librarians. *Library Trends, 55*(1), 202–215.

National Health and Medical Research Council (NHMRC). (2007). *Australian code for the Responsible conduct of research.* Retrieved from http://www.nhmrc.gov.au/_files_nhmrc/file/publications/synopses/r39.pdf.

Nisonger, T. E., & Davis, C. H. (2005). The perception of library and information science journals by LIS education deans and ARL library directors: A replication of the Kohl-Davis study. *College & Research Libraries, 66*(4), 341–377.

Pember, M., & Cowan, R. A. (2009). *Journal quality: An analysis of archives and manuscripts*. Paper presented at the Australian Society of Archivists Annual Conference, Perth, WA, 6–9 August 2008. Canberra, ACT: The Society. Retrieved from http://researchrepository.murdoch.edu.au/2885/1/journal_quality.pdf.

Plimpton, G. (1958, reprinted 2011). Ernest Hemingway, the art of fiction no. 21. *Paris Review, 18*. Retrieved from http://www.theparisreview.org/interviews/4825/the-art-of-fiction-no-21-ernest-hemingway.

Section V

Information Research: Reflections on Past and Future

In this section, the first chapter focuses principally on the future of information research, but links to past and current practices in doing this. Concluding reflections on the research journey concludes the section, and the book.

Chapter 23

The future of information research

Kirsty Williamson[1], Graeme Johanson[2], Alex Byrne[3],
Lisa M. Given[4], Mary Anne Kennan[5] and Gillian Oliver[2]
[1]*Monash University and Charles Sturt University, Australia* [2]*Monash University,
Australia* [3]*Former NSW State Librarian, Australia* [4]*Swinburne University of
Technology, Australia* [5]*Charles Sturt University, Australia*

This chapter is unusual in that it departs somewhat from the pattern of authorship and content in the rest of this book. The editors begin the chapter with a re-examination of some of the key themes of the book, for example, the focus on methodology as the entire framework or design of research: the choice of paradigm, methods and tools or techniques to explore research questions and to create new knowledge. The necessity for rigour in every stage of research is emphasised. Having stated reservations about efforts to gaze into a crystal ball, to predict a specific future for information research, the editors then draw on their own knowledge, as well as that of other expert researchers, specialists in specific areas, to help to identify future paradigms, research methods and data collection tools; the effects of big data; the role of cultural differences in future research; and the delicate (but essential) balance of keeping research relevant to professional practice, and vice versa. The main points of the chapter are illustrated with up-to-date examples, including an account of a fascinating PhD thesis which combines a postmodern paradigm, second generation (constructivist) grounded theory, and innovative data collection techniques.

Research Methods: Information, Systems, and Contexts. DOI: http://dx.doi.org/10.1016/B978-0-08-102220-7.00023-6

Introduction

In this chapter we attempt to gauge the present state of 'information research' and look into what the future might hold. The burgeoning of information technology will undoubtedly have a major long-term impact on future research. It will influence the kinds of questions that can be explored and open up exciting options for answering those questions. Already the possibilities of 'big data' for the growth of information research are recognised. Research questions and methodologies are also likely to be influenced by: developments in other disciplines which are likely to enrich and inform our research; the role of 'culture' in our multicultural society and its impact on information research, especially in relation to professional practice; and the research requirements of, and relationships with, professional practice, in general.

A number of authors have contributed to this chapter. In the first section on research methodology, the editors, Kirsty Williamson and Graeme Johanson – with input especially from Lisa Given, but also from Mary Anne Kennan and Alex Byrne – assess past and current methodologies in the information field and discuss possible future developments. Gillian Oliver discusses the likely role of 'culture' in information research of the future, especially in relation to policy implementation and professional practice and, at the end, Alex Byrne identifies many pressing questions about the future of relationships between researchers and professional practice. An example of a recent innovative PhD thesis is included at the end of the research methodology section of the chapter. It is interdisciplinary and illustrates several modern, fresh approaches to methodology.

Research methodology

The early training of information professionals did not emphasise research or a research mentality. Over time academic interest in methodologies of allied disciplines increased, and were incorporated into serious research projects. Professional practice did not benefit from early development of a research culture.

The past affects the future

Information research, along with social research in general, has developed greater sophistication over the years. Most of the later twentieth century saw an emphasis on quantitative approaches to research in the information field. In a standard reference, Busha and Harter (1980) recommended use of "scientific methods of investigation", only, and careful avoidance of "esoteric problems" which they associated with "theorists in information science" (p. xi). There was little recognition of epistemological or methodological questions. Few researchers were well versed in the philosophical underpinnings of research, including major paradigms; nor showed much interest in how this background knowledge could help to enhance research rigour. The key research method during this time was 'survey' but this was often not treated as a research design, but rather as a synonym for 'questionnaire'. Until 1985, in the library and information science (LIS) field, only 1.6 percent of researchers employed qualitative methods (Järvelin & Vakkari, 1993). For data collection, the emphasis was on questionnaires or structured interviews. As recently as 2015, researchers found that the largest single proportion (37 percent) of research approaches in library cataloguing, published between 2010 and 2014, relied on a survey approach (Terrill, 2015). Research mostly lacked depth, status and quality.

In the LIS field, the 1980s began to feel winds of change. Brenda Dervin's call for a shift of focus from information systems to information users (Dervin & Nilan, 1986) led to the inauguration in 1996 of a specific biennial conference, Information Seeking in Context (ISIC). This, in turn, encouraged research on 'human information behaviour' (HIB), often referred to simply as 'information behaviour', discussed further in Chapter 3: *Information Research*. HIB is one of the research areas where qualitative studies – often framed in the interpretivist paradigm, using methods such as ethnography and grounded theory – gathered momentum. The in-depth or semi-structured interview and observation became popular data-collection tools for qualitative researchers. At the same time, researchers in the field of information systems were initiating qualitative research, framed in both the post-positivist and interpretivist paradigms. The overall result has been much greater diversity in use of research methods and data-collection techniques or tools. Since the 1990s many more people in the information field have undertaken doctoral research and graduated with a PhD, bringing with them much greater understanding and knowledge of research methodology.

Nevertheless, as a paper (McKechnie, Chabot, Dalmer, Julien & Mabbott, 2016), delivered at the ISIC biennial conference attested, there is scope for improvement in terms of rigour, at least with regard to information behaviour research published in the 1996 to 2014 *ISIC Proceedings*.[1] After compiling a long list of possible rigour tactics, McKechnie *et al.* found that "both quantitative and qualitative empirical work is not being reported in ISIC papers in ways that clearly demonstrate research rigour, nor assure replicability". They quoted an article in the journal, *Nature* (Pagan & Torgler, 2015) which offered a succinct and seemingly useful checklist, labelled the 4Rs, for assessing research rigour: reproduction (provision of enough information to allow a study to be reproduced), replication (enough information to allow results in a reproduced study to be replicated), robustness (strong design) and revelation (communicating

---

[1] The ISIC Proceedings are now published by *Information Research: An International Electronic Journal*. http://www.informationr.net/

enough information to allow for accountability and transparency). Strong design is fundamental and is still often lacking in information research.

The question of rigour

This research methods book has attempted to encourage academic rigour in the use of research methodology, which is defined in Chapter 1: *Research concepts* as "the entire framework or design of the research: the choice of paradigm, methods and tools or techniques to explore research questions and to create new knowledge". A yearning for meticulous diligence in methodology and all aspects of research continues to grow in respected disciplines. Thus researchers in information systems write that the aim of information systems is:

> to develop a general conceptualization of truth and correctness that can be applied across all areas of research in IS. Essentially, this will specify criteria for evaluating the rigor and validity of the research whatever its particular philosophy or method [used] (Mingers & Standing, 2016).

While the editors of this book (from a background in LIS) were not prescriptive about how the other key authors (writing about the information systems and knowledge management field and archives and records) should write about methodology, there is a remarkable consistency in approach across all the core methodological chapters – 1, 2, 4, and 5. In Chapter 4: *Archival and recordkeeping research: Past, present and future*, Gilliland and McKemmish summed up the common approach of this book. They postulated that:

> Designing research encompasses identification of the research problem, goals and desired outcomes; selecting the methodology with reference to the philosophical and theoretical approaches that frame the research; selecting and integrating appropriate methods; identifying the most effective techniques of data collection and analysis; and iteratively implementing, evaluating and adapting the research design as the research unfolds.

Similarly, Cecez-Kecmanovic and Kennan, in Chapter 5: *The methodological landscape: Information systems and knowledge management*, a chapter particularly focussed on promoting rigour in research, proposed:

> We emphasise … the importance of methodology as an overall logic of inquiry that includes a set of assumptions or a paradigm as a foundation for conducting research and selecting and applying research methods and techniques. Research methodology thus enables researchers to make knowledge claims and argue contribution to knowledge.

Cecez-Kecmanovic and Kennan provide a very useful figure (Figure 5.1) titled 'The methodological landscape – from paradigms to methods to techniques' which illustrates those three layers and includes detailed commentary on them.

It is important to note that, in professional practice, data are collected to inform decision making and policy development irrespective of the need for the academic rigour espoused in this book. Continuation of this practice, without the compulsion of delving deeper into research methodology, should be encouraged. Rich data sets are being well managed in libraries for a variety of purposes and could be harnessed to support more extensive research projects.

The question of theory

Chu's (2015) study highlighted the rise of theoretical approaches beyond those reported by other scholars in previous studies. However, Julien and O'Brien's (2014) study found that there had been little change in the number of citations of theory in HIB studies, in particular (i.e., approximately 20-30%); overall, they found that the largest proportion (76%) of empirical studies in the field were a-theoretical (p. 244). Nevertheless, it is encouraging that a strongly theoretical paper (French & Williamson, 2016) won the 'best paper' award at the ISIC Conference in that year. In this case, the study combined literature analysis, ethnography and grounded theory analysis to create new theory: the concept of 'information bricolage' as used by welfare workers in their role of helping clients. Other projects have employed established theories to serve as lenses for data analysis or to shape the overall research design. Moring and Lloyd (2013), for example, explored the use of Theodore Schatzi and Etienne Wenger's practice theories as analytic tools for studies of information literacy.

Prophecy: 'From the lush jungle of modern thought' (A. D. Hope, 1975)

Looking into the future is fraught with a host of hazards, not the least of which is the tendency towards exaggerated speculation, even dire dystopias, at the expense of more reliable rigorous prognostications. It is a favourite preoccupation of information professionals to mull over the future (Mathews, 2014). Commendably, they have always peered early into the crystal ball, assessing the advisability of adoption of new information and communications technologies as they emerge (Weller, 2016). Since we do not claim to have a crystal ball, what then can be said of emerging research methodologies: paradigms, methods and techniques?

We know that technology will have a huge impact, as it has done in the recent past. Research stimulated by the availability of 'big data' is more likely to be in the realm of quantitative approaches, but mixed methods are likely also to be part of research where the catalyst is 'big data'. Many researchers still do not confront the 'paradigm' issue and this is likely to continue, although it will remain mandatory for quality PhD research. As intimated above, rigour and depth come from dealing with 'methodology', not just methods and techniques. Methods and techniques explain *how* to conduct research, without discussing *why* we choose to conduct research in a particular way, including the assumptions that underpin the choices. Moreover many researchers do not distinguish between 'methods' and 'techniques'. We acknowledge that the distinction is often tricky, but continue to maintain that, where there are well-established 'methods', with strong theoretical underpinnings (as is the case of those discussed in Chapters 6–14 – not an exhaustive list), then they should be distinguished as such. Our view is that data collection techniques or tools, such as questionnaires and interviews, which can be used in several different methods (e.g., with survey, ethnography, action research, grounded theory), are much better to be labelled as such. Despite our protestations, the lack of precision is likely to continue.

Paradigms of the future

Kuhn's (1970) widely-acknowledged definition of 'paradigm' is included in Chapter 1. Guba and Lincoln (1994, p. 107) discussed a paradigm as dealing with "ultimates or first principles". "It represents a worldview that defines for its holder, the nature of the 'world', the individual's place in it, and the range of possible relationships to that world ...". As indicated in Chapter 5, the three widely known paradigms in information systems and knowledge management are the positivist and post-positivist, interpretive, and critical paradigms. The authors indicate that postmodern, feminist and sociomaterial paradigms (the latter of which explores the interaction of technology, society and organisations) are the less well-established or emerging ones.

In the other two fields specifically covered in this book – archives and record keeping and LIS – the two commonly used paradigms are 'positivist' and 'interpretivist', although it is important to note that Chapter 1 labels 'interpretivist' as an 'umbrella' paradigm, encompassing a range of other paradigms (e.g., constructivism, widely used in the LIS field, and phenomenology). As Chapter 1 warned, research terminology is fluid and poses a challenge for the uninitiated. The postmodern paradigm is likely to become popular in these fields because of its emphasis on flexibility and reflexivity. An example of its recent use, in PhD research in the archives and records discipline, is included below. An example of a study, which draws on phenomenology (Gorichanaz, 2015), is mentioned in Chapter 1 and Chapter 13: *Ethnographic research* (and also in the next section).

It is important to note the ongoing tension which exists between the concept of a paradigm and the theory of postmodernism. The dilemma is illustrative of the type of fuzzy boundaries that can be created by theoretical discourse. The philosophical issue is this: if a researcher wishes to adopt a strict postmodern paradigm, the idea of paradigm becomes anathema altogether. Postmodernism by its nature requires the removal of intellectual (and other) structure. Postmodernism removes itself from epistemological rationalisation (Fuller, 2015): "For the past four decades postmodernism has left a distinctive anti-epistemological legacy that is present today in both the postmodernists and their opponents" (p. 264).

Qualitative research methods of the future

Although ethnography is well-established in anthropology, sociology, and education, this method has not been used as widely as it could be in the information field. It is method which is likely to grow in information research in the future. This is because of the many variants and innovative possibilities that it offers. One recent example is autoethnography. An interesting, innovative PhD study, undertaken in the College of Computing & Informatics, Drexel University, USA (Gorichanaz, 2015), combines autoethnography with phenomenological analysis and systematic self-observation. It is a good example of mixed methods approaches. A staged autoethnographical study (Anderson & Fourie, 2015) is reported in Chapter 13.

Digital ethnography appears likely to be a productive method of the future. It is a branch of ethnographic research which acknowledges the place in human experience of digital media. Digital ethnography conceptualises and studies the mediating nature and function of digital technologies, which may be embodied in the context of a study or be used as tools for researching the social world. An early example of digital ethnography (Al-Saggaf, 2012; Al-Saggaf & Williamson, 2004) is described in Chapter 13.

An exciting initiative is RMIT University's Digital Ethnographic Research Centre (DERC). The Centre examines how people perceive, make sense of and understand their surroundings, often through techniques that use digital technologies or that focus on the use of these technologies. A broad range of project-led research interests is encompassed in the Centre. One focus is on understanding a contemporary world where digital technologies are increasingly inextricable from the environments and relationships in which everyday life plays out. Another is the experience of public spaces during moments of spatial transformation. As a group, the team is interdisciplinary, with wide experience in innovative, reflexive and ethical ethnographic approaches, developed through anthropology, geography, media and cultural studies, design, creative arts and documentary practice, and games research. Joanne Mihelcic who completed her PhD in archival science at the Faculty of Information Technology at Monash University, is currently a researcher at this centre. (http://www.rmit.edu.au/research/research-institutes-centres-and-groups/research-centres/digital-ethnography-research-centre)

A new, emerging method has its roots in theories from urban geography, for example, Lefebvre's spatial dialectics discussed in Leckie and Given (2010), as well as those from other disciplines, including digital humanities and information studies. The end result is a new approach for gathering and analyzing data about library users that is multi-disciplinary and theoretically based. (See Given and Archibald, 2015.)

In terms of foreseeing the information future, the Delphi method is a well-known, systematic approach which could be used more extensively than it has been. The Delphi method asks separate specialists about their views of the likelihood and desirability of prescribed future events or stated future scenarios. An independent facilitator reviews their predictions and feeds them back in summary form to the experts, for a second and third round of reflection and consensus-building. The elicited group view is considered more reliable than individual prognostication (Surowiecki, 2004), a claim which may not apply universally, but which certainly can be demonstrated to apply in many circumstances (Lanier, 2017). The first author's first research methods book provided a chapter on the Delphi method (Williamson, 2002).

The Delphi method functions like recent uses of crowdsourcing, and may well be replaced by it in the near future, because it is based on a fundamental belief in the virtues of the concept of collective wikis and the collation of online opinions. A wiki is a knowledge base created co-operatively by a community of interested people, allowing them to add and edit their own content. In effect, wikis perform the function that the several rounds of surveys perform in the Delphi method.

The advent of 'big data'

Quantitative research is likely to be dominated by the increasing availability of 'big data', an important recent technological and social innovation offering exciting research possibilities. 'Big data' are gathered with little to no human assistance through automatic, remote and networked sensors. Thus the quantity of the data increases exponentially (Gray 2007, cited by Hey, Tansley & Tolle, 2009). Yaqoob *et al.* (2016, p. 1233) noted that "the world's data volume is expected to grow 40% per year, and 50 times by 2020 [so that] data production in 2020 will be 44 times larger than it was in 2009".

Complex issues arise not only about how data can be collected, but they also need to be arranged, analysed, and used transparently and effectively. One question is: Do the data themselves suggest potential topics for investigation or use? 'Big data' will throw up some interpretable patterns, but researchers are still needed to hypothesise from surveillance of the data. Another question, warranting further investigation, is about the intellectual processes involved in selection of one set of data for analysis, and rejection of another. Currently our mental models are guided by questions about what we know already. A lot of data analysis can be automated, but many hypothetical interpretations still require additional human intervention.

The management of 'big data' raises at least three urgent questions for future information research: (1) Do 'big data' embrace and enhance the social sciences and humanities as well as the sciences? (2) Are new paradigms, methods and analysis tools required to make them useful? (3) Will old information theories continue to have relevance? The hope is that information research might fit at the heart of the answers to these questions.

Indeed there is already a role for libraries in maintaining data stores that can be interrogated by researchers. This is most evident among university libraries (e.g., the University of NSW) but data stores are already a feature of state and national libraries, as well as some special libraries. The growing mass digitisation of large collections (especially by the National Library of Australia and the State Library of NSW) is offering to researchers very large data sets which are amenable to a variety of research processes. They include language searching (e.g., to test the emotional character of different periods through the emotive tone of the words used in newspapers); artificial intelligence applied to digitised images or maps (to study various features or simply to generate descriptive metadata); and mashups of diverse datasets to generate new understandings. Libraries' own data, from client interactions and other processes, are already being used to provide more fine-grained understanding of client behaviours and interests, and to improve library processes.

Mashups of diverse library datasets (text, graphics, sound) can produce entirely new creations, which reconfigure digital data sources into fresh history. A multi-media online history of a city is an example (Brown-May, Elkner, & Reeves, 2007). Three-dimensional historical reconstructions of legends also become possible (McKee, 2013).

Data collection and analysis techniques or tools

There are many approaches which may not be 'new' per se, but are now being adopted and adapted by researchers in the information field. It is impossible to say how much they will grow or shrivel. A review of past winners of the Association for Library and Information Science's (2017) ALISE/ProQuest Methodology Paper Award, for example, outlines card-sorting, observational 'traffic sweeps' (discussed above), and vignettes as just a few of the data collection tools to gain attention in recent years. Chapter 17: *Observation*, reported a 'traffic sweeps' project (Given & Leckie, 2003). Examples of other data-gathering tools, recently taken up in LIS, are 'think aloud protocol' and 'transaction log analysis' (Chu, 2015).

The rise in visual approaches in data collection is another trend, both in qualitative studies involving human participants and in quantitative research projects involving analyses of large datasets. Some qualitative researchers, for example, have engaged participants increasingly in arts-based research methods, using photographs, videos, drawings, collages, or other visual tools. Hartel and Thomson's (2011) review article presented a number of strategies for researchers wishing to include photographic techniques in their research designs. Hartel (2014) has also published an overview of an arts-based method she developed to explore people's understandings of the concept of 'information,' where participants engaged in a drawing and writing activity to represent their views. Similarly, Julien, Given and Opryshko (2013) gave participants disposable cameras as part of a photovoice approach, designed to document university students' campus information experiences. Given and Willson (2015) explored humanities scholars' collaborative information behaviours by combining in-depth interviews method with a guided exploration of web-based research visualisation tools. In this study, participants' use of online tools was documented with screen-sharing over Skype, enabling the participants to share their reflections with the research team while using the tools in real time, rather than as part of a purely retrospective interview protocol. The end result is a more robust interview approach with usage examples examined directly at point of use.

Other researchers have increasingly adopted new technologies to explore new information platforms or to extend the usefulness of existing approaches by analysing large, online datasets. Lomborg and Bechmann (2014), for example, discussed the usefulness of application programming interfaces (APIs), particularly for quantitative analyses of social media datasets. The use of these types of tools, alongside webcrawlers and network analysis software, allow researchers to harvest and analyse user data on Twitter, Facebook, and other social networking platforms. Skeggs and Yuill (2016) described the use of four different techniques to harness 'big data' available via Facebook (questionnaires, interviews, custom-designed software tools and data visualisations). The role of 'social networking' in information and communication is likely to be of increasing interest to information researchers. Similarly, Bruns and Liang (2012) discussed the potential of Twitter for gathering real-time user information during natural disasters. Equally Twitter is a primary source of intelligence about terrorists in action (Fiegerman, 2016).

An example of an innovative PhD thesis

Joanne Mihelcic wrote a PhD thesis titled "The Experiential Model of the Person-Centred Record: A Social Constructionist Grounded Theory" (Mihelcic, 2016). This thesis demonstrates some of the emerging methodological approaches discussed above. The thesis was an interdisciplinary work, enabled by the diverse background of the researcher. Joanne's academic and professional experience have spanned: health, education, performing arts, media, knowledge management and archival science. The study involved working with people diagnosed with early stage dementia to understand how their personal stories, and the recording of those stories, supported their memory, identity and personhood. This research was supported by an Alzheimer's Australia Postgraduate Research Scholarship in Dementia.

Joanne's framework embodies the postmodern paradigm and constructivist thinking, with its emphasis on flexibility and reflexivity; these characteristics complement records continuum theory which recognises the layers of context and meaning that can be associated with a record (McKemmish, 2001). Joanne was particularly concerned with "the way relationships between researcher, participant and research data are both inseparable and the product of their combined interactions". (Mihelcic, 2016, p. xiii) The social constructionist paradigm, with its emphasis on socially constructed meanings (discussed in Chapter 1), was fundamental to the research.

The method chosen for the study was second generation grounded theory (constructivist grounded theory), which places an emphasis on reflexive and interpretive practice and is well suited to postmodern and constructivist paradigms. (See Chapter 9: *Constructivist grounded theory: A 21st century methodology*.)

The data collection tools used in the research, apart from the extensive use of interviews, also included some of the most recent and innovative ones being used by researchers in the information field. The constant comparative method and mapping were implemented for the collection and analysis of data, as per Clarke's (2005) discussion of grounded theory after the postmodern turn. Vignettes were created and used for exploring participants' personal stories, events, actions and context. Vignettes offered an opportunity to engage study participants actively in producing, reflecting on, and learning from the data and presenting their stories in their own terms. The final set of vignettes, using each participant's own words and 'voice', with supporting images, formed what Joanne called a 'life book'. Photographs/visual representations were used where possible as part of the vignettes. Some of these came from participants' collections; others were taken during the course of interviews.

Joanne's thesis is well worth a closer look. It is an inspirational piece of work. Below, issues associated with another characteristic of the modern world, in multi-cultural societies, is discussed.

Cultural differences in future information research

In a sense, the prior discussion of 'big data' of itself raised many cultural issues about the implicit social and economic values of large-scale new technologies, bringing with them pressure for umbrella global research projects that will bring fresh attitudes from large multi-disciplinary teams. There are hazards.

The first problem is the threat of excessive homogeneity in data collection and analysis. A degree of homogeneity is necessary for any collaboration, but undesirable if it eliminates entirely 'the interesting underlying' aberrant signals that can emerge from large repositories of data (Randall, 2012). From another angle, in large research teams with representatives from many nationalities and backgrounds, cultural sensitivities must play some role in the formulation and dissemination of research knowledge. It is hard to imagine that the 5,154 physicists who co-authored one single science article were all culturally on the same page (Castelvecchi, 2015). Another social problem with monoculture is neglect of national difference (not in a xenophobic sense). For instance, Australia has for decades maintained a 'universal service obligation' for its telecommunications companies (Nicholls, 2017), as it does for the equitable sharing of other public knowledge (Usherwood, 2016). These are values that may not be widely shared. Such cultural values demand respect from researchers, and often lie unarticulated behind projects.

In the future there will be a need to maintain respect for the habits of traditional disciplinary territories and to ensure permanent digital preservation of small-scale, local cultural memory. These issues, and more, are discussed by Monash University Associate Professor, Gillian Oliver, who wrote the following.

Over the past two decades, trends in internationalism and globalisation have impacted on the development and implementation of information and communication technologies (e.g., facilitating increasing collaborative working and enhanced cross-border data flows). They have both challenged and stimulated research into cultural differences. At the beginning of the millennium it was argued that, despite widespread belief that the globalisation of business would lead to greater standardisation of information technology, local cultures would still lead to organisations adapting standard practices, rules and technologies to suit their own environments (Weisinger and Trauth, 2002).

The strength and resilience of local cultures have attracted the attention of many researchers, particularly those working in the information systems discipline. In 2006, Leidner and Kayworth published a literature review of information technology and culture (Leidner & Kayworth, 2006). Their analysis enabled them to identify research themes addressing culture's impact on information technology and information technology's impact on culture, as well as to formulate particular research challenges associated with cultural conflict. According to *Google Scholar*, their paper has been cited over one thousand times, with over five hundred of the papers citing this article having been published since 2012, thus indicating the extent of research activities that cultural challenges are motivating. Despite this significant body of activity, the need for research into cultural differences and influences is becoming more acute.

The sheer scale of people displaced from their homelands, whether voluntarily or forcibly, is today unprecedented in the history of humankind (UNHCR, 2017). Information professionals cannot ignore such displacement of peoples and populations; there are very clear consequences for the provision of information services. How can public libraries assist and support refugees and migrants? How should their services be promoted to these population groups? What are the implications for collection development, particularly taking language requirements into consideration? Is there a role for mobile phones? These issues are being acknowledged, for instance by the public library sector (IFLA Public Library Sections, 2016), and are motivating research, particularly from an information literacy perspective (Lloyd 2015; Lloyd, Kennan, Thompson & Qayyum, 2013; Qayyum, Thompson, Kennan & Lloyd, 2014).

There is a need to extend and explore this growing body of research, focussed on the implications for information environments of the growing number of refugees, from two main perspectives. Firstly, from the perspective of culture itself, a richer and more nuanced view of the concept of difference is required in order to allow much more than national differences to be taken into consideration. Secondly, consideration of cultural influences and consequences is necessary in many diverse information environments. Both of these perspectives are considered below.

The complexity of culture

Culture is a multi-dimensional and complex concept, providing plenty of scope for misunderstanding and misinterpretation, often as a result of attempts to over-simplify. Dutch social scientist, Geert Hofstede, is most often thought of in terms of his contribution to theory relating to national cultural dimensions. Hofstede (2001) provided the most comprehensive and scholarly articulation of these dimensions. His research has contributed to awareness of multiple layers or levels of cultural influences. In organisational settings, for example, three layers have been identified as significant: national, occupational and corporate. The national cultural layer is the one which has attracted most interest from researchers, and indeed most controversy. There is a very clear danger of associating national cultural differences with caricatures and stereotypes which can result in an understandable hesitancy on the part of information researchers and practitioners to acknowledge, explore or encourage the development of research into differences which might be associated with particular national or ethnic groups.

It is in the cultural arena where much that is of critical importance to the development, implementation, and delivery of information services remains largely unexplored. Within organisational settings, the interplay between national, occupational and corporate cultures remains largely unacknowledged and unexplored. Occupational cultures are associated with different roles and/or professions, and may have profound influences on the way that individuals approach the creation and management of information. Corporate culture is the most superficial layer, is likely to be reflected in management style, and in the choices made for visual representations of an organisation's mission and values, for instance in website design and choice of logos. Similarly, community cultures consist of various levels of cultural influences, with research being needed to understand the complexity of the factors involved.

Consideration of very different preferences relating to the ways in which information is created, managed, accessed and used provides a clear example of the influences of cultural perspectives on the use, re-use, or non-use of information services. The differences which have been associated with cultural dimensions (Oliver, 2008) can be studied from linguistic perspectives (Clyne, 1994; Kelly, 2011). Indigenous views of information are likely to challenge accepted Western norms and attitudes, for instance relating to the ownership of information. Information professionals need to be open and responsive to alternative worldviews. For example, the New Zealand Māori view of archives recognises a spiritual dimension:

> An archive gathers and holds a lingering essence of those who have gone before. Not the whole person, not the entire culture of a person, but only a part of their essence. Some cultures call this gathering together of things the collecting of their ancestral connection, tikanga, whakapapa, cultural heritage, or even what gives them a wairua, their soul. If the originator, from whom those things are collected, ends up not being the holder of the collection, then they might consider such collections, even their souls, as being stolen. ... Most Māori would assert that any archive with an ancestral connection to them is theirs (Tupara, 2005).

Māori cultural memory is active and evolving. Capturing that memory in a western heritage paradigm creates a static representation which is at odds with a Māori knowledge paradigm (Winiata, 2005). Similar issues, relating to information reflecting diverse worldviews, are likely to be characteristic of other Indigenous cultures, but it cannot be assumed that what is appropriate in one setting can simply be applied to another. In every instance, issues and culturally appropriate approaches will have to be identified and developed in partnership with the communities involved.

Engagement with Indigenous peoples and multi-cultural populations is not only about providing better services to both but it can also challenge us to reflect upon and reposition our professional norms and approaches. How do we reconcile our strong commitment to open access to information with expectations of cultural sensitivity, which may require gendered secrecy? Research is needed not only to identify issues and raise awareness, but even more importantly to provide frameworks to assist practitioners to negotiate and develop partnership approaches.

Diverse information environments

The impacts of cultural differences must be considered from the perspective of the purposes for which information, or data, are created, managed, and used. Too often a view of information management is perceived or presented as a holistic one, but represents the perspective of just one group of information professionals (e.g., librarians, or recordkeepers). Cultural impacts may be significantly different when considering freedom of access to knowledge, accountability, or transparency concerns. Thus information research, exploring cultural differences, has to clarify and focus on specific aspects in order to avoid the pitfalls of sweeping generalisation which applies findings regardless to all aspects of information and data management.

Libraries, archives and museums in post-colonial settings such as Australia and New Zealand are likely to expend considerable effort in enabling access to aspects of their collections associated with their Indigenous populations. But evaluating the impact of this effort presents a major challenge and is largely unaddressed. Duff, Flinn, Suurtamm and Wallace (2013) explained impact as "the overall change in state, attitude or behavior of an individual or group after engagement with the service output." (p. 331). The connotations of this far-reaching definition for achieving profound social change, in terms of influencing attitudes, opinions and behaviours highlight the critical role of libraries, archives and museums in a world characterised by increasing nationalism. It also brings into sharp focus the need to develop global assessment of the services provided, moving beyond simply counting numbers of hits or downloads.

The key questions relate to what happens next: How is the information used after it is viewed or downloaded? What impact does it have on the user? Examples of projects under way investigating this emerging research theme are provided by Marsh, Punzalan, Leopold, Butler and Petrozzi (2016) and Crookston et al. (2016).

The globalisation-nationalism paradox

The once seemingly inexorable movement towards globalisation now seems to be turning back on itself (Bloom, 2014) with national sovereignty concerns dramatically marked by such events as 'Brexit' — the outcome of the referendum to withdraw Britain from the European Union. Parallels have been drawn to the dark days of the 1930s (Stephens, 2016) with the stigmatisation of those perceived as outsiders – foreigners, immigrants and other marginalised members of society – accompanied by assertions of national sovereignty and racial superiority. In this climate, knowledge relating to cultural influences on the ways in which people interact with and respond to information has become more critical than ever before. In addition, the very mission of cultural heritage or memory institutions becomes urgent to defend and support, and research must assist in ensuring that activities of cultural institutions are achieving desired impacts. Advocacy and outreach initiatives, focusing on minority or marginalised communities and often involving digitisation projects, provide a critical example for the need for targeted research.

With the movement against globalisation, our information environments are challenged by a paradox of epic proportions. On the one hand there are social, commercial and legislative drivers for ongoing globalisation, coupled with technological developments that are continually enhancing the rapidity and ease of the pluralisation of data, information and information products across the boundaries of time and space. Concurrently, the development of standards not only assist and support cross-border data flow and collaborative working, but also provide a common, internationally agreed basis for practice for information professionals. They attract substantial investment of financial and human resources (Oliver, 2014). On the other hand, the rise of nationalism threatens freedom of movement, and indeed thought, heralding the risk of devastating and destructive history as played out in the 2nd World War repeating itself. The one area of commonality, relevant to both globalisation and nationalism, is cultural. Understanding cultural differences is equally relevant and of critical importance to the two contradictory forces presented by this paradox.

Therefore, information researchers and information practitioners can meaningfully contribute towards ensuring positive outcomes from this dilemma, regardless of the dominance of globalisation or nationalism. This can be achieved in two main ways. Firstly, researchers can investigate the influences of cultural differences on information preferences and behaviours, and implement the findings from such research into the development of services and strategies that do not privilege majority or powerful members of society. Secondly, there is a need to tolerate and advocate for the diversity of our information environments and increase awareness of the potential for the impacts of library, archive and museum services by assisting to meet social justice aims and developing methodologies to understand and document that impact. The role of professional practice, as discussed below, is crucial.

Research and practice

Dr Alex Byrne has been one of Australia's leading library practitioners, as well as a well-regarded researcher. He was the State Librarian and Chief Executive of the

State Library of New South Wales from 2011 to his retirement in 2016 following positions in library and university executive management around Australia, most recently at the University of Technology, Sydney. He is well placed to provide his views on research and professional practice. He begins his piece, which he headed 'Practice-led or practice leading?' by discussing the seemingly symbiotic relationship between professional practice and research.

Practitioners and researchers

Librarianship, information service, and archives administration present as a professional domain that is utilitarian but inspired by passion and a strong ethos. Together, they fulfil the traditional definition of a profession by sharing a body of knowledge, a commitment to provide service to society, and agreed ethical foundations (Oppenheim & Pollecutt, 2000). These features were explored in other contexts in Chapter 3 and Chapter 20: *Ethical research practices*. They have long been highly valued for their enduring roles in keeping the record of communities and societies, making information available and promoting creativity. But they are not immune to change and libraries in particular have changed profoundly through the end of the twentieth century and the first decades of this century. Leaving behind doom-laden claims of their irrelevance in the internet age (Keller, Reich & Herkovic, 2003), they have been early adopters of new technologies, using those technologies to reposition themselves for their communities and organisations, as mentioned already in this chapter.

While guided by high principles of freedom of access to information and an ethos of service, the professional avocations to keep the record, make information available and promote creation, are utilitarian as are the more specific goals of various types of libraries, archives and information services such as promoting literacy, building community, maintaining confidentiality and adding value to parent organisations. Consequently research in the domains is predominantly oriented towards understanding and fulfilling those goals better and is thus inextricably involved with their fulfilment, that is, with *practice*. In this professional environment, research articulates and codifies the 'shared body of knowledge' which lies at the heart of a profession and investigates the challenges of professional practice. It informs the profession and offers shape to professional priorities, applying and deriving theory to inform practice and scope areas for further research.

This intertwining of research and practice demands a symbiotic relationship in which research benefits practice and vice versa. Academic researchers bring objectivity and rigour to set the immediacy of practitioners' concerns in context, to discern trends and paradigm shifts, and to offer frameworks for successful practice. Practitioners bring their understanding and experience of client needs, technological and social change and the constraints of management in order to test theory and expose areas for investigation.

That symbiotic relationship is the ideal but the reality is that most practitioners pay little heed to research, with few who routinely maintain currency with the literature outside formal study. This pattern of uninformed practice pertains despite professional expectations such as those of the Australian Library and Information Association which states that, *inter alia*, "Library and information specialists must be able to ... demonstrate a commitment to the improvement of professional practice through a culture of research, evidence-based information practice and knowledge retention" (ALIA, 2014).

Some practitioners do undertake research and publish their findings, but practitioners' articles in the professional literature are seldom more than reportage with a paucity of analysis, often poorly formulated methodologies, and cursory literature reviews. Research by practitioners undertaken for formal study, especially research degrees, is stronger in these respects but generally limited in scope and the findings lack wider applicability. Few articles endeavour to place findings in a broader context let alone attempt to postulate a model or theory that might inform future practice or research. Chapter 3 provided further detail.

Even reviews of the literature in the field are of limited utility, unlike such sources as the syntheses included in the Cochrane Library in medical fields that are compiled to offer "high-quality, independent evidence to inform healthcare decision-making" (Cochrane, 2016). Reviews of the literature in library and information studies are almost always descriptive with very little synthesis of findings, work which might construct an evidential foundation for practice. Compiling one of the better recent reviews, for example, Brundy (2015) surveys the studies of innovation in academic libraries and attempts to discern the parameters that favour successful innovation, but concludes:

> Due to the wide range of methodologies and rigor employed, it is not clear to what extent many of the results would apply beyond the particular circumstances described ... But taken together, an outline of the innovative academic library as one with a flatter organizational structure that encourages and enables participation in decision making begins to emerge (pp. 35-36).

Despite the hesitancy of this conclusion, it is useful in providing some guidance for practitioners seeking to foster innovation in academic libraries and points to directions for future research. More typical is work like that of Hufford (2013) about the literature on assessment in academic and research libraries, a thorough and well-documented review which falls short on synthesis. It introduces the reader to the literature over the period covered, 2005 to August 2011, with a brief traverse of earlier noteworthy works, but it fails to provide guidance for the busy practitioner seeking a summary to identify best practice in assessment.

This is likely a chicken and egg argument: the quality of studies does not adequately support systematic review or more generalised interpretations that might inform practice and encourage better and more consistent practice across organisations, and the lack of systematic reviews fails to encourage publication of more rigorous studies.

Practitioners may claim that they are too busy to undertake or commission research but without research, the field is stultified and practitioners are unable to learn from properly evaluated experience or to test new approaches rigorously. It is possible to be a practitioner researcher as I have demonstrated throughout my career, employing a wide range of research methodologies and authoring over 300 publications (Byrne, 2017). However, because many practitioners find it difficult to make space for research in a busy professional life, a pragmatic approach is to partner with or commission academic researchers to investigate issues.

Conversely it is unfortunate that few academic researchers appear to be interested in engaging with the challenges and opportunities of practice. Moreover there are significant challenges to be overcome in reconciling motivations, priorities, time frames and funding. Practitioners tend to focus on immediate issues and the delivery of services and projects, often against predetermined schedules and with limited and time-dependent budgets. Academics tend to work on long cycles oriented around teaching and other commitments, including publication and submitting applications for research funding. Practitioners are primarily interested in applicable outcomes while academics are more interested in research questions that will inform understanding, including the development or testing of theory, and that will result in a publication to stimulate further research.

There's the rub. Practitioners do not think of putting their challenges before academics and academics identify research questions and design research projects without consulting practitioners and then wonder why they get lukewarm interest in supporting or engaging with the research.

The tipping point

Taking advantage of the spread of the Internet, a profound reorientation of libraries and information services has occurred over the last two decades. Although it continues to be suggested that libraries are unnecessary in the internet age (Evans & Baker, 2016) and such suggestions can be fanned by incidents such as the closure of public libraries in Britain under budgetary stringency (Anstice, 2017), there is abundant evidence that libraries are prospering because they have been revolutionised.

No longer principally concerned with warehousing printed publications, libraries are now focussed on providing dynamic information services to their communities. Such change is reflected even in the physical design of library space today, where architects design what is known as an open 'knowledge commons', following the research findings of information researchers and modern requirements of practitioners (Mehtonen, 2016). Libraries draw on networked resources – including collections of printed publications but increasingly they focus on the 'born digital', emphasising online resources that can be delivered at all hours and any location. With technical services increasingly outsourced, they are focussing on the 'soft skills' necessary to engage clients, strengthen local or institutional communities and support creation. Library premises have become more welcoming and richer in facilities, aiming to meet the varied needs of diverse communities. They encourage cultural diversity. These are generalisations evidenced by the trends across the range of public, school, academic and special libraries and increasingly in archives. The profundity of the change can be confirmed by considering a few examples.

The first example must be content. The previous model for content delivery was to accumulate the widest possible range of printed and audio-visual material relevant to the clientele's interests and have it available on-site, augmented through collaborative arrangements such as interlibrary loans. Today, a broader range of material can be offered online – 'any time, any place' – by subscribing to aggregating services. Especially in university and research libraries, this dramatic change has had many benefits in terms of range and accessibility to the primary clients. Restrictive licences prevent the libraries from making the materials available to broader communities, such as to the institutionally unaffiliated independent researchers, as they could in the past. This raised broad questions about the role of libraries, questions which have received scant attention by researchers.

A second example is that digital disruption has also changed the shape of the library profession. Formerly there was a need for technical experts, especially cataloguers, but for most libraries today those services are provided by the aggregators or specialist bureaux. Metadata creation is increasingly automated and the algorithms embedded in search engines are incomprehensible to most. These changes challenge the core knowledge of the profession but their consequences for the profession have been decried but not researched.

In a third – and telling – example, libraries around the world have recognised and responded powerfully to the increased need for literacy, including digital literacy in the twenty-first century world (Garner, 2006). They have significantly replaced their previous instructional focus on skills for interpreting bibliographic tools with a broader emphasis on teaching skills in accessing and using online resources. This has been valuable in the school and university contexts where students can be misled by the apparent ease of finding a few resources via a simple search on *Google* or another online tool. Public libraries have also understood that this is increasingly important for the general community as they access ever-broader resources online. For libraries, it has meant a much stronger educational role and a reorientation from a narrow bibliographic focus. Much has been studied and written about information literacy but little about what this development has meant for the profession, our training and our institutions, nor has there been much research on the efficacy of various approaches to information literacy instruction.

We are thus at a tipping point at which the profession and our institutions have changed significantly and we need to examine those changes and inform future directions through research.

Future directions: Both practice-led and practice-leading

As this brief discussion has demonstrated, librarianship and cognate areas are at a watershed, but the rapid change in the roles and services of our practitioners and organisations have received little research focus. Looking forward, we can discern that the opportunities and challenges of digital disruption require academic researchers and practitioners to form partnerships to tackle research questions of importance to our professions and institutions. Such questions will include more effective approaches to practice but also the re-conceptualisation of theory in the always-connected twenty-first century.

The way forward must involve more dialogue to identify strategies that will satisfy the interests of all parties. That must include the fostering of practitioner researchers: research skills development guided by academic researchers and a receptive climate created by library management. Both 'practice led' and 'practice leading', this approach draws on the strengths of both researchers and practitioners and forges mutually beneficial partnerships. The concreteness and urgency of practice can be viewed and refracted through the lens of research.

Communication is another key issue. Research findings need to be accessible to practitioners and practitioners need to be committed to reviewing the relevant – and peripheral – literature. Schemes such as the ALIA Certified Professional membership program (ALIA, 2017) and equivalents promoted by other professional bodies, assist this commitment, and wider participation needs to be encouraged. Time-short practitioners will be assisted by better survey articles and summaries of the literature, perhaps not going as far as the Cochrane Reviews, but certainly pointing to key trends and robust research.

Together, this more systematic and strategic emphasis on research will promote a better-informed and more innovative profession. It will be a profession which is not only willing and able to change, as it has amply demonstrated already, but a profession which is much better informed and evaluative in its approaches to change.

Conclusion

The writing of this chapter has been collaborative, which has the singular advantage that several perspectives have been included: about the implications of likely future scenarios for information research. We were thus able to include pieces written by an expert on the role of culture and its future in library research. Another expert has written from the perspective of someone who has been a leading Australian library practitioner and, at the same time, a serious researcher in the information field. Others have contributed their perspectives on trends regarding paradigms, research methods, and data collection and analysis tools. We do not claim to be thorough-going forecasters. If we can find continuity between current patterns and future trends, then a semblance of foresight informs practical discussion.

The chapter began by drawing together the methodological threads from the chapters initially written from the perspectives of researchers in the three connected fields which are the focus of the book: LIS, archives and records, and information systems and knowledge management. There was a remarkable consistency of approach regarding the notion of 'methodology' as the overarching concept that includes a set of assumptions or a paradigm as a foundation for the selection and application of research methods and techniques. There was agreement on the need for researchers and practitioners to apply rigorous and systematic analysis to problems that will be identified in the future.

To illustrate a plethora of issues that lie ahead, the case of 'big data' is briefly described. 'Big data' has suddenly appeared on the research horizon like a meteorite, and raised its fair share of obscurantist dust. It is hard to tell where and how the dust will settle. Challenges are presented by the enormous quantities of collected data, but equally about their arrangement, management, use and re-use. Many exciting, fortuitous chances will arise for information researchers and practitioners, who are already investigating possibilities. To their advantage, they already curate large repositories of 'big data', and they are well positioned to deploy new as well as tried-and-true research approaches.

The primary changes in culture (now and in future) relate to the growth of globalisation, and in the resistance to it, as well as the implicit culture attached to information and communications technologies, and the threat they pose to local or marginal memory and knowledge. Research thus far has been focused on national, occupational and corporate cultural differences, but very little on the cultures of disadvantage and displacement. We know virtually nothing about the technological and network effects (good or bad) on them. It is all too apparent that the ugly features of nationalism, censorship and xenophobia are biting back, which will be to the detriment of open access to objective knowledge.

The final part of this chapter suggests that information researchers and practitioners should join in solidarity to continue to advocate for professional, ethical values, and to undertake research projects which serve the needs of both groups. Their coming together to share experiences and insights, and to undertake collaborative studies, will enrich the worlds of both groups and enable a bright future for both theoretical and practical information research.

References

Al-Saggaf, Y. (2012). *Online communities in Saudi Arabia: An ethnographic study.* Saarbrücken: LAMBERT Academic Publishing.

Al-Saggaf, Y., & Williamson, K. (2004). Online communities in Saudi Arabia: Evaluating the impact on culture through online semi-structured interviews. *Forum Qualitative Sozialforschung / Forum: Qualitative Social Research, 5*(3). Retrieved from http://www.qualitative-research.net/fqs-texte/3-04/04-3-24-e.htm

Anderson, T., & Fourie, I. (2015). Collaborative autoethnography as a way of seeing the experience of care giving as an information practice. *Information Research: An International Electronic Journal, 20*(1). Retrieved from http://www.informationr.net/ir/20-1/isic2/isic33.html#.WIHhrXrzJnk

Anstice, I. (2017). List of withdrawn libraries. *Public Libraries News; What's Happening to Your Library?* [UK]. Retrieved from http://www.publiclibrariesnews.com/about-public-libraries-news/news-topics

Association for Library and Information Science. (2017). ALISE/ProQuest methodology paper competition – previous winners. Retrieved from http://www.alise.org/index.php?option = com_content&view = article&id = 471#winners.

Australian Library and Information Association (ALIA). (2014). The library and information sector: Core knowledge, skills and attributes. (Adopted 1998. Amended 2009. Reviewed 2012. Amended 9 December 2014.) Retrieved from https://www.alia.org.au/about-alia/policies-standards-and-guidelines/library-and-information-sector-core-knowledge-skills-and-attributes.

Australian Library and Information Association (ALIA). (2017). Professional development. Retrieved from https://membership.alia.org.au/pdinfo/professional-development.

Bloom, P. (2014, October 21). As anti-globalisation politics fail, nationalism sweeps the world. *The Conversation.* Retrieved from http://theconversation.com/as-anti-globalisation-politics-fail-nationalism-sweeps-the-world-33102

Brown-May, A., Elkner, C., & Reeves, J. K. (2007). Taking the rushes on line: The eGold project, a digital encyclopedia. In J. K. Reeves, & D. Nichols (Eds.), *Deeper leads: New approaches to Victorian goldfields history* (pp. 67–83). Ballarat, VIC: BHS Publishing.

Bruns, A., & Liang, Y. E. (2012). Tools and methods for capturing Twitter data during natural disasters. *First Monday, 17*(4). Retrieved from http://firstmonday.org/article/view/3937/3193

Brundy, C. (2015). Academic libraries and innovation: a literature review. *Journal of Library Innovation, 6*(1), 22–39. Retrieved from http://www.libraryinnovation.org/issue/view/33

Busha, C. H., & Harter, S. P. (1980). *Research methods in librarianship: Techniques and interpretation.* London: Academic Press.

Byrne, A. (2017). Possibility and imagination: A personal exploration of research and librarianship. *Library Management, 38*(1), 11–19.

Castelvecchi, D. (2015, May 15). Physics paper sets record with more than 5,000 authors. *Nature News.* Retrieved from http://www.nature.com/news/physics-paper-sets-record-with-more-than-5-000-authors-1.17567#auth-1

Chu, H. (2015). Research methods in library and information science: A content analysis. *Library and Information Science Research, 37*(1), 36–41.

Clarke, A. E. (2005). *Situational analysis: Grounded theory after the postmodern turn.* San Francisco, CA: SAGE.

Clyne, M. (1994). *Intercultural communication at work: Cultural values in discourse.* Cambridge: Cambridge University Press.

Cochrane (2016). About the Cochrane Library. Retrieved from http://www.cochranelibrary.com/about/about-the-cochrane-library.html.

Crookston, M., Oliver, G., Tikao, A., Diamond, P., Liew, C. L., & Douglas, S. L. (2016). *Kōrero Kitea: Ngā hua o te whakamamatitanga. The impacts of digitised te reo archival collections.* Wellington: InterPARES Trust. Retrieved from https://interparestrust.org/assets/public/dissemination/Korerokiteareport_final.pdf

Dervin, B., & Nilan, M. (1986). Information needs and uses. In M. E. Williams (Ed.), *Annual review of information science and technology* (21, pp. 3–33). White Plains, NY: Knowledge Industry Publications.

Duff, W. M., Flinn, A., Suurtamm, K. E., & Wallace, D. A. (2013). Social justice impact of archives: a preliminary investigation. *Archival Science, 13*(4), 317–348.

Evans, W., & Baker, D. (Eds.) (2016). *The end of wisdom? The future of libraries in a digital age.* Cambridge, MA: Chandos.

Fiegerman, S. (2016, August 18). Twitter suspends another 235,000 accounts for promoting terrorism. *CNN Tech.* Retrieved from http://money.cnn.com/2016/08/18/technology/twitter-suspends-terrorism-accounts/?iid = EL

French, R., & Williamson, K. (2016). Conceptualising welfare workers as information bricoleurs: Theory building using literature analysis, organisational ethnography and grounded theory analysis. *Information Research: An International Electronic Journal, 21*(4). Retrieved from http://www.informationr.net/ir/21-4/isic/isic1605.html

Fuller, S. (2015). *Knowledge: The philosophical quest in history.* London: Routledge.

Garner, S. D. (2006). *High-level colloquium on information literacy and lifelong learning* Report of a meeting sponsored by the United Nations Education, Scientific, and Cultural Organisation (UNESCO), National Forum on Information Literacy (NFIL) and the International Federation of Library Associations and Institutions (IFLA), Bibliotheca Alexandrina, Alexandria, Egypt, November 6–9, 2005. Retrieved from http://www.ifla.org/files/assets/wsis/Documents/high-level-colloquium.pdf.

Given, L. M., & Archibald, H. (2015). Visual traffic sweeps (VTS): A research method for mapping user activities in the library space. *Library & Information Science Research*, 37(2), 100–108.

Given, L. M., & Leckie, G. (2003). 'Sweeping' the library: Mapping the social activity space of the public library. *Library & Information Science Research*, 25(4), 365–385.

Given, L. M., & Willson, R. (2015). Collaborative information use with technology: A critical examination of humanities scholars' research activities. In P. Hansen, C. Shah, & C. -P. Klas (Eds.), *Collaborative information seeking best practices: New domains and new thoughts* (pp. 139–164). New York: Springer-Verlag.

Gorichanaz, T. (2015). Information on the run: experiencing information during an ultramarathon. *Information Research: An International Electronic Journal*, 20(4). Retrieved from http://www.informationr.net/ir/20-4/paper697.html#.WHf6uXrzJnk

Guba, E. G., & Lincoln, Y. S. (1994). Competing paradigms in qualitative research. In N. K. Denzin, & Y. S. Lincoln (Eds.), *The handbook of qualitative research* (pp. 105–117). Thousand Oaks, CA: Sage.

Hartel, J. (2014). An arts-informed study of information using the draw-and-write technique. *Journal of the American Society for Information Science & Technology*, 65 (7), 1349–1367.

Hartel, J., & Thomson, L. (2011). Visual approaches and photography for the study of immediate information space. *Journal of the American Society for Information Science and Technology*, 62(11), 2214–2224.

Hey, A. J. G., Tansley, S., & Tolle, K. M. (Eds.) (2009). *The fourth paradigm: Data-intensive scientific discovery*. Redmond, WA: Microsoft Research.

Hofstede, G. H. (2001). *Culture's consequences: Comparing values, behaviors, institutions and organizations across nations*. Thousand Oaks, CA: Sage.

Hope, A. D. (1975). Australia. In *Collected poems*, 1930–1970 (p. 13). Sydney: Angus & Robertson.

Hufford, J. R. (2013). A review of the literature on assessment in academic and research libraries, 2005 to August 2011. *portal: Libraries and the Academy*, 13(1), 5–35. Retrieved from https://www.press.jhu.edu/journals/portal_libraries_and_the_academy/portal_pre_print/articles/13.1hufford.pdf

IFLA Public Libraries Section (2016, June 2). Library services to immigrants and refugees [Blog post]. Retrieved from http://blogs.ifla.org/public-libraries/2016/06/02/library-services-to-immigrants-and-refugees/.

Järvelin, K., & Vakkari, P. (1993). The evolution of library and information science 1965–1985: A content analysis of journal articles. *Information Processing and Management, 29*(1), 129–144.

Julien, H., Given, L. M., & Opryshko, A. (2013). Photovoice: A promising method for studies of individuals' information practices. *Library & Information Science Research, 35*(4), 257–263.

Julien, H., & O'Brien, M. (2014). Information behavior research: Where have we been, where are we going? *Canadian Journal of Information and Library Science, 38*(4), 239–250.

Keller, M. A., Reich, V. A., & Herkovic, A. C. (2003). What is a library anymore, anyway? *First Monday, 8*(5). Retrieved from http://firstmonday.org/issues/issue8_5/keller/index.html

Kelly, M. (2011). *Intercultural communication: An emerging discipline.* University Council of Modern Languages. Retrieved from http://www.ucml.ac.uk/sites/default/files/shapingthefuture/102/14%20-%20Mike%20Kelly%20Inter%20resource%20template_0.pdf

Kuhn, T. S. (1970). *The structure of scientific revolutions* (2nd ed.). Chicago: University of Chicago Press.

Lanier, J. (2017). Digital Maoism: The hazards of new online collectivism. *Edge.* Retrieved from https://www.edge.org/conversation/digital-maoism-the-hazards-of-the-new-online-collectivism

Leckie, G. J., & Given, L. M. (2010). Henri Lefebvre and spatial dialectics. In G. Leckie, L. M. Given, & J. Buschman (Eds.), *Critical theory for library and information science: Exploring the social across the disciplines* (pp. 221–236). Santa Barbara, CA: Libraries Unlimited.

Leidner, D. E., & Kayworth, T. (2006). Review: A review of culture in information systems research: toward a theory of information technology culture conflict. *MIS Quarterly, 30*(2), 357–399.

Lloyd, A. (2015). Stranger in a strange land: Enabling information resilience in resettlement landscapes. *Journal of Documentation, 71*(5), 1029–1042.

Lloyd, A., Kennan, M., Thompson, K. M., & Qayyum, A. (2013). Connecting with new information landscapes: Information literacy practices of refugees. *Journal of Documentation, 69*(1), 121–144.

Lomborg, S., & Bechmann, A. (2014). Using APIs for data collection on social media. *The Information Society, 30*(4), 256–265.

Marsh, D. E., Punzalan, R. L., Leopold, R., Butler, B., & Petrozzi, M. (2016). Stories of impact: the role of narrative in understanding the value and impact of digital collections. *Archival Science, 16*(1), 327–372.

Mathews, B. (2014). Librarian as futurist; changing the way libraries think about the future. *portal: Libraries and the Academy, 14*(3), 1–10. Retrieved from https://vtechworks.lib.vt.edu/bitstream/handle/10919/49667/Librarian_as_Futurist_Mathews_July2014.pdf?sequence=1

McKechnie, L., Chabot, R., Dalmer, N., Julien, H., & Mabbott, C. (2016). Writing and reading the results: The reporting of research rigour tactics in information behaviour research as evident in the published proceedings of the biennial ISIC conferences, 1996-2014. *Information Research: An International Electronic Journal*, *21*(4). Retrieved from http://www.informationr.net/ir/21-4/isic/isic1604.html

McKee, B. (2013). *Animating Yanyuwa narratives: capturing intangible heritage with 3D animation for the purpose of cultural preservation and the cross-generational transfer of knowledge* (Master's thesis). Monash University, Melbourne. Retrieved from http://arrow.monash.edu.au/hdl/1959.1/928173.

McKemmish, S. (2001). Placing records continuum theory and practice. *Archival Science*, *1*(4), 333–359.

Mehtonen, P. (2016). The library as a multidimensional space in the digital age. *Information Research: An International Electronic Journal*, *21*(1). Retrieved from http://www.informationr.net/ir/21-1/memo/memo6.html#.WNnNoBOGPXQ

Mihelcic, J. (2016). *The experiential model of the person-centred record: A social constructionist grounded theory* (PhD thesis). Monash University, Melbourne. Retrieved from https://figshare.com/articles/The_Experiential_Model_of_the_Person-Centred_Record_a_social_constructionist_grounded_theory/4712536.

Mingers, J., & Standing, C. (2016). A framework for validating IS research based on a pluralist account of truth and correctness. Retrieved from https://arxiv.org/pdf/1701.04676.pdf.

Moring, C., & Lloyd, A. (2013). Analytical implications of using practice theory in workplace information literacy research. *Information Research: An International Electronic Journal*, *18*(3). Retrieved from http://www.informationr.net/ir/18-3/colis/paperC35.html#.WL3yfhJ94dV

Nicholls, R. (2017). The Australian telecommunications regulatory environment: An overview. *Australian Journal of Telecommunications and the Digital Economy*, *4*(4), 196–213.

Oliver, G. (2008). Information culture: exploration of differing values and attitudes to information in organisations. *Journal of Documentation*, *64*(3), 363–385.

Oliver, G. (2014). International records management standards: the challenges of achieving consensus. *Records Management Journal*, *24*(1), 22–31.

Oppenheim, C., & Pollecutt, N. (2000). Professional associations and ethical issues in LIS. *Journal of Librarianship and Information Science*, *32*(4), 187–203. Retrieved from http://lis.sagepub.com/content/32/4/187

Pagan, A., & Torgler, B. (2015). Research rigour: Use '4Rs' criteria to assess papers. *Nature*, *522*, 34.

Qayyum, M. A., Thompson, K. M., Kennan, M. A., & Lloyd, A. (2014). The provision and sharing of information between service providers and settling refugees. *Information Research: An International Electronic Journal*, *19*(2). Retrieved from http://www.informationr.net/ir/19-2/paper616.html#.WNEADHrzJnk

Randall, L. (2012). *Knocking on heaven's door: How physics and scientific thinking illuminate our universe*. London: Vintage.

Skeggs, B., & Yuill, S. (2016). The methodology of a multi-modal project examining how facebook infrastructures social relations. *Information, Communication and Society, 19*(10), 1356–1372.

Stephens, B. (2016, March 7). The return of the 1930s: Donald Trump's demagoguery may be a foretaste of what's to come. *The Wall Street Journal*. Retrieved from https://www.wsj.com/articles/the-return-of-the-1930s-1457396236

Surowiecki, J. (2004). *The wisdom of crowds: Why the many are smarter than the few and how collective wisdom shapes business, economies, societies and nations*. New York: Anchor.

Terrill, L. J. (2015). The state of cataloging research: An analysis of peer-reviewed journal literature, 2010–2014. *Cataloging & Classification Quarterly, 54*(8), 593–611.

Tupara, N. (2005). Whose archives are they? *Archifacts*, April, 86-87.

UNHCR. (2017). *Figures at a glance*. Retrieved from http://www.unhcr.org/en-au/figures-at-a-glance.html.

Usherwood, B. (2016). *Equity and excellence in the public library: Why ignorance is not our heritage*. London: Routledge.

Weller, C. (2016, August 25). Libraries of the future are going to change in some unexpected ways. *Business Insider*. Retrieved from http://www.businessinsider.com.au/libraries-of-the-future-2016-8?r = US&IR = T

Williamson, K. (2002). The Dephi method. In K. Williamson (Ed.), *Research methods for students, academics and professionals: Information management and systems* (2nd ed., pp. 209–220). Wagga Wagga, NSW: Centre for Information Studies, Charles Sturt University.

Weisinger, J. Y., & Trauth, E. M. (2002). Situating culture in the global information sector. *Information Technology & People, 15*(4), 306–320.

Winiata, W. (2005). Survival of Māori as a people and Māori archives. *Archifacts*, April, 9-19.

Yaqoob, I., Hashem, I. A. T., Gani, A., Mokhtar, S., Ahmed, E., Anuar, N. B., & Vasilakos, A. V. (2016). Big data: From beginning to future. *International Journal of Information Management 36*(6), 1231–1247.

Concluding reflections

The research journey

Donald Schauder
Monash University, Australia

Introduction

The chapters in this book have offered a range of concepts, methods and techniques that can help information professionals and scholars to undertake the kind of research that extends understanding of how information, the very 'stuff' of communicative action and memory, influences individuals and social collectivities large and small.

For the most part, the research approaches covered in the book can be seen as generic for the humanities and social sciences. In successive chapters, these widely used methods and techniques have been mapped specifically on to information research and reflective practice by presenting examples of research projects that have been undertaken.

Selectively reflecting upon the chapters of the book, this final chapter highlights some issues that the present author − in the light of many years of engagement with research activities − sees as particularly important for information research, and the wider social sciences. These concluding reflections are presented under the headings of five questions facing researchers.

Question 1: Where do I get my background information and my data?

In the Information Age the question of what discourse to interrogate for 'backgrounding' a research project, or as a source of research data, is an ever-mounting challenge. The world has experienced an information revolution characterised by the Internet and the World Wide Web; the advent of blogs, wikis, Facebook, Twitter and other social media; and the proliferation of full-text databases, e-journals and e-books. The power of information searching tools, led by *Google*, is incomparably greater than the analogue catalogues, bibliographies and indexes of the late 20th century.

Boisot (1998, p. 30) described and explained this kind of change as a "shifting isoquant in the evolutionary production function". As socio-technical systems evolve, data increasingly displaces physical resources (for example as digital storage devices replaced paper files in corporate data centres). At a certain point the extent and complexity of data resources themselves becomes a practical and financial burden, and are in turn replaced by more efficient information technologies (for example as cloud storage can replace storage devices in offices or data centres).

The result of this kind of advance for Internet technology means that the amount of informational raw material facing the researcher can now be vast. However, also in line with Boisot's step change model, the techniques and tools available to researchers for selection and retrieval are ever more potent, and usually available from researchers' personal computers or mobile devices.

What is to be done with all this abundance in conducting the phases of research generally called 'the literature review' and 'data collection'?

The categories of literature review and data collection have generally been regarded as separate phases of the research process. However with the information and telecommunications revolution they may both be seen as harvesting of past and present discourses. Especially in the case of data collection, new discourses may be initiated by researchers themselves, for example, by asking questions on a blog.

The information revolution presents many possible new answers to the researcher's classic question, "Where do I get data?" (Gilbert, 2011). In response to the proliferation and popularity of opinion-rich sites, innovative intelligent computational treatments are being explored for opinion mining and sentiment analysis (Pang & Lee, 2008).

All kinds of discourse are worthy of consideration by the scholar as eligible sources for literature review or research data. On the World Wide Web relevance and authenticity are higher criteria than provenance. Having said this, peer-reviewed scholarly discourse does hold a privileged place in reputable research. It is the category of discourse to which information researchers primarily contribute, and by whose benchmarks they are primarily judged.

There are always constraints on what a researcher can attempt, and limitations to searching must always be declared, and the criteria of selectivity explained. The onus is on researchers to seek advice and generally use their best efforts in identifying sources of background information and research data. Researchers are also obliged to make appropriate use of state-of-the-art information technology to aid in analysing and interpreting their data. Moreover, they need to demonstrate that they have done so. It goes without saying that the most complete possible acknowledgement of the words and ideas of others remains fundamental to the quality and integrity of all research.

Question 2: Does my research modelling provide an adequate basis for explaining the phenomena being studied?

Central to the idea of research is to find ways of *seeing*. The very word *theory* derives from the Greek, to see or behold — theatre comes from the same root (Skeat, 1887, p. 503). The great theoretical traditions of positivism and interpretivism are alternative ways of seeing. Researchers need to be self-aware of their own theoretical positioning, and to make this positioning clear to all stakeholders in the research, and in research reporting.

Self-awareness also needs to encompass awareness of any personal values or biases that may influence one's way of seeing, for example, a personal political or religious position, or a financial stake. All researchers approach their tasks of modelling from some prior position of belief. As far as is possible the researcher should strive to understand, and make clear how this might influence their theorising and modelling.

Scholarship in the information disciplines is barren without both theory and observation. Research needs to involve both theoretical perspectives and sufficient specific observation to address the research question. The capacity to choose among a wide array of possible research methods and techniques — as explicated in the preceding chapters — helps us explain social phenomena in the light of theory, and conversely to critique theory in the light of observation. Modelling is crucial to the research process, because models are the bridge between theory and observation.

Information research is particularly tough or complex in that what is studied — information phenomena — are in essence the same as how they are studied — the 'tools' used to study them. Both are constituted of processes of modelling.

What information researchers study is how people selectively take parts of their 'knowledge' — the memories and thoughts that exist in their minds — and *encode* these as representations through 'live' (e.g., conversation) or 'recorded' (e.g., a written letter) information media so that others can decode them and add them, again selectively, to their own knowledge (Burgess & Schauder, 2003; Treloar, 2006, sections 2.1−2.2). In other words they create a model or representation of some aspect of their knowledge.

How information researchers study such phenomena is that they in turn use information models to explicate the communicative modelling processes they are observing!

In both everyday life and research, such externalised modelling of knowledge may also be used to communicate with oneself — for example, writing a diary or notebook — in order to 'refresh' one's memory or knowledge at a later date. In daily life people create information models for all sorts of reasons. These include:

- reminding (e.g., a snapshot of baby in a particular mood);
- proving (e.g., a birth certificate as evidence of baby's birth place);
- explaining (e.g., an x-ray of a baby's broken leg, to explain the injury);
- predicting (e.g., trend statistics about the health of babies);
- discovering (e.g., a psychological hypothesis about developmental stages in babies);
- deciding (e.g., a dietitian's checklist about what you should feed baby);
- entertaining (e.g., the movie *Baby's Day Out* — baby as crime-fighting hero) (Hughes, Johnson, Mantegna, & Boyle, 1991); and
- enculturating (e.g., stories of the baby Moses or Jesus).

The modelling undertaken by information researchers can involve all of the above, even arguably the last two.

A research model need not 'look like' what it represents. It can be a series of equations, a conceptual diagram, or an account in words. Good examples are entity-relationship diagrams in information systems. Such models, that select and represent only high-priority factors and relations, are called homomorphic.

On the other hand a model can look exactly like what it represents. Many baby boomers were inordinately fond of the television series *Star Trek*, and the writer hopes younger readers will forgive references to this ageing, but still relevant, sci-fi classic. In *Star Trek* (2012a) the 'holodeck' is a virtual reality world that looks exactly like what it represents. Such 'total' virtual-reality models are called isomorphic (Beer, Strachy, Stone, & Torrance, 1988).

All models reflect a system. They map the elements of the system. Some information models are static (closed systems) and do not change, while others are dynamic (open systems) and change with feedback. Some are concrete and can be interpreted — or de-coded — largely through the senses (like a pilot-training simulator), while others are abstract and can only be de-coded through the intellect (like Einstein's $e = mc^2$). Some can be causal (as in system dynamics modelling), while others can be associative or probabilistic (like a Chi-square test). Some can focus on only one or a few factors or relationships (like in simple majority decision-making), while others can involve innumerable factors (like explanations of 'the global information society').

As with other conceptual categories used in social science, homomorphism and isomorphism need not be mutually exclusive. There are many hybrid categories of model across the spectrum between these two 'pure' types.

What about Elle Macpherson — the supermodel? Is she a model in the sense discussed? Elle on a magazine cover is indeed an abstraction and codification taken from the publicist's knowledge of the 'whole' Elle Macpherson to enculturate or persuade others into certain values about beauty and fashion. In this sense the magazine-cover Elle Macpherson is a model (a hybrid homomorphic-isomorphic model) while the whole Elle, at home, away from cameras, is not.

What about an elephant in the zoo? To the extent that this is not an elephant in the natural state, but displayed by the zoo to represent a class or category of animal for explanatory purposes — that live elephant is an information model (isomorphic). Return it to the wild, cease using it for education, research or entertainment, and it is a model no longer.

Arguably there is greater congruence between certain kinds of theorising and certain kinds of modelling. For example the preferred setting for research proceeding from an interpretivist theoretical position is immersion in the information phenomena under consideration, as in action research. For action researchers, the information community in which they participate becomes a research model (rather like an elephant selected for study in the wild becomes a model in the context of the research). Interpretivist theorising and isomorphic modelling fit well together, and so do positivist theorising and homomorphic modelling. Once again, powerful hybrid combinations cannot be excluded.

Occam's Razor, otherwise known as the principle of parsimony, is a test of whether a particular model, chosen from many possibilities, is the most appropriate for a given piece of research. Sometimes a model of just two or three factors and their relationships is sufficient to explicate a phenomenon. Sometimes a model capable of accommodating an almost infinite number of factors and relationships is required. Occam's Razor teaches that by limiting to the minimum the elements of a model, making it as tightly co-extensive as possible with the research question or hypothesis, "there is less chance of introducing inconsistencies, ambiguities and redundancies" (Heylighen, 2000).

In summary, information researchers need to ensure that the best possible harmony is achieved between their theoretical perspectives, research questions or hypotheses, and their modelling.

Question 3: In developing my research design, have I deliberately allowed for an intervention effect and consequences, if any?

In 1927 the mechanistic worldview of atomic physics was changed forever when Heisenberg enunciated the 'uncertainty principle', namely that the techniques available to measure the position and momentum of particles themselves affected the values of those variables (Berry, 1988). Around the same time, 1924–1936, experiments conducted in the Hawthorne Works of the Western Electric Company showed that the behaviour of human subjects of observation changes as a result of being observed – the so-called Hawthorne effect (Roethlisberger, 1941).

Similarly, Giddens identifies a phenomenon which he calls 'the double hermeneutic', already referred to in Chapter 4 and elsewhere in this book. It acknowledges the impact of the observer on the observed and vice versa (Giddens, 1986, p. 284). At some level this is an issue for all social sciences, and not least for information research. An understanding of intervention effects is important when designing interactions with respondents, such as questionnaires, interviews or participant observation. There is always the potential for unwittingly changing the situation under study to an unwanted extent. The process of observation, however subtly, changes both the observer and the observed.

In *Star Trek* (2012b) there is the principle of the 'prime directive'. The directive states that crew members of the starship *Enterprise*, in their explorations of space, should not take actions that will distort the development of alien societies with whom they come into contact. The double hermeneutic would suggest that complete adherence to this seemingly worthy principle is an impossible expectation.

By contrast, intervention may be a deliberately desired outcome of a study. Participative action research (PAR) is an example suitable for settings where the researcher and the community at the source of the investigation collaborate as partners in resolving problems and taking actions while the research proceeds. (See Chapter 8: *Action research: Theory and practice* and Schauder, Johanson & Taylor, 2006.) Intervention effects are an issue that must be consciously confronted in good information research, and clearly explicated in a project's research design.

Question 4: How can I ensure that benefit, not harm, will flow from my research?

It is sobering that some of the greatest advances in information technology occurred in the context of totalitarianism, war, or the fear of war. Nazi Germany advanced the cutting-edge information technologies of the day – radio and film – in the service of propaganda. The information technology revolution in large part grew out of the encryption and code-breaking struggles of the United Kingdom and Germany during World War 2. (See, e.g., the role of Alan Turing in Hodges (2012).) The great research databases pioneered by the United States defence industry, and the Internet itself, developed largely by the Defense Advanced Research Projects Agency (DARPA), were products of the Cold War years.

Information research can serve both good and evil purposes. The importance of ethical values in information research cannot be overstated. For the information researcher the Declaration of Principles of the UN World Summit on the Information Society (ITU, 2003) and, in the opinion of this author, J. K. Galbraith's book *The Good Society* (Galbraith, 1996), for example, stand as major ethical guideposts. The important questions for information researchers to address are not only 'What good can this research do?' but also 'What harm can it do, and to whom?'

Question 5: Does my work sufficiently reflect respect for the complexity of my research field and for the contributions of colleagues?

Research almost invariably requires collegiality (the least of which is acknowledging prior work through citation), and collegiality entails respect. The nineteenth century poet Tennyson wrote of the desire of his hero Ulysses:

> To follow knowledge like a sinking star, Beyond the utmost bound of human thought (Tennyson, 1842/1963).

It was a journey Ulysses could make only in company with his peers, and a fitting metaphor for research endeavour. Information researchers need to stay alert to the ideas of colleagues, and honour their contributions to the advancement of their common research quest.

The great 17th century physicist, Newton, was — by reliable accounts — not an easy person to get on with. Contemporaries acknowledged his genius but found him arrogant and difficult. However this intellectual colossus, who transformed humankind's understanding of the universe in so many ways, was humbled by the extent and complexity of the research endeavour:

> I do not know what I may appear to the world, but as to myself, I seem to have been only like a boy playing on the seashore and diverting myself in now and then finding a smoother pebble or a prettier shell than ordinary, while the great ocean of truth lay all undiscovered before me (Grigson & Gibbs-Smith, 1954, p. 303).

While information researchers must go forward with confidence in their research approaches and techniques, they also need the humility to recognise the complexity of their field of study.

Information researchers are privileged to have information as their subject of study — information, the very phenomenon that makes possible the sharing and transmission of knowledge. From the smallest localised group, to collective action on a global scale, the vast and intricate ecology of information flows, resources and systems make possible the patterns of human interdependence that we call society. It is indeed an awesome terrain, but that also makes it exciting and rewarding.

References

Beer, S., Strachy, C., Stone, R., & Torrance, J. (1988). Model. In A. Bullock, & S. Trobley (Eds.), *The Fontana dictionary of modern thought* (Rev. ed., pp. 537–538). London: Fontana Press.

Berry, M. (1988). Uncertainty principle. In A. Bullock, & S. Trobley (Eds.), *The Fontana dictionary of modern thought* (Rev. ed., p. 882). London: Fontana Press.

Boisot, M. (1998). *Knowledge assets: Securing competitive advantage in the information economy*. Oxford: Oxford University Press.

Burgess, S., & Schauder, D. (2003). Spreadsheets as knowledge documents. *Annals of Cases in Information Technology, 5*, 521–537.

Galbraith, J. K. (1996). *The good society: The humane agenda*. Boston MA: Houghton Mifflin.

Giddens, A. (1986). *The constitution of society: Outline of the theory of structuration*. Berkeley, CA: University of California Press.

Gilbert, E. (2011). Social media research, live on the Web, presentation delivered to CS547 Human-Computer Interaction Seminar (Seminar on People, Computers, and Design), May 6, 2011. Stanford CA: Stanford University HCI Group. Retrieved from http://www.youtube.com/watch?v = lo8V8Nvx-HU.

Grigson, G., & Gibbs-Smith, C. (1954). *People*. London: Waverley Book Company.

Heylighen, F. (2000). Occam's razor. In F. Heylighen, C. Joslyn, & V. Turchin (Eds.), *Principia Cybernetica Web*. Brussels: Principia Cybernetica. Retrieved from http://cleamc11.vub.ac.be/OCCAMRAZ.html

Hodges, A. (2012). *Alan Turing: The enigma*. London: Vintage Books.

Hughes, J. (Producer), Johnson, P. R. (Director), Mantegna, J., (Cast), & Boyle, L. F. (Cast). (1991). *Baby's day out*. [DVD]. Twentieth Century Fox Home Entertainment: Beverly Hills, CA.

ITU. (2003). *Declaration of principles, World Summit on the Information Society Geneva 2003 — Tunis 2005* (Document WSIS-03/GENEVA/DOC/4-E). Retrieved from http://www.itu.int/wsis/docs/geneva/official/dop.html.

Pang, B., & Lee, L. (2008). Opinion mining and sentiment analysis. *Information Retrieval, 2*(1–2), 1–135.

Roethlisberger, F. (1941). *Management and morale*. Cambridge, MA: Harvard University Press.

Schauder, D., Johanson, G., & Taylor, W. (2006). Libraries, ICT policy, and Australian civil society: Issues and prospects from national consultations. *Proceedings of VALA 2006, Melbourne, January*. Retrieved from http://www.vala.org.au/vala2006-proceedings/vala2006-session-13-schauder.

Skeat, W. (1887). *A concise etymological dictionary of the English language* (3rd rev. ed.) (p. 503). Oxford: Clarendon Press.

Star Trek (2012a). *Holodeck*. Retrieved from http://www.startrek.com/database_article/holodeck.

Star Trek (2012b). *Prime directive*. Retrieved from http://www.startrek.com/boards-topic/32701605/Prime-directive-_1018877151_32701605.

Tennyson, A. (1963). Ulysses. In *The London Book of English Verse*. (2nd rev. ed., pp. 517–519). London. (Originally published 1842.).

Treloar, A. (2006). The Monash University Information Management Strategy: from development to implementation. *Proceedings of VALA 2006, Melbourne, January*. Retrieved from http://www.valaconf.org.au/vala2006/papers2006/56_Treloar_Final.pdf.

Glossary of terms used in research

This glossary does not include all the terms with which readers may be unfamiliar. Given that some terms represent complex ideas, the definitions below are intended to provide only a starting point of understanding.

Abductive reasoning: a process by which alternative frameworks are applied to data and theory, which are then redescribed and evaluated.

Abstraction: a statement that a thing is a member of a class of things or a class of things is a subclass of another class of things. Abstraction is one of seven principles for interpretivist case studies (Klein & Myers, 1999) and is the ability to abstract empirical findings to the theories used.

Archival science: encompasses theory, methodology and practice relating to records and archives. The field covers recordkeeping and archiving functions such as the creation, management, preservation, retrieval and use of records in and through time; the nature, form and structure of records and archives; the contexts in which records and archives are generated, managed, and used; the social and cultural environment of records; and the role of the record and the Archive in society.

Artefact: a human-made object that is built with the intent it will be useful in some way, or something that occurs as a result of a particular research or technological process that would not otherwise be present.

Autoethnography: is "research, writing, and method that connect the autobiographical and personal to the cultural and social" (Ellis, 2004, p. xix). It is about understanding the relationship between the self and others (Chang, 2008). See also *Ethnography*.

Bibliometrics: "the study of the quantitative aspects of the production, dissemination, and use of recorded information" (Tague-Sutcliffe, 1992, p. 1).

Boundary (design-science research): the set of states and/or events that a theory or model is intended to explain or predict.

Case study: in-depth study of a single 'case', or comparative studies of multiple 'cases', generate rich pictures and insights that might be transferable to other cases. In "comparative archivistics" (Ketelaar, 1997), case studies and ethnographies are used to explore differences in recordkeeping cultures and practice.

Case study research: an "empirical enquiry that investigates a contemporary phenomenon within its real-life context, when the boundaries between phenomenon and context are clearly evident ... and it relies on multiple sources of evidence" (Yin, 2003, p. 13).

Causal variable: see *Independent variable*.

Classical scientific research: research that focusses on building and testing theories or obtaining a deep understanding of phenomena by using various kinds of formal hypotheses, generalisations and abstractions.

Closed system (design-science research): a system that has no interaction with its environment.

Constant comparative analysis: as the process of data collection and analysis proceeds, a grounded theory researcher repetitively compares data with data, codes with codes, and data codes and categories with each other (Birks & Mills, 2011).

Construct: a concept that researchers create as a means of describing and representing some type of phenomena in the world.

Construct validity: extent to which concepts (constructs) being studied are defined appropriately and relevant measures are developed.

Constructivist: qualitative research paradigm which emphasises either the personal, subjective construction of reality and/or the social (or shared) construction of reality produced by humans acting together. The label used for the former is 'personal constructivist' and for the latter 'social constructionist'. The umbrella term is 'constructivist'. See also *Interpretevist* and *Naturalistic inquiry*.

Constructivist grounded theory: application of constructivist approach to grounded theory. Constructivist grounded theory is explicitly not 'objectivist'.

Critical realist: believes "that it is not easy to capture reality directly" as it can "easily become distorted or muddied" (Neuman, 2011, p. 92). A critical realist takes precautions to control the effect of people's interpretations of reality. See also *Critical realist ontology* (under *Ontology*).

Critical theorists: theorists who aim, through the writing of value-laden texts, to liberate groups which are seen to be oppressed, e.g., women or certain racial groups, and to produce transformations in the social order.

Data: "discrete, objective facts or observations ... [without] meaning or value because of lack of context and interpretation" (Rowley & Hartley, 2008, p. 6).

Data archiving: a curation activity which ensures that data are properly selected and stored so that they can be accessed and so that their logical and physical integrity are maintained over time, including security and authenticity.

Data curation: managing and promoting the use of data from point of creation, to ensure availability for contemporary purpose, discovery and re-use. For dynamic datasets this may mean continuous enrichment or updating (Yakel, 2007, p. 338).

Data management: the systematic process of planning and organising activities required to appropriately manage research data throughout its life cycle, curation, preservation and archiving.

Data preservation: archiving activity in which specific items of data are maintained over time so that they can still be accessed and understood through successive change and obsolescence of technologies.

Decompose (design-science research): to break a thing up into its components. Each component will be related to at least one other component.

Deductive reasoning: begins with a generalisation and then moves to inferences about particular circumstances. See also *Inductive reasoning*.

Dependent variable: the factor which is measured to determine how it has responded to a particular treatment or cause. Sometimes called 'effect variable'. See also *Independent variable*.

Descriptive statistics: are used to describe aspects of sets of quantitative data to enable interpretation and comparison.

Design-science research: research that seeks to build, evaluate, and theorise about artefacts.

Design-science theory: "shows the principles inherent in the design of an IS [information systems] artefact that accomplishes some end, based on knowledge of both IT and human behaviour" (Gregor and Jones, 2007, p. 322). The theory is intended to account for the behaviour of some artefact.

Dialectics: argument and discussion that evaluates contradictory facts or ideas, or paradoxical processes, with a view to the resolution of contradictions.

Dialogical reasoning: one of seven principles for interpretivist case studies (Klein & Myers, 1999) requiring sensitivity to the contradictions that emerge between the theoretical preconceptions guiding the research design and the empirical findings with further cycles of iteration.

Diplomatics: body of techniques, theories and principles for analysing the form, function and genesis of documents with a particular view to establishing authenticity.

Discourse: describes written and spoken communications. The term is used in a range of ways, including to describe "the totality of codified linguistic usages attached to a given type of social practice" (Marks, 2001), e.g., legal discourse. 'Discourse analysis' explores the underlying meaning of the phenomenon under study, including its social implications.

Effect variable: see *Dependent variable.*

Element: an individual member or unit of a population.

Emic: insider views, which ethnographers/participant observers, particularly, aim to obtain. See also *Etic.*

Empirical: based on observation or experience.

Epistemology: the theory and nature of knowledge; how it is formed; ways of knowing.

Ethics: a set of moral principles; the rules of conduct recognised in a particular profession or area of human life (*The new shorter Oxford dictionary*, 1993, p. 856).

Ethnography: the study and description of people in their everyday contexts. See also *Autoethnography.*

Ethnology: involves cross-cultural and comparative study of the origin of human cultures, including social structure, language, religion and technology, and social change, often using multiple pre-existing ethnographies (Geertz, 1973; Monaghan & Just, 2000).

Ethnomethodology: "is concerned with how people accomplish their everyday lives ... how everyday life is forged, hence socially constructed" (Adler & Adler, 1998, p. 99).

Etic: reliance on an outsider perspective, which occurs with most positivist research. See also *Emic.*

External validity: refers to the generalisability of research findings, that is, the extent to which they can be generalised to other populations, settings or treatments. See also *Internal validity.*

Framework (research): in the case of sciences and the humanities signifies assumptions, norms, values and traditions that create, perpetuate and institutionalise particular forms of knowledge within a particular field of study (Stanfield, 1998, p. 346).

Generalisability: "the extent to which the findings and conclusions of one particular study can be applied to other similar situations or settings or the population at large" (Gilliland & McKemmish, 2004, p. 172).

Generalisation: a statement that a set of things possess a common property.

Grounded theory: theory which is built from the ground upwards, that is from data observed and collected in the field.

Hermeneutics: an intellectual tradition concerned originally with the interpretation of texts but later of social life. In interpretivist case studies the *hermeneutic cycle* is a fundamental principle (Klein & Myers, 1999) and states that human understanding is based on the iterative sense making of the parts and the whole.

Heuristic search process: the search for a solution to a problem based on rules of thumb or trial-and-error processes.

Historiography: body of techniques, theories and principles of historical research and presentation involving a critical examination, evaluation, and selection of material from primary and secondary resources.

Homomorphic models: minimalist symbolic representations of key factors and relationships.

Hypotheses: specifically formulated and empirically testable statements which predict the relationship between one or more variables in a research study, e.g., the relationship between level of education and library use. In historical research, the hypotheses are used to guide the historian's thinking, analysis and findings, and do not necessarily have the same level of rigour as scientific hypotheses. See also *Null hypothesis*.

Hypothetico-deductive case study (theory-testing): aimed to test theory, where propositions are derived from an existing theory and then tested.

Idiographic: "pertaining to the intensive ... study of an individual case, [such] as a personality or social situation" (*Macquarie dictionary*, 1987, p. 867). Antonym of *Nomothetic*.

Independent variable: the factor manipulated by the researcher to see what impact it has on other variables. Sometime called 'causal variable'.

Inductive case study (theory-building): aims to describe and develop theory. It is used to provide evidence for hypothesis generation and for exploration of areas where existing knowledge is limited.

Inductive reasoning: begins with intense investigation of a particular instance or instances, and concludes with general statements or principles. See also *Deductive reasoning*.

Inferential statistics: used to analyse data in order to draw inferences.

Information systems: a discipline that involves the study of people, procedures, data, software, and hardware that are used to gather and analyse useful information in organisations (Jessup & Valacich, 2008).

Informetrics: "the study [and analysis] of the quantitative aspects of information in any form, not just records or bibliographies, and in any social group, not just scientists" (Tague-Sutcliffe, 1992, p. 1).

Instantiation: a hardware/software system that researchers produce using some method to implement a construct or model.

Internal validity: the extent to which a research instrument measures what it is designed to measure. In experimental design: pertains to the conclusiveness of results, that is, the confidence that observed results are attributable to the impact of an independent variable, and not cause by other unknown factors. See also *External validity*.

Interpretivist or interpretive: from the research tradition, interpretivism, which emphasises natural settings together with individual and group perceptions of events and interactions within those settings. Focus is on inductive reasoning. Examples of interpretivist paradigms are constructivism and phenomenology. See also *Constructivist, Phenomenology* and *Naturalistic inquiry.*

Interval data: measures with order and with equal intervals on a scale, e.g., IQ test scores

Isomorphic models: holistic re-creations of phenomena under study, or 'framing' of actual whole phenomena for the purposes of research.

Iterative: the interweaving of various elements in the research process, where the development of one influences the other, e.g., the interweaving of data collection and the elaboration of theory as researchers move backwards and forwards in a qualitative study.

Likert scale: a rating scale (usually five-point) frequently used in quantitative research, on which respondents are asked to rate their preferences or the frequencies of their activities.

Mean: determined by the sum of the values in the distribution divided by the number of values. The mean is used for interval scale data.

Median: the point on the scale below which half of the values lie.

Metacognition: knowing about knowing; particularly individuals' awareness of their own cognitive processes.

Metadata: most commonly described as data about data (including its structure, content, rights, creation and preservation actions, relationships, context). Metadata can be represented as a catalogue record, a set of business rules, the data dictionary of a database, index entries, or in metatags such as Dublin Core.

Meta-theory/Meta-theorising: concerned with attempts to make sense of different theories that claim to explain phenomena within in a particular disciplinary domain. Meta-theorising examines assumptions behind existing theories in order to achieve a more profound understanding of these theories or different theoretical perspectives.

Method (design-science research): a set of actions (the actions are often ordered) that is used to achieve some outcome (a product or service).

Method: see *Research method.*

Methodology: theory of method; a set of principles of methods. Methodology is the entire framework or design of the research: the choice of paradigm (philosophical underpinnings), methods and tools or techniques to explore research questions and make knowledge claims.

Mode: the value with the most frequent occurrence.

Model: a conceptual object that comprises constructs and associations among these constructs as a way to describe and represent some subset of real-world phenomena.

Multiple realities: see *Social reality.*

Narrative analysis: body of techniques for examining how narrative or rhetorical tropes are used in documents to 'tell stories' or advance particular perspectives or arguments.

Naturalistic inquiry: a complex term, which at its simplest level means the conduct of research in a natural setting. See also *Constructivist* and *Interpretevist.*

Nominal data: measures without order, e.g., *gender.* (Also known as categorical data.)

Nominalist: see *Nominalist ontology* under *Ontology*

Nomological network: a network of related constructs that is intended to account (explain and/or predict) for some phenomena. See also *Theory.*

Nomothetic: "pertaining to the search for general laws" (*Macquarie dictionary,* 1987, p. 1158). Antonym of *Idiographic.*

Non-probability samples: samples which do not meet the standards of probability samples where the probability or likelihood of the inclusion of each element of the populations can be specified.

Norm: establishing a norm (that is, a standard or pattern).

Null hypothesis: "hypothesis that asserts there is no real relationship between or among the variables in question. It involves the supposition that chance, rather than an identifiable cause has produced some observable result" (Powell, 1997, p. 29). See also *Hypothesis.*

Ontology: the science or study of being. In research terminology ontology is the existence and nature of social reality. It is also used to denote a set of concepts and their structural inter-relationships in a particular context.

Critical realist ontology: belief that a 'real world' exists but that "it is not easy to capture reality directly" as it can "easily become distorted or muddied" (Neuman, 2011, p. 92).

Nominalist ontology: belief that experience of the so-called real world "is always occurring through a lens or scheme of interpretations and inner subjectivisty" (Neuman, 2011, p. 92).

Realist ontology: belief that "the 'real world' exists independently of humans and their interpretations of it" (Neuman, 2011, p. 92).

Open system (design-science research): a system that interacts with its environment.

Ordinal data: measures with order or rank. The categories may be numeric but equal intervals between measurement scores on the scale are not established, e.g., activity levels of high, medium, low.

Outliers (data): data outside expected ranges. They may be genuine values that highlight an unusual situation or might be erroneous data values that could distort the analysis.

Paradigm: a set of underlying principles which provides a framework for understanding particular phenomena.

Paradigm incommensurability: the contention that paradigms are mutually exclusive because, although they may blur at the edges, they are based on competing and irreconcilable assumptions.

Participant observation: often used as an alternative term to 'ethnography' where researchers also undertake fieldwork to observe participants. Various forms and levels of participant observation are described in Chapter 17 *Observation.*

Participatory action research: commonly carried out in communities or groups that are trying to overcome negative or oppressive conditions, i.e., it emphasises "political aspects of knowledge production" (Reason, 1998, p. 269). Reflexivity is important, as with all action research. The term may be used differently according to the philosophical bent of the researcher.

Pattern matching: used to compare empirical data collected from qualitative data with outcomes predicted by propositions.

Performance measurement: where output measures are used to determine what has been accomplished by specific programs, services or resources.

Phenomenography: research approach which attempts to find the distinctly different ways of seeing particular experiences by groups of individuals.

Phenomenology: "aims to capture the richness of experience, the fullness of all the ways in which a person experiences and describes the phenomena of interest" (Marton & Booth, 1997, p. 117).

Pluralism: belief that researchers do not have to accept existing or singular paradigms but can develop new ones by drawing on the strengths and weaknesses of the old ones, or adopt alternative, co-existing paradigms.

Population: a complete set of all elements (e.g., people, institutions) which have at least one characteristic in common and which a researcher wishes to study.

Population stratum: a subdivision of a population based on one or more specifications e.g., all Victorian academic librarians under the age of thirty.

Positivist: from the research tradition, positivism, which adheres to the scientific mode of enquiry and emphasises deductive reasoning, measurement, quantitative data and nomothetic knowledge claims.

Postmodern: complex term defying succinct definition. Postmodernists are particularly concerned with issues of 'intersubjectivity', i.e., how researcher and researched affect each other (Glesne & Peshkin, 1992, p. 10). An author is regarded as only one contributor. Discussed widely in Denzin & Lincoln handbooks. Postmodern paradigms emphasise flexibility and reflexivity.

Post-positivist: belief that reality must be subjected to the widest possible critical examination and that qualitative methods are important in achieving this goal.

Probability sampling: the probability or likelihood of including each element of the population can be specified. In true probability sampling, each element must have an *equal* and *independent* chance of being included in the sample.

Problematisation: a process of identifying and challenging the assumptions underlying existing theories and findings (Alvesson & Sandberg, 2011).

Propositions: broad statements drawn from theory or "a theoretical statement about the relationship between two or more variables" (Neuman, 2011, p. 68).

Prototype: a working version or model of an application system (Pratt & Adamski, 1991, p. 807).

Purposeful/purposive sample: selected to suit the purposes of a study — according to what is considered relevant and important.

Qualitative data: data in the form of words but may include other forms, including images. (Note that the description of 'qualitative research', rather than 'data', is complex. It is discussed in details in various chapters of the book.)

Quantitative data: data in the form of numbers or numerical concepts. (Note that the description of 'quantitative research', rather than 'data', is complex. It is discussed in details in various chapters of the book.)

Random sample: each element of a population has an *equal* and *independent* opportunity of being selected in a sample.

Ratio data: measures with order, equal intervals on a scale, and a true zero point (a point at which the trait being measured is totally absent), e.g., *total computer access time.*

Realist: See *Realist ontology* under *Ontology.*

Reality: See *Social reality.*

Relativism: the notion there is no absolute truth and that truth is contingent on the observer, and the time and place of the observation.

Reliability: concerned with obtaining consistent, stable research results capable of replication.

Replication: involves repeating an empirical study, with different participants and in different settings. When using multiple-case studies, each case should be carefully selected so that it either predicts similar outcomes across cases with similar contexts (literal replication), or produces contrasting findings based on theoretical conditions (theoretical replication) to test theory.

Research data: can take many forms depending on the research problem being addressed and the discipline of the researcher. Data are generally gathered or produced by researchers through observations, experiments or by computer modelling. See also *Data.*

Research design: encompasses identification of the research problem, goals and desired outcomes, and selection of methodology, including the choice of paradigm (philosophical underpinnings), methods and tools or techniques.

Research method: provides a major component of the design for undertaking research. Research methods are underpinned with theoretical explanation of their value and use. Techniques for data gathering and sample selection, as well as processing and interpreting data, are usually included as part the research method, e.g., questionnaires are commonly used in the research method 'survey' but can also be used in other methods, e.g., 'case study' or 'experimental design'. (Note that this is the definition employed in this book. Others may adopt different perspectives.)

Research technique: a procedure or tool for undertaking research processes, e.g., selecting samples, collecting and analysing data.

Revelatory knowledge: allows us to 'see' phenomena in the world that previously we did not 'see'.

Sample: a selection of elements from the total population to be studied. A sample is any part of the population, whether it is representative or not.

Sampling error: the degree to which the sample characteristics approximate the characteristics of the population (in probability sampling).

Sampling frame: the list of elements from which a sample is selected.

Saturation: a term that determines when a researcher should stop adding cases (Eisenhardt, 1989), which is the point at which there is no more new information is derived and incremental learning is minimal.

Social reality: how the real world is perceived. The positivist view is that an ordered and stable reality exists out there waiting to be discovered. To interpretivists, reality is personally and/or socially constructed, fluid and fragile, and exists as people experience it and assign meaning to it. The result is 'multiple realities'.

Sociometrics: a quantitative method for studying social relationships, networks and patterns of interactions, and revealing hidden structures such as invisible colleges, subgroups, alliances, ideological agreement, and dominant individuals (Moreno, 1951).

Solution transition path (design-science research): the path chosen by a problem solver from the initial problem-solving state through intermediate problem-solving states to the goal or end state.

State space (design-science research): the space of all possible states that a thing might traverse.

Statistical significance: relates to the level of significance which is the point which the researcher uses to determine whether the observed difference or relationship is too large to be attributed to chance.

Suspicion: one of seven principles for interpretivist case studies (Klein & Myers, 1999) and requires sensitivity to possible biases and "systematic distortions" observed in the stories of the participants.

Taxonomy: (scientific) classification.

Technique: see *Research technique*.

Theoretical drive: is determined by the component (usually positivist/quantitative or interpretivist/qualitative) which will play the more important part in answering the research questions (Morse, 2003).

Theoretical sample: the process of selecting "incidents, slices of life, time periods, or people on the basis of their potential manifestation or representation of important theoretical constructs" (Patton, 2002, p. 238).

Theoretical saturation: the idea (in grounded theory) that the researcher examines, compares and interprets all previous codes, and produces a number of theoretical codes, until no more theoretical codes can be found.

Theory: a viewpoint or perspective which is explanatory. A social science theory is "a systematic explanation of the observed facts and laws that relate to a specific aspect of life" (Babbie, 1989, p. 46). In information systems it is a model with rigorously defined constructs, associations, and boundary conditions.

Transformative knowledge: allows us to 'see' phenomena in ways that are different from those we have used previously to 'see' the phenomena.

Transition path (design-science research): a path from an initial problem-solving state through immediate problem-solving states to a goal or end state.

Triangulation: involves the use of multiple methods of data collection, multiple sources of data, and theoretical constructs.

Unit of analysis: the 'who' or the 'what' that is analysed and researched. It defines the scope and boundaries of a case study (e.g., individual, group, organisation, information systems project).

Validity: see *Internal validity, External validity,* and *Construct validity*

Variable: something which varies. In a research study examples of possible variables are age, level of education, frequency of library use (of respondents in a survey). See also *Dependent variable* and *Independent variable*

References

Adler, P. A., & Adler, P. (1998). Observational techniques. In N. K. Denzin, & Y. A. Lincoln (Eds.), *Collecting and interpreting qualitative materials* (pp. 79–109). Thousand Oaks, CA: Sage Publications.

Alvesson, M., & Sandberg, J. (2011). Generating research questions through problematization. *The Academy of Management Review, 36*(2), 247–271.

Babbie, E. (1989). *The practice of social research* (5th ed.). Belmont, CA: Wadsworth.

Birks, M., & Mills, J. (2011). *Grounded theory: A practical guide.* Thousancd Oaks California: Sage Publications.

Chang, H. (2008). *Autoethnography method.* Walnut Creek, CA: Left Coast Press.

Eisenhardt, K. M. (1989). Building theories from case study research. *Academy of Management Review, 14*(4), 532–550.

Ellis, C. (2004). *The ethnographic I: A methodological novel about teaching and doing autoethnography.* Walnut Creek, CA: AltaMira.

Geertz, C. (1973). *The interpretation of cultures.* New York: Basic Books.

Gilliland, A., & McKemmish, S. (2004). Building an infrastructure for archival research. *Archival Science, 4*(3-4), 149–199.

Glesne, C., & Peshkin, A. (1992). *Becoming qualitative researchers: An introduction.* White Plains, NY: Longman Publishing Group.

Gregor, S., & Jones, D. (2007). The anatomy of a design theory. *Journal of the Association for Information Systems, 8*(5), 312–335.

Jessup, L. M., & Valacich, J. S. (2008). *Information systems today: Managing in the digital world* (3rd ed.). Upper Saddle River, NJ: Pearson Prentice Hall.

Ketelaar, E. (1997). The difference best postponed? Cultures and comparative archival science. *Archivaria, 44*, 142–148.

Klein, H. K., & Myers, M. D. (1999). A set of principles for conducting and evaluating interpretive field studies in information systems. *MIS Quarterly, 23* (1), 67–94.

Marks, L. (Trans.). (2001). *A little glossary of semantics*. Retrieved from http://www.revue-texto.net/Reperes/Glossaires/Glossaire_en.html.

Marton, F., & Booth, S. (1997). *Learning and awareness*. Mahwah, NJ: Lawrence Erbaum Associates.

Monaghan, J., & Just, P. (2000). *Social and cultural anthropology: A very short introduction*. Oxford: Oxford University Press.

Moreno, J. L. (1951). *Sociometry, experimental method and the science of society. An approach to a new political orientation*. New York: Beacon House.

Morse, J. M. (2003). Principles of mixed methods and multimethod research design. In A. Tashakkori, & C. Teddlie (Eds.), *Handbook of mixed methods in social and behavioral research* (pp. 189–208). Thousand Oaks, CA: Sage.

Neuman, W. L. (2011). *Social research methods: Qualitative and quantitative approaches* (7th ed.). Boston: Allyn & Baker.

Patton, M. Q. (2002). *Qualitative evaluation and research methods* (3rd ed.). Newbury Park, CA: Sage Publications.

Powell, Ronald (1997). *Basic research methods for librarians* (3rd ed.). Norwood, NJ: Ablex.

Pratt, P. J., & Adamski, J. J. (1991). *Database systems: Management and design* (2nd ed.). Boston, MA: Boyd & Fraser.

Reason, P. (1998). Three approaches to participative inquiry. In N. K. Denzin, & Y. S. Lincoln (Eds.), *Strategies of qualitative inquiry* (pp. 261–291). Thousand Oaks, CA: Sage.

Rowley, J. E., & Hartley, R. (2008). *Organizing knowledge: An introduction to managing access to information* (4th ed.). Hampshire, England: Ashgate Publishing.

Stanfield, J. (1998). Ethnic modelling in qualitative research. In N. K. Denzin, & Y. S. Lincoln (Eds.), *The landscape of qualitative research: Theories and issues* (pp. 333–358). London: Sage.

Tague-Sutcliffe, J. (1992). An introduction to informetrics. *Information Processing & Management, 28*(1), 1–3.

Yakel, E. (2007). Digital curation. *OCLC Systems & Services, 23*(4), 335–340.

Yin, R. K. (2003). *Case study research: Design and methods* (3rd ed.). Thousand Oaks: Sage Publications.

Author Index

Subject Index

Printed and bound by CPI Group (UK) Ltd, Croydon, CR0 4YY

08/06/2025

01896872-0019